The Impact of Catastrophe

The Impact of Catastrophe

The People of Essex and the First World War (1914-1920)

PAUL RUSIECKI

ESSEX RECORD OFFICE
Chelmsford

Essex Record Office, Wharf Road,
Chelmsford, Essex, CM2 6YT

A catalogue reference for this title is available
from the British Library.

ISBN: 978-1-898529-28-6

Typeset in Sabon by Buffey & Buffey

Essex Record Office Publication Number: 154

Front cover: The skeleton of Zeppelin L.33, which was landed by its crew at Little Wigborough in September 1916.
(ERO: Heritage Education Unit Collection)

For Julie

Contents

Acknowledgements

My first debt is to my father, who first encouraged me in my love of history. As an exile from his own country he was deeply interested in the history of the country which sheltered and adopted him, and I will always be grateful to him for passing on his love of the past to me. To my history teachers at school, Elizabeth Lord and Harry Frear, gratitude for encouraging a lazy boy who had little interest in any other subject at school. I owe a huge debt of thanks to Geoffrey Crossick, who supervised my doctoral thesis, and who more than anyone else taught me exactly what it means when one claims to be an historian. I hope this book is a suitable testimony to the six years of kind and patient work he put in with me. I am very grateful for the help and interest shown by the staff of the Local Studies Department at Colchester Library. It has become almost a second home to me. I would like to thank the staff of the Essex Record Office, and make special mention of Paul Coverley and the staff of the Colchester Branch Office, now sadly closed. My thanks also to Deborah Peers for her help with the publication of this book. I have also been made welcome on my travels at the Chelmsford, Clacton and Southend libraries. Beryl Board kindly gave her time and generously shared her knowledge of Stow Maries during the Great War, and Mabel Jervis gave her kind permission to quote from the diary of her mother, Evelyn Jessie Grubb (née Potter) – my sincere thanks to both. The Archive of the Brentwood Diocese has very kindly granted permission to quote from the diary of Father Patrick Mckenna, for which I offer my thanks. My son Marcus helped me with the research for Chapter 4, and it was great fun as we trawled through the reports of Essex's Military Tribunals. Both he and my daughter Helen have lived with 'Dad's obsession with the past'. Last and most important of all is my wife, Julie. She has tolerated and encouraged me in a life where I have one foot permanently in the past. The debt I owe to her is indeed immeasurable.

Abbreviations

The following abbreviations have been used in the footnotes:

BA	*Barking, East Ham and Ilford Advertiser*
BDA	*Burnham and Dengie Advertiser*
ChBC	Chelmsford Borough Council
CBC	Colchester Borough Council
CG	*Colchester Gazette*
ECC	*Essex County Chronicle*
ECS	*Essex County Standard*
ECT	*Essex County Telegraph*
EEA	*East Essex Advertiser and Clacton Times*
ERO	Essex Record Office
HDS	*Harwich and Dovercourt Standard*
LE	*Leytonstone Express and Independent*
SBC	Southend Borough Council
SE	*Stratford Express*
SSt	*Southend Standard*
WG	*Walthamstow Leyton and Chingford Guardian*
WWN	*Saffron Walden Weekly News*

Before the Storm

CHAPTER ONE

Essex on the Eve of the Great War

The Essex resort of Southend-on-Sea in full swing. This postcard was sent in early August 1914. *(ERO: Postcards Collection, Southend/19)*

BEFORE THE STORM

ESSEX IN 1914 was a county whose scenery and settlement demonstrated both antiquity and the impact of the modern world. The area lacked the scenic grandeur of other parts of England, and despite its strategic location near both the capital and the Continent, an industrial transformation had been wrought only in the areas adjacent to London, in that part of Essex which had become known as 'London over the Border'. Nevertheless, it did possess charms sufficient to attract those who were in pursuit of either its historic past or the hedonism of the time. John Norden, an Elizabethan topographer, perhaps overstated things when he described the county as "the Essex Goshen, the fatte of the Lande: comparable to Palestina, that flowed with milke and hunnye,"[1] although a later author was more restrained, and more accurate, when he portrayed it as

> the scenery of man's devising — the fair prospect offered where man has concentrated his genius through generations on a wise cooperation with nature for the production of crop and stock.[2]

At sixty-three miles long at its widest point (north-east to south-west), and forty-eight miles from north to south, Essex was in size the eleventh largest English shire. In 1911 its population was approaching one and a half million, the result of a truly remarkable level of growth during the previous thirty years. Since 1901 its population had increased by over a third, it had doubled since 1891, and almost tripled since 1881. However, this population explosion was not spread uniformly throughout the county but concentrated in the west, where it bordered on the eastern outskirts of London. The expansion of metropolitan Essex meant that in 1911 over seven hundred thousand people resided in this area, some crammed into the industrial settlements of Barking, or East and West Ham, others living in the more comfortable surroundings of Ilford, Woodford, Walthamstow, or Leytonstone. Over half the county's population was concentrated in less than ten per cent of its area.

Despite the ravages of the Agricultural Depression which had severely affected Essex in the late nineteenth century, the county still had an agricultural base, although its economy could not be described as entirely agrarian. Essex was a county of industry, as well as of farming, and not just in the metropolitan area but in towns such as Colchester, Chelmsford, Halstead, Braintree and Earls Colne, which boasted textile and engineering factories and works. Ports such as Harwich, Tilbury, Burnham, Maldon and Brightlingsea depended on trade, fishing, or ship- and boat-building. The economies of seaside resorts such as Southend, Clacton, Walton, Frinton and Dovercourt were reliant on London's holidaymakers and day trippers.

The growth of metropolitan Essex was the most remarkable feature of Essex's history in the sixty or seventy years before the Great War. This expansion began in

1 John Norden, *The Description of Essex* (1594).

2 C. Henry Warren, *The County Books: Essex* (1959), 3-4.

the 1850s, stimulated by the railway's penetration northwards and eastwards into Essex, and by the opening of the Royal Victoria Dock (1855) and the Royal Albert Dock (1880). This expansion was initially a commercial and industrial one, as chemical industries, shipbuilding, engineering, sugar refining, confectionery and the building trade opened up first in West Ham during the 1850s, then spread into neighbouring parishes, reaching Leytonstone and Walthamstow in the 1870s and East Ham in the 1880s. Residential growth occurred alongside industrial development as employment opportunities beckoned for tens of thousands of workers. Over six thousand were employed at the Great Eastern's locomotive works at Stratford, thousands more at the huge Beckton gasworks in East Ham, the single largest employer in south-west Essex. By the 1890s Barking and Ilford were joined by continuous growth to East Ham; by 1900 East and West Ham, Leyton and Walthamstow were completely absorbed into London's eastern expansion. East Ham, a small village of 2,264 in 1861, had a population of over ninety-six thousand by 1901 and by 1911 it was the eleventh largest town in England. Leyton's population doubled between 1891 and 1911, from sixty-three thousand to one hundred and twenty-four thousand; Ilford's grew by 700 per cent in the same period. A 1904 survey showed that West Ham had over twenty-seven thousand workers within its boundaries, greater than the populations of most Essex towns. Walthamstow, by no means the largest industrial centre in the area, possessed 110 factories, 138 workshops, 458 other places of work and 1,069 outworkers in 1912. Virtually every acre of land in East and West Ham vanished under brick and concrete, although there was still unoccupied land in Ilford, Wanstead and Woodford in 1914. The nature of the settlement and employment, largely unskilled, in East Ham, West Ham and Barking, created a reservoir of casual work, seasonal unemployment, appalling housing conditions and higher infant mortality rates than in other eastern metropolitan parishes. Places such as Ilford, Leyton, Wanstead and Woodford were spared the wholesale industrial transformation of East and West Ham. In these places housing developments were more controlled and restrained, and these parishes developed into residential areas, housing the growing numbers of white-collar office workers who travelled to work in London. At Walthamstow T.C.T. Warner built pleasant housing estates which were not of the traditional terraced variety. Local builders Corbett and Griggs provided houses which were equally appealing to the lower-middle classes who commuted to work in the capital.[3]

Cross-county communications were provided by the railways, which since their inception in the 1830s had crisscrossed the county. In 1914 they were largely in the hands of the Great Eastern Railway Company. Three main lines traversed Essex. Two of them were operated by the Great Eastern Railway; one from London across the north-west of the county to Cambridge, and the other through its heartland from

3 *Victoria County History*, v, 4-6, 10-14, 49, 51-3, 175, 263.

London to Chelmsford and Colchester and on to Ipswich and Norwich. A third line, run by the London, Tilbury and Southend Railway, left Fenchurch Street, and after travelling through east London, wove its way across the north bank of the Thames before reaching Southend and Shoeburyness. Many branch lines radiated from these railways, linking dozens of small villages and every town of even modest size. In the fifteen years or so prior to 1914 several municipalities had also invested in the highly fashionable tramway system, as a speedy, efficient, and supposedly economical way of transporting their citizens between town centre and outskirts. Southend opened its tramway in 1901, Ilford and Barking two years later, West Ham and Colchester in 1904 and Walthamstow in 1905.

However, in 1914 the railways were still paramount and there was, as yet, no serious challenge for either passenger or goods business from the internal combustion engine, which was still in its infancy. Nevertheless cars, omnibuses, vans and charabancs were making their presence felt. In 1908 the county surveyor described the county's roads as being in a fair condition. However, although the number of cars registered had fallen since 1907, the gradual increase in traction engine traffic and heavy cars, especially in the south of the county, was making it more difficult to maintain macadamised surfaces at a moderate cost.[4] During 1903-04 there was considerable support on Colchester Town Council for the creation of a municipal bus fleet rather than a tramway, and the decision in favour of trams was a close one; some councillors were already predicting that buses would render the tramway obsolete. From 1908 the London Omnibus Company ran services to London's Charing Cross and Oxford Circus from Leyton.[5] In Southend taxi cabs appeared in 1908, charabancs in 1910. Bus companies began to develop outside of the capital. Berry's abandoned their horse-drawn service in 1904 and instead operated a Colchester-West Mersea route with a Daimler bus. By 1914 Moore Brothers Ltd and Huntly of Kelvedon and Norfolk of Nayland were running rural bus services through the Essex countryside to Colchester. The advent of the motor car was already threatening horse-drawn forms of transport with obsolescence. In Colchester in 1901 there were ninety-eight horse-drawn hackney carriages, but by 1914 there were less than twenty.[6]

Scattered through the heart of the county were those small towns which, unlike those in metropolitan Essex, had not been urbanised beyond recognition, nor were largely residential in nature, nor dependent upon the sea and the weather for their survival, as were the ports and coastal resorts. Most of these towns had only a fraction of the population of the expanding metropolitan area. Colchester, with forty-three thousand people, was only a third the size of East Ham in 1911. Incredibly three of West Ham's wards — Plaistow, Canning Town and Tidal Basin — had over thirty thousand people in each of them, which made them larger than most of the county's

4 ERO C/DH/10/5

5 *Victoria County History*, v, 28, 183.

6 ECS 31 May, 14 June 1913; P. Denny, *Life in Edwardian Colchester* (1990), 9-11, 24.

municipal boroughs. Billericay, Chelmsford, Braintree and Rochford were in turn only half as large as Colchester. There were nineteen municipal boroughs with populations of less than twenty thousand, and eight below five thousand. With just 1,510 people, the smallest of these was Frinton. The County Borough of Southend, with over seventy thousand people, was the largest non-metropolitan borough in Essex, and with a population increase of over fifty per cent between 1901 and 1911 it rivalled the metropolitan area's spectacular expansion.

Small towns like Chelmsford, Saffron Walden, Romford, Colchester, Grays, Witham and Billericay were market towns set in agricultural areas, but some of them had alternative forms of employment which stood them in good stead during the farming depression. Chelmsford was the county town, home to the headquarters of Essex County Council, and the centre of the new Diocese of Chelmsford which had been created in 1914. It had a varied economy, with Crompton's Electric Light Works, farm machinery factories, iron foundries, a tannery, breweries, maltings, corn mills, ball bearing works and, a sign of the modern world, a car works. Colchester, with its castle, Roman walls and archaeologically rich land (a magnet to practitioners of this relatively new study), gloried in its ancient heritage, although it still smarted from having lost the seat of the new diocese to Chelmsford. Its garrison, a permanent feature of the town since the Crimean War, provided employment and business and softened the impact of the farming depression. Although its footwear industry had suddenly collapsed after 1900, the town's clothing industry provided employment to thousands of people in factories and as outworkers throughout north-east Essex. A sizeable engineering industry was dominated by firms such as Mumford and Paxman. Samuel Courtauld's silk works sustained employment in Halstead and Braintree, at Earls Colne Reuben Hunt's Atlas Works produced farm machinery and employed three hundred and fifty local men. Epping had the Cottis Iron Foundry, there was extensive malting at Saffron Walden, a large lime and cement trade at Grays, and sawing factories, the remnant of velvet weaving and the production of the famous Tambour lace at Coggeshall. Waltham Abbey was the site of Nobel's Explosives Factory and the Royal Gunpowder Factory. Kynoch's explosives factory, and the company-created settlement of 'Kynochtown', dominated the south Essex villages of Coryton and Corringham.

In 1914 Essex farmers were still recovering from the Agricultural Depression which struck in the 1880s and which had ravaged the county for a quarter of a century.[7] Cereal prices had collapsed in the face of foreign competition and farmers and their tenants began to abandon their holdings, or turn from cereals to livestock which resulted in a large increase in pasture and derelict land. In Essex wheat production fell by ten per cent during 1900-01, and during 1903-04 it decreased by twenty-one per cent to just seventy-nine thousand acres. Barley production fell by

7 ERO C/M/Rc 1, County Reconstruction Committee, Chief Medical Officer's Report, December 1918.

about forty per cent from one hundred and three thousand acres in 1890 to sixty-one thousand acres in 1914.[8] In the Unions of Billericay, Rochford and Maldon about eleven thousand acres of soil had ceased to be cultivated in the 1880s and in 1914 the land was still derelict. Turnover in farming was very high as farmers and labourers gave up the struggle, some of the latter moving of their own free will, others forced out by farmers' desperate cost cutting. By 1911 there were only forty-two thousand farm labourers in Essex, less than four per cent of those in employment; in 1811 there had been over one hundred and forty-two thousand of them, forming fifty-six per cent of those in work.[9] Landlords did particularly badly as rents plummeted, and several estates were partially sold off to pay debts. John Fenn, a land agent, described the desperate conditions in the Ardleigh area at the turn of the century. Rents in the area had fallen by fifty to sixty per cent. Some farmers were limping along by working farms let by landlords who could no longer afford to operate them. Farm buildings were deteriorating and the land was being impoverished by improper farming methods. The village's small industries and workshops, and all of its six mills, had vanished by 1910.[10] Cash wages in Essex were low, standing at about 14*s*. 6*d*. a week in 1913. This was lower than in Hertfordshire, but on a par with Suffolk and Norfolk, although this was scant consolation to labourers attempting to raise families with an element of dignity. As people moved from the countryside to find employment in urban areas, rural populations tumbled. By 1900 the populations of eighty-three rural parishes had fallen, and about two hundred had reached their peak by 1851. In the Lexden and Winstree, and the Tendring rural districts village populations had fallen drastically between 1851 and 1901. Six villages had suffered a population loss of up to ten per cent, seven villages had fallen by between eleven and twenty-one per cent, and eight by between twenty-one and thirty per cent. Five others had dropped by between thirty and sixty per cent.[11] By 1906 the author Rider Haggard, speaking at Wilkin's Tiptree Strawberry Feast, was urging a national effort to re-populate the land.[12]

However, Essex farming did not go under. Dairy farming expanded during these years, encouraged by London's insatiable demand for meat, milk and other dairy products, and by the easy transportation of fresh produce along the Great Eastern Railway. Dairying was assisted by the migration to Essex of dairy farmers from Scotland, and to a lesser degree, Devon and Somerset, who were attracted by large farms and low rentals.[13] Others turned to market gardening, mushroom and seed growing, and horse rearing as ways of surviving. Yet other farmers and landowners

[8] ECS 25 May 1901; 22 July 1905; J. Charles Cox, *Essex* (1909), 28; *Kelly's Directory* 1914.

[9] P. Wormell, *Essex Farming 1900-2000* (1999), 12.

[10] ECS 13 July 1901; Ardleigh W.E.A., *Ardleigh of Yesterday* (n.d.), 9-10.

[11] 1901 census.

[12] ECT 7 July 1906.

[13] E.J.T. Collins, 'The Great Agricultural Depression in South Essex', *Panorama*, Spring 1965, no. 9, 17-18.

followed the example of trade unionists and began to combine and cooperate. Lord Rayleigh and Edward Strutt bought up land cheaply with which to create Lord Rayleigh's Farms, and from 1900 were supplying the London market with milk. By 1914 the firm had 770 milking cows producing an average of 728 gallons a day.[14] Earlier in 1897 a group of farmers led by a Captain Whitmore and backed by Essex's leading landowners and agriculturists like Lord Rayleigh, Edward Strutt and Lord Petre, combined to set up East Anglian Farmers Limited which sold its members' poultry, dairy and market gardening produce at Stratford and Covent Garden. In 1911 its sales amounted to an impressive £160,000.[15]

From the Stour to the Thames the coastline of Essex was dotted with the fishing villages and ports of various sizes which had earned the county its maritime reputation. Although in decline by the early twentieth century, Harwich was still the county's largest and most important port. It had been losing trade for years. The packet services had been transferred to Tilbury in 1832 and attempts to open up a steamship route to Antwerp in the 1850s had failed. Harwich's fortunes were revived by the opening of the Scheldt Navigation in 1863, and the creation of the port at the Hook of Holland in 1893. Unfortunately, the reprieve was only transitory. With little room for expansion on its crowded peninsula, Harwich was deprived of its continental traffic when Parkeston Quay opened in 1883. Competition from Grimsby and Hull after 1880 had led to the end of deep-sea fishing from the port by 1914. Although in decline as a fishing and passenger port, its goods trade was still large. In 1910 it exported almost five million pounds worth of British goods, and over two million pounds of foreign and colonial merchandise. The presence of the Royal Navy, like the army at Colchester, helped sustain Harwich's economy. Situated in a vital position opposite the German coast it was the base for the First and Third Destroyer Flotilla, and for a submarine flotilla.[16] Other ports in Essex paled in comparison with Harwich. Only Tilbury, the site of the Port of London Authority's deep water docks, could claim to deal with anything like a substantial trade. Thames Haven operated a modest cattle transportation business, but Barking's fishing fleet had long since expired. Manningtree and Mistley had benefited by the opening of the Stour Navigation in 1730, but their trade had been badly undercut by the railway, although in 1914 there was still a reasonable business there in grain, timber, milling and coal, and a sizeable malting trade supplying breweries in London and further afield. A large part of the populations of Brightlingsea, Wivenhoe, Rowhedge, Tollesbury, Burnham, and Maldon were engaged in maritime pursuits — fishing, yachting, sail-making, and boat-building and repairing. Brightlingsea, Burnham and Tollesbury also cultivated

14 Sir William Gavin, *Ninety Years of Family Farming: The Story of Lord Rayleigh's and Strutt and Parker Farms* (1967), 96-98, 100.

15 Collins, 'South Essex', 219.

16 B. Carlyon Hughes, *The History of Harwich Harbour* (1939), 86; L.T. Weaver, *The Harwich Story* (1995), 114, 122, 137, 140, 148; L.T. Hughes, *Harwich: Gateway to the Continent* (1990), 75.

the oysters, for which, along with Colchester, they were famed. Each of these fishing villages possessed modest fishing fleets which fished for sprats, soles, and dabs in winter and oysters in spring. In the summer the ships' crews could find employment by crewing yachts or trawling for shrimps, mussels and starfish. In most cases their fishing fleets were in decline. Tollesbury's shrimping fleet had shrunk from one hundred boats to a mere twenty by 1914.[17]

Alongside the ports and fishing villages were the seaside resorts which exploited the sea in a different way. Southend was by far the largest and most popular. The resort was visited by about one hundred and twenty thousand visitors on the August bank holiday weekend in 1910, most of them brought by trains and steamers from London.[18] The 1912 August bank holiday figures show that the number of visitors to Southend was more than fifty per cent higher than at Clacton, five times more than those at Dovercourt/Harwich, fourteen times as many as Walton, and over thirty times the numbers at Frinton.[19] As the holiday business expanded in the late nineteenth and early twentieth centuries, the resident populations of these resorts grew accordingly. Southend's doubled from less than thirty thousand in 1901 to over sixty thousand by 1911. Clacton had a resident population of over forty thousand by the turn of the century. Most of these resorts catered for, some said pandered to, the raucous, lively and sometimes vulgar pursuits of the working classes, although all of them had their share of genteel, middle-class and aspirational families who came to take the air. Dovercourt to a certain extent, but Frinton in particular, attempted very successfully to deter the vulgar by restricting the sort of entertainments which were available. Public houses and popular forms of entertainment were not allowed at Frinton, and on the whole day trippers tended to avoid it, preferring the pleasures of Clacton and Walton instead. Other coastal towns and villages with a seafaring tradition, and lacking the sort of glorious beaches available at Southend or Clacton, had set themselves up as centres of maritime activity rather than as seaside resorts. Yachting was immensely popular at Harwich, Tollesbury, Burnham and Maldon. At Walton the yacht club promoted improvements to the local backwaters by channelling and buoying, which attracted many small craft.[20] The coast's seafaring occupations were celebrated in annual regattas at Clacton, Walton, Harwich, Brightlingsea, Burnham, Maldon and Southend, and a joint regatta at Rowhedge and Wivenhoe.

Although the seaside resort was hugely popular, it was not the only form of entertainment available; rural sports and pastimes still survived and drew crowds. Hare coursing was well attended. Ploughing matches were held at Colchester,

[17] Tollesbury Millenium Publishing Group, *Tollesbury to the Year 2000: The Story of a Village and its People* (1999), 52-3.

[18] S. Everitt, *Southend Seaside Holiday* (1980), 121.

[19] ECT 3 August 1912.

[20] ECS 20 April 1912.

Braintree, Fingringhoe, Chelmsford and Dunmow. The Essex Agricultural Show, first held in 1858, was always a sell-out occasion. Gardening and allotment keeping had become popular working-class pursuits as leisure time increased. In the summer months these horticultural activities spawned a seemingly endless round of flower and root shows and competitions. Almost every Essex village had its own show as horticultural societies proliferated from the 1890s, and entries could often be counted in the hundreds. Horse shows punctuated the year. There were well-known ones at Tolleshunt D'Arcy, the Mid-Essex Show at Brentwood and the South Essex Show at Orsett. Hunting was immensely popular with the wealthy. There were four hunts in the county — the East Essex, the Essex, the Essex and Suffolk and the Essex Union — and there were also the Essex Staghounds and Essex Otter Hounds. Shooting, fishing and fowling were carried on along much of the coastline, where the creeks and marshlands of places like Mersea Island provided ample game. Cycling, swimming and, increasingly, motor, clubs could be found throughout the county. The popularity of golf and tennis was also increasing. There were at least twenty golf clubs in Essex, including those at Romford, Ilford, Colchester, Colne Valley and Frinton. Frinton's annual tennis competition was a highlight of the local sporting and social calendar for the middle classes, and by attracting well-known players it rapidly became well known outside of the county. Ice skating was becoming popular and there were at least three rinks in Essex; at Ilford, Leytonstone and Chelmsford. Yachting was the pursuit of the well-off, but there were also many bowls, quoits and athletic clubs. Cricket was played in every town and village in Essex, and ranged from friendly games to the gentlemanly desire to win in local leagues. At the apex of the game was the Essex County Cricket Club. Unfortunately, the club was not in a strong position in the fifteen years or so before the War. Its performances were poor, with the side finishing in the top half of the table only five times between 1900 and 1914. Attendances were erratic, and with only modest membership the management faced a constant battle to ensure the club's survival. An appeal for membership, in 1910 received a poor response and in 1911 the club was £1,100 in debt and forced to open a 'Shilling Fund' to clear the debts and make ends meet. By 1913 the debt was down to £400, but it was only cleared by the generous action of Charles E. Green, the man responsible for the development of the club's fortunes.[21]

By 1914 football, or 'footer' as it was often called, was already established as the most popular sport in the county. The Essex County Football Association, founded in 1882, had a membership of almost three hundred clubs in 1913-14, although many of its members had been in existence before that date; Forest Club (Leytonstone) was founded in 1859, Upton Park (1866), Leyton (1868), Saffron Walden (1872), Colchester Town (1873), Harwich and Parkeston (1877) and

21 ECC 14 April 1911; D. Lemmon & M. Marshall, *Essex County Cricket Club: The Official History* (1987), 116-148.

Harlow Town (1879).[22] The three best clubs in Essex were the professionals of the Southern League; Leyton, Southend United and West Ham United. Below them came several leagues of comparable status and keen rivalry; the Essex and Suffolk Border League, the North Essex and South Essex Leagues. At the next level down came the town leagues of places like Colchester, Chelmsford and Southend. Colchester and Southend had military leagues, and there were several Thursday leagues which played football on workers' half days off. Attendances at games were sometimes very high, especially matches in the F.A. Cup, Amateur Cup, and even the Essex Senior and Junior Cups.

Less strenuous activities included the theatre, music hall and the increasingly popular cinema, which, although it was very much a novelty, was beginning to rival the former. Cinemas were springing up all over the county. East Ham and Harwich had their Picture Palaces, Clacton its Kinema, Halstead the Electric Kinema, and Leytonstone and Southend their Electric Cinemas. Colchester had two Electric Cinemas which appeared shortly before the War.

Politically, Essex was a largely Conservative county. At the 1910 general election eight constituencies returned Conservative M.P.s, three returned Liberals, and only one, West Ham South, elected a Labour member. In most municipal elections too, the political prizes were generally divided between Conservatives and Liberals. In Colchester the Liberals wrested control of the council from the Conservatives and held it until 1907, when the latter regained control and were still holding it in 1914. The relatively new Independent Labour Party made comparatively little headway in Essex outside of the metropolitan area before the War. At Colchester there was just one Labour councillor in 1914. In most municipal elections in the town Labour candidates were defeated with monotonous regularity, and not just in the more prosperous western part of town. When Ernest Maxted stood as a Labour candidate at Thaxted in the 1913 county council elections, he was defeated — but by only 443 votes to 378, a good showing in the Conservative-dominated town.[23] In the metropolitan area, where greater numbers of working-class families lived in squalid, overcrowded homes, faced uncertain opportunities and existed on low wages, Labour support was stronger. In the West Ham South constituency Keir Hardie was elected in 1892, the first ever working man to be elected to Parliament. Although he was ousted three years later, the trade union leader Will Thorne, having lost in the 1900 election, captured the seat in 1906 and retained it in 1910. These were the Independent Labour Party's only parliamentary successes in pre-war Essex.

The Independent Labour Party offered no serious challenge to the political status quo in Essex and the county's trade unions were too moderate to greatly concern the Conservatives. Desultory attempts were made to organise workers in the clothing,

22 C. Barratt, *The History of Harlow Town F.C.* (1998), 1.

23 R. Groves, *Conrad Noel and the Thaxted Movement: An Adventure in Christian Socialism* (1967), 134.

engineering and machine factories before the War, but they were far from successful and many workers from most sectors were not unionised at all in 1914, particularly outside metropolitan Essex. Strikes were comparatively rare, usually of only a few days duration, and were often settled after some sort of compromise settlement had been agreed. In 1910 a week-long dispute at Paxman in Colchester was settled when the management withdrew the 'speediator', a sort of efficiency expert whose suggestions for the improvement of working practices had upset the men.[24] That same year a similar attempt to enforce 'bonus' or 'piece' work at the Hoffmann Manufacturing Company of Chelmsford led to a one-day strike.[25] In 1912 Lake and Elliott's works at Earls Colne were shut by a week-long strike, also over piece work, and the Crittall Manufacturing Company's five hundred men walked out when the management followed Paxman's example and appointed a speediator.[26] Mumford of Colchester was closed when the workers struck after a pay demand was rejected.[27] In 1913 the accumulation of minor grievances, exacerbated by the management's rejection of a pay demand precipitated another strike at Hoffmann; the entire work force of two thousand men, boys and girls coming out on strike for a fortnight.[28] Samuel Courtauld and Company's workers also went on strike in 1913, the 375 workers at the silk mills coming out in sympathy for thirty-six of their colleagues who were sent home for disaffection regarding the imposition of new prices and working conditions. The strike ended when the firm conceded to most of their demands.[29] Agricultural workers in north-west Essex went on strike in the spring and summer of 1914, when farmers, alarmed at the increasing numbers of farm labourers who were joining the Workers' Union or Agricultural Labourers' Union, gave their men an ultimatum — leave the union or face dismissal. When some labourers were locked-out, the men left work and the lock-out developed into a strike. Attempts by the men to prevent imported, blackleg labourers from taking their places provoked threatening responses by farmers, led to police involvement and the countryside had an air of civil strife about it. The dispute was unresolved in August 1914 and was only brought to an abrupt halt by the outbreak of war. Trade unions in Essex were beginning to flex their industrial muscles, and with a measure of success, but in 1914 few employers were greatly concerned.

Although church attendances had been in decline (in the Church of England for one hundred and fifty years), organised religion was still an important force, both nationally and locally. Society demanded high moral standards of its citizens, particularly those holding public office, and these standards were set by the churches.

[24] A.F.J. Brown, *Colchester 1815-1914* (1980), 139-147; ECT 3, 10 May 1910.

[25] EEC 25 March 1910.

[26] ECC 19 April, 7 June 1912.

[27] ECT 4 May 1912.

[28] ECC 11 April 1913.

[29] ECT 22, 29 November 1913.

Essex catered for almost every Christian denomination. The Church of England as the established religion had a church in nearly every village and several in large towns like Colchester and Southend. The metropolitan parishes and boroughs were bursting with Anglican places of worship: East and West Ham had four each, Canning Town had thirteen churches and mission churches, Walthamstow possessed sixteen. Protestant Nonconformity was well represented in the county. There were eighteen Quaker meeting houses, forty-three Baptist chapels, ninety-one Congregationalist churches, and roughly the same number of Methodists — Wesleyans, Primitive and United. The twenty-four Roman Catholic churches formed part of the Diocese of Brentwood. The Plymouth Brethren had eleven congregations, the Salvation Army was particularly strong in the metropolitan area, and there were Unitarian, Swedenborgian, and Christadelphian communities. The Peculiar People, a Christian sect, had developed in the south-west of the county. At Forest Gate, Manor Park and Southend there were Jewish communities.

For Anglicans and Protestant Nonconformists the ten years before the War, much longer in the case of the Church of England, had been turbulent ones, wracked with controversy and bitterness. Since the mid-nineteenth century the Church of England had been torn apart by ritualism, a dispute focussing around, but not exclusively concerned with, the appropriateness and legality of liturgical changes made by some clergy. Opponents of ritualist clergy accused them of undermining the Reformation and threatening the Church of England with Roman Catholic practices and doctrine. The controversy was deep-seated, bitter and very public. Parts of Essex were strongholds of the Anglo-Catholic Party, as supporters of ritualism came to be known, and from the 1890s their actions in churches throughout the county led to vigorous protests from their opponents. Colchester was a particularly strong centre of Anglo-Catholicism and the case of C.C. Naters caused a public scandal, but Conrad Noel, Vicar of Thaxted, was just as unashamed and open in his support of the Anglo-Catholic cause.[30] Shortly before the War Anglicans were also enraged by the Liberal Government's proposal to disestablish the Church of Wales, an Anglican institution, and protest meetings were held throughout the county during 1911-13.

Protestant Nonconformity too had been drawn into controversy and civil disobedience during the decade before the War. The Education Act (1902) swept away the old school boards, and placed all elementary schools under local government control. Anglicans and Roman Catholics were delighted as they were relieved of a huge financial burden. Yet, Nonconformists were appalled that their rates would contribute to the support of denominational schools. A policy of civil disobedience was adopted as the only way to resist the new law. Many Nonconformists refused to pay their rates and some found themselves in the magistrates' courts, where they continued to be hauled until at least 1912.

30 See Chapter 3.

Newspaper reports suggest that there was genuine local concern about the rising international tensions in the decade or so before 1914. In 1912 the *Essex County Standard* voiced fears of a possible Armageddon, portraying Europe in fairly typical contemporary terms as "an open powder-magazine beneath a shower of sparks."[31] Captain Horatio Frasier Kemble, the new High Sheriff of Essex in 1912, expressed what must have been the anxieties of many people when he said:

> We live today in an age of unrest, of wars and rumours of wars, an age in which events move so rapidly that it is quite impossible to predict the future. The dangers which beset Old England are as great, if not greater, than any she has hitherto encountered in all the centuries of her history.

He concluded by warning that "the growing power of Germany is a fact which the blindest of us cannot ignore."[32] Colonel Neville Tufnell, inspecting the Essex Territorials at Braintree on Territorial Sunday in 1912, urged preparedness when he told them:

> I earnestly hope the time may not come when you have to put your shoulders to the wheel, and do the duty your country requires. But you must be ready, and the time may not be far distant, when the whole of you will have to come out to defend your shores.[33]

As it became increasingly clear that Germany, rather than the old rivals France and Russia, was likely to be the foe in any future war, Essex's geographical position opposite the German coast assumed a new significance. Evelyn Wood, the war hero who was living at Wakes Colne Hall, wrote shortly after the War began of his pre-war efforts to prepare the nation:

> I don't fear invasion but consider we should be ready. For five years I have inculcated the necessity of preparedness to the First London Division of Territorials with I am glad to say, conspicuous success — The curse of our country has been the refusal of the people to believe in the German menace.[34]

The increasing use of the term 'German Ocean' instead of North Sea was a vivid

31 ECS 25 October 1912.

32 ECC 29 March 1912.

33 ECC 7 June 1912.

34 ECS 15 August 1914

indication of East Coast anxieties. Writers and playwrights exploited these new fears to produce dramatic and even lurid portrayals of the perilous position of Essex. Major Guy du Maurier's play *An Englishman's Home*, was described as "a powerful exposition of national danger and responsibility." Set in the fictitious village of Wickham, it featured an enemy invasion of the county. The main character was a village resident, a Mr Brown, who was an ardent anti-militarist. However, as the enemy invasion materialised he took up his gun and killed some of the invaders, before he was himself shot dead on his own lawn.[35] The play's moral, the folly of being unprepared, was presumably not lost on its audiences. In 1910 a similar story appeared in *Pearson's Magazine* which described a German invasion and the capture of Colchester. The invaders were shown being assisted by thousands of German agents operating as waiters and tradesmen in Harwich.[36] Two years later, an unidentified 'Essex Man' wrote 'Guns Front! A Story of Essex Territorials.' This too featured a German invasion set in 1925. Incredibly, on this occasion the invading force of one hundred thousand German troops was landed by submarine.[37]

The growing misgivings about German intentions seemed to reach fever pitch in 1909-10 when the actions of some people were in danger of generating what can only be described as an atmosphere of war-hysteria. In January 1909 the *Essex County Standard* reported that a group of cyclists at Walton "were agents of a continental power." It warned that there were some five thousand German secret agents operating on the South and East Coasts, all reporting on England's defences.[38] In May there was a widely believed story in circulation about a mysterious airship hovering over the Essex coast at night which was spying for the Germans. The airship was supposed to have lost part of its superstructure on which was the inscription 'Muller Fabrik, Bremen', which had been reportedly found by a Mr Egerton Fern. The Admiralty was said to have taken possession of the piece of metal and nothing more was heard of it.[39] Egerton Fern clearly had a vivid imagination, for just ten days later he claimed that his house had been spied on for five hours by foreign-looking men.[40] That same spring another Essex man, Charles Lowe, was reported to have spent his entire Easter holiday scouring the county for German spies. Although he found neither spies nor airships, he managed to get the *Daily Chronicle* to publish his story entitled 'A Real Invasion', in which he described how Essex agriculture was being taken over by Scottish farmers.[41] In the following year the alarm was raised when a German student visited the county to carry out

[35] ECS 6 February 1909.

[36] ECS 6 February 1910.

[37] ECS 12 January 1912.

[38] ECS 23, 30 January 1909.

[39] ECS 15, 22 May 1909.

[40] ECS 22 May 1909.

[41] ECS 22 May 1909.

research into the Essex dialect.[42] It was inevitably assumed that there could be no innocent explanation for this. There were similar fears in the spring of 1911 when a German couple, on holiday in Essex for two months, had the temerity to ask for a map of the villages around Walton.[43]

Preparations were being made should war come. No secret was made of the army's military manoeuvres in the autumn of 1904, manoeuvres that were watched by thousands of civilians in north-east Essex. The army successfully landed an 'invasion' force at Clacton, which made its way inland and 'captured' Colchester.[44] Military units launched a similar 'attack' on Harwich in June 1909, and Essex Territorials were involved in another invasion exercise between Harwich and Ipswich in August of the next year.[45] In these last few years of peace there were frequent rumours about Government proposals to strengthen the county's defences. In the autumn of 1909 there was talk of plans to build a naval dock at Tollesbury which coincided with rumours that the Midland Railway Company was about to begin building a new railway line to the port.[46] At least the rumours that Harwich was to be developed into a more substantial naval base turned out to be entirely realistic.[47] In 1912 there were even plans, short-lived as it turned out, to create a military aviation station at Colchester. According to the report, the plans involved the building of accommodation for twenty-five airships sited near the Abbey Field; Royal Flying Corps recruits were to be trained there, and it was planned that scouting flights from the station would patrol the coast.[48]

However, the growing anxieties of these years did not mean that all military measures and defensive precautions were universally popular. In 1909 the chairman of the Braintree Conservative Club, Major G. Barker, expressed his eagerness for war in no uncertain terms:

> I understand that the Germans mean to come and have a go at us as soon as possible, and we must be prepared to kick them out. I understand that the German officers are wishing for the great day when they are to come here, and they actually have the cheek to drink to that great day. I only hope they will come and we shall wipe them out entirely — the German Emperor amongst them.[49]

[42] ECS 15 October 1910.

[43] ECS 22 April 1911.

[44] ECT 10 September 1904.

[45] ECS 6, 13 August 1910.

[46] ECS 9 October 1909.

[47] ECS 28 January 1911, 8 March 1912; ECC 17 January 1913.

[48] ECT 7 September 1912.

[49] ECT 29 May 1909.

The *Essex County Telegraph* dismissed the Major's tirade as 'pestilent nonsense', and dismissed the possibility of an Anglo-German war as "the fancies sometimes entertained in unbalanced minds." That 1909 was the year when Essex was replete with invasion and spy scares might explain the *Telegraph*'s impatience with such comments. The *Telegraph*'s conservative counterpart, the *Essex County Standard*, was equally scathing about the anti-German hysteria gripping the county that year, rejecting out of hand the absurd idea "that Germany has at the present moment any actually matured designs of a sinister character with regard to this country."[50] Shortly afterwards the Colchester branch of the Independent Labour Party criticised the *Daily Mail* for its sensational anti-German articles.[51] Some of the people of Wivenhoe, whilst perhaps not without foreign anxieties in these years, were far more appalled at the prospect of having an explosives factory built in their midst at Lower Lodge Farm. When plans were made public in May 1913, there was a stormy protest meeting, followed by a series of further meetings. Speakers at protest meetings were heckled by those who were in favour of the factory, which would have created jobs for unemployed locals. Those against the factory feared that the local oyster industry would become polluted. Others expressed the worry that in a German invasion, which would inevitably be on the nearby coast, the Germans would first loot the factory and then use the stolen explosives to destroy their main target, Colchester.[52] As it turned out their fears proved groundless. The Lexden and Winstree Justices rejected the application, largely on the petition of Colchester Town Council, which had likewise feared for its oyster beds.[53]

There were other sorts of preparations for a possible war being made in these years. As in every other county, Essex men joined the Territorial Army. This had been created in 1907 by Richard Haldane, Minister for War in Asquith's Liberal administration. Its aim was to create a voluntary military force of county associations, each capable of defending its own territory while the regular army fought abroad.

The Essex Association aimed at a maximum strength of some seven thousand officers and men, but rising international tensions were apparently not a sufficient incentive for men to join, and during these years it consistently failed to achieve a full complement. In 1909 it was 600 men short; the next year 927 men were needed, and by 1911 there was an increased shortfall of 1,285. Only in 1913 does it seem to have achieved its hoped-for size, with a strength of 242 officers and 7,108 other ranks.[54] The difficulties of attracting volunteers led to regular criticism in the press of towns which were not pulling their weight, and produced calls for

[50] ECS 20 March 1909.

[51] ECT 19 February 1910.

[52] ECS 8 May 1909.

[53] ECS 5 June 1909.

[54] ECS 27 February 1909, 9 December 1910, 9 December 1911; ECC 5 September 1913.

conscription.[55] In reality the time involved in territorial work often meant a loss of earnings for some volunteers. Few employers were as generous as the Colchester-based Essex and Suffolk Fire Office, which encouraged its men to volunteer by allotting them between seven to ten days with full pay for territorial duties, in addition to their ordinary holidays.[56] Older ex-soldiers joined the National Reserve to show their readiness and willingness once again to serve their country. At Colchester 840 joined and 120 enlisted at Witham in 1912, when speakers talked forthrightly about the German menace.

The National Service League, which had branches throughout the county, aimed to bring all young people to a better state of physical preparedness and to raise awareness of the danger of war. It had been established by Lord Roberts in the early years of the century, at a time when there were fears that the physical well-being of young people was deteriorating. It also coincided with the beginnings of fears about Germany's growing military and naval strength. Throughout 1910-14 it waged a patient and determined campaign to achieve its aims. It preached the inevitability of a war with Germany and the need for preparedness, especially among young people. To achieve this it advocated a national system of military service as a means of improving the physical and moral efficiency of the nation. The Essex branch of the league had powerful patrons. The Lord Lieutenant, the Earl of Warwick, was its president, and its vice-presidents included the Bishop of Colchester.[57]

Rising international tensions, combined with the very public campaigns of the National Service League and the county Territorial Association, alongside press coverage of the rather eccentric activities of some local people, all helped to keep the possibility of war, and war against Germany in particular, in the public eye for several years before 1914.

Therefore when war broke out suddenly over the August bank holiday of that year, the people of Essex were not entirely surprised.

[55] ECS 16 July 1910.

[56] ECS 27 February 1909.

[57] ECS 23 July 1910.

"The Great Pinnacle of Sacrifice" 1914-1918

CHAPTER TWO

The Start: August 1914

GREAT BRITAIN DECLARES WAR ON GERMANY.

Great Britain has been forced to declare war with Germany through her refusal to respect the neutrality of Belgium.

The British ultimatum expired at midnight on Tuesday, and British and German Fleets face one another in the North Sea, and an engagement may follow at once.

Sir John R. Jellicoe, K.C.B., has supreme command of the Home Fleets as Admiral. Rear-Admiral Charles E. Madden is his Chief of the Staff.

German troops actually entered Belgium on Tuesday.

The Government has taken over the control of all the railways of the Kingdom, and is preparing a scheme to control distribution of food supplies.

The beginning of the War is reported in the weekly *Essex County Standard.*
(ERO: ECS 8 August 1914)

IT HAD BEEN a beautiful summer. Except for a few isolated days of rain, the weather had been glorious. May and June had been exceptionally dry and there had been only one wet day in the whole of July. Denys Yonge, the Vicar of Boreham, a man well into his seventies, found the oppressive summer heat wave intolerable. "All cold drinks were in vain", he confided to his diary, "Would there be some refreshing rain."[1] August was just as sweltering and many farmers were destined to complete their harvest well before the end of the month.[2] The drought was so severe that observers noted that apples, pears and acorns were falling prematurely from the trees.[3] The bank holiday weather of the first few days of August was, with the exception of a light shower or two, equally good.

British summertime pursuits were in full swing. Two dozen or more horticultural societies were preparing for their annual shows on bank holiday Saturday or Monday. Over two thousand of Chelmsford's elementary school children were taking part in their annual sports on the Recreation Ground, there was a hospital fete and gala at Romford and a huge turnout at Maldon's popular Marine Lake for an aquatic display, and later for the Essex Junior Water Polo Championship.[4] At Tollesbury the German Kaiser's yacht, the *Meteor*, was being worked on at the shipyard; its imperial owner destined to never again walk upon its decks.[5] On 28 July the Colchester Archaeological Society took advantage of the weather and embarked on excursions to the Southend area. Frinton's annual and highly esteemed lawn tennis championships were concluding, and the Orsett Horse Show was under way further south. A few ventured further afield under the hot summer sun. The Colchester Touring Club had just completed its annual visit to the German town of Rothenburg on the River Tauber. They arrived back in England on bank holiday Monday, fortunately just one day before war was declared. Trains throughout the county were packed over the weekend; the Great Eastern Railway offered excursions to Maldon, Colchester, Harwich and Felixstowe, while the London, Tilbury and Southend section of the Midland Railway sold cheap third-class tickets to Southend from Romford, Dagenham, Tilbury and Purfleet. During the bank holiday weekend Clacton was visited by between thirty and forty thousand people, the vast majority of them disgorged from trains and coastal steamers. The number of visitors to exclusive and aloof Frinton increased slightly, although at both Brightlingsea and Walton numbers were about twenty per cent down on 1913. As well as holidaymakers, Clacton's population was temporarily increased by the presence of about a thousand men of the Essex Territorials forming

1 ERO 358/27, The diary of the Rev. Denys Yonge 1914-19, 29 June 1914.

2 ECS, 9 January 1915.

3 J. Drury, *A History of Felsted* (1999).

4 ECC 7 August 1914.

5 *Tollesbury to the Year 2000*, 243.

the Essex Territorial Infantry Brigade, who were holding their annual camp near Great Clacton church.[6]

The theatres were busy providing bank holiday entertainment. The Electric Theatre in Colchester's Headgate had a three-day run of *The False Magistrate*; the Vaudeville on Mersea Road presented *The Lighthouse Keepers*, a sea drama. The Brentwood Parade Cinema was showing, perhaps appropriately in view of the events which were unfolding, *Locked in Death*, a Russian military drama.[7] Entertainment of a different sort was being provided in the Moot Hall at Colchester. Parishioners of St James's, unhappy at the Anglo-Catholic practices introduced by the rector, C.C. Naters, had brought a case against him. Their aim was to force him to remove all the ritualistic trappings of Anglo-Catholicism which he had placed in the church, and their protests had resulted in a Consistory Court being held in the Town Hall. Naters and his ritualistic ways had been universally loathed by the more Protestant-minded wing of the Anglican Church since his arrival at St James's in 1895. The court case was considered by some to be an outrageous revelation of the disunity within the Church of England, and the reporting of it caused something of a scandal.[8]

In the Thaxted area the strike by farm labourers demanding a wage increase was entering its sixth week. Wandering strikers roamed the area attempting to dissuade the imported strikebreakers from Cambridgeshire from continuing with their work, and harassing any they found working in the fields. The local police, their numbers boosted by the arrival of sixty police constables from around the county, were equally determined to foil them. Farmers carried guns and burning hayricks lit the rural skyline at night. The Bishop of Chelmsford offered his services as arbitrator but was politely rejected. At the end of July, Sylvia Pankhurst, the well-known suffragette, visited the area to defend the farm labourers' fight for social justice. She addressed a crowd of two thousand from a car which flew the red flag.[9] However, interest in the both the Naters scandal and the Thaxted dispute was about to be submerged in the greatest national crisis since the Napoleonic Wars, as Europe was propelled to the edge of war and beyond.

Since the assassination of Archduke Franz Ferdinand, heir to the Austrian throne, in Sarajevo on 28 June, the possibility of a war in Europe, which later became the threat of a general European war involving Great Britain, had hung over the summer like a dark shadow. Austria's declaration of war on Serbia on Tuesday, 28 July made war more likely, and as events unfolded, Germany's demand for free-passage for her troops through Belgium, delivered on the evening of 2 August, made it less and less likely that Britain would be able to stand aside from the impending war. Indeed, war increasingly occupied people's thoughts in the last days of July. The *East Essex*

6 CG 29 July, 5 August 1914.

7 ECC 24 July 1914.

8 CG 29 July 1914.

9 ECC 3, 31 July 1914.

Advertiser noted that "holiday making and the contemplation of war are rather incongruous topics and yet this is the unfortunate position at the present moment."[10] Newspaper vendors were in great demand with "people chasing and fairly besieging the local agents for papers."[11] The *Colchester Gazette* went even further, asserting that "[the war] has become the all absorbing topic. Never were Colchester people so obsessed with one subject as on Wednesday, when they awoke to find that England was at war with Germany".[12]

The first indication of how serious the international situation was occurred on 29 July, in the middle of afternoon tea and tennis at the weekly garden party at the Colchester Officers' Club. A bugler sounded the alarm, followed by assembly and the announcement of mobilisation. The officers at the garden party abandoned their teacups and were en route to their headquarters within the hour. A former Mayor of Colchester, A.M. Jarmin, added with true literary licence that "the scene was perhaps even more dramatic than that at the Duchess of Richmond's ball on the eve of Waterloo".[13]

Within hours four regiments — the First Somerset Light Infantry, First Rifle Brigade, First East Lancashires and First Hampshires — had departed from Colchester. That same night the men of the Essex Fortress Royal Engineers were called from their homes by messengers who ordered them to report immediately to their headquarters and from thence to Harwich. Mobilisation orders were issued at Southend on the evening of 29 July, and local troops were ordered to return at once to barracks. Between two and three hundred men and non-commissioned officers were out at liberty and needed rounding up.[14] Soon there were armed guards with fixed bayonets posted at the garrison entrance. At Shoeburyness and the Nore there was a great deal of naval activity with warships entering and leaving harbour, or dropping anchor off the coast.[15] Even small towns witnessed dramatic scenes. On 4 August at Braintree the twenty men of the Special Reserve in 'H' Company, the Eighth Essex Cycling Corps, cycled out of the town towards Colchester, cheered by a large crowd.[16] The previous evening, Harold Bartholomew had returned home from a cycle ride with his latest girlfriend to find a long buff envelope waiting for him. The message it contained said starkly: "Report 9 a.m. The Square, Braintree. Full order." Later that day he found himself one of a number of men of H Company stationed along the cliffs, beaches and marshes from Walton to Tollesbury. Companies E, F and G guarded the coastline from Harwich to Walton, and A, B and

10 EEA 1 August 1914.

11 EEA 8 August 1914.

12 CG 12 August 1914.

13 *Colchester War Memorial Souvenir: The Great War 1914-18* (1923), ed. E.A. Hunt, 57.

14 SST 30 July 1914.

15 SST 6 August 1914.

16 ECC 31 July 1914.

C Companies from Maldon to Shoeburyness. There they waited for German invaders to cross the sea.[17] At least one man was lucky to arrive at all. Commander Warren, commander of a submarine based at Harwich, was recalled to duty on 27 July. Driving too fast that night around the roads at Witham, he overturned his car and was fortunate to emerge with only cuts and bruises. He quickly procured another car and was able to resume the last leg of his journey.

There was drama too at Clacton. The Royal Garrison Artillery Band had played at the Pavilion for the week preceding bank holiday Saturday; they had then been replaced by the Royal Marines. However, their afternoon performance on bank holiday Monday was brought to a premature end when the bandmaster, W.I. Newton, received a telegram ordering the band to report back to its depot for mobilisation.

Those who were perceptive enough could see the slide to war; Denys Yonge confided despairingly to his diary on 1 August, "Bella, horrida, bella ... smite, wound, hell, ruin."[18] Others were close enough to these dramatic events to be able to see European peace disintegrating around them. E.G. Pretyman, the Conservative M.P. for Chelmsford, wrote to his friend the Hon. Alwyne Greville, apologising for his inability to attend a function at Danbury. He wrote that

> I have just received an urgent summons to the House of Commons, and must, of course, be there. No doubt we are to vote money and authorise mobilisation. As Germany has attacked Russia and France, I don't see how we can honourably keep out of it ... the odds look in our favour.[19]

News that war had been declared had reached most of Essex by the evening of 4 August. At East Ham the mayor read the royal proclamation declaring war at midnight and posted it outside the Town Hall.[20] At Southend on the evening of 4 August a large crowd, several hundred strong, gathered outside the windows of the offices of the *Southend Standard*. Some cheered loudly, but the *Standard*'s reporter found that on the whole there was a feeling of 'deep anxiety' in the locality:

> Those who watched the faces of the crowd as they scanned the news contained in the windows of the *Standard*'s offices were struck by the absence of any feeling of elation or satisfaction. There was an air of solemnity about as if the issues were too great for levity. There was nothing of the "mafficking" spirit, no horseplay.[21]

17 ERO T/Z 25/625.

18 ERO D/DU 358/27, 1 August 1914.

19 ECC 1 January 1915.

20 A. Stokes, *East Ham: From Village to Corporation*, (1922), 137.

21 SST 6 August 1914.

This gloomy atmosphere was confirmed by Father Patrick McKenna, the Roman Catholic priest of Westcliff-on-Sea, who clearly expected the worst. On 1 August he wrote in his diary, "Awful suspense awaiting news of General European War." Two days later, following the German violation of Belgian neutrality, he noted that "neutral gloom hangs on us all."[22] However, Southend's regulars, as they marched through the town to its railway stations, exhibited more good humour and bravado. "We're twenty-one today, we'll make the Kaiser pay", they sang through streets which were packed with crowds, who, having recovered their nerve, were cheering with gusto. "It's a short way to bloomin' Germany", sang the soldiers to the tune of 'It's a Long Way to Tipperary'. Scenes of "indescribable enthusiasm" greeted them when they arrived at Southend Victoria station.[23] Throughout much of East London though there was said to be "a distinct lack of the accustomed hilarity" over the bank holiday weekend.[24] At Westcliff Patrick McKenna's mood grew blacker as the War progressed in earnest during August. On 20 August he confided a more personal, almost petulant, note to his diary, complaining, "Black Week. My holiday knocked out and our Bazaar abandoned." The next day he claimed that an eclipse of the sun had intensified the "general gloom" which afflicted the local population.[25]

Many Essex people were on holiday when war was declared, some at the county's seaside resorts, others further afield. As news filtered through the county during Thursday, 4 August, Helen Dixon, her husband and four children, walked the four miles from the rather isolated village of Hutton to Brentwood, to see if the rumours of war were true. That same day Sam Ratcliff, who was walking on Sheerness Pier, saw a group of young women approaching. Some were silent, others were crying, a few were very animated and clearly overwrought. They were the wives of sailors who had been disappointed that their husbands had not been granted leave prior to their ships weighing anchor. They had just waved goodbye as the ships of the Home Fleet steamed out to sea.[26]

Meanwhile the Fifth Essex Territorial Infantry Brigade had begun its two weeks of annual training at Clacton on Monday, 27 July. Four days later their adjutants were called to headquarters to receive their standing mobilisation orders. On Sunday, 2 August the men who had attended the camp during the first week went home and were replaced by a fresh contingent. The newcomers' stay was rudely cut short the next day, when at 4 a.m. the men were ordered to strike tents. Their red coats were packed and sent for storage, not to see the light of day again during the coming conflict. The Seventh Battalion left for Walthamstow to await orders, the Sixth departed for West Ham and Southend, and the Fifth, originally ordered to proceed to

22 Diary of Father Patrick McKenna 1859-1937, 1, 3 August 1914, held at Brentwood Diocesan Archive.

23 SST 6 August 1914.

24 BA 8 August 1914.

25 McKenna diary, 20, 21 August 1914.

26 ERO T/Z 25/618.

Chelmsford, had its orders countermanded and at 3 p.m. headed for Dovercourt. The Fourth Battalion left Clacton at 3 p.m. and marched the seventeen miles to Harwich in five and a half hours where it was cheered through the streets and showered with sweets and fruit by excited onlookers. With the Harwich naval flotilla making steam in the harbour there was something of an air of expectancy in the town. That night at 11 p.m. mobilisation papers were issued to all ranks. Those not present were called to the colours and the Essex Battalion was thus put on a war footing.

The Fifth Essex were hurriedly allotted areas along a pre-arranged defensive line west of Dovercourt and worked on those defences for several days. Those men left at Clacton experienced the first invasion panic of the War. At 11.30 p.m. on 4 August they were rousted from their sleep in order to repel a supposed German raid nearby. Each man hurriedly dressed, was issued with twenty rounds of ball cartridge, and rushed to a point two miles west of Clacton. There they remained until 3 a.m. The invasion not having materialised they were ordered to break camp. Within hours three special trains shipped them back to their various headquarters along the Great Eastern line. When the regiment's commanding officer, Colonel J.M. Welch, arrived home at Great Dunmow, he received a telegram ordering the regiment to return to Harwich for immediate embarkation.[27]

The Sixth Battalion had meanwhile been mobilised at its West Ham headquarters. Having arrived back from Clacton on 4 August they were immediately dismissed to their homes for what was to prove their last peacetime visit to their families. A telegram arrived at 8 p.m. that night ordering the battalion to parade at 8 a.m. the following day. That same day £5,000 was paid to the men in wages; post office clerks were in attendance to help the transmission of the money to the men's families. The regimental ammunition reserve was distributed (one hundred rounds per man) and identity discs were issued. On the afternoon of 5 August the regiment entrained at Plaistow for Shoeburyness. On the way detachments were dropped off at the Thames Haven oil works and the Coalhouse Fort. The Seventh Battalion, which had mobilised at Walthamstow, moved across the border into Suffolk on 7 August. Seven of its companies were stationed at the Landguard Fort and in Felixstowe, and two at Harwich.[28]

The Essex Yeomanry was at Ipswich when war was declared. It was at full strength with twenty-seven officers and 441 men. The regiment volunteered for overseas duty although it was not selected for the task until 12 November. On the 29 November it left by train from Ipswich for Southampton, and having crossed the Channel the regiment disembarked at Le Havre on 1 December. The War had started in earnest for the volunteers of Essex.[29]

The pace of military preparations in the county began to quicken. The Colchester

27 ECC 7 August 1914.

28 J.W. Burrows, *The Essex Regiment: The Essex Territorial Infantry Brigade* (1932), 29-30.

29 J.W. Burrows, *The Essex Regiment: The Essex Yeomanry* (1925), 84.

engineering firm of Davey and Paxman received what was in effect their first war order on 1 August, three days before Britain entered the conflict. The Government, sensing the worst, asked the company to rush through a power plant for a wireless station in Egypt, then a British possession, to complete a crucial chain of communication. The firm's workers laboured day and night to complete it. Immediately the War began the Admiralty took over the crucial Marconi Company.[30] After 4 August the port of Harwich was practically closed. All vessels entering or leaving the harbour had to do so between sunrise and sunset and only under certain conditions. Ship owners and local agents had to provide arrival times and give details of the appearance of their vessels to the harbour authorities, and the harbour master's orders were now supreme. All Harwich and Dovercourt were declared to be part of the so-called 'Fortress' area and were placed under martial law. Orders issued by Brigadier-General C.R. Brookes, the commander of Harwich's defences, warned civilians not to use roads, footpaths or fields within one hundred yards of the high water mark between sunset and sunrise. Anyone found there, or on the seashore, during those hours was liable to be shot on sight.[31] Further south, Foulness Island was quickly closed to all except those living there.[32]

At Tilbury the Royal Dublin Fusiliers had been guarding the docks three days before war was declared. The pierhead was manned by a machine gun crew and a six-pounder anti-aircraft gun. The guns of the nearby Coalhouse Fort were manned by eighty-five territorial soldiers, and guns were also in place at Purfleet to protect the huge powder magazine there. Within days of the War starting, a huge tented camp had been built at Purfleet and on the marshes to the west to house the thousands of troops who were flooding in daily. In the event of a German assault up the Thames, a large force of soldiers was in position at East Tilbury. The vitally important Thames Haven oil works and the Kynochtown explosives factory were also under heavy military guard. The inhabitants of several local houses were removed and their properties demolished, so that in the event of fighting the military would have a clear view of the river. In Tilbury docks civilian ships were undergoing conversion to military use or were being armed. The Orient Company liner S.S. *Ophir* was being converted into a hospital ship, as were the S.S. *Oxfordshire* and S.S. *China*.[33]

In north-east Essex military guards were placed on the two railway bridges over the River Stour between Manningtree and Bentley, and also at Marriage's flour mill, the central post office and the Corporation Water Tower in Colchester. At Clacton on 30 July, a seaplane landed on the beach and remained for several hours, its occupants using the nearby coastguard station as a lookout post. The following day a naval

30 W.J. Baker, *A History of the Marconi Company* (1971), 159.

31 HDS 8 August 1914.

32 SST 13 August 1914.

33 R. Reynolds, *Thurrock and the Great War: The Story of the People of Thurrock during the Great War 1914-18* (1998), 9-11, 13, 16-17.

lighter anchored off the pier and its crew began unloading military equipment. As at Tilbury, there were already military pickets at both the entrance to, and at the end of, the pier. The newly created Royal Flying Corps (R.F.C.) had no permanent aerodromes in Essex at the outbreak of war, but the county's proximity to the German coast meant that this soon changed. A detachment of the R.F.C. set up on Clacton's seafront, on West Beach below Marine Parade West. The coastguard station at the Martello Tower became the R.F.C.'s headquarters with a seaplane landing area located on the foreshore at the end of the sea wall to the west of the pier. The base was officially opened on 2 August as one of two substations to the Royal Naval Air Station at Grain in Kent, the R.F.C.'s advanced operational base created to patrol the Thames Estuary and provide air defence for the naval bases at Sheerness and Chatham. On 3 August three Admiralty Type 74 seaplanes arrived as the first detachment, with five pilots on strength.[34] Other coastal preparations occurred which tempted the *East Essex Advertiser* into historical comparisons of a poetic nature:

> Not since the far away days of the Armada, when the men of Brightlingsea faced the Spaniards so nobly and so well, has such a stirring time been experienced on the coasts of the narrow seas.[35]

In fact the only Germans who set foot in Essex in these early days were two unfortunate airmen, Sub-Lieutenant Kaie Wilhelm Kustzn and Mechanic Fritz Otto Grantz. They had been forced to ditch in the North Sea when their hydroplane developed mechanical difficulties, and there they had floated ignominiously for twenty hours until picked up by a Royal Navy vessel. Unabashed, they put on a brave face and although prisoners of war and under military escort they sauntered, apparently unconcerned, through the streets of Harwich, each smoking a cigarette.[36]

It was also through Essex that the last diplomatic formalities were conducted following the outbreak of war. At 9.45 a.m. on Thursday, 6 August, Prince Lichnowsky, the German ambassador in London, his wife and embassy officials, arrived at Parkeston Quay in a special train from Liverpool Street station. Ten large lorries had transported the staff's luggage to the station; the rest of the staff and a few stranded German tourists were ferried there in six motor-omnibuses. At Harwich the ambassador emerged from the train, his wife walking alongside him carrying a small poodle. Walking past a guard of honour formed by the Rifle Brigade, he raised his soft grey travelling hat in response to their salute, and looking

[34] CG 5, 12 August 1914; P.A. Doyle, *Fields of the First: A History of Aircraft Landing Grounds in Essex during the First World War* (1997), 24-26.

[35] EEA 8 August 1914.

[36] HDS 5 September 1914.

"the picture of sadness", he embarked for Germany on the steamer *St Petersburg*.[37] On the evening of the following day the same steamer returned from Germany and brought home the British ambassador in Berlin, Sir Edward Goschen. His arrival at Harwich was accompanied by a large number of destroyers and torpedo boats; a large crowd cheered and on the jetty, true to the spirit of the times, a band played 'Auld Lang Syne', 'God Save the King', 'Rule Britannia', and the 'Marseillaise'. These esteemed gentlemen were rather more fortunate than R.H. Whitcombe, the poor Bishop of Colchester. Holidaying in Switzerland, he was hurrying home through France after the outbreak of war when he was arrested as a spy by a French soldier for some ill-advised use of his camera. His journey was delayed for a couple of days until his identity was verified, thus clearing him of the suspicion of espionage.[38]

The War gathered a momentum of its own. On Monday, 3 August, the day before war was declared, there was a huge demonstration at Hallingbury by the Conservatives of the constituencies of Epping, Saffron Walden, and Hertford. The meeting gave overwhelming support to the Government in whatever action it took "to uphold the country's safety and honour."[39] A meeting in the Margaretting schoolroom resolved to create a 'defence league'.[40] However, there remained isolated pockets of resistance which struggled against being swept along in the War's wake. On the evening of Sunday, 2 August Southend's churches organised a joint service of intercession for peace at the Empire Theatre.[41] At the same time in Chelmsford, with the question of Britain's entry into the War hanging in the balance, a peace meeting was held in front of the Shire Hall. It had been organised by the town's Adult School with the backing of several local churches and was presided over by J. Christy Smith, a local magistrate. We are not told how large the meeting was, but those present agreed to send a message to the Government urging Mr Asquith "to strenuously work for the maintenance of peaceful relations with all European nations and for the preservation of our freedom to act for peace as opportunity offers." The meeting seems to have been a peaceful affair, but the same was not true of a similar meeting held at Saffron Walden. A group opposed to the War and Britain's entry into it attempted to hold a meeting from a car in the market square, but was forced to abandon its plans when a crowd surrounded it and the situation grew ugly.[42] There is no evidence that Colchester's Peace Committee, formed before the War, made any public protest against what was happening.

The so-called 'rush to the colours' began in earnest as soon as war was declared. During August several thousand men were said to have enlisted from Essex, many of

[37] HDS 8 August 1914.

[38] CG 12 August 1914.

[39] ECC 7 August 1914.

[40] ECC 7 August 1914.

[41] SST 13 August 1914.

[42] ECC 7 August 1914; M. White, *Saffron Walden's History: A Chronological Compilation* (1991), 178.

them well before Kitchener's urgent 'Your Country Needs You' appeal.[43] Colchester with its garrison was the largest military town in Essex and Suffolk, and soon volunteers began pouring in from the surrounding towns and villages:

> In the streets were constantly to be seen the men in khaki coming and going. Outside the Drill Halls and the Territorial headquarters there was much bustle and stir. Men came along in motor-cars and carts, on foot and on bicycles, some accompanied by wives or sweethearts.[44]

At St. Botolph station there were scenes of 'great animation' as reservists were shipped away; the goods yard there was illuminated by arc lamps as work went on throughout the night; military departures were often made at night and their destinations kept a secret. At the same time other units arrived ready for shipment to the coast and France. The Essex Royal Horse Artillery returned early from their annual training quarters at Salisbury and by 7 August was camped on the Abbey Field.[45]

Within a week of war breaking out fifty of the six hundred employees of the Crittall Manufacturing Company at Braintree had enlisted, and fifty from the neighbouring firm of Lake and Elliott's Foundry and Albion Works. At Reuben Hunt's Atlas Works at Earls Colne fifty men were called away for service as reservists or in the territorials.[46] Three men of the Clacton lifeboat crew had left on bank holiday Monday to report as members of the Royal Naval Reserve; seven of the town's post office staff had also volunteered within hours of war breaking out. Eighty men, all Special Transport Reservists, were called up from the Seven Kings Omnibus Garage, which necessitated the cutting of twenty-five buses from local routes.[47] On 2 August at Brightlingsea several dozen men of the Royal Naval Reserve had taken trains to join the naval forces at Chatham.[48] In every village men were volunteering. At Tiptree twenty-one had joined up in the first few days; one family was said to have had six men in the forces, and another reputedly had four out of five sons join up.[49] The entire village turned out to see twenty-three territorials depart from Tollesbury.[50] At Burnham one hundred men had volunteered for service within three days of the declaration of war.[51] Five hundred

43 G.J. DeGroot, *Blighty: British Society during the Era of the Great War* (1996), 46.

44 CG 12 August 1914.

45 CG 12 August, ECT 8 August 1914.

46 ECT 22 August 1914.

47 J. Barfoot, *Over Here and Over There: Ilford Aerodromes and Airmen in the Great War* (1998), 3.

48 J.P. Foynes, *Brightlingsea and the Great War 1914-18* (1993), 7.

49 CG 12 August 1914.

50 *Tollesbury to the Year 2000*, 243.

51 BDA 8 August 1914.

men were said to have enlisted within a twelve mile radius of Chelmsford by the end of August. Grays on the other hand, with a population of thirty thousand, was criticised for contributing a mere twenty-eight volunteers.[52] The overheated atmosphere of these early days is easily demonstrated by this report of the send-off given to volunteers from St Osyth:

> Their send off when leaving on Monday was an enthusiastic one, but that word is quite inadequate to express the tremendous feeling shown when on Wednesday at 1.30 the 11 men who had been passed left the Bay Corner in motors kindly lent by Mrs Cowley and Mr Vincent. Apparently nearly all the inhabitants of the village were present and there was an immense amount of cheering as the motors started on their journey to Colchester.[53]

The excitement of these early days was easily matched by the corresponding unease which swept through the civilian population. Rumours spread like wildfire. Robert Bull, the Burnham diarist, reported that he had heard on good authority that seventy trainloads of Russian troops had passed through Chelmsford on their way to the Front, adding that, "they came via Aberdeen."[54] Three days earlier the Reverend Andrew Clark, Vicar of Great Leighs, noted a similar report in his diary, except that his Russians appeared to have originated in Yorkshire. In a second report two days later, he duly noted that other Russians had arrived in Aberdeen from Archangel. This seems to have been the version which Robert Bull heard shortly afterwards.[55]

Civilian unease was most notably manifested by an outbreak of panic buying. The price of sugar, flour and petrol rocketed overnight. In Southend there were rumours that the Government had commandeered all supplies of petrol.[56] At Frinton it was reported that "wealthy residents have gone round the neighbouring villages in a motor car buying bags of flour from the shops."[57] In some places the rush on food stripped many shops bare within hours. At Dovercourt, on the very day that war was declared, one grocer's shop was forced to close at 6 p.m., after which the shopkeeper posted a notice explaining the reason why:

[52] ECC 28 August 1914.

[53] CG 5 September 1914.

[54] ERO T/B 245, Diary of Robert Taylor Bull, 31 August 1914.

[55] J. Munson (ed.), *Echoes of the Great War: The Diary of the Rev. Andrew Clark 1914-19* (1985), 9-10. In February 1915 Colchester people were said to be still clinging to rumours of Russian troops fighting on the Western Front "with undiminished confidence", ECS 6 February 1915.

[56] SST 6 August 1914.

[57] EEA 8 August 1914.

> Residents and visitors will help us greatly, and study their own interests as well, in buying goods in small quantities that is, not exceeding a usual weekly supply. We have large orders for the Government troops, which must be delivered.[58]

Marriage's mill at Colchester's East Bay was faced with unusually high demands for flour, especially from local householders. The manager, Mr Wyncoll, attempted to ease people's fears by explaining that the recent harvest meant that there were sufficient supplies of wheat for three to four months, and he added that he was confident of getting a good supply of American wheat. Nevertheless within three days of the War beginning the price of flour had risen by 8*s*. a sack, wheat had gone up from 10*s*. to 12*s*. a quarter, and bran up 30*s*. a ton. In Bradfield and other small villages, it quickly proved impossible to obtain supplies of sugar and by 5 August prices had risen. Like the grocer's shop at Dovercourt, some shopkeepers attempted to regulate their sales to prevent panic buying. One Colchester grocer pinned a notice to his door saying "We will not accept orders for unusually large quantities from individual customers." Nevertheless, by 6 August about a dozen grocers' shops closed their doors in order to fulfil their orders.[59] The Colchester Cooperative Society raised its flour prices 1*d*. a quarter as early as 1 August, three days before war was declared. The price of bread was pegged for two days, but orders were issued "restricting the sales however to the usual normal orders given by members."[60] Similar instructions were issued at the Tiptree branch, where customers were advised that "the usual weekly quantities of goods can be supplied only."[61] In Southend prices rose so quickly that within twenty-four hours of war being declared they were described as 'famine prices'. Sugar had risen by 2*d*. a pound, bacon had become almost impossible to buy, and tinned food could not be obtained at any price. The town's shopkeepers, to protect their premises from the hordes desperate to buy their goods, locked their doors when they considered their shops were full enough. Some drays, attempting to unload their goods and deliver them to shops, were besieged by the crowds outside them, who demanded instant pavement sales.[62] Southend's shopkeepers' appeal to their customers to continue their support so that shop assistants should not have to be laid off, seems rather extraordinary in the circumstances; for example, the Home and Colonial Stores in Leigh-on-Sea was practically besieged by queues, which formed outside the shop day after day.[63]

[58] CG 12 August 1914.

[59] CG 12 August 1914.

[60] ERO D/Z 175/1/15 Colchester and East Essex Cooperative Society: Management Committee and Members Meeting, minute book 1912-15, 1 August 1914.

[61] ERO D/Z 178/1/4 Tiptree Self-Help Cooperative and Industrial Society Minutes 1913-16, 4 August 1914.

[62] ECC 7 August 1914.

[63] SST 13 August 1914.

The blame for the outbreak of panic buying and the resultant increase in the price of foodstuffs was placed at the feet of shopkeepers and their well-heeled customers. Prominent men like J.J. Crowe, chairman of Brentwood Urban District Council, urged people not to hoard, criticising such action as "wicked, or unpatriotic, or foolish", but there was clearly a groundswell of opinion that this had little impact on those lacking a conscience.[64] The British Socialist Party at Plaistow was in no doubt that the rich were to blame and was equally certain that only Government action could alleviate the suffering of the poor. At a public meeting in the second week of August it urged the Government

> To take immediate steps to purchase, store and control the food to prevent a wild uprush of prices, also the hoggish greed of the rich in piling up stores during this terrible national crisis.[65]

One person, styling themselves 'A Victim', wrote to the *East Essex Advertiser* explaining that the premature departure of holidaymakers from Clacton was the fault of

> the greedy, grasping tradesmen who, the moment there was a war cry raised their prices 50% to 100% and could not guarantee that the prices would not be raised further during the same day.[66]

Another, inspired by the times to sign their letter 'Each for All and All for Each', complained to the *Colchester Gazette:*

> Through the medium of your columns I should like to place upon record my profound disgust at the closing of no less than 8 prominent provision establishments in the town during the whole of yesterday to execute huge orders received from persons, who having the means at their disposal, were thus enabled to lay in a vast stock of food to the detriment of the poorer classes, whose consideration should be none the less than those who can afford to have their bread buttered on both sides.[67]

One correspondent, S.R. Worger, simply accused panic buyers of 'cowardly and unpatriotic' behaviour.[68] The Chelmsford Labour Party held a special meeting to protest at these developments. F. Tyrell Smith voiced the party's view:

64 BA 8 August 1914.

65 SE 15 August 1914.

66 EEA 15 August 1914.

67 CG 12 August 1914.

68 CG 12 August 1914.

> In his opinion there was not a word in the English language bad enough to describe anyone who would penalise the dependants of those to whom they looked for protection or would attempt to make undue profits out of the dire necessities of the people stricken by a calamity such as they were facing.[69]

The party's representations to Chelmsford Borough Council led the latter to form a Vigilance Committee to keep an eye on things. It urged the town's Cooperative Society to set an example in keeping prices down to "the lowest possible level."

This spate of panic buying was just a partial reflection of the fear that the War would have drastic economic implications for the area. There were real worries that the War would bring a collapse in trade, an increase in unemployment, and there were fears that savings might be vulnerable. During the first few days of the War, William Crow, Mayor of West Ham, publicly voiced his belief that it would generate serious distress in East London.[70] The Southend Trades Council and Labour Representation Committee anticipated large scale unemployment and urged the town council to organise relief for the working classes by undertaking house building.[71] Certainly the disruption to trade which followed the outbreak of war meant temporary unemployment for dockers at Tilbury. The secretary of the Colchester Cooperative Society "reported an abnormal number of withdrawals of Share Capital and also that a large number of notices had been handed in." The Management Committee acted quickly to forestall a run on savings and on 5 August limited members' withdrawals of cash to just £1 a week.[72] Fears for the local economy proved relatively short lived. Courtauld's silk factories at Earls Colne and Halstead were on three-quarter's time, and at Braintree half-time work, but all other Braintree factories were said to be in 'full swing'. Crittall of Braintree reported receiving more orders in the week following the outbreak of war than for years. Colchester's tailoring firms viewed their prospects with gloom and anticipated short-time working. However, thanks to the influence of Laming Worthington-Evans, the town's M.P., several firms were placed on War Office lists for the manufacture of uniforms. Wilkin's jam factory at Tiptree, in common with most other British food manufacturers, imported much of its sugar from Germany and Austria-Hungary. Indeed, a consignment of sugar on its way from Germany was stopped by the German authorities at Hamburg when war began. Nevertheless, with a large stock of glass jars and raw materials, the company was confident of being able to carry on its business.[73] The Stratford confectionery factory of Messrs

69 ECT 14 August 1914.

70 SE 8 August 1914.

71 SBC minutes, 31 August 1914.

72 Colchester Cooperative Society minutes, 5 August 1914. The Tiptree Cooperative Society followed suit but not until 15 September.

73 CG 12 August 1914.

Morris, Striemer and Company was closed soon after the outbreak of the War because of the difficulty of obtaining its raw materials. Three hundred girls were thrown out of work, although within a week it had reopened and was operating a three-day week.[74]

It was the Essex coast which bore the brunt of the initial economic dislocation resulting from the outbreak of war. At Mistley trade was very slack, the military authorities refused permission for vessels to leave the port forcing the despatch of freight by rail. However, it was the seaside resorts which were the worst affected. Despite excellent bank holiday weather the number of day trippers was down, and failed to recover throughout August. Many who were holidaying in early August cut short their stay when war began. Worse still, many families who had already booked holidays in hotels and boarding houses stayed away in their thousands. Many were alarmed by the possibility of German coastal raids. Others were worried that they might be stranded, particularly when it became clear that civilian services on the Great Eastern Railway were being drastically reduced. Indeed, the Great Eastern Railway had little choice but to give priority to the military. Between 5 August and 14 September 870 military trains comprising twenty thousand vehicles had been run over the system.[75] Soon hotel managers and lodging house keepers in Southend, Clacton and Walton were bemoaning a severe fall in income and many were threatening legal action against those who had reneged on their holiday bookings. In Southend the numbers of holidaymakers either returning home or simply staying away forced the council to cut the number of bus and tram services.[76]

The local authorities in seaside resorts tried frantically to persuade people that there was nothing to fear and that all was normality. In this they were assisted by at least one journalist who painted a rosy picture of the holiday season at Walton:

> Bathing was in full swing. Hundreds of children were paddling and disporting themselves on the sands, the sunlit waters were dotted with rowing boats, the *Walton Belle* came in and went out on its usual trip, the Band Pavilion esplanade was filled with visitors enjoying the delightful music of the 'White Band', anglers were pursuing their peaceful pastimes on the pier — in fact, there was not a disturbing note anywhere.

Southend's Chamber of Commerce and Clacton's Advancement and Advertising Association placed advertisements in several London daily newspapers stating that their resorts were safe from attack and in full holiday swing. The *Essex County Standard* joined in the defence of the county's coastal resorts, where by mid-August

74 SE August 1914.

75 HDS 10 October 1914.

76 V.E. Burrows, *The Tramways of Southend-on-Sea* (1965), 81.

it noted that "the visiting community has fallen to practically nothing." It launched into a vigorous attack on the rumour-mongers who were damaging the holiday trade:

> It is to be deplored that to a great extent wholly unfounded and extravagant rumours — idiotic and unnecessary lies would be hardly a strong enough description of the stories — seem to have been flying about regarding not only Clacton, but other seaside resorts on the East Coast, with the result that they have suffered beyond all bounds of necessity. It is not, for instance, a fact that all streets are guarded by soldiery or that all entertainments have closed, or that the pier has been destroyed by bombs, or that no trains or boats are running, nor that food is at famine prices, nor that the beach is closed, nor that — but then one could go on ad infinitum enumerating the wild stories that have been heard.[77]

These efforts were in vain, and proved to be so for much of the War. The Belle Steamer Company, whose steamers usually ferried day trippers from London to Southend, Clacton and Walton well into October, announced that its season would end on 30 August. There was simply not enough business to maintain any of its usual services. Things were so slack that by 5 September the *East Essex Advertiser* reported rather glumly that the holiday season was now over — two months ahead of schedule.[78] For Essex's coastal resorts their wartime problems were only just beginning.

Meanwhile the local press performed its duty admirably in whipping up patriotic feelings and anti-German sentiments. The *Southend Standard* placed the blame for the War squarely on Germany's doorstep, while reminding its readers of the economic pressures which lay behind great power rivalry. "It is a struggle for mastery", the newspaper noted, "and for the wealth and power which this mastery affords".[79] Other local newspapers were far less prepared to recognise any extenuating circumstances. The *Essex County Chronicle* condemned Germany as a 'swashbuckler' whose headlong pursuit of irresponsible policies had engulfed all Europe in war. The *Colchester Gazette* was in no doubt about where the blame for the War lay:

> there can be no question that in the history of the future, Germany, whatever excuses she may now make, will be universally credited with the awful responsibility of having initiated the terrible conflagration.

[77] ECS 15 August 1914.

[78] EEA 5 September 1914.

[79] SST 6 August 1914.

The editorial thought that Germany's 'mad ambitions', her dreams of 'destiny', and her "wild notions of overwhelming power" had led to war. Germany was "the Napoleon of the twentieth century." Mark Downe, the writer of the *Colchester Gazette*'s 'Jottings', having just returned safely from Germany by the skin of his teeth, wrote in similar vein that "Germany has rushed madly at all her neighbours." He went on to say that "Germany has long been eager to pounce ... she was eager to let loose the dogs of war and ... she seized greedily on the flimsiest pretext."[80]

A *Colchester Gazette* editorial a fortnight later spoke of dashed German dreams and confidence in ultimate victory: "'The Day' has come, but it has dawned very differently from the expectations of those who dreamed it. They have awakened to find it stormy where they looked for sun, dark where they looked for light."[81] "The cherished ambitions of the aggressive Prussian faction", may have resulted in war, concluded the *Colchester Gazette,* but it was a "prolonged deadlock" that the Allies would win. Such confidence was not universal. Five days before Britain's declaration of war on Germany, the *Essex County Chronicle* cast a critical eye over diplomatic events and pondered what the Government would do. As far as it was concerned the only way to prevent Britain and other countries from waging war was for the people of the democracies to exercise a more direct control over the small political cliques and oligarchies who made the decisions. Some local writers mused anxiously at what the future held:

> Everyone seemed more or less stunned by the dreadful news that the various countries of Europe were entering upon a war which, with the modern and up to date weapons of warfare now in existence, cannot but prove to be one of the most destructive to life and property in the history of the world.[82]

Sadly, these words were to prove tragically prophetic.

[80] CG 12 August 1914.

[81] CG 26 August 1914.

[82] HDS 8 August 1914.

CHAPTER THREE

A Righteous War

GOD SAVE THE KING.

Parish of Gt. Clacton and Lt. Holland

(WITH ST. ANDREW'S CENTRAL MISSION CLACTON-ON-SEA).

HYMNS & PRAYERS

FOR DAILY USE

DURING THE WAR IN EUROPE.

NOTE. There will be special intercession to God in this behalf at Great Clacton Parish Church, at the Daily Service at 10 a.m. and at the Sunday Services at 11 a.m. and 7 p.m.; and also at the Sunday Service at Little Holland Church at 3 p.m.; and at St. Andrew's, Clacton-on-Sea, at 6.30 p.m.

JAMES SILVESTER, Vicar.

"We fight to-day for our honour and for our existence, facing a foe the most ruthless among civilised nations. By God's help we shall win through and shall save Europe from the menace of an intolerable and tyrannical domination." *Evening News, August 5th,* 1914.

GOD DEFEND THE RIGHT.

Potter & French, Printers, Clacton-on-Sea.

Hymns and Prayers for Daily Use During the War in Europe, 1914. *(ERO: D/P 179/28/14)*

THE CLERGY of most Christian denominations found themselves carried away by the spectacular euphoria generated by the outbreak of war. The result during 1914-15 was the delivery of a succession of patriotic and bellicose sermons and addresses justifying the War and demonising the Germans. Anglican clergy in particular, but not exclusively, were swept along by the tidal wave of patriotism which was washing over their parishes. The Reverend Andrew Clark reported that his rector, Thomas Sadgrove, had soon replaced the pulpit-hangings in church with a Union Jack, and that he had preached "a horrifying sermon on the horrible scenes of the battlefield."[1] James Anderson Telford, the Vicar of Harwich, a man who had been noted for his combative pre-war stance on dealing with the Germans, was soon urging that all men between the ages of nineteen and thirty-five "should be knocking at the door of the recruiting officer." "Shouting and flag waving in the streets would not win battles", he declared, "battles would only be won by men carrying arms." With resolute enthusiasm, he embraced the need for the nation's men to step forward and, if necessary, to make the ultimate sacrifice:

> It was a sweet and noble thing to die for one's native land. When wives and mothers were giving their loved ones, when children were losing their fathers, could any young man who was capable of being made a soldier, could any young man bear the shame of holding back?

As far as the Germans' moral degeneracy was concerned he was unequivocal that "there remained a blacklist of callous and barbarous acts of savage brutality that would make the name of Germany stink in the nostrils of all decent people for years to come."[2]

The Vicar of Walton-on-the-Naze, Harold Knocker, spoke in even more grotesque terms when he declared that "God wanted England to be a blessing to the world, but she would only be such as her young men died on the battlefield, fighting to death in the name of God."[3] Such imbalanced utterances were not the exclusive preserve of the Church of England. The Reverend Ernest Greening, Minister of the Cliff Road Congregational Chapel at Clacton, was equally intemperate when he declared "better die than live dishonoured; better war than for the nation to lose its soul."[4] K.L. Parry, of Lion Walk Congregational Church in Colchester, conjured up a Christian image of crusading heroism by quoting from a famous speech made by Lloyd George in September 1914. The War had, he said, taught the nation those things it had forgotten — "duty, patriotism, and clad in glittering white, the great pinnacle of

1 Clark, *Diary*, 30 August 1914.

2 CG 2 September 1914.

3 EEA 30 October 1915.

4 HDS 27 March 1915.

sacrifice, pointing like a rugged finger to heaven."[5]

A conflict between Christian countries in which the clergy of all the combatants claimed that God was on their side, placed some more sensitive individuals in a dilemma: how to be true to one's Christian principles and yet support the War? As a way out of such moral difficulties many people in Britain chose to interpret the War as a righteous war, a just conflict, in which the nation was fighting against a state which had embraced evil, oppression, violence and irreligion. "We go to war as a united nation", said the *Essex County Telegraph*, "with stout hearts and with just cause."[6] Taking up the sword for 'little' Belgium, whose struggle was lauded as "a matchless example for all time" seemed to be eminently justifiable (although those making such claims seemed unwilling to remember the strong-arm methods which had been used to create the British Empire).[7] These themes of honour and righteousness were much used during the first two years of the War. The idea that Britain was innocent of any blame for what might be termed the secular causes of the War was an almost universal theme in 1914. The Reverend P.A. Clements certainly thought so, "England had entered into a fight with clean hands", he argued, in order "to uphold her honour, and succour the weak against the strong." The Bishop of Colchester, Dr. R.H. Whitcombe, made the same point less than a week later when he described war as horrible:

> Yet, he ventured to say, horrible as it all is, if England had not drawn the sword, there would have been something still more ghastly. England would have besmeared her fair name. She would have deserved the name of traitor ... We have drawn the sword, we believe, on behalf of righteousness.[8]

He elaborated on this in a sermon delivered near Christmas, 1914:

> But while Christ was against personal vengeance for selfish ends, it is surely hardly necessary to point out that His command does not involve turning the babies' or the widows' left cheek to be smitten by a ruthless foe. On the contrary, Christianity justifies coercion against cruel barbarity, and no less forcibly commands the strong resistance of evil wrought against the helpless than it condemns a selfish revenge stimulated by merely criminal instincts.[9]

5 ECT 14 August 1917; the reference to Lloyd George's speech is from A. Wilkinson, *The Church of England and the First World War* (1978), 29.

6 ECT 8 August 1914.

7 ECT 12 September 1914.

8 ECT 26 August 1914.

9 ECS 26 December 1914.

Church leaders saw the War as fulfilling the destiny which God had granted to Britain. The Bishop of Colchester was, as usual, able to articulate these sentiments with great lucidity, completely ignoring the fact that the nationalism which he was praising was responsible in no small way for the European catastrophe that was unfolding around him:

> Nationalism, he ventured to say, is planted in the heart of man by God. Just as the love of the family works out for the good of the human race, so the love of country works out for the good of mankind. We have got this spirit of nationalism in our own country. In some respects the history of England is a sacred history. It has had its blemishes, but right from the beginning there has been an upward trend ... He believed the British Empire is the greatest asset to humanity in the world. Anything that lowers the prestige of the British Empire ... would work to the detriment of humanity at large. Throughout the world the British Empire stands for freedom and for great moral principles. The British Empire is bound to take the sword.[10]

Britain and its empire were thus seen as the instrument chosen by God with which to chastise the godless Germans. Bishop Harrison certainly thought so when he declared from the pulpit:

> It seemed too that God had entrusted to this generation, to the English people as a nation, the greatest purpose and hardest task that had ever been entrusted to any generation before.[11]

Dr Nicholas Elrington of Wethersfield, agreed with the bishop. "In all the world's history", he wrote, "it has been God's test of a race whether it could sacrifice itself by taking arms."[12]

During this great crusade Essex people made frequent recourse to the past to inspire, to reassure, and to drum up support for the War. Like the Bishop of Colchester, the Bishop of Chelmsford was an unrestrained advocate of the historic role to which the British Empire appeared to have been divinely appointed. In a sermon at Chelmsford Cathedral on 21 August 1914, the National Day of

[10] CG 26 August 1914.

[11] ECS 9 January 1915.

[12] ECC 4 September 1914.

Intercession, he urged his congregation to "think of how extraordinary it was God had placed this land of ours right in the very centre of the world." God's hand had been at work in creating the "natural convulsion" which created the English Channel, "our security against the armies of the Continent." Even the country's mild climate favoured its island people by promoting trade and commerce. In his view England's history was sacred. Almost echoing the words of his colleague, the Bishop of Colchester, he conceded that "there were blemishes, great blemishes" in that history, "but there was an undercurrent always making for righteousness, always tending to uplift, right from the very beginning." England found itself at war because the nation believed "that for the sake of the human race she must strike."[13] On the National Day of Intercession on 3 January 1915, Bishop Harrison reminded his hearers of the glories of Agincourt, the Armada, Trafalgar and Waterloo.[14] On 13 June 1915, the seven hundredth anniversary of the signing of Magna Carta, the Bishop of Chelmsford again took the opportunity to link the past with the present conflict:

> It is strange that at the very time you are commemorating this great Charter of Liberty and Freedom our nation should be straining itself to the utmost in order to maintain those great principles, not only for Europe, but for humanity at large.[15]

That same week saw the centenary of the Battle of Waterloo. The *Essex County Standard* marked the occasion by musing rather tactfully on how the wheel of international relations had turned in Britain's favour:

> In the commemoration this week of the centenary of Waterloo thought centres rather on the 100 years of peace with France which it inaugurated rather than on the conquest itself. The gallant French nation is now not only in friendly relations with this country, but, by a strange coincidence, is engaged as our brave ally almost on the very same battlefields, but in a struggle of much more Titanic proportions, against a common foe whose ruthless and barbaric modes of warfare are unparalleled in modern history.[16]

The combination of the themes of patriotism, religious faith and freedom, all of them manifested and nurtured in Britain's past, appeared in a poem titled 'The Old

[13] ECC 28 August 1914.

[14] ECT 5 January 1915.

[15] ECC 18 June 1915.

[16] ECS 19 June 1915.

Cause' written in 1914 by the anonymous 'H.M.A.C.' of Brentwood:

The old cause, and the bold cause, the
cause that England made;
The good cause that bent the bow and
winged the goose-shaft true;
The right cause, and the white cause, that
despots made afraid;
Old England taught it to her sons, who
shouted it anew.

For "Freedom!" and "Freedom" and
"Freedom" they did cry;
"'Tis free to live and free to love, to
worship and to die;
And woe to them that dare oppress or
dare to bind the free,
For England's sons are dauntless once, and
serfs they ne'er will be!"

The old cause and the bold cause, the
cause that England made;
It nerved the arm and braced the mind
and made the heart to sing;
It framed laws and it blamed laws – full
sore the tyrant paid;
It wrung the land's Great Charter from
that reluctant King.

The old cause, and the bold cause, the
cause that England made;
For that her children pray to God, their
help and strength, to be;
Protect them, direct them – on Him their
trust is stayed;
O, Lord of Might, defend the right, and
grant them victory.[17]

Viewed in this light, the prosecution of the War was not merely a secular duty but a sacred obligation, a great crusade, which the nation could not, and must not, recoil

[17] ECC 28 August 1914.

from. Indeed the Reverend Parry said "it was a noble crusade to redeem the City of God"[18], a theme repeated by the Colchester Brotherhood, which proclaimed that "out of the battlefields of Belgium would be built a holy temple." [19] Three years later in 1917, the Bishop of Colchester chose the moment of the United States' entry into the War to say that "the whole Anglo-Saxon race is commissioned to set before mankind ... the cause of God and the claims of true religion."[20] However natural and inspiring the use of apocalyptic language may have seemed in the context of this titanic struggle, to a few clergymen it was also dangerous as it encouraged the belief that the War was a simple conflict between good and evil; between the chosen people and the godless. It was this black and white view of the War from which so many people found it impossible to escape.

The perceived righteousness of the cause did not necessarily preclude an assessment of why the War had begun. For some, like J. Farnsworth, it was very simple, as he made clear at a recruiting meeting in Brightlingsea:

> He felt that they were not only fighting Prussian militarism, they were fighting the whole German nation. They had to fight the whole of the German people from the Kaiser to the gutter boy. This great and grave crisis had arisen because the heart of the German people was full of hatred, malice, envy and uncharitableness towards the people of this country and Empire.[21]

The Colchester Brotherhood was of the opinion that the War was being fought "for the freedom of the world against a foul philosophy", presumably Prussianism.[22] Surprisingly, most clergymen were not content to simply lay the blame at Germany's door. Germany's guilt was, of course, taken for granted, but there was also a search for explanations of a more profound nature. The Archdeacon of Colchester articulated the sentiments of those who were trying to avoid simplistic interpretations:

> Whether we believe that war is absolutely at variance with the principles of Christianity, or that it is God's method of punishing nations, or that He wills by this stern discipline to purify and elevate our ideals, we are all quite certain that in the present instance, Great Britain was morally bound to declare war, and is no less bound to carry the war to a decisive issue, whatever the

[18] ECT 5 September 1914.

[19] ECT 17 October 1914.

[20] ECS 28 April 1917.

[21] EEA 12 December 1914.

[22] ECT 17 October 1914.

> difficulties and however great the sacrifice demanded of us. At the same time it is well that we should register our conviction that war between Christian nations is wrong, and that this war is, as has been said, 'the outcome and revelation of the unchristian principles which have dominated the life of Western Christendom', more particularly of the attitude of Germany in claiming the right and duty to make war for the sake of national progress, and of the assertion of her spokesmen that Christian morality is not binding on the State.[23]

Not everyone was prepared to accept that the sinfulness which had precipitated the War emanated entirely from Berlin. Trevor Eddleston, Vicar of Braintree, told his parishioners that God had sent war on England for the same reason that He punished the Jews of the Old Testament, because the country had strayed from Him.[24] The Bishop of Chelmsford, in a sermon delivered at St Paul's Cathedral in the spring of 1916, told his hearers that God had seen fit not to end the War because the people were still steeped in sin.[25] The Peculiar People held no truck with the view that this was a just war. The War "was the work of Satan", said their council, "and absolutely contrary to the principles of the religion of Our Lord and Saviour Jesus Christ and the teachings of the New Testament."[26] Other religious groups saw apocalyptic factors at play. The Dunmow Auxiliary of the British and Foreign Bible Society believed that the War was a precursor of the Second Coming:

> We believe it is in fulfilment of the Word of God, and a sign of the near return of our Blessed Lord, that the great nations of the earth should be thrown into such a struggle for supremacy and world power.[27]

However, some ministers discerned mercenary motives rather than theological considerations. The Colchester Brotherhood saw the War as the result of "the warlords of the earth" attempting to dominate smaller, weaker nations.[28] Roderic Dunkerley, the socialist minister of Colchester's Headgate Congregational Church, found little common ground with Ernest Greening, his Clacton counterpart, in his unambiguously political denunciation of the War. Dunkerley condemned war as "an offence against love and justice." It was the result of "the science of war" and was

23 CDC June 1915.

24 ECC 11 September 1914.

25 ECC 21 April 1916.

26 M. Sorrell, *The Peculiar People* (1979), 51.

27 ECC 23 October 1914.

28 ECT 5 September 1914.

fought "for the sake of gain for gold." It had been caused by "crooks who want war for money, gain and profit." It was not ordinary people who had connived at war but the result of "wickedness in high places." Nevertheless, even Dunkerley had no quarrel with the prosecution of the War itself, for Britain's failure to fight would have left her "on a lower moral level." In the spring of 1915 he reiterated his socialist views on the origins of the War:

> It was not unpatriotic to realise that this and other nations had thought of power and possessions, and it was the war spirit in all commercial and industrial life that had brought the nations to the present state of things. The nations of the world in their commercial and industrial life had been guilty of war day by day.[29]

The solution was, of course, to fight the War to a successful conclusion. Some of the men who went away to fight went armed with their religious principles. Two thousand, five hundred and seventy-five men from the Diocese of Chelmsford signed the War Roll, affirming that

> I hereby pledge my allegiance to the Lord Jesus as my Saviour and King, and by God's help will fight His battles for the Victory of His Kingdom.[30]

The Bishop of Colchester, speaking to troops at Colchester who were destined for France, reaffirmed these principles and the responsibilities they entailed:

> In concluding the Bishop urged them to remember that His promise was to them that loved God, and that it meant putting away sin, and cultivating true Christian manliness, which might be as conspicuous in the self- restraint of those left to guard the country as in the courage and heroism of those at the front.[31]

Clearly for those civilians left at home much would also be expected of them, both physically and spiritually. As we have seen, some clergymen saw the War as a consequence of modern society turning away from God. Bishop Harrison certainly thought so; he preached against "the sin of self-indulgence" and saw the War as a punishment meted out by a dissatisfied God, still set in the mould of the Old Testament:

> Young men and women had thought chiefly about pleasure, neglected worship for it, spent Sunday on pleasure, and their

[29] ECT 8 August 1914; ECS 27 March 1915.

[30] CDC April 1918.

[31] CG 19 August 1914.

> whole lives seem to have been given up to pleasure. But now God had turned pleasure into sorrow, and had reminded us by the sorrow of this war that we must give Him his rightful due.[32]

Harrison's views were widely held ones within clerical circles. The Essex Congregational Union was certainly in agreement. At its annual meeting in 1915 in Maldon, speaker after speaker reiterated the desperate need for the nation to return to God. The Reverend Ewart James from Southend bemoaned the fact that "there had been foolery in literature, in politics, in religion, and what the people loved was pleasure, sport, ragtime music, golf, football, shady novels, and risky plays at the theatre." He argued that the nation was still far too self-centred and quarrelsome, indulging in "racing, drinking, boxing, labour disputes, theatres, nightclubs, betting and gambling." Clearly a moral reformation, a turning away from materialism and hedonism was urgently needed. The people were urged to reject "their luxury and self-indulgence, their neglect of worship, their relaxation of the laws of purity, their commercial intrigues, their class differences, their political bitterness, and their excessive inequalities."[33]

Yet other clergymen were not content to point an accusing finger at society in general without noting the failure of the churches to reach out to these people. The Reverend J.A. Palmer of the Grove Congregational Church at West Ham was one who was prepared to articulate such views:

> When we consider the grave problems which clamour for solution, the growing craze for pleasure, excitement and sport, the disaffection for God's house, the disregard for the Day of Rest, the worldliness and lack of moral earnestness of many Christian professors, the unblushing unbelief which challenges our sacred verities, the perils which menace the young life of these times, the comparatively feeble impression which we appear to make on the teeming crowds around us, surely the time has come for us to abandon ourselves to self-examination, confession of sin, humiliation before God, the renewal of our covenant with Him whose name we bear.[34]

As far as the Bishops of Chelmsford and Colchester were concerned the War could only be survived and won if people sought "a closer and more constant communion with God", which required an acceptance of "the power of intercessory prayer". At St Peter's, Colchester, the bishop pointed out the shortcomings of the nation's prayer life:

[32] ECT 5 January 1915.

[33] ECC 30 April 1915.

[34] SE 9 January 1915.

> how feebly they had prayed to him in the past, how formal their petitions had been, how half-hearted their efforts to learn to pray. What a small proportion of them had prayed at all. But now, in the stress of a great anxiety ... let them turn to Him with all their strength.[35]

Throughout the War these two bishops never wavered from this belief and preached it unflaggingly:

> Therefore the call to the Church today is urgent. Get near to your Lord. It is the only way to obtain power. There must be a return to the old methods of Prayer, Bible Reading and the Holy Communion. It is not sufficient that men should merely join in Intercession in the two or more specified days appointed for the nation but there must be regular, systematic and persistent prayer.

Many churches took this call with great seriousness, as evinced by this plaque, which was placed in Holy Trinity, Colchester, at the conclusion of the War:

> No day passed from August 1914 to November 1918 but Intercessions were offered up in this Church, and the fact is here placed on record.

The Vicar of Margaretting, Sidney Smith, clearly took it to heart. In the parish magazine of June 1915 he berated those parishioners who had been lax in their attendance at church services. "Our lads at the front believe that England is praying for them", he wrote.[36] Another parish priest, Frederick Gardner of Goldhanger, was equally adamant. Less than a month after the beginning of the War he wrote that, "We recognise in it all a stern call to mend our ways and to supplicate in Prayer the Almighty aid of Our Heavenly Father."[37] Repentance was also urged alongside a renewal of prayerfulness. In this, the diocesan viewpoint, though never stated in bald terms, was in agreement with those who saw war as punishment for sin.

Joint prayers with Nonconformists were encouraged, "without any sacrifice of those principles which we, as Churchmen, hold dear."[38] The Church recommended that prayer should be accompanied by restraint in one's personal life, and abstaining

[35] ECT 26 August 1914.

[36] G.M. Baker, *Margaretting: The village with a beautiful name*, volume 2, (1983), 107.

[37] Goldhanger and Little Totham parish magazine, September 1914.

[38] CDC January 1915.

from alcohol for the duration was urged upon the clergy of the diocese.[39] This was music to the ears of Nonconformists; as late as 1917 the Reverend J.R. Mitchell of the Colchester Free Church Council could still identify drink, rather than the Germans, as "England's greatest foe."[40] In keeping with this penitential tone there was some opposition to the celebration of harvest festivals in spite of diocesan approval. Colchester Town Council abandoned its traditional Oyster Feast for the duration on the grounds that "anything in the nature of rejoicing would be out of place."[41] Sporting activities involving young male civilians were criticised mercilessly by clergy and laity alike.[42]

The War assisted in modifying and changing Anglican liturgical practices, a process that had begun in the mid-nineteenth century.[43] The Anglo-Catholic practice of reserving the sacrament had been revived in a limited manner before 1914, although it was extremely unpopular among evangelicals and Low Churchmen. However, as the number of casualties mounted, increasing numbers of Anglo-Catholic priests and military chaplains reserved the sacrament to administer it to the wounded or to troops returning from active service. The Vicar of St Clement's, Leigh-on-Sea, announced that he did not intend to abandon reservation of the holy sacrament, even though the Bishop of Chelmsford had threatened sanctions to curb the practice.[44] The War also led to a much wider revival of prayers for the departed, a practice discredited from the reign of Elizabeth I, but rediscovered by the Anglo-Catholic wing of the Church of England. As the War dragged on and the numbers of those who had died reached catastrophic levels, prayers for the dead, another practice which had fallen into disuse since the sixteenth century, were offered up in most churches. In November 1914 at St Mary Magdalen's in Colchester, prayers were being said for two parishioners who had been killed in action.[45] For the same reason Anglican priests made increasing use of requiem masses, much more so than before 1914, when usage was limited. Clergy who found requiem masses too closely linked to Roman Catholicism and rather distasteful, began to remember the dead during Holy Communion, reading out the names of those who had died. Memorial services for the Fallen became commonplace, although some parishes held them for individuals, and others only as a collective memorial to the parochial dead. The Vicar of St Mary Magdalen's, Colchester, emphasised Christian egalitarianism when he wrote that:

[39] CDC January, April 1915.

[40] ECS 27 January 1917.

[41] ECT 5 September 1914.

[42] See Chapter 11 for a fuller discussion of the impact of the War upon sport.

[43] This section is heavily dependant upon R.W.F. Beaken, 'Wartime Religion in a Garrison Town: The Parish Churches of Colchester during the Great War 1914-18', Lambeth MA (2000), 123-138.

[44] ECC 23 February 1917.

[45] ERO D/P 246/28/31 St Mary Magdalen parish magazine, November 1914.

> We have had no Memorial Services for individuals in our Parish, and it is, in our opinion, better so. All who have fallen should be equally honoured, as far as can be, "high and low, rich and poor, one with another."

The preference for simpler services shown by some parishioners and many servicemen led to modifications being made to Anglican liturgy. The 1662 Prayer Book continued to be used alongside other sources. Litanies, a particular and traditional form of intercession, were used more often. Laypeople were given more of a part to play in the communion service by reading the Old and New Testament. In some churches servicemen actually conducted the whole service by themselves.

There were those both within and outside of the churches who urged restraint in the prosecution of the War, a courageous thing to do in view of the jingoistic passions which the conflict had aroused. These passions were evident for all to see. On 15 October 1914 the pupils of the County High School at Ilford debated the proposition "War is never justifiable." It was rejected by a large majority.[46] "They were Barbarians then, and are Barbarians now", wrote Elizabeth Carolin, the wife of the Rector of Wivenhoe, when describing the German people. "It is astonishing how they still keep their ancient characteristics intact", she added.[47] "Shameless barbarity" was how the *Essex County Standard* described the German air raid on Colchester in February 1915 and after that described them routinely as 'baby killers'.[48] The diarist Denys Yonge condemned the sinking of the *Lusitania* as "a fearful and horrible act of piracy."[49] Going even further than Mrs Carolin, the *Essex County Telegraph* condemned the sinking of the *Lusitania* and stated that "Germany has made the Great War an absolute negation of all those restraints which even the old Pagan civilisations of the Dark Ages regarded as inviolable."[50] The *East Essex Advertiser* used a similar, if equally inaccurate, historical allusion to describe Germany's reversion to barbarism, "Even Attila had his better side. He respected the laws of nations as they were understood in his day, but the modern Attila respects neither the laws of nations nor the laws of God."[51] "Napoleon never stained the French flag with the cruelties and the terrorism with which the German flag had been stained in Belgium", thundered E.G. Pretyman, Conservative M.P. for Mid-Essex, at a huge recruitment meeting on Chelmsford Recreation Ground in September 1914.[52] This

46 *The CHSI Chronicles*: The Magazine of the County High School, Ilford, vol. iv, no.1.

47 ECT 24 October 1914.

48 ECS 27 February 1915.

49 Yonge, Diary, 8 May 1915.

50 ECT 30 May 1915.

51 EEA 15 May 1915.

52 ECC 11 September 1914.

piece of doggerel from the *Southend Standard* by E.M. Naughten perhaps sums up the popular vision of the Germans as barbarians:

The foe must be crushed under,
For his God's a Pagan wonder,
Who thrives on blood and thunder,
And women's hopeless tears.

He uses babies as vanguard,
To his heroic landguard
And waves his bloodstained standard
To the shrieks of children's tears.[53]

During 1915 and 1916 there were those who advocated reprisals and retaliation against the horrors which the Germans were believed to be committing. One letter claimed that reprisals were not "a mere passion of revenge." "To enforce upon a barbarian nation a realisation of its barbarism and a sense of the consequences that will follow unless such tactics are abandoned" was quite legitimate, argued the writer.[54] After being subjected to several murderous air raids by German Zeppelins and Gothas, Southend Town Council urged the Government to state whether or not it would authorise reprisal raids, "and to give an assurance that the engineering of the scheme of reprisal will have little doubt that German civilians shall suffer to as great an extent as the civilians of England have suffered."[55] The resolution passed by a meeting of Walthamstow's inhabitants shortly before the one at Southend was even more uncompromising in its demands for action:

> That this meeting ... calls on the Government to institute immediately a policy of ceaseless air attacks on German towns and cities in order that their population may experience the effects of such methods of warfare, and thus be induced to force the German authorities to cease this wanton destruction of life and property.[56]

However, the calls for revenge were not universal. In June 1917 Barking Urban District Council twice rejected attempts by councillors to pass resolutions regarding German air raids too fierce in tone. The council eventually settled for a more moderate expression of its wishes, "That this Council expresses the continued hope

53 SST 17 September 1914.

54 ECS 5 February 1916.

55 EEC 24 August 1917.

56 WG 7 July 1917.

that the Government will immediately take effective measures to prevent a recurrence of the recent disastrous air raid."[57] This did not mean that the councillors, eager for moderation in some things, could not be tempted away to the extremes in others. In June 1916 and again eighteen months later, they demanded the immediate internment of all those of German and Austrian ancestry "in view of the presence in our midst of so many thousands of enemy aliens."[58]

In was nevertheless clear that in some quarters the English concern for decency, fair play and moderation had been pushed to the limit of its endurance. Some Essex residents of German ancestry, fearful in case local bigotry should overwhelm them, anglicised their names to provide them with respectability, deflect the gossips, and to allow them to assume a new aura of patriotism. A. Langemann of Woodford became A. Langham; D. Oppenheim of Woodford Green changed his name to Openshaw; at Leyton, H.M. Scharm altered his surname to the unrecognisable H. Millington; C.A. Cromff became C.A. Normington; a Mr Hillebrecht became simply Mr Hill, and A.M Schloss became A.M. Castle, thus defiantly retaining his original surname but in an English form.[59] Even the Great Eastern Railway tactfully renamed two of its continental steamers; The *Dresden* and the *Vienna* were renamed after towns in heroic Belgium, the *Louvain* and the *Antwerp*.[60] That the necessity for people of German descent to keep a low profile was not simply a fiction in the minds of the fearful was demonstrated in June 1917. A small group of Germans had been holding religious services in the Marsh Street Congregational Church in Walthamstow for fifteen years. Rumours began to circulate, it is unclear for how long, that the modest congregation met to pray for the success of the Kaiser and Germany. In May 1917 this prompted one outraged local man, J.F. Graves, to interrupt the service. The congregation called for a policeman who promptly ejected Graves. Shortly afterwards the local branch of the British Empire Union held a demonstration urging the authorities to halt the services. How influential the demonstration and the feelings of some locals were is hard to gauge, but the leaders of the Congregational Church gave notice that the services were to be terminated. After permitting the German congregation to use the church during the three years of war they can hardly have had any serious reason to throw them out. Perhaps they thought that discretion was the better part of valour.[61]

The most serious manifestation of anti-German feelings occurred on 12-13 May 1915, and was the combination of both long held animosity and immediate events. Fear of Germany had been preached by politicians, sections of the press, and organisations such as the anti-German National Service League well before the

57 Barking UDC minute, 19 June 1917.

58 Barking UDC minutes, 13 June 1916, 27 November 1917.

59 ECS 22 May 1915.

60 ECS 13 February 1915.

61 WG 1 June 1917.

outbreak of war. Once war started the Germans were portrayed as barbaric and inhuman monsters possessing not a shred of decency or Christian morality. By May 1915 the Germans had been thoroughly demonised in the eyes of most British people and when a series of events coincided over a period of about three weeks, feelings erupted into violence. First, on 22 April, it was learned that the Germans had used poison gas in the trenches at Ypres. Then, just when it seemed as if the Germans had reached an all-time barbaric low, on 7 May a German U-boat sank the Cunard liner *Lusitania*, killing over twelve hundred passengers, including women and children. Evelyn Jessie Grubb, a fifteen-year old girl living in east London, wrote in her diary, "Hundreds and hundreds of people drowned."[62] The *Colchester Gazette* condemned the action as being "entirely outside the pale of civilisation."[63] Three days later on 10 May a German Zeppelin attacked Southend, dropping dozens of bombs indiscriminately on civilian targets, killing a sixty-year old woman, Agnes Whitwell, a resident of North Road, Prittlewell, and severely injuring her husband, George. The German communiqué claiming to have bombed Southend, which was described as 'a fortified place', was greeted with incredulity and anger in South Essex. It was, said the *Colchester Gazette*, the action of a government characterised by a "loathsome and insane inhumanity."[64] Then on 12 May the report of the Bryce Commission into alleged German atrocities in Belgium and France was published. The timing was unfortunate. The commission concluded that the reports of atrocities by German troops were indeed factual, and that Germany stood condemned. On the same day, and the next, there were riots in Southend and in parts of metropolitan Essex. Shops owned by those of German or Austrian extraction, or often simply those with foreign-sounding names, were the targets of angry mobs. At Stratford a mob of some three thousand people wrecked a baker's shop and threw its contents into the street. Crowds ransacked a German barber's shop at Leytonstone, and then after ransacking another shop, threw a piano from the premises into the street. A mob at Upton Park smashed into a butcher's shop, making off with the stock and three carrier bicycles from a back room. Girls even attempted to rip up the linoleum from the shop floor. A mob of two thousand people rampaged through East Ham looking for foreign-owned shops. Evelyn Potter was a witness to some of these chaotic disturbances. "Great riots everywhere in London", she wrote in her diary. She recorded her experiences in her entry on the evening of 12 May:

> Girls coming from "Longthorne" district (Docks, Silvertown) brought news of German owned shops being stoned and entered. They also said mobs were out. About the middle of our [dancing] display people heard banging and shouting

62 Diary of Evelyn Jessie Grubb, *née* Potter, 7 May 1915.

63 CG 19 May 1915.

64 ECC 14 May 1915; CG 12 May 1915.

> outside. Doris Edwards wanted to go home but got as far as the gates and was forced back by the crowds. What they wanted, or thought, is not known. Mr Cyril Hodges and Mr Jennings addressed the people who seemed satisfied and went away. Mr Oliver, our caretaker, locked and bolted all the doors and none of us were allowed out until the end of the display. Rumours Schuarmroffels the bakers being looted, other shops smashed, a Zeppelin overhead, mobs everywhere etc. were flying about. On leaving school about 10 pm (I came home with the Wrights) we were cautioned to form ourselves into parties and keep out of the mob's way, and in the middle of the road. We wished to see if the rumours were right, so we walked up Tennyson Road. Everyone was out of their doors. When we reached Schuarmroffels shop all the windows were smashed to atoms. Glass everywhere. Blinds torn, pieces of framework hanging out, and all the bread and cakes gone! Upstairs windows broken as well. When we arrived at the "Princess Alice" all was comparatively quiet, but people were busy smashing Goebels windows. D'Armes, the florists on the bridge had its windows smashed. A small shop opposite was wrecked.[65]

In Southend on 12 May, where feelings were very raw after the air raid just two days before, a meeting outside the Technical School protested at the non-internment of enemy aliens. When the meeting broke up part of the large crowd moved into Queen's Road, wrecking shops whose owners had German sounding names. Two hundred special constables and the Rifle Brigade were present, but were still too few in number to control the mob. The Border Regiment and King's Royal Liverpool Regiment arrived as reinforcements. Some of the initial banter between soldiers and rioters indicated that some of the troops sympathised with the mob. It was only after being warned by their officers for their apparent indifference to the fate of shop premises that the men moved to disperse them. Shepherded down the High Street by the military, the mob wrecked three more shops before finally dispersing after an hour and a half of mayhem and destruction. At Leyton local councillors intervened to protect the property of a Mr Schmidt, successfully preventing a large crowd from attacking his property. Schmidt, a naturalised British citizen of thirty years standing, had two sons in the army, one of whom had been killed only a few days before. The crowd moved off to find more acceptable targets, and smashed the windows of a baker who was known not be naturalised. At West Ham, John Glasson, who claimed that he and his parents were 'true-born Britishers,' had all four of his shops in the

[65] Potter/Grubb diary, 12 May 1915.

Barking Road wrecked. He estimated the damage at a thousand pounds; with the cost of his stolen goods taken into account, the mob had cost him between three and four thousand pounds.

The *Stratford Express*, although it condemned the rioters as cowardly opportunists, was also prepared to concede that German 'frightfulness' had pushed some people over the edge:

> At last however, the stolid Britisher appears to have been put off his usual imperturbability. The last straw has been added by the sinking of the *Lusitania*, and this latest phase of their barbarity has loosened the restraining influences, and even the self-control of a certain section of the public, who have begun to take the question of reprisals into their own hands.[66]

There were 110 arrests at West Ham, fifteen at Leyton, thirty-eight at East Ham, twenty at Stratford, and four at Southend. On the whole they seem to have been dealt with rather leniently by local magistrates, to the disquiet of some local people and the local press. Most were accused of trivial offences and given small fines. At the West Ham and Stratford police courts about ninety people were charged, largely with looting shops. Thirteen of them were fined £2 each, five were fined £1 each, and six received fines of less than a pound; four rioters were bound over to keep the peace, one was cautioned and three were sentenced to three months hard labour. The four men charged with riotous assembly at Southend, who included a fishmonger, a wine merchant, and an oil and colour merchant, were dismissed with the threat that their behaviour would be monitored. Only one rioter, Thomas Suckling of West Ham, was sentenced to six months hard labour for assaulting a policeman.[67]

However, there were voices urging restraint. In the first fortnight of war the Lord Lieutenant of Essex, the Earl of Warwick, urged tolerance and charity towards enemy aliens:

> They had in their midst friendly Germans, and in their relations towards the Germans in this country he thought they would always preserve towards them the position of honourable gentlemen (applause). We did not want methods of barbarity in this county (applause).[68]

At the same time one of Colchester's leading citizens, Wilson Marriage, wrote a letter to the press urging locals to protect naturalised British subjects, including

66 SE 15 May 1915.

67 ECC 14 May 1915; ECS 15 May 1915; SE 15 May 1915.

68 CG 19 August 1914.

Germans.[69] Other voices too urged restraint. When a Clacton magistrate, G.W. Thompson, publicly expressed the view that he was praying for the Germans to bomb the town as a way of stimulating recruitment, the *Essex County Telegraph* ridiculed this as "patriotism run wild!"[70] There were even those prepared to defend German culture from the philistines. In the first few days of the War a local who preferred to remain anonymous as 'J.T.S.' wrote to the *Stratford Express* to express his dismay at the rapid disappearance of German music from English homes, music halls, and from the repertoire of local bands. "Surely art is international, if it is anything at all", he pleaded, "and recognises no local, racial, or more fundamental boundary marks."[71] A Canon Swallow, the speaker at the Wanstead evening classes' prize-giving ceremony, urged the retention of German in the school syllabus.[72] When it was suggested that German should not be taught in English schools, the *Essex County Telegraph*'s columnist, Junius Minor, attacked the proposal as 'absurd'. Although part of his argument was that learning German was essential if Britain was to understand the mind of its enemy, he also added that:

> The present war will end some time, and to prohibit the children of the present day from studying the German language is to deprive them in the future of an acquaintance with much that is notable in German literature and science.[73]

Courageous words indeed in the frenzied anti-German atmosphere of late 1914.

Throughout the War individual ministers and churches fell foul of public opinion when they seemed to be straying too far from the straight and narrow path of patriotism. In 1916 there were outraged protests at an article in the *Free Church Witness*, the magazine of the Colchester and District Free Churches, when it criticised the Allied economic blockade of Germany for killing German civilians, and condemning it as a morally unjustifiable military tactic. Roderic Dunkerley had public opprobrium heaped upon him for defending the rights of conscientious objectors for whom military service was said to be "disloyalty to the inner witness of God", and for attending tribunal meetings to speak on behalf of a member of the No-Conscription Fellowship.[74] Colchester Peace Committee, which contained some of the town's Quakers, was likewise reviled and ridiculed for its anti-war stance and for publishing a poster entitled 'Peace Will Come'.[75] Anger at those who campaigned that

[69] CG 16 September 1914.

[70] ECT 6 February 1915.

[71] SE 15 August 1914.

[72] ECC 1 October 1915.

[73] ECT 17 October 1914.

[74] ECT 26 February 1916, ECS 18 March 1916.

[75] ECS 20 March 1915.

the War was wrong and that Britain ought not to have taken part led to some people taking direct action. In January 1917 Ramsay Macdonald addressed a meeting at the Cooperative Hall, Walthamstow. Macdonald, the pre-war leader of the Labour Party, had resigned in 1914 as a protest against the party's support for the War. He spent the war years campaigning against the conflict. A demonstration was organised by J.V. Graves, the secretary of the Walthamstow Branch of the British Empire Union to protest against the meeting. The locals who turned up for the meeting gave Macdonald and Val McEntee, from the Amalgamated Society of Carpenters and Joiners, a hostile reception. McEntee was continually interrupted so that he was unable to deliver a coherent message. The meeting was then brought to an abrupt halt when several Canadian soldiers entered and promptly ejected Macdonald and the other speakers. Following their unceremonious departure the audience joined the soldiers in an impromptu patriotic demonstration in favour of the War.[76]

Significantly a year later, when it was proposed "for posterity's needs" to jettison Greek, Latin and algebra from the school curriculum, there was no knight in shining armour to leap to their defence.[77] Indeed in an editorial on New Year's Day 1916, the *Essex County Standard* asserted that "the school curriculum is secondary to the very lives and liberties of the nation." It elaborated on this by advocating a kind of utilitarian imperialism in education as a means of winning the War:

> even the acquisition of the three R's is not prior to that of a sense of the duty of a citizen. The security of the Empire is the first and greatest lesson that needs imparting to every one of her sons and that, until that imperative necessity is realised, all other duties are relatively secondary.[78]

Most schools did in fact place patriotic sentiments firmly in the school curriculum. The established pre-war homage to the Empire continued each year on Empire Day (24 May), when whole schools assembled outside under the Union Jack, sang patriotic songs, particularly 'Rule Britannia' and 'God Save the King', and were subjected to stirring and often jingoistic speeches by the head teacher or chairman of governors. In May 1915 at Tillingham School pupils were given history lessons aimed "to acquaint the children with the lives of important men of modern times." Later that year they were taught about "the work and death [of the] modern martyr", Edith Cavell, who had been executed as a spy by the Germans. On 8 May 1916 the pupils were allowed out for the afternoon to cheer Field Marshal Lord French who was passing through the village, and whose itinerary had been made public beforehand.[79]

76 WG 12 January 1917.

77 HDS 28 August 1915.

78 ECS 1 January 1916.

79 ERO T/P 407/4, Tillingham Church of England School Logbooks 1907-47.

Some individuals tried to focus the public's awareness of the War as a national crusade against military despotism. The Reverend Parry urged no-one to use the War as a means of obtaining material gain from the Germans. He argued that it must not be an opportunity to seize German trade.[80] The virtuous Junius Minor made the same point. "We are fighting for honour", he wrote, "not for cash."[81] Parry was also not alone in urging Christians not to be led into narrow-minded jingoism by "the language of sensational newspapers."[82] In 1915 Colchester's mayor spoke along parallel lines when he rejected the wartime use of "hackneyed platitudes, of which the daily newspapers are daily full."[83]

The churches continued to be at the heart of the public ritual of war. For example, 3 February 1915 was declared a Special Day of Intercession by the Church of England on behalf of "Nation and Empire in this time of war." Services were held in all churches. At St Peter's, Colchester, the civic authorities attended. On 4 August 1915, the first anniversary of Britain's declaration of war, a huge service witnessed by thousands took place on Colchester's Abbey Field. In attendance were the representatives of all the borough's parishes, the wounded and staff from the military hospitals, the mayor and corporation of the town, the borough police, boy scouts, and local residents. The service was conducted from a military wagon parked under a huge Union Jack in the centre of the square formed by the dignitaries and the people. The service was similar to the one being carried out at St Paul's in London. The hymn 'Rock of Ages' was sung, followed by Psalm Fifty-one with its awareness of sin and its plea for forgiveness, "Wash me thoroughly from mine iniquity, and cleanse me from my sin." Prayers were said for the King and royal family, for the armed forces, the wounded and dying, the bereaved, the anxious and the dead. The hymns 'Praise My Soul the King of Heaven' and 'Through the Night of Doubt and Sorrow' concluded the forty-five-minute service.[84]

Individual churches attempted to play their part in the War, largely by providing a source of religious comfort and reassurance for worshippers and parishioners, although there were other aspects to their involvement. St Andrew's, the Anglican parish church at Hornchurch, provides a good example of the Church of England supporting its people at war. The Sportsman's Battalion, based at the nearby Grey Towers Camp, attended church parade every Sunday in the autumn of 1914, as did the New Zealand troops based there until their own camp church was built. St Andrew's remained the parish church of the New Zealanders and its assistant curate, A.J. Parry, together with Reverend Peter Miller, the pastor of the town's Baptist Church, were their honorary chaplains. Like many other Essex churches, within days

[80] ECT 5 September 1914.

[81] ECT 1 September 1914.

[82] ECT 5 September 1914.

[83] ECS 7 August 1915.

[84] ECS 7 August 1915.

of war breaking out, its rather limited number of services had been increased to include a weekday service each day at noon. Herbert Dale, the Vicar of St Andrew's, had established the custom of holding united services on great national or public occasions, inviting Nonconformist congregations and their ministers to attend, and this he continued to do throughout the War. The first opportunity was on 3 January 1915, the day of Solemn Intercession for the Nation and Empire. The vicar preached a sermon and lessons were read by the Reverend Benson Evans of the Congregational Church and the Reverend Peter Miller of the Baptist Church. Further days of Solemn National Prayer (January 1916), and National Prayer and Thanksgiving (January 1918) were held. On 4 August 1915 special services were held on the first anniversary of the outbreak of war.

Inevitably the War intruded into the everyday life of the Church. The casualties began to mount. In Hornchurch the first memorial service for the Fallen was held on 16 September 1915, by which time twenty-eight parishioners had been killed. On 24 October the vicar read the King's appeal to the young men of England to enlist. The congregation stood while his message was read and they sang 'God Save the King' when it was finished. It was at this time that evening services were abandoned because of the lighting restrictions. A generous and resourceful parishioner provided the necessary blackout materials and the services were restored after a fortnight. In September 1916 the church was in the thick of Zeppelin raids, the church bells being rung on the 6 September to celebrate the destruction of the Zeppelin L.31 on 2-3 September. As the German U-boat blockade began to bite, the clergy urged parishioners to consume food responsibly. On 4 February 1917 the Reverend Herbert Dale preached a sermon on 'The religious obligation of economy in food, and self-sacrifice in buying War Loans'. He followed this three weeks later with a sermon on the theme of 'Rationing as a bearing of one another's burdens'. In March-April 1918, as news of the great German offensive portended disastrous consequences, the Bishop of Chelmsford ordered special intercession services to calm the fears of the people. These were held on 14 April.

The final united service of the War at Hornchurch was held on Sunday, 4 August 1918, the fourth anniversary of the declaration of war. The service lasted for nearly two hours, and was attended by all denominations, as well as New Zealanders from the Grey Towers Convalescent Hospital accompanied by their nurses. The altar was covered by the Union Jack and the flags of the Allies hung from the pulpit, reading desk and the easternmost pillar of the south arcade. The sermon was preached by Bishop Neligan, chaplain to the New Zealand forces, who drew on the psalms for his text, 'God is our Refuge and Strength'. 'God Save the King' was sung and the roll of the parish Fallen was read out before the 'Last Post' was sounded by buglers from the New Zealand Army.[85]

Although it was thus able to convey to the public a highly convincing impression

[85] C.T. Perfect, *Hornchurch during the Great War* (1920), 233-45.

of unity behind the War effort, privately the Church of England still writhed under the self-inflicted sore of Anglo-Catholic ritualism. Since the 1870s Anglo-Catholicism had made substantial inroads among the clergy and parishioners of Essex. John Watts-Ditchfield, the first Bishop of Chelmsford, who was enthroned in April 1914, was well aware of the scale of the problem facing him. It was clear that the wide range of churchmanship within the diocese meant that uniformity would be hard to achieve. In his presidential address to the first ever diocesan conference in October 1914 he made it clear that he would not condone what he termed 'disloyal practices'. Although he refused to attend services in churches where incense was used, or where unacceptable liturgical changes had happened recently, he was prepared to visit parishes where such things had been done for years. However, because the issues of ritual, vestments and beliefs were at the heart of Anglo-Catholic priests' search for spiritual integrity they saw no reason to temper either their theology or practices — even during the War.

The Naters controversy in Colchester rumbled on throughout the War and continued even after his death in 1917. When the decision of the Consistory Court went against him in 1914 and he was ordered to remove the illegal objects he had placed in St James's over the previous twenty years, he apparently submitted with a public show of defiance and bad grace. At the time of his death in 1917, Naters had in fact removed none of the offending objects and it was left to his successor, who sought a rapprochement with the Bishop and a return to the diocesan fold, to remove the articles once the War was over.[86] Even during the War liturgical changes were introduced into Essex churches which provoked hostile responses. In 1916 the Vicar of Cressing, William Padbury, introduced incense into his services, conducted the first sung mass in the church, and placed candlesticks on the altar. It was also alleged that he had instructed the pupils at the church school to cross themselves. Padbury had been vicar since 1910, but it was in wartime that he made these controversial changes.[87] George Gresley, Vicar of Shenfield since 1909, also introduced Anglo-Catholic practices into the church in 1916, prompting one churchwarden to resign. Gresley's innovations aroused such hostility that in the autumn of 1917 he resigned, feeling that he could no longer continue his duties in accordance with the principles of the Church.[88] Occasionally inter-denominational disputes flared up. In 1917 the Nonconformists of Ridgewell were outraged when the vicar compelled their children to attend Ash Wednesday and Ascension Day services, and led to their call for a council school for the village after the War.[89] After the War the anti-ritualist Kensitites protested at St Clement's, Leigh, offended by the erection in the churchyard of a life

[86] P. Rusiecki, St James the Great, Colchester: History of a parish church and its people (1996), unpublished typescript.

[87] ECC 4, 18 February 1916.

[88] ECC 7 September 1917.

[89] ECC 29 June 1917.

size crucifix as a war memorial. Here Anglo-Catholic sentiments were evidently very firmly entrenched; in early 1917 the parishioners voted by sixty-one votes to twenty-four to use incense during their services.[90] At Saffron Walden there was an outcry when images of the Virgin Mary were placed in the church. In 1920 the continued presence of the images led to a Consistory Court being held to determine their legality.[91] There was controversy too in Southend. When the Vicar of Prittlewell, E.N. Gowing, invited the Vicar of All Saints', J.L. Weston, to preach in his church, he was appalled by the latter's sermon on behalf of the Anglo-Catholic Additional Curates' Society, in which he explained High Church doctrines and criticised the Anglican Church for going astray. At the end of the service Gowing publicly disassociated himself from Weston's comments.[92] Conrad Noel at Thaxted outdid all other Anglo-Catholic priests in resuming his blatantly provocative actions once the War was over. On 28 June 1919 he organised a Festival of Faith in which he led a large procession of worshippers around Thaxted, making use of incense and holy water, processing the Blessed Sacrament, before which he prostrated himself in the road. Members of the congregation carried a crucifix and images of the Virgin, and several ladies wore multi-coloured hanging veils. In the face of action by an enraged bishop, the parishioners of Thaxted defiantly passed a vote of confidence in Noel.[93]

From 1915 the message of the churches was increasingly one of repentance and renewal as being essential to win the War. In 1915 the Essex Congregational Union urged repentance and cleansing of the nation's social life as a way of focussing on "a holy ... vital and spiritual war."[94] This renewal included the continued exhortations to young men to jump before they were pushed and enlist. In June 1915 Reverend Canon Lake, Rector of the Cathedral Church at Chelmsford, spoke out against the 'regiments of slackers.' On the second anniversary of the declaration of war the Bishop of Chelmsford called for repentance. The nation must cleanse itself of its love of luxury, its social divisions, its neglect of the sabbath, its emphasis on pleasure, the worship of wealth, the relaxation of the marriage laws, the feebleness of their purity and temperance, and religious animosity "which cried aloud our need for repentance and change of heart."[95] The Bishop of Chelmsford and Bishop of Colchester were confident that the War would transform the country. "How this war is going to alter things", said the Bishop of Chelmsford, "we believe a new England will be born." He predicted that it would draw out "the spirit of philanthropy and charity."[96] However, the transformation of the country into the 'new England' which Watts-Ditchfield

[90] ECC 23 February 1917.

[91] ECC 11 April 1919, 5 March 1920.

[92] SST 27 November 1919.

[93] EEC 4, 11 July 1919.

[94] ECC 30 April 1915.

[95] ECT 5 August 1916.

[96] ECT 9 January 1915.

enthused about was evidently not intended to promote women to a more exalted role within the Church of England. Attempts to allow women, who formed a majority in most Anglican congregations, merely to attend rurideaconal and diocesan conferences, led conservative churchmen to throw up their hands in horror in case it provided encouragement to those who were advocates of women priests.[97]

The Bishop of Colchester enlarged on a familiar theme in these years, that of people coming to their senses through suffering:

> In their easy, self-centred lives they were often enervated by luxury and self-indulgence, and thought only of the present and immediate future. The fear of earthly loss and the presence of human suffering, however, enlarged their mental vision and compelled them to think of eternity, the unending spiritual life of which this mortal existence was but a fragment.[98]

The official diocesan view was that as the War dragged on, suffering would increase and intensify and the Church would become more indispensable, and perhaps as a result, it might become less socially exclusive:

> The present prosperity will not last. Work will become less. Receipts from billeting will cease. Deaths of men in the field will become more numerous. Homes will be broken up. The wounded, and the maimed for life, will be in our streets and the widow and the orphan will be found on every side. The Church must keep her head. She must hearten, encourage and comfort. She must leave the favoured few and look after the many. Services must be decreased rather than increased, that Clergy may have more time to go about doing good. The services must be simple and congregational, such as the outsider, driven in by the stress and storm without, can understand.[99]

This penitential theme inspired the Church of England's National Mission of Repentance and Hope, which was launched in the autumn of 1916. This was a response to the apparent failure of the War to stimulate a national religious revival. At first the Church hoped that the War would end and the mission would be implemented during peacetime. However, by early 1916 the Archbishop of Canterbury, Randall Davidson, decided to launch the National Mission of

97 See Chapter 9 for a fuller discussion of this issue.

98 ECS 15 August 1914.

99 CDC, September 1915

Repentance and Hope in October and November of that year.[100] The Church of England was well aware of its own problems and shortcomings. The steady decline in church attendance during the nineteenth century had not been reversed when war broke out in 1914. There was widespread apathy towards the Church throughout the country. Some blamed what was seen as the Church's persistent requests for money; others alleged that the well-educated clergy, many of whom came from privileged backgrounds, were out of touch with ordinary people and unable to respond to their needs. Another reason given for the apathy of the working classes towards religion was that they had become more independently minded, less responsive to the Church's teachings and more attracted to the arguments of trade unions. There were tensions within the Church too, including resentment by some clergy towards an outmoded and inequitable system of patronage which contributed to clerical poverty. In early 1917, J. Anderson Telford, was leaving to take up another living. He was critical of his meagre stipend of £130 a year, claiming that he could not have survived in his living but for sources of income outside it.[101]

Chelmsford, like all other dioceses, was to run its own mission. The Bishop of Chelmsford was appointed to the Central Committee of the National Mission, and he travelled around the diocese promoting the idea. A deanery day of prayer was held; there were special women's meetings; the leaders of the local labour movement were invited to participate. Every parishioner was to be visited by the clergy, a pilgrimage of prayer was planned, there were to be visits by 'flying squads' from the Church Army, and open air meetings held. Meetings were held throughout the diocese in May, and there was a programme of clergy retreats during May, June and July. Quiet days were held for the women of the diocese. The Bishop of Chelmsford's views on the need for repentance were unchanged. At the start of the mission he spoke on the familiar theme of the nation turning away from Mammon and towards God:

> No nation can be regarded as Christian with a drink bill of 160 millions, and an expenditure of some two millions on the evangelising of the world, with a turnover of some 50 millions in the bookmakers' hands; with its reports on Venereal Diseases and the Society for the Prevention of Cruelty to Children, with the appalling conditions of slumland in all our large cities; with the spirit of materialism still in our midst; with the forgetfulness of God as evidenced by the desecration of this Holy Day.[102]

Supported by local Nonconformist leaders the plan was an ambitious one, although it is not easy to measure how successful it was. Services of intercession

[100] Beaken thesis, 140-145.

[101] ECC 19 January 1917.

[102] ECC 13 October 1916.

connected with the mission or the War in general were never well attended, although some special events and certain anniversaries were well patronised. The services on the Abbey Field in Colchester commemorating the start of the War attracted large numbers of people; religious services and concerts held in the open air, as at the Clacton Bandstand, were also hugely popular. Certainly many people in these terrible times were drawn to an ecumenical and congregational spirit of worship rather than anything wrapped up in a denominational straitjacket. This is not to deny that the War did see many turn to the churches. The number of communicants at Anglican churches does seem to have increased, but the spread was patchy. At St Michael's, Kirby-le-Soken, the average annual number of communicants at Sunday worship during 1909-13 was 716; during the war years it increased by only about seven per cent. At St Peter's, Colchester, however, the annual average for 1914-17 was 1,386, an increase of almost thirty per cent on the years 1909-13. Communicant attendances at St Anne's and St Lawrence's, Elmstead, showed an even more remarkable increase, almost doubling in the years 1914-17.[103] Confirmations, a useful indication of the strength of religious feeling, certainly increased during the War. In 1914 there were 4,066 confirmations in the diocese of Chelmsford, during 1915 this rose to 7,797. In 1916 there were over three thousand confirmations in the deanery of Barking alone.[104] Anglican finances however, remained in a generally parlous state. In 1914-15 at Colchester, churches were burdened with financial deficits — St Leonard's, Lexden (£33), St Nicholas's (£11), Holy Trinity (£15), and St Botolph's (£5). The other town churches had generally modest surpluses, ranging from St James's (£35) to St Paul's (3*s*. 9*d*.).

With few exceptions the churches of Essex were wholeheartedly behind the war effort. They saw as their duty the encouragement of the British people to view the War as a national religious crusade against the godless might of Germany. If the utterances of some clergymen seem intemperate and ill-considered to modern sensibilities, their perceptions of the War, fuelled by the invasion of Belgium, allegations of German atrocities, and by contemporary notions of national honour and righteousness, were immensely hard to resist. The churches, particularly the Anglican Church, remained an integral part of the formal and official presentation of the war effort. Their influence was evident throughout the War and Christian theology and imagery were later to play a highly significant role in the war memorial movement from its genesis to its inception.

[103] ERO D/P 169/1/29, D/P 178/1/35, D/P 168/1/13, register of services.

[104] CDC January 1915, January 1917.

CHAPTER FOUR

Volunteers and Conscripts

Guard drawn from the 4th Volunteer Battalion, Essex Regiment in Clarence Road, Southend-on-Sea, 1915. *(ERO: D/DS 229/58)*

He is just a lad in khaki,
But when duty's to be done,
You will find him bravely fighting,
Behind his rifle or his gun.
He is fighting for his country;
He is fighting for his King;
Fighting for his wives and kiddies;
Fighting hard the end to bring.

You may hear him grouse and grumble,
Yet he fights on just the same;
For he knows it is for freedom,
And for England's dear old name.
English, Irish, Welsh, or Scotchman,
Hindu or Colonial brave,
All united in a great cause,
To win honour or a soldier's grave.

Private A. Mansfield of Hutton,
written in the trenches on the
Western Front in August 1915.

THE SO-CALLED "rush to the colours" of August 1914 continued into the autumn and early winter. Throughout Essex the volunteers of August were carted away to Warley barracks for training and consequently Colchester garrison was at normal, pre-war strength until the end of the month. By the end of September however, there were 10,404 troops on strength, 13,973 a month later, 17,172 by the end of November, and a small reduction to 16,901 at the end of the year. These figures, of course, represent an influx of regular army personnel, all recruited and trained in the years before war broke out. However, civilians were also eager to join up. The army recruiting offices in Port Lane were too small to accommodate the numbers trying to enlist; in early September the town council gave the army the use of rooms at the Albert School and the rush continued as over a hundred men a day signed up.[1] Recruiting offices were opened throughout the county; the three main centres were at Colchester, Stratford and Warley. That at Burnham, in the Territorial Drill Hall, was open for two hours a day, three days a week.[2] To stimulate enthusiasm and celebrate local patriotism the local press printed the first list of local volunteers before the end of August; by 17 October closely-packed type crammed two full pages of the *Essex County Standard*.[3] Within a fortnight of Britain entering the War the Essex Territorial Battalions were up to full strength and stopped recruiting because five hundred

1 ECT 5 September 1914.

2 BDA 5 September 1914.

3 ECT 3, 17, 24 October 1914.

recruits had enlisted since 5 August. Individual towns and villages watched as their tally of volunteers for Kitchener's army was listed week by week. Four hundred men were said to have joined up in Colchester on the first three days of September; a thousand from Chelmsford in that week alone. By early September seventy-three men had joined up from Writtle, fifty from Kelvedon, twenty-four from Thaxted, fifty-nine from the Hanningfields, seventy from Hatfield Peverel, over ninety from Felsted and Rayne and sixty from Stansted; five hundred had enlisted from Braintree by the end of the year, and it was claimed that not a single man under thirty-five was left in the village of Pebmarsh.[4] By January 1915, 4,573 men had enlisted from the Harwich parliamentary division. Volunteers in their hundreds had stepped forward from Harwich and Dovercourt (587), Clacton (482), Brightlingsea (288), Grays (287) and even small villages such as Frating (thirteen) and Little Horkesley (sixteen) had contributed a large proportion of their young men.[5] One hundred joined up from the Salvation Army colony at Hadleigh. By mid-1915 it was alleged that Frinton had only fourteen men left who had not volunteered.[6] At Saffron Walden 265 men volunteered in just two days in early September 1914. The local *Weekly News* listed the men's occupations to demonstrate the patriotism of the area's varied military intake:

farm labourers	47	labourers	67
coachman	1	draper	1
gamekeeper	1	butchers	3
chauffeurs	9	footmen	3
dealers	1	decorators	4
hurdlemakers	2	brickmakers	5
milkmen	2	farmers	6
postmen	2	railway porters	5
carmen	7	shop assistants	5
engineers	2	grocer	1
grooms	11	mechanics	2
golf caddie	1	railway clerk	1
hotel porter	1	gas fitter	1
clerks	6	maltster	1
carpenters	9	gardeners	13
drover	1	waiter	1
engine driver	1	platelayers	2
printer	1	horseman	1
bakers	6	whitesmiths	2
stockmen	4	nurserymen	19
stonemason	1	ropemaker	1 [7]

4 WWN 4, 11 September 1914; ECC 18 September 1914.

5 ECS 20 February 1915.

6 EEA 19 June 1915.

7 WWN 11 September 1914.

By the end of October 441 men from the Dengie peninsula had joined the army, and ninety-two had enlisted in the navy. Burnham, for instance, had provided 259 of these men.[8]

Perhaps it is hardly surprising that in the first few weeks of war people's impressions about recruitment erred on the side of generosity. They were overwhelmed by the sense of crisis and occasion, and swamped by the enthusiasm of those who did volunteer, especially as this was often accompanied by the frenzied village farewells which were given to volunteers. The atmosphere of excitement and near hysteria in places such as Colchester, provoked by the constant coming and going of regiments and military units, only added to the belief that local men were volunteering in unprecedented numbers. After three weeks of war Colonel R.B. Colvin stated that there were twelve thousand men serving with the colours.[9] In late September the number of Essex recruits was put at thirty thousand.[10] Three months later at a recruiting meeting, where it has to be said that a concern for the truth was rarely an integral part of the proceedings, the recruiting officer, Captain C.H. Norman, alleged that the slightly lower figure of twenty-five thousand Essex men had volunteered.[11] The military's calculations were on a surprisingly smaller scale. After a fortnight of war the 44th Recruiting Area, which included the districts of Brentwood, Chelmsford, Colchester, Grays, Harwich, Ilford, Romford, Shoeburyness and Southend, reported the enlistment of only about five hundred recruits since 5 August, the day after war was declared. One hundred and thirty-six of these men had been rejected. The announcement noted that there had been a particularly poor response in Ilford and Romford. These figures hardly seem credible and they sit uneasily alongside the claim made in the *Essex County Chronicle* on 11 September, for instance, that 960 had volunteered in Colchester alone in the previous week, or that 500 had joined up within a twelve-mile radius of Chelmsford by the end of August, a further thousand in the first week in September, or with the 265 volunteers who stepped forward in just two days at Saffron Walden.[12] At Harlow between 24 August and 12 September 120 men had enlisted, at Barking 450 men had volunteered, although only 324 had been accepted.[13]

However, enlistment was certainly not uniformly high throughout the county. For instance Rochford hundred's 'Roll of Honour' for August 1914 shows a steady trickle rather than a flood of recruits:

8 BDA 7 November 1914.

9 ECC 28 August 1914.

10 ECC 25 September 1914.

11 ECC 27 November 1914.

12 ECC 28 August 1914; WWN 11 September 1914; BA 19 September 1914.

13 BA 12 September 1914.

Date	No. recruits	Date	No. recruits
6-11 August	40	25 August	16
12-17 August	58	26 August	22
18 August	12	27 August	34
19 August	17	28 August	22
20 August	1	29 August	24
21 August	8	30 August	28
22 August	8	31 August	36
23 August	10	1 September	23
24 August	12	TOTAL	371 [14]

Likewise in the Harlow district recruitment had progressed slowly but steadily until early November when, after three months of war, the figures stood at:

	Population	No. enlisted
Great Hallingbury	490	30
Little Hallingbury	552	38
Harlow	2,980	98
Latton	2,322	8
Hatfield Regis	728	33
Hatfield Heath	645	48
Sheering	664	46
Great Parndon	550	15
Little Parndon	76	1
Matching	554	14 [15]

West Ham proved to be a particularly successful example of voluntary recruitment in the early stages of the War. On 29 December 1914 the mayor received permission to recruit a West Ham battalion, which in due course would become the Thirteenth Battalion of the Essex Regiment. It was to be raised specifically for overseas service as part of Kitchener's army. In mid-January a front page advert in the *Stratford Express* urged men to enlist in the new 'pals' battalion':

> No gas-bag invention can alarm us
> True Manhood will win!
> Join your friends in the WEST HAM BATTALION
> Already enlisted as follows:

A large list of volunteers was added at the bottom of the page. Five hundred men had joined by the end of January 1915, by early March 1,100 had enlisted, and by the end of the month it had met its target of 1,350 volunteers. The War Office was

[14] SST 3 September 1914.

[15] ECC 13 November 1914.

so impressed that the borough was immediately asked to form a second battalion. Shortly afterwards a field artillery brigade was raised in West Ham, and although it only required eighty-six men, 596 volunteered to join. By the end of April, after less than a month, the brigade was created. In May 1915 neighbouring East Ham was asked to form an artillery brigade of 750 men. It was not all plain sailing though. About seven hundred of the First Battalion's volunteers were married men and there was a great deal of local criticism of the apparent reluctance of single men and middle-class men to join its ranks.[16]

In contrast to places like West Ham, some rural locations saw resistance to enlistment. At Stisted local farm labourers were reluctant to respond to the urgings of the local squire, Major Cecil Sebag-Montefiore, who expressed his 'open dissatisfaction' with the fact that only two villagers had volunteered. The Braintree branch of the Workers' Union similarly declined to assist the local recruiting drive because Sebag-Montefiore had previously denied its members assistance, although the particulars of their case were rather vague. He promptly took his revenge by ordering that no eligible man aged nineteen to thirty-five should be employed on his Stisted Hall Estate, nor as beaters in his shooting parties.[17] The Mayor of Southend, Joseph Francis, was determined to send a thousand recruits from the area. Following a football match between Southend United and Southampton in early September, he made a personal appeal to the crowd from the grandstand and had ready a number of cars outside the ground to ferry volunteers to the recruiting station. This was not particularly successful and he launched another appeal at the end of October. However, it was not until early November that Francis's relatively modest target was reached.[18]

Local men were bombarded with patriotic propaganda with only one aim in mind. At Colchester's variety houses and cinemas in late 1914 it was virtually non-stop entertainment with a wartime slant. The *Essex County Standard* claimed that theatre proprietors had discovered that jingoistic patriotism was essential if programmes were to appeal to men in khaki, but such programmes were also an insistent and subtle reminder to male civilians that there was a war going on; one in which they were apparently reluctant to participate. The Theatre Royal showed *Britain's Call*, a tableau in four scenes which included an appearance by Jean Schellermanns, a Belgian despatch rider wounded at Mons. A week later a music-hall evening by the Colchester Operatic Society included the song 'It's a Long Way to Tipperary'. Later that month a concert by the Eighth Norfolk Regiment featured the popular patriotic air 'Your King and Country Needs You'.[19] The Vaudeville Electric Theatre and Headgate Electric Theatre saturated their programmes with wartime features. By the end of

[16] SE 16, 23, 30 January, 6, 27 March, 24 April, 1 May 1915.

[17] ECC 28 August, 4 September 1914.

[18] SST 10 September, 29 October, 12 November 1914.

[19] ECS 7, 14, 21 November 1914.

August 1914 the former was showing film of fighting at Liege; other features included *The Great European War*, *Cavalry Horsemanship*, *In the Wake of the Huns*, *V.C.* and *The Heroine of Mons*.[20] The Headgate Electric Theatre competed with *War and the Woman*, *With the Serbian Army*, *Our Japanese Allies*, *The River Meuse*, *With the Belgian Army*, *Boys of the Bulldog Breed*, *England's Glory* (a naval epic), *The Defence of Alost* (a stirring tale from Belgium), *Kaiserisms* (caricature cartoons), *Your Country Needs You*, *Called to the Front* and an espionage melodrama called *The Enemy in our Midst*.[21] Even the Hippodrome, the theatre least affected by this avalanche of wartime entertainment, showed *Britannia's Honour*, seven tableaux including life studies of Allied leaders such as the Tsar, the French leader Poincaré and the King of the Belgians.[22]

However, as winter began to turn into the spring of 1915, it became clear that the enthusiasm of the early days of the War had not been sustained, and that the number of volunteers was dwindling. Although the local press continued to trumpet the county's recruitment, there is definite evidence of reluctance to enlist on the part of young men. At a recruitment meeting at Galleywood near Chelmsford in early September 1914 only three men of military age attended and many simply refused to go inside. Another meeting at Great Baddow was attended by just twenty elderly men. One of them told the *Essex County Chronicle*'s reporter that of the 110 men in the village eligible for military service, only seven had joined up.[23] A recruitment meeting at nearby Springfield attracted only ladies and a few national reservists, although there was a feeling that many had already enlisted from here.[24] A meeting held at Maldon in late September proved to be equally disappointing and "did not comprise a large number of men eligible for enlistment."[25] In December 1914 there was said to have been considerable disquiet at Frinton in view of the disappointingly low number of volunteers in response the town's recruitment campaign, and the finger was pointed at the town's working classes:

> It is a fact that in the case of Frinton many of those who were the first to respond to the call of duty were men of education, position and used to all the comforts of life – men who did not shrink from the loss of ease and indolence, scratched skins and dirty trenches, men with all to lose and nothing to gain – except the "well done" of their fellows who could not emulate their splendid example.[26]

20 ECS 19, 26 September, 10 October, 28 November, 19 December 1914.

21 ECS 29 August, 12, 19 September, 10, 31 October, 12 December 1914.

22 ECS 5 December 1914.

23 ECC 11 September 1914.

24 ECC 18 September 1914.

25 ECC 25 September 1914.

26 EEA 12 December 1914.

By late February 1915 military personnel were complaining that recruiting meetings in the Colchester division were not well attended.[27] This seemed to be a widespread problem throughout the county, where the Territorial Association bemoaned that recruitment to both its ranks and those of the regular army was in serious decline:

Date	Enlistments to Regular Army	Enlistments to Territorial Association
December 1914	691	791
January 1915	490	545
February 1915	138	176 [28]

There is, however, some evidence that despite the urgent need for men the recruiting authorities were rather selective. A recruiting officer, Captain C.H. Norman, speaking at Springfield in late November, noted that enthusiasm was on the wane and he accused the country of having "lapsed into criminal lethargy."[29] J.J. Crewe, of the Brentwood Patriotic Committee, seemed to be in full agreement with Norman's views. He spoke of the amazing apathy towards the War among the young men of the county.[30] On the other hand, another officer, Colonel W.N. Tufnell, told a recruiting meeting at Writtle that "for recruits they did not want the loafer from the taproom, they wanted men whom they could trust."[31]

In the face of the declining enthusiasm shown by local men further recruitment measures were undertaken. Some of these were decidedly unsubtle. Within a month of the outbreak of war Walthamstow's tramcars carried notices saying simply, "What! Still here?". No one needed to be told who these notices were aimed at.[32] Lieutenant Colonel Fred Taylor, Commander of the 2/5th Battalion, Essex Regiment, appealed for more volunteers from the nineteen to thirty-eight age range and offered a bonus of £1 to the first hundred men to come forward.[33] Shortly afterwards the Essex Territorials, lauded as 'sun burnt warriors', were marched through Essex on a prolonged recruiting parade in order to inspire the county's young men and stiffen their resolve. Just over the border, at Bishop's Stortford some eligible men who were not in uniform were roughly handled by the soldiers, being made "the subject of jibes and ridicule", and one of them was thrown in the River Stort.[34] The march yielded a

[27] ECS 27 February 1915.

[28] ECS 13 March 1915.

[29] ECS 27 November 1914.

[30] ECS 4 September 1914.

[31] ECC 11 September 1914.

[32] LE 12 September 1914.

[33] ECS 27 March 1915.

[34] ECT 8 May 1915; ECC 14 May 1915.

harvest of volunteers – forty-four officers and 1,468 men, but that still left a shortfall of a thousand men.[35]

There was certainly no shortage of eloquent and fervent orators, particularly among the clergy, who were determined to encourage young men into action or to shame them into enlisting. J.A. Telford, the Vicar of Harwich, was one of many clerics who advocated that young men perform their duty:

> It was a sweet and noble thing to die for one's native land. When wives and mothers were giving their loved ones, when children were losing their fathers, could any young man who was capable of being made a soldier, could any such young man bear the shame of holding back? God forbid. Peace! Peace would only come as the result of unflinching fighting on our part.[36]

Since August 1914 Canon Brownrigg, the Dean of Bocking, had been advocating that "things should be made unpleasant, *of course in a very nice way* [author's italics], for young men who did not enlist in the Kitchener army."

Canon Ingles, Vicar of Witham, was completely outspoken in his views about the county's young men. His comments suggest that he too thought that his young male parishioners were not stepping forward to do their duty in sufficient numbers:

> I shall forever be ashamed of my parish if she does not send out all her young men, and those of the proper age to fight. I don't want to see the married men go out first. I want to see all the single men from 19 to 35 years clean out of Witham parish ... I believe this war is a visitation sent from God; and I believe through this war we shall find out what God means for us — and then do it, as Englishmen always have done.[37]

James Silvester, the Vicar of Great Clacton and Little Holland, even wrote a song which was intended to stir men's patriotic souls and which included the following verse:

> Men of the nation so often victorious,
> Sons of your fathers who battled of yore,
> Count life and death to be equally glorious
> As ye contend for the right evermore.[38]

[35] ECC 11 June 1915.

[36] CG 2 September 1914.

[37] ECC 11 September 1914.

[38] ECC 28 August 1914.

On 29 May 1915 Private J. Crowe of Plaistow, lying wounded in a hospital in France, wrote a poem entitled 'The Call' appealing for his fellow county men to enlist. The poem was published in the *Stratford Express* a week later:

> Why are you waiting my brother,
> When your country's in distress?
> Cannot you see you're a "wanted another"?
> Why so hard are you to impress?
>
> Is it the fireside and home ties
> That stop you giving a hand?
> Just think of the men who are fighting
> And left "all" in their native land.
>
> What do their nearest and dearest
> Think of you who are hanging back?
> Buck up! And join them today, lads,
> And help us to shoulder the pack.
>
> For it's weary to see so many
> Who are daily going down
> For the want of you single fellows
> To take up a fighting crown.
>
> It's no use saying there are others
> Who ought to come with me;
> Just weigh it up very clearly,
> And train for across the sea.
>
> Look at it fairly and squarely,
> As a man who has brain and sense,
> And join us today and save us
> From the agony of suspense.[39]

Colchester's M.P., Laming Worthington-Evans, appealed to his audience using the crude methods of emotional blackmail:

> He could only warn them as it were of what might be as the years rolled by. There would be in the future, looking back on today, men who did and men who did not answer the call. The men who did would be honoured forever. The men who did not would be finding excuses for their conduct.[40]

[39] SE 5 June 1915.

[40] CG 23 September 1914.

Such pressure was everywhere. At Great Leighs Andrew Clark noted disapprovingly that the local squire and his daughters were trying to persuade local farm labourers to enlist.[41] The Vicar of Brentwood, the Reverend J. Thomas, was equally keen to urge young men to enlist, and from the pulpit he urged women to put pressure on their menfolk to step forward.[42] When the Reverend F. Kistruck, the Congregational Pastor of Bocking Church Street, said that undue pressure ought not to be brought to bear on young men to enlist, the local M.P., the Hon. Fortescue Flannery, confessed to being "surprised and depressed" by this comment.[43] The local press increased the pressure on young men by constantly listing the number of volunteers from this village or that town, from this workplace or that company. Newspapers were only too willing to print letters sent home by serving soldiers which struck a patriotic tone; printing them could perhaps stir the guilty consciences of those who stayed clear of the recruiting office. One such letter appeared in the *Essex County Chronicle* of 4 September 1914. It had been sent by Private Leslie Clark of Colchester, an ex-grammar school pupil who had joined the Essex Territorials straight from school. He was informing his mother of his reasons for enlisting in the regular army:

> My forefathers before me have won and held this country for us, and now when we are in need of men, one man from each family ought to volunteer. Surely it is better to fight the Germans in their land than to have to fight them on our own doorstep. Now, as I am the eldest son, I wish to fight for my country abroad. All our officers have volunteered. I want to follow their suit, mother dear. I am only asking you because I know an Englishman like father would wish me to go to defend the old flag abroad ... Don't think me selfish; but I want to defend you and England's freedom, and if I don't, who will?

Local government bodies found themselves involved in the fray of recruitment. At a meeting of the Tendring Board of Guardians, one of its members, the Reverend R.P. Tollinton, urged

> That the Board do place on record its intentions as regard the making of contracts in the near future, of giving especially favourable consideration to the tenders of those firms which shall be known to have facilitated the enlistment in the National forces of members of their staff, and in whose employment the proportion of unmarried men, eligible for active service, shall be shown to be the lowest.

41 Clark, *Diary*, 12, 58.

42 ECC 4 September 1914.

43 ECC 21 August 1914.

Tollinton's suggestion was rejected as a number of board members took exception to it:

> Mr Carter said he was surprised to find such a resolution as this being brought forward before a body of gentlemen and Englishmen. It was un-English and partook of the spirit of persecution.[44]

Such setbacks did not dissuade the Lexden and Winstree Rural District Council from passing a similarly critical resolution:

> It was resolved that a protest be made to the Essex County Council against the employment of several able-bodied men on the road at Marks Tey and Copford.[45]

Braintree Rural District Council was also put in an awkward position when it received a critical letter from the Lord of the Manor, Archibald Ruggles-Brise. Ruggles-Brise had taken exception to the council employing two young men on the roads and asked it to sack them. As at Tendring, the council took umbrage at the letter, condemned it, and refused to dismiss them. Whatever reluctance local councils had at participating in the victimisation of young men, they were sometimes willing to identify groups who needed a sense of responsibility forced upon them. In 1917 several boards of guardians joined in an outcry against tramps, who were suddenly identified as a completely untapped reservoir of potential labour or soldiery, all the more so since it was assumed that there were malingerers and shirkers hiding amongst them. H.H. Turner of Barnston Hall, Dunmow, a member of the town's Board of Guardians, referred to them as "Weary Willies and Tired Tims."[46] The Ongar Board of Guardians began the campaign by urging the conscription of all tramps to work on the roads on the Western Front. As many tramps were avoiding workhouses in order to escape registration and conscription, this presumably would entail a round-up of the offending wanderers. Within a month the Guardians at Epping, Billericay, West Ham and Halstead had passed similar resolutions urging conscription of tramps. At Saffron Walden there was anger at the alleged increase in the number of young men tramping, and one councillor urged the creation of a labour colony in the town in order to force them to work.[47] The Essex War Agricultural Committee, desperate to retain its agricultural labourers, also urged the conscription of tramps as

44 EEA 5 December 1914.

45 ERO D/RLw M1/5, Lexden and Winstree Rural District Council minutes 1912-16, 21 July 1915.

46 ECC 12 January 1917.

47 WWN 25 June 1915.

a way of keeping valuable workers on the county's farms. It quoted what it considered to be scandalous figures from the workhouse at Ongar, where it claimed that between fifty and sixty per cent of the 1,052 men who went through its casual wards in the previous nine months were all fit to work.[48] Some, like those at Dunmow, stood aloof from the campaign, but it commanded widespread support and perhaps typified the growing intolerance within British society against those groups who did not conform to wartime expectations.[49]

The views of older ex-soldiers who were returning to active service on the outbreak of war were also given publicity in order to support the recruitment campaign. John George Pearman, a thirty-seven-year-old from Little Canfield, who had previously served for thirteen years in the Royal Artillery in India, Africa and Egypt, wrote that "I have fought with browns, blacks, yellows and whites, and now I am going for the Germans."[50]

Those men that did not enlist in the first wave of recruitment were referred to as 'skulkers', a reference to the belief that, for whatever reason, they were deliberately hanging back. In late November 1914 the *Essex County Chronicle* printed a poem by a local man, Ernest Ellis, entitled 'Fight or Skulk: Which Shall It Be?' Its words echoed the famous poster 'Daddy, What Did You Do in the War?',

> Or will it be you, proved a scorner,
> Of England's need, slunk round a corner,
> To hide the rising blush of shame,
> And stopped your ears from ever hearing,
> The hailing crowds profoundly cheering,
> When came the lads who'd played the game.[51]

R. Woodhouse's mind was running along similar lines when he declared at a recruiting meeting that "It is better that your sons should die if they have to die than that you should have brought forth poltroons."[52] Death rather than dishonour was a theme preached monotonously during the War years. The press printed stories which suggested that it was right to categorise all young men not in uniform as 'slackers'. Five youths appeared at the Ongar Petty Sessions in February 1915 accused of playing pitch and toss on Christmas Day. When the chairman, Mr Tyndale White, asked them why they were not serving, one excused himself on the grounds of poor eyesight, another claimed he had corns, and one alleged he was too young. The moral of the

48 ECC 1 December 1916.

49 ECC 5 January, 2 February 1917.

50 ECC 11 September 1914.

51 ECC 27 November 1914.

52 ECC 11 September 1914.

story, as if the report had not made it obvious enough already, was contained in the following exchange:

THE CHAIRMAN:	If you come up to my place I will cure your corns. Would you join the Army and serve your country then?
THE YOUNG MAN:	I shall go when they come for me — not before.
THE CHAIRMAN:	You are a rotter![53]

Supported by a range of public speakers, the army employed a panoply of recruitment propaganda. To whip up recruits the 2/5th Essex Regiment embarked on a route march through central and east Essex, beginning with Chelmsford and taking in Great Baddow, Sandon, Danbury, Woodham Walter, Maldon and Heybridge.[54] Unfortunately most army recruiting officers delivered their message crudely and tastelessly. "Young men [who are] physically fit ought to be ashamed to stand behind the counter selling calico and buttons, and weighing out cheese and butter", said Colonel Fred Taylor.[55] Another officer, a Captain Newman, targeted un-enlisted men in another occupation and bludgeoned his point home with all the subtlety of a sledgehammer: "All the waiters in every hotel should realise that if they could bayonet a German, it was not their duty to hand round greasy dishes (laughter and applause)."[56] Waiters and, particularly, shopkeepers were frequent targets for recruiting officers who scarcely disguised their accusation that these were men sheltering from the War in rather effeminate occupations. Newman was critical of anyone he suspected of avoiding work, regardless of whether or not they were considered to be engaged in work of national importance: "There were many men who preferred to earn their 30 shillings, 40 shillings, 50 shillings or whatever it was, at Paxmans and Mumfords to enlisting in this great hour of our need."[57]

Shortly afterwards he was berating Essex County Council for failing to inculcate its schoolchildren with militaristic propaganda:

> Why were Essex children not taught something of the glories of their Regiment? Why were schoolroom walls decorated with the pictures of birds and their eggs instead of the roll of honour of their county regiment?

[53] ECC 5 February 1915.

[54] ECC 7 May 1915.

[55] ECC 7 May 1915.

[56] ECC 1 May 1915.

[57] ECS 27 February 1915.

Newman's approach was made to appear almost temperate and considered in comparison with the outbursts of Major Scott-Allen, who could not conceal the contempt he felt for men who had not joined up:

> There are tens of thousands of decadents, called 'nuts' ... who should be ashamed to look upon any woman in the face [sic] until they have put on the King's uniform. These are slackers and shirkers, the softies of the lower middle class. With a view to imparting some backbone to these jellyfish, I should establish the principle that every man's first duty is to his country.[58]

The *Essex County Chronicle* too was in despair at how many young men were evading their duty, and the fact that they seemed impervious to criticism:

> It has unfortunately to be confessed that there are slackers and shirkers ... We all know them. We see them in the train going to the city. We see them in the streets, all gaily dressed on Sundays. They have been hit in recruiting speeches, but they appear pachydermatous.[59]

At a service of intercession on the Essex County Cricket ground, Canon Thornton-Duesbury described shirkers as "scornful and miserable ... when their noble men came back, as pray God, they might, victorious", he told the crowd of two thousand, "these men would shrink back in the crowd, as they had failed to do their duty."[60]

Others were prepared to point the finger of accusation at particular groups within society. At a meeting of the East Ham Battalion of the National Reserve, Colonel Brooker Ward absolved the working class, the aristocracy, and the upper-middle class from guilt, for they had stepped forward in large numbers. In his view the malingerers were the lower-middle class, avoiding their duty by going about their business as if there was no war on. He described them colourfully as "the straw hat brigade, sucking their pipes, smoking fags, reading papers, and talking on the war, which they knew nothing about."[61]

By mid-1915 it was clear that nationally levels of recruitment had fallen below the high levels of nine months earlier. To ascertain just how many men (and women) were available for war service, of whatever nature, the Government ordered a national register of men and women. When the exact number of eligible men who had not enlisted was known, they would be visited and asked to explain why they were not in uniform. Each local council was responsible for organising the register. At Walton

[58] ECS 26 March 1915.

[59] ECC 26 March 1915.

[60] ECC 16 July 1915.

[61] ECC 4 September 1914.

the town was divided into five enumeration districts, perhaps those of the decennial census, with enumerators in each one, aided by special constables; Colchester was divided into ninety-six districts, Braintree into twenty, Saffron Walden into seventeen.[62] In Colchester, as elsewhere, the borough's teachers gave up part of their summer holiday to distribute and collect the registration papers.[63] The register revealed that nationally over two million men eligible for military service had still not enlisted. Popular feeling demanded that these slackers be forced to enlist. The pressure for conscription was becoming increasingly fierce. Prime Minister Asquith adopted a delaying action. In October 1915 the so-called Derby Scheme was launched, headed by the Conservative Lord Derby. It was the last throw of the dice for the voluntary system, a last ditch attempt to stave off the unthinkable — the introduction of compulsory military service. It was something which no British government had ever done, partly because it was regarded by some as being incompatible with the liberal principles on which Britain's greatness was supposedly based, and partly because conscription was regarded as characteristic of the tyranny and militarism which were considered to be the dominating forces at work in continental Europe. As the *Essex County Telegraph* noted, "Prussianism and conscription are synonymous terms."[64]

The Derby Scheme invited men aged eighteen to forty-one to attest or agree to register their willingness to serve in the armed forces when needed. It was understood that the youngest men would be taken first and that single men would be called before any that were married. Eligible men were placed into one of forty-six groups. Groups one to twenty-three for single men, with group one being men aged eighteen, groups twenty-four to forty-six were for married men. In Essex this included a large proportion of the 321,749 males aged fifteen to sixty-five who had been living in the county in 1911.[65] Recruiting meetings under the Derby Scheme were undertaken with a renewed vigour in late 1915. The Recruiting Committee at Harwich, anxious to maximise the chances of the scheme working effectively, issued the following instructions to its urban, district and parish councils:

> We further suggest that in cases where it is desired to hold a meeting, efforts be made to get together singers and, where possible, bands to play and sing patriotic songs, the two most suitable being *It's a Long Way to Tipperary* and *Land of Hope and Glory*.

Essex County Council thought hard about the position of its employees who were

62 ECS 2 February 1918; ECC 13 August 1915; WWN 30 July 1915.

63 ECT 31 July 1915.

64 ECT 21 September 1915.

65 ECS 3 July 1915.

eligible for the Derby Scheme. On 1 November 1915 a meeting of the Chairmen of Committees decided to draw up a list of staff who were considered to be indispensable to the council's operations. They would be urged to attest and then remain in work until called up. The meeting declared that it would "put no obstacle in the way of his [the employee] being enrolled and attested as joining His Majesty's Forces under Lord Derby's Scheme."[66] Incredibly, by January 1916 the council decided that it could continue working at County Hall by retaining only sixteen of its 120 male employees, all the rest being eligible for enlistment.[67]

The scheme was extended two weeks beyond its deadline to encourage those hanging back. On the last day in Colchester there were crowds outside the recruiting office "like a bank holiday theatre crowd." Five doctors, instead of the usual one, were drafted in to examine the recruits. The rush to attest was apparently so great that temporary arrangements were made at the Moot Hall and Borough Social Club.[68] East Ham Town Hall remained open until 1.30 a.m. every day in the week prior to the scheme ending on 11 December.[69] Men who had attested wore white brassards, or armbands, with a letter 'T' on them. In theory this afforded them some protection from those who might have accosted them in the streets accusing them of being slackers and demanding to know why they were not in uniform. The first batch of men called up under the Derby Scheme reported to recruiting offices on 20 January 1916. The men, from groups two, three, four and five, were single men aged nineteen to twenty-two. Single men in group one, those aged eighteen, were not to be considered until they reached the age of nineteen.[70] At Chelmsford the men in each group arrived at two-hour intervals. They had been advised to attend wearing their oldest clothes so as to save the cost of returning them once they had been issued with their uniforms.[71] As the time allocated for the scheme drew to a close, some like Mary Barlow exerted more pressure on the men who had not attested. Her poem, published in the press in October 1915, made it crystal clear where her sympathies lay:

"Come forward! Come forward!
Wait not for conscription,
A roll to your name,
Of a higher inscription;
Come forward at once,
And be noble and brave,
Be true to your Country,
Dear England to save.

66 Essex County Council Reports, 1916, meeting, 22 November 1915.
67 ECC 17 March 1916.
68 ECS 11 December 1915.
69 ECC 10 December 1915.
70 ECS 22 January 1916.
71 ECC 21 January 1916.

What? Wait for the moment
That England is smitten?
How can ye be called
"The True Sons of Britain?"
Come forward! Come forward!
Be noble and brave,
Like true Sons of England,
Dear England to Save.[72]

These efforts made little difference for the Derby Scheme failed to achieve its objective — the attestation for military service of the majority of eligible men in Britain. Of the 2.2 million single men identified in the National Register, only eight hundred and forty thousand attested, and three hundred thousand of these were rejected. A million single men thus ignored the scheme, and the pleadings of the Labour Party, which supported the scheme in order to save the voluntary system, were in vain. Almost 1.5 million married men attested, trusting in the Government's promise to take single men first. The Derby Scheme was no more successful in Essex than it was anywhere else. The Mayor of East Ham alleged that forty-five per cent of the town's unattested single men had failed to attest under the scheme.[73] In Colchester attestation cards were issued to 3,334 single and married men, of these 1,058 had either enlisted or attested between October and the end of December 1915; 645 declared themselves unfit for military service, of whom 209 produced evidence to that effect; 105 said that their employers refused permission for them to enlist; 220 had moved, died or passed the age limit for military service since the register was compiled. Some of those who at first refused later changed their minds, so that by 20 December 1,829 men had attested. This still left fifteen hundred men unaccounted for, comprising largely young, single and older, married men.[74]

The difficulties facing the organisers of the Derby Scheme were also revealed at Walthamstow. There 4,807 single men were canvassed under the Derby Scheme: 446 of them enlisted for military service immediately, 424 attested under the group system and 818 promised to attest. The army rejected 625 of these men on medical grounds, and a further 390 were rejected by other medical authorities. Four hundred and five single men remained in 'starred' jobs, which meant that they were regarded as indispensable to the war effort. Of the 8,649 married men canvassed, 1,795 could give no adequate reasons for declining to attest, although a further 1,287 stated that they would attest if their circumstances were different. Employers refused 242 men permission to attest. The total number of single and married men who were canvassed

72 ECC 15 October 1915.

73 ECS 1 January 1916.

74 ECT 15 January 1916.

was 13,456. Of these four thousand, three hundred enlisted or promised to enlist; 1,578 were men in starred occupations; 1,124 were rejected.[75]

At Braintree about half the munitions workers attested. Between three and four thousand attested at Southend, but based on the national estimate of men who had not attested, the *Southend Standard* estimated that this left about seventeen hundred men in the district unattested.[76] To take a further example, that of Little Clacton, thirty-seven recruiting cards were issued with the instruction that "men who are unwilling to enlist should be requested to give their reasons for doing so." A list of replies had been compiled by 10 November. Of the thirty-seven men, twenty-two had already enlisted, one was ineligible and one had moved. This left thirteen men who did not attest. All were visited at home by lady canvassers. They stated their reasons for not attesting as follows (age, where given, in brackets):

> Has single-handed business which he cannot leave
> Once rejected, "bad teeth, too short"
> Willing but been rejected
> Wait till younger men have gone (39)
> Age (41)
> Managing mother's farm (22)
> Has interests which he cannot leave (38)
> Willing - nearly 41. Not recommended
> Medically unfit (39)
> Willing but father won't give permission (19)
> Post Office (32)
> Not willing. Farming (34)
> Refuses (27)[77]

The eligible men of Saffron Walden also preferred to hang back and wait upon events. Out of 1,707 cards issued to single men, only 709 attested; for married men the figure was 633 out of 1,743 cards; 448 single men and 336 married men simply refused to enlist.[78]

The general awareness that many young men had not attested under the Derby Scheme, seemingly preferring to wait until they were compelled to serve, was sufficient to sustain the campaign against slackers. A letter to the local press revealed the continuing ferocity of feelings against them:

[75] WG 14 January 1916.

[76] SST 13 January 1916.

[77] ERO D/P 80/28/2 Lord Derby's Canvassing Campaign / Harwich Parliamentary Recruiting Committee, 2 November 1915.

[78] ECC 14 January 1916.

> Cannot something be done to stop the scandal in Colchester of young fellows being shelved in factories under the guise of being employed as munitions workers? The young fellows who have joined these since August last as "unskilled" workers should be bundled out, and handed over to the military authorities and not allowed to shirk any longer ... I only hope the military people will yet have power to force these boundersinto the army ... why not a "black list" of "shirkers" who are hiding up as so-called munitions workers to avoid fighting for their country?[79]

In the Walthamstow area it was rumoured that 599 men had been identified as single slackers and these men were reviled in the local press:

> These who have chosen to stand in the ranks of the men who care not a whit for their country's cause, whose souls are so dead that the cry of the weak and the outraged, the sacrifice of the maimed, the blinded and the dead, mean nothing to them.[80]

H.B. Dickinson, a former High Sheriff of Essex, accused the workers of slacking. "It was the most uneducated section of the community that refused to join", he asserted, "men who would not go unless they were fetched."[81] Others continued to blame the pampered middle classes for declining to join up.

The failure of the Derby Scheme, combined with the military commitments which the Government had made for the summer of 1916, resulted in the Military Service Act (January 1916), which came into force in March. This introduced conscription for single men aged eighteen to forty-one, with exceptions for ministers of religion, those medically unfit, men involved in essential work and those with a conscientious objection to military service. As late as 15 January the liberal *Essex County Telegraph* was appealing to single men to rescue the voluntary system by joining up willingly.[82] On the other hand the *Essex County Chronicle* considered that the time for reflecting on whether or not conscription was required was actually harming the war effort. "All talk about the liberty of the subject", it stated, "is on a par with Nero fiddling while Rome was burning."[83] For some people the act came none too soon. The Clacton Chamber of Commerce had demanded the abolition of the voluntary system as early as November 1914; the Essex Territorial Association had unanimously

79 ECS 26 February 1916.

80 WG 14 January 1916.

81 ECC 14 January 1916.

82 ECT 15 January 1916.

83 ECC 7 January 1916.

adopted a similar resolution in favour of compulsory military service in April 1915.[84] The Liberals of Leyton, who favoured the Compulsion Bill, were incensed when their M.P., Sir John Simon, voted against it in Parliament. The two hundred members of the local party voted seven to one in favour of asking Simon to resign his seat.[85] The conservative *Essex County Standard* however, was critical of the Military Service Act, referring to it as "neither compulsoryism nor voluntarism", and urged its replacement with proper compulsion, by which they meant conscription for married men too, on the grounds that the Derby Scheme and the new act had made pledges to them which could not be kept.[86] In this the *Standard* was correct; in April conscription was made universal for both single and married men between eighteen and forty-one. However, conscription was by no means universally popular. The Colchester Trades Council and Labour Party for instance denounced it as a class weapon designed to damage the interests of working people:

> We register our emphatic protests against and determined opposition to the Military Service Bill, and demand that before further conscription of life takes place, the Government immediately takes the necessary steps to acquire the wealth of this country for the people. We record our undying opposition to Prussian methods, militarism and acts of oppression, recently adopted in this country.[87]

On 19 January 1916 the Southend and Shoeburyness Trades Councils, the local Society of Friends, the local branch of the British Socialist Party, the Women's Cooperative Guild, the Gas Workers' and General Labourers' Unions all unanimously approved a resolution condemning conscription. It was condemned because "such a system must destroy the sanctity of human life; betray the free conditions of our country, and hinder its social and industrial emancipation."[88]

The Southend branch of the No-Conscription Fellowship attempted to hold a meeting at Victoria Hall on 17 April. The town's chief constable contacted the Home Office and, presumably, the hall's owner because he withdrew his permission for them to use it. When members of the No-Conscription Fellowship arrived at the Victoria Hall and began issuing anti-conscription handbills, they were dispersed by the police. At about the same time Charles Warner, a Southend Socialist, was arrested for distributing 'Stop the War' pamphlets. His house and three others were searched and "heaps of anti-war literature" were found. A quarter of a million copies of the

[84] ECS 21 November 1914, 17 April 1915.

[85] WG 21 January 1916.

[86] ECS 25 March, 15 April 1916.

[87] ECS 13 May 1916.

[88] SST 20 January 1916.

offending pamphlet were alleged to have been found in Warner's home. Warner was made an example of and found guilty of conduct prejudicial to recruitment. He was fined the very exceptional sum of £100.[89] Grays Urban District Council took a different tack and passed a resolution objecting to conscription unless the proceeds of the profiteers were given over to the nation's war effort.[90] These objections had no effect on the Government and conscription was introduced. Group one's call up date was 28 March. The call-up for other groups was completed by 13 June.

In passing the Military Service Act the Government made a concession to liberal principles by permitting men with a conscientious objection to joining the armed forces the opportunity to state their case before a local military tribunal. Anyone who claimed a legitimate reason why he should not be conscripted had the right to appear before his local tribunal and explain why. These tribunals also determined the eligibility of certain groups of workers. They were authorised to weed out those men in starred occupations who were not, in practice, indispensable. In the same way they were urged to spare men not in starred jobs, but whose work obviously was in the national interest. In Essex there were about twenty-five tribunals, referred to by the *Essex County Chronicle* as the 'Essex War Courts'.[91] They were held at Billericay, Braintree, Brentwood, Burnham, Chelmsford, Clacton, Colchester, Dunmow, Epping, Frinton, Harwich, Lexden and Winstree, Leyton, Romford, Saffron Walden, Shoeburyness, Stansted, Tendring, West Ham and Wivenhoe. Some areas like Epping, Romford, Brentwood, Dunmow, Braintree and Saffron Walden had two tribunals — one rural and one urban. Bumpstead shared a joint tribunal with Clare in Suffolk.

The Local Government Board recommended a maximum of five persons on tribunals, but few kept to this figure. There were fourteen on the Lexden and Winstree Tribunal, the Romford Rural Tribunal had eleven, as did Witham, there were ten at both Dunmow Rural and Billericay Tribunals, and most others had seven or eight members. The responsibility for setting up local tribunals was given to local authorities. They were instructed to choose men of "impartial and balanced judgement", and were free to look beyond local government circles in their selection of suitable men. Chelmsford Borough Council disregarded the Local Government Board's advice. Nine men were nominated, and five were chosen by ballot. Both winners and losers were members of the council.[92] Tribunals were almost always staffed by local government officials or local tradesmen and businessmen. At Barking the six men chosen were all councillors, and there was clear resistance to adding another, working-class, member to the tribunal. Its members tried to insist that if its number was increased to eight, the additional two members should be employers. In the end they were compelled to compromise, with an employer and a labouring man

[89] SST 8, 15 June 1916.

[90] SST 20 January 1916.

[91] ECC 24 March 1916.

[92] ERO D/B7 ChBC minutes, volume 29, 9 November 1915.

appointed.[93] Only two tribunals contained clergymen, the Reverend R.B. Tollinton at Tendring and the Reverend St John Methuen, Rector of Vange, at Pitsea. Military tribunals were generally an all-male preserve simply because it was thought inappropriate for women to pass judgement on fighting men. However, one woman — a Mrs P. Landon — was appointed to the Brentwood Tribunal. The strangest appointment of all must surely have been that of Joseph Smith, a Quaker and therefore a pacifist, as chairman of the Braintree Rural Military Tribunal. Smith saw no conflict between his appointment and his convictions. He argued that the tribunals were civil rather than military institutions, and he stated his belief that he had not had to abandon any of his principles.[94]

The tribunals were controlled locally and staffed by local people. At Dunmow for instance, the first tribunal consisted of five magistrates, including the chairman of the Rural District Council, the chairman and vice-chairman of the Public Elementary Schools Committee, and one of the town's chief landowners. There were two local men who represented the military and two serving officers, as well as a representative of the Board of Agriculture, which was standard procedure in rural areas. Meetings were held in various locations — town halls were a frequent meeting place. The Southend and Braintree Urban Tribunals were held in the towns' police courts, the Maldon Tribunal sat in the boardroom of the workhouse. Sittings were usually open — any member of the public could attend — unless the appellant specifically requested a private hearing. Most did not. Not all military tribunals were prepared to go along with the idea of openness. The Romford Urban Tribunal rejected the attendance of the public on the spurious grounds that there was insufficient accommodation.[95] Usually the tribunals were reported in a more or less abbreviated form in the local press, although the Dunmow and Romford Urban and Rural Tribunals decided not to print the names of appellants in order to retain an element of confidentiality.[96]

Tribunals were authorised to listen to anyone who appealed against being conscripted, and to decide on the validity of each appeal. They could grant absolute exemption from military service, or temporary exemptions of a limited duration after which conscription would occur, although appellants could appeal again once their exemption expired. Alternatively tribunals were empowered to reject an appeal, in which case the appellant had the right to take his case to a higher tribunal, the twenty-one-strong Essex Appeal Tribunal which sat at different times at Chelmsford, Colchester and West Ham. The county appeal tribunal was divided into two sections, one for metropolitan Essex and one for rural areas. As a last resort, appellants had the right to appeal to a Central Appeal Tribunal in London. The military representatives at tribunals were present at the insistence of the armed forces to

93 BA 12 February 1916.

94 ECC 3, 10 March 1916.

95 ECC 14 April 1916.

96 ECC 18 February, 10 March 1916.

ensure that exemptions were kept to a minimum and that the number of enlistments remained high. This representative had an absolute right of appeal if he believed that a tribunal had granted exemption on grounds which he considered inadequate. Tribunals attempted to remain aloof from outside influences. The Dunmow Tribunal had received anonymous letters making allegations against some of the men awaiting a hearing. The chairman announced that "he wished it known that such communications were cast unheeded into the fire."[97] The Epping Tribunal objected to receiving a circular from the No-Conscription Fellowship which was anxious to advertise its views.[98]

Local tribunals sat once or twice a week; the Colchester and Tendring Tribunals held between thirty and forty sittings between July and the end of December 1916. By the end of March the Chelmsford Appeal Tribunal at the Shire Hall had approximately five hundred cases to deal with. A fortnight later it had dealt with 181 cases, but by then there were a thousand cases stacked-up.[99] It was the start of a very busy existence. The Essex Appeal Tribunal at Romford looked back over its first year's work in March 1917; it had held 262 sittings, comprising 250 full days and twelve half-days. It had heard appeals from 7,350 individuals, of whom about five thousand, five hundred, or more than two-thirds, were by then in the army.[100] One thousand, four hundred appellants had been granted conditional acceptance. At that point it still had another 450 appeals awaiting a hearing. During its existence of almost three years it held 567 meetings and heard 12,719 appeals, of which 6,227 were dismissed.[101]

Local military tribunals had no firm rules, instead these tended to evolve during their meetings. The members of each tribunal made decisions based on their own attitudes and judgements, tempered only by their consciences and the attitude of the military representatives. Some guidelines developed only after the tribunals had met and when it became clear that certain principles were needed to inform their decisions on various matters. How to deal with farm labourers was a case in point, because food production was such a vital issue and it was crucial that the supply of farm workers was not restricted. Consequently the Board of Agriculture laid down certain principles governing the matter.[102]

Appeals were sometimes made by employers or relatives on behalf of their employees or sons, who on occasions, particularly in the case of farm labourers, were also their employees. Usually however, individuals presented their own appeals. Appellants sometimes supported their appeals by bringing with them a respected

[97] ECC 25 February 1916.

[98] ECC 10 March 1916.

[99] ECC 14 April 1916.

[100] ECC 23 March 1917.

[101] SST 6 February 1919.

[102] ECC 31 March 1916.

member of the community, usually a clergyman or minister, who spoke on their behalf, particularly if the appeal was on religious grounds. There were several grounds for appeal.

One was that of business hardship, with traders claiming that conscription would ruin their enterprise, as this man did:

> Mr J. Lewsley, fruiterer and greengrocer, High Street, applied for the conditional exemption of his son Joseph A. Lewsley, 40, who manages the business for him and attends the London markets to do all the buying. Refused.[103]

Some men's appeals were based on their 'indispensability', that is, their claim that they were the only employees able to perform jobs which were a vital part of a firm's operations. A horseman named Horner of Hawkwell was appealed for by his employer on the grounds that he was the only able-bodied man left on his farm. However, not all appeals of this sort were successful; William Gibson of Clacton was granted conditional exemption as an indispensable electrician and engineer, until the Clacton Tribunal discovered that "he was merely a stoker." His exemption certificate was revoked.[104] Sometimes the grounds for indispensability were completely ludicrous. The Mayor of Colchester appealed for exemption for his chauffeur, and succeeded in obtaining absolute exemption for him, a decision which was greeted with outrage in the town.[105] A Braintree hairdresser attempted to claim indispensability because he had a contract to provide haircuts for all the workhouse inmates at Braintree. His application caused great amusement at the tribunal:

> Surely they can be allowed to grow beards in the workhouse? Men are badly wanted now, and cutting people's hair is not very important work: with a pair of clippers they can cut each other's hair [Laughter].[106]

The members of the Braintree Tribunal also enjoyed themselves at the expense of a thirty-six-year-old undertaker:

> THE CLERK: Don't you think you would be better employed making coffins for the Germans?
> MAJ. ALLEN: Coffins could be bought ready made.
> MR TANNER: They would not suit my customers.

103 BDA 7 October 1916.
104 ECS 1 April 1916.
105 ECS 24 June 1916.
106 ECC 25 February 1916.

THE CLERK: I would be prepared to have a ready-made coffin if I should become a customer. I certainly would not complain (Laughter).[107]

The father of one applicant produced a dramatic demonstration of his son's indispensability. Mr Claydon, a farmer, appeared at the Braintree Urban Tribunal supporting the claim of his two sons. One was given total exemption, but the other was exempted for just four weeks. Claydon, who had clearly been expecting the worst, was duly outraged and took prompt action:

> Mr Claydon senior, then produced to the Tribunal his wooden leg, which he placed on the table around which members of the Tribunal were sitting.The wooden leg, which thumped with a bang on the table, was seen to be wrapped up in a soldier's khaki puttee ... "You see my wooden leg; well, that gets stuck in the ground when I go to plough, and I cannot get along, especially in wet weather."[108]

Very similar to the claim of indispensability was that of 'in the national interest', which could cover a huge range of occupations. A Dr A. Scott of Braintree appealed on behalf of an employee, saying that it would have been "absolutely impossible to adequately carry out his duties" regarding his five hundred patients without this man. The appeal was allowed. F.G. Andrews, however, had his claim that as a seed grower his work was of vital importance rejected because his seeds were only for flowers.[109] Here too some appeals stretched the bounds of credibility:

> J.E. Went, 43, married, agricultural estate carpenter, employed by Lord Lucas, was claimed on the ground of national interest. It was stated that he was the only man left to carry out all the repairs on an estate of 4,000 acres. The claim was disallowed.[110]

There was a feeling that status was a factor in how a man was treated before a tribunal, and that it might also help to determine how smoothly his application was accepted. This was certainly the case with David Ager, the forty-five-year-old managing partner of Colchester's Vaudeville Electric Theatre. At his appeal Ager:

[107] ECC 17 March 1916.
[108] ECC 3 March 1916.
[109] ECC 1 April 1916.
[110] ECC 5 August 1916.

> urged that these theatres [he managed two] provide relaxation and entertainment for 400,000 persons annually. They were also educational and fulfilled a national purpose in providing propaganda films and rational entertainment in these times of stress. Nothing had ever been shown on the screen which was at all suggestive or demoralising, and pictures of national interest were frequently exhibited, like how to grow and spray potatoes etc. and the military used the place free of charge for lectures, at which it was stated, the men learned more in 2 hours than in many weeks' instruction. Mr Ager mentioned that in taxes to the Government he paid about £5,000 a year.[111]

Ager's appeal, which was based on the grounds of national interest, would be laughable if it were not for the insidious references to favours for the military and taxes paid. Just as appalling is the fact that the tribunal granted him conditional exemption and flattered his already pronounced sense of self-importance by congratulating him as 'a great propagandist'. Charles Mead of Manningtree was granted conditional exemption solely "on the grounds of the numerous public appointments the applicant held." Bertram Young too used this line of approach successfully. He was manager of Manningtree and Dedham Gas Works, the Tendring Hundred Provident Benefit Sickness Society, clerk of Dedham Grammar School, clerk of the Dedham Lectureship, and agent for an insurance society. With these heady and vital responsibilities in mind, the Colchester Tribunal granted him conditional exemption.[112]

Domestic hardship or domestic responsibility was another ground for appeal used by huge numbers of appellants. Men who were the sole support of sickly wives, or of aged and infirm mothers or parents, relatives, or orphaned siblings, claimed that their families would be reduced to destitution if they were conscripted. A typical appeal was this by an appellant from Takeley:

> A widow's son, who manages a public house at Takeley for his mother, who is an invalid, and had a large family of young children, was given conditional exemption.[113]

Not everyone was quite so fortunate. This man seems to have been given a raw deal at the hands of the Burnham Tribunal:

[111] ECT 3 August 1918.
[112] ECS 10 June 1916.
[113] ECC 10 March 1916.

> Elsen Rice, 40 Prospect Place, palm needle hand canvas worker, employed by Messrs T.T. Nethercoat and Co. Ltd. Applicant, who has nine young children, was given six weeks' exemption.[114]

Exemption was also applied for on medical grounds. It was not one which was dealt with sympathetically by tribunals which tended to view such appellants as shirkers. Two cases demonstrate the casual indifference with which such appeals were dealt with. The first was at the Romford Urban Tribunal:

> Applicant had been medically examined and had been passed. He had hardly any sight in his right eye, and his left hand was crippled. The appeal was dismissed, applicant being told that the Tribunal had nothing to do with his physical condition.[115]

Equally unfeeling was the response of the Tendring Tribunal in refusing to exempt the following eighteen-year-old, although

> [he was] only four feet nine inches and weighing six stone. He had been afflicted since his birth, being, according to his medical certificate, pigeon-chested, flat-footed, knock-kneed, and a sleep walker.[116]

However, in many cases, such as that of Joseph Fincham of Marks Tey, it is not difficult to see why tribunals became so frustrated with some applicants:

> Owing to his health he could not do a full day's work, and consequently no firm would employ him. Even the YMCA would not accept his services. Mr Reid suggested that he should go into the Army, as he had been passed for C2.
>
> MR WEATHERALL: That means putting him into the hospital.
> MR REID: Neither you nor I are doctors, who say he is fit for C2.
> MR WEATHERALL: He has never worked before. He lives on milk and could not go into the Army ... It means the hospital if he goes.
> MR REID: Well, let him go into the Army then and then

[114] BDA 23 September 1916.
[115] BDA 3 March 1916.
[116] BDA 19 July 1917.

into the hospital. Other men have to risk their lives in battle. He could do clerical work in the Army.

MR FINCHAM: No. I could not, owing to my head.

Mr Weatherall also said the man suffered from epilepsy. A member suggested he should try farming.

MR WEATHERALL: They won't take invalids because he could not do a day's work. He had no desire to shirk but he has been like this all his life. I know what has been said is true. I will leave it to the discretion of the tribunal.

Conditional exemption was granted.[117]

Occasionally men would offer themselves as substitutes for others who had been conscripted. T. Powell, a golf professional from Braintree, offered to join up if W.W. Waterman, a farm stockman, was exempted. The tribunal "complimented him on his patriotism" and accepted his offer, subject to him passing the medical examination.[118]

The final ground for appeal, and the principal one for which tribunals had been created to deal with, was that of conscientious objection. Tribunals were open to anyone to appeal against conscription on the grounds that their conscience would not allow them to serve in the armed forces. These men, known as conscientious objectors or 'conchies', formed only a tiny proportion of the total number of appellants who appeared before tribunals. Nevertheless conscientious objectors were held in contempt by society at large, and it is perhaps not surprising therefore that their treatment before tribunals was often less than generous. Where the issue of conscientious objectors was discussed in the press, it was usually in the most vehemently scornful of tones, and used the most violent of language permitted in the public arena. The *East Essex Advertiser* scathingly dismissed conscientious objectors,

> 9 out of 10 of whom, we venture to assert, never had a conscientious objection to warfare at all until they observed, or thought they observed, a loophole by which they might possibly escape doing their duty like men ... To listen to their canting humbug is sickening, and one is prompted to turn from them in disgust ... When the war is over their newly acquired consciences will be shed as easily as one discards a worn out jacket.[119]

[117] BDA 24 February 1917.

[118] ECT 4 April 1916.

[119] EEA 18 March 1916.

The article concluded by describing conscientious objectors as "these few miserable cranks and cowards." The *Essex County Standard* labelled conscientious objectors, whom it saw as shirkers, as "a sickening object." The edifice upon which the concept of conscientious objection was built was rejected by the *Saffron Walden Weekly News*, which asserted rather astonishingly:

> No doubt there are a few people who conscientiously object to fight in any circumstances. The whole of Christian tradition is against their view, which, indeed, is capable of no reasonable defence.[120]

Some local men serving in the armed forces had no time for them. One of them, S.F. Watson of Colchester, wrote from the trenches on 19 March 1916 that

> The town of Colchester should be made so hot for these conscientious objectors that they must needs hide their heads in shame, and the surest way to do this is to boycott the tradesmen who employ them.[121]

Clergymen were certainly not above taking shots at conscientious objectors. J.A. Telford, Vicar of Harwich, wrote that

> No doubt there were some who really did believe it was contrary to the teachings of Christianity for anyone to take part in warfare of any kind. It was very evident, however, that in a number of cases this view had been arrived at during the last few months. In some cases there could be little doubt that the religious plea was not sincere — that the real reason of this attempt to secure exemption was cowardice or covetousness; a soldier's pay was not large, and there were many good jobs left by the men who were doing their bit ... Indeed it was a cheap form of religion which consisted in possessing a set of doctrines which enabled one to escape from one of the disagreeable duties of life.[122]

Such was the general odium in which conscientious objectors were held by society, that life was made very difficult for them. When a Mr Portacs, a conscientious objector, was offered the post of headmaster of a Brightlingsea school in 1916, the

[120] WWN 3 December 1915.

[121] WWN 25 March 1916.

[122] HDS 8 April 1916.

Essex Education Committee rejected him. Another teacher was deemed unfit to remain in his post:

> Mr W.G. Fairhead said he thought a man who could teach children on Empire Day and object to taking part in the war could only be a conscientious objector as far as his skin was concerned. He thought he ought not to be allowed to remain in his present occupation, because it was not right for the children, the future guardians of the nation, to have instilled into them the principles held by this gentleman.[123]

Military police were placed outside A.E. Joscelyne's cafe in Colchester High Street, specifically to prevent soldiers entering, because the proprietor was a conscientious objector. According to the Essex War Agricultural Committee, drafting conscientious objectors on to farms was impracticable because the "better class men" refused to work alongside them.

"Cranks Before Walthamstow Tribunal" and "Conscience Cowards" was how the *Walthamstow Guardian* headlined its reports on the local tribunal.[124] The *Essex County Chronicle* had little patience with conscientious objectors, whom it felt ought to be given short-shrift at tribunals. In an article on 21 April 1916 it virtually suggested abrogating their rights and criticised the fact that

> a good deal of the catechising of the conscientious objector seems quite irrelevant ... No, the conscientious objector is having too much of a run for his money and generally speaking, he is not worth it. There must be less talk everywhere if we are to go on and win this war.[125]

Tribunals were almost unfailingly inhospitable towards conscientious objectors. The press records of the interviews between tribunal members and conscientious objectors indicate the extent to which the former attempted to comprehend the views of the latter, but they also reveal the great gulf in understanding which lay between them. The result of these interviews was usually completely inconclusive, with tribunal members being no wiser at the end of the interview about the appellant's real motives than they were at the beginning. Others had the same difficulty. A reporter from the *Southend Standard* scratched his head and mused that "The average man or woman does not know what to make of him or where to place him."[126]

[123] ECS 27 May 1916.

[124] WG 7, 21 April 1916.

[125] ECC 21 April, 22 September 1916.

[126] SST 6 April 1916.

One interview, that of C.F. Barrett, a Colchester ironmonger, demonstrates the incomprehension and frustration of tribunal members, and at the same time Barrett's stubborn, perhaps even courageous refusal to be intimidated into weakening his case:

> Do you say it is contrary to your views to fight?
> — Decidedly.
> Then what do you say to that passage in the Scriptures which says "He that hath no sword, sell his garment and buy one?
> — I think Jesus said that in irony.
> Why? You don't think Christ told them to do that for nothing, do you?
> — I base my whole objection on the principles Christ laid down - to love God and love Man.
> Then what is your remedy for Belgium, as you find it today?
> — Of course, I believe in defending the weak, but my defence is different, I believe in moral force.
> What is your remedy? Is it to stay in England and do nothing or try and help?
> — I believe the Government would be wise to collect all the conscientious objectors and send them over to France to settle the business. (Loud laughter)
> I suggest they make a start with you. (Laughter)
> Do you mean you would stop and argue with the Germans?
> — I should use moral force.
> How would you apply it? Would you stand and argue?
> — I am sure there would have to be talking.
> DR SLIMON: There would if you were there. (Laughter)[127]

The interview above was a later review of Barrett's exemption. At his first appeal, six months earlier, the intolerant attitude of tribunal members was made crystal clear:

> The clerk read a long statement by the applicant on brotherly love to all men etc.
> CHAIRMAN: Is there much more of this nonsense?[128]

Tribunal members remained equally baffled after this interview with A.T. Shippey, a Colchester bookseller:

> In reply to Capt. Howard Shippey said he would object to non-combatant as well as combatant service.

[127] ECS 23 June 1916.

[128] ECS 9 December 1916.

CH: Would you object to helping soldiers who are in agony?
Applicant said he objected to helping soldiers who were wounded because he contended there was no reason for them to become wounded.
CH: You will admit that England is a peace loving nation?
ATS: If we were a peace loving nation we should be in our borders instead of having carried our arms all over the world.
CH: To carry it to a logical conclusion you mean we should be part of the German Empire?
ATS: Our ideas are quite different. The idea of nationality does not appeal to me at all. I consider all as human beings.
CH: Your idea is that we should allow the Germans to come over here, take the country and incorporate it in the German Empire?
No answer.
CH: You consider it quite fair and right to accept money and insure people against Zeppelin raids?
ATS: Yes, because if the people's houses are destroyed and you assist to reimburse them surely you are helping them?
CH: I thought that you would have wiped your hands of everything that had to do with war? Cannot you see that this is a war of right against might?
ATS: It need not be carried on by persons killing each other.
CH: Then you don't believe in self-defence?
ATS: I don't consider it necessary to kill people to defend yourself.[129]

Tribunals showed particularly scant sympathy towards applicants whose defence seemed to them to be transparently dishonest:

Sidney Howard, Thundersley, sand and gravel merchant, said he was a member of the Peculiar People, and could take no part in the war, which he felt was not of Christ, but of Satan.

CAPT. HOWARD:	You took these views after the war started?
	Yes.
CAPT. HOWARD:	What did you belong to before?
	I belonged to the devil then.
CHAIRMAN:	Who was your employer then?
	He was. (laughter)

[129] ECS 12 May 1917.

CAPT. HOWARD: The devil? In what way was he? (laughter)

Appellant further stated that he did not feel that he wanted to die for his country.

CAPT. HOWARD: Then die for your Saviour to endeavour to right wrong ...
CHAIRMAN: We are not satisfied with your bona fides. You must go for full service.[130]

Some conscientious objectors were in fact left-wing pacifists, and their appeals were largely based on political opposition to what they saw as a capitalist war which was not in the interests of the working classes. A press report of such an interview makes this clear:

> Addressing the tribunal, Lee said that he had studied Tolstoi [sic] for many years, and all anti-war literature. He had also listened to men like Philip Snowden and was a member of the ILP, the party which was opposed to all past wars, all present wars, and all future wars, which had taken no part in recruiting and had voted against the Military Service Act.[131]

Tribunal members considered conscientious objectors fair game and as we have already seen, some were particularly fond of attempting to make fun of them and their beliefs. One young man, Albert Lawrence, aged eighteen,

> Asked if he would undertake ambulance work, Lawrence said it depended what kind he was asked to undertake.
> DR SLIMON: And how far it is away from the front. (laughter)

The Colchester military representative, Captain Howard, also tried to impugn the motives of Philip Gammer, aged twenty-three, a grocer's assistant:

CH: Did you say once that it was no use for you to enlist because your chest was below measurement?
PG: Yes, and so it is.
DR SLIMON: Some of the splendid beef they get and dumbbells will bring that up. (laughter)

[130] ECC 14 April 1916.
[131] ECS 18 March 1916.

CH:	When you realised your chest was not so narrow as you thought, did you begin to develop a conscientious objection?
PG:	No. I have had it all my life.[132]

In spite of the hostility and extreme bafflement which tribunal members felt towards conscientious objectors, none were compelled by local tribunals to undertake combatant service. Some were drafted into the army to perform non-combatant duties, usually connected with army medical services, others were ordered to carry out civilian work of national importance which was not directly linked to the military, such as munitions work, or instead laboured in agriculture. However, many conscientious objectors who refused to cooperate either by performing non-combatant service or war work were imprisoned. Ernest Hockley from Barking, a member of the Peculiar People, was sentenced to six months hard labour, commuted to 112 days which he served in Dartmoor Prison in 1916.[133] The same reasonably fair adjudication system was applied to appellants generally. For instance an examination of the Colchester, Brightlingsea, Lexden and Winstree, Clacton, Frinton, Wivenhoe and Harwich Tribunals from 19 February to 18 March 1916, reveals that fifty-five per cent of applicants received some form of conditional exemption. There was a huge range of exemptions — for seven days, two weeks, one, two, three, four, five or six months; some exemptions were granted with the proviso that the applicant remained in his current occupation. Many of the very short exemptions were granted in order to allow the applicant time to put his business in order, which often meant finding someone to run it in his absence. Fifteen per cent of applicants had their cases adjourned or postponed, usually in order that they could obtain medical evidence to support their claim. However, less than ten per cent of these exemptions were absolute, that is, they would not be challenged in future. Seventy-six individuals, about twenty-nine per cent of all cases, had their applications rejected and were conscripted. What must also be borne in mind is that many of the conditional exemptions were reviewed when their time expired, although many individuals received an extension. Eventually in early 1917 the Government, largely at the army's insistence that too many able-bodied young men were being given exemptions, ordered a review of all exemptions which had previously been granted, a huge task. It was an unpopular decision with the civilian members of tribunals, who felt that their judgement was being questioned, and who often resented appeals made against their decisions by the military representative. In this case all their previous exemptions were being called into question.

Although many of those who came before tribunals were viewed with suspicion by tribunal members and by society in general, tribunals were not always seen as the

[132] ECS 24 June 1916.

[133] Sorrell, *Peculiar People*, 52-3.

dispensers of local justice against unpatriotic shirkers. There was a public protest when the Brightlingsea Tribunal granted only three months' exemption to a young man whose parents were dead, and was the sole support of his blind and crippled brother and two younger siblings. The local newspaper commented that "The confidence of the public appears to have been rudely shaken."[134] This certainly seems to have been the case. A month later a protest meeting was held in the town, and those present were convinced that the principles of the Derby Scheme were not being upheld. One speaker commented that

> On some of these tribunals there were gentlemen who decided that other people's sons should go to war while their own skulked at home behind a coward's conscience.

Another speaker said that if these statements were true it was time they were made known in a wider area than Brightlingsea and time they had a new tribunal.

Clearly another cause of this discontent was the belief that "thousands of single men were being exempted on various pretexts", while married men were being conscripted.[135] Other organisations joined in the chorus of criticism against the apparent breaking of the promises of the Derby Scheme. The Grays Traders' Association urged the implementation of the single men first promise.[136] Robert Bull too had heard angry mutterings. He wrote in his diary "Great outcry among the attested married men that they are being called up before a lot of single men who are sheltering inside munitions works."[137] At Saffron Walden there was said to be "seething disillusion" about the treatment of married men.[138] At Southend a mass meeting attended by hundreds of married men was held at the Kursaal to protest at the Government's broken pledges. The meeting passed a resolution stating that "[this meeting] considers that the married men have been grossly deceived and are suffering a grave injustice."[139]

Farmers were particularly critical of tribunals which they alleged were conscripting young farm workers, and leaving them short of desperately needed labour. Four farmers wrote to the press openly criticising other farmers who had secured exemptions for their sons, and the letter also alleged that members of the Colchester Tribunal had done the same thing.[140] Another farmer, whose appeal on behalf of one

[134] EEA 11 March 1916.

[135] ECS 8 April 1916.

[136] ECC 17 March 1916.

[137] Bull, Diary, 13 March 1916.

[138] WWN 26 May 1916.

[139] SST 30 March 1916.

[140] SST 27 January 1917.

of his nineteen-year-old labourers was rejected, reacted angrily with the statement that "Farmers could no more increase the food supply without men than the Egyptians could make bricks without straw."[141] Even the Mayor of Colchester, A.M. Jarmin, took issue with the tribunal's proceedings in this respect, when he wrote to London saying, "The military representative at the Local Tribunals should be instructed not to press his branch of activity in the case of genuine food producers.[142] The Essex War Agricultural Committee also protested at tribunals apparently flouting the Board of Agriculture's guidelines on exemption of farm labourers.[143]

On the other hand, farmers themselves were frequently subject to criticism concerning their attitude towards tribunals. Whilst they saw their appeals as essential to preserve the nation's food supply, outside observers regarded their attitude as self-righteous and self-seeking, particularly when their appeals were on behalf of their own sons. Severe criticism was meted out to a particularly belligerent Lindsell farmer who was attempting to keep all his four sons of military age out of the services:

> THE CHAIRMAN: There is a strong feeling that these young active chaps ought to be doing something for their country. Some farmers are doing too much to it in keeping their sons at home. There is a feeling in the neighbourhood that it would be a better example to your neighbours if you had one [son] in the Army.
>
> APPLICANT: If my boys have to go I shall have to give up the farms, that is all.
>
> THE CHAIRMAN: You must not indulge in threats ...
>
> The Chairman told the applicant that for the sake of public opinion he had better get one of his sons into the Army. In years to come he would be sorry if all his sons stood aside in this national crisis.[144]

Another farmer at Braintree who had four sons working with him was also told that his appeal to retain his sons was creating an 'unfavourable impression' in the district.[145] Other farmers claimed, and this was a common line of approach, that their sons had to be exempted because they could not be replaced by women. "My cattle would not stand a woman to tend them", said one man from Stebbing, "they would

141 SST 24 March 1916.

142 Food Control Campaign, questionnaire, April 1917.

143 ECC 17 March 1916.

144 ECC 25 February 1916.

145 ECC 10 March 1916.

toss her, quick."[146] Other types of work were targeted by those advocating a larger uptake for the armed forces. The Romford, Maldon, and East Ham Tribunals all passed resolutions objecting to the employment of single men in munitions factories.[147] The Grays Tribunal protested at the employment of young men who were accused of evading military service by posing as 'essential' workers at Tilbury docks.[148] Shopkeepers too found themselves subject to criticism, particularly when, like farmers, they attempted to secure exemption for their sons. One Barking businessman who had purchased four new businesses since 1914 with a son in charge of each one, had his appeal dismissed, with the tribunal chairman commenting that "a father had no right to keep his sons out of the army by multiplying shops during war time."[149] In some quarters condemnation of farmers was given an additional impetus in the summer of 1917, when it was proposed to raise the age of conscription to fifty. Dr J.H. Salter, the military representative on the Maldon Tribunal, expressed his anger at the conscription of mature married men while young single men remained at home, particularly on farms.[150]

There were often underlying tensions within tribunals. In April 1917 three members of the Colchester Tribunal stormed out of a sitting in protest at the military representative appealing in several cases where exemptions were granted, in some cases on more than one occasion. One of the three, Councillor Robert Bultitude, protested that "We might as well be in Russia or Germany today."[151] In July 1918 the civilian members at the Southend Tribunal threatened to resign for exactly the same reason.[152] At Witham C.H. Strutt accused the labour representative, Ebenezer Smith, of working to gain the maximum exemption for appellants who were working men. Smith refused to deny the accusation.[153] Tribunals were often unpopular whatever they did. They were criticised for being too zealous, usually by farmers, and for being too lenient. The Ongar Tribunal refused to sit to hear appeals in February 1917 as a protest at the military representative's discourteous treatment of farmers.[154] The Colchester Tribunal was accused by one of the town's Anglican clergymen of neglecting the national interest when it considered exemption for two teachers.[155]

[146] ECC 10 March 1916.

[147] ECC 17 March 1916.

[148] ECC 24 March 1916.

[149] ECC 26 May 1916.

[150] ECC 25 May 1917.

[151] ECS 24 March 1917.

[152] ECC 5 July 1918. However, the military representative of the Lexden and Winstree Tribunal appealed in only twenty-eight cases out of one thousand and two hundred, and succeeded in only ten of these, ECS 25 November 1916.

[153] ECC 27 October 1916.

[154] ECC 2 February 1917.

[155] ECC 29 April 1916.

Few tears were shed once the wartime system of conscription was scrapped. It was accepted by many as a necessity, a regrettable abandonment of liberal principles, something that had to be done in order that the War could be won, but not as a measure that should long outlive it. Others detested it as an affront to liberty, and some Labour politicians and trade union leaders regarded it as an assault upon the working classes. Only five months after the War had ended the Colchester Independent Labour Party called a public meeting to allow people to express their views on conscription. The responses were uniformly hostile. One speaker, Paul Amsden, denounced it as "the sworn foe of democratic institutions, civil liberties, and industrial freedom." It was, he said, part of the "hateful, hideous and devilish system of militarism." The meeting overwhelmingly supported a motion expressing uncompromising opposition to future conscription in any form.[156]

[156] ECT 29 March 1919.

CHAPTER FIVE

Away from the Front: Returning Heroes and Martyrs

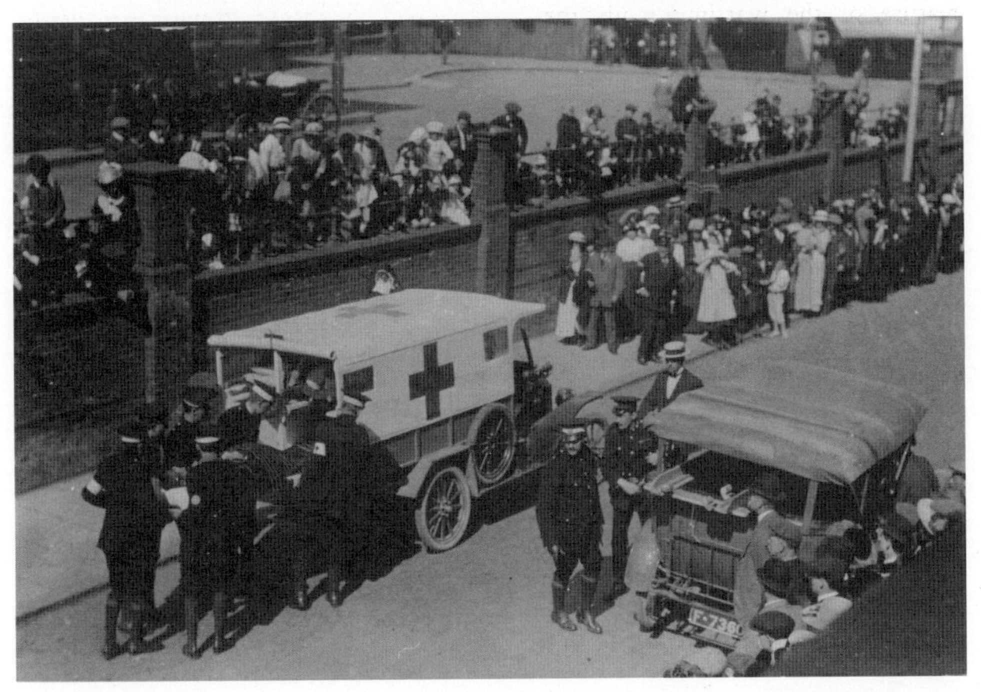

Wounded servicemen arrive at Southend Central Station, 1915. *(ERO: T/S 512/4)*

SERVICEMEN IN MOST WARS have been treated like heroes by their fellow countrymen and -women. In the Great War, which was rapidly reshaped in the popular imagination into a crusade against evil militarism, soldiers, sailors and airmen became its crusaders, and all too often its martyrs — men who had attained 'righteousness' by making the 'supreme sacrifice'. In one very real sense it was hard to avoid noticing men in khaki. The presence of so many servicemen in the county throughout the War had a significant impact on some of its villages and towns. However much the stay of an individual regiment or unit in a particular place may have been transitory, the presence of the military was a more or less permanent feature of the wartime landscape, particularly in certain towns. Colchester, Chelmsford and Warley were the three great recruitment centres of the county, and as such they absorbed the volunteers who had enlisted by the end of September 1914. However, as these troops completed their training, moved out and were replaced by others, accommodation had to be found for them and thus it was that many towns and villages were affected.

Colchester was transformed by the War from a modest garrison town into a huge military camp. By mid-September 1914 there were fifteen thousand men training in the district, thanks to the large number of men who had volunteered nationally since August. Five thousand territorials of the Norfolk and Suffolk Brigade were stationed at Severalls Hospital, artillery units and the Royal Army Medical Corps were at Lexden, the City Battalion at Reed Hall, and many more on the Abbey Field. From the Middlewick Ranges came the sound of troops training on the army's musketry course.[1] Each day hundreds of civilians came to see the trainees in action:

> The Abbey Field is a daily spectacle of human energy. Scarcely a corner is unused as a training ground, and many thousands of men, in companies or squads, may be seen at various stages of the work that makes a soldier.[2]

By mid-November 1914 Colchester's medical officer estimated that the town's population had increased by twenty-five thousand since the outbreak of war.[3] When permitted to leave their barracks and tented camps, these new soldiers flooded into the town, to the delight of some of its traders:

> Trade is very brisk. The amusement houses fill in the evenings, the restaurants, and the public houses have their rushing hours, hairdressers and barbers are run off their feet, and tobacconists have never done so big a trade. Then the larger provisioners and

1 ECT 19 September 1914.

2 ECT 24 October 1914.

3 CBC, Council-in-Committee, 21 October 1914.

> contractors for forage and food supplies are filling enormous orders, and the only fly in the ointment is the fact that the extraordinary demand for household commodities keeps the prices up.[4]

Soldiers seemed to be everywhere in Essex. The average daily strength of the Colchester garrison in 1915 was 12,435, although this very much varied from day to day; there were also estimated to be around two thousand extra women and children, the families of some servicemen who had moved to Colchester to be near them.[5] By the end of 1914 Chelmsford's pre-war population of eighteen thousand had been increased by a third thanks to an influx of six thousand soldiers. Part of Colchester's Recreation Ground was used as an army bakery; trenches were later dug nearby for bayonet practice, and horses were picketed there too.[6] Part of Chelmsford's marketplace was also used to picket army horses. Even relatively small places faced a huge influx of military personnel. A military camp was constructed on Shenfield Common.[7] Hatfield Peverel, with a population of just two thousand, was swamped by six thousand soldiers who were accommodated either in camps or civilian billets. The troops were kept supplied by water only when a second spring was opened in addition to the existing one beneath the swan pond in The Street.[8] At Little Baddow a permanent military camp was built in April 1915 to house the various units who came, stayed for a few months, then left to be replaced by a new regiment. The first of these was the Sixth Battalion of the Gloucestershire Regiment, who arrived in late August 1914 for eight months, having marched from Bristol in seven days.[9]

The presence of the military provided a solution, albeit only a temporary one, to the problem of constructing a bridge across the Colne to link Rowhedge and Wivenhoe. Pre-war attempts by the Colchester Borough Council had failed, but the crisis of war removed any arguments against it. George V was the first to use it on 14 July 1916, after which its use was restricted to the military.[10] By November 1914 a military bridge had also been built over the Thames linking the Tilbury forts with Gravesend. The bridge, a combined effort by the War Office and the Port of London Authority, had a moveable section of 800 feet to accommodate shipping, although it took over five hours to open and close.[11] The Northamptonshire Regiment was also

4 CG 24 October 1914.

5 CBC, Annual Report, Medical Officer of Health, 1915.

6 CBC, Parks and Bathing Committee, 3 March 1915, 9 June 1915; Parks and Bathing Places Committee, 12 May 1915.

7 R. James, *Brentwood Past* (2002), 126.

8 Hadfelda Women's Institute, *Hatfield Peverel, The Street: Past and Present*, undated.

9 Little Baddow Historical Society, *Little Baddow: A Century of Village Life* (1999), 12.

10 N. Butler, *The Story of Wivenhoe*, 214; Rowhedge Village Association & East Donyland Parish Council, *Rowhedge Recollections*, (1977), 8-9.

11 Reynolds, *Thurrock*, 23.

given permission to build temporary pontoon bridges across the River Colne at Middle Mill, Colchester, whenever the need arose.[12]

The invasion of Kitchener's 'new armies' was not entirely welcomed by all citizens. For some the disadvantages of this influx of soldiers in Colchester outweighed the advantages:

> The inhabitant suffers many inconveniences. He gets elbowed out of the tramcar, he gets snowed under by the crowds all day long in the Post Office, he has difficulty reaching his seat in the Theatre or Hippodrome, his long used sitting in church has been occupied by soldiers, and the price of commodities has risen with the increased demands of the district.[13]

However, the arrival of so many troops threatened problems which were potentially far more serious than the mere inconvenience complained of by the above writer. There were severe implications for the health of the towns and villages where troops were stationed. The county's chief medical officer was well aware of this and almost as soon as war was declared he wrote to all medical officers in Essex drawing their attention to the need to supervise billeting, and to check on sanitary arrangements and water supplies. He also secured an agreement about where any cases of smallpox amongst the military were to be sent. Chelmsford's medical officer was horrified at the potential difficulties posed by the arrival of so many soldiers in a town with a limited water supply, an overtaxed sewage system, and what he himself described as an 'old fashioned' method of house refuse disposal. He was also worried by the military's inability to provide exact numbers of those billeted in the town. To encourage healthy habits amongst the troops, and because bathing facilities in most houses were still primitive, the town's public baths were made available to the troops every afternoon. By December 1914 the borough council had also opened up the slipper baths, based on Colchester's model, and these too were available to soldiers. The invasion of troops also aggravated the water shortage which had become acute because of the long, dry summer. During the third week in September 1914 demand had been a record 440,000 gallons of water a day, which exceeded all the borough's supplies, the deficiency only being made good from the Long Stomps Reservoir, which fell to just four feet deep. Only a new borehole at Admirals Park, which produced 120,000 gallons per day, rescued the town from an extremely precarious situation.[14]

Such was the overcrowding in this small market town that the medical officer attributed a severe flu epidemic in March 1915 to a failure by the army to take proper

12 CBC, Parks and Bathing Places Committee, 14 July 1915.

13 CBC 16 January 1915.

14 ERO D/B 7 ChBC, No. 26, January-October 1914, 30 September 1914; No. 27 October 1914-March 1915, 25 November 1914.

care of its men. However, the army was not always to blame when its soldiers were laid low. The medical officer admitted that, given the shortage of accommodation, it was impossible to avoid billeting troops on houses where the inhabitants had infectious diseases. All he could recommend was that the regimental medical officer should visit daily any soldier who became infected. Braintree's medical officer was convinced that overcrowding due to billeting was directly responsible for the increase in the infant death rate, although he felt unable to prove this.[15] Disease among soldiers was held responsible for a series of outbreaks among civilians. For instance, Essex suffered throughout the War from outbreaks of cerebro-spinal meningitis, which caused something of a panic in Chelmsford in the winter of 1914-15; Chelmsford's medical officer believed the disease originated among the military.[16] By the start of 1915 there were seventeen cases in the Chelmsford area, others in Colchester and Hornchurch, and six people had died from the disease.[17] At Halstead in 1916 there was an epidemic of jaundice brought into the town by a single soldier. The county medical officer also ascribed an increased death rate from tuberculosis to a high rate of the disease in the army.[18]

Despite the obvious difficulties associated with billeting, the practice was unavoidable. By December 1914 in addition to the six thousand troops billeted at Chelmsford, eighteen thousand troops had been placed within the borough of Colchester, and according to the town council, "it is gratifying to record that this has been done with complete absence of friction in any quarter."[19] Certainly in most cases the troops were made welcome, as Mrs E.G. Tansley of Manningtree recalled, even when their arrival was at very short notice:

> On a wet, dark evening early in 1916, the Surrey Yeomanry arrived in Ardleigh on their way overseas. An officer came round to see who could put men up for the night. There was no refusal. We had 10 soldiers sleeping on the floor of our large kitchen that night. They were all very wet and cold and I'm sure they welcomed the warmth of our big kitchen range. We were rationed by then so could not offer them much to eat — just home-baked bread, Quaker Oats, cocoa or tea. They were glad of anything hot.[20]

Efforts were made to keep military units together in the same area and the Colchester medical officer reported approvingly that "rowdiness was practically non-

15 Chief Medical Officer, annual report, 1915.

16 ERO D/B 7 ChBC, No. 27, 30 December 1914, 24 February 1915.

17 ECC 19 February 1915.

18 Essex Medical Officer of Health reports, 1916, 1917.

19 CBC, Watch Committee, 20 January 1915.

20 J. Thorogood (ed.), *The Last All-Clear: Essex People Remember Two World Wars* (1989), 6-10.

existent." During 1915 in both Colchester and Chelmsford many huts were built and tents pitched in order to reduce the number of billets. At Wivenhoe troops were billeted all over the town. In October 1914 preliminary enquiries by the Southend police showed that they were anticipating nine thousand troops to be billeted in the area; six thousand in Southend, and a thousand each in Prittlewell, Leigh and Westcliff.[21] To assist billeting officers, the houses of widows, the sick and the elderly were marked with the letters 'EXMT' signifying 'exempt'.[22] At Ardleigh, Leonora Downing's father's bakery was used as a billet when it was not in use. A sergeant and five soldiers used the bakery to cook for troops stationed nearby.[23] Until 1917 billeting was voluntary and involved arrangements between the military and willing civilians.[24] The first inspection of billets by Colchester Borough Council in October 1914 visited 1,042 households and only 551 had soldiers billeted.[25] As a result those households which were apprehensive about accepting soldiers were free to decline. However, during the wretched winter of 1916-17 the army huts in the barracks, hastily constructed in 1915 and which were not weatherproofed, made life miserable for their occupants, and an appeal from the army resulted in many households reopening their doors to the frozen troops.[26]

Troops were of course welcomed for economic reasons. At Saffron Walden in June 1916 a meeting was held in the Town Hall to appeal for the army to billet troops in the town because the earning capacity of its traders had fallen during the War. This was because it was generally assumed by contemporary observers that the practice of billeting was beneficial to the families who participated by bringing additional income into the home, and from there into the shops. At places like Brightlingsea the residents were said to have been protected from the worst economic ravages of the War simply by the presence of so many soldiers and sailors. However, not everyone shared this optimistic view, including some at Brightlingsea where householders complained that soldiers working on pontoons over the River Colne came home wet and very muddy, compelling lighting of extra fires to get them clean.[27] At Clacton the proprietors of boarding houses complained that during the slack winter period, when demand for accommodation was low, billeting was impossible to get, whereas in summer when rooms were scarcer, the army's demands increased. The billeting rate, at least in Colchester, was 2*s.* 9*d.* a day for the first soldier, with a slightly reduced payment for each subsequent man. In August the army proposed to reduce this by 9*d.* a day for the first, and 6*d.* for additional soldiers. Clacton Urban District Council resented this,

[21] SST 29 October 1914.

[22] N. Butler, *The Story of Wivenhoe*, 211.

[23] Downing, *Ardleigh Village*, 17.

[24] ECS 24 July 1915.

[25] CBC, Annual Report, Medical Officer of Health 1914.

[26] Hunt, *War Memorial Souvenir*, 60.

[27] EEA 30 January 1915.

claiming that the current billeting rate was already inadequate and could not compensate for the resort's loss of trade owing to the War.[28] The Colchester Board of Guardians agreed. They argued that some families in receipt of poor relief were tempted into billeting, but because the rate was so low, they ended up worse off.[29] The inexorable rise in the price of consumer goods also had an adverse impact on billeting. One Colchester housewife complained to the press. She received 1*s.* 9*d.* a day for food for each soldier, but by early 1915 she was paying 1*s.* 2*d.* for a pound of bacon, 1*s.* 5*d.* for a pound of butter, 2*s.* per pound of ham, and 8*d.* a quarter for flour. That she claimed to be out of pocket is not surprising as she also claimed that the soldiers were eating five meals a day.[30] Some women found that the billeting interfered with their other commitments. The Colchester branch of the Women's Help Society suffered from declining attendances in consequence.[31] Chelmsford's librarian believed that a decrease in borrowing, particularly of non-fiction books, was because women readers were too busy catering for their military visitors and lacked the time in which to sit and read.[32] Billeting did produce overcrowding, but on a very small scale. The inspections of billets by Colchester's health inspectors found only twenty-nine such cases out of 551 billets.[33] The Billericay Board of Guardians complained that overcrowding in billets was the result of the better-off inhabitants, with larger houses in places like Ingrave, managing to obtain exemption from billeting and thereby increasing the pressure on smaller houses.[34] Others criticised the guardians, like those at Ongar, who cut off out-relief to poorer families once they had troops billeted on them.[35] Nevertheless, the process of billeting was considered to be a success. There were potential hazards, but these failed to materialise in any significant way. Although some householders faced the prospect of insolvency thanks to billeting, only one billet ended in truly disastrous fashion. In the summer of 1916, the Minister of Witham Congregational Church, D.M. Picton, had an officer, a Lieutenant McLagan, billeted on his family. One day, as the Lieutenant was showing the family a grenade, it exploded, killing McLagan and Picton and injuring his wife and daughter.[36] However tragic this incident, elsewhere billeting was unexceptional. As the county chief medical officer commented in 1915, "it is extraordinary how so many men could be billeted in such areas and apparently without any detrimental effect upon their health."[37]

28 ECS 4 September 1915.

29 ECS 3 July 1915.

30 ECT 6 February 1915.

31 ECS 24 April 1915.

32 ERO D/B 7, No. 27, 28 October 1914.

33 CBC, Annual Report, Medical Officer of Health 1914.

34 ECC 12 February 1915.

35 ECC 11 December 1914.

36 M.L. Smith, *A Brief History of Witham Congregational Church* (1965), 36.

37 Chief Medical Officer, annual report, 1915.

Unfortunately, the presence and activities of so many soldiers in Essex played havoc with other aspects of life. In Colchester by early 1915, the continual marching of large numbers of men had damaged Straight Road, Shrub End Road and Drury Road. Although the War Office contributed £606 towards the cost of repairs, these ran at £1,292 by the spring of 1915.[38] The neglect of the county's roads in wartime due to a dearth of young men and because of financial restraint by the county and borough councils was also considered to be a factor in ill-health. It was claimed that the marching of troops and the presence of so many army horses on the roads created excessive amounts of dust, which spread horse manure microbes into the air to be breathed in by troops and civilians alike.[39]

Many local schools were either partly or wholly occupied by the military, although usually for limited periods only. The head teacher of Great Bentley School noted that the military had commandeered the "babies' room" as an orderly room.[40] The schools at Fingringhoe and Purfleet were occupied by the military in 1914. The former school's pupils were transferred to Chapel Hall and other local schools, such as Langenhoe, before the army restored it to the education authorities in February 1915. At Saffron Walden both the Boys' British School and the Friends' School were commandeered. Ardleigh School was commandeered temporarily by the Somerset Yeomanry in August 1914.[41] Colchester's newest school in Hamilton Road had not even seen any pupils before the army took it over early in the War, and retained it for the duration. Culver Street School, recently condemned by the borough, was fortunate to receive a stay of execution as a result of this.[42] Soldiers were not always welcomed by schoolteachers. The head teacher of Manuden Primary School wrote in the school logbook:

> School work much interrupted owing to the village being the centre of a sham fight and field day. Large bodies of troops passed through and [the] children were allowed to see them, the noise etc. making attention difficult.[43]

The logbooks of the head teacher of Benyon School show that she was concerned at how the troops stationed nearby were spoiling the boys and influencing them to be unruly.[44]

The Devonshire Yeomanry took over St Osyth Priory in 1914.[45] Perhaps they took

38 CBC minutes, Roads & Drains Committee, 10, 26 February 1915.

39 Chief Medical Officer, annual report, 1915.

40 J. Watson, *One Hundred Years: A centenary celebration of Great Bentley County Primary School* (1996).

41 L. Downing, *Ardleigh Village Days* (1994), 67.

42 CBC minutes, Report School Medical Officer, 1914.

43 ERO T/P 353/3-5, Manuden County Primary School, logbooks 1878-1953, 14 October 1915.

44 ERO Benyon School, logbooks, 16 October 1915.

45 *St Osyth Parish Council Centenary 1894-1994*, 34.

better care of it than the troops who used Fingringhoe church tower as a lookout post and signalling post. The church had been damaged by the earthquake of 1884, and the church authorities complained that further damage was caused by the soldiers cutting their names and regiments into the lead on the tower.[46] However, this minor vandalism paled into insignificance in comparison with events at Hedingham in September 1918. The military were using the castle keep as a signalling station in case of incursions by German aircraft. The men had built a hut on the roof and they were using a stove. Unfortunately, a fire began which spread first to the roof and then rapidly to every floor, so that the whole place was ablaze. The men made their way to safety, but eventually the floors collapsed leaving just the shell of the keep.

Economically, the presence of the military was not always beneficial. At Wivenhoe the closure of the military bridge for four days in June 1916 closed the Colne to river traffic and threw the employees of Owen Parry out of work. A deputation complained to the Colchester Borough Council that as the workers were in controlled works they were unable to seek jobs elsewhere.[47] The following year, fresh army wire entanglements were placed near the Fingringhoe side of the Colne ferry and produced further complaints about the army's impact on business.[48] Farmers, too, found plenty to complain about. Those at Witham claimed that the army's activities in the district — digging trenches, gunpits and commandeering land as rifle ranges, was making it impossible to cultivate the land without considerable danger.[49] Such was the general depth of concern on the issue of trenching that a deputation of Essex farmers visited the War Office on 23 April 1915. The deputation pointed out that the military's activities, however necessary, had created a twenty-mile swathe of destruction from Panfield to Maldon, involving damage to buildings, fences and ditches, and gave notice that they would require compensation at the end of the War.[50]

There was also a good deal of resentment at Colchester caused by the garrison's apparent disregard for the wartime lighting restrictions, even during times of air attacks, as evidenced by this letter written by a local magistrate to Colchester Borough Council:

> As I walked from this house a short time ago to attend the meeting with regard to National Service, the sky was quite illuminated by the light coming from the Barracks extending from the Military Hospital to the Cavalry Barracks. It is most unfair that the Military should go scot free when they are the most flagrant offenders.[51]

46 ERO D/P 369/6/6, Fingringhoe Church Tower.

47 CBC, Harbour and Navigation Committee, 23 June 1916.

48 CBC minutes, Harbour and Navigation Committee, 20 February 1917.

49 ECC 2 April 1915.

50 ECC 23 April 1915.

51 CBC minutes, Watch Committee, 29 March 1917.

Inevitably, some soldiers could also cause problems of a more unsavoury nature. At Wivenhoe the lack of public toilets resulted in soldiers urinating against the school wall, and in consequence the council felt obliged to build a proper urinal at the council offices.[52] The Chelmsford medical officer sought to provide a toilet for the troops assigned to guard the railway arches. A pail closet seemed to be a temporary solution. The soldiers on duty there had evidently found their own solution, for he was forced to recommend emptying the "accumulated excrement" which was already deposited in one corner of the arches.[53] The army's hooligan element occasionally surfaced. At Great Leighs the soldiery there damaged the schoolmaster's piano when they discovered it was made in Germany.[54] Drunken behaviour by soldiers at Harwich early in the War was only brought to an end by the early closure of public houses which resulted in "decided improvement in the behaviour of the troops in consequence."[55]

The loss of so many men to the armed forces during 1914 created the possibility of real hardship for the families of those soldiers who were married. Within a day of war breaking out C.C. Naters, Rector of St James's, Colchester, wrote to the town council inviting them to a service at his church where, in common with all other town churches and chapels, there would be a collection for the wives and children of the territorials.[56] Individual companies and public bodies made their own arrangements. Employees of Essex County Council were comforted by their employer's guarantee of full pay during their absence, although single men received 7*s.* a week less than married men, unless they had a dependant mother.[57] Both Crittall and Lake and Elliott of Braintree paid 5*s.* a week to the wife of each reservist and territorial called up and 1*s.* per child.[58] Hoffman at Chelmsford made an initial provision of aid for dependants of its enlisted employees.[59] Those employees of the Colchester Cooperative Society who enlisted before 1 September were guaranteed half-wages until the end of the War or until they were disbanded. A guarantee that their jobs would be kept open was also given.[60] However, an employee of the Tiptree Cooperative Society found his employer to be less helpful:

52 Butler, *Wivenhoe*, 213.

53 ERO D/B 7, No. 27, 25 November 1914.

54 Clark, Diary, 45.

55 ECT 26 September 1914.

56 CBC, Council-in-Committee, 5 August 1914.

57 ECC annual report 1914.

58 CG 12 August 1914.

59 ERO D/B 7, Chelmsford Local Representative Committee for the Prevention and Relief of Distress, 31 August 1914-27 April 1916, 31 August 1914.

60 ERO D/Z 175/1/15 Colchester Cooperative minutes, 2 September 1914.

> That in reply to Cranmer's request to be re-instated on his return and for a small allowance to his mother — he be informed that we cannot promise to reinstate him at that time but would find him employment if possible, also, that we consider the Society cannot afford to make an allowance.[61]

However, the Tiptree Co-op does seem to have paid such an allowance, for in April 1917 it was only just deciding to pay 2*s.* 6*d.* to those of its employees serving in the armed forces, backdated to 1 January 1917. This allowance was only paid to those who had been employed by them for five years. An attempt to backdate the allowance to the date on which the men joined up was lost. A further amendment withholding the allowance from men who had not been employed by the Tiptree Co-op on 4 August 1914 was carried.[62] Similar arrangements were made by Colchester Town Council, and these continued even after the recipient was killed:

> Resolved to continue payment of allowance to widow of late Conductor Bland, who was regrettably killed in action on October 22nd 1914, while serving in the Northampton Regt, until such time as she receives Government pension.[63]

Stratford Cooperative Society had called a halt to all the allowances it guaranteed to its workers who enlisted on the grounds that the cost was prohibitive. One former employee, Thomas Budgett, who was serving in the Army Service Corps, sued the Society and at the High Court in March 1916 gained a ruling that his employers were obliged to maintain the payment promised him when he joined up in 1914.[64]

Colchester Town Council claimed that as early as mid-August 1914 it was ready to alleviate local distress with thirteen road widening schemes.[65] Other organisations stepped in with equally practical assistance. The Essex Pharmacists' Association offered to forgo the dispensing fee for the dependants of men who had enlisted, and simply charge them for the cost of the drugs dispensed, a not ungenerous offer considering that the cost of drugs had rapidly increased when war broke out.[66] Chelmsford Borough Council also provided free medical attendance and medicine to dependants of serving troops.[67]

Nationally, the Prince of Wales Relief Organisation was established on the same

61 ERO D/Z 178/1/4 Tiptree Self-Help Cooperative minutes, 3 August 1914.

62 ERO D/Z 178/1/5 Tiptree Self-Help Cooperative minutes 1916-18: 14 April 1917.

63 CBC minute, Tramways Committee, 19 January 1915.

64 ECC 24 March 1916.

65 CBC, Roads and Drainage Committee, 19 August 1914.

66 EEA 29 August 1914.

67 Chelmsford Relief Committee, 29 October 1914.

day that war was declared. Its purpose was to provide financial assistance for anyone suffering hardship directly as a result of the War. Under the oversight of the Local Government Board, local committees were established throughout the country. There was a County Committee which covered all of Essex except for urban districts with a population of over twenty thousand; places like Chelmsford and Colchester organised their own committees. The County Committee consisted of forty sub-committees built around the urban and rural district councils with representatives from the guardians, employers, trade unions, charitable organisations, and the Soldiers' and Sailors' Families Association. A government scale of relief was established in order to discourage the 'lavish' scale of relief which it considered was being was paid out at first. Adults received 6*s*., 10*s*. for two, 1*s*. 2*d*. per child up to three children, 5*d*. per child where there were more than three. Where rent exceeded 4*s*. a week there was an additional allowance to a maximum of 2*s*. 6*d*. The allowance was cut by half if any family member obtained work.[68]

The Executive Committee at Colchester aimed

> to consider what steps can be taken for alleviating the distress likely to be felt by the wives and families of men called on Active Service and of those losing their regular employment owing to dislocation of trade.[69]

Formed by the Colchester Town Council in a meeting at the Town Hall on 7 August, it consisted of the mayor, deputy mayor, two aldermen, five councillors, two guardians and twelve others, including the town's M.P., Laming Worthington-Evans. The committee divided Colchester into ten areas, adopting the ten districts of the Charitable Organisation Society for the purposes of relief. A sub-committee was appointed in each area, with the Charitable Organisation Society and Soldiers' and Sailors' Federated Association forming the nucleus of each sub-committee. A central office was set up in the Albert School in the High Street.[70] The wives and daughters of Colchester's great and good, organised by Miss Marriage, the mayor's daughter, and Catherine Hunt, immediately began organising the collection of donations to the fund. A collection held at this first committee meeting raised £497 10*s*.[71] By 22 August there were eighty ladies engaged in street collections. The first list of donors to the fund was published in the local press on 12 August.[72] Several local firms made

[68] County Relief Committee minutes, 23 October 1914.

[69] ERO Acc. C4, Prince of Wales National Relief Fund: Colchester Branch. Meetings of Relief Executive and Sub Committees 1914-24: Executive Committee minutes 5 August 1914.

[70] Relief Committee minutes, 10 August 1914.

[71] Relief Committee minutes, 7 August 1914.

[72] Relief Committee minutes, 12 August 1914.

their own relief fund collection boxes and placed them on their premises.[73] The local Medical Society made special arrangements for its doctors to attend the dependants of enlisted men. District sub-committees were authorised to defray the costs of prescriptions using medical tickets "in cases where gratuitous attendance to be needful."[74] These sub-committees were also instructed to issue vouchers to any servicemen's dependants in need of free medical attendance. To prevent abuse of this system, recipients were monitored in case a change in circumstances rendered free assistance no longer necessary. No-one was eligible for this aid if they were in receipt of more than the maximum scale of War Office allowances "but special circumstances may be taken into consideration."[75] Chelmsford's Relief Committee met for the first time on 26 August 1914 and consisted of twenty-eight members, including three women and three works representatives — from Hoffman, Marconi and Crompton's.

In reality the fund was neither much needed nor much used in Essex. The presence of tens of thousands of troops in the county was a major factor in this, because by supplementing the incomes of householders, and in stimulating the trade of business and industrial enterprises it helped limit financial hardship. The only area significantly affected by distress arising from the War was the coast, particularly lodging house keepers at Clacton, and to a lesser degree at Walton, whose business evaporated for the duration as soon as war began. The billeting of troops in the area and the opening of the Clacton Workroom, which provided employment for about twenty women, was the committee's response to the crisis. Coastal unemployment in the fishing and yachting industry was tackled by relief work which involved the dredging of public oyster beds in the Mersea Island and Tollesbury neighbourhoods and steps to eliminate the American limpet and other pests.

By late October 1914 the sums donated in Colchester amounted to £3,392. By then the £100 initial donation made by the fund's central organisation had been returned for urgent cases elsewhere — it no longer being required. Between August 1914 and 31 December 1917 only £377 was doled out in relief of distress.[76] As in so many other places, the hugely beneficial presence of the army was of help to both tradesmen and householders alike, and generally succeeded in keeping the wolf from the door. During the War the distinction between the distress affecting the families of servicemen and civilians who had no family members in the armed forces was blurred because the easy availability of munitions work and the scarcity of workers meant that the remaining adult civilians were able to obtain employment. The County Committee's minutes suggest that there were never more than a handful of applicants for relief, about a dozen at the end of 1915, for instance. Very few had to resort to

[73] Relief Committee minutes, 2 October 1914.

[74] Relief Committee minutes, 9 October 1914.

[75] Relief Committee minutes, 21 October 1914.

[76] Relief Committee minutes, 2, 20 October 1914, 22 March 1918.

sending letters like this one, from Annie Cook of Harlow, dated 24 August 1914:

> Kingston Cottages
> Potter Street
> Harlow
>
> I am writing to ask you if you can give me a little help as my eldest son Harry Cook he is in the Harlow Territorials. I am a widow my husband having died since my son has been called up often having been ill for some time. He has been the main[stay] of the family and I have several little ones. Hoping you will try and do your best for me. I am
>
> yours truly
>
> Mrs Annie Cook[77]

For the families of servicemen killed in the War assistance was provided by the long-established Soldiers' and Sailors' Families Association, which stepped in as soon as war broke out. However, by late 1916 the numbers of those who had fallen in the service of their country had become so large that their work was taken over by the Government, which created a national system of War Pensions Committees to tackle the problem.

Alongside the assistance given to the families of servicemen, great efforts were made to provide soldiers with an active and varied social life. Providing entertainment for lonely and bored soldiers away from home was only one reason for this provision. Securing their moral welfare in the face of temptation was of even greater importance. Naturally the religious denominations of the area were at the forefront of this movement. In Colchester, the Society of Friends opened their adult schools to the troops every night, with musical events and impromptu concerts. The Lion Walk Congregational Church, Head Gate Congregational Church, Eld Lane Baptist Church, the Wesleyans, the Roman Catholics of St James the Less, the Salvation Army, St Paul's Men's Club, Holy Trinity and St Martin's all opened their doors to the troops. At Harwich a Local Chaplains Committee was set up to look after the troops' welfare.[78] In the village of Newport the church house was turned into a military canteen.[79] The hall at the rear of the Baptist Church in Hornchurch was transformed into a rest and social room for local troops.[80]

Whatever facilities were established for the area's soldiers, including those provided by non-religious groups, they were always intended to combine entertainment, utility

77 ERO C/DC 14/1 Lord Lieutenant's Emergency Relief Committee Minutes.

78 HDS 11 September 1915.

79 B. Nurse, J. Pugh, I. Mollet, *A Village in Time: The History of Newport, Essex* (1995), 139.

80 Perfect, *Hornchurch*, 207.

and wholesomeness. The Social Club for Troops was opened in Colchester in the old Public Hall in the High Street on 24 September 1914. The electric lighting and gas were provided free until October 1916. The owners of the property, the Essex and Suffolk Insurance Company, let it rent free for the duration. Entry was free. It was designed to allow troops to enjoy a pleasant evening, and the facilities included reading and writing materials, billiards, chess, draughts and dominoes. Light refreshments were available, and cigarettes and stamps were on sale at cheap prices. Refreshments and cigarettes worth £27,000 were sold at the club, with an estimated five million visits being made during its existence. A savings bank was opened there in December 1914 and was in use until April 1917.[81] The club was run by ladies of the Conservative and Liberal Associations who were determined to assist the military:

> Their [the soldiers'] money was not much, and they could not afford to dine at a restaurant, but if they were able to get a cup of coffee or cocoa, and a cake or a sausage roll, it might prevent men going to bed hungry.[82]

The baths at Tendring workhouse were opened to troops in September 1914.[83] In Colchester, where the absence of public baths had been a contentious issue for years, the War speeded things up. In the autumn of 1914 two baths were erected at the rear of the Public Hall near the new social club. Water was provided free by Colchester Town Council's Water Department, twenty minutes was allowed for a bath, with soap and a towel available for four pence.[84] The troops stationed in Colchester also made much of the town's museum. Attendances increased from 29,564 in 1913-14 to 49,689 in 1914-15. Although visits declined in subsequent war years, attendances were never less than forty-four thousand, and actually peaked at 51,496 during 1918-19.[85]

Consideration was also given to the wives of servicemen who managed to reach Colchester to visit their husbands for a short time. In December 1914 a club was opened in the Women's Help Society premises in Osborne Street. It was open from 3 p.m. to 6 p.m. and possessed "a magnificent toy room where they could get rid of the children for a few moments." North Street School also opened rest rooms for a similar purpose.[86]

One form of entertainment beloved of soldiers since time immemorial — the consumption of alcohol — was severely curtailed for the duration. That civilians were

81 Hunt, *War Memorial Souvenir*, 73.

82 CG 16 September 1914.

83 ECT 26 September 1914.

84 ECT 17 October 1914.

85 Annual Reports: Colchester & East Essex Museum 1912-26.

86 ECT 12 December 1914; CBC Education Committee, 28 October 1914.

subject to the same restrictions was little comfort to troops seeking relaxation in a pint of beer. Licensing hours were untouched for the first month of the War. However, the garrison authorities at Colchester, anxious to limit the length of time available to soldiers to over-indulge in drinking, pressed the licensing authorities to force publicans not to serve them after 9 p.m. When some publicans showed a reluctance to comply with this request, they were brought before magistrates for serving excessive amounts of alcohol to the military. The Colchester Justices ordered public houses and clubs to close for the sale of intoxicating liquors at 9 p.m. This came into force on 2 September.[87] However, it was easier to impose the restriction than to enforce it, at least in Colchester. With thousands of recruits in town, many of them not in uniform at first, it proved difficult to ensure compliance. The same closing times were soon enforced in the Clacton, Tendring, and Lexden and Winstree divisions, although it was 10 p.m. at Braintree and Bocking. Chelmsford and district's licensing hours do not appear to have been amended until September 1915, when pub closing times were changed from 11 p.m. to 10 p.m. from Monday to Saturday, and 10 p.m. to 9 p.m. on Sundays. These restrictions had some beneficial results. At Harwich the early closure was said to have resulted in an improvement in the troops' behaviour.[88] Between August and December 1914 there were only four cases of military drunkenness brought before the magistrates in Colchester, and two of them were dismissed.[89] In consequence of similar figures at Clacton, the magistrates there extended drinking hours to 9.30 p.m. in mid-1915, except for the Ramsey and Oakley areas which remained under military control.[90]

Although many people in 1914 anticipated that the conflict would be a short one, facilities for the wounded were being organised almost immediately that war was declared. In fact local preparations were under way even before August 1914. Major C.E. Freeman of Tymperleys, Colchester, convinced that war was coming, was aided by the St John's Ambulance Association in organising and training large numbers of women as voluntary nurses.[91] Not surprisingly, when war did come Essex was well prepared. By the end of 1914 the Red Cross and Voluntary Aid Detachments in the Colchester and Lexden divisions boasted eight women's and one men's detachments. At the outbreak of war, one detachment was ordered to establish a temporary hospital of fourteen beds at Wivenhoe, which was used for six weeks and then disbanded as larger units were set up. St Martin's House in East Stockwell Street was given to the Red Cross in mid-October and used until December, and a further temporary hospital at Woodhouse, Great Horkesley, was used until October. Twenty beds were in use at Stanway Rectory, and a field hospital was set up at Lexden House before being moved

[87] ECS 9 September 1914.

[88] ECT 26 September 1914.

[89] ECS 16 January 1915.

[90] ECS 19 June 1915.

[91] Hunt, *War Memorial Souvenir,* 64-5.

to the Gostwycke Military Hospital in Cambridge Road. The detached buildings at Severalls Hospital were occupied by the military from 19 August.[92]

There were similar developments all over Essex. Halstead workhouse was converted into a Red Cross hospital with sixty beds; the inmates were relocated to an unoccupied part of the workhouse. By the end of 1914 there were twenty-five Red Cross hospitals in the county. They occupied parts of local hospitals and workhouses, such as those at Halstead and Dunmow. Several large houses in Brentwood were converted into military hospitals.[93] These units and their supporters were wonderfully generous in their support for soldiers. The Colchester Red Cross branch sent two £400 motor ambulances to the front.[94] The farmers of Witham, Maldon and Chelmsford raised the not inconsequential sum of £400 to buy an ambulance car.[95] Even small villages were used by the army's medical services. At Newport the church house and parish hall were commandeered as hospitals.[96] The wife of General Byng turned their house at Thorpe over to the military as a hospital in August 1914, as did Frank Hilder, owner of Huskards at Ingatestone.[97]

At Colchester facilities for the wounded arriving back from the front were eventually concentrated into three hospitals — the Garrison Military Hospital, the Essex County Hospital, and Gostwycke Military Hospital. The committee at Essex County Hospital offered the War Office and Admiralty the use of its grounds for tents for the wounded as soon as war began. The offer was quickly accepted, although the military also took over fifty beds, half the hospital's total. By the end of 1914 forty-nine soldiers had been treated there, most of them by Red Cross nurses who were trained on the wards. By 1915 part of the hospital itself was taken over by the military, and the hospital committee rented the Girls' High School to transfer its women patients to, thereby releasing two wards, and the hospital's child patients followed soon after. Two huts were later erected in the grounds for 150 patients, thus increasing the number of military beds to 250. At first the Gostwycke Hospital was used as a clearing station and convalescent cases were sent to the Essex County Hospital. However, in 1915, the military authorities, impressed with the latter's facilities, began to send casualties to the Essex County Hospital directly from the railway stations. During 1914-1918 the Essex County Hospital dealt with 3,997 military patients, with a final flurry during the great battles of 1918 when almost a third of wartime casualties (1,313) were dealt with, necessitating the erection of several marquees in the grounds. Essex County Hospital's pre-war financial difficulties were hardly eased by the pressures of war. In 1915 the War Office provided £2,658 towards the running costs

92 CBC, Committee of Visitors (Essex and Colchester Lunatic Asylums), 1 March 1915.

93 James, *Brentwood Past*, 126.

94 ECT 3 April 1915.

95 ECC 14 May 1915.

96 Nurse, *Newport*, 139.

97 Viscountess Byng of Vimy, *Up the Stream of Time* (1945), 125.

of these hospitals, but there was still a deficit of £8,573; during 1916-17 the War Office's contributions were well over half of the hospital's income, but these contributions fell away dramatically during 1919.[98]

In addition to volunteering for medical duties, civilians, particularly women, also assisted in very practical ways. When war broke out, half a dozen ladies at Colchester, gathered together by Mrs Coats Hutton, organised a group which became known as the War Work Depot. Fifty pounds was subscribed on the spot to purchase materials. Edith Marriage and Ethel Hutton, the mayoress and deputy mayoress, placed an advertisement in the press appealing for garments for the sick and wounded. A committee was set up and volunteers called for. The War Work Depot was responsible for almost single-handedly keeping the Gostwycke Military Hospital supplied with a huge variety of materials. As the demands of the hospital grew so did the number of volunteers. Fifty women worked in the depot's five workrooms in the old School of Art and large quantities of work were farmed out to over twenty working parties. Gifts of all sorts were donated including, "Feathers in sackfuls for pillows, and bags of lavender, walking sticks, and every conceivable garment." Money too poured in, increasing from £354 in 1914 to £1,032 in 1916. The scale of what was achieved by these volunteers can be gauged by what was sent to the military authorities by the Chelmsford War Work Depot in its first two months; it is a list worth quoting in full:

> pyjama suits 125; nightshirts 40; day shirts 2; vests 102; pants 48; day socks 105; bed socks 11; operating stockings 49; slippers 47; skull caps 84; sweaters 6; scarves 9; helmets 7; mittens 16; stump socks 4; treasure bags 3; roller bandages (all widths) 81 doz; slings 3 doz; many-tailed bandages 18 doz; round theatre swabs 91 bags; wool swabs 100 packets; abdominal dressings 3 sets; face washers 10 doz.[99]

Every local town had its own version of these depots. Between August and December 1914 the Walton Working Party, a non-denominational group led by the vicar's wife, Mrs H.C. Knocker, forwarded to the Red Cross Society:

> 16 flannel bedjackets, 20 nightshirts, 15 cotton shirts, 9 flannel shirts, 60 pairs of socks, 10 belts, besides a large number of bandages, mittens, gloves, mufflers, and miscellaneous articles of clothing.[100]

Clearly some of these materials were produced directly for the troops at the front. The

[98] Hunt, *War Memorial Souvenir,* 47-8; J.B. Penfold, *The History of the Essex County Hospital 1820-1948* (1984), 199-203.

[99] ECC 16 March 1917.

[100] ECS 13 February 1915.

Brightlingsea Working Party, set up in 1915, had forwarded thirty-six thousand articles by the end of October.[101]

Provision was also made for the wounded troops at the Gostwycke Military Hospital. Lacking any provision for the soldiers' welfare, Colonel Harvey, medical officer, asked a Mrs W.B. Slaughter for assistance. Modelling the scheme on the one at the base hospital at Boulogne, where she had visited her wounded son, she established her own version called Comforts for the Sick and Wounded Fund. This comprised a basket system in which items were taken round to the men such as

> sweets (especially chocolates), looking glasses and scented soap, tooth brushes and powder, shaving brushes, hairbrushes and combs, all kinds of newspapers — especially illustrated ones — cakes, fruits, and many other things too numerous to mention.

To obtain money Mrs Slaughter organised concerts and other entertainments; she personally canvassed the whole town as part of this fundraising. On similar lines the stationmaster at Colchester North Station, Ernest Wicks, organised the North Station Comforts Fund in May 1917, which provided a free buffet for the wounded arriving there. A Ladies' Committee of War Workers, seeking to improve the lot of British prisoners of war, sent food parcels each valued at 12*s*. to local men in captivity in Germany.[102]

In the early days of the War wounded troops were greeted with rapturous approval when they arrived back in England, as this description at Clacton indicates,

> Everyone cheered and waved their hats or handkerchiefs, and those who were standing in the roadway approached as near as they could to the cars and shouted bravoes to the bandaged occupants. For a considerable distance the road towards the Hospital was lined with people, and although the procession of cars continued for some time, no-one seemed to get tired of cheering and waving.[103]

At the Garrison Military Hospital, those who were sufficiently recovered could be found relaxing outside in the sun where they were visited by relatives and received gifts from influential local people.[104] Red Cross trains packed with wounded were often stopped at Witham, where local women boarded and handed out refreshments. There was certainly no discrimination towards wounded men, even those who had

[101] EEA 6 November 1915.

[102] Hunt, *War Memorial Souvenir*, 65, 78-9.

[103] CG 16 September 1914.

[104] ECT 3 October 1914.

been severely disfigured. In January 1916 a special welcome home meeting was held in the Institute Hall at Tollesbury in honour of Henry Smith, a twenty-year-old private in the Lancashire Fusiliers who had lost a leg in France, and who was lauded as the first man in the village to have sacrificed a limb in the service of his country.[105]

Soldiers who were wounded in action, but whose wounds were not serious enough to merit a return to Britain, often wrote home with startling candour about their experiences. Instead of being appalled by these revelations, often full of tales of blood and death, their families seem to have taken a patriotic pride in these escapades, and were often only too happy to pass their letters on to the local press. This one was sent by a Burnham man:

> Our biggest casualties occurred when we did an advance to take up a hitherto unoccupied position. We were ordered to go 300 yards, I understand, but actually went about 1400 yards, under a heavy fire. We are continually losing men here, most of them from shrapnel bursts, as the whole of this part of the peninsula is under fire. Shrapnel is whizzing about me as I write.[106]

This letter, written to the Vicar of Goldhanger, Frederick Gardner, by a soldier who had served with his son who had been killed in action, provided a graphic account of his death:

> We went "over the top" on the 15th Sept. between Trones Wood and Flers. I was not in your son's platoon, but in the preparations I was put under his command. We started at 6 am and took the three German trenches, Lieut. Gardner leading the way. About half a mile from the last taken trench, he was hit in the leg with a piece of shrapnel, as I was behind, I asked him if I could help him. I bound his leg up and was helping him to a shell hole for cover, when a shell exploded, and a piece went through his body, he was killed immediately. I was wounded also in the head and thigh, the piece coming with such force as to pass through your son's body into my thigh. I hope you will forgive me if I have caused you any pain, but when I read in the *Ipswich Star* of your great loss, I felt it would relieve you to know that he did not suffer.[107]

A letter from Private Davis, Albert Street, Colchester, who was serving with the King's Royal Rifles in France, gave vivid descriptions of how his fellow soldiers were

[105] ECC 26 January 1916.

[106] BDA, 18 September 1915.

[107] Goldhanger parish magazine, Nov. 1916.

killed by shellfire. His comments home reveal the astonishing optimism which could only be generated by a very localised awareness of the fighting:

> If we caught any prisoners they seemed quite pleased, and would tell us they are fed up with this life, and don't know what they are fighting for. Poor fellows! They are getting starved to death and are glad to surrender, for they are cut off from supplies. We are simply all around them and they do not know which way to turn. I think their army is about finished, and the Kaiser does not know what to do. He will throw it up shortly and ask for peace. At least the war will be over in about a month's time, and I shall be home for Christmas.[108]

However, the optimism of men like Davis began to evaporate as the fighting continued through the winter of 1914 and into the new year. Casualties began to appear in the local newspapers, with officers frequently awarded full obituaries, while the 'rank and file' casualties received conspicuously fewer column inches. Typical of the latter was the following, written in April 1917:

> Pte Henry B. Mann, King's Shropshire Light Infantry, killed in action, was 32 years of age, and lived at 33 College Road, Little Thurrock. He leaves a wife and four children. His father is Mr Keen, a signalman at North Thurrock.[109]

By July 1915 the *Essex County Chronicle* announced that it would be printing a full casualty list of Essex men on the first Friday of each month. On 19 July it listed twelve hundred fatalities; in just over a week it rose to fifteen hundred. During 1915 the battles of the Ypres area led to a steady increase in the numbers of men listed as prisoners of war, wounded, missing or dead, and for the next four years there was no let up. By late 1916 shopkeepers were unable to obtain sufficient mourning materials to keep up with demand.[110] Most of those killed in action were buried abroad and bereaved families had to make do with letters of regret written by commanding officers or by a friend of the deceased, as in the case of Lieutenant Gardner above, or this letter from a comrade of Private Hugh Smith of West Mersea, killed on 15 February 1916. Both letters made a sincere attempt to assuage the feelings of the family of the bereaved:

[108] ECC, 3 October 1914.

[109] ECC 13 April 1917.

[110] Clark, *Diary*, 165.

> Dear Mrs Smith,
>
> Undoubtedly you have by now been notified of the death of your son Hugh. He was killed by a shell on Tuesday last, February 15th, while doing his duty as a true Englishman. It may slightly comfort you to know his death was instantaneous. He was carried back to a village near the trenches and properly buried in a British cemetery. The NCO's and men of the platoon join with me in expressing our very deepest sympathy. He was liked and respected by all who knew him, and for myself, he was my chum, and I loved him almost as a brother. I am afraid there is nothing I can say to comfort you, but the One above who ordains all things for our good also gives us strength to bear these terrible burdens. His personal property, less his watch and cigarette case, which of course were smashed, were handed in at headquarters, and will be forwarded on to you shortly. I can assure you I sympathise with you with all my heart, as I myself miss him terribly.
>
> Believe me to remain,
>
> Yours respectfully,
>
> Albert A. Branch.[111]

At Tillingham Church of England Primary School the headmistress recorded in the logbook the names of former pupils of the village school who died in the War. Lieutenant Dougal Sewell was the first. He was killed at Mons. A month later she recorded the name of Arthur Skeats, drowned when H.M.S. *Cressy* was sunk. When in January 1916 Ernest Perrin was drowned on the *Persia*, she added that he had been "brutally murdered." Harold Drakeford, killed at Gaza in Palestine, Charles Bateman and Claude Taylor were all included in the logbook before the War was over.[112]

Many of the wounded who were brought back to Essex did not survive their wounds and were buried locally. For those killed abroad, influence and position in society was often used to ensure that the body was returned to England. Lieutenant Claude N. de Crespigny, son of a leading county family, was killed in action on 1 September 1914. His body had been buried, but was later disinterred. Laid with seventeen others, it was only recognisable by the name on the neck band of his shirt. It was brought home and laid to rest at the Crescent, the private family mausoleum at Champion Lodge in Heybridge.[113] One death in particular so affected the Colchester medical officer that he was moved to comment on it in his annual report, in rather less plodding terms than was usual for such documents:

111 ECT 11 March 1916.

112 ERO T/P 407/14, Tillingham Church of England Primary School, logbook 1907-47.

113 ECC 13 November 1914.

> Most pathetic and forlorn is the last death. The formal and official death certificate bears his only epitaph, "apparently a soldier." His rank, his name, even his nationality, all gone. Among other wounded from the front he was brought in; he was never able to speak; his clothes not his own and no mark to distinguish him; he had been grievously wounded and came from the field of battle; and so he passes, bringing the grim reality of war a little closer — wounded unknown, "apparently a soldier."[114]

There were comparatively few reports of military funerals in the local press. One occurred in May 1915. Lieutenant Gerald Piggott, only eighteen years old, was buried in Doddinghurst churchyard. The church was full of flowers and there was a large attendance. The Union Jack, the symbol of national unity, was hung in the church and his sword and helmet were placed on the altar. He was an only son. More usual were memorial services, which became increasingly popular during the War, held for a family member who had been buried abroad. One such service was held at Braintree on the evening of 23 May 1915. Corporal Frederick Seabrook had been killed at Ypres, nine days earlier. His last letter had been written the day before. At the end of the morning service in church on 23 May the Dead March from Saul was played. At the memorial service the congregation sang Hymn 595 on its knees, and this was followed by 'Abide With Me' and 'God Save the King'.[115] One rather unusual funeral was that of a Belgian officer, Lieutenant Ferdinand Bandour. Aged only nineteen, he had been wounded by shrapnel. Following his transfer to the Garrison Hospital at Colchester gangrene set in and his leg was amputated. Failing rapidly, he died on 31 October 1914. Typical of the frenzied patriotism of these early months of the War, was the report, perhaps apocryphal, perhaps not, that with his last breath he asked to be shown the Belgian flag, and then "he peacefully passed away." He was buried with full military honours on 2 November. The cortege wound its way from St James the Less Roman Catholic Church to the town cemetery. His coffin, placed on a gun carriage, had a crucifix at the head, and was covered with the Belgian flag. The band of the Royal Fusiliers and a firing party of ten soldiers from the same regiment preceded the gun carriage. Behind it came twenty English and three Belgian officers, one of the latter with his head in bandages and bearing a wreath with the words "A leur regrette compagnons" written on it. A large number of off-duty recruits marched at the rear. In the cortege were a Roman Catholic priest, Dean Bloomfield, and Father Clarke, accompanied by a crucifix bearer and surpliced acolytes. At the graveside the first part of the service was conducted in Latin according to the rites of the Roman Catholic Church, followed by commendatory prayers in English. Three rifle volleys

[114] CBC, Medical Officer of Health, Annual Report, 1915.

[115] ECC 28 May 1915.

were fired over the grave and a bugler played the 'Last Post'; the band concluded the service by playing the Belgian national anthem. The *Colchester Gazette*'s reporter completed his account of the funeral with his own thoughts concerning the significance of what he had just witnessed:

> and thus ended a unique ceremony in the history of Colchester, a ceremony eloquent of self-sacrifice and heroism, as well as of sadness and solemnity, which seemed to be accentuated by the autumn aspect.[116]

[116] CG 4 November 1914.

CHAPTER SIX

The Defence of the County

The German air raid on Colchester lampooned. *(ERO: ECS February 1915)*

ONCE WAR BROKE OUT, general apprehension about the security of the county manifested itself in both official concern and public panic. The former was sustained throughout the War. The latter, however, occurred periodically, for instance during the autumn of 1914 when there were rumours of German U-boats in the River Blackwater. There were said to be three, six, or seven depending on who was telling the tale. The despatch of territorials to support the local coastguard on 15 November suggested that the rumours were taken moderately seriously. Such panics reappeared briefly in the spring of 1918 in the wake of the final great German offensive of the War.[1] This apprehension centred on several worries. Firstly, there was the fear of a German invasion. Anxiety about the close proximity of the German fleet had already been revealed in pre-war contemporary references to the North Sea as the 'German Ocean'. The invasion panic in August 1914 was sufficient to wreck the Essex coastal holiday season and threaten the livelihood of those who were dependant upon it. There was also concern at the presence of enemy aliens, and the possibility that they may have carried out sabotage or spying. We have already seen that in August 1914, in response to these concerns, both the military, and incredibly the boy scouts, were used to guard 'vital' installations and patrol lines of communications throughout the area. Such were the fears of invasion, that in 1915 the Anglican Church Congress being held at Southend was hurriedly abandoned for fear of the Germans descending upon their deliberations.[2]

However, it was clear that a more structured and long-term solution was required if the county was to be secure from enemy action of whatever kind. One Essex gentleman, Claude Moffatt Bailey, soon suggested the creation of a 'national guard' on the lines of the French model of 1871, and within a week of war being declared a meeting at Maldon attended by over a hundred men established its own town guard.[3] In reality, the solution to home defence was to be centred on the police rather than a multitude of town guards, although the creation of local volunteer groups was also given official sanction as part of an overall structure. In 1914 there were only four hundred and fifty men in the Essex Constabulary, and if the police were to carry out the additional wartime duties assigned to it, far more men would be needed. This meant the introduction of special constables. The Special Constabulary was organised by a Captain Ffinch, who operated directly from his home at the Mill in Maldon. Ffinch was given the rank of assistant chief constable by J.A. Unett, who replaced E.M. Showers as chief constable in 1915,[4] when the latter reached the statutory retirement age.[5]

1 BDA 21 November 1914.

2 CDC August 1923.

3 ECC 14 August 1914.

4 Showers then became Chief Constable of Colchester during the War.

5 This section is largely based on ERO D/P 77/1. Some orders, reports and letters relating to the Colchester Division, Essex Special Constabulary, during the Great War 1914-18, volume 1 1915-16, and D/Z 137, the logbook of Special Constable H.J. Gripper.

The duties of special constables were the same as those of regular police officers with the addition of wartime responsibilities. They were empowered to stop and challenge anyone they were suspicious of, and instructed:

> to take notice of all passers-by and stop and question all who look like foreigners or suspicious persons, and if the Special Constable suspects them to be either German or Austrian to demand their permits ... and unless produced to detain the suspects.

A directive of 15 September 1914 also allowed them to challenge "any evilly disposed people", a sufficiently vague description to cover just about anyone.

Full instructions were issued to all special constables on 2 September 1914. These ordered that "they should carry out their duties with energy, promptness and determination, and obey the orders of those over them, using great tact and good temper at all times". Their duties included guarding all "vulnerable points liable to outrage", such as "Railway and other bridges, Waterworks, Reservoirs, Lighting Works, Magazines, Churches, Town Halls, and other large buildings." Individual sentry duty was not permitted, all duties had to be doubled up, although dogs could also be used to accompany their masters. Sentry duties were on the basis of two hours on, four hours off. When challenging strangers the phrase "Halt, who comes there?" was to be used. On 10 September Ffinch authorised that special constables be issued with "about two yards of rope to be taken ... in case it may be required to use it as a handcuff." By 1915 they had also been issued with torches.

Special constables were initially sworn in for a year. Their uniform consisted only of an armlet. Sergeants and corporals had an 'S' or 'C' embroidered on them. Training was minimal; the constables were to be drilled twice a week by corporals, and once a fortnight by a police sergeant. Ffinch restructured the Special Constabulary on a more organised footing in 1915. The Colchester Division was organised into fifteen groups of parishes; for example, Group One comprised the villages of Wivenhoe, Alresford and Elmstead. In small villages, such as Ramsey, four special constables were appointed.[6] At Colchester seven were enrolled for the River Colne patrol.[7] By the end of 1914 the town had eighty special constables enrolled, including many 'notable' professional and commercial men. Alderman Wilson Marriage, the deputy mayor, was enrolled as 'Special Constable Number 1', complete with armlet, staff and whistle.[8] There were 120 men in the Southend Special Constabulary by the end of 1914. This rose to 571 during 1915, stood at 472 in 1916, and was 368 in 1917-18, the gradual decline being explained by the absorption of some of the men into the

6 HDS 9 January 1915.

7 CG 9 September 1914.

8 ECT 12 December 1914.

regular armed forces once conscription was introduced in 1916.[9]

Recruitment rates throughout the county were very high. Within a month of the outbreak of war there were fifty-five special constables at Burnham, and eighty at Southminster.[10] The experience of the Special Constabulary at Hornchurch was probably typical of most places in the county. Hornchurch, which was part of the Romford Division, had nine men sworn in on 4 September 1914 in the Old Schoolroom on Church Hill. A week later a further forty-six were sworn. George M. Horey was elected as parish officer with the rank of sergeant. On September 29 the Hornchurch section began its duties by patrolling the roads and lanes within the parish. Such patrolling was part of a national network, and was carried out within a six mile radius of the coast and tidal rivers along the entire South and East Coasts. At Hornchurch these patrols were organised in three shifts, with three patrols to each shift, from 8 p.m. to 5 a.m. With seventy-nine men in the section at full strength, this meant a patrol for each man every third night and in this way eighty miles of road was patrolled each night.[11] Not all special constables adopted a cooperative approach. In early 1915 a number of them were sacked at Witham for failing to meet the required standard. They had failed to attend drills and had proved to be averse to discipline. One of those dismissed described the work as "absolute piffle" and said that their duties were best left to soldiers.[12]

The Special Constabulary was among the unsung heroes of the War. Its duties were arduous, monotonous, and conducted relatively anonymously. In the words of one author,

> during the four and a half years of their service the public saw very little of the Special Constables, except, perhaps, when a careless householder happened to be showing too much light, and then he was promptly acquainted of the fact by one of them, and duly warned of the consequences. Their measured tread was, however, often heard in the dead of night. Often, too, they were out in strong force awaiting the consummation of a first warning of approaching enemy aircraft, and ready either to take up their air raid posts, or, in the event of a threatened raid not maturing, the order to resume normal conditions, in which case those not on actual patrol duty would be free to go back to their homes and beds, and the general residents would be unaware that anything out of the ordinary had happened.[13]

9 SST 13 February 1919. The 571 in 1919 consisted of 121 at Southend, Westcliff 176, Leigh 123, Southchurch seventy, Thorpe Bay forty-six, and Prittlewell thirty-five.

10 BDA 5 September 1914; SST 20 August 1914.

11 Perfect, *Hornchurch* 188-189.

12 ECC 14 May 1915.

13 Perfect, *Hornchurch*, 191.

Special Constable Gripper of Chelmsford sat down on a January night in 1919 and totted up the duties he had completed during the War. He had done sixteen all night guards, attended fifty-four drills, completed 152 patrols, during which he calculated that he had walked approximately seven hundred and forty miles, and had been on duty for 752 hours. Gripper was sufficiently impressed with a poem written by one of his colleagues, Special Constable 353, whose name unfortunately he did not provide, to copy it into his logbook. In a light-hearted way it welcomes the end of their duties and celebrates their achievements:

No more in icy blackness
The Reservoir to guard
Or tramping round the viaduct
And the smelling railway yard

No more in midnight watches
We wait the Zeppelin's hum
Or watch the bursting shrapnel
As the raiding Goths come

No more our worthy Sergeant
Will send us out at night
To watch and ward the Borough
And see to lights too bright

We may not get a medal
We cannot win VC
We have only done our duty
Without reward or fee.[14]

Complementing the introduction of the Special Constabulary was the Volunteer Force, an organisation designed to allow boys and men who were either too young or too old for the regulars or territorials to train, drill, shoot and be ready in any emergency such as invasion. In Colchester Charles Clarke, secretary of Colchester Town F.C., proposed a "Home Defence Force" of serious intention; "it must be understood", he said, "that the Corps was not to be a comic-opera affair, but a businesslike, patriotic force".[15] This came into being on 22 September 1914.

The Volunteer Corps, as they came to be known nationally, were eventually organised into a national organisation overseen by the War Office. In January 1915 the Colchester Volunteer Corps received official instructions from London. Although

14 ERO D/Z 137 Gripper logbook, 15 January 1919.

15 CG 2 September 1914.

volunteers were forbidden to wear badges of rank, uniformity of dress was permitted. The approved uniform was a Norfolk jacket with shoulder straps, made in a green-grey rainproof drill, breeches or trousers made of whip cord or cloth, brown leather gaiters and boots. On the head an ordinary peak cap or forage cap was to be worn. An officer's rank was indicated by white braid bands on the cuffs. Given such suggestions, based on assumptions about the resources which might be available to corps members, it is not surprising that most were from the middle classes, although this was not exclusively so. In Colchester, as well as municipal assistance, a public subscription was launched to raise funds for uniforms, suggesting that they were beyond the means of some members. Edgar Hunt recalled a touching story about one such donation:

> It was in 1915, and Mr Coats Hutton, the Mayor happened to open the door himself. A little shabby old man, a total stranger, handed him a bag with 5 sovereigns in it, towards the Voluntary Equipment Fund. He simply said "A Message from Mars", and disappeared into the night.[16]

Local authorities often stepped in with donations. Maldon gave £100, Colchester £250 and Witham an impressive £500. Chelmsford Town Council was accused of being unpatriotic when it contributed nothing to its municipal force.[17] The town's Volunteer Corps was reduced to placing an advertisement in the *Essex County Chronicle* appealing for £400 for uniforms for its five officers and 258 men. Since its establishment the company had come up with £1,174, all raised by its own efforts, except for £399 donated as a result of a variety of entertainments performed by supporters. However, in spite of these efforts the company was £250 in debt, and without the council's aid, it had little choice but to resort to an appeal.[18] Barking Urban District Council also refused to make any donations to the local volunteers, rejecting their requests on two occasions in 1917.[19]

It is clear that a good many young men of near military age joined the Volunteer Corps, prompting the War Office to authorise recruiting officers to visit its meetings at any time to recruit anyone eligible, particularly if he has "no good and sufficient reason" for being there.[20] By the spring of 1915 the Colchester battalion had some two hundred and fifty men in it; at its height it had seven hundred. Yet by the summer of 1916, its numbers had shrunk to two hundred because so many of its members had either volunteered or been conscripted into the armed forces.[21] The same problem

16 Hunt, *War Memorial Souvenir*, 57.

17 ECC 30 March 1917.

18 ECC 1 June 1917.

19 Barking UDC minutes, 13, 27 February 1917.

20 ECS 16 January 1915.

21 ECS 27 March 1915, ECT 1 July 1916.

affected other local battalions, such as those at Lexden and Wivenhoe.[22] What began as an organisation designed to provide a sort of First World War 'Dad's Army' ended as a training unit for the forces. Individual firms organised their own drills. Davey and Paxman's employees who were over military age borrowed the rifles of the Colchester Grammar School's Cadet Corps, until the firm made its own arrangements.[23] At Woodford, a rifle range was opened for the Volunteer Corps on private land. The owners of Burgess's factory at Brentwood provided an indoor rifle range for the local company; drills were carried out at the grammar school and parochial hall.[24] Alderman Martin, of Southend Borough Council, offered £100 towards the provision of rifle ranges for the town's Volunteer Corps. Eventually, in September 1914, a rifle range for the Southend Rifle Club was opened at Sand Pit. This opened daily from 2 p.m. until 6 p.m.[25] In some towns, particularly when much waste ground was absorbed into allotments, it became hard to find spaces on which to drill. There was an outcry in Southend when it was suggested that cricket pitches were the perfect solution.[26] Schools were involved in the preparations too. At Bancroft's School in Woodford at Easter 1915, a miniature rifle range was set up in the school's cellars, where the Cadet Corps, which was created that summer, learned the art of marksmanship.[27] At Leyton, fourteen of the seventy teachers who were beyond military age formed their own rifle company in September 1914.[28]

The likelihood of an air raid or naval bombardment being launched against England had been accepted as a possibility since the deliberations of the Hague Convention in 1899. The great powers present at the conference all agreed to outlaw the use of aeroplanes to drop bombs. However, by the time of the second Hague Convention in 1907, such unanimity had been abandoned as the military potential of aviation became increasingly apparent. Consequently, in 1908 the Government set up a parliamentary committee to investigate the dangers posed by military aviation and before long both the army and navy were alerted to the problem. Two years later the Home Ports Committee, staffed by representatives of the Admiralty and the War Office, reiterated the parliamentary committee's suggestion that the most effective defence against air attack was for the Government to construct airships and aircraft. Government action was not slow in coming. Airfields and naval air stations were built and in 1912 the R.F.C. was created. When war broke out almost all of the R.F.C.'s squadrons were sent to France and from 3 September 1914 the defence of

22 ECS 6 March 1915, 15 July 1916.

23 CG 2 September 1914.

24 ECC 22 January, 5 February 1915.

25 SST 3 September 1914.

26 SST 7 January 1915.

27 D.C.R. Francombe and D.E. Coult, *Bancroft's School 1737-1937* (1937), 96.

28 LE 12, 19 September 1914.

England against air attack devolved upon the Royal Naval Air Service, which had just fifty aircraft at its disposal.[29]

An editorial in the *Harwich and Dovercourt Standard* raised the possibility of Zeppelin raids as early as mid-October 1914, largely because of the German occupation of Belgium.[30] The German naval raids on the Norfolk coast on 2 November, and the naval bombardments of Scarborough, Hartlepool and Whitby on 16 December, which were so shocking to the English imagination, provided ammunition for those who claimed that Essex was vulnerable to enemy action. So too did the gunfire on the Western Front which could be heard in Essex over the course of the springs and summers of 1915-18.[31]

In January 1915 the *Essex County Telegraph* poured scorn on those who it thought were over-reacting to the threat of air raids with an editorial headlined "Silly Zeppelin Scare in Essex". However, it was this danger, rather than the possibility of sea bombardment which turned into reality for Essex. On 9 January 1915, the Kaiser gave permission to begin air raids against Great Britain. Although the first targets were to be military ones, the purpose of German raids was soon changed. With its Grand Fleet bottled up in harbour and its army stalemated on the Western Front, the Kaiser saw his air force as the spearhead of a new tactic to break the military deadlock by using it to destroy the morale of the British people. Although the resources of the German air force were inadequate to begin operations in 1914, its strength grew sufficiently to launch this entirely novel type of warfare early in 1915.[32]

Sunday, 21 February 1915 was a fine moonlit night, clear enough for the first German air raid of the War. A single German aircraft, having crossed the North Sea, was reported over Clacton. It reached Braintree where it dropped two incendiaries, and returning to the North Sea via Coggeshall it offloaded a high explosive bomb. By 7.55 p.m. it had reached Brightlingsea and by 8.20 p.m. it was over Old Heath, flying very high and in the direction of London. At 8.40 p.m. a single high explosive bomb was dropped which landed in the back garden of 41 Butt Road, Colchester. This one bomb had a powerful impact on local sensibilities. Windows were smashed in nearby Denmark Street and a shell fragment was picked up 250 yards away in Crouch Street. The bomb left a crater five feet in diameter and two and a half feet deep. The kitchen was wrecked, the door of an adjoining sitting room was splintered and there were bomb fragments embedded in the wall. House windows nearby were smashed and corrugated iron sheds were crumpled. The bomb turned the garden shed at 41 Butt Road into matchwood and pulverised a baby's pram which was inside it. At the back of the house a small baby lay sleeping, but in fact the only fatality from all this

[29] H.T. Sutton, *Raiders Approach* (1956), 5-7.

[30] HDS 17 October 1914.

[31] ECS 1 March 1919.

[32] J. Morris, *The German Air Raids on Great Britain 1914-18* (1969), 6, 11.

wreckage was a thrush, found dead nearby. At Coggeshall, the wife of an agricultural labourer died of shock. Colchester was busy and town centre streets were crowded. Householders were quickly aware that a bomb had been dropped, but most were unsure where it had fallen. Many people dived for shelter in cellars and cupboards, although the town's tram services continued unimpaired. The garrison, which as many observers had commented, had so far studiously ignored the blackout restrictions affecting the rest of the town, was rapidly plunged into darkness. Inevitably, given the paranoia of the times, there were rumours that a car with bright headlights had been driven along local rural roads, guiding the plane to Coggeshall and Braintree.[33] The Reverend Reeves of Stondon Massey also thought a pro-German fifth column was at work, "the belief was that the course of the Zeppelins was directed by strong lights on the roads below, handled by aliens or by unworthy payees of Germany, acting as the enemy's scrats and informers".[34] There were wild suggestions that cars everywhere should stop running at dusk. The local press reacted to the lone raider with immense anger. The *Essex County Standard*, in a vitriolic editorial, denounced the raid as part of "a reckless policy of uncontrolled fury ... a diabolical outrage ... [an act of] shameless barbarity", and saw it as evidence of the Germans' "petulant frenzy." Although the child at 41 Butt Road was uninjured, the *Essex County Chronicle* denounced the Germans as 'baby killers'.

The local authorities had already prepared rudimentary instructions for use in an air raid. Those concerning Harwich were issued on 30 November 1914. Civilians were advised not to congregate in the streets, but to shelter in their cellars and basements. In the case of a sea bombardment arrangements were made for teachers to disperse schoolchildren to their homes, but it is unclear if the same arrangements were to apply in an air raid.[35] In fact, probably fewer people dived for cover than appeared outdoors as onlookers during most air raids. At Burnham the diarist Robert Bull, his wife and many neighbours, when roused from sleep by the sound of Zeppelins, donned dressing gowns to watch from outside their homes. Four days later when another Zeppelin flew over the town, they did exactly the same thing.[36] Evelyn Potter was certainly not intimidated. On 10 September 1916 she dashed outside to see an air raid at first hand, an experience which she described romantically in her diary:

> I had a fine view of the Zeppelin. It seemed to stand still, lit up
> bright with search lights against the dark sky and the shells
> were bursting all around like stars.

[33] ECT 23 February 1915; ECS 27 February 1915; Morris, *German Air Raids* (1969), 208.

[34] Reeves, Stondon Massey MS.

[35] ERO D/Z 77/1, instructions from Ffinch.

[36] Bull, Diary, 27, 31 May 1915.

A fortnight later she witnessed the destruction of the Zeppelin L.32:

> A raid on tonight. 1.30 a.m. After a terrible din of guns, then a silence, we heard people shouting and clapping. Rushing out we saw a great red glow, like a Chinese lantern in the sky, over towards Avenue Road and in the centre — voila — Monsieur Le Zepp, burning from end to end! Slowly it sank down, a burning shape. What a terrible fate for the men inside! Sirens going — shouting — people's feet — am going out to the front door again.[37]

On 24 September 1916 Conrad Noel, the Vicar of Thaxted, along with other clergy, was on retreat discussing the problem of social democracy within the Church of England. They too adjourned their discussions to watch the L.32 shot down and crash in flames at nearby Great Burstead.[38] When Zeppelins bombed Southend on 10 May 1915 thousands of people "overcoats over night attire", coolly watched things from the insecurity of their streets and front doors.[39] Sightseeing could hardly have been more dangerous for the workers of the giant Kynochtown explosives factory than sheltering in the dugouts and haystacks that were available for them.[40] Only at Tollesbury did some inhabitants feel safe from attack. With the Kaiser's yacht, the *Meteor*, in dock there since 1914, it was rumoured that Germany's supreme warlord had given express orders that the town was not to be attacked.[41] Time and the increasing severity of German raids did not deter these sightseers. The chief constable reported that when, on 5 June 1917, Romford's sirens wailed out a warning, it resulted in hordes of onlookers rushing into the streets rather than diving for cover.[42] Only when bombs fell close were people shaken out of their complacency. Mrs E. Shead recalled that after one bomb landed near houses at Braintree, she, as a nurse, spent the whole night treating people for shock.[43] In late May 1915, after an air raid on Southend, Father Patrick McKenna wrote how he and others sheltered in his church in Westcliff. "We stood shivering in Church awaiting death", he noted in his diary, "while incendiary bombs fell all round us and our guns firing uselessly at the foe. Thank God we escaped."[44] People were not the only ones to suffer, particularly when bombs fell on the countryside. In April 1916 several bombs fell at the junction

[37] Potter/Grubb diary, 10, 23 September 1916.

[38] R. Groves, *Conrad Noel and the Thaxted Movement: An Adventure in Christian Socialism* (1967), 177.

[39] ECC 14 May 1915.

[40] W.N. Scott, *Coryton: The Story of a Village* (1981), 23.

[41] *Tollesbury to the Year 2000*, 243.

[42] ERO J/P 12/2, Essex police notes, 9 June 1917.

[43] ERO T/Z 25/619.

[44] McKenna, diary, 26 May 1915.

of the parishes of Stondon, Blackmore and Kelvedon Hatch leaving craters fifteen feet in diameter, and between three and nine feet deep. The Reverend Reeves recalled that one old man described to him the strange blending of noises which resulted from the explosion:

> I never heard, said he, such a harmony: — bullocks, cows, calves, lambs, sheep, horses, dogs, fowls, rooks and pheasants: all might be heard calling in the night: all terrified, and wondering what was the cause of the sudden crash into the silence.[45]

Coastal towns had been subject to a blackout from the first day of the War and these restrictions soon covered the whole of the 'prohibited zone', which included Colchester as a vital military centre. Air-raid arrangements tended to develop piecemeal rather than as a fully thought out plan. Car lights were ordered to be covered at night, and it was forbidden to shine torches skywards. There were even fears that the overhead sparkings of Colchester's trams at night might be visible to German raiders miles away.[46] In some Essex towns, like Colchester, the kerbs on street corners were painted white to ease the darkness during blackouts.[47] The ringing of church bells was limited and the use of clock chimes, such as those on Colchester Town Hall, were discontinued on the grounds that they might be heard by enemy aircraft and used as beacons to guide them on their raids.[48] Following the February air raid, the bells of St Peter's, Colchester, were silent after 7 p.m.[49] A high barometer reading, which supposedly increased the likelihood of Zeppelin raids, meant a 'period of vigilance', and although later abandoned, a system of rocket signals was initially instituted with the Essex coastguard to give warning of incoming raiders. It is unclear what form the air-raid warning of Colchester took in the early years of the War, although Colchester's Special Emergency Committee authorised the use of factory and works hooters in January 1915.[50] However, in June 1917 a new siren, nicknamed 'Bellona', was wired up to the Borough Electricity Station. It was sounded every day at 12.30 p.m. to ensure that it worked.[51] At Brentwood the air-raid siren was fitted on the gasworks; at Chelmsford the works hooters of prominent businesses — Hoffmann, Crompton and Clarkson (the National Steam Car Company) — were mobilised when the borough's gasworks siren proved to be unreliable. The warning

45 Reeves, Stondon Massey MS, 15 April 1916.

46 ECS 6 November 1915.

47 ECS 8 May 1915.

48 Amendment to Defence of the Realm Act, 30 March 1916.

49 ECS 24 April 1917.

50 ERO Acc C4, Colchester Special Emergency Committee 1914-18, minutes, 27 January 1915.

51 Hunt, *War Memorial Souvenir*, CBC, Council-in-Committee, 9 June 1917.

sign of an air raid was three short blasts followed by a continuous blast, repeated three times. Industry was mobilised at other places too. At Braintree, Lake and Elliott, and Crittall used their factory hooters, at Halstead both Courtauld and Portway used the works bell. Clacton was warned by the council's steam siren in its works yard. Romford's siren was a klaxon horn operated from the top of the police station.[52] Southend Borough Council used a steam hooter to warn of incoming raiders. Colchester's shopkeepers were asked to allow their customers to shelter in their shops during a raid; those willing to cooperate pinned up notices to that effect.[53] During the warning of a daylight raid Colchester's trams were to continue running, but were ordered to head for the nearest terminus with the words 'hostile aircraft approaching, seek shelter' on their headboards. If a raid actually materialised, tramcars were to be stopped and their occupants were to be instructed to seek shelter.[54] Later, different warning methods were adopted. Once a warning had been received, observers were used on the tops of buildings, the Guildhall at Maldon for instance, and only when raiders were actually sighted were sirens used. This was to avoid alerting enemy aircraft to the fact that they had reached a large town, and to lessen use of sirens, the too frequent use of which was said to be making people "jumpy and nervous."[55]

Although air raids had been a reality since early 1915, Colchester Town Council did not withdraw permission for large meetings in Castle Park until July 1917. The Salvation Army were advised that if they persisted with large open air meetings, their organisers would be responsible for any tragic results. It was fortunate that no large-scale air raids did occur, because by mid-1917, thanks to the military's policy of commandeering animals, the town's Fire Brigade was no longer able to obtain horses. If the worst came to the worst it was reliant upon borrowing horses from the Royal Field Artillery at the barracks, an arrangement which was not designed to speed up the process of fire extinguishing.[56] The arrangements in other parts of the county were even less polished. A Mrs Haggis, a resident of Holland-on-Sea, recalled that during an air raid "the police cycled round the streets with a placard on their chest and back saying 'take cover' and they shouted it through a megaphone; at the all clear a whistle blew".[57]

At Chelmsford the possibility of air raids was taken extremely seriously. On 17 May 1915, Chelmsford Town Council held a special meeting to consider the steps to be taken in such an emergency.[58] The chief fire officer stated that in his opinion the town's Fire Brigade could deal with two fires at once, but he feared that the Germans'

[52] ECC 8 22 June, 6 July 1917.

[53] CBC, Watch committee, 2 June 1917.

[54] CBC, Tramways Committee, 17 July 1917.

[55] ERO J/P 12/2, Essex Police notes 1915-18, 30 May, 15, 19 June 1917.

[56] CBC Watch committee, 10 July 1917.

[57] ERO T/Z 25/624.

[58] ERO D/B 7, Borough of Chelmsford: Fire Brigade Committee minutes 1903-19.

use of incendiaries might result in several fires which would stretch the brigade's capabilities beyond breaking point. The resulting discussion led to the recommendation that the Fire Brigade be enlarged by use of military personnel, special constables, the incorporation within its ranks of other local brigades, or an appeal to former brigade members to rejoin the service for the duration. The need for more equipment was recognised, as was the need for greater mobility than was provided by horse-drawn fire engines. Within twenty-four hours of the meeting fifteen volunteer firemen had offered their services — without pay. Although the town council noted that it was not legally obliged to insure its volunteers against accidents, it nevertheless did so. By 1917 Barking Urban District Council had three motor-cycle messengers permanently on station, with two of them in communication with the fire station. Once a state of alert was declared, warnings written on cards were taken by boys to all the local schools with instructions to show them to the first teacher they met. Head teachers were given permission to dismiss all pupils when the Woolwich siren was heard. Sandbagging of all first floor windows of public buildings and schools was undertaken during 1917, and all public buildings were placed in readiness to shelter the public during an air raid.[59]

By October 1915 the Chelmsford Fire Brigade had been called out five times in connection with air-raid alarms, although the town itself had not been targeted directly by the Germans. In January 1916 Chelmsford Town Council followed the lead of other municipalities in agreeing to purchase a motor tractor to pull the fire engine. The decision was made with some reluctance, and was forced upon it because of the difficulty in obtaining horses. The need for urgency in the event of an air raid, led the council to ban the use of its fire engine outside of the borough boundary. The only exceptions to this rule were the Isolation Hospital on Baddow Road, Hylands Park, or where there was a existing written agreement concerning the wider use of the fire engine.[60] The town's special constables were also organised for action during air raids. In June 1917 the Chelmsford area was divided into five groups or 'piquets'. One was located at the police station, one in St John's Church at Moulsham and there were two watching posts, including one on the cathedral tower.[61] Every settlement in the county was expected to set up its own arrangements for air raids. Shenfield Parish Council circulated its own air-raid precautions to inhabitants in June 1915. To combat fires there were already three specially marked boxes containing fire hoses in the parish, and a fourth was added that year.[62] When air raids commenced the Special Constabulary at Hornchurch was trained to be ready to provide first-aid, and to assist anyone rendered homeless by bombing. Several householders volunteered to shelter

59 Barking UDC minutes, 26 September, 9 October, 9 November, 11 December 1917.

60 ERO D/B 7, Fire Brigade Committee minutes, 19, 26 May, 15 October 1915, 14 January, 10 March 1916.

61 ERO D//Z 137 Gripper logbook.

62 ERO D/UBn/12 Shenfield Parish Council minutes.

these unfortunates, although it did not prove necessary.[63]

There were even plans to create a squadron of anti-aircraft motor cars. No mention was made of the armament to be used on them, perhaps because only rifles were available, but the colouring of the cars was minutely detailed. Each car was to be painted white on top, green in the middle, and red on the lower half. It would be marked with a small white ensign and fly a red, white and green pennant.[64] Whether these armed knights of the road ever saw service is highly questionable.

The single aircraft raid on north-east Essex in February 1915 was the precursor of nine German airship raids affecting the county that year. Airships attempting to reach London, crossed the North Sea and generally made landfall over the Suffolk or Essex coast, before following the line of the Great Eastern Railway south-west directly to the capital. Some Zeppelins raided in a less focussed way and flew over Essex en route to raid other counties. Many never reached London. Deterred by the concentration of anti-aircraft guns ringing the capital, and by the possibility of attacks by British aircraft, many turned back dropping their bomb loads indiscriminately as they retired. Airships raided Essex on the night of 15-16 April. A Zeppelin hugged the Essex coast from Clacton to Walton, Burnham and Maldon. Maldon was raided rather ineffectually. Two bombs fell in the town, but did little damage; twenty incendiaries landed in nearby fields killing three hens.[65] Bombs were also dropped on Tillingham. Southend was hit twice on 10 and 26 May. The raid on 10 May was one of three attacks planned as a preliminary raid to the first on London. Airship L.238, commanded by Hauptmann Linnarz reached Southend, dropped its bombs and then retired when fired on over Canvey Island, re-crossing the sea over the River Crouch. Linnarz dropped a card which said "You English. We have come and we will come again. Kill or cure. German." A dozen houses were destroyed and other properties damaged, including a timber yard which was set alight. One woman was killed during the raid. Agnes Whitwell, aged sixty-six, of North Road, Prittlewell, died when an incendiary crashed through the roof of the house, setting fire to the bed she and her husband were sleeping in. He was unable to save her and was himself badly injured. Four high explosive bombs were dropped, but only two went off, one in Leigh, and one near Southend's Great Eastern Railway station.

On 26 May Linnarz returned as he had promised. At 10.30 p.m. his airship crossed the North Sea at Clacton and flew south-west to Southminster, where it was fired on. Linnarz retreated to Burnham, reaching there by 11 p.m., was then fired on over Shoeburyness, but reached Southend before heading out to sea over the Blackwater. Five R.F.C. aeroplanes were deployed to locate him, but he evaded detection and escaped. He dropped seventy incendiary bombs from between two and six thousand feet; these landed on Southend, Westcliff and Leigh. Unlike the raid of a fortnight

63 Perfect, *Hornchurch*, 190.

64 ERO D/Z 77/1, anti-aircraft motor cars, 9 June 1915.

65 ECC 23 April 1915.

earlier there was little material damage, although a young woman visiting the town was killed and two people, including a seven-year-old girl, were badly injured.[66] Raiders reached east London for the first time via Essex on the night of 31 May-1 June. Linnarz was once again among the raiders. He reached landfall at Shoeburyness and flew via Billericay, Brentwood and Wanstead, before bombing several locations, including West Ham and Walthamstow. There were five further raids in June, August and September. A few bombs were dropped on the outskirts of Harwich on 12-13 August. On 17 August the airship L.10, following the well-established Great Eastern Railway route, bombed Leyton, Leytonstone and Wanstead and on its return dropped two bombs on Chelmsford. A month later twenty-two high explosive and five incendiary bombs were dropped on villages between Colchester and Woodbridge. In terms of damage of military significance the effect of the raids was negligible. Just over six hundred bombs were dropped; the largest number in one night was the 124 unloaded on Southend on 10 May, a total which included 120 incendiaries. Loss of life was slight: twenty-seven people were killed and 113 injured in these raids.[67]

By the end of 1915 there had been three airship raids on London, and there was a corresponding growth of official concern. Since 1914 responsibility for the capital's air defences had been divided between the Admiralty and War Office and this had delayed effective planning. However, in March 1916 defence matters were handed to the R.F.C. and things moved forward. By then there were eight fighter airfields around London, including Hainault Farm in Essex. There were also other airfields in the county; Clacton, Chingford, Burnham, Rochford and Writtle were all established in August 1914. Following the air raid on north-east Essex on 20 February 1915, a night emergency landing ground was set up on Blackheath Common at Colchester, designed to support the R.F.C. Home Defence Squadrons patrolling Essex against incoming raiders. Other bases were added in 1915 at Goldhanger, Horndon-on-the-Hill, Widford, and Sutton's Farm near Hornchurch.[68]

During 1916 German airship crews, building on their previous experience, raided more persistently, more successfully and inflicted more material damage resulting in a greater loss of life. To the people of Essex they became known as the 'silent raiders'.[69] There were five large airship raids on Essex between March and September. Nearly thirteen hundred bombs were dropped, killing 101 civilians and injuring 247. On 31 March the L.14 flew in a wide arc over the county, dropping bombs on Braintree, Blackmore, Doddinghurst, Springfield, Stanford-le-Hope and Thames Haven. Only the latter, with its oil refineries, could be categorised as a legitimate military target. A month later the L.297 bombed Harwich to little effect, after being turned back from the outskirts of London at Seven Kings by anti-aircraft fire. The

66 ECC 14, 28 May 1915; ECS 29 May 1915.

67 Morris, *German Air Raids*, 21-23, 25-26, 28, 30-32, 49, 51, 59.

68 Doyle, *Fields*, various pages.

69 ERO T/Z 25/601.

airship raids in early 1916 threw the Government into something of a panic, and the result was the creation of a rash of even more airfields in Essex and the home counties, all designed to strengthen London's defences. By April nine new airfields and landing grounds had been created in Essex at Beaumont (near Clacton), East Hanningfield, Easthorpe, Fairlop, Mountnessing, North Benfleet, North Ockendon, North Weald Bassett and Sible Hedingham. By the end of the year another six had been built at Fyfield, Little Clacton, Orsett, Shenfield, Stow Maries and Wormingford.

After the April raids there was a three month lull in German raids. They then resumed in earnest in the great airship offensive which began at the end of July. On 17 August a Zeppelin dropped bombs around Leyton Midland Station and more on its way to Wanstead Flats. Some five hundred houses were damaged, eight people were killed and forty injured.[70] On the night of 2-3 September the Germans sent sixteen airships, twelve naval and four military, to form the biggest ever raid on London. This great enterprise — the largest planned attack on Great Britain since Napoleonic days — was a failure, none of the 363 bombs dropped fell on London. Worse still was the disaster which befell the S.L.11. The airship crossed over Essex at Foulness, flew northwards just east of Witham, before striking west above Great Bardfield. From Saffron Walden she flew westwards over Hertfordshire, then south hoping to approach London from the north-west via Luton. After being driven back northwards by heavy anti-aircraft fire the airship dropped sixty bombs, causing little damage. She was then caught in the defenders' searchlights and subjected to heavy anti-aircraft fire before being engaged by Lieutenant W. Leefe-Robinson, who had flown from Sutton's Farm airfield, near Hornchurch, to intercept her. At 11,500 feet he attacked the Zeppelin and it burst into flames, crashing near Cuffley in Hertfordshire. The disastrous end of the S.L.11 was witnessed over much of western Essex. It was seen very clearly miles away at Leyton. All the crew perished. The crews of several of the other German airships were nearby and they witnessed the terrible end of their comrades. All of them abandoned the raid and headed for the sea, dropping their bomb loads indiscriminately as they left.

The shooting down of the S.L.11 heralded the death knell of the Germans' airship war, although there were two further airship disasters in the skies over Essex before the strategy was abandoned. Three weeks later, on the night of 23-24 September, eleven naval airships, including three of the new so-called 'super Zeppelins', L.31, L.32 and L.33, crossed the North Sea. These aeronautical monsters had a capacity of two million cubic feet compared with the 1.3 million cubic feet of the S.L.11. Unlike the latter, these super Zeppelins were built with a metal superstructure and driven by six engines with a total of 1,440 horse power. The L.33 was the first of the new airships to reach London. Over the East End she was engaged by anti-aircraft guns

[70] W. H. Watson, *The Story of Leyton and Leytonstone* (1921), 215.

and hit by a shell. One of her propellers was damaged and her gas bags were punctured by shrapnel. After being hit by a second shell her commander, Kapitanleutnant Bocker, decided that discretion was the better part of valour and headed for home. Reaching Chelmsford via the line of the Great Eastern Railway, the L.33 was engaged by a British aeroplane flown by Lieutenant A. de B. Brandon. In a running fight lasting ten minutes Brandon was astonished to see his bullets hitting the target without any effect. Brandon, low on fuel, gave up the chase and returned to base. However, time was running out for Bocker. Losing gas and height, he had his men jettison everything they could to maintain altitude. Over the next few days many of the items that they desperately threw overboard were recovered from the fields of Essex. These included a machine-gun, two cases of machine-gun cartridges, a machine-gun belt, an electric battery in a leather case, an instrument box, a celluloid screen, two packages of aluminium sheeting, two portions of maps, a metal tube and a canvas bag.[71] By 1.15 a.m. the airship had limped to the coast, crossing it at West Mersea. By now it was obvious that there was no chance of the L.33 crossing the North Sea and reaching home. Bocker reluctantly reversed course and re-crossed the English coast, safely bringing his airship to ground between Little Wigborough and Peldon. The airship landed within thirty feet of two farm cottages, one occupied by Thomas Lewis and his family and the other by Frederick Choat; both men were workers at nearby New Hall Farm. Bocker rapidly made plans to set the airship alight to prevent it from falling into the hands of the military. He spoke English very well, and in the dark he shouted his intentions through the doors of both cottages, thereby giving them an opportunity to escape the imminent conflagration. Lewis, however, unsure what reception he would get if he left the cottage, pushed his terrified family into the back room, where they hid and remained silent. Bocker gave up on them and torched the airship. Unfortunately for him, but fortunately for the cottages and their inhabitants, the airship had leaked so much gas that only its covering was destroyed. Dawn revealed the frame intact, deposited like a beached whale. The only damage to the cottages was a few broken windows and burnt paintwork.

Bocker and his crew then began to trudge off in the darkness to hand themselves over to the authorities. A tragedy now unfolded. Alfred J. Wright, a seed grower and owner of nearby Grove Farm, answered the call when one of the Germans was injured. He reached the German crew but unsure whether or not they were armed, he returned to his farm and getting on his motorcycle he set out for West Mersea to rouse the military authorities there. In the darkness he was hit by a car. His leg was badly injured and was later amputated at Colchester Hospital. He never recovered from his injury and died two months later on 13 November. He was buried in Little

71 ERO J/P 12/7, Zeppelins at Great Burstead and Little Wigborough, police reports, September 1916. The police report does not, of course, identify these items as coming from the L.33, but they could not have originated from any other airship that night; the L.32 came to grief further west, and its crew is unlikely to have seen jettisoning equipment as a means of saving their stricken airship.

Wigborough churchyard. Bocker and his crew surrendered and spent the rest of the War in captivity.

Meanwhile the L.31 raided London and escaped. The L.32 was not so fortunate. After dropping her bombs between Aveley and South Ockendon, including one on Sutton's Farm, she was shot down by a British aircraft and crashed in flames, Conrad Noel and his fellow clergymen watching, coming to ground at Snails Farm, Great Burstead, just south of Billericay. The blazing airship passed over several villages as it descended to its doom. Helen Dixon of Hutton heard the screams of the crew as they were incinerated aboard the disintegrating airship, which crashed about two miles away from her home. Mary Blakeley of North Ockendon saw it pass directly over her house, so close that she was aware of the "heat and the stench". Catherine Brown and her workmates at Kynochtown also saw the blazing hulk of the L.32 slowly descend to earth. The next morning, some of them who lived near Billericay went to see the crash site. They reported that some of the dead crew "only looked about fourteen." Years later she recalled that, "We could not help but feel for their mothers in Germany."[72]

Unfortunately, what followed the airship's demise reflected no great glory on either the locals or British soldiery. Sergeant Wolverton of the Billericay Constabulary had been alerted at 9.15 p.m. that airships were approaching. At about 10.35 p.m. he saw what was presumably the L.32 pass over on its way to London, and from the Billericay police station he saw its return at about 1.10 a.m., under heavy anti-aircraft fire and attack by a solitary aircraft. Like so many others that night, he saw the airship catch fire at the rear; at first just a tiny flicker of light which grew and expanded until it engulfed the entire airship, which then began to descend in flames. Wolverton got hold of a car and drove to the crash site, which was about a mile from the centre of Billericay. The L.32 was still blazing when he arrived. The bodies of some of the twenty-two crew members were still in the wreckage, but several had fallen away from it and lay in nearby fields within a 250 yard radius of the airship. One lay head first in a ditch. Most of them had had their features burned away and some were headless and limbless. Three of them, including the commander, were still recognisable; he was said to have had a peaceful expression on his face, although the top of his head had been singed and his neck was broken. Within minutes of Wolverton's arrival, men of the Billericay Special Constabulary arrived and he ordered them to cordon off the airship. Soon a further thirty men arrived from Hutton, fourteen from Brentwood, and one from Chelmsford. The men remained on duty until daybreak, by which time Captain Ffinch, commander of the county's Special Constabulary appeared on the scene, as had troops of the Irish Guards, who were stationed in the vicinity.

As the flames died down and darkness descended, Wolverton and his men had great

[72] ERO TS 54.

difficulty in keeping sightseers and looters away. Locals, using the cover of darkness, attempted, many successfully, to take away souvenirs, particularly pieces of the airship's superstructure, which, being made of aluminium, were light and easy to carry off. The penalty for absconding with items of potential military importance was a fine of £100 or six months hard labour, but this proved to be no deterrent. Corporal Albert Harrington was ordered to stop passing cars and search them. In one he found the occupants had accumulated a bag full of Zeppelin parts and one of its wheels, which he promptly confiscated. One young lad named Freeman got away with a chart from the wreck, which he gave to his employer, who sent it to London to be framed before the police came to claim it. Some of the local firemen who arrived on the scene were warned off when they attempted to remove things from one of the bodies.

Wolverton and his men had begun to gather the bodies, until he was told that the coroner would want them left where they had fallen. The bodies that were collected were put in a shed. Wolverton's men claimed to have seen Irish Guardsmen removing items from the bodies. One officer took an Iron Cross from one of his men after he had attempted to hide it. One R.F.C. officer threatened a group of them with his revolver when they seemed reluctant to move away. Wolverton swore to Ffinch that the bodies had not been interfered with when they were placed in the shed. Shortly afterwards, when he returned to the shed with the coroner, he found that the German commander's silk waistcoat had been torn or cut away, and all his buttons were missing. From other bodies which were not badly burned a fur collar and fur gloves had been taken, and possibly a gold watch. These items were never recovered, despite extensive police inquiries in the area. Many were sold on as souvenirs. One of the stolen articles was the airship's ballast book, which only came to light in 1932. The partially filled book showed that the L.32 was on its thirteenth voyage. This was supposed to have accounted for the story told by some locals that they could hear the German commander shouting loudly as he was dying, "Dreizehn! Dreizehn! Dreizehn! (Thirteen! Thirteen! Thirteen!)" The crew of the L.32 were buried together in Great Burstead churchyard in a shared grave, although the Zeppelin's commander was interred separately. Men from the R.F.C. acted as pallbearers.[73]

On the day after the L.32 was destroyed, another raid again hit Leyton. This time eight hundred houses were damaged. Six more people were killed and twenty-six injured. However, by the end of 1916 German airship raids were abandoned. London's defences now covered even the originally exposed northern flank, and the combined anti-aircraft and aircraft defences were simply too fierce for the vulnerable airships to challenge. For the Germans, airship raids had become too costly. Following the abandonment of their airship war, the Germans turned to aeroplanes as an alternative weapon with which to bludgeon British morale. They had built large

73 ECC 29 September 1916.

military aeroplanes, the Gothas, in 1915, but it was not until early 1917 that they were used in a systematic way. Gothas were three-seater biplanes, thirty-eight feet long with a seventy-two feet wingspan. They were armed with three machine guns and carried seven 50 kg and six 12½ kg bombs. Between May and October 1917 there were fourteen aeroplane raids on various parts of Essex. The first raid, on 5 June, featured twenty-two Gothas in an attack on Sheerness and Shoeburyness. Eight days later, fourteen reached and bombed London, their bombs raining down in the vicinity of Liverpool Street station. East Ham was bombed on 13 June, in the first daylight raid on the capital. At times the raids by aeroplanes could be as disruptive as the earlier attacks by Zeppelins. In June 1916 Evelyn Potter was at school when an air raid began. The following extract from her diary shows that there was no panic:

> About 11.30 a.m. at school heard a buzzing noise like aeroplanes. Then thuds and guns. Got nearer till it was overhead. A raid, I felt sure. We went on with the lesson, though the noise was dreadful. Miss Graydon advised getting away from windows.

The disruptive effect of an air raid is vividly illustrated in another of her diary entries, from January 1918:

> Long raid last night. Lasted from 9.30 p.m. to 1.15 a.m. We heard the siren, then went into Aunt Hettie's house. Stood at her gate and saw the maroons go up — reports, then red stars which slowly sank. Like fireworks. Beattie played the piano all the barrage time so it kept things lively. At times the noise outside was deafening, drowning the playing inside. They had a mobile gun running up and down the road.

The following day, after another night raid, she noted that "there was an awful smell of sulphur in the air."[74] Harwich was the target twice, on 4 July and 22 July, and there were four further raids in early 1918 before the German air war faded away. Again the growing strength and ferocity of the capital's defences had defeated the attackers. By early 1918 the capital was ringed by a circle of gun stations and searchlights, and an outer ring of searchlights and barrage balloons, in places such as Snaresbrook and Wanstead Flats.[75] Inside this defensive ring were aeroplane patrol lines. Nevertheless the raids had been costly. Nearly two thousand bombs were unloaded in raids that attacked Essex as well as other counties. Four hundred

[74] Potter/Grubb diary, 12 June 1917, 29, 30 January 1918.

[75] R. Layton, Epping Forest and the Military during the Great War, *Essex Journal*, Spring 1988, vol. 23, no. 1, 5-8.

and seventy-eight people were killed and almost fourteen hundred injured by the Gothas. It was a remarkably slight loss of life in the face of the Germans' determined and sustained air offensive.

The February air raid on north-east Essex prompted local authorities, private businesses and individuals to hastily reassess their insurance arrangements. In late August and early September 1915, ten thousand pounds was handed over to insurance agents in Colchester alone to secure "government insurance". Coastal resorts, where prosperity had evaporated in 1914, now had to pay for insurance, and there were complaints about "the further fleecing of the shorn lamb".[76] Colchester Borough Council had already formed a War Risks Committee, which, only three weeks before the February air raid, had recommended that the council insure its properties. The value of the suggested properties was as follows:

Public Elementary Schools	£79,200
Town Hall	£57,300
Electricity Supply Station	£28,000
Water Tower & Pumping Station	£27,900
Tramway Cars	£11,250
Library	£8,900
Osborne St Depot	£7,000
Tramways Depot	£6,600
Total	£226,150 [77]

In view of the Government's refusal to provide financial relief for any raids other than those which had already occurred, the council had little choice but to take out a Lloyd's policy for its properties, as listed above. Over the next fifteen months, perhaps on the premise that it was better to be safe than sorry, the fire station, fire engine, Albert Museum and Art Gallery, Infectious Diseases Hospital and sewage outfall works' buildings were all added to the council's policy.[78] The Harwich Education Committee similarly insured all its schools against air raids and sea bombardment. The schools, valued in total at £25,260, were insured at a cost of £37 18*s*. The risk, however slight, of someone having their house bombed by the Germans, was a possibility. In late 1917 the Chelmsford branch of the Society of Amalgamated Toolmakers suggested that Chelmsford Borough Council construct air-raid shelters for the women of the Borough. This opened up a debate within the council, which, having considered the matter, decided that no building or shelter was bombproof and therefore opted not to build air-raid shelters. Instead, it recommended

[76] CG 22 September 1915.

[77] War Risks Committee, minutes, 5 February 1915.

[78] War Risks Committee, minutes, 20 July 1915, 8 May 1916.

its citizens to stay in their homes during raids.[79] At Southend too, the town council, after voting to spend £1,000 on building air-raid shelters in the gravel pit at Guildford Road, eventually decided to take no action. Instead, it persuaded the owners of a number of businesses in the town to permit their use as shelters. Each place so designated was marked with a large red circle and the words 'Air Raid Shelter' were written outside in large lettering. The public toilet at Thorpe Bay was transformed into a shelter when sandbags were placed on its roof.[80] Workers at Chelmsford's Crompton's and Marconi's works were more fortunate, as their employers had air-raid trenches dug.[81] Chelmsford Borough Council was, however, extremely critical of the Government's refusal to meet the costs of insurance against air raids for East Coast residents, particularly as the latter were not only particularly vulnerable to attack, but many were experiencing "severe financial loss and depression" in consequence of the War.[82]

The safety of school children during air raids was given considerable thought by the local authorities. In 1916, the Colchester town clerk informed head teachers that they could use their discretion as to whether to continue lessons or dismiss pupils after the warning of an air raid had been received. The head teacher of St John's School noted that "any parent who calls is to be given charge of their children." This followed an air-raid warning on each of the two previous days. The head teacher commented that the town siren was not easily heard at the school. On 14 June only one parent arrived to take her children home and school continued without interruption.[83] At Orsett Church of England School, one mother, fearful of a threatened air raid, caused a disturbance until she was allowed to take her child home.[84] A year later an air-raid warning before school began ensured a poor attendance for the day at Dovercourt New Central School, although the logbook also recorded "children wrongfully ordered home by military police." Those boys who did arrive were eventually sent home "a trifle earlier", thanks to a series of alarms.[85] The previous day, the head teacher of a Clacton school seems to have taken less exception at official intervention, noting in the school log book:

> At 3pm special constables called to inform me that as enemy aircraft were reported to be approaching the police considered it

[79] HDS 31 July 1915; ERO D/B 7, Minutes of Chelmsford Borough Council Special Purposes Committee 1920-21, 13 March 1918.

[80] SBC minutes, Health and Works Committee, 22 November, 6 December 1917, 21 January 1918.

[81] ChBC minutes, volume 32, 31 October 1917, 27 March 1918.

[82] ChBC minutes, volume 29, 23 February 1916.

[83] ERO M/L 143/3, school logbook 1908-37, 13-15 June 1916.

[84] ERO Orsett Church of England School logbook, 2 October 1917.

[85] ERO E/ML 138/2 school logbook 1887-1922, 15 June 1917.

> desirable to disperse the scholars at once. In accordance with these instructions all the children were dismissed.[86]

Schools in south-west and metropolitan Essex were more vulnerable to aeroplane raiders in 1917, and some school staff had an uncomfortable time of it. Barking Urban District Council even mooted the idea of removing what it defined as "extremely nervous children" to other districts during an air raid, although ultimately it took no action.[87] By 1916 schools in south-west Essex were carrying out regular air-raid drills. At Creekmouth School, Barking, the entire school was expected to be in "safety positions" as soon as possible. On 29 November 1916, it took just twenty seconds to achieve this.[88] The pupils of Westbury Council School took three and a half minutes.[89] The pupils of Becontree Heath Boys' School held daily drills in the summer of 1917. The children marched to the fields at the back of the school, where they sheltered in the ditches that were prepared there.[90] On 13 June at Bridge Road Upper Standard School, Grays, the air-raid warning was heard at 11.20 a.m. The head teacher noted that precautions were taken:

> The children were removed as far as possible from the windows and outside walls and work was continued although the heavy firing and the noise of aircraft took the children's attention. There were no signs of alarm, only of great curiosity. A few parents called for their children and they were allowed to take them away.

On the following day another alarm occurred shortly before the end of the school day. This time things were very different:

> The same arrangements for the safety of the children were adopted as on the previous day. Within five minutes however, the school was besieged by a crowd of anxious and hysterical mothers, alarmed by the deaths amongst London schoolchildren on the 13th. It was impossible to resist them and it was with the greatest difficulty and exertion that they were prevented from rushing into the school. They were supplied with their children as quickly as possible, but the work of the school was completely disorganised. There was however, no alarm amongst the children and some refused to go home with their mothers.

86 ERO Acc. A 6391, Clacton St Osyth Road Council School logbook 1914-25, 14 June 1917.

87 Barking Urban District Council minutes, 5 February, 5 March 1918.

88 Creekmouth School logbook, 29 November 1916.

89 Westbury Council School logbook, 15 June 1917.

90 Becontree Heath Boys' School logbook, 18 June 1917.

On the next day, the head teacher, determined to avoid a repeat of the previous day's hysteria, gave instructions that in future, on receipt of an air-raid warning, the children were to be sent home immediately, and the few children who lived some distance away were to be sheltered in the school cellar. On the 4 July attendance was low because the Kent air-raid sirens had been heard across the Thames. The head teacher went to the police station to ascertain whether or not it was safe to let the children on to the streets. Assured that this was so, he sent the older pupils to round up the absentees from their homes, and within a short time 137 appeared in school.[91]

This was not an isolated case of parental hysteria in the face of enemy raids. On 14 June, the same day that parents at Bridge Road tried to storm the school, there were similar scenes at nearby Quarry Hill County Junior School:

> The signal for a daylight air raid was sounded today again at 2.40pm. The Infants and Girls Departments having been immediately dismissed — the parents came up to the Boys School in large numbers and demanded that their boys should be handed over to them. As the parents appeared the boys were called, and sent home with their mothers. The school was so much depleted, that it was considered wise to send the remainder home in batches of 10 or 12 according to the separate streets or direction in which they lived, in view of the increased and persistent demand of the parents, and of the desirability of avoiding a great concentration of human life within such a small area at a time of grave risk. The school was completely cleared within ten minutes.[92]

Schools in the south-west part of Essex were certainly much harassed by German air raids during 1916-17. The head teacher at Benyon County Primary School recalled the impact on the school of the Zeppelin raids of late September 1916:

> The recent Zeppelin raid has had an effect on [the] children. Many of [the] parishioners, after the terrifying affect [sic] of [the] week end, have refused to go to bed in case of another visit, and consequently some are suffering from shock and sleeplessness. Exam papers have been prepared for half-year exams but owing to [the] disturbed state of [the] children's minds and [the] absence of staff, it will have to be deferred for [a] few days.[93]

91 ERO E/ML 23, Grays Bridge Road Council School logbook, 1898-1925.

92 ERO T/P 440/1-7 Quarry Hill County Junior School, Grays Thurrock, logbooks 1903-36, 14 June 1917.

93 ERO Benyon School logbooks, 29 September 1916;

At Hamstel Junior School, near Southend, the logbook noted in July 1917 that "Boys did not go swimming today because of the presence in the vicinity of hostile aircraft."[94] Pupil attendance could be severely affected by air raids. The day after an air raid on 6 September 1917, only seventy per cent of the pupils at Barking's North Street Girls' School attended. Following another attack attendance fell to just forty per cent on 2 November, and after three other raids in 1917-18 attendances never exceeded sixty-nine per cent.[95] At Creekmouth School, Barking, on 1 November 1916 only nineteen of the seventy-six pupils came to school after the previous night's raid. An air raid on 5 December 1917 resulted in only forty-three of the seventy-five pupils being present.[96] In February 1918, Leyton Education Committee published figures showing that following two air raids only nine thousand of the borough's twenty thousand pupils attended school the next day.[97]

However, although the air raids caused considerable consternation, an Essex man attempted to portray the courage that he assumed must also have been displayed by county residents in the face of the German air war:

Why Jane, her mistress said, "You look
As if you'd quarrelled with the cook."
"No please, your la'ship", stammered Jane,
"They dropped a bomb here in the lane.
Last night at one, it was, I think,
Since then I never slep' a wink."

"What!" Cried the other from her bed,
Her eyes protruding from her head,
"The German airships came last night,
And I not only missed the sight,
But never heard a sound before
Your knuckles rapped upon my door!"

"If you a grain of sense had got
You would have waked me on the spot."
While Jane, retreating, muttered "hor!
I never saw her cry before."

A German invasion of Essex was an eventuality well rehearsed by authors and playwrights before the War and inevitably it was taken seriously by many Essex

94 ERO T/S 607/1 Transcripts of Hamstel Junior School.

95 North Street Girls School logbook, 7 September, 2 November, 7 December 1917, 21 January, 18 February 1918.

96 Creekmouth School logbook, 1 November, 6 December 1917.

97 LE 23 February 1918.

people and the authorities after 1914. The Vicar of Stondon Massey, Edward Reeve, was both impressed and disconcerted by the large entrenchments being dug in the area. "Stondon is becoming honeycombed with trenches", he noted in early November 1914. He claimed to have information revealing that forty thousand men were engaged in digging trenches around the whole of London, with Stondon forming part of these defences. His febrile imagination working overtime, he added that

> It is quite clear that vast stores of arms have been kept in concealment, and that even concrete emplacements for large guns have been for years prepared under the guise of foundations of tennis courts etc. etc.[98]

Although Reeve exaggerated the scale, there is no doubt that a considerable number of entrenchments were dug in order to create defensive barriers against a German advance towards London, following a landing on the coast. The village of Danbury, for example, had long been recognised as occupying a crucial strategic position to repel any invaders who had landed on either the River Blackwater or River Crouch. It was made into a strongpoint in 1778 when Britain and France were at war during the American War of Independence. The earthworks around the village were then strengthened in 1803 during the Napoleonic invasion scare, and in 1914-15 the fields south of Frettons were once more fortified, this time against German invaders.[99]

Other steps were taken to strengthen the security of the Essex coast from attack. When war broke out the War Department moved quickly to buy Foulness and the nearby New England Islands, completing the purchase in 1915. Squire Finch, the principal landowner on Foulness, sold his four thousand acres for £70,000. After 1915 there were no longer any tied cottages on the island; those permitted to remain in residence rented them from the War Department.[100] Osea Island in the River Blackwater was taken over by the Admiralty in 1917 in order to use it as the base for a fleet of coastal torpedo motor-boats. Construction began in the summer of 1917. Wooden huts were constructed, a pier was built into the river with concrete slipways to accommodate up to fifty torpedo boats, and workshops to service them. The first of them arrived in early 1918, having been constructed on the Thames, at Portsmouth, Lowestoft and the Isle of Wight.[101]

[98] ERO T/P 188/3, E.H.L. Reeves, MS notes for a *History of Stondon Massey* (1919), 30 October, 10 November 1914.

[99] M. Hopkirk, Danbury: *Historical Notes and Records of the Village of Danbury in the County of Essex* (1945), 86-87.

[100] J.S. Dobson, *Fowlness: The Mystery Isle 1914-39* (1996), 29, 43.

[101] J. Wise, *The Story of the Blackwater Sailing Club: The First Hundred Years* (1999), 56; A. Agar, *Baltic Episode: A Classic of Secret Service in Russian Waters* (1963), 17-18. I am grateful to Richard Shackle, formerly of Colchester Central Library, for drawing my attention to Agar's book.

The possibility of a German invasion occupied the attention of the military, police and local authorities throughout the War, as plans and preparations were formulated and continually modified. In the view of local seafaring men, an invasion was unlikely simply because the sand banks and shallow waters off the Essex coast would prohibit German warships from operating effectively.[102] Others were of the opinion that the possibility of an enemy invasion was less dangerous than the complacency of ordinary people. These views were not shared by all civilians or by those in authority. As late as the spring of 1916 Ffinch wrote, "the possibility of a German invasion of Essex is considered by no means improbable or remote".[103] The sound of gunfire from the Western Front was a frequent reminder that decisive land battles were being fought not that far away from Essex. Mr Miller Christy of Chignall St James heard the sounds from Flanders during the early part of the War, and when he realised what they were, he kept a meticulous record of them until the Armistice. The gunfire was only heard during spring and summer months. He described the sounds as

> quite faint, though easily perceptible and quite unmistakable. There is no sharp explosion, as when a gun is fired close at hand. What one hears resembles more nearly a dull and distant thud, which one seems to feel, rather than to hear.

On 24 June 1916 he heard, without realising it at the time, the beginning of the week-long British artillery bombardment which preceded the Battle of the Somme. "From 8pm till 11.30 (when I went to bed), firing very violent", he noted. "It was not very loud, but exceedingly rapid — the most rapid, beyond comparison, I have yet heard." His final tally of what he described as the "Periods of Audibility" showed that between 1 May 1915 and the end of August 1918, the sound of gunfire was heard for sixty-seven weeks and five days.[104]

Detailed plans were put in place to deal with the unthinkable. Special Emergency Committees were appointed by the Army Council. The primary duty of these committees was the evacuation of the civil population during an invasion, in order to remove them from the front line and presumably, in view of the rumours of atrocities perpetrated by German soldiers in Belgium, to prevent a repetition of such acts in Britain. The schemes they were expected to draw up were prepared under the direction of a Central County Committee presided over by the Lord Lieutenant, the Earl of Warwick, who in turn was responsible to the Home Secretary.

The Central County Committee for Essex met for the first time on 22 October 1914, in the County Hall, Chelmsford. The committee consisted of twelve men, eight

[102] EEA 9 January 1915.

[103] ERO T/Z 77/2, Essex Special Constabulary papers, volume 2 1917-18, Ffinch to Chief Superintendent of Special Constables, 22 April 1916.

[104] ECS 1 March 1919. In 1915 gunfire was heard for seventeen weeks three days, in 1916 for fifteen weeks, in 1917 for nineteen weeks four days, and in 1918 for fifteen weeks five days.

from the army and four county luminaries. Several of them had already been to meet the Home Secretary, Arthur Balfour, who was anxious to implement some scheme to prevent the civilian population "acting as a drag"[105] on the military in the event of a German landing. By then the creation of county and local committees had already been decided on. News of an invasion was to reach them via the chief constable, who would be informed at the same time as the general officer commanding, South Midland Division, whose command included East Anglia. It was accepted that the involvement in the planning of so many people in each county meant that secrecy was impossible. Once the news leaked out that invasion plans were being considered it would have an unsettling effect on civilians and Balfour promised to write a reassuring statement for the press.

What the authorities feared most of all was civilian panic; both the panic resulting from news of the creation of emergency committees, and the nightmarish prospect of the panic generated by a German landing. Colonel Colvin said that in his opinion "there would be a panic, especially among women and children, in the event of a landing." The Earl of Warwick believed that if German forces shelled any town there would be "a stampede of the inhabitants." For these reasons Sir Edward Troup urged that the committee must make its objects public, which in fact it did. Shortly afterwards the Central County Committee for Essex met, chaired by Lord Warwick, and after due deliberation, decided that the final destination of Essex refugees during an invasion was to be Oxfordshire.

The Colchester Emergency Committee met for the first time on 20 November 1914, with eight (later nine) members.[106] Information from the county committee was transmitted to the Colchester Emergency Committee, which in turn despatched it to the village emergency committees in the outlying areas. The Tendring, Lexden and Winstree, and Witham areas were reckoned to be the ones likely to receive removal orders first, probably with no more than six to eight hours notice.[107]

The authorities devised three warning periods prior to, and including, an invasion. Firstly, there was a 'Special Vigilance' period when the German fleet was active. This would remain in force until the fleet dispersed. If it did not disperse and seemed to be menacing the coast, a 'Prepare to Move' alert was to be declared. If an enemy landing was made, the third period 'Move' was put into force. Red posters would be put up by the armed forces in those places where the civil population was in the greatest peril. Each village was instructed to prepare a list of tools available for the construction of defences and a list of able-bodied men capable of building them. These were to include "spades, shovels, picks, billhooks, reaping hooks, axes, forks, crowbars, adzes, wire cutters, wire of all sorts, sacks, rope, hammers, nails, staples, hedging gloves".[108]

[105] ERO L/P 3/1.

[106] ERO D/Z 77/1.

[107] ERO D/Z 77/2, 22 April 1916.

[108] ERO D/P 88/28/3, from Charles Gooch, chairman of Lexden and Winstree Local Emergency Committee, March 1917.

Clearly defined evacuation routes were decided by each committee. For those living in Colchester's north and east wards their initial destination was to be Saffron Walden, reached via West Bergholt and Bures; those in the west ward were destined for Clavering via Great Tey and Thaxted; citizens of the south ward were to head for Bishop's Stortford via Easthorpe and Felsted.[109] The inhabitants of the Lexden and Winstree petty sessional division were to be evacuated along seven routes, which terminated at the initial destinations of Messing, Tolleshunt Knights, Coggeshall, White Colne and Bures.[110] Individual villages were given their own directions; the people of Alresford were under orders to assemble at the corner of the road by the Pointer Inn, and then head for Bures via Ardleigh and Dedham.[111] For some communities there was to be no evacuation. The military refused to sanction the removal of Harwich's civilian population, because it regarded it as unfeasible to attempt to move seventeen thousand people along just one main road. It was also deemed impracticable to remove the populations of Chelmsford, Maldon and Rochford, because any attempt to direct them northwards would interfere with the west-east movement of the army.[112]

Colchester's committee was not happy at the choice of routes for its townspeople. The town clerk wrote to the military authorities on 25 April 1916 complaining that an examination of the suggested routes revealed some of them to be "mere narrow country lanes", impassable for any form of "vehicular traffic", lacking adequate water supplies at any point, and effectively doubling the journey to the initial destinations because of "the circuitous ways to be traversed." The committee felt that "they could not undertake the responsibility of sending people to encounter the dangers which would inevitably ensue and requests that more direct and open roads should be made available".[113]

Of course, the military had chosen these routes precisely because they were little more than country cart tracks. The main roads would be occupied by the army, as troops were ferried to the coast to repel the invaders. The committee also suggested that it be allowed to use empty troop trains at Colchester to more quickly evacuate women, children, and the old and infirm. This idea met with equally short shrift: "the slowness of evacuation by road is held to be a lesser evil than the confusion which would result from the possible miscarriage of a scheme which from the nature of the case cannot be worked out in detail beforehand".[114]

The plans assumed that there would be about a thousand refugees per mile of road, probably travelling at a maximum speed of two miles per hour, although wheeled

[109] ERO Acc. 4, general instruction booklet issued to civilian population.

[110] ERO D/Z 77/1, February 1915.

[111] ERO D/P 336/30/1.

[112] ERO L/P 3/9, Papers for Emergency Committee meeting, 10 September 1915.

[113] ERO Acc. C4, minutes 31 May 1916.

[114] ERO D/Z 77/2.

traffic might manage twenty miles a day. Marks Tey was designated as the rendezvous point for Tendring, Colchester, Lexden and Winstree, Halstead, and North and South Hinckford for "mechanically propelled and other vehicles of military value."[115] Not that many would have avoided being commandeered by the army. The Colchester committee complained that the military had earmarked most of the vehicles in the borough, and there would be few left at the disposal of refugees.[116] In effect, all refugees would have to walk or be carried to safety, regardless of their age or the state of their health. The instructions stated that "all able-bodied persons must walk, taking with them food for forty-eight hours, money, jewellery, and a pair of blankets if they can carry them". [117] The committee at Alresford added "weatherproof boots and clothes" to the instructions issued to their villagers.

On the journey refugees were to be organised in groups of about fifty people. They were to be billeted on villages en route. Once their two days' supply of food was exhausted, they were instructed to buy more from the villages they encountered.[118] The Colchester committee decided it was not feasible to attempt to organise a population of about fifty thousand in groups of fifty because "they are unable to take upon themselves the responsibility of issuing directions to the townspeople which in their view can only lead to chaos and disorder."[119]

Numerous other instructions were hurled at the population. During November and December 1914 every household received a copy of a leaflet entitled 'What to Do in Case of Invasion'. This was followed in February 1915 by small cards, colour coded for each area, or in Colchester's case, each ward, which outlined what needed to be done to evacuate the population if an invasion occurred.[120] The instructions ordered civilians not to attempt to carry furniture with them; people were authorised to empty cycle shops and commandeer their contents; private firearms had to be handed over to the police in case belligerent civilians taking potshots at Germans resulted in the latter taking reprisals; all deserted houses were to be left open; civilians were ordered not to attempt to use the railways; all intoxicating liquors were to be poured away, which presumably referred to stocks in public houses and hotels; and all supplies of grain, hay, straw, petrol and livestock were to be destroyed.[121]

Individual village committees struggled to be prepared. At Alresford a list of conveyances, wagons and drivers was compiled; in 1915 there were sixteen wagons available to carry the 200 parishioners out of the total village population of 249 who needed transporting. The village's wealthiest inhabitant, probably as in other villages,

[115] ERO D/Z 77/1, Chief Constable to Captain Tuffnell, Garrison Adjutant, Colchester, 2 January 1915.

[116] ERO Acc. C4, letter from Home Office, 24 March 1915.

[117] James Round, Chairman, Lexden & Winstree Emergency Committee, February 1915.

[118] ERO D/Z 77/2, Ffinch to Chief Superintendants of Special Constables, 22 April 1916.

[119] ERO Acc. C4, minutes, 3 May 1916.

[120] ECS 2 January, 6 February 1915.

[121] ERO Acc. C4, general instruction booklet.

was unlikely to be affected by these arrangements, as the minutes of the Arlesford Emergency Committee pointedly record: "Mr Marriage has two motor cars and a chauffeur. He will probably make his own arrangements".[122]

Early plans to sound the invasion alarm by ringing the church bells were later prohibited, and it was left to a messenger or despatch rider to bring the news. By 1916 Arlesford's population had fallen, and there were only 177 people in need of conveyance; ten wagons were available along with four others from local dealers which would carry the villagers' provisions. Plans were made to carry out official instructions and kill the village stock. Shotguns were to be used to destroy the 500 sheep, 60 pigs and eighteen steers, although the minutes record that "there were not enough men to kill such numbers in reasonable time'.[123] At Wakes Colne the village committee made an impressively comprehensive list of what was available for refugees and what would need to be destroyed, "107 horses, 112 cattle, 175 sheep, 313 pigs, 135 quarters threshed grain, 606 in stack, about 200 implements. 3 cars, 14 bikes, 115 wagons/carts, horsed vehicles".[124]

The Saffron Walden area would have had a huge job of destruction on its hands had the Germans invaded. An agricultural census revealed that there were 3,142 horses, 6,371 cattle, 12,905 sheep and 10,107 pigs in the locality, as well as 26,000 quarters of grain, 13,362 tons of hay, 17,414 tons of straw, and 1,448 tons of flour. To convey its inhabitants to safety there were available 142 cars, 48 motor bikes, 659 bicycles, 1,298 farm carts, 549 wagons and 3,077 gallons of petrol. Two thousand and eight hundred males were available to dig ditches, destroy animals and assist in removing civilians. The evacuation route west was to be marked out by arrows. Civilians were advised to take with them food, forage, rugs or a blanket, a bucket, a lantern and matches, rope and shoulder chains. To help guide them there were ten special constables, six men on point duty, four despatch riders, eight local guides, four men responsible for collecting tools, six to drive the stock, twelve slaughterers and eighty-two men to dig ditches. It was a superbly organised plan in theory; fortunately, it was never put into operation.[125]

The Colchester committee was also concerned at how such a huge exodus of refugees would be fed, for it considered that the requirement to carry enough food for forty-eight hours was insufficient. When it enquired about what arrangements had been made to feed Colchester's refugees upon arrival at Saffron Walden, it was informed that no such arrangements had been made, probably because it was realised that the locals would have hoarded or carried off with them whatever was available. The War Office's reply to the committee seemed to suggest that it was not unduly anxious about the possibility of a German invasion, "the contingency of such a step

[122] ERO D/P 336/30/1.

[123] ERO D/P 336/30/1, minutes, 5 January, 1, 8 February 1915, 27 March, 10 May 1916.

[124] ERO D/P 88/28/3, Summary of Wakes Colne Parish, 29 December 1917.

[125] ERO T/B 384/1 Ashdon Emergency Committee minutes.

being necessary is too remote to justify its adoption at present".[126] The Tiptree Co-op, however, was taking no chances. In September 1917 the society resolved "that should any unrest appear amongst Members owing to the reported rumour of Enemy Invasion, Share Withdrawls be paid out as usual".[127]

According to Chief Constable J.A. Unett, he and his colleagues were informed on more than one occasion that the Germans were on the point of invading, and they were issued with 'standby' orders.[128] Nevertheless, the years from 1914 to 1917 passed uneventfully with no serious public alarms. However, on 21 March 1918 the Germans launched a highly successful spring offensive, their last desperate gamble to defeat the British and French armies before the arrival of American troops turned the tide of war against them. The offensive swept all before it and within weeks their forces were once more poised at the gates of Paris. There was panic in the south-east of England; invasion fears were resurrected, as the *East Essex Advertiser* noted, "never since August 1914, has the population of this country followed the War with such a tense interest, such an anxiety to know from hour to hour how the battle goes".[129]

Such was the level of concern that in mid-April Lord Warwick called a meeting of Essex mayors and town clerks at Chelmsford. In his address to the assembled dignitaries he told them that

> The great German offensive of March 1918 attained such a measure of success in its opening stages that the Channel ports were gravely threatened and the Secret Service reports indicated that there was very great danger to this County of invasion or at least of an attempt to land a powerful raiding force which would have for its object the devastation of the district.

A Colonel Barclay noted that "confidential reports" showed that the Germans had completed preparations "to convey an army across the North Sea." He added with a dramatic flourish that "if the attempt materialised it would be on the Essex and Suffolk Coast and the objective would be London taking Colchester on the way". He warned that as the German invaders moved inland "the Colchester district must be prepared to deal with crowds of fugitives and also to evacuate our own population if the landing succeeds on the Essex coast".

A revised scheme was thought up to deal with the apparent new threat. In this the military authorities and the Home Office decided not to evacuate all the civilian population, nor would the livestock and food supplies be destroyed. Civilians were to

[126] ERO Acc. C4, letter from Home Office, 24 March 1915.

[127] ERO D/Z 178/1/5, Tiptree Co-op minutes 1916-18, 11 September 1917.

[128] ERO D/Z 77/1.

[129] EEA 30 March 1918.

be encouraged to stay at home unless they were under direct enemy bombardment, although all able-bodied men were to be placed at the disposal of the military.[130]

According to Lord Warwick, depots of provisions would be placed every ten miles to feed the refugees, seemingly a significant step forward from 1915, when no such steps were under official consideration. The first depot was at Colchester. However, had the Germans invaded and thousands of coastal refugees left their homes and descended tired and hungry upon Colchester, they may have been disappointed. For the only supplies available there, safely stored in the basement of the Town Hall, were forty tons of army biscuits and ten tons of cocoa.[131] At Chelmsford Central Store things were hardly more promising. To feed an anticipated one hundred and fifty thousand refugees fleeing from the coast, the store held a mere sixty-seven tons of army biscuits and four tons of admiralty cocoa. Each refugee was to receive one pound of biscuits and an ounce of cocoa.[132]

Fortunately the fears of a German invasion, nurtured for years before the War, were never realised, and the wartime plans devised to counter this event never had to be put into effect. These plans did not have the full confidence of local government officials, and as late as 1918, the evidence suggests that had they been implemented they may not have been a resounding success. There is also evidence that had an enemy landing been effected cooperation between local emergency committees might not have been as efficient as was anticipated. At Freshwell, the local emergency committee bemoaned the fact that "It is extraordinarily difficult to get any of the farmers to look at the matter seriously."[133] The reluctance of emergency village committees to provide the necessary information led the chairman of the Tendring Emergency Committee, W.H. Slimon, to resign in June 1917. "Indeed during the past 12 months", wrote Slimon, "several [committees] have been, to put it moderately — offensive." He added, "The officer in charge of the Area Walton to Brightlingsea, is quite ignorant of, I may say, all the work of the Emergency Committee." It was only with great reluctance that he was persuaded to retract his resignation by the Lord Lieutenant.[134] There were no enemy naval raids on the scale of those on the towns of the north-east coast in 1914, and the air raids which did materialise were on a relatively small scale and inflicted no significant military damage, no significant damage to the region's infrastructure, and resulted in comparatively few civilian deaths. In this respect, most of Essex endured a relatively comfortable war against that portion of the might of the German war machine which was hurled against it.

[130] ERO L/P 3/35.

[131] ERO Acc. C4, Notes re Conference of Essex Mayors and Town Clerks called by Lord Lieutenant at Chelmsford, 15 April 1918.

[132] ERO L/P 3/1, County Committee minutes.

[133] ERO L/P 3/20.

[134] ERO L/P 3/35.

CHAPTER SEVEN

Sustaining the People

MINISTRY OF FOOD.

NATIONAL RATION BOOK (B).

INSTRUCTIONS.

Read carefully these instructions and the leaflet which will be sent you with this Book.

1. The person named on the reference leaf as the holder of this ration book must write his name and address in the space below, and must write his name and address, and the serial number (printed upside down on the back cover), in the space provided to the left of each page of coupons.

Food Office of Issue .... *Date* ....

Signature of Holder ....

Address ....

2. For convenience of writing at the Food Office the Reference Leaf has been put opposite the back cover, and has purposely been printed upside down. It should be carefully examined. If there is any mistake in the entries on the Reference Leaf, the Food Office should be asked to correct it.

3. **The holder must register this book at once by getting his retailers for butcher's meat, bacon, butter and margarine, sugar and tea respectively, to write their names and the addresses of their shops in the proper space on the back of the cover.** Persons staying in hotels, boarding houses, hostels, schools, and similar establishments should not register their books until they leave the establishment.

4. The ration book may be used only by or on behalf of the holder, to buy rationed food for him, or members of the same household, or guests sharing common meals. It may not be used to buy rationed food for any other persons.

Continued on next page.

N. 2 J (Nov.)

IF FOUND, RETURN TO ANY FOOD OFFICE.

A ration book issued in October 1918. *(ERO: D/DS 321/2)*

ON 4 AUGUST 1914, the day that Great Britain entered the Great War, David Lloyd George, Chancellor of the Exchequer, promised the country's business community that the Government would do all it could to promote "business as usual". Lloyd George's statement was clearly intended to reassure businessmen, but it was also an expression of confidence in liberal principles, at least as far as the economy was concerned. The Government intended to wage war by preserving free enterprise, intervening on an ad hoc basis only when it was considered to be absolutely necessary. However, slowly but surely, as the conflict dragged on, and as preserving the people from starvation and defeat became an ever more precarious task, the demands of total war gradually eroded confidence in the efficacy of free enterprise in wartime.

The mounting pressures of war and subsequent government intervention had an enormous impact on the local economy. The outbreak of war precipitated a spate of panic buying throughout Essex (see Chapter 2). Essex County Council appealed to employers not to panic by cutting wages, reducing hours or by sacking their employees. It urged "no scares, no attempt to corner the necessities of life, no private hoarding of supplies, no waste in any shape or form."[1] These appeals went largely unheeded, but fortunately the panic was short-lived. The fears that the enemy might attack the Essex coast, coupled with the belief that the military operation of the railways might leave holidaymakers stranded in resorts, had long lasting effects on the tourist industry. Thousands of holidaymakers, largely from London and the South-East, decided that discretion was the better part of valour and stayed away, mostly without informing the hoteliers and boarding house keepers who were expecting them to arrive. The number of day trippers visiting Essex's coastal resorts was badly affected during the August bank holiday weekend, when many would-be visitors were deterred by the widespread rumours of war. The number of visitors at Frinton fell by about ten per cent, those at Walton and Brightlingsea by a quarter.[2] As fears of a German invasion began to recede, some of the less timid holidaymakers did arrive. However, the vast majority stayed away, and newspaper appeals by organisations such as the Clacton Advancement Association, emphasising that there was nothing to fear, were unsuccessful in tempting them to return. Although a few individuals who had defaulted on their holiday bookings were taken to court, it was impracticable to take legal proceedings against the thousands who had neither arrived nor paid in full.

The absence of full holiday bookings in resorts like Clacton, Frinton, Harwich and Walton during August and September 1914 robbed them of two-fifths of their lucrative holiday season. The Belle Steamers, which traditionally brought London day trippers to the north Essex coast, were faced with drastically reduced numbers of passengers and revenue, and so concluded their sailing season on 30 August, several

1 ECC 7 August 1914.

2 EEA 8 August 1914. Walton's Bank Holiday numbers dropped from 5,340 (1913) to 4,237; Brightlingsea's from 1,612 to 1,340. These figures are based on the number of visitors arriving by train.

weeks ahead of schedule. By mid-September Brightlingsea's yachting season had also been terminated, some six to eight weeks early. Harwich too, was badly hit by the decline in holiday bookings, particularly as holidaymakers' perceptions of the town were that it had been taken over by the military and was an obvious target for German maritime raids. The knock-on effect of the huge reduction in anticipated income and anticipated spending by holidaymakers and day-trippers was significant. Hoteliers and boarding house keepers were badly affected, and so too were the shops and stores which relied on a good summer's financial takings to see them comfortably through the winter months.

The disastrous late summer and autumn experienced by Essex's coastal resorts was only part of the deleterious impact of the War on the coastal economy. Plans for a Colchester to Southend railway, first mooted in 1904, shelved and renewed later in 1910, were finally allowed to lapse because of the War. Instead the exigencies of war now suggested that a Colchester to Mersea Island line might be viable, providing a rapid route from the town's garrison to the coast should the Germans invade. The depth of water at Mersea at low tide (forty-five feet), which was sufficient to accommodate ships of various sizes, was used to try to induce the War Office to support the scheme. Unfortunately, it came to nothing.[3] At Brightlingsea the premature demise of the yachting season left local shipwrights facing a reduced living, and here, as elsewhere, the fishing industry was said to be "at a standstill".[4] The town's annual regatta, horticultural show and local ploughing matches were all abandoned in the late summer of 1914, and trade generally was hit very hard.[5]

Brightlingsea's fishermen were soon anxious to know whether the Admiralty would permit them to carry on with their customary sprat fishing between late October and February. About a hundred fishing smacks were engaged in this trade, which provided one of the main sources of income in the winter months. During the previous year fifty thousand tons of sprats were landed; much of which was sold in Britain, but some went to Swedish and Russian ports where it was used in the sardine and anchovy trade. The problem was that sprat fishing was done at night, with the smacks at anchor and an anchor light up, making it potentially a very hazardous occupation in wartime. The Admiralty did grant permission for sprat fishing, although for naval reasons it was prohibited west and south of the area known as the Mouse and in the Barrow Deep. It was, however, completely prohibited in the Thames Estuary, thereby causing a great deal of resentment in Essex, as the naval anchorage which was supposedly being protected by this move remained largely empty throughout the War.[6] The activities of Essex fishing fleets were further handicapped by the positioning of protective booms between the sandbanks in the

3 ECT 17 October 1914.

4 EEA 19 September 1914.

5 EEA 2 January 1915.

6 EEA 17 October 1914; J.P. Foynes, *Brightlingsea and the Great War*, 64.

Thames Estuary. The booms were put together in the creek at Brightlingsea and towed into position from there.[7] However, within a couple of weeks a request that fishermen be allowed to fish in the Barrow Deep during daylight was rejected.[8] This too put an almost intolerable strain on the town, which was only rescued by the arrival of military and naval forces in late 1914. Large-scale billeting and the spending of servicemen provided a much needed boost to the local economy.[9]

Not every town was as fortunate as Brightlingsea. By December 1914 things at Burnham were so bad that seventy-two local tradesmen signed a memorandum and presented it to the urban district council, asking them to attempt to get troops billeted in the town. The traders claimed that with between two and three hundred young men having enlisted, their businesses had been badly affected by a reduction in spending.[10] By late 1914 the Essex and Suffolk fisheries were complaining of the enormous drop in the quality and quantity of the fish being caught, which was ascribed to the military prohibitions on many of the more lucrative areas of the fishing grounds and the enlistment of many young sailors. One channel along the Essex coast, known as the Swin, had been sealed off by the authorities using big steel nets, although local fishing smacks continued to fish alongside them.[11] The fishing catch of 1915 was only half that of 1914, but the shortage sustained prices; the catch of shrimps in the Thames was also very good.[12] The Colne oyster fishery was also badly hit by the War. Most of its produce was exported, but its continental market had largely evaporated in late 1914, as had the public and private dinner parties which consumed its fare.[13] By early 1915 some oyster growers were selling their produce at what was deemed to be the ridiculously low price of 2*s*. a ton. Transport difficulties resulting from the military's extensive use of the Great Eastern Railway made it difficult to get oysters to London markets.[14] The company's trade improved in 1915 with sales exceeding those of 1914 by a third, largely because the domestic market did not completely collapse, and as demand exceeded supply, the price was maintained.[15] Harwich too suffered, as its holiday trade, yachting business and fishing fleet were all adversely affected.[16] Harwich's merchant fleet, a vital part of the town's economy, was seriously affected by the increase in admiralty moorings as the port became increasingly used as a naval base. By March 1915 the Harwich Harbour

7 E.P. Dickin, *History of Brightlingsea* (1939), 160.

8 EEA 31 October 1914.

9 EEA 2 January 1915.

10 ECC 19 December 1914.

11 ECS 3 March 1917; M. Leather, *Saltwater Village* (1977), 130.

12 EEC 17 March 1915.

13 ECS 28 August 1915.

14 ECS 27 February 1915.

15 ECT 3 March 1917.

16 ECT 13 March 1915.

Board reported that since the outbreak of war its harbour dues had fallen by nine hundred pounds. To offset this disastrous fall in revenue, the board requested that the Admiralty pay the dues on all ships carrying government cargoes during the first eight months of war and in the future. The Admiralty turned a deaf ear to such requests.[17]

Some local fishermen successfully diversified their interests which had been so badly affected by the War. Sailors from Mistley abandoned their usual practice of coastal coal carrying, which fetched only 10*s*. a ton, and instead carried coal across the Channel by barge for the British Expeditionary Force on the Western Front. This more dangerous route brought in the far more substantial sum of £6 10*s*. a ton.[18] At Wivenhoe several private boats were requisitioned by the Admiralty. The *Venetia* and the *Vanessa* were commandeered early in the War and the *Rosabelle* in 1915. The *Miranda* and the *Lady Blanche* were transformed into armed patrol boats. Whatever individual hardships resulted from these requisitions were more than offset by the fact that Wivenhoe's shipyards were soon working full-time manufacturing naval vessels.[19]

Essex's seaside resorts, in common with resorts throughout the region, were not in the enviable position of being as adaptable as local fishing towns and villages. In the spring of 1915 they were faced with the possibility of another dearth of holidaymakers in the summer. At Walton a committee was set up to arrange advertisements as far afield as London.[20] A special advertising scheme was instituted, funded by subscribers anxious to ensure a successful holiday season. One result of this was a poster featuring a young girl pictured on the beach entitled 'Sister Susie Seeking Sand and Sunshine'. However, the advertising campaign brought meagre results. At Frinton the number of visitors over the May bank holiday 1915 fell by about a third; at Clacton the difference was disastrous; there were only 2,581 visitors compared with 11,917 the previous year.[21] The whole summer was a very lean one. Three months later, the August bank holiday attracted only 2,659 visitors to Walton, a fall of about forty per cent since 1913. Once more Clacton came off worst. Although the number of visitors was over three times as great as the May bank holiday, the figure of 7,888 visitors was almost two-thirds down on the 22,623 who came in 1913.[22]

Southend was more fortunate in retaining a greater share of its pre-war visitors. This can be partly explained by the resort's close proximity to London, and partly by the fact that its railway was less used by the military than those which ran between London and north Essex resorts, and served the strategically important port of Harwich, and which was thereby dominated by military traffic. In 1915 Southend

[17] Carlyon Hughes, *Harwich Harbour*, 104-5.

[18] R.J. Horlock, *Mistleyman's Log: Chronicles of a Barging Life*, (1977), 76.

[19] Butler, *Wivenhoe*, 213.

[20] ECS 3 April 1915.

[21] EEA 29 May 1915.

[22] EEA 7 August 1915.

welcomed 105,000 visitors, a drop of only 15,000 on 1910, though probably a good deal fewer than in 1911-14. During Easter 1917 twenty-three thousand visitors arrived by train, only a third as many as in 1914, and a drop of almost sixty per cent from 1916. That same year, the number of August bank holiday visitors fell to 82,000, and reached a low of 63,000 in 1917.[23] Even at Southend there was no unequivocal success.

One tactic which seaside resorts used repeatedly, and usually fruitlessly, was an attempt to persuade the Great Eastern Railway to reduce its fares so as to attract desperately needed visitors. The railway company was regretful, but adamant, that fares could not be reduced. Use of its track by the military and munitions manufacturers, the loss of valuable railway workers to the forces, and the need to maintain a large number of engines and rolling stock in reserve for the military, were some of the reasons given for its policy on fares, which actually increased in 1915.[24] In 1915 Southend Town Council attempted to offset the decrease in population caused by voluntary enlistments and the consequent decline in trade by appealing to the War Office to create a military depot in the town. The councillors stated that the appeal should:

> set forth the extreme salubrity of the Borough and its huge outlay for sanitary purposes; the broadness and disposition of its streets and boulevards; the opportunities which still exist of obtaining lands and spaces for training troops; the advantage and vicinage and the connection both by water and rail with London and the Country generally.[25]

In 1917 Southend's councillors attempted, and failed, to secure exemption from season ticket increases which came into effect in that year.[26] At Clacton hoteliers counteracted increased railway fares by reducing their prices.[27] During the summer, a further blow was received by Clacton when the military cut billeting rates.[28] In January 1916 the Clacton Chamber of Commerce renewed its efforts to persuade the Great Eastern Railway to cut its fares, and combined this with an accusation that local magistrates were compounding the difficulties of local traders by imposing fines for breaches of the lighting order which were higher than in other danger zones. It claimed that Clacton traders "are unanimously of the opinion that the fines inflicted on the traders and other members of the community by the Clacton Bench in respect

23 Everitt, *Seaside Holiday*, 121; ECC 13 April, 6 August 1917.

24 EEA 27 March 1915.

25 SBC Special Committee minutes, 22 February 1915.

26 SBC minutes, March 1917.

27 ECS 26 June 1915.

28 EEA 4 September 1915.

of lights are out of proportion to the offences committed".[29] Convinced that their plight was being ignored, various municipalities in East Anglia combined their efforts to lobby the Government. In October 1915 a conference of local authorities was convened by the Corporation of Lowestoft on the theme of 'The War and East Coast Distress'. The conference discussed issues which were familiar to all the representatives present; the collapse of the holiday trade and the adverse impact of the War on fishing, which were the region's main industries. It was claimed that municipal receipts in East Anglia had fallen on average by fifty per cent, and that the number of passengers on the Great Eastern Railway had fallen by forty-one per cent compared with 1913, which was having a seriously detrimental effect on the region's economy. The conference appealed for aid for local authorities, for resorts, and for towns whose fishing fleets were suffering; it demanded municipal grants, assistance with rates, interest-free loans, and relief from war taxation for East Coast resorts whose distressed condition was the result of the War. A deputation was despatched to Westminster to argue the case for relief.[30]

By the early winter of 1916 the situation in the county's resorts was deteriorating at an alarming rate. The *East Essex Advertiser* reported that the area was experiencing an abnormal number of furniture sales, as lodging house keepers had given up the fight to stay in business and were selling their belongings.[31] Walton Town Council decided not to carry out its annual mosquito destruction scheme — it was argued that there were simply too few visitors to justify the expenditure.[32] The Government's decision to declare Harwich a closed port in 1916 further reduced the harbour revenues. A deputation of dock and harbour authorities saw the Prime Minister, but no action resulted from this. In May the port was closed by the Admiralty, although it claimed that its normal trade would be interfered with as little as possible. Six months later, the Harwich Harbour Board was owed £1,168 in harbour dues. Matters had so far deteriorated that by early 1917 the board's liabilities exceeded its assets by £560. In September the board was given £1,200 by the Government as an interest-free loan, but it was not until August 1918 that a final financial settlement was reached with the Admiralty.[33] Fortunately, the Government recognised the region's pleas that local circumstances were quite unique. In February 1916 the Treasury provided grants to East Coast towns with hugely increased liabilities. Clacton alone received £4,000.[34] Help was also forthcoming from an unexpected quarter. In late 1915 a grant was provided by the Government and people of Canada to assist those lodging house keepers in east and south-east coastal towns

[29] ECS 15 January 1916.

[30] EEA 9 October 1915.

[31] EEA 8 January 1916.

[32] EEA 4 March 1916.

[33] Carlyon Hughes, *Harwich Harbour*, 106-8.

[34] EEA 12 January 1918.

who had suffered a financial loss because of the War. Essex resorts received the sum of £19,500. Southend, the county's premier resort, received £7,250; Clacton was awarded £1,875, Walton £500, Harwich and Frinton only £75 and £50 respectively.[35] The catch was that in order to qualify for the grant, lodging house keepers had to persuade their landlords to reduce their rent, not an easy task given the economic circumstances in their towns.[36] By late 1917 the Canadian fund was nearing exhaustion. Treasury grants, which were still available, provided some compensation for this, with East Coast towns receiving £70,000 to cover the year ending 31 March 1918. Nevertheless, a further conference of East Coast towns was held in November 1917, which later sent a deputation to the Government Committee on the Relief and Prevention of Distress, hoping to obtain grants from the Prince of Wales Relief Fund.[37]

Some fishing communities in Essex, faced with what they perceived as the unreasonableness and intransigence of the Admiralty and the disinterest of the Government, took radical, unilateral action to try to alleviate their distress. In the spring of 1915, fishermen at West Mersea, frustrated at what they saw as the unethical and unpatriotic activities of local fish merchants, who bought their fish at rock-bottom prices, then sold them on to local people at inflated prices, decided to eliminate the middle-men by creating a fishing cooperative.[38] Other fishing communities eventually followed suit. At Brightlingsea too, the unpopular activities of local fish merchants, like Musson, stimulated the creation of a fishermen's cooperative in June 1917, and at Walton another cooperative was established in the same month.[39] Led by the left-wing Dr Jameson, the district representative of the Fisheries Board, a small informal meeting at Brightlingsea led to the formation of the cooperative, with a representative committee to oversee every aspect of its operation. The cooperative aimed to sell all its catch locally wherever possible. Operating along cooperative lines meant that its members received a dividend which was dependant on the scale of their business. With a nod in the direction of Abraham Lincoln, Jameson stated the aims of the cooperative quite unequivocally, "It was by the people and for the people, and for eliminating that shoal of sharks, the middlemen and wholesalers". He went on to praise the growth of cooperatives in Russia since the overthrow of the Tsar in February, and expressed the hope that they and English cooperatives might work together.[40]

Although they consistently sought to play down the extent of the economic dislocation along the Essex coast, the authorities in Essex did recognise that there

[35] CG 22 December 1915; EEA 1 January 1916.

[36] HDS 15 January 1916.

[37] EEA 10 November 1917, 12 January 1918.

[38] ECS 27 March 1915; EEA 9 June 1917.

[39] Foynes, *Brightlingsea*, 64; EEA 16 June 1917.

[40] ECS 9 June 1917.

were difficulties in that area. Other parts of Essex were more fortunate in that the economic impact of the War was far less severe. Indeed, the War actually boosted some local economies within the county and created employment on a large scale. Billeting was a shot in the arm for the economies of many towns and villages. Colchester, Chelmsford, Southend, Braintree, Romford and Hornchurch were just some of the county's towns that benefited. Even quite small villages played host to a succession of army units. Local craftsmen were set to work building, and often sustained in work extending, repairing and maintaining, the military camps which were springing up all over the county. Unskilled labourers, who had a hard time of it in some areas at the start of the War, were able to find employment in the munitions industry. The port of Tilbury was said to have had more work than at any other time because ships were being diverted there from elsewhere.[41] At Chingford some unemployed men obtained work at the Government Smalls Arms Factory at Enfield Lock; Nobel's Explosives Factory at Waltham Abbey was employing one thousand men and one thousand, five hundred women by early 1915. The Essex Relief Committee was informed by the person who wrote to them about local conditions that "I do not think Walthamstow was ever better off or [has had] more money coming into the place." The explosives factory known as Kynochtown, near Thames Haven, employed hundreds of men and women. Further employment opportunities were opened up as firms abandoned the manufacture of peacetime products and changed to producing weapons and uniforms. Two hundred people were employed at the Pitsea Explosives Factory, which had been built twenty years before war broke out. The factory covered 130 acres and consisted of 200 buildings. Materials were brought in and finished explosives shipped out via nearby Holehaven. It manufactured nitro-glycerine, dynamite, blasting glycerine, gelatine dynamite, gelignite and cordite.[42] Hunt's Atlas Works at Earls Colne, which had manufactured agricultural machinery before 1914, was turned over to making shells and munitions. The labour shortage caused by large numbers of men enlisting in the armed forces in 1914, made it possible for the unemployed and unskilled to be absorbed into work. Many military hospitals were created throughout the county, all of which helped to generate local employment and boost the sales of local shopkeepers and retailers. Small villages benefited too. By 1917 sixty-four people from Great and Little Leighs were cycling daily to the munitions factories built at Braintree and Chelmsford.[43] At Margaretting, a railway halt was built against the crossing at the parsonage. A train stopped there every day at 7.30 a.m. to pick up villagers who worked at Hoffmann's munitions factory in Chelmsford, and another returned them home every evening.[44]

41 ECC 4 September 1914.

42 SST 5 June 1919.

43 Clark, *Diary*, 183.

44 Baker, *Margaretting*, 111.

The effect of the War on the Essex coast was patently severe, but its impact on local business communities was also of great significance. At first, the War provided an unexpected boom for shopkeepers in towns such as Colchester. All business enterprises, whether large or small, were affected, first by voluntary enlistment, and then by the conscription of their employees. At the outbreak of war firms like Bentall of Heybridge feared short-time working. Bentall anticipated a three-day working week because of the loss of its foreign trade, especially with Russia.[45] The Colchester Borough Tramways Department had lost twenty-eight men, or sixty per cent of its outside workers by October 1914.[46] By May 1915 the borough's Water Supply Committee regretted that owing to the number of enlistments it was unable to release men for munitions work.[47] Advertisements in the local press for tramway employees combined a sense of urgency with an unsubtle hint about who ought not to apply for the jobs: "Colchester Tramways are urgently in need of motormen and Conductors. Preference given to men over or under military age or medically unfit for the Army".[48]

After a year of war the borough's male education staff, teaching and non-teaching, had largely enlisted. Even so the Education Committee's attempts to gain exemption from military service for two of its seven attested teachers was criticised in rather extravagant terms by Canon Brunwin-Hales as "fiddling while Rome was burning."[49] Private firms were hit just as severely. At the start of the War the Colchester Brewing Company had 134 male employees. By mid-1916 more than eighty of them were in the forces, twenty-seven had attested and were awaiting call-up, eighteen men had been rejected on health grounds, three had been granted exemption, and only one employee had not attested. The shortage of manpower was so acute that the company considered it essential to appeal on behalf of the three men who were called up.[50] Daniell and Sons, brewers of West Bergholt, were similarly affected; forty-two employees were in the services by March 1916, and six months later all the company's seventy-one eligible men had been called up, to be replaced by women, or men who were over military age.[51]

At Tiptree, Wilkin, the jam manufacturer, had lost twenty-five of its seventy-seven eligible men by the spring of 1916, and most of the others were called up over the next year.[52] By January 1917 the Colchester Manufacturing Company had lost half of its men, and it too resorted to appealing against the conscription of its remaining male

45 ECC 7 August 1914.

46 CBC Tramway Committee, 17 November 1914.

47 CBC Water Committee, 8 May 1915.

48 ECS 23 October 1915.

49 CBC, Report of Education Committee, 30 September 1915; ECS 29 April 1916.

50 ECS 1 July 1916.

51 West Bergholt Local History Cooperative, *Bergholt in Living Memory: Aspects of Life in West Bergholt 1850-1950,* no pagination.

52 ECS 1 April 1916.

employees as a matter of course. By the spring of that year Sainsbury's in Colchester had just one man left; all its other employees were women. It successfully appealed against the conscription of its sole remaining male worker on the grounds that he was the only one capable of carrying out the heavy duties which were considered too strenuous for females. Tweeds, the Colchester bakers, had by then lost its entire male staff of ten; the ironmongers Blomfield had just two men remaining out of twelve; J.G. Church, the Crouch Street butcher, had lost three men and two boys, and had just one man remaining. Wallace and Company, plant and bulb-growers, employed sixty-one men in 1914, of whom thirty-nine were of military age; by 1917 twenty were in the forces and most of the others had migrated to better paid jobs in munitions. The workforce in that year had dwindled to twenty-six males, females, and boys; five of these men had been rejected by the army as medically unfit and two were above military age.[53] Cullingford and Blaxill in Colchester lost most of their male staff during the course of the War.[54] Small, or even one-man, businesses were particularly badly affected.

By 1917 Colchester's butchers, bakers and undertakers were pooling their resources, which in some cases meant that they themselves offered particular individuals for conscription. The town's butchers held a meeting in March and decided that six men from their businesses would have to go. Undertakers were told to combine in order to continue operating. However, bakers were criticised by the military representative on the town's tribunal for attempting to exploit pooling in an effort to minimise the impact of conscription on their trade.[55] In 1917 there was even a suggestion that the shops of men who were in the forces should have a special distinguishing mark put on them to encourage their customers to continue using them; the assistance of other shopkeepers was sought to achieve this, but it is unclear whether anything resulted from it.[56] Colchester Town Council held a series of conferences with one-man businesses in the town to encourage pooling and hopefully ensure the survival of the businesses of those who were conscripted.[57] The Clacton Chamber of Commerce, presumably motivated by the same concerns as Colchester Town Council, protested at exemptions granted to the managers of large companies and 'multiple' shops, while men operating one-man businesses were conscripted.[58] As in other spheres, it was extremely difficult for shopkeepers to construct a credible argument that their business was of national importance to the war effort. H. Cole, a cycle agent of Colchester, claimed that his business was of vital importance on the grounds that he enjoyed large sales to munitions workers who had been forced to give

53 ECS 13 January, 24 March, 14 April 1917.

54 *A History of Cullingfords 1885-1985* (1985); N. Blaxill, *A Family Firm in Colchester 1838-1988*, 27.

55 ECS 24 March, 19, 26 May 1917.

56 ECS 9 June 1917.

57 ECT 4 May 1918.

58 EEA 11 November 1916.

up their cars and horses, as well as the Army Cyclist Corps. By January 1917 he had lost twelve of his twenty-seven male employees to the armed forces, replacing them with youths and girls. Nevertheless he failed to hang on to those of his young men who were still employed by him.[59] Some tradesmen attempted to minimise their staffing difficulties by employing young boys in their shops. These boys were usually under age, and shopkeepers were regularly hauled before the magistrates for this, including a number of barbers, milk vendors and newsagents in 1917.[60] By the early summer of 1915 Colchester's traders had lost so many of their assistants to the armed forces that they introduced a novel experiment — a lunchtime closure — from 1 p.m. to 2.15 p.m. in order to provide the remaining assistants with a break.[61] Throughout the county shops began to close earlier than usual, a step taken partly because of the shortage of labour and partly because of the lighting restrictions.

During the War, tradesmen and shopkeepers were affected by much more than just the loss of many of their young male shop assistants. Lighting restrictions were imposed on everyone from October 1914, and tradesmen were compelled to reduce the amount of lighting expended on shop window advertising.[62] In November the restrictions were relaxed somewhat, with traders permitted to place one shaded lamp of twenty-five candle power in a shop window, although all lights had to be extinguished by 8 p.m.[63] Failure to observe the new lighting regulations led to a succession of prosecutions. In August 1915, for instance, the Colchester police court played host to a gentleman's outfitter, the manager of Woolworth's, a greengrocer, a schoolroom caretaker, the manager of a cooperative store and a cycle agent.[64] As the need for the people to reduce food consumption accelerated during 1917, and as government intervention became more wide-ranging, shopkeepers were faced by a myriad of food orders. The Brewers' Sugar Order fixed the price of sugar and the Price of Milk Order did the same for milk; the Potatoes Main Crop Order limited the price that could be charged for the 1916 potato crop; the Feeding of Game Order prohibited the feeding of wheat, pulses and grains to game birds; the Sugar (Confectionery) Order fixed the price of chocolates and sweetmeats, and prohibited the use of chocolate and sugar in cakes; the Bread Order restricted the sale of new bread and laid down rules governing the weight and shape of loaves; the Tea Order prohibited the sale of tea by net weight; and the Public Meals Order established strict regulations concerning the food that could be served in hotels, inns, restaurants and clubs. By the spring of 1917 the Reverend E.H.L. Reeve of Stondon Massey was complaining that at Ongar confectioners refused to serve 'sit-down' meals, and that

59 ECS 6 January 1917.

60 ECS 30 January, 13 March 1915.

61 ECT 29 May 1915.

62 ECT 10 October 1914.

63 EEA 14 November 1914.

64 CG 1 September 1915.

at Brentwood tea and light refreshments were available only between 3 p.m. and 6 p.m. There was also, he noted, "a famine in Lucifer matches."[65]

Although retailers were no doubt exasperated by wartime restrictions, they were nevertheless anxious to parade their support for them. Advertisements in the local press were used to demonstrate their patriotism and simultaneously attract customers impressed by their earnestness. W.R. Simkin, a Colchester cabinet-maker and upholsterer, urged his clients to continue their custom in order to display their patriotism and preserve his employees' jobs:

> Do your part in helping to find employment during the war. He is anxious to be in a position to keep his staff employed. If his customers will realise this, and will continue to place their orders as usual, they will be doing a service to some, without loss to themselves.[66]

In a similar vein A. Owen Ward urged people to "keep on buying to keep the flag flying." At Christmas 1914 Owen Ward's theme had not changed:

> Christmas and our brave boys at the Front.
> Now is the Time to send your presents.
> This Christmas let us Remember the men who are fighting for
> The Defence of our Country and the Protection of our homes.[67]

Wilkin of Tiptree urged people to buy its preserves by noting that "dry bread is proverbially unpalatable, but dry bread with Tiptree Jam is food for kings."[68] B. Chawner, who sold watches in Colchester, advertised his products as "not an Ingersoll or a German, but a general Swiss wristlet watch".[69] The Colchester Cooperative Society urged its members to continue their loyalty with a rather laboured wartime allegorical advertisement:

> ANOTHER VICTORY! ALLIES ADVANCING.
> The ALLIES of THRIFT and INDUSTRY are forging
> Ahead and working out a revolution that leaves no tears of sorrow
> Behind but HAPPINESS CONTENTMENT and PEACE.
> NEW RECRUITS urgently wanted to hold the ground
> Recently occupied, and for a further advance.[70]

65 ECC 1 June 1917; ERO T/P 188/3.

66 ECS 31 October 1914.

67 ECS 7 November, 12 December 1914.

68 ECT 18 March 1916.

69 ECT 11 April 1916.

70 ECS 1 January 1916.

Of all retail business, the licensed trade was the one which harboured the most persistently deep-seated grievances during the War. The Government restricted opening hours, limiting them to between 11 a.m. and 3 p.m., and 7 p.m. and 11 a.m. The manufacture of alcoholic drinks was limited — in effect the brewing industry was the first to be subject to rationing, and very early in the War. Before the War the industry produced thirty-six million barrels of beer, but this had fallen to fifteen million by the end of 1917.[71] The difficulties facing brewers can be understood by examining the proceedings of the annual meeting of Daniell and Sons, a brewing company from Colchester. It bemoaned the impact of the War which had hit its seaside outlets particularly badly as the population had declined. It complained of a heavy beer tax and reduced hours, although its losses had been partially offset by the consumption of troops billeted in the area.[72] Those in the industry were incensed by government intervention. S.C. Butler, a Colchester licensed victualler, resentful that he was paying what he considered to be an excessive licensing duty, saw licensing controls as a step too far:

> it is treatment like this that creates internal enemies for a State; because it generates the feeling that if the King's enemies did occupy our land, they would not serve its greatest revenue producing trade worse that the King's officials do.[73]

Like Butler, Harry Blewchamp, the secretary of the Colchester and East Essex Licensed Victuallers' Association, warned of dire consequences and of the resultant inability of brewers to contribute to local war funds. In January 1915 Daniells took out a half-page advert in the *Essex County Standard* defending the continued manufacture of alcohol. It criticised what it regarded as "the unreasonable nature of the [anti-drink] agitation", and then produced an astonishing statement which seemed to remove all reason for drinking their product. According to the advert, "The alcohol in modern beer is only just sufficient quantity to entitle it to rank as an alcoholic beverage at all."[74]

Although the restrictions on the licensed trade were controversial and unpopular with people from all classes, there was support for them. There was a vigorous, persistent and vocal temperance movement in Essex which focused on two things. First, that it was morally wrong to permit the use of valuable resources, such as grain and sugar, in the manufacture of alcoholic drinks in a time of national crisis. Second, that alcohol consumption would damage the war effort through the loss of working hours and days caused by over-indulgence. The campaign against alcohol was

71 ECC 4 January 1918.

72 ECS 20 March 1915.

73 CG 16 September 1914.

74 ECS 23 January 1815.

possibly coordinated by the Essex Temperance Council, which had been founded in 1895, although a county-wide wartime temperance campaign does not seem to have been launched until May 1915.[75] In 1916 the Essex Temperance Council criticised the continued importation of foreign materials used in the drink industry, while the importation of fruits and sugar was being cut.[76] George V had called for abstinence early in the War and he was supported by many clergymen. In April 1915 the Bishop of Chelmsford urged abstinence on all Christians in the diocese.[77] Local people shared these views. The War was only a few days old, when Jenny Walker of Manor Park condemned drink as a dangerous, morally disruptive influence. "There are no greater destroyers of these qualities of character and demeanour," she wrote, "than drink, drink bars, and drink customs."[78] Some people were unconvinced by the complaints of the publicans, as this extract from a poem written in 1914 makes clear:

> And this is why our drinks are dear,
> And daily after nine
> We cannot get the brewers' beer,
> While still we get their whine.[79]

However, not everyone shared these opinions. In 1915 the leadership of the National Union of Clerks was displeased when its Plaistow branch supported the Government's restrictions.[80] Early in 1917 a working-class correspondent wrote to the *Essex County Standard* denouncing the latest round of restrictions on the brewing industry as class legislation directed against the working classes. "It leaves the rich, the teetotaller, the smoker with all their wasteful extravagances," he asserted, "and denies the toiler his modest refreshment, and it will sooner or later provoke a revolt."[81] Neither the drinks industry nor its customers, nor the county's temperance advocates, actually embarked on an open revolt, but the issue remained a contentious one to the end of the War and beyond.

Shopkeepers and publicans were not the only businesses affected by the War, larger companies and public utilities too were enveloped in its grip. The Colchester Equitable Building Society considered that it had done quite well in spite of the War and was able to maintain its pre-war dividend of four per cent throughout 1914-18. It did, however, note that large numbers of its members had withdrawn shares and deposit capital, which it presumed had been used for patriotic purposes.[82] The

[75] ECC 14 May 1915.

[76] ECC 24 March 1916.

[77] ECC 9 April 1915.

[78] SE 12 August 1914.

[79] CG 5 December 1914.

[80] ERO D/Z 107/1, minutes, 3, 17 December 1915.

[81] ECS 3 February 1917.

[82] ECT 13 February 1917.

Burnham, Colchester and Halstead gas companies seem to have experienced contrasting fortunes. At Burnham the company's profits fell by twenty-eight per cent, thanks to an eight per cent fall in sales. At Colchester however, the gas company's supply increased by seven per cent largely because of the increased consumption of the garrison. Gas consumption also increased at Halstead.[83] In 1914 Wilkin of Tiptree feared that their sugar imports, which came largely from Germany, would be blockaded and would bring their business to an abrupt end; fortunately, alternative sources were secured. The company was also alarmed by the Government's threats to stop exports of jams because of an anticipated shortage of sugar supplies, but this was never enforced. Nevertheless like all companies, the firm was affected by sharp increases in wages and rates.[84] Shortly before war broke out, Arthur Hartley of Coggeshall introduced double-decker omnibus services between Coggeshall and Colchester, replacing his horse-drawn coaches. As petrol restrictions for civilians became severe in 1915, Hartley was forced to abandon his buses for the duration and to reintroduce his horse-drawn vehicles.[85] Other transport firms were compelled to do the same. The National Steam Car Company of Chelmsford blamed its falling profits on the petrol shortage, increased prices and wages, and the delay of its efforts to bypass petrol by converting its bus fleet with coke-powered motors.[86] Daniell, the Colchester brewers, also identified price increases, the difficulty of obtaining labour, as well as major government intervention in the industry as the reasons for its declining fortunes and bleak future.[87] In Colchester Laming Worthington-Evans, the town's Conservative M.P., used his influence to arrange to have several local firms placed on the War Office's lists for the manufacture of military uniforms.[88] At Rowhedge a company opened a new factory in 1915 which made army officers' uniforms; the jackets were made at Rowhedge and the trousers at Colchester. Outworkers, as well as factory workers, were employed by the company.[89] Some companies did extremely well out of the War, and were indeed rescued by it. In 1914 the Dunmow Bacon Company faced an adverse bank balance of £1,999. However, as the War progressed, its produce not only became much more in demand, but increased significantly in price and the company's fortunes revived. The result was that by 1917 its deficit had become a credit of £542.[90]

[83] BDA 20 March 1915; ECS 27 February, 20 March 1915.

[84] ECS 20 March 1915, 13 March 1920.

[85] E. Axton, *Public Transport in the Halstead District* (1980), 51-52.

[86] EEC 4 January 1918.

[87] EEC 17 March 1916.

[88] CG 19 August 1914.

[89] ECS 6 November 1915; Rowhedge Village Association & East Donyland Parish Council, *Rowhedge Recollected* (1977), 12.

[90] EEC 23 February 1917.

The companies that flourished most of all were those that became involved in large-scale munitions work for the Government. Nobel's Explosives Factory at Waltham Abbey employed one thousand men and fifteen hundred women. Business was so good that the Lord Lieutenant's Emergency Committee found that there was no distress in the area. The cooperative production of munitions was coordinated by the East Anglian Munitions Committee, created in May 1915 of nineteen companies in East Anglia, including Davey and Paxman, R. Hunt and Company of Earls Colne, Stone Brothers, and Stanfords of Colchester. The committee's first government contract was for two hundred thousand 18-pounder shells at 22*s.* per shell for the first twenty thousand, and £1 each for the remainder. An Executive Committee was formed on 15 June 1915, with P.A. Sanders of Colchester firm Davey and Paxman representing Essex. A further contract to produce 4.5 inch shells was arranged with seven firms, including Davey and Paxman, and one million were manufactured.[91] The firm of Davey and Paxman was perhaps typical of these firms, who were conveniently able to combine patriotism with increased profits. Its first war order was actually made on 1 August 1914, three days before Britain entered the conflict — a power plant for a wireless station in Egypt which was intended to complete a chain of communications in the Middle East. The majority of the company's work was for the Ministry of Munitions and the Admiralty, although it also completed large orders for the War Office, the Ministry of Air, the Ministry of Food, the Ministry of Shipping, and the Department of Mechanical Warfare. In the early days of the War it was one of only three firms engaged in secret work for the Admiralty, and throughout the War the company carried out secret work on submarines. In 1915 as a national crisis over shell production threatened to imperil the prosecution of the War, the company installed plant to manufacture 18-pounder, 13-pounder, and 6 inch and 4.5 inch shells. Hundreds of women from the Colchester area were employed at the factory, many of them working on the night shift, at weekends and even during air-raid warnings. Its fully equipped canteen produced meals for employees twenty-four hours a day.[92]

As we have already seen in Chapter 2, food prices shot up in the initial panic surrounding the outbreak of war in August 1914. Although the scale of these initial rises quickly stabilised, prices continued to rise throughout the War. By the beginning of 1915 food prices were already twenty per cent higher than at the start of the War, and general consumer prices were ten to fifteen per cent higher. During the course of the War household food bills increased by about sixty per cent, which averaged out at about two pounds a week for a working-class family.[93] By early February 1915,

[91] W. Stokes, *A Short History of the East Anglian Munitions Committee in the Great War 1914-1918*, 5, 6, 9-10.

[92] ERO D/F 23/1/23, D/F 23/1/78.

[93] deGroot, *Blighty*, 205-6.

the *East Essex Advertiser* noted that prices had risen "at a truly alarming rate".[94] Colchester Borough Council made the same point at the same time. It noted that bread prices had increased by fifty per cent and other main foodstuffs were increasing beyond the pay of both working- and middle-class families.[95] Flour, which had sold at 27*s*. a sack in August 1914, was selling for 43*s*. a sack by January 1915.[96] By the summer of 1915, Harry Wadley, a shopkeeper in Layer Marney, was concerned that the price of flour had increased so much that he felt unable to pass on the full cost to his customers.[97] Local organisations were also concerned at the rising cost of living. The Romford Board of Guardians was urged to increase the cost of out-relief to the poor in view of price rises, but after a discussion the suggestion was rejected.[98] At Tendring the guardians, in view of their observations that prices had risen by twenty-five per cent by March 1915, decided to continue the extra relief issued throughout the winter for a further fourteen weeks. As prices continued to rise they extended this relief for a further period on 3 July.[99] Colchester's Royal Eastern Counties Institution, which relied entirely on voluntary donations, expressed its growing alarm at price rises which threatened its future. By June 1915 it noted that its difficulties were the result of price increases of almost every commodity. Meat prices had doubled, and other goods had increased in price — bread, groceries, clothing, boots, leather goods, coal, coke, even the cost of lighting. It estimated that its overall bill had increased by at least two thousand pounds, and the final figure was possibly nearer to three.[100] The Lexden and Winstree Board of Guardians' provisions bill was £286 for the second quarter of 1914; in the same quarter of 1915 it had risen to £372. Here too, the guardians felt particularly aggrieved at the price rises for beef, milk, cheese, butter, tea and coal.[101]

It is possible to get some idea of the difficulties facing retailers by looking at how the Colchester branch of the Cooperative Society dealt with the problem of bread and flour prices. It had increased the price of flour by one penny on 1 August 1914, three days before war was declared, when it immediately raised the price of bread. By mid-August it was short of flour, perhaps unsurprisingly in view of panic buying earlier in the month. The society increased the price of its flour and bread in February and May 1915, although in June it was reduced by 1/2*d*. However, the price was increased by 1/2*d*. in July and again in August 1916. In October the price of both bread and flour was raised, again by 1/2*d*., as it was again in March 1917, but a further 1/2*d*. cut

94 EEA 6 February 1915.

95 ECS 6 February 1915.

96 HDS 16 January 1915.

97 ECT 8 June 1915.

98 ECC 19 February 1915.

99 ECC 19 February 1915.

100 ECS 12 June 1915.

101 ECS 24 July 1915.

followed in April.[102] Constant price rises and shifts were only brought to a halt by the introduction of rationing.

Price increases were bitterly resented by working people, and they were often interpreted as the result of the greed of suppliers and retailers. In October 1915 people at Braintree became particularly incensed when they believed that local shopkeepers had increased their prices ahead of the imminent budget, particularly the price of tea, sugar, tobacco and cigarettes. At a public meeting held to protest at these rises, one speaker called for the internment of those shopkeepers who were responsible and urged a boycott of their businesses. The local branch of the Cooperative Society was accused of being the first to raise its prices. In a return broadside local shopkeepers complained anonymously through the press that local people had in fact sparked a panic by attempting to buy large food stocks ahead of the budget. The society, anxious to refute allegations that it had been profiteering, announced that it too had been seriously hit by inflation. It claimed that since August 1914 it had paid an extra two hundred pounds for flour, nine hundred pounds for bacon, five hundred pounds for tea, seven hundred pounds for sugar, and six hundred pounds for butter, which amounted to an extra cost of three pounds per society member, or four pounds if the cost of coal was added.[103]

The remorseless increase in food prices put great pressure on working-class budgets as well as those of the middle classes who relied on fixed salaries. Employers seem to have been generally sympathetic towards their plight, and throughout the War pay increases, often referred to as 'war bonuses', were paid to prevent employees from falling too far behind inflation. Chelmsford Borough Council granted its first pay increase to its employees following a petition in March 1915, as inflation began to bite. The council recommended paying a war bonus of 1*s.* a week to those earning between 22*s.* 6*d.* and 29*s.* a week, and 2*s.* to those earning less than 22*s.* 6*d.* A further war bonus of 1*s.* 6*d.* was paid in March 1916, and its carters received 3*s.* in November. In January 1917 its sweepers, gardeners and baths handymen received 1*s.* 6*d.* a week, and 2*s.* 6*d.* a week was given to its labourers and dustmen. The borough's teachers received a pay rise of £4 a year in January 1917 for those not earning more than £100 a year. Further increases were given to various groups of employees in September, October and December 1917, and in May and July 1918.[104] Similar steps were taken by Colchester Borough Council in order to protect the interest of their employees. It granted pay rises or war bonuses in November 1914 and March 1915. As they had done in Chelmsford, borough employees, represented by the Workers' Union, requested further pay rises in October 1915 in view of the unprecedented rise

[102] ERO D/Z 175/1/15, CCS minutes, 1, 19 August, 10, 17 February, 12 May, 15 June 1915, 2 February, 25 July, 9 August, 10 October 1916, 18 April 1917.

[103] ECC 8 October 1915.

[104] ChBC minutes, 9, 31 January, 26 September, 31 October, 31 December 1917, 29 May, 31 July 1918.

in the cost of living. The council agreed, and granted additional increases in May, June and September 1916, and in March and October 1917.[105]

The teaching profession proved to be a particularly troublesome body as far as local authorities were concerned. They were especially insistent about their pay increases, claiming that they had been unswervingly patriotic in giving up their time, often during school holidays, to assist in the organisation of various government schemes such as the Derby Scheme and the compilation of the National Register. In both cases teachers delivered leaflets and forms, and canvassed residents. Chelmsford Borough Council increased teachers' salaries in March 1915.[106] Essex County Council did the same in September 1916, after being petitioned by uncertificated and supplementary female teachers.[107] Colchester teachers aired their grievances in June 1915, describing their salaries as "inadequate". In January 1917 Essex County Council's teachers earning less than £100 a year received a war bonus of £4 a year.[108] Teachers claimed that by then some of their number were in dire financial straits. A new salary scale was introduced in September 1917 which increased salaries for all teachers, and which cost the county council an additional £15,792.[109] Despite these salary increases, Essex teachers were still not happy with their lot. In mid-October 1918, just as the War was grinding to a close, teachers held a mass meeting to express their "intense dissatisfaction with the unjust treatment of Essex teachers by the Essex Education Authority." They accused the county council of operating less as "educators" and more like "rate savers." Suggested pay rises on offer were derided as "extremely meagre" or "entirely unsatisfactory."[110] Essex County Council rejected the teachers' accusations, pointing to the huge cost of the increase in their salaries, from £158,533 in 1914-15 to £195,948 in 1917-18.[111]

Ratepayers were sometimes critical of local authority pay increases, and this was a major factor in the post-war creation of the Middle Class Union, which was anxious to restrain council spending, especially the spiralling growth in wage levels. In October 1918 there was severe criticism of the county council when it granted the county accountant a pay rise of two hundred pounds, leaving him with a salary of one thousand pounds. This was unfavourable compared with the £175 a year salaries earned by some of the county's head teachers.[112]

[105] CBC minutes, 11 November 1914, 17, 18 March 1915, 13, 22 October 1915, 26 May, 19 June, 7, 12, 27 September 1916, 6 March, 16 October 1917.

[106] ChBC minute, 31 March 1915.

[107] ECC 22 September 1916.

[108] ECC 19 January 1917.

[109] ECC 14 September 1917.

[110] ECC 18 October 1918.

[111] ECC 5 July 1918.

[112] ECC 18 October 1918.

Local authorities, businesses and householders faced additional difficulties as a consequence of increases in the cost of fuel, and the transport problems which stemmed from it. The Government's commandeering of thousands of horses affected farmer and retailer alike. Within three days of war breaking out, the army commandeered two of the Colchester Cooperative Society's horses and served notice that it was likely to take another sixteen. By October 1914 the Society had lost so many of its horses that it was considering the use of steam wagons as an alternative. Nevertheless, in mid-November 1914 and January 1915 more of its horses and some of its carts were commandeered.[113] Unsurprisingly, by December 1914 the Society was already experiencing problems with its coal deliveries. The shortage of horses and the decrease in the number of trains available for civilian use was further aggravated by the loss of a number of its men to the forces.[114] Coal prices increased in January and February 1915, and by March it was in sufficiently short supply that the Colchester Cooperative Society restricted its members to 1½ hundredweight per week.[115]

In London coal merchants had reached agreements with local authorities in order to maintain supplies and to limit price increases. In November 1915 Colchester coal merchants reached a similar agreement with the borough council. After agreeing that coal merchants could adjust prices to take into account railway costs from London, it fixed prices at an upper limit of 8*s*. to 10*s*. a ton. Coal supplies to north Essex were erratic throughout the War. By June 1917 Colchester Borough Council was said to be "seriously concerned" about the town's coal supplies. A month later it asked the coal controller for one thousand tons that could be stored by coal merchants until needed in the autumn and winter. The Board of Trade did allow five hundred tons to be delivered for the poor, but only "if ordinary supplies fall short of the demands", and it was not to be used without the express approval of the coal controller. The council continued to appeal for one thousand tons, but in September only five hundred tons were delivered, although a further two hundred and fifty tons arrived in October. Nevertheless by November 1917 stocks were said to be "dangerously low" and six months later they were said to have been "very much depleted", with some coal merchants dangerously short.[116]

Petrol shortages quickly snuffed out bus services throughout Essex, services that in most cases had been established only just before the War. Most returned to horse-drawn services, although as in retailing, a shortage of horses made life difficult for them. By late 1916 the National Steam Car Company was attempting to convert all its vehicles into coke-driven buses, particularly in view of the fact that petrol cost 2*s*.

[113] ERO D/Z 175/1/15, CCS minutes, 7 August, 7 October, 18 November 1914, 6, 16 January 1915.

[114] ERO D/Z 175/1/15, CCS minutes, 2, 22 December 1914.

[115] ERO D/Z 175/1/15, minutes, 20 January, 17 February, 10 March 1915.

[116] ERO Acc. C4, CBC minutes, 19 November 1915, 20 June, 16 July, 7 August, 15 October 19 November 1917, 22 May 1918.

a gallon, while coke cost only 25*s*. a ton, which amounted to a saving of 1*d*. a mile to the company. It was a slow, and ultimately an unsuccessful, attempt to thwart rising fuel prices and shortages. By early 1918 the Company's reduced profits were being blamed on the shortage of oil fuel, increased prices and wages, and the continued delays in the production of the company's new coke-powered motor buses.

By 1915 it was becoming increasingly evident that the War would not only be fought by the armed forces of the combatants, but would involve civilians who would be called upon to make significant sacrifices to ensure victory. Germany's U-boat war threatened to cut Britain's trading lifeline. Shipping losses meant that imports, even of essential foods, would be reduced, and that civilians would have to adapt their lifestyles accordingly. However, until 1917 the Government was reluctant to introduce any form of food rationing and called instead for people to make economies in their food consumption. George V, who had already announced that he would abstain from alcohol for the duration, made it known that the royal family would enjoy a modest table as well. In April 1915 the King urged all households to cut their bread consumption by a quarter. His proclamation was read in churches and chapels on four successive Sundays, and also outside the Town Hall in Colchester.[117] The Bishop of Colchester, Dr Whitcombe, publicly pledged to eat no more than four pounds of bread or three pounds of flour a week, saying that "liberty was always better than compulsion", a reference to the possibility of rationing being introduced should voluntarism fail.[118] In December 1916 Lloyd George, the Prime Minister, appointed Lord Devonport as food controller, although he proved rather ineffectual, and less than six months later he was superseded by Lord Rhondda. In February 1917 Devonport urged all adults to restrict themselves to four pounds of bread, two pounds of meat, and twelve ounces of sugar a week, and recommended meatless days, although he subsequently retracted this unpopular suggestion in the spring. The appeal for reduced bread consumption asked a great deal of working-class families, who were more likely to depend on bread, rather than meat, for their sustenance. In November 1917 Lord Rhondda asked for a further tightening of civilian belts, when he brought in a new scale of voluntary rationing. The weekly meat ration for adults was reduced to two pounds, together with twelve ounces of cereals, ten ounces of butter, margarine or lard, and eight ounces of sugar. He urged restrictions on the consumption of milk and cheese and it was recommended that people should make more extensive use of fruit and fresh vegetables, especially potatoes.[119] As a further encouragement to economise in food consumption the officially produced 'Rhymes for the Times' were circulated during 1917. These included such catchy sayings as:

[117] ECS 4 May 1917.

[118] ECS 12 May 1915.

[119] ECC 16 November 1917.

A Christmas truce in every larder
Means making all our troops fight harder.

When Christmas is over, the War will last —
And the greater the feast, the larger the fast.

Just think of this at Christmas, when you carve
The Nation's S. O. S. is "Save or Starve."

If your MENU the U-MEN is to beat
You must be mindful when and what you eat.

We will be traitors without thinking
If we heed not our eating and drinking.

Public bodies were also anxious to publicise their own contributions to national economy. In May 1915, shortly after the King's proclamation on thrifty eating, a municipal kitchen was opened in Colchester, its purpose being to provide cheap, wholesome meals, and simultaneously demonstrate how to make the best use of existing resources.[120] In August 1915 the Colchester Board of Guardians, who had recently been criticised for extravagant expenditure, debated inconclusively whether or not to stop the beer allowances granted to the workhouse officers, both male and female. In November beer was indeed no longer served to inmates, although this was temporarily rescinded at Christmas.[121] In January 1916 the guardians were again heavily criticised for purchasing foreign condensed milk which was cheaper than domestic milk. Economising was acceptable, but only as long as it did not conflict with patriotism.[122] The Ongar Board of Guardians reduced the amount of bread to workhouse inmates and gave them vegetables, boiled rice, porridge or pease pudding instead.[123] Faced by dwindling supplies and rising prices, the guardians at Chelmsford served stewed fruit and custard instead of the traditional plum pudding and mince pies on Christmas Day. At Braintree workhouse apple dumplings were served in place of plum puddings.[124] Halfway through the War, the Orsett Board of Guardians decided that the workhouse chaplaincy would be an honorary position, rather than a paid post, in order to save money.[125]

As meat became more expensive and the better cuts harder to obtain, people turned to what had become unfashionable alternatives. Rabbit became a sought after commodity once more, with a thousand of them being sold at Braintree poultry

[120] ECS 19 May 1915.

[121] ECT 20 July 1915; ECS 7 August 1915; CG 15 December 1915.

[122] ECS 22 January 1916.

[123] ECC 30 March 1916.

[124] ECC 28 December 1917.

[125] ECC 10 March 1916.

market in February 1918.[126] In the opinion of the *Essex County Chronicle*, by early 1918 horseflesh was also increasing in popularity. To conserve flour, more and more bakers used potato in their bread. Twenty-one of Chelmsford's thirty-one bakers were doing so by early 1918, and by May only one baker was continuing to use nothing but flour.[127] Leonora Downing, whose father ran a bakery in the village of Ardleigh, remembered her father having to use a flour substitute called 'standard', the use of which became compulsory. "It looked and tasted like the sweepings from a flour mill after the men had cleared up", she recalled.[128] It was hardly surprising that in April 1917 'Argus' of the *Harwich and Dovercourt Standard* felt able to say that, "we are getting nearly used to see our daily bread get darker every week."[129] It may have been more nutritious than pre-war bread, but it was not popular. Mrs E. Stead from Braintree remembered that standard bread tended to go mouldy in the middle and that her family threw it away, preferring instead to eat biscuits and porridge.[130] In view of such unpalatable choices and because of the depth of concern over food shortages, in June 1917 the Executive Committee of the Essex Farmers' Union called for a cull on dogs to conserve supplies.[131]

In November 1915 there were howls of protest when the chief constable was found to have spent fifteen guineas on his chauffeur's livery, an action which was considered to be a gross extravagance in wartime.[132] Colchester Borough Council was accused of failing to economise in the spring of 1918, after it increased the rates by four pence for the half year. The *Essex County Standard* pointed out that this rate rise came in spite of the increased use of the much maligned tramway, which for once was not making a loss, the reduction in the lighting bill as a result of the Government's restrictions, and the fact that the increased salaries of its employees had been offset by the loss of well-paid staff who had enlisted.[133] The borough council's economising had ensured a fall in the rates from 7*s.* 4*d.* in 1914 to 7*s.* 1*d.* in 1915, 6*s.* 10*d.* in 1916, and 6*s.* 9*d.* in 1917; only in 1918 did the rates increase for the first time in the War to 7*s.* 1*d.*[134] Clacton Urban District Council set a half-yearly rate of 1*s.* 4*d.* in 1915, the lowest rate since 1900. In 1916 Frinton Urban District Council's economies led to a reduction of two pence in the rates, although it was unable to maintain this in 1917.[135] Essex's metropolitan councils, with larger financial commitments and

[126] ECC 8 February 1918.

[127] ECC 27 February, 10 May 1918.

[128] L. Downing, *Ardleigh Village Days*, 1994, 15.

[129] HDS 21 April 1917.

[130] ERO T/Z 25/619.

[131] ECC 8 June 1917.

[132] ECC 3 December 1915.

[133] ECS 28 April 1917.

[134] ECT 27 April 1918.

[135] EEA 6 November 1915, 18 March 1916, 13 October 1917.

bigger workforces, struggled to sustain economies in the face of demands from workers for pay increases and war bonuses. By the spring of 1918, Leyton Urban District Council faced a deficit of £4,483, largely incurred by the Highways Committee which granted war bonuses to its staff and had little choice but to pay hugely inflated prices for materials.[136]

It was during the War that daylight saving (putting the clocks backwards or forwards) was introduced in order to make use of a greater number of daylight hours in spring and summer. The idea had been first seriously suggested by William Willett, a London builder whose father had been a Colcestrian. He wrote a pamphlet entitled 'Waste of Daylight' in 1907, urging that the clocks should have twenty minutes added to them on each of four successive Sundays in April, and twenty minutes taken off on four successive Sundays in September. A bill to enact this was introduced in Parliament several times after 1909, but failed to make passage. Willett himself spoke about his ideas at Colchester in February 1914, and the town council voted in favour of it before the War; Willett died a year later without ever seeing his idea brought to fruition. However, faced with the need for farmers and allotment holders to have more time to spend at work, and with Germany and Austria having already adopted the scheme, the Government passed Willett's proposal on 17 May 1916. The idea met with considerable resistance, but in his home town Willett was hailed as a national hero, and there were even plans to erect a statue to him outside Colchester Town Hall.[137]

Food Control Committees were created in the summer of 1917, when disillusionment with the voluntary system of food control was beginning to assume significant proportions. Their establishment was a half-hearted admission by a reluctant Government that the system of food supply and distribution was in need of regulation. The idea emanated from the Ministry of Food, headed by the dynamic Lord Rhondda. The new committees, like the military tribunals, were to be created by local authorities, but their membership was more wide-ranging. They inevitably included members of local councils, and Lord Rhondda advised that no more than a third of committee members should be from the business community. Each committee was urged to include a female member as befitted a structure created to oversee what were considered to be domestic matters. A single woman was to be found on the committees at Halstead, Colchester, Rochford and Stansted, although there were two women on the Chelmsford committee.[138] As well as the two women, the Chelmsford committee contained two borough councillors, a representative of the Cooperative Society and a member of the town's traders' association.[139] However, additional representatives could be co-opted on to committees, sometimes creating an imbalance

[136] LE 2, 30 March 1918.

[137] ECS 6 May 1916; EEA 20 May 1916.

[138] ECC 7 September 1917.

[139] ChBC minute, 29 August 1917.

in favour of traders. At Chelmsford representatives were added from Crompton's, Hoffmann, Marconi and the National Steam Car Company.[140] Such moves were bitterly resented by local people who felt, not unreasonably, that traders might have divided loyalties, and not necessarily have the best interests of the population at heart. Such was the hostility and suspicion of the townspeople of Chelmsford towards the Food Control Committee, that within weeks of its creation they were holding a "food vigilance meeting" to protest at the number of traders that had been included on it.[141] Similarly, Brentwood Cooperative Society protested to the committee that that it was failing to adhere to Rhondda's instructions relating to the inclusion of a labour representative.[142] A deputation of Colchester's working people made the same point in January 1918.[143] At Braintree public censure forced the resignation of the committee's chairman, C.H. Howard, a grocer, after a two-hundred-strong petition alleged that he could not avoid a conflict of interests if he remained as chairman.[144]

By late 1917 it was evident that the public perception, particularly the perception of the working classes, was that voluntary restraint in food production was not going to be sufficient to achieve the twin objectives of staving off the German U-boat campaign and feeding the people equitably. Compulsion, in the form of food rationing, seemed to be only a matter of time. In reality, the introduction of rationing was a response to the dissatisfaction of the general population. During the winter of 1917-18 there was serious social unrest throughout the county, resulting, people believed, from food shortages, incompetent organisation, inept supply and distribution, and corrupt traders, all of which combined to create a system which discriminated against the working classes. By August 1917 the *Essex County Chronicle* had already expressed its belief that it was common knowledge that meat prices were prohibitive for working people, who were being debilitated by its absence.[145] The Barking Ratepayers' Association certainly felt so, for in September it demanded an investigation into meat prices in the town. The Mayor of Chelmsford, as chairman of the Food Control Committee, personally visited all the town's butchers after complaints that meat prices were excessively high.[146] Working-class discontent in Barking was particularly high. In July 1917, a deputation to the Urban District Council was organised by the town's trades council and ratepayers' association following a mass meeting in the park. The resolution passed by the meeting tried to influence the imminent creation of the Food Control Committee, and it provides an excellent insight into the fears of local people. The meeting insisted on

[140] ChBC minute, 30 January 1918.

[141] ECC 19 October 1917.

[142] ECC 31 August 1917.

[143] ECS 9 February 1918.

[144] ECS 7 September 1917.

[145] ECS 31 August 1917.

[146] ECS 21 September 1917.

the inclusion of local bodies which in some way represented working-class interests; it demanded a more equitable distribution of supplies, especially sugar, margarine, bread, flour, meat, potatoes and coal; it called for the regulation and fixing of prices for all the necessities of life; and sought the creation of a mechanism to permit the distribution of food to small purchasers, which would therefore eliminate the need for queuing.[147]

By the winter of 1917-18 there was seething public discontent and anger against the system of supply and distribution of food, and not even the growing evidence that the Government soon intended to introduce a complete system of rationing was sufficient to calm things. At Chelmsford there was resentment against milk retailers who were seeking to increase the price of milk. The shortage of butter in the town was blamed on butchers, who were suspected of hoarding supplies in order to drive up prices. What was particularly galling for working-class people was the belief they had to spend much of their day queuing at shops whenever meagre food supplies were available. By January 1918 queues at Canning Town were said to be seven thousand strong; queues of three to four thousand people could be seen at Barking, and thousands queued for margarine at Ilford.[148] At the same time margarine queues at Brentwood were said to be a scandal, with hundreds of women standing in the freezing cold for hours. Thanks to the poor distribution of supplies by shopkeepers, some women were able to get all they wanted, but then supplies ran out leaving others with nothing. It led to serious disturbances in the High Street. Middle-class women, who were angry that the Food Control Committee had put an end to them sending in orders to shops, were even more annoyed when they were among those who ended up with nothing. According to the committee's chairman, he received more verbal abuse from "this type of woman" than from any other social group.[149] At Chelmsford people in meat queues were incensed when they saw meat orders, including legs of mutton, being sent out through side doors — the assumption they made was that these were being delivered to well-off households who not only had the money to buy such things, but were also able to avoid the necessity for queuing because of the collusion of shopkeepers. There were also complaints that well-off families were obtaining more margarine than was fair, and that the distribution of cheese was not being carried out equitably.[150] Working-class residents of Braintree also complained of the unequal distribution of butter and margarine, and both there and at Halstead cheese was said to be extremely scarce.[151] Paul Amsden, a Colchester

[147] BA 28 July 1917.

[148] SE 30 January 1918; BA 9 February 1918.

[149] ECC 25 January 1918.

[150] ECC 25 January, 22 March 1918.

[151] ECC 1 February, 15 March 1918.

resident, expressed working people's disquiet and dissatisfaction with things in this pithy little verse:

> One thing the people won't excuse
> Is that the poor must wait in queues,
> While wealthy folk need only give
> Orders for wherewithal to live.[152]

This poem, which appeared in the *Essex County Telegraph* four weeks later, was equally bitter about the situation:

> They've raised the price of whisky,
> And they've raised the price of stout,
> And sometimes when you want a glass
> The Landlord's stock's run out.
>
> The price they say is maximum,
> But all of us do know,
> That maximum means minimum,
> For nothing's sold below.
>
> Our local food committees say
> No food must be reserved
> For customers most regular
> "All comers" must be served.
>
> So the queues folks still continue
> To crowd at every spot
> Where there's margarine or butter
> And quickly buy the lot.[153]

An anonymous wit at Brentwood also waxed poetic, although the poem they produced contained an undercurrent of social criticism:

> I said, "I want a little tea,
> A couple of pounds will do.
> And sugar and bacon and butter and lard."
> But the shopman said, "No poo!"
> But just at the moment we've quite run out.

[152] ECT 22 January 1918.
[153] ECT 26 February 1918.

I said, "Then give me some margarine."
And he answered with honest pride,
"We are selling that by the quarter ounce,
Will you join the queue outside?"
But having no more than an hour to spare,
I tried – with no better luck – elsewhere.[154]

The Epping Food Control Committee was faced with angry residents as meat supplies ran out. The committee's explanation that shortages were due to butchers supplying meat to nearby army camps, the town's hospital, and to private London schools to the detriment of local people did nothing to mollify opinion. Allegations that traders were giving preference to well-off people from outside the town only served to aggravate the situation.[155] It was the same at Colchester in January 1918. The town's market had only fifteen bullocks to supply the whole district, instead of the usual weekly quota of sixty. The Colchester Food Control Committee was also forced to commandeer a large part of the district's margarine supply to stock the town's shops. In early February, following the raid on margarine vans by residents the previous month, there were rumours circulating that workmen were intending to raid food shops in the town.[156] Residents of East Ham attended a meeting arranged by the town's Trades Council and Vigilance Committee to protest at high food prices and at the unequal distribution of food. The Leyton Food Control Committee was faced with three deputations from the town's postal workers, the Amalgamated Society of Engineers, and the women workers from Temple Mills. All of them threatened strike action unless they and their families were provided with adequate food supplies. The railwaymen from Temple Mills representing their families, three hundred women and children, complained that they were unable to survive on a diet of bread and butter. They too hinted that strike action might be forthcoming unless the committee remedied the situation. The Leyton Food Control Committee had already taken steps to ameliorate the plight of people in the town by commandeering margarine supplies and limiting people to just half a pound per person. In the committee's opinion this was the only way to ensure equal supplies for all, particularly the poor, who often found it difficult to get time off work to stand for hours in queues.[157] The Chelmsford Food Control Committee also commandeered supplies of butter and margarine, and asked grocers not to sell more than a pound to each person.[158]

The West Ham Food Control Committee, like that at Leyton, was also compelled to allow the workers to let off steam by meeting a deputation of railwaymen on

154 ECC 4 January 1918.

155 ECC 8, 15 February 1918.

156 ECT 29 January, 5 February 1918.

157 SE 2 January 1918.

158 ECC 25 January 1918.

25 January. However, in some places such meetings were not considered to be sufficient. At West Ham a crowd stormed into the Town Hall to protest at rumours that ten hundredweights of margarine stored in the Maypole shop had been sold outside the area, and demanded that it be sold locally. The crowd virtually took over the Town Hall and the work of the Food Control Committee was seriously disrupted.[159] On 12 January at Walthamstow local people also took matters into their own hands. Crowds met vans bringing food supplies and commandeered the contents, distributing them amongst themselves before they could be delivered to the shops.[160] At the same time margarine vans were stormed at Colchester, the crowds dividing up the supplies in the streets. Members of the local committee and the police had to be present when the next delivery came, in order to forestall a repeat of the incident.[161] The frustration of Colchester's working population was indicated at a meeting at the town's Cooperative Hall when those attending demanded "national control of all food supplies, the abolition of profiteering and equal rations for rich and poor." There were allegations that much of Colchester's food supply was finding its way to the wealthier west end of the town.[162] When a government minister, Sir Arthur Yapp, the Director of Food Economy, visited Chelmsford in early January 1918 to speak at a public meeting he received a very rough ride from some in the audience. Yapp argued that food shortages were caused by nothing more sinister than defective distribution and urged that this could be remedied if people were patient, and thus avoid the need for rationing. The audience noted that it was only the working classes who were languishing in queues, because the rich were able to obtain all they required. Yapp dismissed these comments as "exaggerated", and he unwisely advised people to watch themselves not their neighbours. When E.G. Pretyman, Conservative M.P. for the town who was sharing the platform with Yapp, claimed that the War had seen an absolute equality of sacrifice between the classes, a member of the audience replied, "As long as the rich have the money they get the food." It was evident that people had reached breaking point.

The authorities had been aware for some months before the incidents of January 1918, that something more than voluntary food reductions might eventually be necessary. In early 1917 the *Essex County Chronicle* added its voice to those appealing for rationing; by April the newspaper was urging the immediate introduction of rationing. Alongside the continued exhortations to the nation to reduce food consumption, to grow more of its own food, to observe meatless days, to economise and make use of waste by rearing animals, the Government was reluctantly planning to introduce rationing. The pace of change was increased following the resignation of Lord Devonport, and the appointment of the more determined Lord Rhondda as his

[159] SE 30 January 1918.

[160] SE 16 January 1918.

[161] Hunt, *Souvenir*, 53.

[162] ECS 26 January 1918.

successor in April 1917. Rhondda was fortunate. He was able to be more effective because he had the good fortune to exercise authority at a time when the Government had decided to challenge the power of the production and retail industry, which had for so long set its face against rationing. Rhondda moved to ensure a steady supply of bread, recognising its importance in the diet of the working classes, and took steps to prevent the price from rising too fast. The controls that were introduced in September actually reduced the price of a loaf.[163]

The instruments of Rhondda's plans were to be the much reviled food control committees which he created in the summer of 1917. These were to operate under the direction of fifteen divisional food committees that were empowered to control prices, register all retailers and inspect the premises of all producers and distributors. These committees established smaller regional food control boards; one was created for Hertfordshire and Essex, and these in turn delegated their powers to urban and rural food control committees. The Colchester Food Control Committee divided the town into ninety-six districts, corresponding to those of the National Registration Scheme.[164] The scale of the operation is indicated, for example, at Burnham. In this relatively small town 2,425 adult ration books were issued, 268 to children under six years, sixty-four to soldiers for margarine and butter, forty-five supplementary ration books for adolescent boys, and 202 supplementary ration books to adults.[165] The scope and complexity of the government rationing scheme facing food control committees can best be understood by looking briefly at Chelmsford's experience. The Chelmsford Food Control Committee was set up in August 1917. By June 1918 the committee had seven hundred orders from the Ministry of Food to implement; by the end of October that number had doubled to one thousand, three hundred. By the summer of 1918 some twenty thousand ration books had been issued together with two thousand supplementary ration books. Its first meetings were held in the municipal offices, but the pressure of work forced it to move to rooms at the back of the Corn Exchange. On 22 January 1918 a full-time executive officer, Ethel Hawkins, was appointed, and the volume of work meant that she was helped by three lady assistants. The committee was also in charge of the Food Economy Committee, part of a national organisation created at the insistence of the Government when it appeared unlikely that world harvests would meet British requirements. The task of the Food Economy Committee was to encourage and to educate the public about the reduction of food consumption and the more effective use of existing food resources.[166] Food economy committees became largely superfluous once full-scale rationing was introduced in early 1918.

[163] DeGroot, *Blighty*, 91.

[164] ECS 2 February 1918.

[165] BDA 27 July 1918.

[166] ChBC minutes, 26 June, 30 October 1918.

The introduction of rationing was done steadily from late 1917 onwards. Some food control committees decided that they could not wait, and stole a march on the Government by introducing their own systems. The Braintree Urban Food Control Committee adopted a ticket system in January 1918. At Halstead a card scheme was adopted whereby all householders were guaranteed an equal supply of tea, margarine, and butter.[167] Even small communities took steps to obtain a fairer and more consistent food supply. At Woodham Ferrers a public meeting debated the issue and resolved to begin its own rationing scheme.[168] However, not everyone was convinced that cards or ticket systems were the solution. The Brentwood Food Control Committee urged the immediate imposition of government controls. It was also unconvinced that the commandeering of supplies by some committees was worthwhile.[169] Where possible, committees operated with the cooperation of retailers, reaching agreement on prices through negotiation rather than simply by imposition. For instance, the Halstead Food Control Committee fixed meat prices after meeting with the town's butchers. At Leyton, the committee and the town's butchers reached an agreement that committed the latter to serve only residents of Leyton, and which banned the prior ordering of meat by customers.[170]

By the end of 1917 sugar had been rationed. The scheme was introduced in a manner that was to be repeated for other foodstuffs over the next year. Sugar retailers were registered, householders had to register with one of the retailers, the quantity to be allocated to each shopkeeper was decided, and rationing cards were issued to all householders. There were nine thousand applications for sugar cards at Colchester, 2,256 at Halstead, three thousand at Billericay, and six thousand in the Braintree district.[171] When milk was rationed, priority vouchers were issued to infants and invalids. In December, the West Ham Food Control Committee forwarded to the Ministry of Food a resolution urging the rationing of tea, butter, margarine, meat and other essentials.[172] The Government already had this in mind, and in February 1918 rationing was introduced in London and the Home Counties, and was extended throughout the country in July. The weekly allowances were: 1½lb of meat per person, 4oz of butter or margarine, 8oz of sugar, 7lb of bread for men and 4lb for women.[173] Supplementary ration cards were issued in March for groups who were considered to be in need of extra food, such as children under five, adolescents, and those involved in heavy manual work. Three thousand supplementary cards were issued in Chelmsford alone.[174] At Braintree

[167] ECC 4 January 1918.

[168] ECC 1 February 1918.

[169] SE 2 January 1918.

[170] LE 9 February 1918.

[171] ECT 10 November 1917; ECC 24, 31 May, 5 July 1918.

[172] SE 12 June 1920.

[173] deGroot, *Blighty*, 203.

[174] ECC 29 March 1918.

several hundred women workers applied for supplementary cards, although there is some doubt about whether they received them.[175] Special ration cards were also issued to invalids, Jews and vegetarians. For the first time in months food queues were reduced, and in many cases disappeared altogether.

However, if rationing finally provided fair and equal access to food supplies for the working classes, thereby easing social tensions, it exacerbated the strains which existed between retailers and food control committees, and consumers inevitably became involved in these difficulties. The root of the problem lay with the reluctance of retailers to recognise that they no longer had absolute freedom to impose their will on consumers, whose interests were now being defended by the food control committees. These committees had the authority to set food prices, often for several months ahead. Retailers almost always regarded these prices as having been fixed at levels which discriminated against their interests.

The most intransigent and disaffected group were the milk retailers, who considered themselves to be particularly oppressed. Their belligerence had unfortunate consequences. Not everyone was as fortunate as the villagers of Hutton, where the incumbent, P.L. Claughton, took on a herd of Jersey cows to provide his parishioners with milk.[176] Milk retailers were discontented about prices by the spring of 1917. The Ongar branch of the National Farmers' Union, angry that the price of a quart was less than *6d.*, argued that the producer and retailer should be left alone to make their own arrangements. A year later the branch was arguing that because the cost of milk production was higher in Essex than elsewhere, they ought to be allowed to charge higher prices.[177] These were not popular views. By October 1917 food control committees were pegging milk prices and were being met with opposition from retailers. In September the Chelmsford Food Control Committee set the price of a quart of milk at *6d.* for October and November. A deputation of the local milk retailers' society tried to blackmail the committee by threatening that this would create milk shortages because they could not operate with milk prices kept at such a low price.[178] The committee refused to budge. Halstead's milk retailers had a similar request rejected. At Brentwood and Billericay milk retailers threatened that if their request for an increase in the milk price was rejected they would make only one delivery a day. It was the start of a cycle of control and protest which soured relations between some milk retailers and food control committees. Things reached a head in September 1918. Maldon's milk retailers were incensed when the food control committee set prices for September at *6d.* a quart for the first two weeks, and *7d.* for the last two weeks. They nevertheless managed to negotiate *7d.* a quart for three weeks. At Chelmsford the price per quart was set at *8d.* to the end of December, and

[175] ECC 19 April 1918.

[176] ERO T/Z 25/614.

[177] ECC 30 March 1917, 29 March 1918.

[178] ECC 2 November 1917.

then *9d.* to the end of April 1919. The town's retailers considered that these prices were too low and on 1 October they stopped making deliveries. Supplies continued to be issued at retailers' dairy shops, but the Cooperative Society was the only business which maintained deliveries to customers' homes. The retailers' action, which in effect amounted to a milk strike, was immensely unpopular. Factory meetings throughout the town expressed their support for the food control committee. Employees of the National Steam Car Company expressed the view that dairymen were making a fair profit and were behaving unreasonably. The Trades and Labour Council condemned the strike, as did workers at Marconi, and a memorandum from 330 workers at Crompton's supported the committee's actions. In fact, although there was little public sympathy for the retailers, it was the farmers as milk producers who were seen as the villains of the piece. J. Gowers, Chelmsford's mayor, was critical of the food controller's action in fixing the wholesale price of milk for producers at 2*s.* 3*d.* a gallon, denouncing it as exploitation by farmers because milk prices were two hundred per cent above the levels of 1914.[179] The strike was ineffectual. It was brought to a halt after a week when it became abundantly clear that the Food Control Committee had no intention of making any concessions. Milk retailers in Burnham resorted to similar actions. They too objected when the food control committee refused to increase the price of milk from 2*s.* to 2*s.* 4*d.* a gallon. A.B. Croxon, one of the area's main milk producers and retailers delivering five hundred gallons a week, brought all of his deliveries to a halt in protest. The food control committee stepped in, took over his business, and delivered his milk for him.[180]

The years 1914 to 1918 were difficult ones for both the civilian population of Essex and for those who sought to provide them with the means of sustenance. In one respect, a combination of circumstances ensured that there was comparatively little hardship resulting from the enlistment and conscription of male bread-winners. The contributions of the Prince of Wales Relief Fund, the Canadian Relief Fund, and later government grants to seaside resorts, which felt abandoned in 1914, combined to salve the worst effects of the War. The establishment of war industries throughout the county filled economic gaps in both town and village, and the rising cost of living was offset by wage increases and war bonuses. However, the problem of how to sustain the people was a persistent one, and one which became intensely acrimonious. Popular perception was that both food production and distribution were managed incompetently. Worse still, was the belief that the food industry was manipulated for the benefit of profiteers. This explains popular anger against milk producers in 1918 and the intense feelings towards local government officers in charge of rationing. On the other hand, many of the county's business communities felt themselves to be the unfair victims of official discrimination and public resentment. The seaside holiday

[179] ECC 4, 11 October 1918.

[180] ECC 6 September 1918.

industry felt abandoned in 1914, and was disgruntled at first that it was rescued by Canadian assistance rather than by its own Government. Within the licensed trade there was a firm belief that both central and local government were pursuing a vendetta which was intended to weaken, or even destroy, the trade. Rationing satisfied no-one; the working classes remained convinced that the better off retained access to more and better quality food, whilst producers were convinced that their operations were being reduced to unprofitable levels because of official neglect or hostility.

CHAPTER EIGHT

Farmers, Food and Friction

The school garden at Ford End. *(ERO: I/Mb 383/1/53)*

WHEN WAR BEGAN, Great Britain, as an island nation, was vulnerable to an enemy whose surface and underwater fleets had grown to menacing proportions in the previous twenty years. The Government was slow to recognise this threat. Although Germany's surface raiders had been swept from the seas by the end of 1914, her U-boat campaign, which began in early 1915, proved to be infinitely more damaging and dangerous, particularly to Britain's foreign food supplies. In the face of such a weapon the country needed to increase its production of home-grown foodstuffs. Unfortunately, as we saw in Chapter 1, Britain was only slowly emerging from the depression which had crippled its farming since the 1880s. Confronted by cheap imports of foreign food, British farmers had responded by turning over four million acres of arable land to pasture, and resorting to dairy farming instead of cereal production. At the outset of war British-grown produce was capable of feeding the nation only one day in every three.

During 1914-15 the Government, as in so many other areas, was slow to recognise the weakness of British agriculture. Although farming was labour intensive and virtually unmechanised, Asquith made no attempt to restrict the number of farm labourers enlisting during 1914-15, nor was the army prevented from commandeering tens of thousands of horses from farms. At the same time, nitrogen and phosphates, previously used in fertilisers, were now the first call of the rapidly expanding munitions industry. Although research has demonstrated that the drain on farm labourers through enlistment was less drastic than might be supposed, with a fall of only seven per cent during 1914-16, this was certainly not the perception of farmers at the time.[1] At the annual meeting of the Essex branch of the National Farmers' Union in April 1915, members complained of the difficulties of replacing men who had joined up. The meeting called on the Government to prohibit further enlistment in rural districts, or face the consequences of a drastically reduced food supply. They urged that boys be permitted to leave school early to work on farms as a means of compensating for the loss of labourers. The Government took little notice.

In 1915 the Milner Committee, established in order to consider ways in which the harvest could be increased, presented two reports. It recommended, rather obviously, a drastic conversion of grassland to arable. Farmers were to be guaranteed a minimum price for wheat of 45*s*. a quarter, and county and district agricultural committees were to be created to report on the capacity of farms to produce more food, as well as to advise farmers on how to do this. The recommendations amounted to a national agricultural policy, a sensible step given the circumstances, but the Government declined to implement them. Buoyed up by favourable domestic and foreign harvests and a belief that the submarine menace had been neutralised, them saw no need to enact what in some cases were controversial measures involving excessive state control of farming. However, by the

1 P.E. Dewey, 'Agricultural Labour Supply in England and Wales during the First World War', *Economic History Review*, 28 (1975), 100-109.

autumn of 1916 the Government's complacency had crashed about its ears. Germany's U-boats were sinking an ever-increasing tonnage of Allied merchant shipping which British shipbuilding was unable to replace. Britain's access to foreign food supplies was being increasingly squeezed. America's harvest, upon which Britain particularly relied, had been disappointing at below pre-war levels, as had those of her other suppliers, France, Italy, Canada and Argentina. Germany's military successes cut off much of what came from Russia and Romania. Adding to this catalogue of disaster, Britain's own potato crop had also been dissappointing in 1916. Lloyd George, by now the Prime Minister of a coalition government, acted promptly in the face of this grave crisis. He appointed a new Minister of Agriculture, R.E. Prothero, and finally decided to employ Milner's recommendations as the basis for increasing the nation's food production. From early 1917 Prothero's agricultural committees were empowered to enter any farmer's land, inspect it, specify the crops to be grown, require the use of fertilisers, and force the break up of grassland into arable. There was no right of appeal against their decisions. Not surprisingly, the committees were extremely unpopular with farmers, who considered that they alone knew what was best for their holdings.

Farmers had already struggled for over two years to overcome the difficulties which they believed had been heaped upon them by the Government's short sightedness. Pressure from farmers' unions led local authorities to consider permitting young boys to work on farms. Colchester's Borough Education Committee did relax their regulations in this respect, but drew the line at allowing the employment of boys under the age of twelve.[2] At Ilford the Education Committee also refused to allow the employment of under-twelves. Those over twelve were able to work between Lady Day (25 March) and Michaelmas (29 September), but it was stipulated that the boys' work had to be genuine agricultural labour.[3] In February 1915 Essex County Council agreed to similar measures. Boys were permitted to work on farms for six weeks, working a maximum of eight hours a day, and they were to be paid no less than 3*s.* 6*d.* a week. In May the county council extended its initial time limit on these measures from May to the end of July, and continued to do this throughout the War.[4] In some rural areas employment for teenage lads was now plentiful, as the head teacher of a primary school in South Ockendon noted, "several boys have been marked [as] left this week. They are now much sought after in employment as men are getting short. Our upper standards are becoming miserably short in numbers."[5]

The employment of boys was not universally welcomed. E. Lambert of Romford urged farm labourers to resist employment of boys because it would lead to a worsening

2 ECS 4 March 1916.

3 ECC 24 March 1916.

4 ECC 19 February, 14 May 1915.

5 ERO T/P 434/4-6 Benyon County Primary School, South Ockendon, logbooks 1898-1938, 1, 2 December 1915, 7 January 1916.

of their already appallingly low wage levels. Instead, he argued that labourers ought to join trade unions, so that pressure could be put upon farmers to pay higher wages, and thus halt the exodus of men from farms to better paid jobs in munitions factories.[6] The socialist Vicar of Tilty, E.G. Maxted, carried out a protracted letter-writing campaign in the press urging the abolition of such schemes.[7] Others favoured the employment of boys, but advocated that they be drawn solely from the sons of farm labourers. "[Only] those who have been bred and born to the land", argued Hugh Ward of South Hanningfield, "are best suited to the land." He predicted that the employment of boys from public schools would signal disaster for Britain's crops.[8]

Worse was to follow. Farmers and their union leaders were driven into paroxysms of fury when the introduction of compulsory military service in 1916 led to the conscription of large numbers of farm labourers. At first it seemed as if the Government would heed the despairing lament of the farmers. In March 1916 Mr Dent, a representative of the Board of Agriculture, arrived at a meeting of the Essex County Appeal Tribunal to inform it of the principles to be used in guiding military tribunals when dealing with farm workers. He assured those present that sufficient men would be left to work the land. To ensure an adequate supply of milk, two men would be permitted to remain on each dairy farm. On arable farms the ratio was set at one man and a pair of horses per fifty acres of land. For the purposes of threshing, the gangs of men employed might vary in number, although the three key men, the driver, the sacker and the feeder, would be placed in reserved occupations. Three men and a driver were permitted to each steam plough.[9]

In reality the Board of Agriculture's principles were often ignored, subverted or subjected to interpretation by the county's military tribunals, and individual farmers saw their farm workers forced to enlist. The result was an ageing workforce on many farms. At Armoury Farm, West Bergholt, for instance, eight of the nine farms hands were aged between fifty and seventy-nine, and the other was a sixteen-year old boy.[10] Young farm workers were also conscripted under the Government's substitution scheme. This scheme demanded farmers give up their Class 'A' men to be replaced by returned soldiers categorised as Classes 'B' or 'C', who were less suited to agricultural work, particularly if they had not been farm labourers. Appeals by farmers were not always successful, as in this case, which was put before the Rochford tribunal in February 1916:

> A horseman named Horner, of Hawkwell, applied for total exemption. Mr Montgomery, his employer, said the man was

6 ECC 5 March 1915.

7 ECC for example see ECC 5, 19 March 1915.

8 ECC 7 May 1915.

9 ECC 31 March 1916.

10 ECS 18 November 1916.

> indispensable. Witness had already lost two men. Temporary exemption for three months was granted, so long as Horner remains in his present occupation.[11]

Farmers continued to protest. In late 1916 Tendring farmers repeated their union's earlier warnings about the dire consequences of putting food production in jeopardy. One man declared that "it was more important that they [farm workers] should be retained here producing food than that they should be sent to the trenches."[12]

The Essex War Agricultural Committee, the body which stood at the point of contact between the Government and farmers and their organisations, repeatedly stressed the need to curb conscription of farm workers. By early 1917 it was in despair, pointing out that men who had previously been granted exemption from conscription to 1 January 1917 were now also being called up, thus paring to the bone the number of farm workers left on the land.[13] In the spring of 1917 B.S. Wood of Bocking, perhaps a farmer, protested at how tribunals were reviewing their previous exemptions of farm labourers, but seemed to be ignoring the numbers of young men still engaged in producing luxury goods such as silk.[14] The Essex War Agricultural Committee in January 1917 expressed its anger, frustration and despair at the Government's policy of reviewing the exemptions of farm labourers:

> That this meeting ... cannot understand how the War Office can claim any additional men from Essex, as representatives of the War Office and the Essex War Agricultural Committee have gone through the census returns together and found there was no general excess of labour in Essex over the minimum scale agreed to, and it seems the War Office has made a grievous mistake in calling on further men without going into the matter with the Essex War Agricultural Committee, as they were promised by the substitution offer that no further men would be taken until substitutes were found.

The resolution was carried unanimously by the committee, as indeed it was at a farmers' meeting a short time later.[15] Unfortunately, farmers in many areas of the county weakened their own position by resisting the employment of women as replacements for male labour on arable farms, and adamantly refusing to allow them to work in dairying.

[11] ECC 25 February 1916.

[12] ECT 28 November 1916.

[13] ECC 26 January 1917.

[14] ECC 27 April 1917.

[15] ECC 26 January 1917.

Alongside its advocacy of the employment of boys to replace farm labourers, the Essex Farmers' Union suggested the inclusion of milking training in the elementary school curriculum. Two hours of milking practice before and after school was suggested in early 1915. The county's Education Committee agreed to institute a scheme to train both women and children aged twelve to fourteen years old in milking. By July 1915 it had selected six elementary schools in the county's milk producing districts where farmers tutored pupils. Tuition was given by using an 'artificial cow' rather than the genuine article.[16] Such schemes were not restricted to local government; private individuals combined their own initiative and sense of patriotism. Lady Petre of Thorndon Hall organised her own milking scheme at Home Farm, where twelve-year-old children were instructed once a week. Within a couple of months of the scheme starting over eighty children had been trained.[17] However, resistance to the employment of women in dairy farming was strong. It was not until late 1916, for instance, that two 'lady milkers' were appointed in the Ongar district to teach young girls how to milk.[18]

Some schools took the initiative and began to incorporate horticulture into the curriculum. At Coggeshall School, a Mr C. Wakeley, described as a "horticultural expert", was a regular visitor. The older boys, aged between eleven- and twelve-years-old, were instructed in gardening classes, and in November 1916 thirty children were driven to Kelvedon, not an insubstantial journey in those days, for a lecture on poultry keeping. To encourage fruit growing in the school, Seabrook and Sons, a Chelmsford firm, delivered five apple trees, two plum trees, a pear tree, eighteen blackcurrant bushes and a gooseberry bush to the school.[19] A Felsted Preparatory School student noted that "work on the land in term time is in full swing, and the purpose for which we are primarily sent here has for the moment taken second place".[20] The boys of the Junior House went pea-picking and dock-pulling, and potatoes and strawberries grew in the school gardens instead of flowers.

The conservatism of Essex farmers made them suspicious of, and resistant to, the Government's interference with their work. Nevertheless, as Germany's resumption of unrestricted U-boat warfare in 1917 brought appalling losses of merchant shipping and threatened a national disaster, the Government embarked on an unprecedented level of intervention in farming. The Corn Production Act (1917) guaranteed minimum prices for wheat and oats. Farm labourers were guaranteed a minimum wage by a wages board, and the Board of Agriculture was authorised to use county agricultural committees as a means to impose changes on farmers.[21] The Essex

16 ECC 23, 30 April, 30 July 1915.

17 ECC 26 November 1915, 28 January 1916.

18 ECC 5 January 1917.

19 ERO T/A 593 Coggeshall School logbooks, 21 September, 2, 3 November, 1 December 1916.

20 D.J. Armour, *Felsted Preparatory School: The First Hundred Years 1895-1995* (1995), 16.

21 P.E. Dewey, 'British Farming Profits and Government Policy during the First World War', *Economic History Review*, 37 (1984), 378, 387.

Agricultural Committee consisted of just three men — W. Hasler, C.N. Brooks and F. Dent. It met four or five days a week to organise the increase of the county's food production.[22] In Essex the committee's inspections of farmers' holdings frequently brought angry reactions. Farmers at Wakes Colne objected to what they saw as a superficial survey, and were affronted by subsequent comments that their farms were being badly run.[23] Government intervention in the potato market in order to stabilise prices also met with an indignant response. Essex farmers had been selling their potatoes for £10 to £12 a ton, which they argued was a fair price, and were highly critical of the Government's decision to peg prices at £8 a ton, with seed potatoes at £10 a ton. A protest meeting organised by the Colchester branch of the National Farmers' Union complained bitterly at the inadequate amount of petrol being allocated to them and the military commandeering of hay, straw and wool. They also made the, by then customary, complaint about the shortage of farm labour.[24] At about the same time, the Ongar branch of the National Farmers' Union passed a resolution urging the Government to see that farmers had sufficient labour and ample artificial fertiliser at a reasonable price.[25] However, what the Government seized with one hand it tried to return with the other. Farmers had been encouraged to use mechanical methods of ploughing and harvesting since at least as early as 1915, with one demonstration of tractors at Moulsham Lodge Farm near Chelmsford attracting four hundred farmers.[26] In February 1918 at Colchester's Layer Road football ground a demonstration of the "Eros" tractor attachment, which fitted to the back of a Ford car, was hailed as a marvellously efficient method of ploughing.[27] However, it was not until 1917-18 that this began to produce results, and then only in a very modest way. In the autumn of 1917 there were only twenty-seven tractors in use in Essex.[28] One rather novel way of encouraging farm mechanisation ended in failure. In 1918 the Essex War Agricultural Committee passed on to the county's farmers several large caterpillar tractors. These had originally been intended for use in Russia where they would have pulled Howitzers over snow. When Russia collapsed and left the War, the tractors were re-allocated to British farmers. Unfortunately, they were far too large for use on Essex fields; moreover, the instruction book was written in Russian, and as the soil got into the gearbox it destroyed the machines very quickly.[29]

[22] ECC 12 January 1917.

[23] ECS 24 February 1917.

[24] ECS 28 April 1917.

[25] ECC 5 January 1917.

[26] ECC 23 July 1915.

[27] ECT 2 March 1918.

[28] ECC 21 September 1917.

[29] D. Smith, *Finchingfield Tales: A book of country gossip in bygone years* (1983), 113.

Although the Government's pegging of farm prices seemed to guarantee an escape from the economic difficulties of the preceding half century, the evidence suggests that farmers were unable to loose the skein of vulnerability which tied them to the past. The Corn Production Act, lauded by the *Essex County Chronicle* as "the Magna Carta of Agriculture", guaranteed minimum prices for wheat and oats until 1922. However, it failed to persuade many farmers to invest in mechanisation. It also intensified farmers' sense of dissatisfaction by guaranteeing a minimum wage of 25*s.* per week for farm labourers, which farmers believed was too high. At the same time the Agricultural Wages Board, which was created to ensure a minimum wage for farm labourers, was demonised by their employers as an organisation trying to squeeze more out of farmers than they could afford to pay. When in early 1918 the Government-controlled Essex District Wages Committee proposed that farm labourers' wages be increased from 25*s.* to 30*s.* a week for a fifty-four-hour working week, with forty-eight hours in winter, farmers reacted angrily. The Ongar branch of the Farmers' Union wanted their labourers to work fifty-four hours all year round, and opposed the granting of a half-day holiday on Saturdays. They argued that if labourers' wages were increased by order of the Government, farm prices, now also controlled by the Government, should be revised more generously in favour of farmers.[30] Farmers were dejected when the Central Wages Board rejected the Essex District Wages Committee's suggestion and fixed farm labourers' wages at 32*s.* per week, based on the county's proximity to London. Feeling that its recommendation had been unfairly disposed of, it was only with some difficulty that the committee was persuaded not to resign en masse.[31] In September 1918 the Central Wages Board further infuriated farmers by increasing the wages of horsemen, stockmen, cowmen and shepherds to 38*s.* a week. Braintree farmers protested that this would lead to lay-offs and would be prejudicial to food production. At Ongar the National Farmers' Union urged its members to ignore the new ruling and promised to support any who were prosecuted for doing so.[32]

There were other bones of contention too. Farmers believed the Government's milk pricing structure discriminated against their interests. They reasoned that the cost of milk production in Essex was higher than elsewhere, and therefore they should be permitted to charge higher prices. In late 1916 the Braintree branch of the Workers' Union had already protested at a price increase by the town's milk vendors, who justified the increase by citing the rising cost of cattle feed.[33] Six months later in June 1917, Braintree's milk producers and dairymen decided not to raise their prices from 6*d.* to 7*d.* a quart, as permitted by the Government's new Milk Order. Recognising the delicacy of the situation they left their price at 6*d.*, resolving to reconsider in the

30 ECC 29 March 1918.

31 ECC 31 May 1918.

32 ECC 20 September 1918; BA 28 September 1918.

33 ECC 22 December 1916.

winter if the price of animal feed increased.[34] At Ongar too, farmers complained that they were unwilling to sell their milk prices below *6d.* a quart. As summer passed into autumn, Chelmsford's milk producers sent a deputation to the town's food control committee. They appealed that they be allowed to increase their price to *8d.* a quart, claiming that this was necessitated by the rising cost of shoeing, harnessing and horses. Their appeals fell on deaf ears.[35] In the face of what they saw as the Government's indifference to their plight, farmers' unions began to urge greater collaboration to add muscle to their protests.[36] A speaker at a meeting of the Southminster branch of the National Farmers' Union spoke of farming's "disunion and ruin" in the face of government action. His solution, already adopted by some as an escape from the pre-war farming depression, was the creation of small-scale cooperative societies in the district which could handle farm production and produce to the advantage of farmers.[37] There was further dissent between the General Workers' Union and National Farmers' Union over the traditional settlement of harvest pay rates in 1918. The latter reluctantly agreed to pay harvest wages of 32*s.* per week for a fifty-four-hour week, with overtime at the rate of 1*s.* 9*d.* per hour. Farmers resented paying such wages, while the Workers' Union seethed at its lack of representation on the wages boards.[38]

Part of the solution to the problem of Britain's food supply was to produce more home-grown produce by turning more land over to arable farming. By the end of the War, seven and a half million acres had been added to cultivation. In Essex this process was overseen by the County Food Production Committee. As Essex was a largely arable county there was only limited scope for the conversion of grassland. Yet, by 1915 almost fifteen thousand extra acres of corn crops had been cultivated. Two years later, a thousand extra acres had been added in Lexden and Winstree, and six hundred in Tendring alone. Although the national average increase in arable acreage was 5.2 per cent, in Essex it was a mere 3.5 per cent, amounting to about thirty thousand acres of the sixty-two thousand acres it had been expected to convert from grassland.[39] Local farmers were contemptuous of the prevailing ignorance among those who so readily advocated the conversion of unused land to arable. At Ongar, where farmers were told to plough up between seven and eight thousand acres of grassland, they believed they would be lucky to get a thousand. Firstly, the four thousand cows in the district required a large amount of grassland to be kept in use. Secondly, and more importantly, the prevalence of wireworm in the soil meant that it would be impossible to plant wheat and bring it to fruition for several years. Instead

[34] ECC 8 June 1917.

[35] ECC 26 October 1917.

[36] ECC 30 March 1917.

[37] BDA 21 September 1918.

[38] BDA 10 August 1918; ECC 2 August 1918.

[39] ECC 19 April 1918.

of impractical suggestions for ploughing up land badly needed by flocks and herds, they advocated increasing the yield of existing arable land by using much more artificial manure and greater numbers of farm labourers.[40]

With labourers conscripted, the number of school boys available to work limited by local authorities, and resistance to female labour lingering in parts of Essex, other sources of labour were tapped. Over eight hundred German prisoners of war were employed on farms, part of a labour force of thirty thousand nationally. Working a nine-hour day, they were paid 5*s*. a week, well below the going rate for British farm labourers.[41] Other work was done by British troops during 1917-18, when the army drafted men on to farms. During 1918 Danish agricultural workers and students also worked on Essex farms.[42]

The importance of encouraging private citizens to grow more of their food as a way of lessening demand for imported food was recognised early in the War. In the spring of 1915 the Colchester Rose and Horticultural Society was urging the area's allotment holders to grow vegetables on their plots rather than roses. Apart from the obvious economic benefits which this would have, food growing was deemed to be patriotic. A.E. Clark of Frinton, encapsulated these two points of view:

> Just a passing word remember:
> Those of us who can, must toil,
> There are many ways of helping —
> One is tilling of the soil.
>
> All at last can make an effort,
> Talent God has given to man;
> Just a bit of dear old England —
> Make it fruitful while you can.[43]

Colchester's rose growers contemptuously dismissed their own livelihood, declaring as part of their attempt to influence public opinion that "Roses and horticulture are suggestive of peace."[44]

In 1916 the Food Production Department was established, a sub-department of the Board of Agriculture, this was given the responsibility of encouraging home-growing of foodstuffs. It devolved the task of organising food-growing schemes to local authorities, assisting them in their task by issuing the Cultivation of Lands Order under the Defence of the Realm Act (1914) which allowed them to take possession of

40 ECC 8 June 1917.

41 ECC 29 June 1917.

42 ECS 13 May 1915, 12 January 1918; ECT 8, 15 January, 1 June 1918.

43 EEA 19 January 1918.

44 ECT 9 March 1915; ECS 1 May 1915.

vacant land without any liability to pay rent to the owner, and to sublet it to individuals as allotments. Parish councils were at first excluded from the scheme, but after much pressure were eventually admitted. Hornchurch Parish Council was the first in the country to receive powers under the new order.[45] By the end of the War there were over two thousand allotment holders in Colchester, occupying 227 acres of land scattered around the town; forty of these plots were in the Castle Park. There were sixty allotments at Wivenhoe, 104 at Harlow, 300 in Chelmsford, 400 in Romford, 500 at Brentwood spread over twenty-eight acres, and 215 covering thirty acres at Clacton.[46] Hornchurch added 256 wartime allotments to the 254 which existed in 1914.[47] Southend had 3,712 allotments situated in 317 acres. There were three thousand in Barking and twenty thousand in total in East and West Ham, Barking, Ilford, Leytonstone and Walthamstow.[48] In early 1918 there was a list of several hundred people awaiting an allotment in Ilford. In December 1916 the borough council there identified thirty-three allotment sites which it was prepared to rent at 1*s*. a week to individuals and 9*d*. a week to members of allotment societies. In January 1917 it added a further seventeen sites, and ten more in June. By March it had received 1,648 applications for allotments and already approved 1,500 of them.[49] In 1917 both West Ham and Leyton Corporations were permitted to use forty acres of land in Epping Forest as allotments. During 1917-18 five other Essex corporations and urban district councils were granted use of a further forty-three acres. Attempts by West Ham and Leyton to obtain more land were subsequently rejected.[50]

Local authorities were empowered to order the seeds of various vegetables and distribute them to allotment holders. At Colchester twelve tons of seed potatoes were distributed in June 1917, twenty more tons in December, as well as twenty thousand cabbage plants, and more than a hundred fowls for breeding and egg production. Chelmsford Borough Council purchased nine tons of seed potatoes in March 1917, and Romford Town Council ordered fifteen tons in May. Colchester allotment holders were also offered the chance to have their plots sprayed with insecticide at a cost of 1*s*. 6*d*. per ten rods of potatoes. Southend Borough Council ordered fifty tons of seed potatoes in February 1917, and a further sixty-three tons in May, at a total cost of £1,502. It also purchased ten tons of lime, eight tons of superphospate, and two tons of sulphate of ammonia. By September, the council had spent £54 spraying

45 Perfect, *Hornchurch*, 219.

46 CBC Parks Committee 7 February 1918; ECC 30 March, 11 May 1917, 7 June, 26 July 1918.

47 Perfect, *Hornchurch*, 219-20.

48 ECC 28 June 1918, 13 April 1917; BA 2 November 1918.

49 SBC minutes, Town Planning Committee, 21 December 1916, 22 January, 9 March, 4 June, 7 September 1917.

50 R. Layton, 'Agriculture in Epping Forest during the Great War', Essex Journal, Winter 1986, Vol. 21, No. 3, 61-64.

crops on allotments, a further £1,269 buying and delivering seeds and manure, and £65 ploughing up vacant land in the borough. It spent £18 on hand cultivators and six spraying machines, which where then hired to allotment holders.[51] Wivenhoe Urban District Council bought eighteen pigs and a sow for its employees. Chelmsford Town Council rejected the idea of a system of food waste collection from householders in order to feed pigs, but Southend Borough Council instituted such a scheme, although it only involved large firms in the town.[52] Church cadets at Ilford collected the town's domestic waste which was used for pig feed.[53] At Clacton the Chamber of Commerce attempted to arrange one morning a week off work for its shop assistants, so that they could tend their allotments or assist local farmers. Unfortunately the attempt failed.[54]

Some church leaders gave their blessing to Sunday allotment working only hesitantly and with reservation. The Bishop of Chelmsford did not share the enthusiasm of the Archbishop of Canterbury, who exhorted his flock to dig on Sundays. He was anxious lest the patriotic fervour for allotments might set an unfortunate precedent that would be hard to break once the War was over.[55] Other clergymen were less reserved in their enthusiasm. The Rector of Little Braxted, Bernard Rooke, cancelled his Sunday afternoon and evening services for several weeks in the spring of 1917 to dig church land. The Reverend H.J.W. Karslake went one step further. In early 1917 he gave up the living of Kirby-le-Soken in order to farm 340 acres of land at Hurstmonceux in Sussex.[56] Rogation Sunday, when the church traditionally called on God to bless the crops, was especially observed in Romford in 1917. There were evening processions through the parish, praying for God's blessings on its gardens and allotments.[57]

The cultivation of allotments was not the only way in which people sought to increase food production, or protect and utilise produce. Tendring War Agricultural Committee and the Essex War Agricultural Committee tried to assist farmers by appealing to Colchester Borough Council to suspend its byelaws restricting dung carting.[58] The mounting necessity of increasing domestic food production also led to a campaign of extermination against any rodents or 'pests' which might damage crops. Local authorities offered bounties on certain rodents and other undesirable creatures to encourage their destruction. In 1918 alone, over eighty thousand

51 SBC minutes, Town Planning Committee, 9 February, 4 May, 7 September 1917.

52 SBC minutes, Town Planning Committee, 5 April 1917.

53 LE 23 March 1918.

54 CBC Special Lands Cultivation Committee, 28 June 1917; ECT 8 December 1917; ECC 30 March, 11 May 1917.

55 ECC 6 April 1917.

56 ECC 23 March 1917.

57 ECC 18 May 1917.

58 CBC, Health Committee, 4 April 1917.

butterflies were destroyed by Colchester school children in order to protect cabbages. One boy, Alfred Scrutton of Old Heath, killed 1,500.[59] In Lexden and Winstree *3d.* was paid for a dozen heads of mature sparrows and *3d.* for sparrows' eggs. L.R. Tippin of Mistley wrote to the *Essex County Standard* advocating "Persistent nest-robbing" to eliminate the "sparrow plague." F.J. Coverdale of Ingatestone wrote to the *Essex County Chronicle* on 25 April 1917, recommending the use of wheat soaked in strychnine to kill sparrows. He noted that a pint of the poison cost just *2d.* and was sufficient to kill two thousand sparrows.[60] The *Essex County Standard* supported such methods with enthusiasm and suggested organised shoots as a way of destroying pigeons.[61] Southend's allotment holders appealed to the council for permission to shoot rooks which were eating their seeds.[62] Likewise wasps were targeted to preserve fruit supplies. Between March 1917 and September 1918, 53,644 rats had been killed within the jurisdiction of Tendring District Council alone.[63] At Wivenhoe 282 rats were killed between February and April 1917. Wivenhoe Parish Council paid *2d.* on the production of each rat's tail, Rowhedge paid *1d.* a head. Some crafty individuals cut the rats in two, and then took the appropriate half to each parish council, thus earning *3d.* per body.[64] At Braintree and Witham an unusually large number of cats died in January 1916 and this was put down to the unfortunate felines killing and eating rats which had recently consumed rat poison.[65] Numbers of pigs were in decline because the high cost of food and the decline in human food wastage resulting from greater economy in people's eating habits. The Essex Farmers' Union saw a solution to this problem in suggesting a national cull of the 1.9 million dogs in England which consumed food which would otherwise be fed to pigs.[66] Even fox-hunting was a patriotic activity, since killing foxes supposedly reduced their depredations of poultry. In 1915 the East Essex Hounds had killed a record number of twenty-seven foxes during the season to March.[67]

Human depredations were no less unwelcome. Both Southend Borough Council and the Colchester Association for the Protection of Property issued a *10s.* reward for information about anyone who damaged crops around their towns. On a less adversarial note, Colchester Borough Council attempted to encourage people to preserve fruit and vegetables by purchasing bottles and jars from the Essex War Agricultural Committee and selling them on at *5s. 4d.* a dozen. The borough council

[59] ECT 5 October 1918.

[60] ECC 27 April 1917.

[61] ECS 24 February 1917.

[62] SBC minutes, Town Planning Committee, 5 April 1917.

[63] ECS 8 March 1919.

[64] ECS 14 April, 26 May 1917.

[65] ECC 4 February 1916.

[66] ECC 8 June 1917.

[67] ECC 5 March 1915.

ordered 408 dozen jars which were bought by 114 applicants.[68] At Hornchurch the council supplied 5,760 glass jars at cost price.[69]

The role of farmers in helping to keep the country fed and in staving off starvation and defeat was rightly recognised and lauded. However, they were also perceived as a selfish pressure group, eager to exploit their special position in order to preserve their profits. Their attempts to keep their labourers, and in many cases their sons, from military service, caused great resentment amongst other working groups and led them to question farmers' patriotism. On the other hand farmers saw them themselves as ill-used. They believed that they were being asked to perform heroic feats of food production without the means to achieve them. They complained at the commandeering of their horses; they railed against the conscription of their farm workers; they criticised the pegging of their prices and at laws forcing them to pay higher wages to farm labourers. Perhaps not surprisingly, farmers were seen as both heroes and villains during the War.

68 CBC, Special Lands Cultivation Committee, 11 July, 18 September 1917.

69 Perfect, *Hornchurch*, 220.

CHAPTER NINE

Women and the War

Catherine Brown (née Mackintosh) in her Kynochtown uniform, 1916.
(ERO: T/Z 162/1)

PRIOR TO THE WAR, most women held a private rather than a public role in Edwardian society. Amongst the landed, business and professional classes who ran the county, wives could be regarded as either decorative or as a guarantee of her husband's social conformity and moral stability. Their public utterances were rare, their appearances were invariably silently supportive. Even when these relatively privileged women met in some sort of official capacity, for instance when the Conservative Primrose League held its meetings, the chief speaker was usually a man of local or national standing and political experience. At such meetings the organisers of the local branch would introduce the speaker and applaud him as he rose to his feet. They, like the rest of the audience, were then relegated to the role of polite and passive listeners. A brief concluding commentary by the branch secretary on the wisdom and appropriateness of what the gentleman had said was the nearest that the meeting came to being a dialogue between female listeners and male speaker. Women's intellectual potential or achievements were rarely celebrated in public, because it was generally assumed by men that they possessed little of either. Even an educated man such as P. Shaw Jeffrey, Headmaster of Colchester Royal Grammar School, could declare in 1912 that a woman's interests "did not lie so much with her mental as her physical education."[1] Women were still largely excluded from the universities and the professions, and the education of women of all classes was designed to equip them for life as a companion, wife, mother and housekeeper. As we shall, see the Great War was far from successful in breaking down these male prejudices. In 1919 a Mr Beecroft felt able to tell a ratepayer's meeting at Leigh that "it was unsatisfactory to have girls employed as messengers in place of boys — boys had more intelligence than girls."[2] Although women had been managing households for centuries, in 1915 the *Essex County Chronicle* could still condescendingly trumpet a new series of articles entitled 'Women and the Home', as being designed to assist women and their daughters "in a practical way by showing how, especially in times like the present, economies may be effected and money made to go as far as possible." One female reader wrote tartly to express the hope that "we are not to have a repetition of the views of men who think themselves well informed as to what really interests women."[3]

Women in Essex were employed in many different occupations prior to the First World War. Thousands of them were in domestic service, many more in the factories and sweatshops of the growing metropolitan area. Scattered throughout the small towns of Essex were industrial concerns such as Lake and Elliott at Earls Colne, Crittall at Braintree, Paxman at Colchester, and Crompton's at Chelmsford, which employed hundreds of women workers. Several thousand toiled for long hours as outworkers in the textile trade based at Colchester. In some parts of the county seasonal work was available in farming and market gardening, for example in the

1 ECT 16 January 1912.

2 SST 12 June 1919.

3 ECC 9 April 1915.

Tiptree area there was summer fruit picking. An army of women earned their living as hoteliers or as lodging and boarding house keepers, catering for the weekend visitors, day trippers and holidaymakers who descended upon Southend, Clacton, Walton and Frinton between May and September. Other women could be found employed in traditional roles as nurses and midwives. Large numbers of women worked in the retail industry as shop assistants; others were waitresses or in catering; towns like Southend and Colchester offered an enormous range of employment opportunities in this area. Increasingly there was female employment as office workers — secretaries, typists, and filing clerks. Educated women filled many teaching posts, although the moral standards of the day dictated that they give up their posts once they became engaged to be married. Part of the problem was the generally held assumption that a woman's working life would automatically end when she married, although many married, working-class women continued to work out of necessity. Attempts were made to organise women workers into trade unions. These were generally desultory and far from successful, although female workers at Courtauld's silk mills in Halstead had been organised in the Women's Federation since 1897. Courtauld's workers then organised into a branch of the Workers' Union shortly before the War, when several hundred women signed up.[4]

Colchester women had been granted the vote in municipal elections as early as 1869, but all women were denied the vote in parliamentary elections, and were therefore unable to play even a minor role in national politics. A married woman might be seen to support her husband's political role, but even those who were married to politically active or influential men were rarely expected to air their views in public. The suffragette movement had made some inroads into the county in the years preceding the War, but apart from occasional speaking campaigns in Chelmsford, Clacton and Colchester from 1908 onwards, they were not much in evidence. When they did appear, their meetings were subject to heckling, abuse and occasionally rough treatment at the hands of male opponents. In 1912 Colchester Town Council voted by twenty to three in favour of extending the franchise to women "at the earliest opportunity" but many did not share this enlightened view.[5] As late as 1916 the *East Essex Advertiser* was still dismissing the suffragette movement as the work of "a few extremists", and argued against women's suffrage as "such a leap in the dark so fraught with uncertainty and danger that [it] should be condemned by all reasonable people."[6] Even the suffragists, who were committed to securing enfranchisement by peaceful means, were not immune from male hostility. At a public meeting held in Colchester to welcome their fellow members who were embarked on the East Anglian Suffragist Pilgrimage, they were pelted with rotten eggs by young

4 ECC 9 November 1917.

5 ECS 8 June 1912.

6 EEA 11 November 1916.

men.[7] In the churches women played a largely secondary and submissive role. The clergy was an all male preserve, and churchwardens and sidesmen were also men. Women played no active part in the ritual of Anglican services, and in most churches were not even allowed to speak in church meetings.

The outbreak of war produced an immediate and significant change in the lives of thousands of women throughout Essex, as their husbands, sons, brothers and fathers marched off to enlist. Most employers quickly guaranteed the employee's family a set amount each week and usually promised them that their job would be left open for them at the end of hostilities. Crittall of Braintree for instance, paid 5*s*. a week to the wife of every reservist or territorial who had been called up from their works, and 1*s*. for every child. Lake and Elliott also offered 5*s*. a week to wives and 1*s*. for each child under fourteen.[8] The Colchester Cooperative Society offered families of employees half of their wages for the duration and promised that their jobs would be kept open.[9] The Prince of Wales Relief Fund was also established in 1914 to assist wives and families reduced to destitution by their husbands enlisting. However, as we saw in Chapter 5, the fund was not much used in Essex. The only group of women who required regular assistance was the seaside landladies whose livelihoods were badly affected by the War. Government assistance and help from the Canadian Relief Fund provided some aid, but the War years were hard for the county's seaside towns.

Middle-class women with time on their hands, no financial imperative to earn a living, and who were eager to demonstrate their patriotism, flung themselves into the war effort with gusto. Before 1914, partly in anticipation of a calamity such as war, many women had already been trained as nurses in the voluntary aid detachments which had been created throughout the country under the auspices of the British Red Cross Society. The Essex branch of the society consisted of seventy-three voluntary aid detachments with a personnel of over two thousand, seventy-five per cent of whom were women.[10] Eight of these women's detachments, along with one men's, were found at Colchester, and involved 201 individuals. Other women created the war work depots which sprang up all over Essex in 1914, with the aim of manufacturing medical articles and surgical dressings for the troops. At Hornchurch for example local women initially set up a branch of the Queen Mary's Needlework Guild, but as women from nearby Upminster joined the group, it became known as the Hornchurch and Upminster War Hospital Supply Depot and Working Parties. Staffed at first by thirteen women, the depot eventually consisted of 148 volunteers. It worked just three hours a day, from 2 p.m. until 5 p.m. on Monday, Tuesday and Thursday afternoons. Its funds amounted to £1,166 raised in collections, and the value of the sixty-five thousand articles they produced during the War exceeded five

7 ECS 19 July 1913.

8 CG 12 August 1914.

9 ERO D/Z 175/1/15 Colchester Co-op minutes, 2 September 1914.

10 ECC 14 August 1914.

thousand pounds. As well as sending their finished hampers of articles to domestic locations, they also dispatched them directly to the Dardanelles, Egypt, to prisoners of war in Germany, and to troops in France and Serbia.[11] The East Ham Women's War Help Society worked to provide parcels to British prisoners of war. Its aim was to send three parcels a fortnight to each man. Each parcel initially cost 10*s*., and consisted of tea, cocoa, sugar, butter, biscuits, corned beef, tinned sausage, Oxo, baked beans, condensed milk, soup powder, cigarettes and sweets.[12] These depots were the perfect means by which women were able to demonstrate their patriotism, feel valued and useful, and confident that they were achieving something significant. By operating as a closely knit group it also nurtured that most valuable of wartime commodities — civilian morale.

Wealthy, middle-class women with social standing were assured of a prominent role in women's war effort. Lady Gooch of Hylands Hall at Chelmsford helped to organise the hospital created on her and her husband's property. Lady Petre of Thorndon Hall assisted in the creation of the county milking scheme at her home and presided over the meetings of the Essex Womens' War Agricultural Association. Lady Rayleigh was the President of the Essex branch of the Soldiers and Sailors Federation. Others organised collections to raise money for worthy wartime causes and appeals. In 1915 the "ladies" of Chelmsford raised £200 by selling the Queen Alexandra's rose.[13] In August 1914 there were eighty women on the streets of Colchester collecting money for the Prince of Wales Fund.[14] Britain celebrated the National Festival of France on 14 July 1915. At Chelmsford, Clacton and Colchester, dozens of female collectors sold buttonhole flags saying "*Vive la France*" for a penny, as well as larger flags for display on cars and bicycles.[15] Women up and down the county rattled their tins and collected for Belgian and Serbian refugees, Romanian soldiers, British prisoners of war, Britain's Russian allies, and many others. One woman, a Mrs Godley, the wife of a territorial officer, grasped the War with eager hands when she took it upon herself to scour Dovercourt for German spies, and acted when she believed she had found two:

> She went behind a hedge, heard the men speaking in broken English to a little boy whom she had sent to ask the time. Leaving them she went and "flagwagged" her white parasol, which attracted the attention of the patrol near Dovercourt Church.[16]

11 Perfect, *Hornchurch*, 199-205.

12 Stokes, *East Ham*, 235.

13 ECC 14 August 1914.

14 CG 26 August 1914.

15 ECS 17 July 1915.

16 HDS 15 August 1914.

What became of those she had arrested is unknown. In all likelihood they were released when they were able to establish their identity.

As the troops poured into the barracks of Colchester and Warley and the camps scattered around the county, women were busily engaged in organising rooms where wives could visit their soldier-husbands, have their children cared for, and be given refreshments during their stay. Southend had a Servicemen's Wives Club which opened each day from noon to 8.30 p.m., complete with meeting rooms and a cheap two-course dinner.[17] Of course, neither the refreshments nor the dinner included alcohol. Many women threw themselves into their patriotic activities and brought a fervour for temperance with them, a fervour heightened by the War. Many women were already members of local temperance branches, with those at Chelmsford, Colchester, Ilford and Southend being particularly active.[18] There was a very large membership, for instance, of the Chelmsford Women's Total Abstinence Union.[19]

Many middle-class women showed their commitment to the war effort and their patriotism by joining either the Girls' Patriotic League or the League of Honour for Women and Girls, two pre-war organisations which were marshalled as part of the war effort. A branch of the league was set up at Colchester in November 1914. Each member swore the following oath:

> I promise, by the help of God, to do all that is in my power to uphold the honour of our nation and its defenders in this time of war, by prayer, purity, and temperance.[20]

By early 1915 there were seven hundred members at Colchester, and over two hundred and twenty thousand across the country. The league saw itself as the guardian of the nation's reputation by attending to the morals of its young women. It was "to watch over girls and young people to see that the honour and purity of womanhood was upheld." The social pedigree of its leaders was impeccable. Ethel Hutton, the wife of the mayor was the president, its secretary was the wife of K.L. Parry, a Nonconformist minister, and the wives and daughters of other Colchester worthies, such as the daughter of Wilson Marriage, formed the rest of the committee.[21] The Colchester branch of the Girls' Patriotic League opened its premises in 1916. It opened daily from midday until 2 p.m., and each evening until 9.30 p.m., although it was also available from 10 p.m. to 11 p.m. for women who had just finished a shift at the munitions works in the town.[22]

[17] SST 14 January 1915.

[18] ECC 23 March 1917.

[19] ECC 23 March 1917.

[20] ECT 21 November 1914.

[21] ECS 13 March 1915.

[22] ECS 8 July 1916.

The league's emphasis on the purity of British womanhood reminds us that these women (and many men) believed that their sex had a vital role to play in the war effort, a role which transcended raising the children of absent fathers, or of taking the places of male workers in munitions factories or tramcars. That role was to preserve and sustain the purity of its young women, and by doing so, to preserve the moral fibre of young people as a whole. Just as the War was being fought as a crusade against evil, so the moral standards of those young people left behind ought to be beyond reproach. Both young girls and young men needed protection from the temptations of the flesh in order to preserve the purity of the cause. That reality did not always follow such high-minded philosophy is evinced by the Girls' Aid Society in Chelmsford, a home for unmarried mothers which had forty-six residents in 1916. While on a visit the Bishop of Chelmsford declared himself pleased that none of the forty-six residents' children were the result of liaisons with servicemen.[23] This must have been something of a relief for him, as in April 1915 he had rejected newspaper reports that there were two hundred "war babies" in Essex, stating that there was, in fact, only one.[24] The Vicar of Goldhanger, F.T. Gardner, warned of the perils facing young girls, particularly from lascivious servicemen:

> And then there are such places where no good girl should be seen. Good Mothers will see that their daughters avoid late hours at night, and above all be more than ever careful over the perilous intimacy that arises between those who are "Keeping Company".[25]

His remarks were a reference to his fears about the dangers facing young women whose families had servicemen billeted on them. Older women faced the perils of increased independence resulting from the War. One woman war worker who travelled by train to Colchester, complained that Sunday train services in Essex were inconvenient, "to say nothing of the temptations they meet with while wandering about for hours in a strange town."[26]

As far as Gardner was concerned, women who had troops billeted upon them also had the additional responsibility of setting before them the example of Christian family values:

> In a house where grace is said before and after a meal — no bad words, no queer talk allowed because you are not used to it, where the men are encouraged to wait on themselves on Sunday

23 ECC 15 June 1917.

24 ECT 1 May 1915.

25 Goldhanger and Little Totham parish magazine, September 1915.

26 ECS 24 June 1916.

> morning because your church and communion calls you. You will be doing your part to help these men, as nothing like the influence of a good woman can, to become purer and better fitted to carry out what their country expects of them.[27]

Certain limited wartime roles were considered ideal for women, but there was considerable resistance to allowing women to undertake any which were not of a traditional nature. When invasion fears led to the creation of county emergency committees, a deputation of women saw the Lord Lieutenant to request that they be allowed to serve on them. They argued that women should be permitted to assume leadership roles in matters concerning food, shelter, children and evacuation of civilians in the event of invasion. Their arguments made little impression on the Lord Lieutenant who fobbed them off with a vague assurance that in the case of a "serious raid" the county's women could be "of assistance." He deftly avoided making any direct commitment.[28] When food committees were established in 1917 women were admitted to them on the grounds that the committees were concerned with what might be described as a domestic matter. Nevertheless, in every case women were in a definite minority. There were only two women on the Chelmsford Food Committee, which was untypical because most had only one, as at Halstead, Colchester, Castle Hedingham, Rochford and Stansted.[29] The only exception to this male domination of wartime committees was at Chelmsford, where the food committee was run by a female chief executive assisted by three other women, although all four of them were not committee members but operated in an administrative capacity. Military tribunals, which dealt with masculine concerns, were an almost exclusively male preserve. It is surprising then, that one woman, a Mrs P. Landon, sat on the Brentwood Tribunal at one point.[30]

The War did not lead to a radical reappraisal of the role of women in the Anglican Church. When the planning for the National Mission was in full swing in the late summer of 1916, the Bishops of London and Chelmsford let it be known that they were prepared to allow women to speak in churches during the mission. However, such a suggestion struck horror in the hearts of the more conservative members of the diocese, whose fertile imaginations saw such an innovation as the first step along the road leading inexorably towards the ordination of women. The strength of the opposition to his proposal stunned the Bishop of Chelmsford, and compelled him to backtrack very quickly to prevent the mission being wrecked by a huge schism before it had even begun. It was pointed out that his comments had been misinterpreted. He had, in fact, mentioned "special gatherings" which comprised entirely women and

[27] ECS March 1916.

[28] ECC 7 May 1915.

[29] ChBC minutes, 29 August 1917; ECC 7 September 1917.

[30] ECC 11 February 1916.

girls as the only places where women could speak. If a woman was invited to speak by an incumbent, the hardliners were mollified by the reassurance that "the speaker was not to use pulpit, lectern, or chancel steps", but was "to stand in some unofficial place." Recognising what lay at the root of the opposition, the Bishop stated categorically that, "This, of course, will not cause any assumption of the priestly office, which would be contrary to all Apostolic and Catholic teaching." At the time that the storm broke the bishop was on holiday in Teignmouth; having been contacted by the *Essex County Chronicle* which sought to apprise him of the "unseemly discussions" taking place in Essex which appeared to threaten the mission, he penned a prompt response which the newspaper printed. Although he conceded everything that the opposition wanted, his frustration at their narrow-minded attitude appears to be obvious:

> Women will not be allowed by the Bishop of London or myself under any circumstances to speak at ordinary or official services in Church. The opposition is founded on an absolutely wrong conception of what is proposed, and is illogical unless they refuse women the right to speak anywhere on religious matters.[31]

The bishop followed this up by withdrawing his permission, which he had earlier granted, for women missioners, whose role had been interpreted by conservatives as that of women preachers. Once again he expressed his frustration, regret and sadness, and almost incomprehension at those who opposed his plans, although he was prepared to sacrifice the wider needs of women in order to preserve the National Mission. The last sentence was a firm metaphorical slap in the face for those whose opposition was based on "ignorance and prejudice."

> It seems incredible that such a course would have been opposed, but so it is. Party passions have been aroused, controversy encouraged, and all this on the eve of the great movement which has been in our thoughts and prayers for months. Surely this has been the work of the Devil.
>
> Yet, what is to be done? The natural man would say, "Resist unfair agitation, largely begotten of ignorance and prejudice." But such a spirit would surely wreck the Mission, for no blessing could rest upon it conducted on such lines. *I have therefore decided that during the Mission I shall not sanction any woman telling her sisters of the Saviour's love in any Church in the Diocese of Chelmsford* [author's italics].[32]

31 ECC 11 August 1916.

32 ECC 25 August 1916.

The Canewdon and Southend Rurideaconal Conference voted to allow women to attend rurideaconal and diocesan conferences, but such views were not widespread.[33] At the 1917 Chelmsford Diocesan Conference there was support for a motion which favoured amending the regulations for rurideaconal and diocesan conferences which at that time excluded women communicants. Others saw any softening of the rules as the thin edge of the wedge and liable to give succour to the women's ordination movement. The Bishop of Chelmsford prefaced his views on the matter with a warm tribute praising the role of women in the War:

> in the last three years the women of this country had displayed a heroism unsurpassed by men, which had been an inspiration to the whole of our national life, and they had destroyed for ever the traditional view as to the place and function of women in the life of both Church and State.

However, he was not sufficiently inspired by women's war effort to signal a change in how they were treated in his diocese. He added that the Church needed to be cautious against "too sudden and too progressive alterations." An amendment tabled by him was passed by the conference. It advocated waiting until there had been further discussions on the subject at convocation. Like many men, the bishop's advocacy of delay was probably influenced by his views on women's abilities:

> In the national life it would be the women of power and intellectual force who would make her influence felt, whereas in many parishes the girls and women would be, for some years to come, least equipped for governing powers.[34]

The War did not reduce the intense hostility which still remained towards the idea of the ordination of women. At a meeting in Southend in 1920, speakers argued that women's ordination was not sanctioned by scripture, and would destroy any chance of a reunion with the Roman Catholic Church. Mrs. J.J. Whitehouse, wife of the Vicar of St John's, believed that such unwarranted action would strike at the heart of the Church and weaken the life of the country. There was strong opposition to women's ordination from many women at the meeting. A Miss Beay stated that "they did not want women to preach to them when they went to church."[35]

Although tens of thousands of men had enlisted and there were unfilled vacancies in many areas of employment, employers were reluctant to employ women in large numbers. By April 1915 Colchester women were meeting in the Town Hall to protest at the dilatory pace at which female employment was being planned, although by

[33] ECC 6 July 1917.

[34] ECC 12 October 1917.

[35] SST 11 November 1920.

then a government scheme to place women in munitions factories was under consideration.[36] This reluctance by male employers was not easily overcome. Certainly by the second half of 1915, there was a noticeable shortage of young men who had been employed in various occupations and employers were compelled to advertise for female replacements:

> Wanted. Young Lady with knowledge of Boot Trade. Apply Stead and Simpson, Colchester.
>
> A woman of business habits and ability may hear of good appointment at Singers, Colchester.
>
> Wanted at once, one or two smart Young Ladies to learn Photography; small salary to begin, with good prospects to applicants showing ability and taste.[37]

Small shopkeepers had little choice but to seek female replacements as soon as possible. Larger concerns hung on for as long as they could. By the summer of 1915 Colchester Corporation was experiencing a severe shortage of tram drivers. Over sixty per cent of its outside workers in the Tramways Department had enlisted by October 1914, and as enlistments continued, the borough's need to replace them became more acute. By May 1915 shortages were affecting services and the *Essex County Standard* was speculating that it was only a matter of time before female drivers and conductresses were employed. In July the Tramways Department conceded as much in its annual report.[38] However, the corporation refused to countenance this, and six months later advertisements were still being placed in the press which avoided appealing to women:

> Colchester Tramways are urgently in need of motormen and conductors. Preference given to men over or under military age or medically unfit for the Army.

The campaign failed to attract enough young men and three weeks later the council bowed to the inevitable in an advertisement which reeked of bad grace:

> The Colchester Tramways Committee are prepared to consider applications from suitable women for the post of Tram Car Conductresses. Wages to be on par with men. No war bonus available.[39]

36 ECS 24 April 1915.

37 ECS 14 August, 18 September, 4 December 1915.

38 CBC minutes, 31 July 1915.

39 CBC minutes, 5 June, 23 October, 13 November 1915.

Southend Town Council was even more grudging and procrastinating in its employment of women as tram drivers. Like the National Steam Car Company, it employed women as conductresses in 1915, by which time the council was hiring thirty-eight overcoats and fourteen oilskins for its new female workers.[40] However, employing women as tram drivers seems to have been seen as more damaging to male egos than women as conductresses. The council did not get round to discussing the issue until April 1916, when its Light Railways Committee decided not to hire women as tram drivers. This was grudgingly rescinded in January 1917, when it was decided to employ them "as a temporary expedient." In February an attempt to delay implementation by getting the decision referred back to the full council was defeated. Women were finally recruited when only six men could be found to be tram drivers, which left thirty-five vacancies.[41]

Resistance to the idea of employing married women as schoolteachers was overcome during the War, but once more it was a slow process and conceded to reluctantly. Male opposition was based on the belief that it was inappropriate for a married, and therefore a sexually active woman, to be given the charge of children. There were, of course, no such scruples regarding married, male teachers. Harwich Education Committee was countering male teacher shortages with married women as early as September 1914, but elsewhere it was a different story.[42] By mid-1915 teacher shortages in Essex were beginning to bite. Essex County Council had just granted leave to enlist to four head teachers, nine assistant teachers and a handicraft teacher, and was being forced to consider married women as replacements. One councillor, Dr Murray Aynsley, strongly disapproved, supporting his misogynist views with the allegation that "it has been found that women teachers do not bring up boys to be as manly as the men teachers."[43] Nevertheless appointments were made in the teeth of serious opposition. Colchester's Education Committee took the unprecedented step of extending contracts to women who became engaged to be married:

> They [the Committee] also recommend that, in view of the exceptional circumstances, Miss W. Moss, an assistant teacher at East Ward School, whose marriage was impending, and whose engagement would terminate *ipso facto* on marriage, should be retained as a teacher on supply at the salary she is receiving.[44]

The "exceptional circumstances" mentioned was a reference to the eleven

40 SBC minutes, 21 July, 22 September, 17 October 1916.

41 SBC minutes, 19 January, 20 February, 9 March 1917.

42 HDS 3 October 1914.

43 ECC 2 July 1915.

44 ECS 31 July 1915.

vacancies caused by enlistment that the committee had to fill with only four female replacements found from college.[45] In 1916 an even greater staff shortage forced the committee to abandon wholesale its reluctance to employ married women. From then on, married women who had earlier resigned upon marriage were allowed to return on supply for the same salaries they had received before their resignation.[46] Although teachers were relatively well paid there was, as in other professions and jobs, a significant difference between male and female salaries. When the Essex County Council salary scale was amended in October 1917, male head teachers were paid £200-£300 a year, female head teachers only £150-£240. Assistant male teachers received £110-£175, assistant female teachers £100-£135.[47] Not surprisingly with these sorts of differentials, thirty female uncertified and supplementary teachers employed by Chelmsford Education Committee requested a pay rise that took into account the rising cost of living.[48]

In agriculture there was determined opposition to female employment throughout the War, regardless of the severe labour shortage which farmers constantly complained about. Farmers objected to the drafting of women on to farms for a variety of reasons — they could not do hard work, they were unused to working with animals, they were not mechanically minded and could not be expected to handle threshing machines or the new tractors which were appearing on farms.[49] Much of the opposition was misogynist and based on a belief of the physical and mental inferiority of women. The Essex War Agricultural Committee believed that it had a more measured appreciation of women on farms, classifying them into three categories — "Women accustomed to work on the land", "partly trained women of education", and the "hopelessly inefficient amateur".[50] Farm labourers also feared that if farming was flooded with cheap, female labour their wages would be at risk. For this reason labourers in the Braintree area refused to teach women their job unless they were paid the same wages.[51] However obdurate they might have been the labour shortage forced most farmers to become reconciled to female labour. By the spring of 1915, the Essex Education Committee had started a scheme to train women, girls and boys in milking. The scheme failed to attract local working-class women, but did draw in large numbers from "the educated classes, who came forward from patriotic motives."[52] Working-class women often rejected farm work, which paid 24*s.* a week, because munitions work paid 30*s.* In the Tiptree and Coggeshall areas, where women

45 ECT 3 August 1915.

46 CBC minutes, Education Committee, annual report, 1916.

47 ECC 14 September 1917.

48 ECC 22 September 1916.

49 ECC 23 April 1915.

50 SST 13 July 1915.

51 ECC 23 March 1917.

52 ECC 30 April 1915; ECT 6 January 1917.

had for years been employed in the soft fruit industry, female employment in farming was more widespread, particularly on the more progressive Strutt and Parker estates at Feering. There women were employed hoeing, harvesting peas and hay, cutting beans, picking and sorting potatoes, and spreading manure.[53] In Orsett and Romford too, farmers were prepared to place women in jobs vacated by male labourers.[54] The numbers of women employed in agriculture began to increase. According to the Essex War Agricultural Committee, at the beginning of 1916 there were only 409 at work in the county. By June the number registered was about three thousand, five hundred; with 368 at work in: Ongar (158), Billericay (30), Braintree (102), and Bishop Stortford (78). In Rochford there had been almost two hundred women employed on farms before the War, by 1917 there were three hundred. During 1917 registration increased exponentially, and by the end of August there were some seven thousand women at work full-time, in addition to a large number of part-time workers.[55] There was at least one slightly eccentric offer. In 1917 the ladies of the Metropolitan Academy of Music offered their services at harvest time. The Essex Farmers' Union, anticipating that their talents lay elsewhere, turned down the offer.[56] The general trend towards employing women was reasonably successful, but it failed to draw into farming the numbers of women for which the authorities had hoped.

Despite resistance to women's employment, they were drafted into several spheres of work. Chelmsford Corporation appointed a female gas meter inspector in 1915, and two years later employed two women workers in the gasworks yard.[57] Colchester Corporation gave permission for five female taxi drivers to ply their trade in 1917.[58] The first two female assistants to be employed at Colchester Library were working by February 1915, and the town's first postwoman, a Miss Page, appeared on its streets in the summer of the following year. By the end of 1916 several postwomen were employed.[59] Although the town's rose growers were prepared to employ young boys, it was not until 1916 that women were hired. Essex's police forces on the other hand, were more reluctant to employ women, either as clerks or police officers, and it was not until 1917 that a small number of women were accepted at places like Colchester. Even after this there was a rather bemused debate in the local press about whether women could be sworn in, could arrest anyone, or if they had the same authority as men.[60] Thousands of women were employed at Braintree, where it was said that "they have invaded every sphere of labour." They were also working in large numbers

53 ECC 19 November 1915.

54 ECC 24 March 1916.

55 ECC 18 February, 28 April, 12, 26 May, 9 June 1916, 31 August 1917.

56 ECC 8 June 1917.

57 ECC 28 December 1917.

58 ECS 6 October 1917.

59 ECS 10 June, 16 December 1916.

60 ECS 5 January 1918.

in the seed growing industry around Coggeshall.[61]

Thousands were employed in munitions factories at places like Kynochtown and Waltham Abbey, and at the military engineering establishments created when firms manufacturing peacetime products turned to military production. Catherine Brown and her sister worked from 1915 to 1917 at Kynoch's munitions factory.[62] She worked from 6 a.m. to 6 p.m., Monday to Saturday, alternating each week with night duty. In 1915 she was paid 4½*d.* an hour, with time and a half on Saturday nights, although when she left in 1917 the hourly rate had increased to 7½*d.* Some of the workforce were local girls who arrived daily in lorries, others came from further afield and lived in lodgings in nearby Corringham or Stanford-le-Hope. Catherine Brown shared a room in Corringham with two other Kynoch girls, the landlady providing them with a packed lunch, although the works canteen provided tea and it was possible to obtain a hot meal there too.

They were transported to work on a light railway which ran from Corringham to Kynochtown. Once they had clocked-in, the women changed into their "danger clothes", which were khaki faced with red, and when they arrived at their designated place of work they put on overshoes to avoid carrying grit into the workroom.

Catherine Brown worked on 20 Range making cordite using ether and alcohol. The trays of cordite had to be taken outside of each room periodically and stored, because the fumes which they gave off were capable of causing anesthesia if they were allowed to build up. On one occasion her sister was rendered almost unconscious by the fumes and she had to be placed in the Ambulance Room for most of the night. As the needs of the War increased, the company expanded and employed more and more women, which resulted in the building of the Colony at Corringham. The Colony, an additional workers' settlement, was run by other women. Catherine Brown and her sister moved there. The charges were inexpensive, lunches were provided and these could be heated up at work. When the women returned from work, they were served with a hot meal. The Colony had a recreation room and many social events were organised, including an historical pageant.

The work was far from pleasant and exceedingly dangerous. Catherine Brown later recalled two accidents that occurred while she worked there. One of them was an explosion during the manufacturing of cordite which resulted in one girl losing her right hand. Until the accident she had been a keen pianist. The explosion also caused a fire and the whole factory had to be evacuated.

In a continuation of pre-war practices women were generally paid less than men. Female schoolteachers, for instance, were paid significantly less than their male counterparts. This is demonstrated by the figures from the Colchester Education Committee, which show pre-war salaries for male and female teachers, alongside the

[61] ECC 23 March 1917.

[62] This account is dependant on Catherine Brown's recollection of her time at Kynoch's, which she wrote in 1977, ERO T/Z 169.

revised salary scale introduced in the summer of 1918:

	Pre-war	1918 Scale
Headmasters	£170-320	£270-400
Headmistresses	£130-170	£185-300
Assistant master (certificated)	£140	£230
Assistant mistresses (certificated)	£60-70	£100[63]

In 1915 female clerks employed by the Essex Education Committee complained at the county's reluctance to raise their salaries. Southend Town Council's female deckchair collectors were paid 20*s.* a week while their male counterparts received 25*s.* The borough's bus and tram conductresses were also paid less than the men. A male champion, Almey St John Adcock of Leigh, accused the council of sweating women in its employ. He also urged working men to re-evaluate their attitude towards women workers:

> Just so long as the working man regards the working woman as his enemy in the labour market, just so long will she continue to be used as an unwilling tool to undermine his wages by the bulk of the employing classes.[64]

The Braintree Urban Military Tribunal discovered that West & Sons, a firm of brush manufacturers, opposed the conscription of their employees because the men refused to train women workers as replacements unless they were paid the same wages as the men. The company claimed it could not do this because the women's work was inferior. The Braintree and Bocking branch of the Workers' Union alleged that West & Sons employed women merely because they were cheap labour.[65]

Most women felt aggrieved that their pay never approached that of men. Women workers at Courtauld's silk mills were disgruntled that their war bonus was 9*s.*, well below the 12*s.* 3*d.* awarded to male employees.[66] There were other more obvious injustices. At Braintree, with its high concentration of women war workers, the Urban Food Committee received hundreds of requests from women who claimed that the nature of the heavy work they did entitled them to receive supplementary rations. None of their appeals were successful.[67] On the other hand, some men saw working women as undermining the whole concept of the primacy of male employment. In late

63 ECT 1 June 1918.

64 SST 27 April 1916.

65 ECC 23 March 1917.

66 ECC 2 November 1917.

67 ECC 19 April 1918.

1917, the Southend branch of the National Federation of Discharged Soldiers and Sailors protested at the borough's employment of conductresses on trams while discharged soldiers were unemployed.[68]

Although women were led to believe that the granting of the vote in 1918 was a reward for their war work, local women were not satisfied that those under thirty were still disenfranchised. "Are 19 year-old men better able to use the vote than a professional female graduate?" asked the Chelmsford League for Women's Suffrage. Despite the disappointment, individual women achieved some modest successes in the first post-war elections. In the Epping Urban District Council elections of 1919 the town's branch of the Workers' Union returned two female councillors out of the four elected. The next year saw a woman, a Mrs Allan, supported by the town's Women's Institute, come top of the poll.[69] In 1920 a candidate for the non-party Women's Freedom League stood in Southend's Chalkwell ward. Before the War ended, Colchester had two female councillors. The Colchester Women's Citizenship Association, which was affiliated to the National Union of Societies for Equal Citizenship, was a non-party organization which aimed to support any woman standing for parliamentary or local government elections, provided their "feminist principles" were put before their party political views. When a Colchester councillor gave up his seat after being made an alderman, the vacancy was filled by Catherine Hunt, both as recognition of her long-term service to the town and her stalwart war work. In the November elections of 1920 a Mrs E.M. Green stood as a Labour candidate in the town's South Ward, but was defeated.[70]

It would be an exaggeration to say that the War effected a permanent transformation of the lives of most women in Essex, or anywhere in Britain. Nor did it result in a significant change in the way that women were viewed by many men, particularly in the job market. Thousands of Essex women, both single and married, had worked full-time before 1914. For many women work in factories and workshops was not unusual. What was new, was the fact that tens of thousands of women had to deal with the absence of their husbands, sons, brothers and fathers, and in many cases cope with a permanent loss. In many cases war work was both a financial necessity and a social godsend. War wages for most women were higher than in peacetime, and billeting too played its part in ensuring that there was little economic distress outside of the coastal resorts. However, for many men, whatever the sacrifices and heroism of women's war effort, female incursions into traditionally male spheres of employment was but a temporary phenomenon, to be tolerated during the War but definitely not to be approved of, or continued beyond the Armistice. Many employers were at first reluctant to employ women, and when they did they paid them lower rates than men, and as soon as demobilised men began to

[68] ECC 14 December 1917.

[69] ECC 2 April 1920.

[70] SST 14 October 1920; ECT 10 January 1920.

return home they dismissed their female employees with unseemly haste. Where there was insufficient speed in the dismissal of female employees, demobbed men's organisations were quick to urge a return to pre-war 'normality'. The vote was granted to women, supposedly as a reward for their wartime patriotism, but only to women over thirty. The Church of England lauded the role of women, and granted them equal rights with men on the new parochial church councils, but refused to countenance any moves towards the ordination of women. In many respects the War left women exactly where they had been in 1914.

CHAPTER TEN

Enemies Within: Spies, Aliens and Criminals

ALIENS IN ESSEX.

HOSTILE DEMONSTRATION AT SAFFRON WALDEN.

A large number of aliens were arrested in various parts of the country on Thursday.

At Ilford two 'bus loads of Germans were taken to a concentration camp. Several German tradesmen have closed their shops. Arrests were also made at Barking.

Strong feeling against Germans has been manifested this week at Saffron Walden, where Cr. Midgley's house in London Road was attacked by a crowd in the belief that he was entertaining two Germans—a man and wife. Mr. Midgley's visitors, acting an advice, left before the hostile demonstration took place.

There have been demonstrations also against tradesmen with German names in the Leyton district.

HARWICH, FELIXSTOWE AND CLACTON.

In Harwich, Dovercourt, Felixstowe and Clacton-on-Sea the sweeping up of aliens began immediately the war was declared. Between sixty and seventy alien enemies of military age were intercepted by Special Service officers of Scotland Yard as they attempted to board steamers from Harwich to the Continent, and these were handed over to the military authorities and interned.

Harwich is a prohibited port. The recent Government order for the removal of alien enemies called for no special further action. It is reported that there are only two or three enemy aliens now in Harwich, and one of these is an old lady of about eighty who married an Englishman and is unable to leave her house.

'Aliens' in Essex were soon the subject of newspaper articles and worse.

(ERO: ECS October 1914)

AS WE HAVE ALREADY SEEN in Chapter 7, the start of the War raised genuine fears about the possibility of a German invasion of Essex. The precipitous collapse of the holiday season for the county's seaside resorts was a significant result of these fears, as both Essex people and Londoners cancelled their bookings en masse. In those early days and weeks of the War there was both official concern for, and widespread public alarm at, the possibility of the Germans being assisted by spies and aliens. A secret register of aliens living in this country had already been compiled by the Government before the War. It revealed the presence of over twenty-eight thousand people of foreign extraction, or 'aliens', over eleven thousand of whom were of German or Austrian extraction. The 1911 census had revealed that 5,248 aliens lived in the county, including 2,437 Germans and 555 Austro-Hungarians, of whom 1,970 were aliens, the rest being naturalised British citizens.[1] Consequently, the day after War was declared, the Government, armed with these facts, passed the Alien Restrictions Act, making it necessary for aliens to register with the police, restricting their movement and giving the police the power to remove them from prohibited areas.[2] As we have already seen the Essex coast and certain inland areas were classified as part of this prohibited zone, either because of their military and naval importance, or because of their proximity to the coast. These changes, together with the rapidly enforced lighting restrictions in those areas, probably unintentionally fuelled the fears of the local population. Within days of the outbreak of war, boy scouts were being used to patrol road and rail routes on the assumption that the large number of enemy aliens in Essex threatened the county's telegraph lines.[3] Captain Ffinch, the man in charge of the county's special constables, had a decidedly jaundiced view of Essex residents of German or Austro-Hungarian descent when wrote that

> The Authorities think a German raid is possible — in which case undoubtedly Germans and pro-Germans in England will try to help by committing crimes and damage in Essex.[4]

Certainly some individuals were genuinely alarmed by the potential harm that could be done by enemy aliens, those who in the Second World War would be described as 'fifth columnists'. The fear of spies was felt in even the smallest community; Marion Todd of Wickham Bishops expressed her concerns:

> I would not harbour any spies knowingly. I despise them too much — it seems the East Coast is not clear of them yet, I think

1 CG 28 October 1914.

2 DeGroot, *Blighty*, 157.

3 Hunt, 60.

4 ERO D/Z 77/1, letter from Ffinch, 12 November 1914.

> stronger measures should be taken for good natured tolerance of Germans may mean death to some of our men. I may be wrong, but I think they should be well looked after.[5]

Newspaper reports give us some idea of both the paranoia which gripped individuals and of the type of unfortunates who fell victim to it. Within a day of war breaking out two men were arrested at Clacton for flying a kite with wire suspiciously thin enough to suggest that they might be attempting some sort of telegraphic transmission to German vessels in the North Sea.[6] At Harwich, one man named Stesel was apprehended on the day before war began. Like the Bishop of Colchester in France, he was in possession of a camera and was further regarded with suspicion because "he had somewhat the appearance of a German."[7] After investigations, the Clacton kite flyers were released and Stesel, who turned out to be an American, was allowed to continue on his temporarily interrupted journey to New York. In January 1915, Charles Vorwerch, a seaman, and a registered German, was sentenced to six months imprisonment with hard labour for entering the Royal Albert Dock without a permit. He claimed that he was merely seeking work. Gustav Plock received three months hard labour for the same offence.[8] Ernest Pierce, the stage manager of the visiting production of *Princess Caprice* at the Colchester Theatre Royal, was arrested at Wivenhoe for sketching, but released two hours later.[9] Anyone, it seems, who did not possess what were considered to be the archetypal facial features of an Englishman, whatever they were perceived as being, was immediately suspected of malevolent intentions. At St Botolph station a "foreign looking man, over six feet high, with a military bearing" was arrested for supposedly looking over boxes of ammunition. Further enquiries revealed that he was a Norwegian. He too was released.[10] Harwich, with its important naval installations, was definitely the place to avoid for those with heavy moustaches, swarthy complexions or unshaven faces. In the first week of war several 'spies' were arrested there, and quickly released without charges being made.[11] At Dovercourt one accusation resulted in a sensational court case. William Whitehead, a naturalised German, and the popular proprietor of the Victoria Hotel, was arrested on suspicion of using carrier pigeons to convey information to the Germans regarding the arrival and departure of ships at Harwich.

5 ERO D/DGd/C44.

6 EEA 8 August 1914.

7 ECS 5 August 1914; EEA 8 August 1914. As we saw in Chapter 2 the Bishop of Colchester was briefly detained by the authorities in France for a similarly unfortunate use of his camera whilst on holiday there.

8 ECC 5 February 1915.

9 ECT 7 November 1914.

10 ECT 8 August 1914.

11 CG 12 August 1914.

The evidence against him seemed to be either entirely circumstantial or completely invented. He was apparently seen, "by persons conversant with pigeons", releasing the birds, which were then observed flying off, "probably to Holland". The Guildhall, Harwich, where Whitehead's case was heard a fortnight later, was crowded with people. When the case against him was dismissed his discharge was accomplished "amid cheers from the crowded court."[12] At Basildon, Henry Ubele, a local resident, was also arrested by the military on suspicion of using carrier pigeons to convey messages to the enemy. Five soldiers took him away. His barn, from where a solitary pigeon was seen to fly, was searched, but nothing incriminating was found. Ubele neither kept not bred pigeons, nor was there any proof that the offending bird was even a carrier pigeon. Not surprisingly, the case against him was dismissed.[13] Nothing can convey the hysteria of the time and the belief that local people were attempting to communicate with the enemy better than the story of what happened to poor Henry Harmer of Maldon. The police report of the incident notes that:

> Considerable suspicion was aroused amongst the residents at Maldon at 8.15 p.m. 13th June 1915 by a pigeon which had settled on the roof of Harmer's house, causing a crowd of 200-300 persons to assemble. The police endeavoured to catch the pigeon but on being disturbed it flew away in the direction of Purleigh and was lost sight of. Harmer's house was subsequently searched but nothing was found there to incriminate him. P.C. Bolden made further inquiries and ascertained that two pigeons had escaped from the premises of John Ewers, Market Hill, Maldon, one had returned but the other had not.[14]

Rumours of the supposedly frenzied activity of German spies and their agents was even covered in the *Daily Express* on 29 April 1915, in articles headlined "Signals from the East Coast" and "German agents at work in Essex".[15] The extent of the public's gullibility in accepting the more ludicrous stories provides an astonishing indication of their fear of German treachery. In the summer of 1915 one story going the rounds in Colchester was that the demolition of Middle Row and St Runwald's Church years earlier could be directly attributed to German spitefulness. The story had it that at the time that a committee was debating what to do with these properties, Colchester was visited by a high-ranking member of the German royal family. His chance remark in the High Street, that it was a pity that it was disfigured

12 ECT 22 August, 5 September 1914.

13 ECC 23 April 1915.

14 ERO J/P 12/6, Essex Police Investigations.

15 ECS 1 May 1915.

by these ugly buildings, was said to have been influential in their destruction.[16]

Distance from the prohibited zone was no guarantee that cooler heads would respond more rationally to the appearance of strangers. In the small village of Great Leighs in September 1914, an itinerant lace seller was arrested and spent the night in gaol because his accent was thought to sound suspiciously like that of a German. A few weeks later in the same area a surveyor employed by the Ordnance Survey was also arrested by troops because his accent did not fit with that of the locals. Over the next few days during the course of his work he was questioned on several occasions by soldiers, police and local busybodies. He was actually arrested on six different occasions by the six special constables in the six districts of Great Waltham. He was only rescued from further harassment by pleading the protection of Colonel Tufnell, a local magistrate.[17] At Braintree, a foreigner who lacked any command of English, was arrested in a barber's shop after gesticulating that he required a haircut.[18] Throughout the county unwary artists and camera enthusiasts found themselves unexpectedly enjoying the pleasures of a police cell for a few hours. The Halstead Union Workhouse had been turned into a barracks for German prisoners of war. The Germans were hired out to local farmers and others to the unease of some of the local population. They travelled unescorted or with a very small escort on the Colne Valley Railway, taking up seats that would have been occupied by civilian passengers. The fact that they worked on local roads and engaged in conversation with passers-by was considered by some to be scandalous. One person was outraged that the prisoners worked in a nursery garden at Marks Tey, not far from English women workers:

> The Germans are themselves with the civil population. People seem to forget that these prisoners are the fellows of the men who commit every kind of atrocity in Europe, and who murder from submarines our people at sea ... The German under strict discipline is a very good servant, but given a free hand is a dangerous master.[19]

Such was the alarmist atmosphere of these years, that even British soldiers came under suspicion. An anonymous person wrote to the Maldon District Emergency Committee expressing their concerns about a labour gang of about one hundred and fifty men of the 31st Middlesex Regiment located in Purleigh and Cold Norton. The letter they wrote alleged that many of these soldiers had been heard expressing pro-German sympathies, adding that "many of them are men of German origin, and that, in case of invasion of this District, these men would be of grave menace to the

16 ECS 11 September 1915.

17 Clark, *Diary*, 19-20, 24-5.

18 ECC 7 August 1914.

19 ERO L/P 3/35, Harlow Emergency Committee.

Realm."[20] The committee forwarded the letter to the War Office which dismissed it with the note that "Local rumours were exaggerated."

Wartime suspicion offered the perfect opportunity for local busybodies to settle old scores, to exact revenge for past, or even imagined, slights, and it gave free rein to anyone to indulge in malicious accusations, whatever their real motivation. Distanced by time from their historical context, the activities of such busybodies may now appear to be rather amusing, perhaps even farcical. However, they were far from comical to those individuals who had their ancestry and loyalty impugned in a far more subtle, but no less insidious way; those who were the victims of innuendo and sly, malicious rumours. Councillor Arthur Midgely's house in Saffron Walden was attacked in September 1914 because he entertained two German friends there. A religious man, he held regular meetings in the market square, but on the day that his German friends left he was heckled and booed, and he and his associates were advised by the police to leave. A crowd of about five hundred people followed him to his home and despite the presence of the police, missiles were thrown which broke several windows and damaged his greenhouse.[21] At Clacton, a local resident, Mr G.L. Hoffman, almost certainly targeted because of his name, felt compelled to place a notice in the local press saying "Being a true-born Britisher, I wish to give the lie to the malicious report in circulation in this town, that I have been deported for being a German."[22]

George Waldeck, postmaster of the North Station Post Office in Colchester, placed a similar notice from his solicitor in the *Colchester Gazette*, aiming to refute rumours that he too was a German.[23] One wonders whether or not those who spread these rumours felt differently about their actions when Waldeck's brother, Frederick, was lost aboard H.M.S. *Aboukir* only three weeks later. At a meeting of the Colchester Brewing Company oblique questions were asked probing the nationality of a Mr Rothbarth, a director of the company. Other directors sprang to his defence, pointing out that he had lived in England since childhood and that he was a naturalised Englishman whose son was a serving officer.[24] Local clergymen with suspiciously foreign sounding surnames were not exempt from the hysteria. G.M. Behr, priest-in-charge of St Stephen's, Colchester, used his parish magazine to broadcast his defence:

> may I just say I am not a German — that I was born in England and have never set foot on German soil, not even for a holiday; that my mother is English, born and bred. My father was indeed of German nationality, but was naturalised on coming to England somewhere back as far as the "sixties."[25]

20 ERO 3/35, Maldon District Emergency Committee, May 1917.

21 White, *Saffron Walden*, 179; WWN 28 October 1914.

22 EEA, 12 September 1914.

23 CG 16 September 1914.

24 CG 14 October 1914.

25 ECS 22 August 1914.

The Mayor of Maldon, Alderman H.A. Krohn, had to resort to the columns of the *Essex County Chronicle* to deny rumours that he was German and that he had been asked to resign as mayor.[26] Allegations were made in the Southend Council Chamber that Councillor H.W. Cooney was a director of a German-controlled company. It also came to light that the two directors of the Southend Steam Packet Company were both naturalised citizens and had lived in England for almost twenty years.[27]

Even local entertainment failed to elude the clutches of this anti-alien hysteria. At the conclusion of their Friday performance at the Clacton Pavilion on 28 August 1914, Mr Vale Lane's White Band had their rendition of 'God Save the King' interrupted when someone in the audience took exception to the band's tympanist remaining seated. An unpleasant argument resulted. The next day Mr Lane issued circulars stating that every member of his band was of British stock, and that the tympanist in question had remained seated for practical reasons rather than a lack of patriotism.[28] Misplaced local enthusiasm was sometimes complemented by official fervour in an attempt to root out those who presented a possible hazard, however unlikely. In December 1916 Emily Ramspott, a music hall artiste who was appearing at the Hippodrome, Southend, was fined 10*s*. for each of two offences — entering Southend without an identity book and failing to register as an enemy alien. Miss Ramspott's mother was married to a German who had been interned at Wakefield, and the male half of her parentage meant that she was regarded as a security risk.[29]

The eager willingness of seemingly public-spirited and patriotically-minded individuals to do their duty in rather unfortunate ways was perhaps unwittingly sanctioned by officialdom. The instructions issued to special constables on 2 September 1914 were deliberately vague and susceptible of a wide interpretation. They were ordered

> To take notice of all passers-by and stop and question *all who look like foreigners or suspicious persons*, and if the Special Constable suspects them to be either German or Austrian to demand their permits ... and unless produced to detain the suspects. [author's italics][30]

A few months later the chief constable amended earlier instructions to give his officers even greater freedom of action:

> In times such as the present the Police will be well advised to look upon everything with suspicion until their loyalty is proved

26 ECC 30 October 1914.

27 SST 22 April 1915.

28 CG 2 September 1914.

29 ECC 29 December 1916.

30 ERO D/Z 77/1, Unett to police superintendents, 29 July 1915.

> *and not start by assuming that everyone is loyal until something occurs to show they are otherwise.* [author's italics][31]

Clearly when it came to the political control and the security of the nation in wartime, the much vaunted principles of British liberalism were not regarded as sacrosanct. Two West Mersea men, Leonard Weaver and his son Leonard, probably thought not. The two men, keen to begin the construction of a light railway from Mersea Island to Colchester, obtained the permission of the Board of Trade to begin sketching out maps and plans of the route. Unfortunately, they omitted to obtain the permission of the military authorities, who promptly arrested them for carrying out dangerous activities in the prohibited area. The case against them was eventually dropped, but the elder Weaver was severely criticised for defending his actions in a letter to the *Essex County Telegraph* in which he revealed details about the depth of water and potential dock facilities locally, details, which it was alleged, could easily have fallen into the hands of the enemy and been used in the event of an invasion.[32]

Some of the incidents noted above might be ascribed to the heightened emotions resulting from the onset of war, which gripped people with an over-zealous and fearful patriotism. The playing out of these emotions led to the embarrassing arrest of many unfortunate individuals who looked 'foreign', or who had inadvertently wandered into a prohibited area, or were seen using a camera, particularly in urban areas. These public displays of local panic either died out, or were simply no longer reported in the press by the middle of 1915. As people's nerves settled and as no upsurge of alien sabotage manifested itself, there was less need to see spies around every corner.

However, this did not mean that everyone was convinced that the danger from aliens and spies was past, and throughout the War citizens of Essex continued to be accused of either unpatriotic or potentially treasonable behaviour. Many of them were blissfully unaware of the accusations that had been levelled against them, but some were all too conscious of the fact. Dozens of these accusations were made throughout Essex. Almost all of them were based on information provided by other Essex residents, which arrived on the doorsteps or through the letterboxes of various police stations, or were simply voiced to the local bobby.[33] Had England been an authoritarian state similar to Revolutionary France, the Third Reich or Stalinist Russia, one might be tempted to describe these actions as 'denunciations'.

Although the original notes and letters sent to the authorities do not appear to have survived, the police comments on them have and they provide sufficient evidence in many cases that such information was almost wholly unreliable. Victor Montgomery,

31 ERO D/Z 77/1, Unett to Police Superintendents, 29 July 1915.

32 ECT 17 October 1914; ECS 24 October 1914.

33 The following section is based on ERO J/P 12/6, which is a file entitled simply, 'The War: Suspects'.

a resident of West Mersea, fell under suspicion when reports were made of someone allegedly signalling to the enemy at Tollesbury. Special Constable Trim "and others" stated that they "believed him to be an Austrian *but no definite reasons are given*" [author's italics]. Perhaps of greater significance to the accusation was the additional comment added by a police officer at Chelmsford, "Friction exists between Mrs Montgomery and Special Constable Trim." The often absurd basis of these denunciations is exposed in this report of a police interview with a Mrs Carpenter of South Essex, who was reported by a neighbour:

> I thought I know what you mean. Some days ago a woman living in the neighbourhood, who is a busybody and always interfering with other peoples' business, said to me, "Mrs C. you are not a German are you?" I jokingly replied, Yes, I think I must be a Prussian. I thought no more of it and had no idea that she would say anything about it or I would not have said it. I had no idea it would cause all this trouble.

Maurice Goodrick of Romford was investigated by the police after various allegations were made about him. He too fell foul of a malicious individual who exploited the opportunity presented by the War to vent her spite on him:

> Enquiry was made but none of the allegations could be verified and it was found that they emanated from a Mrs Romaine James, a journalist of 103 Etchingham Road, Church End, Finchley, out of spite, she having had to make a written apology to Goodrick in 1915 for stating that he was a German spy.

Police dismissed equally unfounded allegations against Alfred Pawle of Burnham, ascribing them to jealousy of him among local fishermen "caused no doubt by the fact that he is superior to the professional fishing class."

Distance proved to be no barrier to the desire to inform on the locals. Frank Gourlay, postmaster of Tendring, fell under a cloud because he was married to a German woman. Neither the fact that she had already been relieved of her duties as postmistress, nor the common knowledge that the couple had a son serving in the Royal Navy and another in the Third Suffolk Regiment, was a deterrent to gossip. Private G. Sherring, presumably a Tendring resident, was serving with the West Somerset Yeomanry when he passed information through the Yeovil police alleging that Mrs Gourlay "has German connections and sympathies and in his opinion requires watching."

As in the witch crazes of the sixteenth and seventeenth centuries, suspicion quickly fell upon those who did not seem to conform to the accepted norms of social behaviour of the time. William Harper, Clacton's postmaster since 1911, was described as being "of so austere and of unapproachable manner that nobody appears to know anything about him". The police dismissed out of hand the allegation that he was a German. William Harrowers of Little Kirby was described as "a suspicious German who wanders about at all hours of the night". A police check refuted this and revealed that Harrowers was a "Scotchman". At Dovercourt an "elderly maiden lady" named Sara MacDonald, born in Canada of Scottish parents, was said to have been behaving suspiciously. Perhaps significantly she was described as "a very eccentric person." Mrs Campbell-Ogilvie of Manningtree was alleged to be a German and "violently anti-English". The police decided that she was no risk at all, but their comment that she was "an interfering woman" probably got nearer to the truth about why she was accused. Harry Rome, of Canvey Island, was expelled from Essex because as well as appearing to be under the thumb of his German wife, he was "at times ... very eccentric [and] of drinking habits." Three other Essex residents were investigated seemingly because of unconventional habits. J. Birchenough was said to be "very reserved in his manner." A man named Bedingfield was informed on because "He does not associate with the people of the District and on this account is regarded with suspicion." A man by the name of Smith was also condemned because "he does not associate with the people of the district."

Life could be equally dangerous for those who placed themselves outside the bounds of conventional respectability. Dr Cecil Bowman, a weekend resident of East Mersea for some six years, was said to be "regarded with some suspicion by the Military Authorities who state that he is addicted to drink and mixes with undesirable company." F. Farr of Little Oakley was informed on by Sir Henry Earle, who was probably impugning his sexuality, because whilst a resident at Harwich, he "is said to have consorted in an odd way with sailors and talked to them."

C.B. Norman of Brentwood was described in the police report as "a black sheep." It was alleged that he had been cashiered from the Army in 1877, had committed various "financial irregularities" and spent time in prison. He was accused of being a Turkish spy. In his trips abroad he was said to have used "every opportunity of establishing cosmopolitan relations, and especially with Germans." Although he was over seventy years of age, the report concluded that "his former history cannot be ignored at this juncture and that he is a potential danger to national interests who should not be lost sight of." A Mrs Booth fell foul of local informants when she moved in with the elderly and practically blind Reverend Swinerton of Tolleshunt Major in order to assist him with his parish work. Her large grey car was said to have been driven around the area guiding German airships on their bombing raids. The police concluded that since her arrival there had been "some trouble between local officials and the Vicar", and that, "Ever since [Mrs Booth's arrival] rumours and idle gossip have been quite common."

There were a variety of other accusations levelled at Essex people, usually by anonymous informants. Connections with Germany or Austria, whether in the past or present, and no matter how feeble, were always investigated. Margaret Mounsey and her daughters, of Dedham, were "supposed to be in Communication with Germany in some mysterious way." The core of the allegation was that Margaret Mounsey, an American by birth, had spent three winters in Dresden prior to 1893 and had lived in Berlin as a child. It was alleged in a letter of 24 November 1915 that Agnes Wadley of West Bergholt had German sympathies. As with the Mounseys, it was time that she had spent as a maid in Brussels that was used against her. Margaret Paton, an elderly resident of Tolleshunt D'Arcy, was denounced for supposedly receiving payments from German banks in England. Here too the tenuous thread of information behind the allegation was fuelled by the fact that her sister had been a lady's companion in Austria. Almost equally incredible was the allegation against John Etty of Frinton, based on his receipt of £2 by money orders from the Hague, a neutral capital. George Beneke of Earls Colne, born in Hanover but naturalised in 1882, and for many years a captain in the East Lancashire Regiment, was accused because "a great many people" thought he was a spy. "Plans of fortification", it was alleged, "have been seen in his possession." Harold Picton of Ugley was denounced because he befriended a young German boy who had been ill-treated by his stepfather, and because he sent the boy parcels after he was placed in a civilian internment camp. Picton too, "was of a quiet disposition and associates with few persons in the district." Aloysia Brennfleck, Mathilde Hoffman, Jacob Langer, and Frederick Rawwais, all elderly persons of German birth, were accorded deferred internment. For each of them the police notation was similar, stating that the deferment was on the grounds of long residence in their home districts. They were plainly not above suspicion though, as the records show, "the fact that she is German born and can speak the German language leads to the possibility that important information could be extracted from her once she was accessible to the enemy."

Equally dubious was the evidence concerning Tom Powell of East Mersea. A letter sent on 20 July 1915 from a Mrs Margaret Wilson alleged that Powell had German sympathies and besides, was "always prowling about". The police report commented that

> The writer when interviewed by the Police was unable to refer to anyone who could give information but said that there were rumours about him which had probably been circulated in consequence of his having resided in Berlin for a short time.

Incompetent seamanship got Fritz Challis of Leyton, a young man of German parentage, into trouble. He owned a yacht and regularly sailed at Burnham, where unfortunately he frequently ran aground. He was reported on suspicion of using his reputation as a poor sailor as a cover for taking soundings in coastal waters preparatory to invasion. The police report was more realistic and attributed his behaviour to "carelessness and inexperience".

In accordance with Chief Superintendent Unett's instructions the police were obliged to investigate any and all allegations. The evidence suggests that this was usually carried out in a subtle and sensitive way. It does not seem as if all the victims of these allegations were confronted by the police. Rather, it seems likely that they were never aware that a friend or neighbour had made such a hurtful accusation against them. In cases where the police were not entirely convinced that an individual was not a potential security risk, but where the risk was not thought to be serious, they were placed in the *Scheme for Dangerous Persons in an Emergency*. The individuals concerned were not informed of this, but in an emergency, such as the threat of, or actual, invasion by the Germans, they were liable to arrest, removal and internment. Eugene Scheel of West Mersea was placed in the scheme. Born in Germany in 1874, he came to England in 1894, and had been a naturalised British citizen since 1908. Similar action was taken against Rosalie Abberfield of Clacton, even though she had lived in England for over thirty years, and had two sons in the armed forces. She had been born in Hungary in 1854, and as part of the Austrian Empire, Hungary was now at war with England. Charles and Florence Strauss, also from Clacton, were placed in the scheme even though Charles's brother was M.P. for Southwark West.

Others were not kept in such fortunate ignorance. Frank Gourlay, the Tendring postmaster, his German wife and two daughters were ordered to leave the prohibited area of Essex in January 1917 and were sent to Surrey. The order enforcing their exile was not revoked until January 1919. About Bertha Tebbutt, a German woman married to an Englishman and living in Clacton, it was alleged that "She has always been very pro-German and has spoken foolishly about this and her native country. She is looked upon with suspicion by her neighbours." She was expelled from the prohibited zone in June 1915, and although the order was later rescinded, it was enforced for a second time in January 1918, remaining in place for a further year.

Some police methods left much to be desired. Archibald Triggs, a painter at the explosives works at Great Oakley, was under suspicion because of his "foreign appearance". According to the police report

> He has been under observation and while absent at work his belongings at Robert Ollis's house with whom he lodged were searched but nothing of a suspicious nature could be found.

The unfortunate Reverend Swinerton was subjected to similar treatment, even though, as we have seen, the police were convinced that the accusations against his assistant, Mrs Booth, were based merely on hearsay. The report indicates that "Unbeknown to the Vicar we have searched the whole of the buildings." Against poor Sara MacDonald, accused of pro-Germanism because she was a "very eccentric person", there was apparently not a shred of evidence. Nevertheless, the police decided that "Miss MacDonald's letters should be censored."

Only one person was successfully able to thwart the system. Christopher Cordsen, officially a German alien living in Brightlingsea, attended Colchester police station on 11 August 1914 to register as an enemy alien. On the 19 August he was ordered out of the prohibited zone. However, he reappeared at the police station the next day claiming that he was a naturalised American citizen with a master mariner's certificate to support his claim. His 'proof' was rejected as inadequate by the police, and he was again ordered to remove himself to London. He was back on the 21 August with more proof — a certificate from the American ambassador certifying his American citizenship. Three days later Cordsen received official War Office approval allowing him to remain in Essex.

The police file of evidence on Essex's informers and their victims is mercifully thin, and fortunately contains only a minuscule number of names from the county's huge population. Nevertheless it does reveal a darker side to the English character in wartime. Many of these allegations were directed against those who were vulnerable; the old, the unconventional, those who stood out from the crowd and who did not conform to accepted notions of united social behaviour in wartime. The picture it paints of English 'patriotism' is not a pretty one.

In a country where people were locked in a life or death struggle, we have already seen that in the case of those people seeking to avoid military service, for whatever reason, their behaviour was regarded at best as anti-social, and at worst, unpatriotic, even treasonable. It is not surprising that criminal behaviour came to be regarded in the same way. It is not easy to assess whether or not criminal activity decreased in the war years. Enlistments and conscription undoubtedly swept up many of the individuals whose activities placed them on the margins of social respectability. There is evidence that the restrictions on drink led to a decline in drunkenness and in drink-related criminal activity. In Essex, cases of drunkenness did decline, but this was probably part of a trend which had begun before 1914. There were twelve cases of drunkenness in the Lexden and Winstree Hundred in 1913 and 1914, this fell to seven in 1915, four in 1916, and three in 1917 and 1918. At Witham prosecutions fell from thirty-five in 1915 to just seven in 1916.[34] This trend can be observed all over the county during 1914-1918. In late 1917, when a new police inspector was welcomed at Halstead, the chairman of the local police court, C.E. Brewster, felt able to declare

[34] ECC 9, 16 February 1917.

that there was no crime in the town.[35] On the other hand, in that same year Colchester's mayor bemoaned the "great prevalence of crime among young persons and children", and local justices unanimously recommended birching as a suitable punishment.[36]

What is certainly true is that the new wartime regulations, either under the Defence of the Realm Act (D.O.R.A.) of 1914 or the multitude of various orders that were enacted, criminalised activities that until 1914 had been perfectly legal.[37] Inevitably some of these activities now fell foul of security arrangements which had been put in place. Hundreds, if not thousands, of otherwise law-abiding citizens were prosecuted for showing lights from their houses which might have aided German airships or aeroplanes. Although many of these prosecutions occurred in 1914-15 as people struggled to come to terms with the blackout rules, such cases continued to the end of the War. For the same reason Henry Wicking of Ardleigh and H.G. Linsell, a Finchingfield farmer, were prosecuted for allowing a fire they had lit in the daytime to smoulder on into the evening. With pigeons often used by the military to carry confidential messages, it was not surprising that Mabel King was summonsed for shooting two of them. Frank Wallis, a visitor to the county from Finchley, was found photographing in a prohibited area, namely a headland at Walton. When questioned he said that the photograph was to have been used by his bedridden wife to produce a painting. Other such breaches of D.O.R.A. were potentially more serious in view of invasion fears and the hysteria concerning German spies and aliens among the population. W. Oldridge of Hull was fined for sailing his boat after dark in a prohibited area. Armang Dubois, a waiter at the Frinton Hotel, was fined for being an alien in a prohibited area without an identity book and without the permission of the military authorities. Hotel and boarding house keepers such as Henry Wicking of West Thurrock were fined for failing to keep a register of aliens over the age of fourteen years who were among their guests. Samuel Mills, a boatswain from Parkeston, was prosecuted for having in his possession three letters from Holland and bringing them into the country without declaring them. Holland was neutral, but it was feared that espionage materials might find their way into Britain through its ports.

Those who assisted individuals to evade military service were fined for participating in unpatriotic activities. George Carter, a car proprietor from Grays, was fined for helping one of his employees to avoid military service. A Clacton employer, George Mann, was convicted of failing to fill in the appropriate form which revealed that an employee was eligible to join up. Deserters were regularly rounded up. Some of them exploited their military status to take advantage of the gullible.

[35] ECC 2 November 1917.

[36] ECC 11 May 1917.

[37] The following section is based on an examination of press reports of court cases, largely during 1917, with some from 1918.

Francis Atkins, a sailor, was found guilty of fraudulently obtaining credit at Chelmsford. He persuaded families to give him meals, shelter and money by pretending to be severely wounded. He was a particularly convincing war 'casualty'. He appeared in an overcoat, his left sleeve empty, with his left arm hanging down uselessly. He claimed to have been injured at the Battle of Jutland, where he said he had lost two ribs and had a silver plate inserted in his abdomen. At one house the family were so taken in by him that they even cut up his meat for him. William Downey of Thorpe obtained 10*s*. by false pretences. He took people in by pretending to be a destitute, discharged soldier trying to get to Harwich to see his sister. To appear convincing he wore two gold wound stripes on his jacket, as well as two medal ribbons.

Shopkeepers faced a huge number of government orders and it was perhaps not surprising that some accidentally fell foul of the legislation, although undoubtedly sharp practice and dishonesty also occurred. William Patrick, a Danbury dairyman, was just one of many who were prosecuted for tampering with their milk. He was found to have sold milk that was deficient in milk fat by thirteen per cent, and for having watered it down. Milk was not the only product that tempted traders into misdemeanours. Alfred Smith of Burnham was found guilty of selling loaves weighing less than a pound or which did not weigh an even number of pounds. Such sharp practice was considered to be unfair to other bakers. William Symes, a baker from Epping, was taken to court for selling bread that was not twelve hours old. The time restriction was an attempt to prevent shopkeepers selling fresh bread, which might have tempted people to favour one shopkeeper rather than another. Many traders, like William Deeks, a Tilbury grocer, were fined for selling their goods at a price that was above government regulations. Martha Bailey, a Westcliff shopkeeper, was fined for selling potatoes, Quaker oats and self-raising flour at prices that were in violation of the food orders. Restrictions on bakers were particularly arduous in their limitations of the use of sugar and other ingredients. A Goodmayes baker, Charles Warren, was fined for selling currant buns and tea cakes in violation of the Bread and Pastries Order. As food shortages began to assume serious proportions in late 1917, restrictions were placed on opening times to ensure fair competition. Shopkeepers like John Baker, a fishmonger of Braintree, was fined for keeping his shop open after the official closing time of 8 p.m. It also became illegal to pressure customers into buying more than they required. Many shops contravened this, for instance the Sainsbury's branch at Colchester was fined after one of their shop assistants, Rosa Nicholls, tried to sell sugar to someone on the condition that they also bought tea, coffee or cocoa. Restaurants too frequently breached government restrictions. Henry Mahoney, proprietor of the Marlborough Hotel, Southend, was taken to court for serving potatoes on a day when they were prohibited. They could only be served on Wednesdays and Fridays.

The importance of preserving the nation's food supplies meant that farmers too were faced by an enormous number of regulations. Some of them were merely continuations of pre-war agricultural policy, but they assumed a new significance during the War. George Carrington, a Colchester dealer, was severely criticised by the bench for allowing his donkey to trample vegetables on newly dug allotments. Reginald Marriage of Springfield was fined for failing to notify the authorities that one of his pigs had swine fever. Alfred Askew of Loughton was taken to court for failing to report a case of parasitic mange — an outbreak of disease was something which the county could ill afford. For the same reason Frank Stock of Dunmow was summonsed for transporting a pig from a sale yard without a licence. George Carrington was fined for failing to keep five newly purchased pigs separate from his other animals for twenty-eight days after the purchase. Alfred Blomfield from Gosfield was fined for misuse of foodstuffs for a different reason — a teetotaller, he fed barley flour to his pigs rather than allow it to be used in the manufacture of beer. Thefts of virtually any kinds of foodstuffs, whether home grown or shop bought, was a common occurrence. Arthur French, a young boy from Witham, was birched for stealing eight cabbages from an allotment. Individuals who had stolen from their employers were frequently brought before the courts. James Porter, a labourer, stole two pounds of meat, ten ounces of sugar, two ounces of tea, and nine pies from his employer, a restaurant owner. Robert Green, an assistant cook at the Colchester garrison canteen, stole bacon, beef, mutton, sugar, tea and a pot of paste. Given the nature of the stolen goods, it was assumed that they were not intended for his personal consumption but to sell on at a healthy profit. Civilians were often fined for receiving stolen goods from soldiers. In March 1917 at Grays, twenty-one people were fined for possessing army clothing sold by soldiers from the camp at Purfleet.

Even normally law-abiding and seemingly respectable people were tempted into breaking the law as the food situation deteriorated, and as opportunities presented themselves. Aileen Campbell Johnson, a well-heeled resident of Epping whose husband was an officer serving on the Western Front, was fined for food hoarding. Local suspicions were raised when she had a seventy-pound cheese delivered to her house from a source outside of the town. The police were informed and they searched her house. The search revealed that she had just ten pounds of the cheese left; she claimed to have cut up the rest and delivered it to twenty-one of her neighbours. She was also found to have stored around the house twenty-three pounds of macaroni, forty pounds of tinned fruit, thirty-five pounds of shop bought bottled fruit, 132 pounds of home bottled fruit, seventeen pounds of shop bought jam, sixty-five pounds of home made jam, and large quantities of oatmeal, cornmeal, semolina and other items. The bench took a surprisingly lenient view of her extensive larder and she was fined only for her possession of the sugar and macaroni. Mrs Johnson's case was an exceptional one in terms of the enormous quantities she had amassed, but food hoarding was not unusual, inevitably among those who could afford to do it. Other women were tempted into trying to find a way round the preserving restrictions. Individuals were permitted to apply for extra sugar for preserving fruit and jam making, providing they grew fruit on their own property. The temptation to obtain the much desired commodity was often too much for some women (it was usually women who were prosecuted for this offence). At Epping, for instance, Amy Cook, Emily Wright, Emily Rowland, Alice Potter, Emma Cordell, and Kate Wallis were all fined for giving false statements in order to obtain sugar. The ridiculous greed of one of them who applied for a hundredweight of sugar when she had no fruit trees on her property, was simply asking to be found out. The following week at Epping another nine people were fined for the same offence, and all over Essex in 1917 there were hundreds of similar cases.

The temptations of war involving greater freedom of movement for men, and to a certain extent, for young women, may have contributed to several prosecutions for bigamy. Between late 1917 and mid-1918 there were at least six cases in Essex courts. Queenie Smith, for instance, a respectable twenty-year-old woman, was said to have "conceived an infatuation for various officers and went through a form a marriage with three of them."[38] Two of the other five offenders were women.

Breaking the law was no longer the preserve of criminally-inclined individuals, but became an activity involving people of all backgrounds, and one which was engaged in despite the risk of social humiliation if discovered. Much of this criminal activity revolved around the new government regulations concerning food, which effectively criminalised all sorts of hitherto legal behaviour. One is tempted to think that the number of individuals who were brought before the courts was only a small proportion of those who were actively involved in trying to circumvent these regulations.

[38] ECC 2 November 1917.

CHAPTER ELEVEN

Sport: A Casualty of War

Military sporting events remained acceptable, even when those with civilian participants were decried as unpatriotic. *(ERO: I/MB 383/1/50)*

> It was no time for games, no time for watching games, for amusing themselves, they were called to sterner things.

SO PREACHED the Reverend James Telford, Vicar of Harwich, on 30 August 1914, in a lengthy sermon on the necessity for young men to do their duty and, if necessary, lay down their lives for their country.[1] Telford was not alone in this rather stark view that sport had suddenly been rendered redundant by the outbreak of war. Colonel R.B. Colvin, the chairman of the Essex Territorial Force Association, and a former master of hounds in the county, urged a drastic reduction of sporting activities:

> It is of no interest to anyone now if Essex beats Hampshire at cricket, or if Tottenham Hotspur beats Aston Villa at football. What we want to know is if these athletes can tackle the Germans. And as to hunting we don't want to know if a man can run a 10-mile point — we want to know if the "thrusters" of the Hunt can chase the Germans.[2]

However, not everyone was prepared to publicly endorse these views, even in the first flush of patriotic enthusiasm. The outbreak of war coincided with the onset of the 1914-15 football season, and the *Essex County Telegraph* reported a groundswell of local opinion that the sport should take place as usual:

> with the hope of producing a distraction for the people, and replenishing the ranks of trained men, who shall be physically fit and ready when their time comes to bear arms.[3]

The Football League would have agreed wholeheartedly with the *Telegraph*'s assertion. In early September 1914 its Committee of Management issued the following statement urging the commencement of the football season as usual:

> Any national sport which could minimise the grief, help the nation to bear its Sorrow, relieve the oppression of continuous strain, and save the people from panic and undue depression is a great national asset. We therefore appeal that our great winter game shall pursue its usual course.

Yet, even the Football League was aware of the need to pacify those who were critical of the continuation of the professional game, and its statement concluded with a

1 CG 2 September 1914.

2 ECC 4 September 1914.

3 ECT 1 September 1914.

patriotic appeal — "every player should specially train to be of national service at least in his country's defence."[4]

There stood the two patterns of thought confronting each other: one believing that in a time of national crisis the pursuit of sport involving young men who should be serving their country was, at best, a distraction, and at worst a national disgrace; the other insisting that sport in time of war was an honourable way to prepare young men for the rigours of military life, and one which helped to distract civilian minds from the fears and fancies of war.

In reality the dilemma facing sport was not quite as simple. Many sporting activities folded fairly quickly simply because many of the young men who participated in them enlisted during August and September. Football was a case in point. The Essex Society of Association Football Referees was in no doubt that football had to be sacrificed for the good of the nation:

> The Council of the above Society are very desirous of bringing before the members and referees generally the importance of every individual doing his share towards the defence of the country, and in the preservation of peace and order during the present grave crisis in the country's history. It is fervently hoped that they will uphold the prestige of footballers in particular, and sportsmen generally, by doing their share and joining, where possible, one of the several bodies now forming, in answer to the appeal of the King and country. The selection of the particular branch can best be left to your own discretion and the time at your disposal. Be sure and do something for the sake and honour of England.[5]

Faced by pressures from within, hostility without, and by the actions of young men who voted with their feet by enlisting in the armed forces, it is hardly surprising that football bodies quickly abandoned attempts to start the new season. The officials of the Essex and Suffolk Border League, meeting at the Sea Horse public house in Colchester on 20 August, suspended the league for the 1914-15 season because seven military clubs had pulled out and several others had lost players to the armed forces.[6] The North Essex League, the Woodford and District League, and the Harwich and District League soon followed suit. Some clubs, either swept up in the tide of patriotism engulfing the nation or feeling compelled to make a virtue out of necessity, did not wait for official notification of suspension. In north Essex, Braintree Albion, Burnham Ramblers, Chappel and Wakes Colne, Clacton Town, Coggeshall,

4 ECC 4 September 1914.

5 ECC 28 August 1914.

6 CG 26 August 1914.

Colchester Town, Dovercourt Athletic, Earls Colne, Halstead, Maldon, Manningtree Red Star, Manningtree United, Mistley, and Harwich and Parkeston had all suspended their clubs' activities for the duration.[7] Colchester Town placed its by now redundant ground at the disposal of the newly formed Volunteer Force for its rifle shooting and drills.[8] Nine of its team — W.E. Wheeler, R.H. Morley, R. Burton, T.W. Coles, A. Heron, C. Thompson, J. Coote, A. Berryman and R. J. North — had already enlisted.[9]

West Bergholt F.C. was crippled by the enlistment of eleven of its players. During the 1914-15 season only one match was played, against the 4th Suffolk Regiment, and after that the club loaned their ground to the military for the rest of the War.[10] Ongar F.C. had lost nine of its first team to the army by the end of August, Chelmsford had lost eight, and Braintree Albion was missing seven of its first team players.[11] By early October, the *Harwich and Dovercourt Standard* felt able to declare that "Footer is practically dead in the Borough of Harwich." Without doubt organised league and cup football in north Essex had become dormant.

However, not all clubs were eager to sacrifice themselves on the altar of patriotism. Some players and spectators looked forward to the new season with anticipation and there was a feeling that it should be started regardless of the grim international situation. Clacton Town's decision to suspend its activities was not a popular one with either its supporters or its officials. When the committee voted on whether or not to suspend the club for the season, the result was seven in favour and seven against, and it was only the casting vote of the club's chairman, H. Sergeant, which decided in favour of suspension.[12]

Views for and against carrying on with the season as normal were aired at the meeting of the Executive Council of the Essex County Football Association (E.C.F.A.) which was held at the Great Eastern Hotel in London on 9 September. There was clear acceptance that military recruitment had hit the sport badly. One hundred and sixteen clubs had not renewed their membership of the association, several competitions had been called off, and the sport had been virtually wiped out north of Chelmsford. Not surprisingly, it was suggested that all competitions be abandoned for the time being. Clubs in the south of the county and in the metropolitan area, the strongholds of professionalism, were adamantly against this idea, especially as many of them had heavy ground rents to pay and matches attracting paying crowds were essential in order for them to survive. Unsure about what action to take, the council chose procrastination and deferred until 9 December the decision on whether or not to run the Essex Senior and Junior Cup competitions that season, although it did

7 ECC 18 September, ECT 5, 12 September 1914; BDA 12 September 1914.

8 CG 2 September 1914; ECS 5 September 1914.

9 ECS 5 September 1914.

10 ECT 5 September 1914.

11 ECC 4, 11 September 1914.

12 ECS 22 August 1914.

resolve not to play any inter-county matches. In effect, it left the choice of whether or not to play matches to the clubs and leagues themselves, stating that it saw no reason to interfere with their decisions, although it expressed the rather pious hope that a proportion of all gate receipts would be donated to the Prince of Wales Relief Fund, and that teams should be selected from those who, for whatever reason, were unable to enlist.[13] However, public disapproval may have encouraged the Essex County Football Association to steel itself to take a decision much earlier than it had planned. Less than a fortnight after shuffling responsibility for a decision on to member clubs, it declared that although it had no intention of interfering, "teams will be confined to players precluded through physical unfitness or home ties from serving their King and Country."[14] In reality the E.C.F.A. had probably been waiting to see which way the wind blew at the headquarters of the Football Association (F.A.) and Football League. When the latter decided to press on with its new season, and the F.A. opted to run the F.A. Cup and F.A. Amateur Cup competitions as usual, the E.C.F.A. was emboldened to invite entries for both the Essex Senior and Junior cups. Of the twelve Essex entrants in the F.A. Cup only three came from outside the metropolitan area (Chelmsford, Hoffmann Athletic, and Shoeburyness Garrison), and in the F.A. Amateur Cup there were only two out of six Essex entrants in a similar position (Hoffmann Athletic and Grays Athletic).[15] In the event there were insufficient entries to warrant proceeding with the Essex Junior Cup, but presumably bound by its own stipulations about the eligibility of players, the first round of the Essex Senior Cup went ahead on 30 January 1915. There were no sides in it from north Essex, and with the exception of Chelmsford, all of the clubs (eleven of them) were from the metropolitan area.[16] As an act of appeasement towards the critics of the competition, the E.C.F.A. decided not to issue the two finalists with medals and instructed the clubs, Grays Athletic and Clapton, to do the same.[17]

Several metropolitan clubs and a few leagues had already decided to play a full season for 1914-15. At the end of September, the South Essex League decided to carry on, claiming that this was in response to the pleas of those clubs who had enough players with which to play. This was in spite of the fact that over two hundred players and officials had enlisted. Its first division comprised five teams, and there were seven in its second division, although only nine of these teams actually saw the entire season through.[18] The London League and the Southern League, the latter containing Essex's two premier professional clubs, West Ham United and Southend

[13] ECT 12 September 1914.

[14] ECT 22 September 1914.

[15] ECC 25 September, 6 November 1914.

[16] ECT 23 January 1915. The competition was won by Grays Athletic, who beat Clapton two-one in May 1915.

[17] ECC 22 January 1915.

[18] SE 22 May 1915.

United, also decided to play for the full season.[19] West Ham's officials tried to deflect criticism by pointing out that the club and its players made weekly subscriptions to the Prince of Wales' Relief Fund, and that the players were also involved in weekly rifle practice.[20] Southend United played on until the end of the 1914-15 season, ignoring the criticism that arose from its charging serving soldiers full price to see its matches.[21]

North Essex was not entirely devoid of football during the War. The Harwich Charity Cup, a popular local competition, did take place, but it was competed for entirely by military teams, with the 34th Siege Battery eventually defeating the Bedfordshire Regiment one-nil in the final.[22] Specifically military cups were introduced, like the Cruiser Cup competition designed for Royal Navy crews. In the 1916 final, the crew of the *Dido* defeated that of the *Aurora*, two-nil.[23] It was service teams also who competed in the Training Centre League and the Colchester Military or Garrison Cup, held annually throughout the War. Sixteen teams took part in the first cup competition. In the first wartime final in March 1915 the rather exotic-sounding finalists were the 13th Cavalry Reserve Regiment and the 10th (City of London) Royal Fusiliers, the former emerging as winners by four-nil.[24] There was still a large reservoir of football fans eager to watch anything which was organised. On one afternoon in mid-January 1915, large crowds turned up on Colchester's Abbey Field to see a selection of games: the 10th Fusiliers beat the 265th Battery, Royal Field Artillery eight-nil; Royal Engineer Signallers drew three-three with the 13th Cavalry Reserve Regiment; the 8th Suffolk Regiment was routed eight-nil by the 83rd Brigade, Royal Field Artillery; and the 8th Battalion Norfolk Regiment narrowly defeated the 18th Division Ammunition Column two-one.[25] A friendly game between Harwich and Parkeston and a team of "Kitchener's Troops" had earlier attracted a crowd of twelve hundred.[26] A military match at Frinton attracted several hundred spectators because the teams contained players who before the outbreak of war had played for two of the top teams in Southern England, Bristol City and West Ham.[27]

However, not even concessions such as those made by the football authorities were sufficient to satisfy those who demanded a complete cessation of footballing activities. R.C. Fowler of Witham wrote that "Every man fit to play football is fit to enlist in Lord Kitchener's new army." "It will be a national disgrace", fumed

[19] ECC 2 October, 6, 13 November 1914.

[20] SE 2 September 1914.

[21] P. Mason & D. Goody, *Southend United FC: The Official History of the Blues* (1993), 19.

[22] ECT 8 May 1915.

[23] HDS 10 June 1916.

[24] ECS 13 March 1915.

[25] ECS 16 January 1915.

[26] ECT 3 October 1914.

[27] EEA 30 October 1915.

F.N. Charrington of Mile End, Colchester, "if we have our best athletes charging one another on the football field instead of charging the Germans on the battlefield."[28] The Hon. C.H. Strutt, one of the most influential men in the county, had clearly been influenced by a certain famous recruiting poster when he addressed a meeting at Witham:

> History was now being made, and he asked the young men who were hesitating about making up their minds about whether they could stay at home. When their children asked them in years to come what they did during the great war, could they say: — I went to watch some football matches?[29]

Percy Shaw Jeffrey, the headmaster of Colchester's Royal Grammar School, was so incensed by the sport's continuation that he wrote to the *Morning Post*:

> There is only one way to get recruits. Stop this pestilential League football, which many of us older footballers think is a disgrace to the nation. While the boys in every decent public school in the country are cutting their matches and learning to drill and shoot, hordes of stalwart young fellows, who ought to be with the colours spend their weekly half-holidays not in "playing football"— this at least would teach them the meaning of British grit and pluck — but in emitting discordant yells, punctuated with blasphemy and shrouded in the rank smoke of the emasculating cigarette.[30]

The letter, reeking of assumptions about class, honour and duty, may well have presented a rather extreme view. Nevertheless, the *Essex County Telegraph* deftly supported Jeffrey, wrapping its opinion in a footballing metaphor by saying that a young man should be "learning to do his little bit in helping the country to score the winning goal in the greatest tussle in history."[31] The Bishop of Chelmsford joined in the fray, condemning the continuation of football matches, especially professional ones, as "incongruous and unworthy" in wartime.[32] Others took more direct action. Frederick Charrington, the owner of Osea Island, took his protests to football matches and was ejected from more than one ground for his pains.[33] Some were

28 ECC 4 September 1914.

29 ECC 11 September 1914.

30 Quoted in ECS 21 November 1914.

31 ECT 21 November 1914.

32 ECC 4 December 1914.

33 ECC 11 September 1914.

unconvinced. One correspondent, signing himself 'Plebian', wrote to the press condemning Shaw Jeffrey's letter as "intemperate", and full of "bitterness, invective and vituperation." Picking up on Shaw Jeffrey's criticism of professionalism and working-class participation in the game, Plebian added that his letter

> is not that of a recruiting sergeant, but is the recrudescence of the old Amateur Football Association intolerance which led to the revolt against the parent association, and is an attempt to utilise public sentiment in hitting an honourable and successful opponent beneath the belt.[34]

Football at the highest level survived for a season. Everton won the First Division Championship, and Sheffield United the F.A. Cup in 1915, beating Chelsea three-nil at Old Trafford. However, this concluded wartime football at a national level and both competitions went the way of their less illustrious rivals. The sport did continue in north-east Essex, but after 1914 it was only acceptable if matches were between military teams or the odd game between local works teams, particularly if the companies concerned were involved in vital war work. For that reason the military leagues at Colchester and Southend were perfectly acceptable and their fixtures were watched by large crowds. Nor was there opposition to a Colchester match between Paxman and Culver St Ironworks, or between Paxman and the 10th Bedfordshire Regiment, both played in October 1915.[35] Football matches in Essex during 1916-17 raised £2,286 for the football battalions raised by the F.A. However, falling attendances, the result of spectators being in the forces or because individuals chose not to watch football matches as a matter of principle, caused severe financial problems for many clubs. By the end of the 1914-15 season, English clubs had estimated debts of a quarter of a million pounds. West Ham United showed a loss of £175 on the previous season. The club's average Southern League gate was £259, a decrease of £73 on 1913-14. Leytonstone Football Club had lost twenty-nine players to the forces. Their income for 1914-15 was a mere £261, a loss of £543. By the autumn of 1915 Barking F.C. had just £8 with which to meets its liabilities of £94, which included rent of £50.[36] However, all these clubs were fortunate to avoid the fate of Southend United. By the spring of 1915 the club was one thousand pounds in debt. The F.A.'s decision to cut players' maximum wages to three pounds a week and its abolition of summer (inter-season) wages had not really assisted the club's desperate plight. Its shareholders resisted the slide towards liquidation for as long as possible, but in October 1915 its footballs, players' jerseys,

[34] ECS 28 November 1914. The Amateur Football Association had broken away from the F.A. in 1907-8 in protest at the F.A.'s attempt to compel all county football associations to accept the affiliation of professional clubs. The breach was not healed until 1914.

[35] CG 6, 13 October 1915.

[36] ECS 3 September 1915.

corner flags and goalposts were auctioned off. When the lease expired on the club's ground at Roots Hall in June 1916, the remaining fixtures and fittings were also auctioned. The grandstand was sold for £92 10*s*., including the dressing rooms and the club office. The 1,100 feet of fencing around the ground was sold for £15. The auction raised the grand sum of £137. A few days later the land that had been Roots Hall football ground was converted to allotments to support the war effort. Southend United was the most notable sporting victim of the War in Essex.[37] There were other, smaller fry too. By mid-1917 fifty clubs had been struck off the membership roll of the E.C.F.A. for non-payment of its annual subsidy.[38]

Football was not the only sport to suffer from the onset of war; the local cricket season was also brought to a slightly premature close, although county fixtures were seen through to the bitter end without the same degree of condemnation which was heaped upon footballers. Local clubs attempted to continue as normal, but as their footballing counterparts were soon to discover, a large number of their personnel had enlisted. At the end of August the Colchester and East Essex Cricket Club was still playing, in this case against West Bergholt, but within a fortnight it gave up the ghost, cancelling the remainder of its programme "out of respect for public feeling", which perhaps hinted at opposition to the club continuing to play. Besides, the War had already reduced what was left of the club's season to a shambles — since 4 August ten of its games had been scratched.[39] The Tendring Hundred Cricket League decided as early as March 1915 that there would be no competition that summer.[40] The Essex County Cricket Club hoped that its loyal following would allow it to survive. In April 1915 over eight hundred members had promised to continue paying their dues.[41] In the spring of 1915 Colchester and East Essex decided to resume playing matches during the summer, particularly against military teams, although it was careful to stress that the club had a number of players who were ineligible for the armed forces, either because of age or business commitments.[42] However, there were limits to what the club was prepared to tolerate. Suggestions that the cricket pitch be ploughed up and used to grow potatoes provoked a storm of protest, with one correspondent to the *Essex County Standard* decrying the suggestion using a variation on the famous 'playing fields of Eton' theme, "the athletic grounds of England and the Colonies had made the manhood of the Empire what it is."[43] Witham Cricket Club suspended its fixtures for the 1915 season. The decision was taken to continue running the club and keep the ground in good shape, but this was to be done by three committee members

[37] Mason & Goody, *Southend United F.C.*, 19-20.

[38] ECC 8 June 1917.

[39] ECC 12 September 1914.

[40] EEA 6 March 1915.

[41] ECC 23 April 1915.

[42] ECS 17 April 1915.

[43] ECS 6 May 1916.

who were ineligible for military service.[44] Other clubs, like Saffron Walden, decided to continue playing, but insisted that players were above military age.[45]

Even hunting had a far from easy time attempting to sustain its activities. The Committee of the Masters of Foxhounds Association resolved to press ahead with hunting, although it solemnly urged its members not to view it as a sport until the War was over.[46] In consequence the Essex and Suffolk Hunt decided to carry on as usual, even though many of its members were serving as officers in the armed forces and half its horses had been commandeered by the military. The joint masters decided to maintain the pack and preserve its traditions rather than see the hunt go under. However, the loss of paying members meant that within three months of war being declared the hunt faced a deficit of £356 on its subscriptions.[47] Its rather self-important justification for carrying on was the fact that

> It was the hunting field that made their cavalry and battery officers, and if they were to have good officers in future they must keep hunting going in England.[48]

As it turned out, the nature of the fighting in the First World War, particularly on the Western Front, rendered this justification rather obsolete. The Essex Foxhounds continued its activities, although the Essex Farmers' Staghounds abandoned things for the duration and dispersed its pack.[49] The Essex Hunt lost its master, Seymour Gosling, to the army, but his brother took his place. However, with far fewer horses its meetings were fewer and of shorter duration.[50] Even among the hunting fraternity opinions were divided about whether it was appropriate to continue its activities. Colonel Colvin, the chairman of the Essex Territorial Forces Association, a huntsman and former master of hounds, urged that all sport be reduced to a minimum, with fox hunting's upper class setting the example. At the quarterly meeting of the Territorial Association, he stated that,

> We cannot expect the workmen to make sacrifice and enlist if the wealthy stop at home and enjoy their selfish pleasures. All must work and many must fight, and the man who does nothing to keep his country in its need must receive the treatment accorded to a parish dog.[51]

44 ECC 26 March 1915.
45 WWN 14 May 1915.
46 ECC 28 August 1914.
47 ECS 21 November 1914.
48 ECT 17 November 1914.
49 ECC 11 September 1914.
50 ECC 26 March 1915.
51 ECC 4 September 1914.

Others defended the sport, claiming that it trained horses for the army. Edward Barclay, master of the Puckeridge Foxhounds, wrote to the press stating that he intended to hunt as much as possible with the horses he had left. Two weeks later he declared that as a last resort he would continue to hunt foxes on his bicycle, or even on foot (Barclay resigned the mastership in January 1915). Meanwhile Colvin severed his links with his hunt, but other members chose not to follow suit.[52]

Other sports too were affected. In 1914 the annual Essex Lawn Tennis Championships were held at Colchester. They began on 4 August, the day that Britain declared war on Germany, and continued until the 7 August. The men's tournament was badly hit by the call-up of territorials, and the ladies' tournament was drastically reduced. Of the two lady finalists, one reached that stage of the tournament by playing only one match, and the other had not played any.[53] At Maldon the Promenade Tennis Club abandoned its attempt to persevere in the spring of 1917, and handed over its courts to the corporation for the duration, with the latter taking half of the fees.[54] Pigeon fanciers in the county were compelled to put patriotism before racing. At its annual meeting in November 1914, the Colchester Racing Pigeon Society abandoned plans for its forthcoming fifteenth annual gathering because all the society's best birds had been given to the army.[55] The Dengie Show for 1915 was called off. Yachting, a very popular pastime and coastal sport, expired very rapidly once war began. The restrictions placed on the sailing of yachts and pleasure craft on the Rivers Colne, Blackwater, Crouch and Roach killed off the activity. At Brightlingsea the season finished some six to eight weeks earlier than usual.[56] In the early summer of 1915 the vast majority of yachts were still in their winter berths, and were to remain so until the War ended.[57] All sailing regattas and athletics meetings disappeared. Southend Harriers had little choice but to abandon its activities when forty-three of its men were either called up as territorials or had enlisted by mid-August 1914.[58] The Essex Cycling Association put away its bicycles for the duration. Leytonstone Rugby Club had lost fifty-five of its sixty players to the armed forces by early October 1914.[59] Even sporting activities which might have been able to carry on because part of their membership were probably over military age, were not unaffected by the War. The Rochford Hundred Golf Club was forced to abandon its plans to extend the clubhouse because it anticipated a significant decline in income.[60]

52 ECC 4 September 1914.

53 ECS 8 August 1914.

54 ECC 11 May 1917.

55 ECT 14 November 1914.

56 EEA 19 September 1914.

57 ECS 26 June 1915.

58 ECC 14 August 1914.

59 ECC 16 October 1914.

60 ECC 19 February 1915.

The Essex Bowling Association decided against holding its usual gala day for its finals and opted for a quiet day instead.[61]

However, other leisure activities continued as normal. Coursing continued at several venues in the county such as Southminster. Quoits matches were carried on. Bowling was carried on because most of its players were above military age. Where this was not the case, organisations laid down certain ground rules. The Braintree Anglers Association specified that no-one of military age would be permitted to participate in its fishing competitions.[62]

And so the opportunities for watching young men at play faded almost completely from the locality, unless of course one was content to watch those in uniform. Large crowds did turn out to see almost every piece of organised military sporting activity imaginable. In March 1915, for instance, hundreds were present at the Abbey Field in Colchester to watch the start and finish of an eight mile race comprising eight military teams, totalling three hundred runners.[63] Equally large crowds watched troops engaged in boxing and, perhaps not surprisingly in view of widespread war fever, bayonet fighting.[64] Hylands Park, Chelmsford, was frequently packed as people flooded in to see military sports. In August 1916 a crowd estimated at between twenty and thirty thousand watched an athletics meeting of the 65th (Lowland) Division, an event which also included a huge re-enactment of the Zulu attack on Rorke's Drift in 1879, and a grand tattoo featuring twenty military bands.[65] More sedate sports continued throughout the War, largely for the benefit of those who were too old to don a uniform. Colchester had a Billiards League, Draughts League and a Bowling League, all of which pre-dated the War.[66] Tennis tournaments, such as the prestigious one at Frinton, continued, but here too the action was a good deal slower than before 1914. Frinton Golf Club remained open for those of its members who were not of military age. Of course, these did not include any aliens — in October 1914 the club secretary issued a circular "suggesting" that members of German or Austrian nationality should not frequent the club.[67]

Given the immense upsurge in patriotic feeling generated by the outbreak of war, it was perhaps unsurprising that sport soon fell victim to ferocious wartime hostility. Sporting pursuits which were essentially the realm of the young, were firstly damaged by the departure of young men, and then condemned as unpatriotic. It was thought to be inappropriate that those of an age to bear arms should not only have avoided their duty, but be seen besporting themselves at play, particularly in a garrison town

[61] ECC 11 September 1914.

[62] ECC 25 June 1915.

[63] ECC 20 March 1915.

[64] ECT 9 March 1915.

[65] ECC 11 August 1916.

[66] CG 6 October 1915; ECT 20 February 1915.

[67] J. Bond, *Frinton Golf Club: The First Hundred Years* (1995), 22.

like Colchester, a naval base such as Harwich, or a town swamped with soldiers like Chelmsford, where the call of duty was everywhere and obvious. Resistance to those intent on eliminating civilian sport was not widespread. In most, though not all instances, it was abandoned willingly and ungrudgingly. Those who were too young or too old to compete were deprived of their entertainment, and the large attendances at military sporting events throughout the War were a testimony to the insatiable demand for such events among the people of Essex. Their loss was but a temporary irritant. For others it had far graver consequences. Many of those who forsook their sporting pursuits to follow the call of King and country were never to set foot on a playing field again.

CHAPTER TWELVE

The Finish: November 1918

Patients of Witham Voluntary Aid Detachment Hospital celebrate the end of the War. *(ERO: Postcards Collection, Witham)*

NOVEMBER 1918 saw Essex trudging through the start of its fifth year of war. There were torrential downpours on the first two days of the month. The county was once more plunged into autumn darkness at night as shop and street, railway station and army camp, coast and village observed the blackout. Bonfire night came and went, and for the fourth year in succession there were no evening celebrations, no bonfires and no fireworks. It was cold, and the continuing severe shortage of coal only made matters worse. Large numbers of men were still overseas in the armed forces; some had come back injured, and several thousand would never return. The *Essex County Standard* for 2 November recorded the deaths of fifteen men, with two wounded. These included: twenty-year-old Reginald Eves, who died in a French hospital after being gassed; Private Albert Firmin, a former employee of Woods Mineral Waters in Colchester, who left a wife and child; Lieutenant John Turner of Coggeshall, killed in action in France; and Tom Bagley, a member of Colchester Town F.C., who died of pneumonia in a French hospital. Others died at sea, in Italy and in Palestine. The number of widows, orphaned children and grieving families continued to grow. Food supplies were still being rationed, and luxuries involving the cooking of buns or cakes with chocolate or sugar were a rarity. The Colchester Meat Traders' Association met to complain bitterly about unfair price fixing by the Government and falling profits. The opening hours of public houses were still shortened. Over and above all of this, the county was being ravaged by a lethal flu epidemic which was sweeping across much of Europe and spreading far beyond it. The disease had not struck the area with such ferocity since 1890 when Russian flu hit Colchester, infecting a thousand people, followed by a similar epidemic two years later which killed forty-three people in one week alone in mid-January.[1] In 1918 Colchester people queued daily for disinfectant at the health office in Stanwell Street. Foxearth School treated its pupils with a mixture of pure paraffin and menthol.[2] Essex's medical officer recommended that children be sprayed with a two per cent mixture of formalin.[3] Bradfield was not unusual in having whole families sick in bed.

The county's schools were devastated by the outbreak. Chelmsford's elementary schools were closed during October, and after being reopened were forced to shut again because of the huge number of teachers taken ill. All but two of Epping's schools were closed, as were most of those in Burnham. All the elementary schools in East Ham, Romford and Halstead were closed. At Southend in early November there were over three thousand children ill and over fifty teachers absent from school. During September and October over a thousand schoolchildren were ill in Barking, and Leyton's schools were closed by late October. All of Ilford's schools were closed because a large proportion of its eleven thousand school population had succumbed. The village school at Bradfield, and those of nearby Mistley and Manningtree, were

1 ECS 2 November 1918; SE 26 October 1918.

2 ECS 2 November 1918.

3 ECC 1 November 1918.

closed, and indeed at one time or another between October 1918 and January 1919 virtually every village school in the county was affected. The absentee rate in rural schools in late October was fifty per cent.[4] Dovercourt Central School was so badly hit it was ordered to be closed for three weeks on Armistice Day. Birch school, on the other hand, which had been closed on 18 October because the head teacher and sixty children were ill with flu, actually had the good fortune to reopen on Armistice Day. Other schools, like Clacton St Osyth Road, remained open for longer. It struggled on until 6 December when the outbreak of flu became so severe that it was closed until the end of the Christmas holiday.[5]

Official precautions were ineffectual and the outbreak reached epidemic proportions; seventeen people in Colchester had died by the end of October, a further twenty-four by 2 November, and over forty more by the time the War ended on 11 November.[6] These figures paled in comparison with those of metropolitan Essex, where there were thousands of cases reported. By the end of November there had been 267 deaths from flu in East Ham, 126 in Ilford, 200 in Leytonstone, 234 in Walthamstow, and 570 in West Ham.[7] The situation was considered so serious that in order to stem the spread of the disease, Colchester Town Council banned children and youths under sixteen years old from attending local cinemas and theatres.[8] At East Ham the Borough Licensing Committee acted in a similar fashion, banning all under-fourteens from theatres, music halls and cinemas.[9] So many people were hospitalised by the disease that an emergency ward was set up at the Colchester workhouse. In Ilford the town's undertakers were hard-pressed to keep up with the many deaths from the disease, and the military were brought in to assist with grave digging at the Manor Park Cemetery. At one doctor's surgery in the town there was said to have been a queue of over seventy people. When Dr M. Davis died in late October, Roydon lost its only doctor. Two hundred cases were registered at Saffron Walden. Eleven of the forty hospitalised cases in Epping died at the end of October. Hundreds of cases were reported at Maldon in the first week of November. The epidemic claimed the lives of the great, the good, and the unfortunate. British wounded, home from the front to be nursed in hospital, and German prisoners of war were among the victims. The daughter-in-law of Colchester's mayor, Councillor Jarmin, died of flu; tragically she died within hours of her husband, who had recently been returned to England after recovering from being gassed at Ypres.[10]

4 ECC 8 November 1918; BA 2 November 1918.

5 ERO M/L 138/2, school logbook, 11 November 1918; E/ML 242/2 school logbook, 18 October, 11 November 1918; AA, A6391, school logbook, 6 December 1918.

6 ECC 7 December 1918.

7 ECC 1 November 1918.

8 Acc. A6391, 7 December 1918.

9 ECC 1 November 1918.

10 Hunt, *War Memorial Souvenir*, 61.

Nevertheless, there was hope in the air. Bulgaria had collapsed by the end of September and the resolve of both the Austrians and the Turks was crumbling. From mid-October peace rumours surfaced regularly. On one occasion the *Essex County Standard*'s offices were besieged by people who believed that Turkey had surrendered.[11] By early November it had, and the end was not far away. On 9 November, the Kaiser abdicated and his war-weary generals sued for peace. News of the Armistice reached the *Essex County Chronicle*'s offices at Chelmsford at 9.30 a.m. on Monday, 11 November. Lloyd George confirmed that the Armistice had been signed at 5 a.m. and that hostilities would cease at 11 a.m. On 11 November rumours of the Armistice led to crowds besieging the offices of the *Leyton Independent*. As rumour was confirmed as reality, the town's fire stations sounded their sirens and fired maroons at 11 a.m. Union Jacks appeared on houses throughout the borough, and on trams and buses. Drapers' shops were thronged with people buying tricolour ribbons. The November weather was unable to defeat the people's spirit and the streets were packed with celebrating crowds. As darkness set in against the wintry sky, the trams continued to run fully lit for the first time since 1914.[12] News of the Kaiser's abdication was pinned up in the windows of the *Southend Standard* on Saturday night. Rumours that there was to be an armistice on Monday was viewed with scepticism until confirmation arrived. At 10.43 a.m the air-raid siren wailed for seven minutes. It was a cold, damp and overcast day with drizzly rain but no-one cared — the War was over. What happened next is best left to the *Southend Standard*'s reporter, who brilliantly captured the unrestrained enthusiasm of the moment:

> When at 10.43 the syren [sic] blared out, men, women and children paused to listen. No sooner was its import grasped than word flew swiftly from street to street; the armistice was signed. Suddenly, as by the stroke of a magician's wand, flags appeared at innumerable windows; men emerged at housetops and ran up the Union Jack, the Stars and Stripes, the White Ensign, or other victorious emblems; people were heard cheering far down the street. Folk appeared by all points of the compass wearing patriotic colours ... the colours of the Allies flew bravely from above Messrs Garon's premises in High Street; Union Jacks were thrust in haste from over shop doorways and from the windows above; infants in prams shook their flags as they passed ... Horses appeared bright with favours, dogs ran to and fro ablaze with red, white and blue; cats were held up at windows and balconies similarly adorned. Far as the eye could reach a blaze of many colours met and mingled — there was no mistaking the local outburst of feeling ... Boys marched in little groups shouting

[11] ECS 19 October 1918.

[12] SE 16 November 1918.

> "The war is over", a huge blue ensign fluttered and flapped over Messrs Brightwell's premises in High Street which closed its doors at noon ... Another group of boys passed presently shouting "The Yanks are coming everywhere." Employees gathered at doorways and shouted "Hip, hip, hooray." Others took up the strains of "It's a long way to Tipperary."[13]

Further north at Walthamstow the celebrations were just as wild and unrestrained:

> 11 a.m. Over the bank at Wanstead I heard a siren and then maroons and guns by the dozen, just like a raid. We rushed out and everybody cheered and shook hands; some were overcome; could not realise that this was an end to four years of fighting and anxiety. Everyone rushed to buy flags, me included. Soon all the High street had huge flags hanging out ... I tied a large bow of red white and blue around Jack the dog and Mee-wee the cat. Everyone went mad, shaking hands all round with Barclays (the employees). Mrs Chew came in from the house with cups of coffee and biscuits. Guns were still going off and Mr Joliffe's boy was riding up and down blazing away on a bugle fit to blow his lungs out! Later on a huge lorry flew past crammed with R.F.C. men ... The men had mouth organs and tambourines ... Mr Clark, manager at Barclays, brought out some champagne.[14]

The news arrived in the north of the county late that morning. Crowds packed the streets of Colchester and gathered in great numbers outside the Town Hall. The town council was holding its quarterly meeting when the news was brought. At this the entire council donned their robes, stood and sung the national anthem in the council chamber and then crowded onto the Town Hall balcony where George Wright, who had begun his year of office only two days earlier, sought to stamp a mayoral and civic mark onto this momentous occasion:

> Fellow citizens, rejoice with me this day — the greatest day in the world's history. An armistice has been signed (loud cheers). Congratulate yourselves on this marvellous victory. The fighting is over (loud cheers). Thank God for the victory. May we have a world's peace and may all those waiting for their dear and loved ones have them soon returned to their homes (cheers).

The crowd sang the national anthem and gave three cheers for the King.

[13] SST 14 November 1918.

[14] Potter/Grubb diary, 11 November 1918.

Within minutes of the news percolating through to town and village there were frenzied celebrations all over Essex. Soon the band of the 6th Volunteer Battalion of the Essex Regiment was marching around Colchester. Soldiers and munitions girls formed processions through the town, the bells of St Peter's rang out, other troops appeared in fancy dress and "the scenes of jubilation continued unflagging." Munitions workers were given a three-day holiday. On the day after the Armistice, the Culver Street Ironworks Band led a procession, once again to the Town Hall, where they were received genially by the mayor who once more addressed the crowds from the balcony. That same day both he and the corporation processed in state to the thanksgiving mass at St Peter's. The Reverend Parry gave the address, the first time in Colchester's history that a Nonconformist minister had spoken from an Anglican pulpit. Two thousand people had to be turned away and an 'overflow' service was held at Lion Walk. Parry spoke of how the nation was awakening from "a night of restless sleep disturbed by hideous dreams." Continuing a theme which he and other church leaders had voiced throughout the War, he said that the death of young men performing their duty, "was not tragedy, nor cause for tears, unless of envy." In his hopes for the future, he urged his listeners to "be done with all that was mean, selfish, and ignoble, and try and imitate their goodness and strength."[15]

B. Carlyon Hughes witnessed the celebrations in Harwich harbour, and they had such an impact on him that he was able to recall them vividly over twenty years later:

> When that longed-for hour arrived there was the most gorgeous spontaneous demonstration of joy that it has ever been my lot to see. All the ships switched on their lights and searchlights and blew their sirens. All up and down the harbour was a continual blaze of Verey lights, rockets, and coloured signals. As the night was a flat calm and clear, but very dark, the effect was beautiful.[16]

At Brightlingsea the sirens and hooters of all the vessels in the estuary put up a deafening cacophony; bunting appeared everywhere, and rockets and maroons, presumably stored for years, were set off all over the town. In Ladysmith Avenue residents trampled a German flag in the middle of the road. A great procession through the town, headed by motorcycle outriders of the Australian Engineers' Depot, was followed by a thanksgiving service at All Saints', attended by army and naval officers, councillors and the families of those who had lost their lives. Masses were held in a field by Cinque Port Deputy-cum-Swedenborgian minister Harry Deans and the Australian military chaplain. Later on, Australian troops held a mock trial of the Kaiser, following which they disguised themselves as aborigines and did a "bush dance" in Victoria Place.[17] The Gloucester and London regimental bands

15 ECS 16 November 1918.

16 B. Carlyon Hughes, *Harwich Harbour*, 108-9.

17 Foynes, *Brightlingsea*, 63-4.

toured the streets of Clacton and huge crowds turned out to see them play at the Pavilion bandstand. At Harwich the night sky was lit by two hours of fireworks and a spectacular display by scores of military searchlights. For those children at schools which were not ravaged by flu and who were still at their desks on 11 November, there was a bonus, as at Clacton St Osyth Road:

> At 2.15 the Chairman of the Managers (Rev. J.H. Peabody) visited school and authorised the dismissal of the children for the afternoon to celebrate the cessation of hostilities.[18]

At Great Bentley a thanksgiving service broke all records:

> Never before in living memory has the old historic church of St Mary been called upon to accommodate as many worshippers as on Tuesday night.[19]

Those in the works and factories of Chelmsford downed tools and poured onto the streets. Hoffmann was rapidly emptied. At Hunt's Atlas, Crittall's and Lake and Elliott's works emptied at 11.10 a.m. Bells, bunting and flags appeared at Braintree, and led by all the town's bands, a mile long procession of factory workers snaked its way around the streets. Everywhere bands donned their uniforms and led thousands of jubilant, relieved and near-hysterical crowds in prolonged and noisy marches around town and village. At Romford, the crowds were led by the New Zealand Expeditionary Force band.

Rumours of an armistice reached Saffron Walden just after nine in the morning. Crowds, undeterred by the thick fog which lay over the town, gathered around the board of Messrs Hart and Sons. At 12.45 p.m. the mayor, Alderman A.N. Myhill, was seen heading for the post office and the crowd, alerted to this, followed expectantly. From the windows of the Magistrates' Room Myhill read the telegram which he had been expecting to the assembled throng — "Armistice signed at 5 o' clock this morning. Hostilities ceased on all fronts at 11 o' clock (official)."

The mayor's attempt to follow this up with his own significant remarks was drowned in a cascade of cheering, so instead he began to sing the national anthem and everyone joined in. At two o'clock the town's Company of Church Ringers marked the occasion by ringing one thousand rounds. At the nearby village of Wimbish, the blacksmith celebrated the news and entertained everyone else by striking gunpowder on his anvil to make six huge explosions.[20]

As a tangible symbol of victory captured German field guns began arriving in Essex towns as trophies of war. At Colchester one such prize was placed outside the castle.

[18] ERO Acc A 6391, logbook, 11 November 1918.

[19] ERO Acc A 6391, logbook, 11 November 1918.

[20] WWN 15 November 1918.

Even more dramatic was the scene at Harwich, where 114 surrendered German U-boats could be seen stretching for a mile and a half up the River Stour; thousands of sightseers came to gaze at the craft which had almost brought England to her knees. The awareness of this and the realisation of the enormous cost of the War, meant that there were few English voices urging generosity or moderation in the treatment of defeated Germany. This editorial from the *Burnham and Dengie Advertiser* is probably typical of the nation's sentiments at this time:

> There are many people who think we ought to let the Hun down lightly, kill him with kindness, and so forth, but he is not made that way. By upsetting his deeply laid plans we have earned his undying hatred and sooner or later he will try to get his revenge. What we have to do is to render him helpless as far as his power of doing mischief is concerned for the next one hundred years.[21]

Although there was much anger and hatred in the air it was the feelings of relief and gratitude that were uppermost. The Billericay Board of Guardians recorded "its deep thankfulness to Almighty God that the Great European War has victoriously terminated and that peace is now imminent."[22] However, let us leave these first few heady weeks following the Armistice with the words of Frinton-on-Sea Urban District Council. Aware of the historic significance of the moment, its record of the Armistice was written in a rich vein of purple prose, and perhaps summed up the feelings, not just of the people of Frinton, but of most of the inhabitants of Essex at the end of the Great War:

> That the members of the Frinton-on-Sea Urban District Council on the occasion of its first meeting after November 11 1918, on which ever memorable day the armistice was signed ending the great war with the Germanic powers, desires to place on the record of the Council's Minute Book their profound gratification at the splendid triumph of the arms of Britain and its noble Allies, their deep gratitude to all those who fought the battle of right against might, of liberty, humanity and justice against despotism, brutality and ruthlessness; to the statesmen who so honourably and so successfully directed the policy of their country during years of unprecedented stress and unparalleled difficulty; to all those who, in any way whatsoever, helped our gallant and devoted soldiers and sailors to fight and suffer and to endure, and finally, their heartfelt sympathy with all those who suffered the loss of husbands, fathers, sons or brothers, dying in the noblest of all causes.[23]

21 BDA 16 November 1918.

22 ECC 15 November 1918.

23 ECC 15 November 1918.

The Post-war World
1919-1920

CHAPTER THIRTEEN

Winding Down the War

The 'official' peace celebrations in Witham held in July 1919. *(ERO: T/P 339/26)*

ONCE THE ARMISTICE WAS SIGNED, and the War was over, which was how most people perceived the ceasefire, there was an expectation that normality ought to be achieved in the shortest time possible. The *Essex County Telegraph* voiced the views of many when it stated shortly after the ceasefire, "War, we believe, will be banished for generations, perhaps for ever, so far as the civilised nations are concerned."[1] The deep wounds, the scars and the psychological damage caused by the War would take years to heal; for some they never would. However, the trappings of war, those administrative details and wartime organisations which had governed and plagued people's lives for over four years, were very largely swept away within eighteen months of hostilities coming to an end.

The most pressing need as far as most people were concerned was for their loved ones in the armed forces to be returned home. At first this seemed unlikely, thanks to an ill-considered government scheme for mobilisation, which was bitterly unpopular with the troops and prompted mutinies both in France and England. There was certainly unrest at Fairlop aerodrome. On 7 January 1919, orders arrived for the transfer of ninety R.F.C. men to other bases. The orders were soon known throughout the camp and in a short time the entire complement, some four hundred men, paraded and asked for a meeting with the commanding officer, Colonel Ward. He met them and listened to their grievances. After deliberation, and presumably after contacting a higher authority, he decided that all those who could prove that they had a business or employment to go to, could have a day's leave to return home to get their papers and then return to present them. If the papers were satisfactory, they could then await demobilisation at home.[2] The Government too saw sense and following the "coupon election" of December 1918, Winston Churchill at the War Office devised a more equitable and practical scheme, and by the summer of 1919 over three-quarters of the armed forces had been demobbed.[3] It was perhaps fitting that tens of thousands of demobbed soldiers made their first steps back into civilian life at Tilbury and Purfleet, where many of them had been processed into the army in 1914. Here a large number of temporary buildings were erected to accommodate the two to three thousand men who arrived each day once demobilisation was in full swing.[4] In Colchester sufficient numbers of the "Comrades of the Great War", as they styled themselves, had been returned home for them to hold a Victory Ball at the Moot Hall on 20 February 1919, when 250 comrades and their ladies celebrated their good fortune.[5] Most prisoners of war were repatriated within weeks of the ceasefire. The Mayor of Harwich was holding a welcome home dinner for a hundred of the town's repatriated men in early

1 ECT 28 December 1918.

2 ECC 11 January 1919.

3 DeGroot, *Blighty*, 253-7; Taylor, *English History 1914-45*, 138-9.

4 ECC 17 January 1919.

5 ECS 22 February 1919.

January 1919, and 150 men were treated to a similar occasion at the Troops' Social Club in Colchester, where they were invited to bring along their 'wife or lady friend'.[6] At Harold Wood about two hundred and fifty men and their ladies were treated to a dinner at the Village Institute paid for by Sir Joseph Brookbank. These occasions were an early opportunity to pay a tribute to those who had survived, as well as to the Fallen. At Harold Wood 206 men had served; forty were still in uniform at the time of the dinner, 140 had returned safely, and twenty-six had been killed. "Their achievements were all the greater", said Brookbank, "because they had never murmured or desponded under temporary defeats or boasted in the hour of victory, and they never knew how truly noble they were in it all." At Hornchurch the returning servicemen attended a garden party on 28 June 1919, the very day that the Treaty of Versailles was signed with Germany's representatives in Paris. Three days later, they were invited to a church parade and drumhead service on the Millfield, and on 18 October, 220 of them sat down to a dinner provided by Joseph Lyons and Company. The Reverend J. Benson Evans, Vicar of Hornchurch, proposed a toast to "Our Absent Comrades", which was received in silence. Remembering them, he said, "Our dead comrades, I feel, are with us in spirit, and are still associated with all that is high, noble, and gallant, as they were in life."[7]

The administrative organisation whereby the people of Essex had played their part in the war effort was not dismantled with as much rapidity as demobilisation was effected, but this too had been very largely accomplished by the end of 1919. Military tribunals ceased to meet as soon as the Armistice was announced. With an end to the fighting there seemed no justification for continuing to draft young men. The Burnham Tribunal, which had temporarily exhausted its quota of conscripts, had been due to hold its last meeting on 15 November 1918, when two appeals would have been heard. The Armistice and subsequent instructions from the Local Government Board put an end to its deliberations for good.[8] Lighting restrictions in the prohibited coastal areas were effectively abandoned on the night of Armistice Day, when street and shop lights and fireworks lit up the sky for the first time in over four years, although by early December about one-third of Colchester's town lights were still not in operation at night.[9] With the threat of invasion finally banished, barbed wire began to disappear from local coastal resorts well before Christmas 1918. The barrier erected around the Harwich fort was dismantled, and the fort itself and the beach area where unwary trespassers had run the risk of being shot, were once more open to all.[10] The trenches around the Hadleigh-Wickford area were filled in and

6 HDS 18 January 1919; ECT 11 January 1919; Collection of Local Material 1917-18 by Arthur Jarmin, Colchester prisoner of war welcome home invitation card.

7 Perfect, *Hornchurch*, 256, 324-5.

8 BDA 23 November 1918.

9 ECS 7 December 1918.

10 ECT 21 December 1918.

Southend's barbed wire and sandbags disappeared.[11] More dangerously, German mines continued to be swept ashore for some years after the War ended. A controlled explosion of one such mine in February 1919 was alleged to have been heard as far away as Wakes Colne.[12] Another was washed ashore as late as October 1922 at Walton.[13] The last night of duty for the special constables of Southend was 6 February 1919. The Hornchurch section attended the National Peace Thanksgiving Service on Sunday 6 July 1919; this was its last parade, for it was disbanded a week later on 14 July.[14] Unfortunately, the cessation of hostilities generated practices which appalled local fishermen as the military began dumping surplus ammunition in the waters off the coast of Essex.[15] The R.A.F. aerodromes which had ringed the capital and been scattered through the county were soon dismantled. That at Rochford closed in mid-1922 and all its effects were put up for auction on 7-8 June. Between two and three thousand people attended and the sale raised £7,000.[16] Some memories were worth keeping. In July 1919 the battleships and battle cruisers of the Atlantic Fleet visited Southend and presented a wonderful sight to the inhabitants, who flocked to view them in their thousands. The last visit of the fleet had been exactly five years earlier, just days before war began.[17] In September the boys and girls of Hamstel Junior School at Southend went a few steps further when they were taken onboard the captured German U-boat, *Deutschland*, at Harwich.[18] Within six months rusting hulks like the *Deutschland* were sold for scrap and were being towed away from the resort to be broken up.[19] Those ships of Essex's ports and fishing villages which had been commandeered for naval service began to return. In the spring of 1919 two Wivenhoe yachts, the *Rosabelle* and the *Lady Blanche*, returned home after several years of patrol work.[20] Brightlingsea's naval base, which had served its country so well, was closed on 31 October 1921.[21] The town's Bayard Recreation Ground, which had been taken over by the military and closed to the public since 1915, had already been reopened six months earlier.[22] Clacton's pigeon owners, who had sacrificed their birds to the service of the nation, were duly

11 SST 1 June 1922.

12 SST 15 February 1919.

13 ECS 28 October 1922

14 SST 13 February 1919; Perfect, *Hornchurch*, 191.

15 SST 19 June 1919.

16 SST 15 June 1922.

17 SST 17 July 1919.

18 ERO T/S 607/1.

19 EEC 7 March 1919.

20 EEC 8 March 1919.

21 ECS 5 November 1921.

22 ECS 9 April 1921.

rewarded with certificates for the birds' meritorious service.[23]

By mid-December 1918 the Cake and Pastry Order, which had effectively starved the nation's sweet tooth, was withdrawn, theoretically in time for Christmas. Light and fancy pastries, muffins and crumpets, and cakes iced with sugar or chocolate were now permitted, although in practice it took longer for sugar supplies to arrive in sufficient quantities to make this possible. Milk controls were not withdrawn until February 1920, and restrictions on other items, such as eggs, were not lifted until March.[24] On 30 June 1920 the Braintree Food Control Committee, which had dealt with 270 retailers and met twice a week since its inception in August 1917, was brought to an end.[25] Two days earlier the last meeting of the Harwich Food Control Committee was held, exactly six years after the assassination of Archduke Franz Ferdinand at Sarajevo had precipitated the Great War. The end of the food control committees effectively drew a line under local wartime food organisations, although food restrictions continued for some time afterwards.[26] There was certainly an immense weariness about all aspects of the bureaucracy concerning food. At Maldon the town council flatly refused to set up a 'profiteering tribunal' on the grounds that the local populace were heartily sick of tribunals and committees, as well as arguing that its existence would be a slur on the honesty of local retailers.[27]

By the spring of 1919 most of the voluntary organisations which had developed during the War to render assistance to the war effort had also been consigned to history. Where they existed, air-raid shelter committees were wound up. That at Southend's St Helen's Road concluded its meetings in March. The war relief committees, which in reality had had little to do, were also concluded. South Benfleet's closed in May. Hornchurch's committee, which had been formed on 12 August 1914, was wound up in 1919, with £150 of its funds remaining. The town's savings committee was terminated on 31 July.[28] The War saw a proliferation of local war hospitals, all of which had been made redundant by the Armistice. The 43rd Essex V.A.D. was disbanded a fortnight after the Armistice. It had dealt with some twelve thousand patients, transporting the sick and wounded to various hospitals throughout the Southend area.[29] The last group of wounded soldiers was discharged from the Essex County Hospital at Colchester on 3 March 1919. Female patients, who had been banished to the school building adjacent to Hospital Road in August 1914, were once more allowed to return to the former female wards.[30] Local Red

23 EEC 14 June 1919.

24 HDS 10 January 1920; ECS 15 March 1920.

25 EEC 6 August 1920.

26 HDS 3 July 1920.

27 EEC 12 September 1919.

28 SST 1 May 1919; Perfect, *Hornchurch*, 209-11.

29 SST 5 August 1920.

30 ECS 15 March 1919.

Cross depots, such as the one at Thorpe were closed, and when Woodhouse Hospital, Great Horkesley, was closed in April, it was the last of the auxiliary hospitals in north-east Essex to be shut down.[31] On 16 February 1919 at St Michael's, Braintree, the Red Cross flag and Union Jack which had flown over the town's V.A.D. hospital during the War, were taken down and hung in the church. The alabaster plaque below them reads "Inasmuch as ye have done it unto these my brethren, ye have done it unto me."[32]

The local war work depots, whose female workers had done such magnificent work in making, amassing and despatching comforts for the troops, also wound up their activities; those at Southend and Woodford closed in March 1919, that at Clacton closed in April, Colchester's in June. Hornchurch's depot closed on 19 July; it had been created just four days after war was declared. A Mrs Gardner, co-founder and leader of the depot, wrote a poignant farewell to those who had worked in it for five years:

> Ladies, the good-bye brings with it a tone of sadness; sadness that you and I, who have been working here together, have now to part. Our work is finished, and we can set aside our needles and thimbles, feeling that we, who have met here each week, have done our little bit to help others during this sad war and anxious time. I think, in times to come, many of us will look back with pleasure on the work we have done here, and to our bright, happy little meetings — meetings which I trust have made us all fast friends for life — but I cannot say good-bye without first thanking you one and all for the kind and willing help you have all given me during these past years. Without your help this little Depot could not have been the success it has proved to be![33]

That same month the Social Club for Troops in Colchester closed its doors for the last time, and the Colchester Sick and Wounded Soldiers' Comfort Committee disbanded itself and distributed its remaining funds to various charities. One month later, the East Anglian Munitions Committee, which had performed such sterling war work for the Government, was officially terminated.[34]

However, there were those for whom the War could not be considered at an end until peace was properly restored. The Allied naval blockade of Germany and her defeated allies was maintained throughout 1919 as an incentive for the new German government to sign the peace terms which would eventually be offered to it. There is no doubt that

[31] ECS 12 April 1919.

[32] I am grateful to Gordon Cornell, churchwarden of St Michael's, for providing me with this information.

[33] Perfect, *Hornchurch*, 203.

[34] ECS 14 June 1919; ECT 5 April, 17 May 1919.

the blockade continued to cause enormous suffering in Germany and Central Europe. The Armistice having brought hostilities to an end, there were those who were affronted at the retention of a policy which now seemed to be vengeful and vindictive. The Quakers of Kelvedon wrote to the Government appealing for the blockade to be lifted "to prevent the starvation of millions."[35] Edith Marriage, wife of former Colchester mayor, Wilson Marriage, wrote a letter to the local press appealing for material assistance for the people suffering in central Europe.[36] However, few people were prepared to entertain such qualms of conscience where the Germans were concerned. Many would have agreed with this uncompromising poem by Isabella Pearson, who was in no doubt that post-war German pleas for leniency should be ignored:

"A blockade is inhuman,
Our children must be fed,"
Thus whimpering wails the German,
His prestige lost and dead.

But what of loud explosions,
Torpedoes 'neath the waves,
'Gainst merchant vessels speeding,
With orders none to save?

The food supply of Britain,
Was good and lawful prey,
The "Fatherland" is sacred,
Or so they seem to say.

The massacre of Britons —
Old men, and children, too —
By dropping bombs, was only fair,
'Twas just and right to do.

The prisoners from Britain,
Could slave, and starve and die,
The Belgians' food is stolen;
The Hun says, "What care I?"

And now the tide is turning,
The blood-red tide of war,
And those cry out for mercy,
Who showed no ruth before.[37]

[35] ERO T/A 434/1/9 Kelvedon Friends, 16 March 1919.

[36] ECS 5 July 1919.

[37] ECC 22 November 1918.

In late June a hoax telegram announcing that the treaty had been signed arrived at Colchester garrison, and prompted hundreds of soldiers to appear half-dressed in the streets of Colchester, before heavy rain drove them indoors again. It was a short time after these premature celebrations, that the Germans eventually signed the Treaty of Versailles on 28 June 1919 and the War officially came to an end.[38] The news reached the area by the evening of that day and wild celebrations, of a far less restrained nature than on Armistice Day, went on late into the night. The *Essex County Standard* described it as "among the unpleasant episodes of the war."[39]

With the War now at last completely over, the nation's peace celebrations, which had been gestating since the ceasefire, could begin. To the great delight of pupils and staff, the school summer holidays were extended by one week as part of the celebrations.[40] Colchester Town Council had already formed a Special Celebration of Peace Committee and by March had come up with ideas for the 'Peace Week' proposed by the Government. The committee's suggestions were along similar lines to the celebrations of George V's coronation in 1911, with a procession, or "march of triumph", through the town, a united service of thanksgiving, a tea and entertainment for the borough's children, a cycling carnival and athletic sports, other entertainments and concerts and a firework display.[41] The borough planned its celebrations for August, but when the Government set aside 19 July as a national day of rejoicing, the events were brought forward.[42] Sunday 6 July was designated a National Day of Thanksgiving for Peace. In Colchester a united service was held in Castle Park, preceded by a fifteen hundred strong procession of civic and military dignitaries. At Clacton, six thousand people congregated around the band pavilion for the thanksgiving service there. At Brightlingsea naval base every ship in port was decorated with bunting. During the so-called Peace Week, the Colchester Board of Guardians doled out 3*s.* to every adult recipient of outdoor relief, and 1*s.* 6*d.* to each child. The workhouse employees were given a week's holiday with pay. The Colchester celebrations on 19 July went very much according to the plans of the Celebration of Peace Committee. A triumphal march of a naval detachment from the Colne, together with troops from the garrison, and joined by demobbed ex-servicemen, marched through a town bedecked with hundreds of Union Jacks, before standing in massed ranks in front of the Town Hall — the military to the right of it, the demobbed men to the left. Above them was a huge banner stretched across the High Street between the Town Hall and shops opposite, which read "Peace with Victory: Colchester Thanks You." A large flag bearing the town's arms was draped over the balcony, and above this was the flag of St George. The mayor and council stood on a slightly raised

38 ECC 28 June 1919.

39 ECS 5 July 1919.

40 Reynolds, *Wilson Marriage School*, 55.

41 ERO, minutes of Special (Celebration of Peace) Committee, 26 March 1919.

42 ERO, minutes of Special (Celebration of Peace) Committee, 2 July 1919.

platform erected outside the Town Hall steps, flanked by two lamp stands which were adorned with large wreaths. The Town Hall balconies were crammed with people, and every window on the High Street side was crowded with others peering to get a glimpse of the historic occasion. The High Street itself was packed with thousands of people.[43] George Wright, inaugurated as mayor only two days before the ceasefire, and who had rapidly become known as the 'Peace Mayor', addressed the crowd as he had done on November 11:

> Commander Mahon, General Towsey, Sailors, Soldiers of His Majesty's Forces, Demobilised and Discharged Men, Nurses and all who have taken part in this great War for Liberty — I offer you, on behalf of this ancient and loyal borough of Colchester, our heartfelt thanks for all your heroic efforts that have enabled us to meet to-day to celebrate a great and successful victory. (Cheers.) Many of us, some too old, some too young, and others for various reasons, could not take part with you in the great war; but hour by hour, day by day, we watched you as you went forward with bravery in the field of battle fighting for this your native country, and although at times the issue may have seemed doubtful, yet we placed our reliance of the bravery of the lads, the justice of our cause, and we prayed for you, and knew God would give us the victory. (Cheers.)[44]

A town hall reception at 11 a.m., was followed by a 'Grand Free Fete' on the Abbey Field and an athletics meeting at Land Lane, both at 2 p.m. At 3 p.m. and 6.30 p.m. special peace celebration music and national airs were played in the Castle Park by the Colchester and District Musical Society. At 10.30 p.m. an enormous crowd gathered at the Abbey Field to see the lighting of Colchester's bonfire, one of many lit to create a chain of bonfires across the land. The day's entertainments were concluded with a fireworks display.[45] Four days later on the Recreation Ground, 6,117 children of the borough were entertained with a 'peace treat'. Children throughout north-east Essex were treated to peace souvenirs; those at Ramsey received a peace mug, although they did not get them until November.[46]

The peace celebrations in the larger towns may have been lavish, but every other town and village indulged themselves, albeit on a more modest scale. The celebrations at Harold Wood revealed the same unashamed joy as elsewhere. A school treat was held, decorations were everywhere, and the village was illuminated at night. There

43 ECT 26 July 1919.

44 Hunt, *Colchester War Memorial Souvenir*, 41.

45 ECT 26 July 1919.

46 HDS 8 November 1919.

were races, tugs-of-war, a fancy dress event and a beauty contest. Tea was served to hundreds of people in the institute, there were evening concerts, and the whole day was brought to a close with a fireworks display.[47] Hornchurch's celebration, "in the field between Harrow Drive and Grey Towers Camp", was a riot of activity. An "old folks and widows dinner" was the only sedate item on the day's agenda. There was a fancy dress carnival, and a host of games — sack, egg and spoon, four-legged, obstacle, "sweep and miller" and "blindfold driving" races, a "bun struggle", "tilting the bucket", tug-of-war and wrestling on horseback. Dancing began in the drill hall at 7.30 p.m. and there was a concert in a large marquee, as well as a country fair, swings, roundabouts, and at least two bands.[48] At Wrabness, which only had a population of about two hundred and fifty, the parish council decided on "tea and sports" for the children, and "a meat tea for all the inhabitants of Wrabness, with Sports for Adults and Juveniles on the Rectory Lawn." It was decided to spend about £20 on food, with £10 for prizes.[49] The village celebrations on 19 July were recorded in the parish council minutes:

> Wrabness was in holiday garb on Saturday when a capital programme was carried out. Mrs Robinson kindly lent the Rectory Lawn, where a most enjoyable and pleasant time was spent.
>
> The Committee of management deserves great praise, for truly there was not a dull moment throughout the proceedings ...
>
> Tables were laid to accommodate 250, spread with white cloths, tastefully decorated with flowers, and when spread with the good things provided presented an appetising appearance. The menu was, bread and butter, ham, beef, sausage rolls, salads, cake, buns, tarts, tea and fruit. The weather was all that could be desired. The success of this long-to-be-remembered and eventful day was due largely to the villagers themselves, who met the appeal for finance in a liberal way ...
>
> So abundant was the provision that the surplus was disposed of by a Tea for all the children of the Parish on the following Monday.
>
> Now let us sing God bless ye, Peace
> May bloody war for ever cease
> May health and wealth join hand in hand
> To bless the people of this land.
>
> God bless the King.

47 Perfect, *Hornchurch*, 255.

48 Perfect, *Hornchurch*, 322.

49 ERO D/P 6/30/2, Wrabness Parish Council Minutes 1895-1933, 7, 11 July 1919.

So much was collected for this feast that even after such magnificent celebrations there was still 10*s.* 7*d.* left over. It was duly donated to the village war memorial fund.

On a more sombre note, the end of the War saw the return to Essex of the remains of Captain Charles Fryatt, executed by the Germans on 27 July 1916 for his attempt to ram a U-boat. On 12 July his remains were ferried to Dover, after which a special train carried his body to London, where it was greeted by representatives of the King and the Government. It was then carried to St Paul's on a gun carriage by naval blue jackets, his coffin draped by the Union Jack and the medal of the Chevalier of the Order of St Leopold, which had been pinned on the head of the coffin by the King of the Belgians at the start of its journey. A special train took the coffin from Liverpool Street station to Harwich; the funeral cortege included the Mayor of Harwich, the town's M.P., Harry Newton, representatives of the R.A.F., Royal Marines, of the ships in harbour, the Great Eastern Railway, and the Naval Training School at nearby Shotley. The Bishops of Chelmsford, Colchester and Barking were in attendance, and music was played by the Salvation Army and naval bands. Two carriages contained floral tributes, including one from the King and Queen of Belgium made of white roses and lilac. Thousands of people lined the route from Dovercourt station to the churchyard, and thousands more were crammed in and around the churchyard itself. The funeral service was conducted by the Reverend T. Grey Collier, Vicar of Dovercourt, at the end of which the coffin was lowered into a grave lined with evergreens and flowers to the strains of 'Abide with Me'. In view of the great feelings which Fryatt's death had roused, the Bishop of Chelmsford's sermon was remarkably restrained, although he too saw him as "a victim of ignoble spite", and said that in shooting Fryatt, "Germany sounded the lowest depths of her national ignominy."[50] On 18 June 1920 an obelisk was unveiled to his memory in Upper Dovercourt churchyard.[51] Two months earlier another martyr's body had passed through Colchester, that of Edith Cavell, executed as a spy by the Germans in October 1915, her body carried on a special train bound for burial at Norwich. The employees of the Great Eastern Railway stood silently on the station platform as the train, with the white carriage containing her remains, passed slowly through.[52] In both cases these ceremonies marked the beginning, rather than the end, of the memorialisation of those who had lost their lives in the Great War.

50 HDS 12 July 1919.

51 EEC 25 June 1920.

52 ECT 17 May 1919

CHAPTER FOURTEEN

Memories of the Past, Visions of the Future: The War Memorial Movement in Essex

The unveiling of the war memorial at Maldon.

(ERO: Postcards Collection, Maldon)

THE BRAVE WHO DIE

Not theirs the victor's wreath of classic bay;
Not theirs the acclaim of myriad voices clear.
The feast, the laughter, the triumphant song.
Their guardian shines a crown of brighter ray —
Unfading glory, glistening with a tear,
Whose light shall glow the ages all along.

Written by "H.M.A.C." of Brentwood,
Published in the *Essex County Chronicle*,
2 July 1915.

THE DESIRE TO COMMEMORATE the service and sacrifice of individuals and communities was not a phenomenon that was unique to the Great War. Public monuments in England were rare before 1800, but this changed dramatically in the early nineteenth century. The prolonged wars against Revolutionary and Napoleonic France stimulated the growth of nationalist sentiments, and produced a population eager to celebrate both the country's victory, and the heroes who had brought about that victory. New towns in the industrial North and Midlands that sought to express their civic identity, willingly erected statuary and monuments along neo-classical lines. The trend reached its culmination in the 1830s and 1840s with the erection of the national monument to Nelson in Trafalgar Square, funded entirely by voluntary subscriptions.[1] With a precedent firmly set, the role played by Essex men in national events was commemorated locally during the course of the next sixty years. At Birch, stone flags were placed in the church wall in memory of an officer killed in the Cawnpore massacre during the Indian Mutiny.[2] Robert Thornhill, his wife, two children and their nurse perished in the same horrific disaster and are commemorated in Liston church. Another victim of the Indian Mutiny, a Captain Gordon, is remembered at Wethersfield church. On a wall in Saffron Walden church are banners and helmets carved in memory of two sons of Lord Braybrooke, who died in the Crimean War, one killed at the battle of Inkerman, the other a week later at Balaclava. Fifty years later the South African, or Boer, War gave rise to a new generation of memorials. While the Boer War was still being fought, a marble tablet was placed in St Botolph's church in Colchester in memory of Private Ben Cheer, a twenty-four-year-old Colcestrian member of the City of London Imperial Volunteers, who died at Pretoria in 1900.[3] Another tablet to a soldier killed in this war had an epitaph from *Macbeth* included on it. Jack Watney, a nineteen-year-old young man

1 A. Yarrington, *The Commemoration of the Hero 1800-64: Monuments to the British Victors of the Napoleonic Wars* (1988), vi-xi.

2 A. Mee (ed.), *The King's England, Essex: London's North Sea Neighbour* (1942), 164.

3 ECS 23 February 1901.

was killed in 1901; his memorial is in Birchanger church. One hundred men of East Ham who died in this conflict are remembered in the Town Hall.[4] In 1910 the county's own monument to those who fought in the South African War was unveiled in Chelmsford. At about the same time, Dovercourt church acquired a memorial window featuring Christ and a centurion. It commemorated the German soldiers who died fighting alongside British troops in the disastrous Walcheren expedition against Napoleon in 1810.[5] In view of events only four years later, it was somewhat ironic that the window was a gift from the German Kaiser, Wilhem II.

As we have seen in Chapter 3, the Great War rapidly acquired the status of a religious crusade against the brutish and irreligious Germans. The near religious nature of the War, the accompanying demonisation of the enemy, the titanic scale and perceived significance of the conflict, and the immense loss of life and suffering which it involved, made it inevitable that it would burn itself into memories of the people and make it impossible for them to forget the enormity of what had happened. Equally inevitable, was the fact that those who had lived through and survived the War would seek to commemorate their part in it, and more importantly, the sacrifice of those who had not survived.

The public manifestation of grief and remembrance occurred throughout the War. Widows wore black, notices were placed in the local press relating the death of local men, and memorial services were held for dead servicemen, particularly where they had been active in church affairs, or in villages where the deceased was known to everyone. In January 1917 at Burnham, for instance, a memorial service was held for the thirty-three men of the town who had been killed. Both the pulpit and the communion table were draped with a Union Jack.[6] As we saw in Chapter 5, the headmistress of Tillingham School faithfully recorded in the school logbook the deaths on active service of former pupils from her school. A few families, we can hardly call them fortunate, were able to conduct burial services for their sons or husbands and witness them interred in their home churchyards and cemeteries. Thanks to the Germans setting a headstone over the grave of David Keith-Johnston of the Royal Naval Air Service, who was killed over Ostend in August 1915, his parents were able to bring his body home for burial in Felsted churchyard.[7] Very few were able to act similarly, particularly when in late November 1918 the French authorities clamped down on the unofficial exhumations which were occurring throughout the burial grounds on the Western Front. This effectively closed off the method by which well-off families had attempted to recover the bodies of their loved ones.[8]

4 Mee, Essex, 36, 118-119, 165, 223, 301, 377.

5 Mee, Essex, 114-115; V.G. Ballance, *A Short History of the Parish Church of Dovercourt*, 66-7.

6 ECC 26 January 1917.

7 M. Craze, *A History of Felsted School 1564-1947* (1955), 273.

8 J. Winter, *Sites of Memory, Sites of Mourning: The Great War in European Cultural History* (1995), 24.

For much of the War, death notices were short, simple and factual. A typical entry was this one from the *Essex County Chronicle* of 1 May 1915:

> Srgt G.J.F. Greenwood ... was a son of Mr Greenwood, of Colchester, who for many years has been foreman to Messrs Brackett and Co., engineers, Greenstead Road. Srgt Greenwood was married to a daughter of Mr and Mrs Wood of Colchester, and was at home on leave only three weeks ago. He leaves a widow and two children. He held an important position with Messrs Brown and Co., timber merchants, Ipswich. He was a native of Colchester and was educated as a bluecoat boy in the Colchester National Schools.

However, by 1917 this pattern of remembrance was changing. Instead of placing purely factual entries which had traditionally been pigeonholed under 'Births, Marriages and Deaths' as the 'Roll of Honour', it became more and more usual for families to include a sentiment as part of the message, which then tended to appear under 'In Memoriam'. Many of these sentiments were of the utmost simplicity, concluding the remembrance with 'At Rest', 'Until the Day Break', or 'Sadly Missed'. Others included more overtly Christian sentiments such as 'Thy Will Be Done', 'Greater love hath no man than this that he lay down his life for his friends', or 'God hath given and He hath taken away'. Alongside brief sentiments such as these, there began to appear verses of mourning and remembrance. These verses seem rarely to have been composed by the families themselves. Instead, they were selected from a wide choice of in memoriam cards, produced, for instance at Colchester by Benham, the owners of the *Essex County Standard*, and available from the *Standard*'s offices, at the price of 2*s*. 6*d*. Initially announcements were limited to four lines, but as the practice of inserting verses became increasingly popular, this seems to have been dropped.[9] The practice of purchasing in memoriam cards as funeral cards which were sent to family and friends went back to Victorian times. However, for the vast majority of bereaved families during the Great War there were no funerals to attend, no graveside goodbyes to be said. Some individuals and families clung to the hope that their loved ones might have survived long after the futility of such hope was obvious. On Christmas Eve 1918, the *Southend Standard* printed this forlorn note:

> Mrs Cross, of 38 Cromwell Road, Prittlewell, would be grateful if any repatriated prisoner-of-war could give her any news concerning her husband, 30601 Private L.C. Cross, 1st Essex Regiment "X" Company, who has been missing since April 14th, 1917.

9 ECS 13 April 1918.

Most families who lost a loved one abroad had to rely on letters written by their commanding officer, military chaplain, or comrades for information about how they died. Stanley Victor Lamb, aged just nineteen years old, of Burlington Road, Colchester, was injured on 23 May 1917 when a shell exploded in his trench. He died shortly afterwards in a dressing station. Several of his company died with him. He had enlisted in the Bedfordshire Regiment on 31 October 1916 and been sent to the trenches in March 1917. His chaplain wrote to his parents:

> The next night we buried him ... with all the respect and reverence we could pay to gallant men who had given their lives for their country. Record is kept of the place where they lie, and these British cemeteries are going to be preserved and kept sacred by the French government for ever. Each grave is marked temporarily with a wooden cross, and after the war I understand that permanent memorials will be erected, bearing the names of the brave men who sacrificed themselves in the cause of right and justice.[10]

The desperate anguish caused amongst bereaved families by the absence of a body or a funeral is all too evident in the verses selected for inclusion in the press.[11] Their inability to participate in any ritualised farewell for husbands, fathers or sons is expressed more often than any other sentiment and is typified by the following verse:

> Two years have passed and still we miss him
> Never shall his memory fade,
> Though far away our thoughts will wander,
> To the place where he is laid.

This same heartbroken theme of the inability to have been at the graveside appears in this verse:

> Could I have stood beside his grave,
> And seen him laid to rest,
> The blow would not have been so hard,
> For me, who loved him best.

Many relatives had not only to come to terms with the death of loved one, but also with the realisation that they may have had no resting place of their own:

10 ECS 9 June 1917.

11 The following selection of verses are drawn from the *Essex County Standard* and *Essex County Chronicle* in 1915, 1916 and 1917.

He sleeps on the blood-stained fields of France,
A gallant lad so brave;
No loving hand may place a wreath,
Upon his unknown grave.

Grief made worse by ignorance of how someone died, compounded by acceptance that they lay in another country, appeared frequently and was expressed in various forms:

The unknown grave is the bitterest blow,
None but aching hearts can tell
We often sit and think of him
And wonder how he died.
And wish we could have said good-bye,
Before he closed his eyes.
Could we but kneel beside his grave,
And shed a silent tear,
But no! He lies in a foreign grave,
The only boy we loved so dear.

Another family chose a similar theme for their remembrance card:

I often sit and think, dear son,
And wonder how you died;
With no one else who loved you dear
Before you closed your eyes;
Sleep, dear son, in a foreign land;
In a grave we may never see
But as long as life and memory last
We shall always remember thee.

Some families took consolation in their Christian faith and in traditional Christian language and imagery, "We have lost, heaven hath gained, / One of the best the world contained". The idea of death as but a temporary separation had an immense hold upon the popular imagination:

I picture him safely returning
And longed to clasp his dear hand,
But God has postponed the meeting
Till we meet in the better land.

These verses too, all contained a stated trust in God and the consolation of Christian resurrection:

> God gives but does not take away,
> He only safely keeps above,
> For us the treasures that we love.
>
> The cross was heavy, the blow severe,
> To part with him we loved so dear,
> But we must bear and not complain,
> But trust in Christ to meet again.
>
> From our happy home and circle,
> God has taken one we love.
> Borne away from sin and sorrow,
> To a Happier home above.

Some sentiments, like this one chosen by a Colchester widow, expressed comfort in the belief of the spiritual survival in this world of her dead husband:

> I miss you and mourn you in silence unseen,
> And dwell in the memories of days that have been.
> Unknown to the world he stands by my side,
> And whispers these words, "Death cannot divide."
> God has taken my loved one from my home.
> But never from my heart.
> Gone, but not forgotten.

Most secular sentiments, devoid of any obviously spiritual content, contained a despairing tone, "Death divides; memories cling". The following verse sounded even more despairingly:

> We think of him in silence
> And his name we oft recall,
> But there is nothing left to answer
> But his photo on the wall.

This then, was how some grieving families publicly expressed their loss. The sentiments which were expressed were comparatively few in number — his duty done, he died for a noble cause, a brief parting, not dead but gone before, memories linger, not dead but sleeping, without a goodbye, gone but not forgotten. Despite the apparent artificiality of the production and selection of these sentiments, for many they gave voice to their loss, and as such they were to have a significant influence on the war memorial movement.

From the outset the War was regarded as a struggle between good and evil, and the very future of civilisation was seen as depending upon its outcome. Embroiled in a war of such significance, the memorialisation of the part played by local people occurred almost immediately. The compilation of town and village rolls of honour, the lists of men who had volunteered for active service in the autumn of 1914, was a celebration of local gallantry and patriotism. It was also the genesis of the war memorial movement, the first attempt to record the local contribution to the War at the front. Later, as the tragedy of the War acquired a far more grim significance, these rolls of honour were transformed from a record of voluntary service into a catalogue of those who had made the 'supreme sacrifice'. For instance, by the end of 1916 the roll of honour for communities in the Dengie peninsula listed the Fallen as follows:

Burnham	33	Southminster	13
Althorne	4	Bradwell	2
Dengie	1	Latchingdon	2
Tillingham	4	St Leonard's	1
Asheldham	4[12]		

Rolls of honour were compiled by practically every community and organisation which lost men to the services; the action of the Colchester and East Essex Cricket Club, which hung its roll of honour prominently in its pavilion, was not unusual.[13] Most churches compiled lists of their parishioners and placed a copy in the building. These rolls of honour were often regarded with great awe and reverence. The one at Braintree was deposited in the church porch. At Little Clacton, the roll of honour, which by 1917 comprised the names both of volunteers and those who had died, was stored in the church and placed on the church's original Reformation table. Above it was a picture of the Crucifixion, and over that hung the Union Jack. A prayer desk was positioned in front of the table. It is evident from this that the roll of honour had clearly already taken on a patriotic, symbolic, religious, and perhaps even a mystical, significance.[14] The most appropriate expression of the significance of rolls of honour is perhaps to be found in the wording that was written to accompany that at Walthamstow:

> They whom this roll commemorates were numbered among those who, at the call of King and Country, left all that was dear to them, endured hardness, faced danger, and finally passed

[12] BDA 30 December 1916.

[13] ECS 24 July 1915.

[14] ECS 2 June 1917.

> out of the sight of men by the path of duty and self-sacrifice,
> giving up their own lives that others might live in freedom.[15]

Before what might be termed an 'official' war memorial movement gathered pace in 1918-19, some individuals attempted to express their own feelings about the Fallen in a very public way by erecting what became known as 'war shrines'. These shrines, which were invariably wooden, were a distinctly religious expression of remembrance, and were probably deliberately modelled on the wayside crosses, or *calvaire*, which are found in many Roman Catholic countries in Europe. Southend Town Council approved of at least three shrines erected by private citizens in 1916. Sir Charles Nicholson placed one at the entrance to his premises at Porters, Southchurch Road. Another was put in the centre of the road at Bournes Green. It was understood that they were to be removed at the end of the War.[16] One made of black oak was erected in Wanstead.[17] C.C. Naters, the controversial Rector of St James's, Colchester, who introduced the trappings of Anglo-Catholicism into his church, had no qualms about setting up war shrines in his parish. In October 1916 he suggested the creation of five such shrines.[18] At Ardleigh the war shrine, donated by a Mr and Mrs J.A. Josselyn, and erected in 1917, was made of oak and inscribed with the words "To the Glory of God. Ardleigh Roll of Honour." At the foot of the shrine were the words "Brethren, pray for us".[19] That at Little Leighs was donated by the daughter of a former rector. It was a triptych of wood from H.M.S. *Britannia*, a broken-up training ship. Its doors opened out to reveal the twenty-seven names of the Fallen, and underneath was a cross.[20] The Rector of Rayleigh erected a memorial to the Fallen in his churchyard.[21] There were four in Romford — at Squirrel's Heath, Mawneys, St John's, and All Saints'.[22] By 1918 shrines containing the names of volunteers and the dead had been placed in the lychgate at St James's, Brightlingsea. Others were erected in places such as Sandon, Tillingham, Feering, All Saints' and St Martin's, Colchester, Lexden, Parkeston, Roxwell, Sible Hedingham, Stebbing and Wickford. Kirby-le-Soken was unusual in that it had two shrines; one was placed inside the railings surrounding the Primitive Methodist Church, and another outside the entrance to the parish church. Both were built of battleship teak.[23] At Great Wakering a temporary wooden cross was put up in preference to a shrine. On either

15 WG 28 March 1919.

16 SBC minutes, 27 October, 22 December 1916, 8 March 1917.

17 LE 19 October 1918.

18 ECS 4 November 1916.

19 ECS 6 June 1917.

20 ECC 27 April 1917.

21 ECC 13 April 1917.

22 ECC 18 May 1917.

23 EEA 15 September 1917.

side empty shell cases were used as flower vases.[24] In 1918 a twelve foot high war memorial cross was unveiled on the green in front of the church at West Mersea.[25] War shrines, alongside the rolls of honour, formed the earliest examples of war memorials. In design they were remarkably similar in their efforts to capture a medievalism appropriate to a situation where the War was viewed as a crusade and its soldiers were regarded as warriors.

The public process of commemorating those who had lost their lives occurred throughout the War. Rolls of honour and war shrines were a significant part of this process. Commemoration was also undertaken by the families of those who had been killed. A marble tablet was unveiled in Harwich parish church in April 1917 in memory of Sub-Lieutenant George Paterson, an Australian naval officer killed at the Battle of Jutland.[26] In that same month the parents of a sailor from Southend erected a Calvary at Stornoway on the Isle of Lewis. Their son had worshipped in the church there when he had been stationed on the island prior to his death.[27] In June a memorial window was installed in St James's, Clacton-on-Sea, for Charles Nicholson, a twenty-year-old Clacton man killed on the Somme in September 1916.[28] Memorial services for the dead became a regular feature of memorialisation, especially where the deceased had been a regular worshipper at a church or where he belonged to a close-knit community, such as a small village. One such service was held at Braintree on 23 May 1915 in memory of Corporal F. Seabrook, who had been killed in action nine days earlier. He had been a member of the church choir and his father was a former churchwarden. That same day a memorial service took place in Doddinghurst church for Gerald Piggott, an eighteen-year-old Lieutenant and an only son. The church was bedecked with flowers, and the Union Jack and his helmet and sword were placed on the altar.[29]

The end of the War accelerated the momentum of the war memorial movement which was well under way in many parishes and workplaces before 1918. The parishioners at St Mary's, Walthamstow, had discussed the possibility of a war memorial as early as November 1916, fully two years before the War ended.[30] A meeting of former pupils of Felsted School to discuss a war memorial occurred in London in September 1917. Two months later fundraising towards a war memorial was already under way at St Alban's, Southend. Individuals were commemorated in tablets at Hatfield Broad Oak and Coggeshall in early 1918.[31] The parishioners of St Mary Magdalene's, Colchester, were busy organising a sale of work to raise money for their war memorial on the very day

24 EEA 16 November 1917.

25 *Essex Review*, xxvii, (1918), 42, 101.

26 HDS 7 April 1917.

27 ECC 4 May 1917.

28 ECS 23 June 1917.

29 ECC 28 May 1915.

30 P.H. Reaney, *The Church of St Mary's, Walthamstow* (1969), 68.

31 ECC 7 September, 16 November 1917, 11 January, 15 February 1918.

that the Armistice was signed.[32] Not all these commemorations were of military personnel. A memorial was erected at Southend in November 1917 in memory of Gladys West, a resident of the town who had been killed in a German air raid.[33]

The language of memorialisation both during, and after, the War helped to cloak people's thinking about the dead in an atmosphere of reverence and romanticism, and reflected people's perception of the War as a historically significant and religious crusade against a barbaric enemy. The dead were referred to in romantic, medieval and euphemistic terms which were designed to dignify the sacrifice of those who had died, as well as disguising the often dreadful nature of their sufferings and death. For instance, only a few days after the War ended, a memorial was dedicated at Warley to Frank Sturch, who was described as having "passed from the battlefields of France to perfect peace in the immediate presence of the Saviour he loved and served."[34] It must have been a great comfort to the man's relatives to believe that his transition from the horrors of war and life to eternal bliss was portrayed as such a painless, seamless transition. This medieval, almost knightly, tone can be found in the wording on the war memorial at Clavering, an obelisk erected in 1921, which immortalised the Fallen "who went forth to the Great War and returned not again." The war memorial at Beaumont-cum-Moze portrayed a knight kneeling before the crucified Christ with the city walls of Jerusalem in the background. The 'Children's Window' at St Mary the Virgin's, Prittlewell, featured King Arthur wielding Excalibur; The Jesus Guild's window in the same church portrayed medieval knights.

The dead, when mentioned in public, were overwhelmingly referred to as 'the Fallen', but quite often the terms 'the Glorious Dead' or simply 'Warriors' were also used. When Dr Edgar Hunt wrote to the local press in Colchester on Christmas Day 1918, he referred to "our beloved fallen."[35] Less frequently public speakers told of 'The Great and Silent Company', a term suggestive almost of a spiritual presence or even a ghostly survival of dead servicemen. At the dedication of the war memorial of All Saints', Vange, on 28 February 1920, Brigadier-General H.R. Aldair spoke in similar terms of spiritual survival:

> There was no waste in God's economy and they could not think of those bright and radiant spirits passing into the void, but rather living on in another sphere. They were now free to be the men God desired them to be, unhampered by infirmity of will and frailty of flesh.[36]

Those servicemen who died were said to have made the supreme sacrifice.

32 ECS 16 November 1918.

33 ECC 23 November 1917.

34 ECC 15 November 1918.

35 ECS 25 December 1918.

36 SSt 4 March 1920.

The planning and bringing to fruition of war memorials throughout Essex was not achieved without debate, and in some cases controversy and acrimony. There was little disagreement about the purpose of war memorials. Few would have taken issue with W. Gurney Benham, who said in the Moot Hall during Colchester's inaugural public meeting to discuss a war memorial for the town that, firstly, it was to be a memorial to the dead, but also

> to those who risked their lives, those who had endured untold hardship, suffering, wounds, sickness, who had sacrificed their livings, given up their comfort and had endured and fought and conquered.[37]

Edgar Hunt echoed these thoughts when, at the same meeting, he said that a memorial should be a celebration of thankfulness at being saved, it should perpetuate the memory of the Fallen, and be an expression of sympathy with their parents and relatives. There were also those who felt instinctively that a war memorial, however much it inevitably harked back to a specific event in historical time, also pointed to the future; that it spoke not only to those who had lived through the Great War, but to unborn generations yet to come. Alderman Wallace of Colchester articulated these sentiments when he advocated a monument containing

> the figure of a soldier on a plinth containing scenes of the war. He would be looking out towards the new world he had helped to create, with his back to the past — the best of the past.

The Reverend E.L. Lewis, Pastor of Burnham Congregational Church, also set his thoughts on the future when he told people that the Fallen had not died merely to preserve England's appearance, nor its traditions. They died, he said "not for the land they knew but for the land they hoped it would be." "The old world was not what these men died for", he continued, but "for a new world, a new future, where war would be no more possible."[38]

Entwined in thoughts such as these was the feeling of immeasurable gratitude felt by those who had lived through the War to those who had not survived. The Reverend J. Benson Evans, speaking at the unveiling of the Hornchurch Congregational Church war memorial on 30 May 1920, said that

> This memorial, handed down to posterity, will show that the people of 1920 were not ungrateful to those who, abnegating themselves, gave *all* in the cause of liberty amongst Nations. No

[37] CG 5 February 1919.

[38] BDA 3 September 1921.

> tablet or memorial can adequately express what we owe to them ... We do not forget those who fought and suffered hardships and were able to return to their homes when the war was over, but this evening we concentrate our thoughts in grateful memory of those who gave their lives for their country ... They gave all. What can a man do more? We thank God to-day for what they did, and we shall thank *them* some day when we shall meet them in the glorious reunion in the Home above. [author's italics][39]

A sense of gratitude was required, perhaps even demanded, of the survivors; that they should consecrate their post-war lives to being worthy of the sacrifice made by the Fallen. This is what Canon Brunwin-Hales, Rural Dean of Colchester, whose sons were both killed in the War, felt when he wrote:

> I hope we shall not have a memorial which will have two purposes or more, but a beautiful monument which will say with no uncertain voice to every passer-by: "These men served their country well. Go and do thou likewise in the liberty and peace which they died to gain for you."[40]

The same themes of honouring the dead by constructing a monument and by living a life worthy of their sacrifice runs through Edgar Hunt's letter to the local press of Christmas Day 1918, in which he sought to initiate and influence debate on the issue in Colchester:

> Now, in the first instance and before any other consideration, what should a war memorial be? It should be obviously erected to the memory of those who have fallen in the Great War, something obviously erected to honour the dead, a mark of love for and devotion to those who have made the sacrifice than which there is none greater, an object lesson of their devotion to duty, of their service to their King and Country, of their patriotism — a tangible proof of what this generation did at a great crisis in our history as an example and an incentive to future generations to emulate them in their day when they are called, as they surely will be sooner or later, to bear their part in some crisis yet to come.[41]

[39] Perfect, *Hornchurch*, 266.

[40] CG 5 February 1919.

[41] Hunt, *War Memorial Souvenir*, 17.

However, unanimity about what war memorials were for, did not necessarily lead to agreement about what form they ought to take. In general, people were divided along two lines of thought. There were those who thought that war memorials ought to be noble, uplifting and inspiring monuments forever associated with the sacrifice made during the Great War. On the other hand, there were those who preferred them to be entirely practical and utilitarian. The Church of England, conscious that many war memorials would be placed inside its churches or on consecrated ground, sought to influence the debate at an early stage. In 1916 the Bishop of Chelmsford urged parishes to avoid memorials "which lack artistic merit." None ought to be erected, he added, without a faculty application.[42] In his view it was impractical to seek to commemorate all the Fallen individually; churches would simply be overwhelmed. Instead he urged the erection after the War of a single roll of honour.[43] That same year the Convocations of Canterbury and York passed resolutions recommending that dioceses set up advisory committees consisting of those with a knowledge of art as groups whose advice could be sought by those seeking to create war memorials. Sixteen were quickly established, although the Diocese of Chelmsford did not institute one.[44]

The notion that the sacrifice of the Fallen could be commemorated by an entirely practical undertaking was abhorrent to many people. Edgar Hunt condemned the idea. Councillor F. Chapman of Colchester stated that he would not contribute one penny to establish a school of art, which was one proposal, but that he would donate £100 towards a sculptural monument. J.H. Round, Lord of the Manor of West Bergholt and a leading figure among local gentry, stated that

> the commemoration of the dead should not be made a mere excuse for demands by the living for something that they would like to have.[45]

Canon Brunwin-Hales spoke against using war memorials as "a subterfuge to obtain some convenience",[46] but he nevertheless attempted to reconcile the two divergent viewpoints in a diplomatic letter to the first public meeting held in Colchester to discuss its war memorial:

> In my small way I shall be ready to support any scheme in the way of a memorial you and your colleagues decide upon after public consultation, whether I like it or not. My own decided

42 A faculty is the official authorisation required to place a memorial in a church or its grounds.

43 CDC November 1916.

44 CDC Magazine May 1918, August 1919.

45 CG 16 April 1919.

46 ECS 7 August 1920.

> wish is for the erection of a noble monument, unmistakeable in its meaning and conspicuous in its position, symbolising the sacrifice of the fallen and the fruit of their sacrifice, the liberty of the world in general, and our own empire in particular. A monument like that appeals to me as immensely practical. It was the spirit of our gallant boys and others which won the war, and anything calculated to perpetuate that spirit will be of the utmost advantage in the future.[47]

When a disabled ex-serviceman complained that looking at a monument would do him no good at all, Brunwin-Hales wrote that:

> a visible memorial could do him and his brave wife some "good" directly by strengthening their spirit to bear their sore burden and indirectly by its teaching others to ease their burden by rendering them sympathy and substantial assistance.[48]

At Colchester the sub-committee entrusted with the task of considering a monument as a war memorial concluded their report by noting

> That no final scheme for a War Memorial for the Borough would be complete which does not include a Monument worthy of the occasion and the Borough as part of that scheme.[49]

The other side of the argument had its adherents too. The author of the *Colchester Gazette*'s 'County Notes' wrote that:

> A war memorial should not in short be merely a dead and ornate funerary monument but a living and lasting testimony to public spirit and patriotism and gratitude.[50]

At Burnham J.W. Booth thought the same thing when he urged the creation of a "living monument not a lump of stone".[51] The Reverend T.M. Mundle pulled no punches in his dismissal of monuments at Chelmsford's inaugural meeting. He agreed that:

[47] CG 5 February 1919.

[48] CG 12 February 1919.

[49] Report of Monument Sub-committee, 23 April 1919.

[50] CG 8 January 1919.

[51] BDA 22 February 1919.

> there should be a memorial to perpetuate and keep fragrant in all the years to come the names of the heroic dead, but he was afraid that monuments did not achieve that end. He did not think people studied monuments ... he was sure from his experience that a monument was about the worst thing in the world to perpetuate the memory of those they wished to honour.[52]

Colchester Town Council's War Memorial Committee, set up shortly after the Armistice, unanimously recommended that the memorial "should be practical and permanent in character." It recommended the creation of a war museum and general museum "supplementary to the existing museum of local antiquities in the Castle", a public art gallery, and a school of art and art library.[53] A few months later the committee appointed to investigate the idea that the memorial should take the form of a memorial hall and art school reported that, in its opinion,

> there is a feeling amongst the townspeople generally, and especially amongst the working population, that in Colchester — as in most other towns of any size — the local war memorial should take a practical form, and be of some permanent benefit to the Borough and to future generations.[54]

At the public meeting held to discuss the memorial on 29 January, the voices favouring a practical memorial made up a majority of the speakers. By that time the deputy mayor stated that the council had already received ten proposals and several were aired that evening. J. Carter, a wounded soldier, said that his fellow ex-servicemen wanted a utilitarian memorial. In his view, "the memory of the 'living dead' required no monument except a monument that should be of material advantage to those who had survived the trenches".

A Mr Harris advocated cottages for disabled soldiers and their families, or for those suffering from consumption. Cottages could be occupied at a peppercorn rent, and servicemen's children could be assisted by establishing scholarships. A Labour councillor, Timothy Smith, favoured the building of two hundred houses "for the free use of the soldiers' widows and disabled soldiers, under the control of the Council." These need not be regarded as almshouses, he argued, "but as a war memorial as a free gift of the citizens to those who had done so much for the country and the town."[55] Following the meeting, further suggestions continued to roll in to the press.

[52] ECC 20 December 1918.

[53] ECC 20 December 1918.

[54] Report of Memorial Hall & Albert School Site Sub-committee, no date.

[55] CG 5 February 1919.

William Harper suggested that the memorial should take the form of swimming baths, which had long been campaigned for in the town. Edwin Merrick was in favour of spending about £40,000 of public money aided by private enterprise to revitalise the ailing Vineyard Street area and the placing of a war memorial there.[56]

These divergent views were mirrored in other towns and villages throughout Essex. At a meeting at Walthamstow it was suggested that a Y.M.C.A. branch be created, as well as a cottage hospital, or a modern factory which would be designed to employ men who had been discharged from the armed forces because of injury or illness.[57] At Epping several suggestions were put forward at the inaugural meeting, including a calvary, a cross, swimming baths and a hospital wing. The cross was chosen, but on a more practical note it was decided that:

> the second part of the memorial take the form, if sufficient pecuniary support be forthcoming, of a fund, the income from the investment of which shall be used to assist the children of fallen men in their upkeep and education, and in placing them in a position to earn their own livings, and to give such occasional assistance to the mothers or other guardians of such children as may be found to be desirable.[58]

Southend's War Memorial Committee narrowed down the suggestions it had received to four; an extension to the Victoria Hospital, gardens at Prittlewell, cottages for disabled ex-servicemen, and a monument. The latter was eventually chosen, but as at Epping, the aim was to use any surplus funds to assist the children of the Fallen by providing educational scholarships.[59] At Lexden the ornamental suggestions which were made were matched by those advocating utilitarianism. A Mr Cadman suggested two almshouses be built, a Mr Tanner favoured a scholarship for young men "starting in life", and a Mr Hurnard preferred something useful rather than £300 spent on marble.[60] At Maldon the Workers' Council favoured a library; swimming baths were also suggested, as well as a monument placed in an extension to the churchyard.[61] The parish meeting at Thorpe-le-Soken came up with the idea of a new organ for the church, or a reredos, together with a memorial tablet. Clacton's War Memorial General Committee suggested a clock tower "on a prepared garden on the greensward, as an artistic adornment to the front, and at the same time a useful one", a new wing to the town's hospital with its beds endowed in memory of the

56 CG 12 February 1919.
57 LE 2 November 1918.
58 ECC 10 January 1919.
59 SSt 6 March 1919.
60 CG 8 January 1919.
61 ECC 11 April 1919.

fallen, an artistic creation on an appropriate site, or a playground, public park and sports ground. Here too practicality vied for acceptance with nobility. T.J. Price, the Wesleyan minister, urged that the memorial:

> serve to elevate and ennoble the lives of future generations and [he] would like to see something adopted which would have its influence on the development of the intellectual well being of the future men and women.[62]

At West Bergholt the parish meeting decided that if sufficient funds could be raised, a monument, a parish institute, and a recreation ground would be built.[63] At Frating the parish chose a village hall as their war memorial. When communities made their choice of war memorial, the limited availability of funds dictated that most of them chose some form of tablet, although as the following table shows, there was a large variety in the type of war memorial finally selected.

Breakdown of the type of war memorials found in Essex

	Number	%
Tablets	512	47
Cross	130	12
Church furniture/ornamentation	88	8
Rolls of honour	66	6
Stained glass windows	60	5
Obelisk/monument	47	4
Memorial halls/village halls	18	2
Cenotaph	18	2
Calvary	11	1
Statuary	10	1
Others	c.140	12

The mechanics of planning, organising and building a war memorial were, in most towns and villages, extremely simple. In general, the groundswell of opinion in favour of community war memorials was so overwhelming that it needed little encouragement. Local town and parish councils, responding to, rather than spearheading, public opinion, organised public meetings open to all residents irrespective of religious or political affiliation. At these meetings, inevitably chaired by a member of the clergy or a local dignitary, suggestions were put forward by anyone with an idea. At this point a committee would be formed, and entrusted with

[62] ECC 12 March 1919.

[63] ECS 10 May 1919.

the task of deciding which suggestion was most suitable and how it would be brought to fruition. An appeal for funds was usually necessary, although in some places wealthy local benefactors provided either a generous share of the required funds, or donated the land for the memorial free of charge, which was helpful as in most cases purchase of the site was the single largest expense. At Great Holland for instance, the war memorial was the gift of Mr and Mrs Samuel James, who were already well known for their generosity to the village. Meanwhile at Great Wakering £700 of the £880 raised for the memorial was contributed by one person.[64] Local employer and philanthropist, W.J. Courtauld, gave £3,000 and donated the fifteen acre site for the Peace Memorial Recreation Grounds at Braintree and Bocking.[65] Colchester's elegant war memorial site was only made possible thanks to the generosity of Charles Round, the owner of the castle, Hollytrees mansion and adjoining properties, and Lord Cowdray. In May 1919 Round agreed to sell the castle to the borough, which led the town's War Memorial Committee to decide to site the memorial near the castle. Lord Cowdray then stepped in, and in order to create a more open aspect with a view from the memorial to the castle, he purchased the castle, Hollytrees and its grounds, meadow, and other properties and roadways from Round for the sum of £18,000, threw in another £2,000 to create a new entrance, and added a further £3,000 to pay for the erection of railings and gates at the entrance. The only proviso was that Captain Davison, the tenant of Hollytrees, was allowed to remain in residence during his lifetime.

Once fundraising had begun, an architect, and perhaps a sculptor, needed to be contacted, or in many cases the expertise of local people was sought and utilised, local building firms approached, and plans drawn up. A second public meeting was then usually held to approve the preliminary work done, and, if more than one suggestion for a memorial had been considered, a final choice would be made, sometimes after a heated discussion. In some cases the committee was told to go back and reconsider an alternative suggestion. Not surprisingly, in some places where there was a lack of unanimity repeated meetings were held over many months, or even years, before a decision was finally made. Once approval had been given, the work was proceeded with and ultimately a date set for the dedication ceremony. The whole process might take months, or in the case of more elaborate memorials, or where funds accumulated slowly, years might pass before everything was completed.

Most war memorial committees consisted of only a small number of people, perhaps half a dozen to a dozen in most villages or small towns. Larger towns, feeling the need to create committees which were representative of the community and those who had played a part in the war effort, acted on a larger scale. Colchester's inaugural public meeting authorised the creation of a selection committee to debate the merits

[64] SSt 27 January 1921.

[65] ECC 8 February 1924.

of whatever memorials were suggested. Its membership was unusually large and consisted of people from the following organisations:

Scouts Association	1	Comrades of the Great War	2
National Association of Discharged Soldiers & Sailors	2	Secondary Schools	4
Married Women	2	Art Club	2
War Pensions	2	War Work Depot	2
Catholic Church	2	Chamber of Commerce	1
Special Police	1	Master Builders' Association	1
Freemasons	1	Nursing	1
Free Church Council	4	Head Teachers' Association	2
Trades Council & British Labour Party	3	Established Church	4
Oddfellows	1	Foresters' Society	1
Buffaloes	2	Hearts of Oak	1
		Board of Guardians	2

Various workplaces were permitted to nominate a representative, each to be chosen at an employees' meeting; those workplaces eligible to nominate were:

Colchester & E. Essex Cooperative Society	Messrs Leaning & Co.
Davey & Paxman Ltd	Marriage & Sons
Colchester Manufacturing Co.	Spottiswoode's
Mumford Ltd	Hart & Levy
Myam Manufacturing Co.	Britannia Engineering Works
Stanford Co. & Woods	Hollingtons
Owen Parry	Crowther Bros

One representative was also allotted to the employees of

Colchester Corporation	Colchester Post Office
Great Eastern Railway	Colchester Gas Co.[66]

The Selection Committee was made up overwhelmingly of the commercial middle class, either as those engaged in business at the time, or those who had made their money, retired or moved into borough politics. Working men were represented, but they were in a distinct minority, and only a handful of women were to be found within its ranks. At Colchester the two representatives of married women were the

66 ERO Acc. C4 Minutes of Colchester Borough War Memorial Committee and Sub-committees, 1919-25.

deputy mayoress, and Mrs Gurney Benham, both well known local benefactresses and society hostesses.[67]

A general committee was set up which met on 3 March 1919 to consider the six schemes which had survived beyond the public meeting in January. One suggestion, that for public baths, was eliminated from the running and sub-committees were established to investigate the merits of the five surviving proposals — the memorial hall/school of art, purchase of the castle, a memorial house, an additional block for the Eastern Counties Hospital, and a monument. During the next few months each of the five committees reported back, and the executive committee voted by nine to seven in favour of a monument. Three weeks later the huge general committee voted by forty-eight votes to five to adopt the executive committee's resolution, and imposed a ceiling of £3,000 on the cost. A vote was taken on what to spend any surplus funds on, resulting in a tie of twenty-two votes each for the memorial hall and the Eastern Counties Hospital block.[68] On 6 June a second public meeting endorsed the decision on the monument. An amendment to build the memorial hall instead was lost. The hall was also thrown out even as a recipient of surplus funds when the meeting opted to devote all such funds to the hospital.[69] Finally on 30 June the Monument Sub-committee selected the castle as the most suitable site, providing that the demolition of adjacent property, including the Castle Inn, could bring the castle and monument "well into view from the High St."[70] In July an appeal was launched in the town, and the scheme finally commenced.

Colchester's war memorial took over four years to come to fruition, but even those in small villages could take just as long. The villagers at Althorne decided very early on that the war memorial, which would be a "plain, simple, dignified memorial of oak", would not be built until all the money was raised. By mid-1922 £63 had been raised, the rural district council had given permission to utilise a piece of its land, and the idea of a monument accepted. Eighteen months later the amount raised had risen to £85 and the land was in the process of being purchased. In order to raise the final sum, seventy-five residents pledged to give 2*d.* a week for a year.[71] The patient and painstaking effort which must have been required to raise the money is indicated in this account from September 1924, by which time over £150 had been collected:

[67] Vice-Presidents were Viscount Cowdray (High Steward of Colchester), Sir Laming Worthington-Evans M.P., James Paxman, Mrs H.G. Egerton-Green, Charles Round and George Courtauld.

[68] ERO Acc. 4 General Committee minutes, 23 May 1919.

[69] ERO Acc. C4 Report of public meeting, 6 June 1919.

[70] ERO Acc. 4 Monument Committee minutes, 30 June 1919.

[71] BDA 6 May 1922, 13 October 1923.

Althorne war memorial fund account:

	£	s.	d.
Donations	52	19	6
Concerts & dramatic performances	45	6	9
Lantern lectures	6	2	0
Dances	5	4	6
Whist drives	22	1	8
Bargain sale	3	14	3
Sale of handicraft	1	1	0
Collections at flower show etc.	1	10	0
Sale of stamps	10	7	0
Sale of postcards	1	1	6
Interest banked	1	6	4
TOTAL	150	14	6 [72]

At the time of these accounts, the village was still attempting to raise the final £100 of the cost of £250.

Many towns and villages raised astonishing sums of money for their war memorials. The more modest ones, usually involving a tablet in church, were relatively inexpensive. The monument at Christ Church School, Warley, cost just £36, that at Black Notley £50. At Dedham by the end of 1919, £430 of the £500 needed had been collected. Birch had raised £1,376 towards its memorial in January 1920. Clacton's War Memorial Committee presented the town with several alternatives, all very expensive — a statuary priced at £2,000, a clock tower and ornamental gardens costing £5-6,000, an extension to the cottage hospital at £4-5,000, building a larger hospital at a cost of £10,000, a recreation ground costing £6,000 with £200 a year upkeep, a reading room at £5,000, and an institute costing £8-10,000. The public meeting which considered these options chose the cheapest one, the statuary.[73] At Colchester in just over a year £7,599 was subscribed to the memorial appeal. Of this, £3,000 was allocated to the erection of a war memorial, although subscribers earmarked only £1,090 of the total amount for such a purpose, whereas £2,188 was donated specifically to the hospital scheme.[74] In most other places fundraising was a long-winded and laborious process. Ilford's ambitious scheme, which was expected to cost twenty thousand pounds, had raised just £6,200 by June 1921. Some communities met or exceeded expectations very quickly, even when extremely high. Brentwood, for instance, raised £6,455 of the £6,500 required, the residents of Great Baddow were left with a surplus of £140, those at Dunmow, £325. Stock collected all of its £400, Moulsham its £200 and Theydon Bois £500 of the £550 needed.

[72] BDA 20 September 1924.

[73] ECS 12 July, 6 December 1919, 17 January 1920.

[74] ERO Acc. C4 Executive Committee interim report, 19 October 1920.

Although many Essex war memorials took a long time to come to fruition, they were usually achieved with comparatively little controversy and acrimony. At Colchester various suggestions were put forward, but there was little competition between those who favoured one suggestion rather than another. The *Colchester Gazette* feared that the public meeting in June 1919 might have been packed with Labour Party "irreconcilables" who wanted the war memorial to be a cottage hospital, but its fears proved groundless.[75] In fact the opposite was the case. There were fears that the people of Colchester were apathetic about the war memorial, and with only about one-eighth of the memorial fund subscribed directly to the war memorial itself, there may well have been some truth in this.

Other towns and villages in the county were not so fortunate, and the causes of the difficulties and controversies which surrounded war memorials were varied. At Lexden things began well enough. Support for a churchyard cross as a war memorial was very strong. Of the thirty families whose relatives had been killed, twenty-six signed a petition requesting such a memorial. The committee set up to consider the matter voted six to three in favour of a cross. At a parish meeting in March 1919 C.H. Morton, the originator of the idea of a cross, said that Lexden was not a poor parish and that the money was there to build a cross costing between £150 and £500. An alternative proposal to erect a brass tablet in the church was rejected, and the cross approved unanimously. Morton was delighted. As far as he and others were concerned, a tablet hidden away in church, was:

> not sufficiently dignified, not becoming, for such a parish as theirs, and it was only suggested, he believed, because it was cheaper — did it not make them shiver and their blood run cold? He did not think that Lexden was sufficiently awake to her enormous obligations in this matter. Let the more fortunate ones think this over.[76]

An appeal was begun and £200 was raised. Then the whole scheme seemed to falter and by October nothing had been done to move things on, to the anger of those who blamed this on the selfishness of those who had escaped the sufferings of the War.[77] At a parish meeting on 2 October, it was revealed that the committee, which had earlier approved the cross, had now reversed their decision, and intended to use the funds raised for a tablet in church. Members of the committee had even visited Great Wigborough to view such a tablet, and they produced a plan for the meeting's approval. When those present declined to agree to this, the committee, rather than reopen the debate about the churchyard cross, closed the meeting. C.H. Morton, the chief supporter of the cross, missed most of the meeting, having being stranded at

[75] CG 4 June 1919.

[76] CG 26 March 1919.

[77] ECS 11 October 1919.

Frinton by the railway strike that day. Thanks to a lift from Weeley by a Colchester motorist, he finally arrived, but too late to influence events. However, by now the supporters of the cross were up in arms. A further meeting was called for early November and here relatives of the dead and ex-soldiers spoke vehemently against the committee's high-handed attitude. In a further vote, there was once again a unanimous response in favour of the churchyard cross and there matters lay. The scheme for a tablet was abandoned.[78]

Tensions between Anglicans and Nonconformists were the cause of several controversies. At Myland not everyone was enamoured of the choice of a granite cross as a war memorial; some villagers would have preferred a memorial hall as a more useful commemoration. There was certainly a feeling that the memorial had been an exclusively Anglican choice, "a juggled up affair between the Rector and his confederates" as a Mr Harvey of the Workers' Union complained, and from which he alleged that the Nonconformists had been deliberately excluded. The proposed site of the memorial, on land owned by Mr Cant, the rose grower, and the fact that the memorial was to be built of Italian granite, which, because of the favourable exchange rate, would be cheaper than British materials, only added to local discontent about the whole affair.[79] A similar denominational dispute occurred at St Osyth, where failure to resolve whether or not the memorial should be erected in the churchyard resulted in the building of two memorials, one in the churchyard and another on the recreation ground.[80] At Springfield there was some disapproval of a war memorial in Holy Trinity church, possibly disapproval which was denominationally based, but this was overcome because forty-nine of the village's fifty war dead had been Anglicans.[81] Great Baddow's Nonconformists objected to the use of the £140 surplus in the war memorial fund to restore the Anglican-controlled almshouses, although a compromise agreement was eventually arrived at.[82]

Controversy sometimes arose where it was suggested that war memorials take the form of a cross or a calvary. The dedication ceremony at St Erkenwald's church, Southend, was briefly interrupted by a man with a trumpet who tried to disrupt the proceedings because he objected to the cross as idolatrous.[83] One man at a war memorial meeting at Saffron Walden objected to the placing of a cross at the top of the memorial.[84] There were similar objections to a proposed calvary at Epping, where objectors saw it as too Roman Catholic and liable to offend Protestant sensibilities.[85]

78 CG 12 November 1919, ECS 8 November 1919.

79 ECT 28 February 1920.

80 CG 28 May 1919.

81 ECC 6 December 1918.

82 ECC 30 July 1919.

83 SST 24 July 1919.

84 WWN 12 December 1919.

85 EEC 10 January 1919

The perceived high-handedness of Anglican clergy created difficulties and not just with local Nonconformists. The longest running dispute over a war memorial occurred at Stow Maries. Some residents of Stow Maries were mistrustful of their rector, Gordon Smythe, probably because of his Anglo-Catholic style of worship and his rather old-style, imperious churchmanship. The parish meeting rejected several of Smythe's suggestions which included a shrine, an organ, and new school buildings, even though he had offered glebe land on which to build a memorial, but it did agree to erect a reading and recreation room. However, even after this Smythe had to reassure villagers that he would hold no religious meetings in either the room or on the land he was conveying. The choice of a reading room caused "much friction" and contributed to a long, drawn-out tussle over several years. By 1922 four years had passed since the decision to build a reading room had been taken, and no progress had been made to bring it to fruition. Smythe, attempting to reconcile the warring parties, proposed a war memorial institute on glebe land, which the parish meeting accepted. A year later the parish meeting rescinded this decision, probably irritated by his having already erected a war memorial tablet in the church as part of a re-ordering of the sanctuary, including the installation of a reredos and a tabernacle for the reservation of the sacrament. The War Memorial Committee held its last meeting in 1924, still with no tangible result to show after five years. The meeting stated its opposition to using the £70 raised to help rebuild the Anglican church school, which was already earmarked for closure. In consequence Smythe set out to build a new village school, which was eventually opened in 1927. This, with its tablet inside, can also be considered part of the village war memorial.[86]

At South Weald the Reverend A.G. Kirby was accused of ignoring the wishes of his parishioners, as expressed in a public meeting, by unilaterally deciding to place a monument in the churchyard, a decision which led to the abandonment of alternative plans such as a village institute, and caused a great deal of ill feeling.[87] Some villagers objected when in 1923 Kirby attempted to use the war memorial fund for the upkeep of the church school, which was threatened with closure. To forestall this move, a meeting voted by twenty-eight to one to appoint the parish council, not the rector, as the trustees of the fund. By the end of 1924 there was still no institute. The War Memorial Committee, of which the rector was no longer a member, rejected a second attempt to use the fund to rebuild the school. Resentment of Kirby was so strong that the committee passed a resolution stating that, "no clergy should be elected for Committee or Trusteeship." At Ardleigh there was a dispute over the war memorial, but not between village factions, in this case the memorial fell foul of the church authorities. The Josselyn war shrine, donated by the Josselyn family, was erected outside the church in 1917. However, when plans were submitted for a permanent

[86] ERO D/P 391/30/6 Stow Maries war memorial minute book; B. Board, '"A Venture of Faith": The building of a school in Stow Maries', Essex Archaeology and History 32 (2001), 228-236.

[87] EEC 28 February 1919

memorial to be built inside the church, the proposed wording, "Brethren pray for us", which had been on the original shrine, came in for ecclesiastical censure. A letter was sent on behalf of Sir Arthur Bray Kempe, Chancellor of the Diocese of Chelmsford, explaining the thorny doctrinal problem involved:

> He presumes that the roll of honour will contain the names of those who have fallen in the war. If so, the inscription is a request to all those who look at the Roll of Honour to pray for the Dead there scrolled — in view of the fact that the Church of England — while not suggesting that those who think it right to do so may not properly privately offer prayers for the dead — has deliberately struck out such prayers from its public offices, it seems to him to be very questionable whether an ecclesiastical judge can properly authorise the public request on a War Shrine that such prayers should be offered up. It may be added that the words "Brethren pray for us" were not used by St Paul as requesting prayers for the dead.[88]

Acrimony and controversy surrounding war memorials also stemmed from the concerns of post-war society and which affected the perception of whatever war memorial proposals were made. There were those who looked at the need for reconstruction and the problems this would cause, and who concluded that war memorials ought not to add to the financial burden of future generations. There was opposition particularly to war memorials which took the form of institutes, village halls or recreation grounds, and which might have incurred an ongoing cost in the form of upkeep and repairs, or which required ongoing commitment to paying the salary of a groundsman or caretaker. At Burnham there were complaints that some suggestions would incur a charge on the rates. The Felsted branch of the Workers' Union debated the war memorial and urged that improving the village's social conditions deserved at least as much priority.[89] At Chelmsford the plan to incorporate the war memorial into the rebuilding of the town's 'unworthy' municipal buildings was criticised by those who regarded the cost as too great, and who saw the building of working-class housing as the priority for the town. When a special meeting of the town council voted sixteen to one to proceed with the scheme, the dissenting councillor accused the others of "reckless expenditure".[90] The debate about whether war memorials should or should not be utilitarian boiled over into a major controversy at Witham. Charles Knight, a doctor in the town, along with others, was incensed at the town council's appeal for £750 for a cross and campaigned for the building of a cottage

[88] ERO D/P 263/6/20, response to Ardleigh request for a war memorial in church.

[89] ECC 31 January 1919.

[90] ECC 21 March, 4 March 1919.

hospital or a nurse's house as a more practical and fitting memorial. He claimed a great deal of support from the town's working population. The Co-op subscribed £100 towards a hospital and the town's branch of the Federation of Discharged Soldiers and Sailors supported the idea. The War Memorial Committee, having raised £600 towards the project, was not about to abdicate. A bitter public meeting, called by Knight, was held in May 1919. This ended with Knight and his supporters storming out, although a new chairman was chosen who succeeded in obtaining a twenty-six to eighteen vote in favour of a hospital. A further public meeting a month later debated the issue, with supporters of the cross defending it on the grounds that a cottage hospital was too great a burden and was unnecessary in view of the number of local hospitals which the town's inhabitants had access to. Five months later in November the issue was again debated at yet another public meeting.[91]

Arthur Walker of Braintree was enraged by the suggestion that the town's war memorial should be a recreation ground. He objected to the idea of a sports ground as a memorial as crass, but his anger had its roots in the War too:

> Should the "memorial" for them [the Fallen] be a sports ground where "conchies" and "aliens" could congregate for enjoyment? Spirits of the Departed, Relatives of the Fallen, do I not hear you say, God Forbid?[92]

At Black Notley too there were very strong objections to a village hut because it was felt that obtaining a source of entertainment as a war memorial was inappropriate.[93] The new egalitarian spirit which was abroad after the War led to a dispute at Springfield. The vicar, F.S. Paynter, was in favour of placing the names of the Fallen on the village's memorial according to their military rank, with officers listed first, followed by non-commissioned officers and other ranks. Some villagers objected to what they saw as the perpetuation of class division and wanted the names placed in alphabetical order. The vicar stood his ground, and the church's tablet also listed the Fallen according to which arm of the service they had been in, with the Royal Navy first, then the army, led by the Essex Regiment, and then other regiments.[94]

The climax of months, and in some cases, years of work, was the day on which the war memorial was unveiled and dedicated. Very few of these ceremonies actually occurred during the War. In 1919 about a dozen were held but it was in 1920, by which time villages had had time to complete their preparations, that the overwhelming majority of dedications took place. A handful were carried out in 1921, 1922 and 1923, but by then most communities had completed their plans.

[91] ECC 28 March, 23 May, 6 June, 21 November 1919.

[92] ECC 18 April 1919.

[93] ECC 5 May 1922.

[94] ECC 25 July 1919, 12 November 1920.

These ceremonies, regardless of whether or not they were secular or religious in spirit, were always carried out with deep solemnity and, outside of the larger towns, with measured unpretentiousness. Not one of the hundreds of dedication ceremonies which took place throughout Essex resulted in the occasion being exploited in order to glorify war or to celebrate victory in an overtly triumphalist way, and at only a handful were there any recriminations against the Germans or the behaviour of some English people during the War. They were inevitably rather mournful occasions, an opportunity for communities to contemplate the terrible cost of the War. Few families had had the opportunity to visit the graves of their loved ones, and although at the time of their loss, grief was shared amongst family and friends, this mourning was carried out in relative isolation from other bereaved families. The dedication ceremonies now offered an opportunity for communities to share their collective grief, and to express this in a temporary recreation of wartime unity and community spirit. They were cathartic and redemptive occasions, which allowed communities to recall the self-sacrifice of the Fallen, demonstrating this by honouring their memory and expressing their eternal gratitude for their actions, and they permitted both the bereaved in particular, and communities in general, to take the final farewell which had been denied to most of them during the War.

The essence of what these occasions meant to individuals and communities can be examined by studying the six key aspects of the dedication ceremonies — the arrangement and ritual of the ceremony; the biblical readings and texts chosen at ceremonies, which had a distinctly Christian ethos; the choice of hymns; the choice of speakers; the addresses given by the speakers; and the words which were placed on the war memorials themselves.

The dedications of war memorials were occasions when the local clergy, Anglican and Dissenting, often showed great solidarity in expressing the Christian significance of the event. For instance at Weeley's dedication ceremony the Anglican clergy of Weeley, St Paul's Clacton, St James's Clacton, St Osyth, Brightlingsea, and Alresford, together with a representative from the Clacton Primitive Methodist circuit, were present.[95] At Tiptree there were almost a thousand people present. Prior to the unveiling ceremony a large procession made its way to the war memorial. In it were the Tiptree Band, the War Memorial Committee, drummers of the 2nd Suffolk Regiment, the village's ex-servicemen, the Salvation Army, the Sons of Temperance, the Oddfellows, and some three hundred naval cadets.[96] Such elaborate processions were not unusual even in the smallest villages. The unveiling of the war memorials of larger towns like Colchester, Chelmsford and Southend were the occasion for considerably more pomp and ceremony. At Colchester Field Marshal Sir William Robertson, who was to carry out the unveiling, travelled from Liverpool Street with a special party including Lord Lambourne, the Lord Lieutenant of Essex, Viscount

[95] ECS 9 October 1920.

[96] ECS 10 July 1920.

and Viscountess Cowdray, Sir Laming Worthington-Evans, M.P., and his wife, together with a party of alderman who had journeyed to London to accompany them. The party travelled by motor car from North Station to the Town Hall, where the rest of the procession was waiting. The Welsh Regiment and band formed a guard of honour as they entered. At 2.15 p.m. the procession left the Town Hall and made its way down High Street to the war memorial. Men of the 1st Norfolk, 2nd Suffolk, and Bedfordshire and Hertfordshire Regiments lined both sides of the High Street, which was crammed with thousands of people. The massed choir, band and buglers of the 2nd Battalion, Suffolk Regiment, played solemn music. Colour parties from battalions of the 18th Division raised in Colchester during the War, and a detachment of the R.A.F. were also present.[97]

At Chelmsford the ceremony on 11 November 1923, the fifth anniversary of the Armistice, was an equally grand affair. The whole corporation were present in their robes. They were preceded to the cenotaph by the surpliced cathedral choir and the London Road Congregational Church choir. Men of the 5th Battalion Essex Regiment formed a guard of honour at the memorial opposite the Prudential buildings. Also in the procession was the Chelmsford Fire Brigade, representatives of the Essex County Constabulary, 120 boy scouts and girl guides and over three hundred ex-servicemen. Many in the crowd of thousands who lined the route of the procession and massed around the memorial wore the medals and decorations of departed loved ones. The hymn 'O God Our Help In Ages Past' opened the dedication service, followed by prayers for the Fallen read by Canon Lake. The mayor, Alderman Frederick Spalding, then spoke:

> On behalf of the subscribers, I, as Mayor, accept the trust of the memorial, and charge my successors in office, the aldermen and burgesses of this town, to maintain and preserve it for all time, so that future generations may be reminded of the great sacrifice these men made for us, and the great principles for which they died.

At this point Sir Roger Keyes, Deputy Chief of the Naval Staff, pulled the cord to release the huge Union Jack which draped the cenotaph. It was then dedicated by the Bishop of Barking. The Reverend W.H. Pace said further prayers and the hymn 'For All the Saints' was sung. The 'Last Post' was played, followed by a minute's silence and then 'Reveille'. Various dignitaries and representatives of a number of organisations laid wreaths at the foot of the memorial, and after the blessing the national anthem was played. The ceremony was concluded when Keyes inspected the ranks of the ex-servicemen assembled there.[98]

[97] ECS 30 May 1923.

[98] ECC 16 November 1923.

Clearly the measure of ceremonial and ritual, from the simple to the very grand, was intended to convey to those present the great social and historical significance of these events. On the whole the simplicity of dedication ceremonies reflected the generally held view that an excessive display of ritual would have been unbecoming and in poor taste, completely inappropriate to a commemoration of the self-sacrifice of men who had given their lives as patriots.

Unlike the choice of hymns on these occasions, where there was a good measure of unanimity about what was chosen, the selection of biblical readings or texts as the basis of an address was far more eclectic and idiosyncratic. Where the local press reported which texts were chosen, many different texts were selected. At Beaumont the Bishop of Colchester chose I Ephesians 8.12, with its revelation of the ultimate awareness of God's love, "For now we see through a glass, darkly; but then face to face: now I know in part; but then shall I know even as also I am known." The self-sacrifice of the Fallen was a frequent theme, as at Margaretting, where the reading was from John 15.5-13, which included Christ's words prophesying his own death, "Greater love hath no man than this, that a man lay down his life for his friends." Others chose texts which affirmed some of the basic tenets of the Christian faith, such as John 11.27, selected at Tiptree: "She saith unto him, Yea, Lord; I believe that thou art the Christ, the Son of God, which should come into the world."

The Christian belief in eternal life, with its consoling promise that death was but a temporary separation, was very much in evidence, as at Colchester St Mary Magdalene's, where Revelation 22.1-5, was chosen, with verse five ending:

> And there shall be no night there; and they need no candle, neither light of the sun; for the Lord God giveth them light: and they shall reign for ever and ever.

Equally appropriate was I Thessalonians 4.13-18, which was the reading at Epping, "For if we believe that Jesus died and rose again, even so them also which sleep in Jesus will God bring with him." With its apocalyptic vision of new beginnings Revelation proved a popular choice. At St Botolph's, Colchester, it was 21.1-7:

> And I saw a new heaven and a new earth: for the first heaven and the first earth were passed away; and there was no more sea.
>
> And God shall wipe away all tears from their eyes; and there shall be no more death, neither sorrow, nor crying, neither shall there be any more pain; for the former things are passed away.

Psalm 23 was chosen on many occasions, as at St Giles's, Colchester; its words were eminently appropriate:

> Yea, though I walk through the valley of the shadow of death, I will fear no evil: for thou art with me; thy rod and thy staff they comfort me.
>
> Surely goodness and mercy shall follow me all the days of my life: and I will dwell in the house of the Lord for ever.

The choice of hymns revolved almost exclusively around those whose theme was the promise of eternal life. Two hymns outstripped all other choices in the minds of those who selected them — 'O God, Our Help in Ages Past' and 'For All the Saints, who from their Labours Rest'. The first of these, whose theme was centred on God's love for his creation since time immemorial, was incontestably appropriate:

> O God, our help in ages past,
> Our help for years to come,
> Our shelter from the stormy blast,
> And our eternal home;
>
> Beneath the shadow of thy throne
> Thy saints have dwelt secure;
> Sufficient is thine arm alone,
> And our defence is sure.[99]

The use of the word 'saints' in the second verse is instructive. It reminds us that those who died in the War were frequently lauded, and not just by the clergy, as canonised martyrs who had merited such exalted status by virtue of their self-sacrifice in a great holy war against an evil foe. 'For All the Saints', with its martial and medieval nuances, its images of resting 'warriors' and vision of heavenly glory, was admirably suited to the post-war beatification of the Fallen:

> Thou wast their Rock, their Fortress, and their Might;
> Thou Lord, their Captain in the well-fought fight;
> Thou, in the darkness, still their one true light.
> ...
> The golden evening brightens in the west;
> Soon, soon to faithful warriors cometh rest:
> Sweet is the calm of Paradise the blest.[100]

[99] *Hymns Ancient and Modern*, no. 165.

[100] *Hymns Ancient and Modern*, no. 527.

The same medieval imagery of warriors released from life's cares, their duty done, invulnerable in God's safekeeping, reverberates through 'The Saints of God! Their Conflict Past':

> The Saints of God! their conflict past
> And life's long battle won at last,
> No more they need the shield or sword,
> They cast them down before their Lord:
> O happy saints! forever blest,
> At Jesus' feet how safe you rest!
>
> The Saints of God! their wanderings done,
> No more their weary course they run,
> No more they faint, no more they fall,
> No foes oppress, no fears appal:
> O happy saints! for ever blest,
> In that dear home how sweet your rest! [101]

Another popular choice, 'O Valiant Hearts' is rich with the same insistent tone of medievalism, laced with images of patriotic self-sacrifice:

> O Valiant hearts, who to your glory came,
> Through dust of conflict and through battle flame;
> Tranquil you lie, your knightly virtue proved,
> Your memory hallowed in the land you loved.
> ...
> These were his servants, in his step they trod,
> Following through death the martyred Son of God;
> Victor he rose, victorious too shall rise
> They who have drunk his cup of sacrifice.[102]

'Peace, Perfect Peace' with its emphasis on the peaceful certainties of heaven, meshed well with the contemporary need for spiritual comfort:

> Peace, perfect peace, in this dark world of sin?
> The blood of Jesus whispers peace within.
> ...
> Peace, perfect peace, death shadowing us and ours?
> Jesus has vanquished death and all its powers.[103]

[101] *Hymns Ancient and Modern*, no. 572.

[102] *Hymns Ancient and Modern*, no. 584.

[103] *Hymns Ancient and Modern*, no. 358.

The choice of individuals selected to unveil and dedicate war memorials, and to deliver the address, again demonstrated, perhaps inevitably, that these ceremonies were dominated by both religious sentiments and by the military events which gave rise to them. In country parishes, where the memorial was often placed in the church or churchyard, the vicar or rector frequently performed the ceremony and delivered the address, although to emphasise the importance of the occasion local dignitaries were also invited to perform the honours. The memorial at St Erkenwald's, Southend, was unveiled by Lady Gwendolin Guinness; Upminster Congregational Church's community hall by Lady Griggs. Others like Alresford, Beaumont, Messing, Stebbing and Bocking invited the Bishop of Colchester to do the honours. The dedications at Great Wakering, Southend, Chigwell school, Willingale and Shellow Bowells, amongst others, were performed by the Bishop of Chelmsford. The Bishop of Barking dedicated the memorials at Steeple, Althorne, Epping Upland and Gidea Park. The Archbishop of Canterbury was the honoured guest at Chelmsford Cathedral. Many parishes preferred to emphasise military considerations by inviting retired or serving officers to perform the ceremonies. The great local war hero, General Lord Byng of Vimy, who had led the Canadian Corps in that battle, and who lived at Thorpe for a while before moving to Canada as Governor-General, presided at Little Clacton, Halstead, Thorpe-le-Soken, and at the Walton memorial to Private Columbine V.C. Field Marshal Sir William Robertson unveiled the Danbury memorial, while Lord Horne, Commander-in-Chief, Eastern Command did the same for that at Saffron Walden's memorial. Brigadier F.W. Towsey of the Colchester garrison, appeared at Fingringhoe, Kelvedon, Marks Tey, Christ Church and St. Nicholas's, Colchester and at the unveiling of the Old Colcestrians' memorial. Other communities stressed the significance of their ceremonies by inviting civic dignitaries or public figures. At St John's, Moulsham, the memorial was unveiled by the Mayor and Corporation of Chelmsford in state. Sir Philip Sassoon M.P, the Vice-Secretary for Air, and Katharine Stewart-Murray, Duchess of Atholl, M.P. for Kinross and West Perthshire, and the first female to hold ministerial office in a Conservative government as Parliamentary Secretary to the Board of Education, were at the unveiling of Stow Maries school memorial. The Mayor of Colchester unveiled the grammar school's swimming bath memorial; Laming Worthington-Evans, M.P. delivered the address at St Mary-at-the-Walls, describing the Fallen as "Crusaders within the sight of the Holy City". Those at Grays, Brentwood Grammar School, Loughton, and Dovercourt were unveiled by the Lord Lieutenant of Essex, Lord Lambourne.

The addresses which were delivered on these occasions were intended to provide a keynote for the ceremony. It is unlikely that the speakers were actually instructed what to say. The themes of most addresses suggested themselves naturally enough given the nature of the event, and this is borne out by the fairly narrow content of most of them. The *Southend Standard* was doubtful whether there could be a true appreciation of the War at that time:

> We are too near the rigour and ardour of the conflict, the bloodshed and the loss; the mental stress and poignant anxiety fully to realise the immensity of the effect or the value of what was achieved.[104]

However true this may have been, most speakers at war memorial ceremonies attempted to make sense of the recent cataclysmic events. Some speakers attempted to provide comfort to their listeners by assuring them that the Fallen were now at rest with God. One officer, a Colonel Hilder, made this point very picturesquely at Horndon-on-the-Hill:

> Their spirits had gone through space millions of miles behind the sun, which had set in the west with its glorious halo and promiseof eternal life.[105]

Some speakers reminded their listeners of the past. At Little Clacton Lord Byng spoke of the Fallen having achieved righteousness, a theme which occurred in many addresses:

> They had fought for freedom and righteousness and he would rather emphasise the latter objective of the great struggle than the former, which was the more material side of the war, for if they had obtained nothing more than righteousness, then the war had been worth fighting for.[106]

Others urged those present to be thankful that the country had not been invaded, or as General Towsey put it at Kelvedon, "The foot of no foreign invader had trodden the soil of our dear land."[107] The Rector of St Leonard's, Colchester, put it in even more blood curdling terms when he said that England had saved the world from "the Christless spirit of Prussian militarism."[108]

However, most addresses, whilst not neglecting the sacrifice of the Fallen, tended to draw their hearers' attention to the present and future. The idea that those who had survived the War were in some way indebted to the Fallen, and that in order to honour this debt they should live lives which were worthy of their sacrifice, was a

[104] SST 17 November 1921.

[105] ERO T/Z 43/2, Press cuttings Thurrock area.

[106] ECT 24 May 1919.

[107] ECS 26 February 1921.

[108] ECS 14 February 1920.

common one. The Rector of St Leonard's voiced the idea when he urged his parishioners to:

> live worthy of the lives laid down, and to carry on unfalteringly the great aims and ends they gave their lives for. This will be our best tribute, and let us see to it that we do not play them false.[109]

The speaker at Brightlingsea Wesleyan Church echoed these sentiments, which were fortified by the hope of eternal life:

> Though they could not come back, those who revered the memorial could go forward with brave hearts and brave hopes, realising that if they lived their lives as the departed had lived and died they would stand together at the same Throne.

General Atkinson of Mistley Hall, when unveiling the war memorial of his home village, was perhaps uncharacteristic of military speakers when he expressed the hopes of the brave new post-war world:

> Let them make a solemn covenant to live their lives a little better, to put away all evil speaking and uncharitableness, and try to think and speak the best of one another — not the worst. Let them find the only way to find true happiness — to work, not for personal gain, but for the sake of duty well and truly accomplished.[110]

Sir William Robertson's theme of a man's sacrifice having an impact on those who knew him was to become a familiar one, although when he spoke at Willingale in April 1918, such dedication ceremonies were still in their infancy:

> We believe, and we know, that a man cannot live to himself alone. We know that a great act does not perish with the life of the man who performs it, but that it lives and grows up into the lives and acts of those who survive him and cherish his memory.[111]

Many speakers, particularly military men, interpreted the survivors' indebtedness to the Fallen as including the care of ex-servicemen. At Coggeshall, General Shute used

[109] ECS 14 February 1920.

[110] ECS 22 January 1921.

[111] ECC 19 April 1918.

his address to bemoan the fate of ex-servicemen, neglected by an uncaring, ungrateful and self-serving nation;

> Thousands of ex-soldiers were wandering about the country practically homeless, maimed and helpless and no-one doing anything to help them, but certain sections of the community were doing their utmost to prevent these men earning their living. Was that the way they paid their debts? What had these men come home to — to a country torn to pieces through selfishness; everything they fought for was being thrown to the winds by selfish people who never went out of the country. England, he said, was going down and Germany was gaining more and more, helped by the selfishness of those people who took jolly good care to save their skins and not go out to fight.[112]

In his speech at Weeley, Brigadier-General Metcalfe also emphasised the need to care for those who were maimed or unemployed; Captain St John of the Royal Navy urged his listeners not to forget the "maimed and disabled", particularly those facing starvation and unemployment. At Christ Church, Colchester, General Towsey urged people to aid ex-servicemen, "Was England going to forget her sons to whom she owed so much? He trusted not, but signs were not wanting that the public memory was short".

Towsey was not alone in expressing his pessimistic view of the post-war world. Convulsed as it seemed to be by industrial disputes and strikes, challenged by a rising left-wing political party which was seen as alien by men like Towsey, it was not surprising that he and others chose to use dedication ceremonies as a platform from which to warn their listeners of contemporary social trends which they believed were undermining British society. This is what the Bishop of Chelmsford had to say at St Mary Magdalene's, Colchester:

> In these days of strife and division, and hatred and bitterness between various sections of society, of strikes and rumoured strikes, it might be questioned whether they were showing their appreciation of the love of those who had laid down their lives on their behalf ... let the tale of their dear brothers, the inspiration of their example, the record of their sacrifice, be handed down not only in tablets of stone but also in hearts of flesh which were going on from strength to strength, from stage to stage, growing in grace and in the knowledge of the Lord.

[112] ECS 11 September 1920.

This theme was reiterated by the speaker at St Martin's, Colchester:

> In a time when a spirit of selfishness seemed to be succeeding that spirit of self-sacrifice which led these men to give themselves for their wives and children, might the nation always look to the men who had counted nothing in comparison with the safety of their country.[113]

At High Beech Field Marshal Evelyn Wood spoke of the need to organise a united effort "to overcome the plague of anarchy" which was assaulting the country, a clear reference to militant trade unionism.[114] A speaker at Heybridge lashed war profiteers whom he believed "were for the most part foreigners, or in the pay of foreign countries, who wished to ruin England and the Empire that they might enrich themselves".[115]

Other military men saw the solution for the nation's troubles in the cultivation of discipline, especially among the young. Major-General Sir Charles Harington, speaking at Lexden, was of the opinion that:

> The best way to prevent war was to preserve the comradeship and association found during the years of war and instil discipline and loyalty into the young and stamp out the bad element whenever it appeared. Without discipline in the home they could not have the good citizenship so essential to the welfare of the nation.[116]

One speaker, Ernest Dilliway of Burnham, used the occasion of the dedication of the memorial in the Forester's Hall as an opportunity to attack the League of Nations and all it stood for, and instead advocated an England-First policy:

> A great deal of sloppy sentiment was talked about internationalism, which in too many cases meant that those who professed it were always ready to believe that every country was right except their own.

In his view those who had died in the War had subscribed to a very simple ideal, "Our country, in its intercourse with foreign nations may it always be in the right, but our country, right or wrong".[117]

[113] ECS 19 June 1920.
[114] ECC 6 June 1919.
[115] ECC 25 July 1921.
[116] ECC 24 July 1920.
[117] BDA 28 October 1922.

The words which were placed on war memorials were of great significance and not simply because they were chosen as embodying the feelings of the communities who erected them. Long after the wreaths had faded, memories dimmed, and when eventually, as has almost occurred in our day, these events have passed out of living memory, it would be these words which successive generations would read, and the meaning of which they might perhaps ponder. As with the ritual of dedication ceremonies themselves, these words usually expressed a simple sentiment without affectation. None attempted such a sweepingly comprehensive commentary of the War as did the wording on the cross of sacrifice in the East London Cemetery at Plaistow:

> To the memory of the sons of the British Empire.
> In Sympathy with the Orphan, the Widow, the Sonless Parent.
> To Commemorate the Righteous Alliance of the British Empire/France/Russia
> Japan/Belgium/Serbia/Montenegro/Italy/Rumania/Portugal/United States.
> In gratitude to our maimed and broken heroes by whose
> anguish we have peace.

The wording on other war memorials was less ambitious, although the war memorial of the Frinton Golf Club did see their members' sacrifice in rather more grandiose terms, the dedication reading: "In honoured memory of our gallant members who fell in the Great War for the Freedom of the World 1914-1919".

The same belief in the global significance of the War was found in the sentiment on the war memorial at Colchester:

> Our beloved Fallen took up their cross under
> the banner of Christ, and fought and fell in
> the greatest crusade in the world's history.

At Boxted the memorial had a patriotic theme; its words included the phrase, "For Britain Honour Freedom Righteousness". At Frating too, patriotic sentiments were very much to the fore, "in honoured memory of the men of Frating who gave their lives for their homeland 1914-1919." The words on the memorial tablet in St Michael's, Braintree, commemorating the Preston brothers, Ralph and Philip, contains both biblical imagery and an adamant assertion that their deaths were not in vain:

> The Angel of Death has been abroad throughout the Land.
> You may almost hear the beating of his wings.
> Dulce et decorum est pro patria mori.

The repudiation of such sentiments by soldier-poets like Wilfred Owen clearly had no place in the Preston family's remembrance of their sons' sacrifice.

However, it was the scouts' memorial in St George's Club, Colchester, which perhaps recaptured the jingoistic sentiments of the War:

> Only the Coward dreads,
> Such deaths as these have died,
> Lift up O Scouts, your heads,
> Look wide, look wide.

The great honour associated with the sacrifice of the Fallen was also remembered at Dedham:

> We that survive perchance may end our days,
> In some employment meriting no praise;
> They have outlived this fear, and their brave ends
> Will ever be an honour to their friends.

The familiar theme that the sacrifice of those who died should inspire the lives of those who survived the War is found at Bures, "Pass not this shrine in sorrow, but in pride / And may you live as nobly as they died." For some communities religious sentiments were of paramount importance. On the cross at Layer-de-la-Haye, on the simple wooden crosses at Birch and in St Andrew's, Greenstead, are Christ's words from John 15.13: "Greater love hath no man than this, that he lay down his life for his friends".

The conclusion of these ceremonies was the laying of wreaths on the newly dedicated memorial by the families of the Fallen. The words on these wreaths were often poignant. At Weeley one wreath said simply "In proud memory of our dear sons, from their parents". Three months later in the same village, a slab was placed at the foot of the war memorial, subscribed to by the village's ex-servicemen. It contained the sorrowful words, "To our fallen comrades, from those left behind". At St Martin's, Colchester, a wreath once more combined proud patriotism with a sense of indebtedness, "They hazarded their lives unto death; for England and the Right".

The war memorial movement was not just a cultural phenomenon tacked on to the end of the Great War. Its conception and evolution began in the very early days of the War, in the autumn of 1914; its appearance a wholly understandable outcome of the immense significance of the War, and the enormous number of casualties which resulted from it. War memorials form part of the interpretation of the War by those who lived through it. They remind us of how many in this generation viewed the War as a righteous struggle against evil, a crusade against ungodliness, and how the great sacrifices that had been made were not in vain, because victory had been achieved. Many people in Essex would probably have agreed with the assessment of the War by the Bishop of Chelmsford, who said in October 1920:

> "Was it worth it? What has been got out of the war? Apart from the men who had defiled their hands with ill-gotten gains, they had got mothing materialistic out of it. Not in pounds, shillings and pence did they reckon; if they did it would be Loss! Loss! Loss! What had they got? The things without which the world would have become hell. They had got freedom; they had preserved their honour; they had retained their self-respect, and were conscious that they had done their duty.[118]

We see how sentiments such as this influenced the view of those who fought in the War, and led to their deaths being interpreted as a sacrifice to attain righteousness, to save all that was good, to maintain freedom, and to preserve democracy, the nation and the Empire. War memorials were the response of a nation struggling to come to terms with the historical recollection of collective grief on a scale never before experienced in Britain. However, war memorials were not simply the product of communities wallowing in sentimentality and self-indulgence. Instead they were conceived as the visual embodiment and permanent reminder of the debt owed by the survivors of the Great War and future generations to those who had died in it. The ceremonies at which war memorials were unveiled and dedicated were used by those leading them to direct the minds of their communities, however fleetingly, to the achievements of the nation made possible by the sacrifice of its dead. For a few short moments there was a pause; a time for communities to recollect, to pray, to praise, and to weep. A few moments of calm in a nation already beleaguered by a renewal of political divisions, social problems, and by the spectre of class conflict.

[118] SE 16 October 1920.

CHAPTER FIFTEEN

A Land Fit for Heroes?

These soldiers' fates are denoted by the symbols marked by each man.

(ERO: T/Z 232/1)

THE POST-WAR WORLD 1919-1920

EVEN AS THE GREAT WAR was stumbling to its bloody beginnings some local commentators were distressed, not by the prospect of Armageddon, but by the end of the existing order and the uncertainties of the post-war world. J.A. Bolton of Brightlingsea, in an article entitled 'The New Europe' in December 1914 said that,

> It is idle to imagine that out of the raging seas of bloodshed and destruction there will spring complete in form and beauty the consummation of a world at peace.[1]

Even the usually sanguine Junius Minor, depressed that the War had dragged beyond Christmas 1914, could find no comfort at all in contemplating a world which might eventually find peace, as his doom-laden vision shows:

> There will be a mass of discontent throughout this land immediately after the end of the war. Old industries paralysed, new industries not yet in being, unemployment on an unprecedented scale, women and children clamouring for bread, the humble taxpayers unable to make ends meet ... There will be civil commotion and turmoil and travail in this land, as in many lands.[2]

Once the War was over, other observers also fretted about the failings of this supposed new world. The Bishop of Chelmsford bemoaned the "growth of lawlessness and the defiance of authority", which he ascribed to the absence of fathers and working mothers.[3] The *Burnham and Dengie Advertiser* also found that "the old discipline is very much relaxed."[4] Sir Fortescue Flannery M.P. was appalled that returning troops "found a land of discontent, of dissatisfaction, and of unrest — in every house a grievance, in every man's breast some unusual longing."[5] The Countess of Warwick, wife of the Lord Lieutenant of Essex, wrote in *Lloyd's Weekly* of her fears of post-war "social chaos". There was a lack of love and romance, she bemoaned; war had hardened society, making it vulgar and degraded.[6] Like her ladyship, F.H. Owers of Chelmsford was equally disgusted at what he saw as the declining moral standards of the day:

> We have in Chelmsford — no worse than in any other town — walking about in our midst, sin unblushing, rampant, unashamed, in our streets, corrupting the boys, ruining the girls.[7]

1 EEA 5 December 1914.
2 ECT 29 December 1914.
3 ECC 19 April 1918.
4 BDA 28 May 1921.
5 BDA 27 September 1919.
6 ECS 27 January 1917.
7 ECC 14 March 1919.

A letter from Southend was critical of the lack of manners and general politeness in society. The correspondent in question cited the prevalence of smoking on trams, unfair tram charges, overcrowding on public transport, the presence of those under fourteen years old on licensed premises, and the upsurge in drunkenness as examples of what he perceived as this new depravity.[8]

However, in the short term the end of the Great War produced less of a dispiriting atmosphere, and more of an upsurge in public and private sentiment urging the creation of a better post-war world, both domestically and internationally. After all the suffering, the horrors and the losses, and particularly the self-sacrifice of the heroic Fallen, it was felt that those who had survived the War had an obligation to build a more charitable, noble and united country. The Reverend Parry of Colchester urged that people "must be done with all that was mean, selfish, and ignoble, and try and imitate their [the Fallen's] goodness and strength."[9]

Yet, there was also a general feeling in society that, having won the War, it was equally important not to lose the peace. There was a general acceptance by people of all political complexions that the post-war reconstruction of society needed to pay particular attention to the needs of the working classes, but in fact peace, or reconstruction, which was the term applied to the post-war reshaping of Britain, meant different things to different groups. It was soon evident that their particular objectives, usually of a selfish nature, tended to lack the nobility which was so piously expressed in public utterances at this time. The Conservative Party's objective, shared by the more prosperous elements in society who tended to vote for them, was to limit social and political change and retain their wealthy supporters' control of the way the country was run; turning the clock back to 1914 to erase the wartime gains of organised labour. The Labour Party was committed to gaining control of local and national government on behalf of the working classes, even if the latter showed in the 1918 election that they preferred a Conservative to a Labour government. Trade unions were determined to acquire greater strength and influence, and use them to ensure a continuation of the wage rises and improved working conditions gained as a result of the War. The middle classes, on the other hand, at least as typified by the recently-formed Middle Class Union, aimed to influence public opinion to urge restraint on the leaders of both employers and trade unions. The churches, maintaining the stance they had adopted in wartime, hoped for a return to earlier values, marked by a renewal of commitment to God, a greater emphasis on moral values, a hope for improved church attendance, and continued resistance to women playing a wider role in the life of the Church. The organisation representing demobilised servicemen, quickly named by its members the Comrades of the Great War, was determined to protect the interests of the demobbed, particularly as regarded employment. It too was hostile towards females, in so far as they seemed

8 ECC 26 September 1919.

9 ECS 16 November 1918.

entrenched in jobs at the expense of unemployed ex-servicemen. Farmers and other employers anticipated that a brake would be put on the escalating costs and wage rises which had occurred throughout the War. They were particularly adamant that they would resist the imposition of a forty-eight-hour working week for farm labourers, and were anxious to slow wage rises for their employees. Brewers and publicans expected that the wartime restrictions on opening hours, and the Government's tampering with drink, would be brought to an end. One correspondent to the *Essex County Standard* urged the abolition of drinking restrictions, those "fetters on freedom". The Clacton Chamber of Commerce's rather insular views, supported by the urban district council, nevertheless spoke for many retailers and shopkeepers when it urged compulsory early closing of shops, cheaper postal rates, increased and cheaper railway facilities, and the speedy demobilisation of men who ran one-man businesses.[10] Shopkeepers in metropolitan Essex, as in Leyton and Leytonstone, were urging an end to the street markets which had grown up at the end of the War and which they believed were damaging their interests.[11] The working class themselves tended to demonstrate less of an interest in the sort of political radicalism espoused by Labour Party and trade union leaders, and a more immediate concern for wage levels and the rising cost of living. Clearly some groups were keen to retain the changes of the wartime world, while others preferred to try to turn the clock back to 1914. In terms of politics, these views were rather blurred during the country's first post-war general election.

The gunfire of the Great War had hardly died away before local political parties prepared for a resumption of a different kind of hostilities. Indeed three months before the Armistice was signed, the Maldon Conservatives were already accusing the local Liberal and Labour parties of breaking the electoral truce.[12] Certainly, the Labour Party in the Mid-Essex constituency was lining-up its candidate and extending its organisation for the general election, whenever it came, well before the War ended.[13] The haste with which a general election was called, the first one since 1910, helped to intensify the ferocity of some of the contests in Essex and ensured the speedy, though only partial, collapse of the wartime political truce. The date set for the election was 14 December, just over a month after the Armistice. Although the case for an early general election was considered overwhelming in some places, not everyone was convinced. E.W. Tanner, the Liberal candidate at Maldon and E.G. Pretyman, the Conservative candidate for Mid-Essex, both believed the election was too rushed.[14] Along with many other Liberals, Arthur Goldfinch, the prospective candidate for Colchester, described the election as coming at "an inopportune time".

[10] ECS 7 December 1918.

[11] SE 13 November 1920.

[12] ECC 26 July 1918.

[13] ECC 23 August, 6, 13 September 1918.

[14] ECC 29 November 1918.

The general election was to be fought in a new political landscape. The Representation of the People Act of 1918 produced a major redistribution of parliamentary seats, including those in Essex. In 1910 the county had eleven constituencies; the 1918 Act increased this to twenty. Eight new parliamentary divisions were created at Chelmsford, Colchester, Epping, Harwich, Maldon, Romford, Essex South East and Essex South West. There were six other parliamentary boroughs; East Ham, Leyton and Walthamstow each had two M.P.s, Ilford and Southend had one each, and West Ham had its number of M.P.s increased from two to four. Three new constituencies — East Ham North and South, and Ilford — were carved out of the huge Romford division. Three others — Leyton East and West and Walthamstow East — were created out of the equally large Walthamstow division. Eleven of the twenty Essex constituencies lay within eight miles of London and occupied less than one-fortieth of the county's area. The redistribution reflected the demographic changes in the county in the previous fifty years by transferring electoral power to the south-west and metropolitan area.[15] Not everyone was pleased with the new parliamentary boundaries, some of which, like Maldon, were described as "grotesque" in their unwieldiness. There were also significant differences in the population of these new constituencies. Harwich contained fifty-seven thousand people, whilst Romford had seventy-eight thousand, and Epping over eighty thousand.[16] The majority of the constituencies were three-cornered contests, with supporters of Lloyd George's government, the Coalition Liberals and Coalition Conservatives, ranged against the Labour Party and non-Coalition Liberals, and at Southend, Leyton East and Plaistow, independent candidates stood as well. In some constituencies, such as Colchester and Leyton West, the Liberals declined to contest the seat because local party leaders supported the Coalition and opted not to challenge the Conservative Unionist candidate. At Colchester and Maldon a Labour candidate appeared for the first time in a parliamentary election.

The Representation of the People Act of 1918 increased the electorate from eight million to over twenty-one million. The residency requirement of at least one year in the same dwelling, which discriminated against soldiers and industrial workers, was reduced to six months, and widened to cover residency in the same general area rather than one dwelling. Men aged nineteen or twenty who were on active service were enfranchised in recognition of their contribution to the war effort. All conscientious objectors were punished for their 'disloyalty' by being disenfranchised for five years, unless they could prove they had done work in the national interest. The franchise was also extended to women over thirty who were ratepayers or who were married to ratepayers. As a result about eight and a half million women and almost thirteen million men were enfranchised.

The election was called by Lloyd George's coalition government to obtain a

[15] G. Caunt, *Essex in Parliament* (1969), 98; ECC 20 December 1918.

[16] ECC 20 December 1918.

mandate from the British people to continue governing in the post-war world, and in particular, to deal with the defeated Germans and their allies at the peace talks planned for 1919. The parliamentary candidates of all parties therefore based their campaigns on the issue of the suitability of their party to assume this historic burden. Labour's candidates championed the moderate socialist programme with which the Labour Party was making its bid for power. Andrew Conley, the Labour candidate at Colchester, and George Dallas at Maldon, advocated the nationalisation of land, mines, shipping and the railways. They urged "social reconstruction", by which they meant a better deal for the working classes, educational reforms leading to equal opportunities for all, shorter hours and a living wage. Men such as these had sprung from the working class themselves and they had learned their political craft in the trade unions. Dallas had worked in Essex supporting the interests of farm labourers, Conley, although not a local man, had helped to organise women workers in the garment trade in north-east Essex in 1912-13. They believed that they alone were qualified to represent the workers.

The Conservative Unionists tirelessly hammered home their argument that only the coalition could be entrusted to guide Britain through the peace talks and ensure that Germany got its just desserts. Labour was constantly accused of being soft on the Germans. The *Essex County Standard* shuddered at the thought of a Labour government in charge of the peace negotiations:

> A Ramsey MacDonald or a Philip Snowden would be entrusted to represent this great nation at the round table and to the everlasting disgrace of Britain terms would be advocated which would expressly avoid any guarantees for the future and would encourage Germany to prepare for another and mightier effort in time to come to redeem her lost fortunes and plunge this nation into surrender to her base ambitions.[17]

Like Labour, the Conservative Party presented itself as a moderate, reasonable, reformist party with working-class interests at heart. Its candidates advocated social reconstruction, a widening of educational opportunities, improved living conditions, improved wages and increased leisure for the working man. Sir J. Fortescue Flannery, their candidate at Maldon, supported local authority housing, equality of education and aid for discharged ex-servicemen.[18] Frank Hilder, the candidate for South-east Essex, said that wages "must be the highest consistent with national prosperity." R.B. Colvin, at Epping, wanted labour to receive a fair share of profits, equal pay for men and women, and "the inclusion of women in any profession for which they are suited." A key plank of the Conservative campaign was that Labour's 'wild' schemes

[17] ECS 14 December 1918.

[18] ECC 13 December 1918.

for nationalisation and increased taxation could not deliver the improvements for working people which they were promised. Labour's economic competency was questioned and its lack of government experience derided. In Mid-Essex E.G. Pretyman's theme was a familiar one:

> A Labour Government could do something but it could not make a new Heaven and a new earth, or make or spend money until that money had been earned.[19]

R.B. Colvin was undoubtedly thinking of the Labour Party when he warned voters of the dangers of the "poisonous seeds" of Bolshevism.[20]

Most candidates were agreed that Germany had to be dealt with firmly and decisively. However, their solutions to the German problem were expressed in various degrees of intemperateness. At Harwich, the Conservative candidate, Harry Newton, urged that Germany be excluded from the League of Nations until she was "a civilised and regenerated nation." Laming Worthington-Evans, the sitting Conservative M.P. at Colchester, demanded that Germany be made to pay "The fullest and most complete reparation." "Germany would have to pay every penny that she could possibly be made to pay", he stated. Maldon's Liberal candidate, E.W. Tanner, urged "drastic" treatment of Germans, but perhaps not as drastic as that being advocated by Frank Hilder when he referred to Germans in Britain. Hilder said that, "The Hohenzollern tribe must be outlawed for ever ... Every German, man, woman, boy and girl must be despatched to Hunland immediately, ships are available to take them and good riddance."[21]

On the whole the campaign was fought in a restrained and decent manner, although that at Colchester was an exception to this. The Conservatives, clearly alarmed at the level of support Conley was receiving, campaigned tirelessly to prove that the Labour Party was unprincipled, incompetent, untrustworthy and unpatriotic. Conley was criticised for allowing the red flag to be flown outside his headquarters, and his supporters were accused of intimidating the opposition at meetings up and down the constituency, accusations which had not a shred of evidence to support them. On the day of the election the Conservative *Essex County Standard* issued a 'Last Word to Electors'. The newspaper began: "Let every voter ask himself the question "How should I vote if I were a Hun? This is the test question." The answer to this question was apparently self-evident. Only Lloyd George and the Coalition could secure an appropriate peace; Labour could not be trusted. Indeed, since Labour represented disunity, a vote for Labour was tantamount to aiding Germany:

19 ECC 29 November 1918.

20 ECC 6 December 1918.

21 ECC 6 December 1918.

> Shall I vote as Germany desires or shall I support the Government with its fixed purpose of securing an era of peace unendangered by the revengeful desires of our still unrepentant enemies?

Just to make sure that its readers knew exactly where the *Essex County Standard* stood it rounded off its anti-Labour tirade with its *pièce de résistance:*

> Before Voting ask yourself
> THIS FINAL QUESTION
> HOW WOULD THE GERMANS
> LIKE ME TO VOTE?
> TO VOTE FOR WORTHINGTON-EVANS
> is to support LLOYD GEORGE, which
> Will not please the Germans,
> who would like to see our National Unity broken and the Lloyd George Coalition Government overthrown

The day of the election was very cold and drizzly. This may have affected the turnout which was disappointingly low. In the county's boroughs only 48.8 per cent of the electorate voted, and it was only marginally higher in county constituencies, at 50.2 per cent. Of the seven thousand or so soldiers entitled to vote, only 2,427 did so, and according to the Liberal *Essex County Telegraph* at Colchester they voted solidly for Worthington-Evans. At Chelmsford women were believed to have outnumbered men at the polling booths. Farm labourers at Notley refused to vote as a protest at a local beer shortage. In High Roding, because the polling station was three miles away, only about thirty of the village's two hundred voters turned out.

The election was a triumph for Lloyd George's Coalition, but particularly for its Conservative members. Four hundred and seventy-three Coalition M.P.s were returned against a mere twenty-six non-Coalition Liberals and fifty-nine Labour. Of the 473 Coalition M.P.s, 339 were Conservatives. It was a Tory-dominated government, an indication that the political climate had moved to the right, and was more in harmony with the wartime inclinations of the Conservative Party rather than with those of the Labour Party. In Essex too, the Coalitionists practically swept the board, winning eighteen of the twenty seats. Twelve Conservative Coalitionists were returned, four Coalition Liberals and two members each of the Coalition National Democratic and Labour Party. The Labour Party won the two newly created seats of West Ham Plaistow and West Ham Silvertown. Some Coalition victories were very comfortable; their majority at Epping was over ten thousand, eight thousand at

Southend, nearly seven thousand at Chelmsford, five thousand at Leyton West and Romford, and four thousand at Colchester. Coalition Liberals won handsomely at Romford (five thousand majority) and Saffron Walden (over five thousand majority). Will Thorne achieved the largest electoral success in Essex by polling over twelve thousand votes against the independent candidate's 657. There were close finishes in only three constituencies. The Coalition Liberals won Leyton East by only two hundred votes against an independent challenger; at Maldon Labour's George Dallas came close, polling 6,315 votes against Fortescue-Flannery's 8,138. At Harwich it was even closer with the Coalition Conservative just fighting off the Lib-Lab pro-Coalitionist Aylmer Digby, who polled 7,064 votes against Harry Newton's 8,281, a majority of only 1,197. Labour's first joust at these parliamentary constituencies had ended in failure, but as the Coalition swept the board nationally, this was not a great surprise. Labour was far from demoralised by these failures, and the bedrock of support which had been shown to exist in the East End, and at Chelmsford, Colchester, Romford, Saffron Walden, Ilford and Maldon gave encouragement to the campaigns which would be fought later at municipal level. However, as the bulk of the area's working-class voters would continue to prefer Conservatism to Labourism throughout the inter-war decades, the latter had its work cut out to convince them to change.

In spite of working-class reluctance to embrace the moderate left-wing policies of the Labour Party, let alone communist extremism, the Conservative Party and conservative-minded local people saw the threat of Bolshevik revolution, as represented in Britain by the Labour Party and trade unions, at every turn in the years after the War. The growth of trade unions, which were beginning to flex their muscles in pay demands and industrial disputes, the wartime creation of fishermen's cooperatives with their socialist overtones, the public espousing of socialism by men in apparently respectable professions, all allegedly spearheaded by the Labour Party, sent shivers down the spines of local Conservatives. In their view they had not defeated the Germans and preserved Britain and her Empire, only to hand them over to Labour extremists who had been inspired by the horrors of the Bolshevik revolution in Russia. William Kimmond, a Colchester Conservative from Lexden, sounded off to the *Essex County Standard*, condemning trade unions as "this hydra-headed monster", and urged the Government to make them illegal. He declared that the only effective way to help the working class was to encourage them to help themselves, "not by giving them a reward which is really the robbery of what abler and more industrious and frugal men have earned." Warning of the dire consequences of union power, he feared that "the whole valour of our best fighting men will be impotent against these foes of the nation."[22] Later in the year Kimmond was again writing to the press, warning of the consequences of irresponsible trade union power, or as he put it, "mobocracy." The same fear-mongering appeared at the 1919

[22] ECS 29 March 1919.

Colchester Oyster Feast. General Towsey, the local military commander who saw left-wing extremism lurking around every corner, declared that unemployment was the most effective recruiting agent of the Bolsheviks, alias the British Labour Party and trade unions. He condemned the latter as:

> the people, who, having nothing, risked nothing, and whose methods, judging by the state of Russia, appeared to be a combination of robbery and murder.[23]

Laming Worthington-Evans struck the same doom-laden note when he speculated that the imminent miners' strike of 1920 "would be the first step towards the revolution which so many of the hotheads who desired to form a Soviet government had been planning."[24]

T.G.B. Kay, the Vicar of Southminster, preached to his congregation that Bolshevism was "a false freedom" and contrary to Christianity. With tales from Russia in mind, he said that "Bolshevism led to murder and starvation."[25] Essex sailors, returning from service in the Russian Civil War, related horror stories of the Bolsheviks. Charles Gain of Burnham described the atrocities they committed at the port of Odessa; George Baerselman from Southend, was relating similar stories six months later.[26] Far more virulently anti-Labour was the utterance of Herbert Harris, a Colchester councillor, who alleged that the workers, having demanded state control, now claimed that it had not sufficiently transformed society:

> They were squealing under it. Let them squeal on. They had brought forward no solution to bringing down the cost of living: the only thing they had in their minds was class hatred, pure and simple ... The Trade Union movement claimed to stand for freedom and liberty, but it was freedom and liberty only for themselves ... The solution for high prices was to cast aside for ever this class hatred ... to sweep away State control and Government interference, the encouragement of private enterprise, and open competition coupled with increased output.[27]

The Colchester Unionist Women Workers' League, although claiming to represent the whole country, likewise condemned the Labour Party for preaching "narrow class

23 ECS 25 October 1919.

24 ECT 28 August 1920.

25 BDA 7 June 1919.

26 BDA 11 October 1919; SST 15 April 1920.

27 ECT 10 July 1920.

hatred." In view of this anti-Bolshevik hysteria it was not surprising that a meeting was held in Chelmsford in October 1919 urging the authorities to make arrangements for future emergencies such as left-wing instigated coups and strikes. At Burnham there were plans to set up a Citizens Guard to be prepared for left-wing sedition and violence.[28]

The Conservative Party was not the only organisation to issue apocalyptic warnings about the consequences of the Labour Party and the trade unions acquiring national power. The Middle Class Union was a national organisation of 150 branches which had been set up in 1919 to defend the interests of the middle class. Its aim of offering resistance to "extreme measures by capital or labour" appeared to be even-handed. In Essex branches were established at Brentwood, Chelmsford, and Colchester. The inaugural meeting at Colchester in 1920 promised to denounce excessive expenditure by central or local government which led to increased taxation, rates or price rises, and aimed to expose profiteering where it occurred. It also urged pay restraint on all employees. The union claimed that excessive profits by employers and the doubling of wage levels for employees, had combined to damage middle-class interests. At Chelmsford the branch identified the greed of both rich and poor as the cause of their problems:

> Both manual labour at the bottom, and Capital at the top, were highly organised, and when the great Trade Unions got advances in wages, the capitalists passed it on, and the middle classes paid the bill ... In municipal government they found all kinds of people getting on the Councils, ignorant, knowing nothing about Economics or finance, who had no outlook beyond their own front door, and had the idea that money fell like manna from heaven.[29]

Resentment of trade union power was a commonplace of meetings of the Middle Class Union. "Education was becoming a farce", said J.O. Thompson at Chelmsford, "a man who was educated could not get half so good a living as the uneducated man who was organised."[30]

However, although the union frequently criticised town councils for their debts, their failure to impose economies on their workforce, and for escalating rates, its most ferocious condemnation was always reserved for the working class and trade unions. This is hardly surprising. The Middle Class Union's leaders can usually be identified as Conservative supporters or businessmen who detested the Labour Party. It was essentially a reactionary group, which in its own words aimed to "quash

[28] BDA 11 October 1919.

[29] ECC 19 March 1920.

[30] ECC 11 June 1920.

revolution or attempted revolution", a phrase which could only have been directed at the Left. The Union's inaugural meeting at Colchester flinched at the mention of Russia's "resolute desperadoes", and in the same breath condemned "the wild men of labour."[31] "They wanted to back up the honest working man to see he got every penny he earned", said one speaker, "but they also asked him, as an honest working man, to earn every penny he got", a comment which insinuated that wartime, working-class pay rises had not necessarily been earned.[32] At Brentwood, the trade unions were condemned as "the extremists who desired to seize everything for themselves and hand the country over to riots and revolutions."[33] The same branch saw the imminent farm and gas strike in 1920 as "darkness and chaos". The political inclinations of the Brentwood branch were made clear when, at the same meeting, J.F. Gibbs, the manager of the beleaguered gasworks in the town, asked for volunteers to resist those trying "to wreck society."[34] At a Colchester union meeting six months later, Captain C.J. Round accused the working classes of becoming comparatively well-off at the expense of the middle classes. Incredibly he described the miners as "the new rich, wanting nothing, and living in many cases in luxury." He too warned of the Labour Party's Bolshevik tyranny. In September 1920 the imminence of a threatened miners' strike drove all impartiality out of the collective minds of Colchester's Middle Class Union:

> this meeting deprecates the threatened strike of the miners as being an attack against the community: and condemns the action of the political labour party in attempting to usurp the powers of constitutional government by threatening to use the forces of industrial organisation for the purposes of dictating the policy of the nation.[35]

A few weeks later a Middle Class Union meeting described the dispute as "the most ghastly strike the country had ever seen".[36] At the inaugural meeting of the union's Ilford and Leytonstone branch, a Captain P. Ashford asserted reasonably enough that "the union was not a class union, but one which represents all those who believe in work and in enjoying the reward of their work." However, in common with speakers from other Essex branches, he quickly made it clear that his branch too saw working-class idleness as the most pressing danger facing the country:

[31] ECS 6 March 1920, ECT 12 June 1920.

[32] ECS 6 March 1920.

[33] ECC 16 April 1920.

[34] ECC 25 June 1920.

[35] ECT 7 September 1920.

[36] ECS 23 October 1920.

> But it did not attempt to represent anybody who wanted to live on the work of other people. Neither did it represent anybody who wanted to lean against a lamp post to keep himself upright. In other words it represented the manhood of the country, the thrifty and the industrious. It represents the people who tried, and execrated the loafer and the ca'canny. It believed that the world was built up by people who tried, and that if these people were to be taxed out of existence there was a poor outlook for the people who were left to get a living out of the efforts of those who did as little as they could. In plain English it represents the patriotic, industrious citizens.

At the Colchester Oyster Feast, the Recorder of Colchester, Sir Richard Muir, also criticised the idleness of the working class whilst praising the industriousness of the middle class:

> The bourgeoisie on the other hand, were the backbone of all order, the people who were not idle, who did not live upon wealth acquired by somebody other than themselves, and who added it to the wealth of the nation. The working classes were, so their leaders seemed to think, going to acquire better things for themselves by working shorter hours and doing less for it.

It was evident that Muir was perturbed by what he saw as unwelcome changes in the social order, and saddened by the apparent ebbing away of deferential attitudes:

> With regard to the relations between employers and employed, why did not the masses of the working men trust their educated employers as the men at the front had trusted their educated officers?[37]

In his view of the situation, the election of a Labour government could only spell disaster for the country. It would mean handing over "all finance of the country to people who could not run a cookshop at a profit on Blackpool sands." It would also lead to revolution and chaos which he pledged to resist to the end:

> As long as they had the power to use their brains the Royal Standard and the Union Jack should never be torn down and trampled in the dust, to be replaced by the red flag of Socialism, starvation, murder and anarchy.

37 ECT 25 October 1919.

How realistic were these dire forecasts of the growing power of the Labour Party in Essex? The radical Independent Labour Party (I.L.P.) and local trades councils in metropolitan Essex had campaigned against the War as a capitalist war used by the employers to exploit the workers. With Russia's withdrawal from the War in 1917, following the Bolshevik Revolution, these groups had a further grievance against the Government. In 1918 it had joined other Allied countries in despatching armies to Russia to help overthrow the Bolsheviks and install a government which would re-enter the War. The East Ham Trades Council was outraged at the Government's intervention and passed a threatening resolution urging the National Labour Party to organise meetings and demonstrations to protest against, and demand the withdrawal of, the Allied forces from Russia, and if necessary to call a general strike, even if civil war resulted from it. Furthermore, the resolution considered that the Allies' action was a violation of neutrality equal to that perpetrated by Germany against Belgium. The resolution also asserted that the Government's real aim was to destroy the Russian Revolution, a purpose for which the men of England did not volunteer. In August and September 1920 there were demonstrations in East Ham against intervention in Russia. The mayor, G.P. Dean, congratulated the people of Russia on gaining their freedom, seizing the land of the wealthy, and he condemned stories of Bolshevik atrocities as "an abominable lie".[38] In the spring of 1919 the East Ham Trades Council also accused the Government of inhumane actions by maintaining its economic blockade of Germany, arguing that no-one with humane feelings would try to gain an advantage through the starvation of infants, and that the faults of Prussian militarists were no excuse for the action undertaken by the Government. In June of 1919 the Trades Council was still urging the evacuation of British troops from Russia so that it could effect its internal economic and political emancipation. Should the Government fail to act, the council urged that it should be forced to do so by direct action.[39] In reality these were empty threats, for neither the East Ham I.L.P. nor the Trades Council possessed the political strength nor the economic muscle to carry them out.

The Labour Party itself, judging by its public pronouncements, was pursuing a moderate political agenda in these early post-war years. At Colchester five thousand people turned out for a bank holiday party rally on the Recreation Ground in August 1919, during which the following resolution was passed:

> That this demonstration voices the demands of labour for an end of militarism in this country, only to be obtained by the abolition of conscription, by rapid discharge of all soldiers not volunteering, and the immediate withdrawal of our forces from Russia; and declares that profiteering can only be ended, and

38 SE 21 August, 4 September 1920.

39 East Ham I.L.P minutes, 11 August 1918, 2 April, 18 June 1919.

> fair conditions of labour, housing, and reduced cost of living attained, by the end of militarism, the nationalisation of mines, the effective organisation of agriculture, and the advent of a Labour Government.[40]

This resolution had varied little from the one made four months earlier at a May Day rally in the town, when conscription, Russia, and the nationalisation of "land, railways, mines and all monopolies" had been urged.[41] A year later the objectives of the branch remained very much the same in demanding:

> the drastic reduction of the cost of living, the immediate building of houses by direct labour employed by the local authorities, the opening up of trade with Russia without equivocation or reserve, the withdrawal of troops from Ireland, and the release of all political and military prisoners. Realising that these objects cannot be obtained from the present or any other capitalist government, we hereby pledge ourselves to do all in our power, by practical, moral, and financial support, to secure the return of Labour representatives to Parliament, and to all local governing bodies.[42]

Chelmsford's Labour Party protested at the Government's assistance to the Poles in their war against Russia. The Labour Party at Southend also leapt to the defence of Lenin's Bolsheviks when it called upon the Government "to withdraw immediately the British forces from Russian soil, and leave the Russian people to decide for themselves what form of government they desire." Both the Chelmsford and Southend branches created a Council of Action to campaign against Britain's intervention in the civil war raging across Russia.[43]

These then were the policies pursued rigidly by local Labour parties during 1919-20. The party's *raison d'etre* was its championing of the working classes, both domestically and internationally, hence its concern for Ireland and Russia. Daniel Hughes, the party's parliamentary candidate for Colchester, criticised the Government's military campaign to crush Irish republicanism and urged self-determination for the Irish, "We bled for Belgian self-determination; we bleed to deny Irishmen the same boon."[44]

Throughout these years the Labour Party denounced the profiteering of business owners and shopkeepers. Both the Braintree and Colchester Labour Parties criticised the

40 ECS 9 August 1919.

41 ECS 3 May 1919.

42 ECT 8 May 1920.

43 SST 9 January 1919, 12 August 1920; ECC 20 August 1920.

44 ECT 7 February 1920.

inadequate Labour representation on profiteering committees. The Colchester branch also criticised employers who seemed to be paying wages below what it considered to be acceptable levels, taking the Colchester Board of Guardians to task in September 1919.[45] The Southend Trades and Labour Council objected to the removal of two Labour members from the town council's Education Committee.[46] It attempted to keep the rising levels of post-war unemployment in the public eye. At Clacton labour representatives met with the urban district council and local employers of labour to discuss the issue.[47] Working-class pay rises were urged and justified at every opportunity, and whenever possible, the defects of working-class housing and the housing shortage were discussed publicly and in the press. When in February 1920 Colchester Town Council purchased 150 police truncheons, Labour councillors were swift to denounce it as a plot to use repressive measures on workers who were successfully asserting their rights to wage bargaining.[48] The party also made loud protests when Colchester Town Council rejected a request to use the Castle Park for its May Day demonstration, suggesting the Recreation Ground instead.[49] A few prominent clergymen joined Labour's ranks. A.E. Ley, Vicar of Manningtree, declared that he would rather see Labour in power than an aristocrat.[50] K.L. Parry wrote that "I believe today ... that some of the sublimest ideals of human liberty and progress are to be found within the Labour movement."[51]

Conservative fears that these thousands of new voters might be seduced by the Labour Party and used as socialist fodder by its supposedly Bolshevik propagandists proved to be largely groundless. The Labour Party's failure to capture more than a handful of Essex constituencies in the 1918 election was merely the start of a whole crop of failures in subsequent local elections during 1919-20. The area mirrored national political apathy, with only fifty-six per cent of the electorate turning out to vote in the 1919 municipal elections in Colchester, which was nevertheless a significantly higher turnout than at either Chelmsford (thirty-seven per cent) or Harwich (thirty-three per cent). At Colchester the Labour Party received less than a third of the votes cast and only one of its eight candidates, Frederick Billington, a millwright, came top of the poll in the East Ward, the Labour stronghold in the town. In the other three wards Labour was trounced; in the well-heeled West Ward it polled a mere 525 votes against the 3,363 cast for its opponents. Even more galling for the Labour Party was the fact that in the South Ward, Herbert Harris, a boilermaker's assistant, was elected in second place as the Conservative Party's first working-class

[45] ECC 7 November 1919.

[46] SST 20 November 1920.

[47] ECS 11 December 1920.

[48] ECS 28 February 1920.

[49] ECS 10 May 1919.

[50] ECS 14 February 1920.

[51] ECT 21 September 1920.

councillor. At Wivenhoe it had been a similar story in the spring elections to the urban district council; the party's four candidates polled only 426 out of the 1,374 votes cast and they came bottom of the poll. At Brightlingsea only one of the four Labour candidates, Hazell Polley, secured election.[52] Three of its five candidates were defeated at Dedham, and all were beaten at Burnham. Elsewhere Labour's fortunes were more satisfactory, four of its eight candidates secured election at Chelmsford, and after winning a municipal by-election a month later Labour's supporters sang the 'Red Flag'. Four Labour candidates were elected at Leyton; its two nominees were returned unopposed at Harwich, three at Shoeburyness, four at Walthamstow, and all its candidates were returned at Grays. The party's three successes at Southend gave it four members on the town council. At West Ham, Labour won seven of the nine wards, gaining four seats and winning a majority on the town council.

Labour's fortunes deteriorated in 1920. Labour strength in metropolitan Essex stood firm, but it faltered badly in the rest of the county. The Halstead Urban District Council elections in April saw all four Labour nominees defeated; at Wivenhoe J. Frostick came top of the poll, but his running mate, T. Chamberlain, came bottom.[53] In early October there was an early municipal contest in the Colchester East Ward, which had a concentration of working-class voters, to replace H.J. Everett who had resigned. Labour's candidate, Edwin Kerry, who had been defeated several times in previous elections, including that of 1919, was again beaten, this time rather surprisingly, albeit by the narrow margin of 133 votes — 1,140 against 1,007. In the November elections all Labour's candidates but one were defeated. Only Timothy Smith secured election, coming top of the East Ward poll with 1,526 votes. As in 1919, its share of the vote was no more than a third. The regional municipal elections generally were an unmitigated disaster for the Labour Party. It was defeated at Maldon and at Chelmsford, where, after its moderate success in 1919, all eight of its candidates were beaten. Labour fielded seven candidates at Southend, but here too there was no repeat of 1919 and all were defeated. Four out of five candidates lost at Harwich, all four lost at Saffron Walden and at Halstead. Coalition candidates had campaigned on a platform of retrenchment, which largely meant they urged limiting the cost of social reform. Not surprisingly the *Essex County Standard* interpreted Labour's defeat at the polls as a rejection of its "reckless disregard for extravagant expenditure."[54] Only in the West and East Ham municipal elections was there any encouragement for Labour. The party won nine of the eighteen seats contested in East Ham, and its supporters sang the 'Red Flag' in the town hall grounds to celebrate their successes. It was indeed seen as a great success, winning wards in both municipalities where ten years earlier such victories would have been unthinkable. However, such successes could not be taken for granted at that time. After the municipal elections in

[52] Foynes, *Brightlingsea*, 66.

[53] ECT 3 April 1920.

[54] ECT 6 November 1920.

November 1920, the elevation of a number of councillors as aldermen in East Ham led to eight by-elections only three weeks later. The Labour Party contested all eight seats, but was defeated in six of them.[55]

There was little about the Labour Party in these early post-war years which suggested dangerous success or recklessness. In reality the party was quite conformist. The brass band of the Colchester branch entertained the crowds in Castle Park on nine occasions in 1920, although there were some on the town council who expressed a preference for the more traditional military bands. Far from being a party of revolutionaries, its adherents showed a firm attachment to traditional forms of employment. When a meeting was held at the Colchester Corn Exchange concerning domestic service, it was Mrs P.R. Green, a Labour councillor, who chaired the meeting and described it as "an honourable and congenial occupation."[56]

If the Middle Class Union and the Conservative Party were seemingly horrified by the prospect of Labour advances, they were equally appalled by the growing assertiveness of the local trade union movement. Local trade unionism had made moderate gains before and during the War and was determined to retain these in the post-war years. Combination seemed to be the way forward in order to reinforce pay demands with industrial muscle. In April 1919 the Colchester guardians, and more reluctantly, the Lexden and Winstree guardians, bowed to pressure from the Poor Law Workers Trade Union to establish a forty-eight-hour working week for its members.[57] With similar prompting from the Workers' Union, Colchester Town Council adopted the forty-eight-hour week in May. With examples such as these before them during 1919-20, various groups of workers formed their own trade unions. In April 1919 a meeting of medical practitioners was held in Colchester to establish the local medical profession on the basis of a trade union (the Medico-Political Union).[58] The United Garment Workers urged garment trade workers in north-east Essex to join their union, claiming that since 1914 it had increased its members' wages to 18*s.* 9*d.* a week for men, and 12*s.* 6*d.* for youths and women.[59] Branches of the British Gardeners' Trade Union and National Union of Shopkeepers were established at Colchester in November 1919. The Southend and Westcliff Chambers of Commerce amalgamated in 1920 to more effectively represent trade interests in the town.[60] The Colchester and District Newsagents' Association complained that its members were working an eighty-four-hour week. At a meeting its members urged the association to join the National Federation of Newsagents and supported the need to be "thoroughly organised." Even the town's Bank Officers'

[55] SE 6, 27 November 1920.

[56] ECS 12 April 1919.

[57] ECS 12 April 1919.

[58] ECS 5 April 1919.

[59] ECS 26 April 1919.

[60] SST 15, 22, 29 January 1920.

Guild was lobbying for combination to force up wage levels.[61]

The Conservative Party and Middle Class Union dreaded that Labour power and trade union muscle would lead to runaway pay awards for the working classes which would place an intolerable burden on middle-class ratepayers. Not surprisingly, Conservative candidates in local elections tended to make their stand on pay restraint and economic retrenchment as the issues which would sway the electorate. Electoral successes by the Right were usually greeted as evidence that voters preferred to put their trust in tried and tested businessmen rather than the supposedly economically inept Labour Party. There is no doubt that in these post-war years local government finances made for grim reading and an even grimmer reality for ratepayers. Colchester's rates had actually fallen between 1913 and 1917, exceeding pre-war rates only in 1919, and then by less than *6d*. Since 1911 the town's debt, the legacy of a large programme of municipal improvements in education, health and sanitation since 1890, had been cut by almost twenty-five per cent from £408,000 to £300,000.[62] These improvements were continuing in 1919-20, but inevitably at a cost to local ratepayers. Rapidly escalating rates were unpopular with middle-class property owners on fixed incomes who resented the pay rises being given to their working-class tenants. Rates were increased in April 1920, largely the result of increases in police and teachers' pay, and the cost of dredging the River Colne. By then the town's rates stood at 19*s*. 4*d*. in the pound. Unfortunately, the accumulation of rate increases was making life harder for those who had to pay them. The county's poor rate rose by more than £10,000 during 1919-20, and the Colchester guardians half-yearly rates for April 1920 increased by £11,717 to £27,483, an increase put down to the rising cost of pauper maintenance.[63] The town's poor rate had almost trebled since 1916. In November the guardians at Chelmsford, Colchester, Tendring and Lexden and Winstree protested in vain to Essex County Council's Finance Committee. Faced by rate increases of this magnitude, it is not surprising that at a meeting of the Middle Class Union in October 1920, its members urged the council to restrain its expenditure and resist what one person described as the "idiotic advances" which it had recently granted to its employees.[64] Such attitudes were not confined to Colchester. At Walton the ratepayers' resistance to the council's proposal to spend £600 on public lavatories, forced the holding of a public inquiry to investigate the matter.[65] At Harwich a debate on teachers' salaries was critical of the rising cost, resulting, said one councillor, from "the Government's Utopian schemes."[66] In metropolitan Essex ratepayers' associations and municipal alliances

61 SST 22, 29 November, 5 June, 31 July 1919.

62 ECS 25 October 1919.

63 ECS 17 April 1920.

64 ECS 23 October 1920.

65 ECS 30 October 1920.

66 ECS 10 April 1920.

contested elections in virtually all municipalities, often as the sole rivals of the Labour Party. In 1920 fears of socialism led to the reforming of the Wanstead Ratepayers' Association, which had lapsed in 1914. The West Ham Municipal Alliance feared the possibility of Labour victory, as being likely to bring with it extravagant expenditure which would be extremely damaging to ratepayers.

There is no doubt that wage levels had risen significantly under the pressures of war; most workers' pay levels had almost doubled since 1914. The cost of the salaries of the county council's teachers had risen by almost sixty per cent during 1917-19 from £155,000 to £240,000.[67] Chelmsford Education Committee was appalled that teachers' salaries had increased by £9,375 during 1919.[68] During 1918-19 the wages bill of teachers employed by the Colchester Education Committee had risen from £21,500 to £26,500.[69] A further pay rise in April 1919 took this figure to £29,000, and when the Burnham salary scale was introduced the following year the annual wage bill stood at £40,000.[70] At Harwich, the Burnham award increased the wages bill from £9,715 to £14,670. In 1914-15 it had stood at a mere £5,310. The overall cost of education in the borough of Harwich had increased from £9,735 in 1914-15 to £21,423 in 1920.[71] At Colchester, the Education Committee suggested that graduate salaries be increased by £20 above the existing scale. However, the pay rises which had been granted to teachers led to the town council rejecting this attempt to attract recruits in an increasingly competitive market.[72] The public sector was not the only area to be affected by wartime wage rises. The National Steam Car Company's Chelmsford business lost almost £18,000 in 1919, partly because of the high cost of paraffin and the failure of its coke-fired buses in London, but also because of large wage increases. Between 1917-18 and early 1919 wage payouts had increased by £18,000.[73]

Local government was faced with the greatest pressure to insist on pay restraint and to exercise financial prudence among its employees. Colchester Town Council, which had paid a generous war bonus to its employees during the War, and conceded several pay rises, attempted to resist further wage demands in 1919-20. Although belligerent at first, they were forced to give way, granting further wage advances in March and September 1919, and February 1920. On one occasion their concession narrowly averted a strike. Chelmsford Town Council found itself in a similarly awkward position. In February 1919 they conceded a pay rise to their employees in the gasworks who were threatening to walk out. The resultant pay settlement increased

[67] ECC 27 June 1919.

[68] ECC 16 January 1920.

[69] ECS 8 March 1919.

[70] ECS 27 March 1920.

[71] ECS 10 April 1920.

[72] ECS 29 May 1920.

[73] ECC 3 January 1919.

the borough's annual wages bill by over £2,000. In 1914 its wages payouts amounted to £2,500, but by 1919 it stood at £7,200.[74] At Southend the town council also attempted to keep the floodgates closed, but a single settlement of 7*s*. 6*d*. a week for all employees in August 1920 added £12,500 to the town's rates.[75]

Local Conservative fears that trade unionists might inflict industrial anarchy on the area never approached realisation, although relatively small-scale and short-lived disputes littered the early post-war years. In August 1918 a strike by Colchester Town Council's tramway workers was narrowly averted when the council granted them a 4*s*. a week pay rise.[76] Bus conductors and conductresses at Chelmsford walked out in January 1919 because of the loss of their Christmas bonus and resentment over low pay levels in comparison with wage levels in London. That same month Rochford shipyard workers also went on strike to attempt to force their employers to concede London wage rates.[77] Shortly afterwards the three to four thousand employees at Hookers of Walthamstow went on strike for a day. In March 1919 the largely female workforce at the Pinkham glove factory at Witham went on strike to press for higher wages. Only sixty of the 320-strong workforce were unionised, and the factory was never entirely shut down. By the summer of 1920 Pinkham paved the way to resist further industrial action by opening a new factory in Belgium, where he claimed to be doing more business than at Witham.[78] In June the moulders of Colchester and Braintree went on strike as part of a national strike, and threw the local engineering industry into disarray. Although in January 1920 the men voted to return to work, the national ballot was almost two to one in favour of continuing the strike, which dragged on to become the county's longest strike of 1919-20.[79] At Walton there was a clash of wills between the owners of Robert Warner and Company, an engineering firm, and the Amalgamated Society of Engineers. Warner and Company were reluctant to recognise the union and in January 1920 it dismissed all its employees, refusing to re-employ anyone who was a trade unionist. The firm continued to keep its foundry running by using blackleg labour organised on its own "model" workers' scheme. For a while railway and transport workers cooperated with the strikers by refusing to handle Warner's goods, which caused some disruption to the firm's very significant foreign trade. It was not until July that the two sides were able to break the deadlock and reach a mutual agreement to end the strike. The company agreed not to blacklist trade unionists and all those men and boys who had participated in the strike were reinstated, although some were only given unemployment pay rates by the firm until its business had recovered.[80]

[74] ECC 7, 14 February 1919.

[75] SST 22 July, 5 August 1920.

[76] ECC 3 January 1919.

[77] ECC 24 January 1919.

[78] ECC 15 March, 3 July 1920; ECS 15 March, 19 April 1919.

[79] ECC 27 June, 5, 26 December 1919.

[80] ECT 24 January, 10 July 1920.

Local authorities continued to be affected by industrial action too. Colchester Town Council's refusal to abide by the terms of the Whitley Council, a national arbitration award which affected its electricity supply workers, threatened a further strike in September 1920. The council was reluctant to agree to honour the award in case it opened the way to further pay demands by the Workers' Union. In the end the council avoided a strike by agreeing to go to arbitration to determine how much of the Whitley Award it ought to pay.[81] Ilford, Chelmsford and Southend's municipal workers went on strike at different times in the summer of 1919. At Southend the corporation workforce struck in early July after having several grievances unresolved since April. They had demanded a forty-eight-hour week, a guarantee that wages would not be cut, the merging of temporary bonuses into permanent pay, one week paid holiday after one year of service, and, as was being demanded elsewhere at this time, the payment of London pay rates at Southend. When their demands were not met following a meeting with the council in June, they increased their demands to a forty-seven-hour week, a £3 a week minimum wage for all council employees, and improved rates of overtime pay. The council's claim that they were awaiting the result of the National Industrial Conference before making a decision failed to avert the strike, which lasted for a week.[82] The Chelmsford and Southend branches of the National Painters' Union had already gone on strike in 1919 claiming London rates. In August 1920 a similar walkout by Leigh gas workers was averted by a hastily arrived at settlement. Along with those at Southend, the gas workers made new pay demands in December. Essex postal workers were balloted about a strike, and Tilbury building workers downed tools in August.[83] Even Essex doctors were threatening to go out on strike in support of the Medico-Political Union.[84] Strike fever spread to schoolchildren, with older boys at Braintree schools refusing to work and absenting themselves from school claiming the right to a week's holiday like their fathers.[85]

Two strikes, both of which formed part of wider national disputes on the railways and in farming, had by far the greatest impact on the area during 1919-20. The railwaymen went on strike in late September 1919 in order to resist a wage reduction. The Prime Minister, Lloyd George, intervened to impose a settlement favourable to the railwaymen. The strike lasted only four days and during that time two things became apparent — firstly, that there was considerable opposition to the strike amongst the public at large, and secondly, that the working classes who, according to the Conservatives and Middle Class Union, were spearheading industrial anarchy, were in fact divided as to the merits of the strike.

Most of the Great Eastern Railway Company's employees in Essex refused to work,

[81] ECS 20 November 1920.

[82] SST 10, 17 July 1919.

[83] SST 26 August, 16 December 1920.

[84] ECC 28 March 1919.

[85] ECC 8 August 1919.

although the company managed to maintain a much reduced service. The Braintree line was closed during the strike and the station shut at night. A goods train travelling from Bishop's Stortford to Dunmow was stopped by strikers, and the engine driver was compelled to return it to Bishop's Stortford, where it remained for the duration of the strike. Another goods train was deliberately abandoned at Kelvedon in order to disrupt main line workings. However, such incidents were the exception. About forty railway workers at Shoeburyness broke the strike and ran trains to, and from, London. All the staff at Takeley station worked throughout the strike and at Colchester two non-union porters, as well as clerks and women ticket collectors, continued working. Many ex-servicemen actually strove to defeat the strike by driving the lorries which ferried food supplies into Colchester. So much for Conservative fears of the dangers of revolutionary working-class solidarity. The *Essex County Standard* had no sympathy whatsoever with the railwaymen and compared their tactics with those of Germany in 1914. Even the more supportive *Essex County Telegraph* was forced to admit that the strikers had little support locally.[86]

The goods train abandoned at Kelvedon was moved by volunteers who helped to maintain services throughout the county. Special constables were reactivated during the strike. Able-bodied men stepped forward at Harwich after a municipal appeal; twenty-five were sworn in at Witham. Members of the Romford branch of the Discharged Soldiers and Sailors Federation offered to assist the local police. At Wanstead inhabitants met and resolved to resist an attempted takeover by any single group in society. The strike resulted in a huge increase in road traffic from London, and at Colchester local motor bus companies engaged in fierce competition to ferry workers to the capital, initially at £2 for the return journey, although this soon fell to 15*s*. At Southend commuters were brought in by firms only too eager to exploit the opportunities presented by the strike. Both of Hadleigh's bus firms ran services to London, the Southend Charabanc Company made a daily return journey, and a number of private cars crammed with commuters set off before breakfast each day from Leigh, Westcliff and Southend.[87]

Food distribution was maintained with comparatively little inconvenience. Southend's area distribution officer organised the collection of flour and milk. Dairymen from the town collected milk from the countryside using vans. Workers unloaded packets of fish landed by steam drifters into waiting lorries. Crittall used its own lorries to collect materials which were essential for its works. Several trains containing freshly landed fish or fresh fruit were stranded at Colchester, but the wartime Food Control Committee intervened, putting the produce into cold storage and selling it cheaply at the Corn Exchange. Goods from outlying farms and market gardens were brought into Colchester and Harwich by lorry and sold. Colchester's trams were withdrawn to save coal. The town's huge number of clothing workers

[86] ECS, ECT 4 October 1919.

[87] ECC 2 October 1919; SST 2 October 1919.

were threatened with being laid off unless supplies could be obtained, but the short duration of the strike rendered this unnecessary.

The agricultural labourers' strike in the following year caused far less disruption. Agricultural workers, who before the War had been amongst the lowest-paid workers in the country, had seen their wages almost double since 1914, but this was still significantly behind the cost of living. With a weekly wage of around 42*s.* 6*d.*, their wages were much less than a railwayman's average of 56*s.*, or a general labourer's 62*s.* Neither did they benefit from the general rise in farm profits. Besides, there was also the looming fear of increased unemployment for farm labourers. During the War wages increased and formed a much larger share of farmers' costs; in response many sought to decrease their wages bill by cutting back arable farming, thus reducing their need for as much labour. However, the labourers' organisation had improved and expanded. In Essex farm workers had flocked to one of two trade unions — the Workers' Union, which had so effectively pressed for increases to the pay of Colchester's council employees, or the Agricultural Labourers' Union. By 1919 there were some ten thousand Essex farm labourers in the Workers' Union, ten per cent of its total membership, and eight thousand in the Agricultural Labourers' Union. These unions were now pressing farmers and the Government for a minimum wage of 50*s.* a week, which the Farmers' Union was vigorously opposing. The latter eventually offered to increase weekly wages to 46*s.* 6*d.* which was unacceptable to either trade union. The Church of England, anxious to avoid industrial strife, urged both employers and workers "not to strive for mastery."[88] It expressed its concern at what it saw as the manipulation of farm labourers by left-wing political activists. "The Class War will bring nothing but harm to everyone concerned", wrote the Bishop of Chelmsford, "and has brought about the utter ruin of Russia."[89]

Both sides had engaged in an uneasy truce during the War but by 1919 a showdown was near. The two farm workers' unions were organising and recruiting furiously and farm workers were becoming belligerent. In November 1919 threshing machine workers in the Rochford area went on strike when the local farmers attempted to cut their wages by a shilling a week.[90] Farmers too were preparing for the coming conflict and were organising to resist their employees' demands. A new branch of the National Farmers' Union was formed at Braintree in March 1917 with forty-five members. The Wickford branch's 161 members were adamant that farmers should not concede more than 32*s.* a week for a fifty-four hour week.[91]

On 17 June 1920 the Workers' Union issued notice of a strike by its members to begin on 26 June. About ninety-eight per cent voted for the strike. The Agricultural

88 *Chelmsford Diocesan Chronicle*, March 1918.

89 *Chelmsford Diocesan Chronicle*, September 1918.

90 SST 20 November 1919.

91 ECC 14 February 1920.

Labourers' Union, a keen rival of the Workers' Union, was not consulted about the strike and an opportunity for united action was forfeited. The strike was a fiasco. On 25 June, the day before the strike was due to begin, the Workers' Union suspended strike notices for a week. Many of its members were not informed however, and went on strike, which then rapidly fizzled out. Trade union rivalry destroyed any chance of an effective demonstration of strength by farm labourers in Essex. This strike, like the rail strike a year earlier, carried little public support, although in response to a plea by the Farmers' Union for volunteers to milk cows during the dispute, only forty-five women and girls stepped forward from the area.[92]

Although there was trade union discontent during 1919-20 it never reached significant proportions and, with the exception of the very brief rail strike in September 1919, industrial disputes achieved little disruption to the region's economic life. Membership of trade unions was still extremely small, about a thousand in the Colchester area, a tiny percentage of the number of men and women employed in north-east Essex. In general, local workers, facing their own problems with jobs, pay and housing, tended to be relatively unsympathetic to strikers, particularly when the coal dispute threatened widespread layoffs in the clothing industry and many other industrial concerns. The fact that some of the buses ferrying people to and from London during the rail strike were driven by ex-rank and file soldiers indicated a lack of sympathy with what were scathingly referred to as 'Bolshevik' or 'Hun' tactics, depending on one's political point of view.[93]

It was not only employers and trade unions who began to adopt more assertive attitudes during 1919-20, individuals and groups became more independent and aggressive. Ratepayers had banded together before the War to create pressure groups or to demonstrate their dissatisfaction with local matters. Some ratepayers' associations had entered candidates in local elections, though in a rather piecemeal fashion. After the War ratepayers' associations sprang up throughout the county, many of them seeking election of members to local office as a way of protecting their own interests. There were ratepayers' associations in Hadleigh, South Benfleet, Leigh and Wickford. The Leigh association was instrumental in purchasing the Belfairs estate, and in having the Food Office reopened in the town as a protest against rising food prices. It supported the local Vacant Land Cultivation Society which was alarmed that it might lose its allotments in post-war house-building schemes. During the Southend municipal elections in 1920 it was influential enough to hold a meeting at which the local candidates thought it prudent enough to explain their policies, although it was also running its own candidate, as was the Westborough ward's ratepayers' association. The association was also at the centre of a move to refuse to pay water rates as a protest at spiralling rates.[94] The Hadleigh association pressured

92 ECT 3 July 1920.

93 ECS 4 October 1919

94 SST 20 November 1919, 14, 21 October 1920.

the parish council to seek urban powers in conjunction with Rayleigh, South Benfleet, Thundersley and Canvey Island, believing that this would give it a greater say in its financial affairs.[95] The ratepayers of Epping, frustrated by what they saw as rising local government expenditure, met to pass a unanimous resolution demanding that the urban district council reject all housing tenders unless they were below £1,000.[96]

Ratepayers' associations were not alone in taking more direct action. In the 1920 Southend municipal elections, ratepayers' candidates jostled with the Women's Freedom League, a non-party organisation, the Labour Party, the local Chalkwell Bay Association, the Discharged and Demobilised Soldiers and Sailors Association, and the Westcliff Chamber of Trade. There was also the newly-created Municipal Alliance, which performed the same role at Southend that the Middle Class Union performed elsewhere. It aimed to raise interest in education, to counsel "moderate and economical expenditure", proper control of municipal undertakings, and to draw attention to Southend Corporation's debt and increasing rates. Its opposition to left-wing politics also meshed with those of the Middle Class Union; the Municipal Alliance claimed to be non-party and non-sectarian, but one of its aims was "to combat the growth of Anarchic Socialism."[97] Like the Southend Municipal Alliance, a "Progressive" party was created at Ashdon which aimed to encourage voters to participate in local and parliamentary elections. Although in 1919 it failed to get any of its candidates elected in the rural district council elections, the party claimed a moral victory.[98] At Great Baddow the residents organised a vigorous campaign against the county council's housing scheme, which they claimed was threatening to swamp the village. Those of the villagers who tended allotments were also angry that the proposed building scheme was likely to destroy their plots.[99]

Although ratepayers' associations and various political groups and non-party organisations were adopting more active policies, it was ex-servicemen who felt that they had particularly pressing reasons to adopt a more militant and direct approach to tackling their problems. Many ex-servicemen who had survived the War sufficiently healthy in mind and body to be employable found themselves without a job and with diminishing prospects of obtaining one. In most Essex towns ex-servicemen formed a majority of the unemployed. By the end of 1920 seven hundred of the thirteen hundred unemployed men in Colchester were ex-soldiers and ex-sailors, many of whom were said to have been living in a "semi-starved state."[100] At the same time of the year in Southend most of the nine hundred unemployed men were demobbed servicemen.[101] Consequently, in places like Colchester and Romford

[95] SST 8 July 1920.

[96] ECC 12 March 1920.

[97] SST 30 September 1920.

[98] WWN 11 April 1919.

[99] ECC 20, 27 June 1919.

[100] ECT 16 October 1920.

[101] SST 11 November 1920.

there was an insistent campaign led by ex-servicemen's associations against the employment of women in jobs which had formerly been regarded as male occupations. Witham's branch of the Comrades of the Great War, on the other hand, was especially critical of war profiteers, who had enriched themselves under the flag of patriotism while they and their dead comrades had suffered and died under it.[102] There was particular bitterness about the plight of disabled ex-servicemen, those men physically and mentally scarred by their wartime experiences, whose numbers were considerable in these post-war years. Although at Chelmsford 362 men were registered as disabled, many of these were more fortunate than in other towns because local employers hired them in large numbers. Hoffmann employed 175, Marconi 100, Cromptons forty, and the town council fifteen.[103] Elsewhere it was a different story. At Southend in January 1919 there were 1,551 disabled ex-servicemen registered with the War Pensions Committee, thirty-eight of whom were receiving hospital treatment. A month later this figure had risen to 1,630, by May there were 1,866 men registered, and by October this had increased by almost sixty per cent to 3,055. As time passed the effects of the War on men's health meant that more were classed as disabled in some way. By the end of 1919 there were three thousand, four hundred disabled ex-servicemen in Southend, and by the end of February it was almost four thousand.[104] Able-bodied ex-servicemen were incensed at what they saw as the nation's neglect of these men and this contributed greatly to the resentment which they harboured. The treatment of their disabled comrades led Chelmsford's ex-servicemen to refuse to participate in the victory celebrations in July 1919, a decision which was also made by those at Maldon.[105]

At Burnham the dissatisfaction felt by ex-servicemen was particularly acute. Firstly, they were unhappy about the disposal of surplus monies from the town's United Services Fund. The men had been promised that it would be used to help build hot and cold baths and they were angered when it was announced that the surplus was to be distributed to them at just a few shillings per man. Secondly, they felt keenly that the town's urban district council had bungled the plans for the war memorial. The men felt that the council's War Memorial Committee had not listened to their views, that its proposals lacked public support, hence the poorly attended public meetings, and that the process was taking far too long. A meeting between the committee and a deputation of ex-servicemen failed to mollify the men, and in late June and early July 1920 their anger boiled over. In common with many towns and villages throughout the country Burnham was in receipt of a war trophy, thousands of which were distributed by the War Office as a tangible reminder of Britain's defeat of the Germans. These trophies were intended for display in some public place.

[102] ECC 3 October 1919.

[103] ECC 25 July 1919.

[104] SST 6 February, 6 March, 8 May, 9 October, 4 December 1919, 26 February 1920.

[105] ECC 27 June, 11 July 1919.

Burnham had received a German field gun and a machine gun, which were being stored in the fire station yard. The men's patience, already strained by the slow progress on the war memorial, snapped shortly after the guns arrived. The presence of German guns only aggravated the sense of betrayal at the lack of a war memorial. One night a large crowd of people, led by ex-servicemen, broke the fire station gates, dragged the artillery piece and carried the machine gun off, and hurled them off the quay into the River Crouch. The council dredged up the field gun and took it back to the fire station yard where, a few days later on the night of the 2-3 July it was again removed from the yard by "a large crowd of men disguised in various ways, accompanied by a number of women." The gun was pulled along the High Street and Silver Road, and at the rear of Wycke Cottages it was tipped into a ditch. The wheels were removed and hurled into the river. At this point the council decided to leave the gun where it was for the time being. The ex-servicemen then formed their own War Memorial Committee, and publicly announced that they would organise their own memorial.

The growing assertiveness of trade unions was not simply a response to the escalating cost of living and their desire to ensure that wage levels kept pace with it. Behind both of these issues lay the dreaded spectre of unemployment, which was rising alarmingly during 1919-20. On the eve of the War there were only 132 persons officially listed as unemployed in the Colchester district, probably about one per cent of those in work. The demands of war saw this fall to ninety-six in 1915 and a mere forty-five in the following year. However by March 1919, four months after the Armistice, the borough's jobless total was 290, and 666 by May. By the new year of 1920 the number of unemployed stood at 1,684. Unemployment figures for the Colchester and district employment area, which included the Tendring district and other areas, were much higher, and persistently so. Between October 1919 and 10 January 1920 unemployment increased by over fifty per cent from 1,645 to 2,548; within three weeks it had shot up to 2,951. Although the number of people out of work then fell steadily, it still stood at 1,303 at the end of the year. By the end of the summer of 1920, 256 of Southend's 500 unemployed had found jobs, but by the end of the year the number of jobless had more than quadrupled, with 850 men and 260 women seeking work, the majority of the men being ex-servicemen.[106] Romford had 240 unemployed in the autumn of 1920, but this had risen to over seven hundred by the end of the year because of sackings at the town's Roneo works.[107] There were between seventy and eighty unemployed at Burnham, including about fifty men from the Mildmay Ironworks.[108] There were 480 men out of work at Barking, where the council was providing relief work on a park extension. The 161 unemployed at Brentwood included many employed by Hoffmann in Chelmsford. The unemployed

[106] SST 5 August, 25 November 1920; BA 8 January 1921.

[107] BA 15 January 1921.

[108] BDA 15 January 1921; ECC 24 September 1920.

were being given work on a weekly basis, although the council only had sufficient funds to employ two hundred of the men. As local hardship increased so did the cost of poor relief. By late 1919 the Rochford guardians found that the cost of relief had grown by £4,000 a year, and by Christmas towns such as Colchester and Southend were organising funds to assist unemployed ex-servicemen.[109] At Colchester, as efforts to assist the unemployed foundered for lack of financial support, there was talk of applying for distressed area status.

Colchester Town Council's solution to the problem of unemployment was to seek financial support to revive the pre-war idea of a programme of improvements to the River Colne between Brightlingsea and the Hythe. In the short term it was hoped that this would provide employment for some four to five hundred of the town's jobless, and in the long-term it would help to ensure the town's trade and prosperity as a port by permitting larger vessels to reach the Hythe. The original plans, devised shortly after the War, were estimated to cost £120,000, but significant government assistance was anticipated.[110] Unfortunately, after a considerable period of waiting the council's application for financial assistance was rejected by the Ministry of Transport in March 1920, and later by the Director-General of Civil Engineering.[111] Southend Town Council proposed an unemployment scheme to improve East Road. The scheme, presented in December 1920, was expected to cost in the region of £40,000, funded by a hoped for government grant of £20,000 and a loan for the same amount.[112] Although post-war levels of unemployment in Essex during 1919-20 were very low compared to those of industrial Britain, they were nevertheless perceived as a disaster by local people and were a rude awakening after the full employment of the wartime years. In metropolitan Essex the unemployed, frustrated at what they regarded as official inaction, took matters into their own hands, and in December 1920 they took over the Walthamstow public baths to draw attention to their plight. The men handed in a "mandate" to Walthamstow Town Council saying that they were in possession of the baths and that they intended to hold them. There were claims that there were between twenty and twenty-five thousand unemployed in the West Ham area, and in Walthamstow unemployed and homeless former soldiers were said to be sleeping in Epping Forest.[113]

As well as growing unemployment, housing was recognised as a problem which urgently needed to be tackled. "Homes fit for heroes" had been on most candidates' lips during the election of 1918. Under Christopher Addison, Minister of Health, the Housing Act of 1919 was designed to ensure the construction of half a million houses within three years and relieve the depression of the building industry. Addison's plans

[109] SST 4, 24 December 1919.

[110] SST 7 December 1918.

[111] ECS 20 March 1920; ECS 4 December 1920.

[112] SST 9 December 1920.

[113] SE 4, 11 December 1920.

were later abandoned by a cost-cutting Conservative Government and he himself was out of office by 1921, but a start was made on tackling the problems of rural and urban housing in Essex during 1919-20.

The fact that the nation's rural and urban working classes had fought heroically for their country refocussed public attention on the appalling state of many of the homes to which they were expected to return. In the small village of Bradfield on the south bank of the River Orwell, all of the workmen's cottages were described as being in a disgraceful condition. Of the village's 186 houses, ninety were permanently unfit for human habitation, and only twenty were said to be repairable. A detailed description of the conditions at Bradfield makes sorry reading:

> The old cottages contain permanent defects, such as damp floors, walls, and ceilings and low rooms. The kitchens were often dilapidated, dark and unwholesome, cold in winter, and warm in summer, with no ceilings, but with the roofing tiles exposed on their undersides, from which the rain dripped into the kitchen in wet weather. In most of the cottages there was no proper food pantry. The stairs were steep, tortuous, twisty, and often dark. The bedrooms were mostly attics, low and inadequately ventilated, and seldom had fireplaces. The walls and roofs were mostly in bad repair. The windows and doors were old and draughty, and let in wind and rain. The sanitary arrangements were condemned ... Water was obtained in most cases from shallow wells, usually open at the top and insufficiently protected. Some houses were grossly overcrowded.[114]

Urban housing was sometimes little better. At Colchester some houses were criticised as "absolutely unsanitary and unfit for working people to live in", and one councillor said that "some of the existing places were not fit to put pigs in." Councillor Mrs Alderton, who voiced these criticisms, elaborated her statement by describing the town's overcrowding:

> In Colchester men earning good wages are crowded with wives and families into a couple of rooms. Married couples are living with their parents. Soldiers, who gave up their homes, cannot now get a house at all. Weary, overstrained mothers have to give birth to their babies in indecency and discomfort, and if a child dies, who can blame the mother if she drearily feels "It's all for the best."[115]

[114] ECT 22 February 1919.

[115] ECT 8 May 1920.

In early 1919 the town's medical officer was of the opinion that between sixty and seventy houses would need to be condemned. At Harwich too, the conditions in many working class homes were described as "scandalous."[116]

The appalling condition of working-class homes was partly the result of the inadequacies of the original design and construction, and often the studied neglect of landlords. However, it was clear that the War had been responsible for aggravating the local housing shortage and the resulting problem of overcrowding. At Clacton half of the town's 2,613 houses were small, working-class buildings; during 1910-14 about twenty of this sort of house was built each year but then the War brought this to a complete halt. In 1919 the wartime retreat of residents had left thirty houses empty and forty-one larger houses unoccupied, but although it was hoped that peace would result in these being filled, it was still estimated that Clacton would require the construction of an additional thirty houses, especially as many demobilised soldiers had married but were living with parents or in-laws.[117] Colchester faced a similar problem. Three hundred and seventy houses had been built during 1910-13, but none had been constructed during the War, when it was estimated that ordinarily about four or five hundred might have gone up in those years. At Coggeshall the problem had been decades in developing; since the 1880s about a hundred cottages in the town had been demolished, and only ten new ones built, resulting in acute overcrowding.[118] A few highly publicised incidents of homelessness highlighted the scarcity of housing. For instance, in September 1919 Sergeant George Batchelor, a recently demobilised soldier, his wife and six children aged between one and eighteen years old, had to be temporarily housed by the Vicar of Southchurch, after they had wandered for a month, sleeping rough in a railway carriage, a bell tent and a tennis pavilion. Homelessness was so acute in the Chelmsford area that the *Essex County Chronicle* suggested using the town's prison, which was empty at the time, as a hostel for homeless people. The borough council inspected the prison, but decided that it was unsuitable to be used as a boarding house.[119]

At Colchester the Housing Committee planned to build eight hundred new houses and by the summer of 1919 had preliminary plans to construct two hundred of them in various parts of the town. The medical officer estimated that five hundred houses of four to six rooms would be required, together with a hundred larger houses. He thought that some three to four hundred houses could be built on the Harwich and Ipswich Roads alone. The prices, ranging from £971 to £1,081, were very expensive and reflected the high cost of both wages and materials which hampered the economic recovery of the building trade. Some houses in the west end of Colchester were even more expensive, costing £1,550 to construct. The Ministry of Health

[116] ECT 14 February 1920.

[117] ECS 9 August 1919.

[118] ECS 10 January 1920.

[119] SST 25 September 1919; ECC 19, 26 March, 2 April 1920.

sanctioned loans of £192,480 to purchase land for road building and to construct houses. The first of the new houses in Colchester's post-war housing development were opened on 17 February 1921 at Defoe Crescent. Eighteen homes had been completed and nine were ready for occupation at that point. Rents were set at 16*s*. 9*d*. a week, although had the rent been set at truly economic levels, the council might have charged over 30*s*.[120] At Frinton the council had plans to build thirty-two houses costing £28,364. At Wivenhoe plans to construct villa-type houses costing £550 were revised upwards to £940, and as this was considered prohibitive it was decided to concentrate on building parlour houses at about £800 each or bungalows, although it was eventually forced to accept tenders at £889 and £896, much higher than it wished.[121] Chelmsford Town Council intended to purchase sixty acres in the Springfield ward on which to build workmen's houses. At £225 an acre the cost of the land was £13,500. However, opposition to what was seen as the excessive cost of the land forced the council to drop its plans and instead purchase 118 acres at £100 an acre in the North ward. This site too fell through, and it was not until the spring of 1920 that one was acquired. Nine hundred and thirty-five houses were to be built, and with a rent suggested at not less than 15*s*. a week, the council anticipated a loss of £38,000 a year on the scheme. After the delay acquiring the site there were complaints about the slow pace of the building. In July the Mayor of Chelmsford actually called for building work on the town's new cinema to stop, on the grounds that it was less essential than working-class homes.[122]

At Burnham the urban district council identified nineteen houses which were uninhabitable amidst a severe housing shortage. At the end of 1919 it devised a housing scheme with houses costing £925. As at Chelmsford, it was estimated that it would result in a heavy loss running at about £900 a year. The first pair of houses was ready for occupation by October 1920. The council set its rent at 8*s*. a week, and waited for the Ministry of Health to approve it. Like many local authorities in Essex, the urban district council sought to set rents which were affordable for local people. Frequently the housing commissioner overruled them. The 8s. a week rent set by the Burnham Urban District Council was rejected in November 1920 when the housing commissioner suggested that a rent of 10*s*. a week, 13*s*. 8*d*. with rates, would be more appropriate. Burnham's council rejected this and took the issue to arbitration.[123] Braintree Urban District Council planned to build 120 houses, ninety of which would be constructed by private firms and in early 1919 Maldon Rural District Council presented plans to build four hundred working-class cottages.[124]

Private companies as well as local authorities were building housing developments

[120] ECT 19 February 1921.

[121] ECT 15 May, 19 June 1920; ECS 14 August 1920.

[122] ECC 3, 31 January, 7 February, 28 March, 31 October 1919, 16 April, 18 June, 2 July 1920.

[123] BDA 29 November, 6 December 1919, 10 January, 30 October, 27 November, 11 December 1920.

[124] BDA 15 February 1919.

in these post-war years. Using the Government's public utility scheme, Braintree's major employer, F.H. Crittall, was spearheading the construction of a hundred houses using government funds, his own company's money, and assisted by private individuals in the town anxious to obtain a home. The public utility society which was created — Braintree Cooperative Houses Limited — began building sixty-eight concrete block houses with flat roofs, a concession to the scarcity of timber at the time, and steel staircases and cupboards. The houses were said to be fireproof and seasonally hot and cold; they also had a vivid appearance, being built of concrete using the bright red sand which underlay the estate.[125] At Southend, the Southend Estates Company planned to develop the Wick Estate, a new, so-called garden city at Thorpe Bay. The estate was to be fashionable and conservative. No licensed premises were planned and street hawking was prohibited. There was to be a bowling green, public and private tennis courts, a children's playground, public gardens, a shopping centre and a cinema. A free site was provided for the Church of England to build a church. At only twelve houses to the acre there would be plenty of space for each house.[126] The Chapmansford estate at nearby Leigh was begun in June 1920 with the construction of sixty-four houses. It too was built under the Government's public utility scheme.[127]

Housing developments were also taking place in rural districts because the problem of rural housing was a common one throughout the Essex countryside. Great Baddow, for instance, was seventy-eight houses short, and many of its old one- and two-roomed cottages were said to be unfit to live in.[128] Rochford Rural District Council's area suffered from poor housing and at Stambridge it was described as particularly disgraceful. In its Reconstruction Plan the county council had already identified 1,982 cottages requiring demolition, as well as a need for 2,170 immediate replacements. The whole of the county was set to receive these much needed cottages — Lexden and Winstree and Tendring 250 each, Chelmsford 200, Maldon 170, Rochford, Saffron Walden and Ongar 150 each, Dunmow and Halstead 120 each, Epping ninety, Stansted and Belchamp fifty each. By late 1919 houses were under construction all over Essex. Lexden and Winstree Rural District Council had formulated plans to build houses at Birch, Boxford, Dedham, Fingringhoe, Little Tey, Abberton, Langham, and Layer-de-la-Haye. Construction costs were far more expensive than in Colchester; non-parlour houses cost £1,483, those with parlours £1,558. Tendring Rural District Council, with twenty-seven parishes, a population of 21,957, and some five thousand houses in 1920, proposed to build an additional three hundred houses on thirty-seven sites. The costs facing it were significantly lower than for Lexden and Winstree; four cottages at Kirby cost £3,540, twelve cottages at

[125] ECC 29 November, 6 December 1918, 26 September 1919.

[126] SST 1 July 1920.

[127] SST 16 September 1920.

[128] ECC 15 August 1919.

Great Oakley cost £13,252, twelve at Ramsey £13,464. Houses at Tendring were tendered for at between £836-896, Weeley £800, St Osyth £778 and Beaumont £789. There were clearly important differences in the quality of houses being built throughout the region. It was under Tendring's housing scheme that the very first houses in Essex were completed under the Housing Act (1919). Two pairs of houses were opened at Frating Green in July 1920. The houses, the cost of which had risen from £830 to about £1,000, comprised a kitchen, parlour, scullery, pantry, three bedrooms, a coal house, tool shed, a quarter of an acre of land, and a covered well providing water, eventually for eight pairs of houses. There were no bathrooms — only a small proportion of Tendring's houses possessed these.[129]

Part of the county council's Reconstruction Plan was the revitalisation of trade and industry by carrying out improvements at ports and building new light railways. Mistley, St Osyth, Brightlingsea, Mersea Island, Heybridge, Bradwell and Burnham were identified for port reconstruction. Nine new railway lines were suggested, Ongar -Sible Hedingham, Ongar-Chelmsford, Rainham-Stanford-le-Hope, Rochford-Paglesham, Southminster-Bradwell, Heybridge-Tolleshunt D'Arcy, Stanway-Mersea Island, Kelvedon-Coggeshall, and Colchester-Boxford.[130] None of these proposals came to fruition and instead it was motorised transport, which had stagnated during the War years because of petrol restrictions, which was resumed in earnest during 1919-20. A county council traffic census carried out at Little Clacton and St Osyth, eighteen hours a day between 9 and 15 August 1920, revealed a total of 14,167 vehicles using these roads. The total tonnage of these vehicles was 12,696 tons. Petrol-driven vehicles were not yet in complete control. Of these vehicles 6,059 were bicycles and 1,257 were light or heavy horse-drawn vehicles. Motor cars and charabancs accounted for 2,796 vehicles, there were 1,386 motor cycles, and 727 buses, vans and lorries.

Colchester's trams continued to run but they faced increasing competition from buses, and were vying for street space with more and more cars and motor cycles. Pre-war bus services disappeared during 1914-18, being replaced by horse-drawn omnibuses, but they rapidly reappeared after the Armistice. Blackwells opened a bus service from Earls Colne to Colchester in 1918; Moore Brothers of Kelvedon began a Coggeshall-Earls Colne-Halstead service in 1919, and another from Halstead to Colchester via Tiptree. Silver Queen of Clacton ran charabancs and buses to Colchester. Berry's Motor Omnibuses, 'The Brown Buses', ran four services a day from Colchester to Rowhedge. In 1920 the first 'company' operator — the National Omnibus and Transport Company Limited — began bus services in the area, running daily Colchester-Halstead and Chelmsford-Halstead services.[131] By early 1919 the

[129] ECT 17 July 1920.

[130] ECC 21 February 1919; ERO DDU 746/12.

[131] B. Everitt, Moores: *The Story of Moore Bros, Kelvedon, Essex: Passenger Carrying through Five Generations* (1998), 28; E. Axten, *Public Transport in the Halstead District* (1980), 54-55; ECT 12 June 1920.

Clacton and District Motor Service Limited ran a route to Colchester, as did the Clacton-based Raglan Red Motor Buses, journeying via Weeley, Frating and Elmstead. However, the National Omnibus Company, having built a garage at Colchester, opened up services from the town throughout the area — to Braintree, Coggeshall, Halstead, Wivenhoe, Dedham, Witham, Brightlingsea, West Mersea, Clacton, Boxted and Nayland. Soon bus services had become so extensive that they were threatening the viability of Colchester's trams. In 1920, under strong pressure from the town council, bus operators were persuaded to charge fifty per cent more to passengers picked up by buses in the borough along routes served by the tramways. Meanwhile the number of companies vying for business was creating cut-throat competition. The West Mersea-Colchester route was particularly affected by such competition. One of the firms involved in this competition, the Mersea, Colchester and District Transport and Bus Company, was formed in September 1919. By early 1920 it was running five motor buses, two steam lorries, a petrol lorry and several trailers. In its first four months it carried eight thousand passengers and provided important haulage facilities for farmers and coal contractors. In January 1920, at its first annual meeting, its 250 shareholders, many of whom were from West Mersea, but included people from Colchester and neighbouring villages, received a five per cent dividend. To increase the company's capital 5,000 new shares were offered at £1 each.[132] The bus industry was already turning out to be a potentially lucrative prospect. The Mersea and Colchester Bus Company was even offering holidays by bus, to places such as Scarborough at a cost of £10 10*s*. As bus companies prospered only one ran into financial difficulties. The National Steam Car Company, which had its Moulsham bus works at Chelmsford, had ended the War in difficulties. In late 1919 it gave up its operations in the capital and decided to limit bus workings to the provinces. Still struggling to restrain its escalating costs, within a short time it had closed the Moulsham works, throwing over a hundred men out of work.[133]

Competition between bus companies was not the only road transport issue causing concern and acrimony at this time. Road accidents involving motor vehicles, which had been increasing in number before the War, were once again a controversial issue. Between June and the end of December 1920 there were thirteen press reports of traffic accidents, with two fatalities at Clacton and one at Tiptree. At Colchester there were calls for a speed limit to be imposed. In September 1919, following the death of a young child cyclist, a jury in the town called for a speed limit of ten miles per hour on all cars and motor cycles. In January 1920 during a lively debate in the council chamber a speed limit of fifteen miles per hour was suggested and opposed by some councillors, one of whom objected to it as an example of "old womanishness." Letters to the press complained of the activities of "gasoline juggernauts" in quiet country lanes. Tendring Rural District Council took matters into its own hands and

[132] ECS 17 January 1920.

[133] ECC 3 January, 7 November, 26 December 1919.

actually banned motor vehicles, heavy lorries and charabancs from roads which were less than sixteen feet wide. Billericay Rural District Council followed suit.[134] For some, what was perceived as excessive speeding was also linked to the clouds of dust raised up by motor vehicles in dry weather, especially in summer. The issue had been a perennial one before 1914 and refused to go away. On the other hand local authorities were also embracing the new transport. In late 1919 Colchester Town Council trialled steam refuse wagons, although trials were abandoned after only a month.[135]

Motorised transport was also beginning to create traffic problems and congestion in towns. By mid-1920 the large number of bus companies picking up passengers in Colchester High Street was causing congestion. When they were moved to Stanwell Street the same problems resurfaced. The appearance of taxis in large numbers also led to controversy. In 1918 when passengers complained at the excessive fares being charged by taxi drivers the council passed by-laws regulating the taxi trade which included the compulsory use of 'taximeters' to record the distances travelled and to allow passengers to monitor their fare. The taxi owners and their drivers, many of them ex-servicemen, responded belligerently and refused to fix taximeters, thereby risking prosecution. On 19 May 1919 a deputation saw the town's chief constable in an attempt to get the by-law removed. Although taximeters were compulsory at the High Street cab rank, the Great Eastern Railway was not insisting on their use at the cab rank at North Station. However, the obduracy of the taxi companies was ultimately in vain. Although sympathetic hotel owners allowed taxis to pick up fares in their yards, and although the taxi owners threatened to take their case to the Local Government Board, the council refused to budge and taximeters came in. As a concession the council agreed to a request from the taxi owners to add 6*d.* to each fare to account for maintenance and repairs to the taxi and the cost of petrol.[136]

Essex was also becoming attractive to the infant aircraft industry. An air charter company applied to Southend Borough Council for the exclusive right to fly four-seater biplanes from the beaches. However, it was an industry which was growing at a snail's pace at this time. The Central Aircraft Company already had a business based at Shoeburyness. In September 1920 it appealed to the urban district council to reduce the rent it paid on the land where its hangar stood. Its appeal was based on the fact that in seven weeks it had carried only fifty-seven passengers and taken a mere £70, whilst facing an expenditure of £774.[137]

Sports and entertainments which had been mothballed by the War gradually reappeared as the area's young men returned from the Front and as things got back

[134] SST 1, 22 July 1920.

[135] ECT 7 June, 6 September 1919, 10 January, 8 May 1920; ECS 2 September, 6 December 1919, 24 January, 8 May 1920.

[136] ECT 12 July 1919.

[137] SST 24 January, 16 September 1920.

to normal. The Essex County Football Association moved to revive the game. During 1919 it was already urging the Football Association to lobby the Government to restore the pleasure party railway fare, previously used by clubs on away fixtures, and to modify the entertainment tax in their favour. In January 1919 only about eight of the clubs affiliated to the County Football Association in 1914 had reformed.[138] However, by 1920 the association had 446 affiliated clubs, 180 of which had entered the fold since the Armistice. Attempts to form a new senior league in north Essex were abandoned in favour of an extension of the existing Essex and Suffolk Border League, whose premier section was increased from twelve to fifteen clubs. The Border League had to rebuild itself after the carnage of war. Of the 1,095 players registered with it in 1914, 480 had been killed, and the league had shrunk from thirty-two to twenty-six clubs. With no garrison sides in town in 1919 Colchester Town was the only side available to play in Division One and the reformation of the league in full had to wait. Other local leagues — the Braintree and District League, Tendring Hundred League, Harwich Y.M.C.A. League, and Harwich and District League — were all reformed during 1919-20. The South-East Essex League was reformed with eight clubs elected to it — Burnham Ramblers, Mildmay Ironworks, Southminster St Leonard's, Tillingham Hotspur, Wickford, Billericay, Maldon St Mary's, and Sudd's Athletic.[139] The East Anglian League was reformed with a proposal to create a first division of just six clubs, all located on or near the main railway line to London to ease travel and travelling expenses. The Colchester and District Junior Cup was one of the first competitions revived and completed soon after the War. Clubs like Clacton Town and Parkeston G.E.R. were allowed to enter the competition provided they paid the excess expenses incurred by clubs travelling more than ten miles to play them. The final in April 1919, between Britannia Athletic and Culver Street Ironworks, ended in a one-one draw. The crowd was large enough to result in gate receipts of £47.[140]

Individual clubs were reformed as soon as it was feasible to do so. Colchester Town held its first post-war annual general meeting at the Red Lion on 27 May 1919. The club's pre-war purchase of its Layer Road ground by the sale of debentures had in effect left it £800 in debt, although this had been reduced to £650. Far worse was the fact that the 1914 team had been devastated by the War; Ellison had been killed, R.W. Chapman had been lost at sea, Knox (the goalkeeper), Walker, Smith, Pitchford and T. Bailey had also lost their lives. Manfully, the club tried to rebuild itself. Its first post-war fixture, against Ordnance Sports Club, ended in a three-three draw, watched by a large crowd cheering on the team which contained only a few familiar faces who had survived the War. However, its attempt to compete in the reformed East Anglian League during 1919-20 had to be abandoned because the club was unable to meet the

[138] ECC 24 January 1919.

[139] BDA 20 September 1919.

[140] ECT 19 June 26 August 1919, 1920; ECS 26 April, 28 June, 6 September 1919, 8 May, 19 June 1920; HDS 4 January 1919.

hefty travelling expenses required of them. Proposed new improvements at the Layer Road ground included a terrace on the 'popular' side of the ground made up of railway sleepers on a bank of clinkers and a new stand opposite the old one. The aim was to increase the ground capacity to five thousand. The pitch was to be railed in on all sides. To help create a reserve or second team the grammar school was scouted for up and coming talent, although the collapse of the successful Colchester St Nicholas team in 1919 resulted in the majority of its players being absorbed into the Colchester Town set-up. Admission prices were set at *5d.* on the popular side, and 1*s.* on the enclosure and stand side, and it cost 1*s.* to become a club member.

Harwich and Parkeston, like nearby Ipswich Town, was unable to compete in the East Anglian League because prolonged military occupation of their grounds had rendered them completely unfit for football. Their decisions were made even though the East Anglian League offered to waive the customary entrance fees to the league for that season. Due to these difficulties Harwich and Parkeston F.C. was not reformed until May 1920. Witham F.C., the Braintree and District League Champions, was reformed on 5 July. Clacton F.C. was looking to reform, but because of problems concerning the ownership of the club's ground, it was estimated that £200 would be required to restart it.

Southend United rose from its wartime ashes once hostilities were over and was again accepted into the prestigious Southern League. Unfortunately, the club was in desperate straits at the time. Although it had sold its ground in 1916 to try to meet its debts, this had failed to erase the amount outstanding, which stood at £5,000 in 1919. Lacking a ground was bad enough, but the club had no team and only a handful of directors. In its searches for a pitch, the Kursaal was suggested as a possible location. Time was running out however. In February 1919 the club was unable to assure the Southern League that it would be able to begin its fixtures in September. They were given until early May to sort things out, but it was not until April that the Kursaal was acquired as a ground. It was a close run thing, but the club was able to compete, playing a 'plum' tie against Sheffield United in the F.A.Cup first round, and ending the 1919-20 season with a profit of £329. Signings such as Tom Mather from Manchester City, who was appointed secretary and manager, and Joe Walters, a former Aston Villa and Oldham Athletic player, boosted the club's fortunes.[141]

Cricket too was quick to reform. In 1920 Colchester, together with Southend, was permitted to resume its county cricket week, first granted only weeks before the outbreak of war, and then cruelly snatched away. The cricket week, involving matches against Hampshire and Gloucestershire, was held in Castle Park. In an inauspicious start to post-war county cricket at Colchester, Essex was thrashed in both games; Hampshire scored 415 runs for 9 declared, before dismissing Essex for 87 and 266;

[141] SST 30 January, 13 February, 20 March, 3 April, 8 May 1919, 26 August, 23 September 1920.

Gloucestershire too had little trouble, scoring 421 runs, and bowling Essex out twice for 121 and 244. Local interest was keen with five thousand people watching the first day's play against Hampshire. The local Colchester and East Essex Club also got off to a shaky start. In 1919 they played few games owing to a shortage of players and the poor state of the ground.[142]

Other sporting activities were resuming in a big way during 1919-20. In April 1919 the Colchester Swimming Club held its annual meeting, its first since 1916 and rapidly resumed its activities.[143] Colchester Rovers Cycling Club, which had lost thirteen of its members in the War, was likewise reformed in 1919, as was the Colchester and District Motor Club.[144] The town's Billiards League, which had continued until 1916, when it was abandoned, was reformed late in 1919 with twelve teams. Golf continued to enjoy its growing pre-war popularity with the wealthier classes. Colchester Golf Club was established on a five-year tenancy at Braiswick in 1919. To join as a playing member cost three guineas, no small amount. However, by March there were 104 members, and in just over a year this had doubled to 209.[145] The Colchester Sea Angling Club began again in 1920. Three bowling links were opened up at Frinton during the Spring. The Walton and Frinton Yacht Club began its post-war activities with a flourish by opening a new clubhouse in July 1920. There were of course entertainments of a different nature. After performing at the town's peace celebrations in the summer of 1919, the Colchester Musical Society began regular activities that autumn. New styles of dancing were becoming increasingly popular. J.A. Waldron, "Colchester's well known dancing professor", ably aided by his daughter, "at once graceful, pretty, interesting and an eloquent disclaimer to the attacks made upon this class of dance" gave the first demonstration of jazz inspired-dancing. Undeterred by the War, Waldron had performed in the town for sixteen successive years. At the fancy dress ball he held on St Patrick's Day at the Co-op Hall, several hundred people crammed in to dance and cavort the evening away.[146]

The end of 1920 is not the ideal point at which to assess how far the War had changed Essex, but there is no doubt that there was a feeling that some things had deteriorated. Perhaps not surprisingly for many people who had heralded the end of the Great War as the dawn of a new beginning, the first two years of peace proved to be a bitter disappointment. The difficult state of the country's economy saw a significant rise in unemployment. Unemployed ex-servicemen, having risked their lives in the War, were embittered by what they perceived as both public indifference to their plight and official inaction on their behalf. In their eyes both of these injustices seemed to be aggravated by the retention of women in jobs that they

[142] ECS 3 April 1920.

[143] ECS 5 April 1919.

[144] ECS 10 May, 7 June 1919.

[145] ECS 22 March 1919, 31 July 1920.

[146] ECT 24 January 1920, 22 March 1919; ECS 15 May 1920.

perceived as theirs by right. Outside of metropolitan Essex, the Labour Party, having energetically wooed the working classes by posing as their most genuine suitor, was deeply disappointed at their reluctance to embrace it. Even the victorious Conservatives, keen to turn the political, economic and social clock back to 1914, were faced with growing union assertiveness, political indifference, and the intractable nature of post-war unemployment. Trade unions viewed the future anxiously, fearful in case the financial improvements made during the War should be eroded by a deteriorating economic climate. Employers, reluctant even to maintain the wage levels of 1914-18, let alone enhance them, were alarmed at the growing willingness of trade unions to embark on damaging, and sometimes prolonged and costly, strikes. The churches, having spent the war years urging the people to walk more closely with God as the only way to rescue themselves from the secular evils of the modern world and as the key to winning the War, found that a weary and disillusioned population seemed to be no more reliant on organised religion than it had been before 1914. Women found that after making what they regarded as substantial sacrifices during the War, they were being harassed for remaining in 'male' jobs, and were still subject to restrictions in both church and politics. As the wartime decade drifted to a close in December 1920, many of those who had welcomed Armistice Day as the dawn of a new age looked to a future laced with bleak uncertainty.

The Survival of the Great War

CHAPTER SIXTEEN

Shadows of the Past

Great Horkesley war memorial.
(ERO: D/DU 1264/13)

THE MEMORY OF THE GREAT WAR did not die out when the last local war memorial was completed and dedicated. That was hardly surprising since war memorials were not envisaged as a transient phenomenon, but as a timeless commemoration of human sacrifice. Unlike the wreaths which the relatives of the Fallen had laid at the memorials, the memory of the War did not immediately fade but was sustained by those who had experienced the War. This idea was articulated by Sir William Robertson on 21 April 1918 at the dedication of the war memorial of the village of Willingale:

> We believe, and we know, that a man cannot live to himself alone. We know that a great act does not perish with the life of the man who performed it, but that it lives and grows up into the lives of those who survive him and cherish his memory.[1]

These sentiments are a timely reminder to we who now stand almost a century beyond these events. It reminds us that the established perception of the Great War that many people now accept almost as a fact, as truth — it was a tragic event, a criminal waste of life that sacrificed a whole generation — was not a view that would have been shared by the generation which lived through it. The discussions held then about why Britain fought, about war memorials, their purpose and significance, the sacrifice of the Fallen, reveal that the War was perceived as a noble, necessary and entirely worthwhile endeavour, and that its victorious conclusion was a magnificent achievement. This does not of course mean that there was no national outpouring of grief and sense of loss, no awareness that a monumental tragedy had just been experienced. However, the sense of anger at those responsible for the War was often directed outwards, towards Germany. Frederick H. Keeling, a local man, wrote with some bitterness that,

> To some survivors the honour and glory of death in action is some consolation. For me, probably to many others, the whole tragedy is unrelieved by the thought that the shoddy vainglory of two diseased Emperors and the folly and criminality of their subjects should have bled Europe of her best lives.[2]

In the months and years immediately following the Armistice the War continued to claim lives. On 17 September 1919 the funeral took place at Stanway, near Colchester, of Lance-Corporal George Kettle, who had died less than a fortnight earlier. Kettle had been wounded on 1 June 1918, but he had lingered on for over a year before he died. Edgar Dunlop of St Osyth died in November 1920. He had been

1 ECC 26 April 1918.

2 ECS 3 February 1917.

discharged in 1917 after being severely wounded. He was just twenty-four years old.[3] In late December 1918, several weeks after the War had come to end, the Ellerman-Wilson liner, the *Gitano*, was sunk en route from Hull to Gothenburg. It was sent to the bottom by a mine which had not yet been cleared. A young Colchester schoolboy, Geoffrey Gabbitt Barnes, who had only left school in the summer of 1917, lost his life in the sinking.[4]

The focus of the official post-war remembrance of the Great War was the annual Armistice Day service, held at the country's war memorials on 11 November. Throughout the years between the Great War and World War Two the nation came to a standstill that day at 11 a.m., the exact time that the Armistice of 1918 had begun. It was an occasion of great solemnity and great importance, a simple act of worship which united the country in remembrance of what had gone before, and of those who had not survived it. This was best summed up at Colchester in 1926, when the mayor said:

> Heroes of Colchester, once more we salute you, and today we pledge ourselves to strive for the ends which you visualised when you went from us. We will work for righteousness among the nations, and goodwill to all people, that peace may ever remain with us.[5]

A similar concrete expression of the memory of the sacrifice of the Fallen occurred on Palm Sunday in 1924, in a special service that occurred at Lexden. It featured a number of the original wooden crosses which had stood on soldiers' graves on the Western Front. These had been collected by members of the Church Army and were presented to the relatives of those whose graves they had marked.

For many the idea of the Armistice Day service was meant to be timeless. The Mayor of Colchester, Gerald Benham, speaking in 1936, expressed these sentiments in a way which echoed back to the first post-war dedication ceremonies:

> The ceremony of Armistice Day is a profoundly religious and patriotic one in spirit and intent, in which the British nation throughout these islands and throughout the whole of the British Empire pays homage to those who gave all they had to give in serving our nation in the Great War.
>
> It is a pilgrimage of remembrance and thankfulness made by the highest and the lowest, a sacred acknowledgement to those brave fellow countrymen and women who made the supreme sacrifice.[6]

3 ECS 20 September 1919, 13 November 1920.

4 ECC 11 January 1919.

5 ECS 13 November 1926.

6 ECS 14 November 1936.

At the same time, just as the addresses at the original dedication ceremonies had been used to deliver what were considered to be meaningful commentaries on the post-war nation, so the annual Armistice Day ceremonies came to reflect the nation's changing mood and circumstances. Gradually bitter wartime memories began to mellow. In 1927 the Mayor of Colchester, E.H. Turner, used the occasion to appeal for international understanding:

> They were not unmindful of those amongst them who still bore signs of wounds and sickness, but they were hopeful that the sores of war were now slowly, but surely healing, and that the nations engaged in that terrible four years' struggle were now working together for a better mutual understanding in the interests of peace and prosperity.[7]

However the modern world soon began to intrude on what was, for some, a sacred occasion. In 1928 wireless sets were installed in the churches at Great Tey and Little Tey so that the congregation could follow the Armistice Day service at the Cenotaph in Whitehall from 10.30 a.m. to 11.02 a.m. The novelty of wireless operation was evident as the rector, Reverend R.E. Corbett, "explained to them something of the rudiments of wireless reception." "All remained standing during the time", noted the *Essex County Standard*, "an atmosphere of marked reverence being observable." At Colchester the occasion was still used for soul searching. Various speakers questioned whether their listeners were living lives worthy of the dead, or whether they were doing enough to kindle the spirit of comradeship. It was still common practice in some places for the names of the Fallen to be read out at these ceremonies. Suggestions that the public's commitment to Armistice Day might be in decline were met with indignation:

> The observation of the Armistice anniversary at Clacton on Sunday must be counted as a direct demonstration that, so far from the solemn celebration waning in the succeeding years since the Armistice was signed, it has grown in intensity of interest and of meaning.[8]

However, by the early 1930s the optimism of the late 1920s, stimulated by international agreements such as the Dawes Plan and the Kellogg-Briand Pact, and by Germany's admission to the League of Nations, was already evaporating in the face of escalating international violence and economic depression. From 1929 it was increasingly clear in Armistice Day addresses that many people's hopes of peace were

[7] ECS 12 November 1927.

[8] ECS 17 November 1928.

being pinned on the League of Nations. In 1933 the Reverend F.S. Hopkirk, Vicar of Layer de la Haye, was noting pessimistically that "the world is beginning to crack and is threatened with chaos."[9] At Colchester in 1934 A.H. Cross the mayor, bemoaned "misunderstandings among the nations, wars and rumours of wars; economic and tariff conflicts." "The vultures of greed, revenge, avarice, suspicion" were, according to Cross, the aftermath of the War, "It left the economic depression and disturbances that paralysed industry and commerce, with all the anxieties and worries of unemployment."[10] Indeed, by 1936 confidence in the future had fallen so low that the pre-Armistice Day ceremony at Colchester's Albert Hall was the setting for open criticism of the victorious peace settlement of 1919:

> I am not attempting to defend what the present regime in Germany has done ... but I ask you to face this fact — those things which we dislike the most in the Germany of today are our own creation. They are the direct result of the post-war policies of the allied powers, and of having missed the opportunity presented to us 18 years ago of making peace. If we had sown the seeds of peace in 1918 by now we should have raised up in a better world order a worthy memorial to those whom we commemorate today.[11]

Two years later a speaker at an Armistice Day eve service at Colchester's Culver Street Methodist Chapel was even blunter in allocating blame for the rapidly deteriorating situation in Europe:

> We are so fond of talking about what are called the gangster nations, but it is not only the totalitarian nations which have done wrong and are doing wrong. We see again the foe we thought was utterly vanquished and downtrodden, and we see the conditions we imposed by force being broken by force or threat of force. Such ways of evil cannot lead either to peace or prosperity.

That same year H.H. Fisher, Mayor of Colchester, invited his listeners to ask themselves whether or not the concept of remembrance had become meaningless and sentimental, and whether the sacrifices of the Fallen had been in vain.[12] Such a question, voiced publicly at the war memorial, would have been unthinkable twenty years earlier.

[9] ECS 18 November 1933.

[10] ECS 17 November 1934.

[11] ECS 14 November 1936.

[12] ECS 12 November 1938.

The Second World War proved to be a watershed in the public remembrance of the Great War. Owing to the fear of German air raids there were no official remembrance ceremonies in Essex towns in 1939, or indeed for the rest of the hostilities. Instead, in that year the two minutes silence was kept at Colchester as usual and a number of residents, including the mayor and mayoress, gathered at the war memorial at 11 a.m. There was no general stoppage of traffic as in all other years since 1923, although one or two buses and a few cars came to a halt. The borough's poppy wreath was laid informally. At Brightlingsea it was the first time that the service had been held inside St James's Church rather than outside.[13]

This second world conflict was seen by many British people as a situation in which the nation just had to roll up its sleeves and get on. Even the ultimately horrifying revelations about the evil nature of Hitler's Nazism, which dwarfed in criminality the actions of Germany's leaders in 1914-18, failed to transform the Second World War into another crusade against godlessness. Religion was simply no longer that significant to increasing numbers of British people. At the end of the conflict there was no movement clamouring for the dead to be memorialised. There were, of course, far fewer deaths among British servicemen than there had been in 1914-18. The dead were no longer referred to as the Fallen. In most cases a simple, small tablet listing the dead was placed in village churches and words and names were affixed to the existing war memorial. Most of the ceremonies in which this took place were not subject to the same avid press interest as had occurred in 1919-23, when those held in even the smallest village were occasions of great significance for the community and were covered in copious detail by local newspapers. The *Essex County Standard*'s report on the Armistice Day commemoration at Colchester in 1945 was scaled down to a single column of writing. In 1946 written coverage disappeared altogether and was replaced by a couple of photographs of the occasion, accompanied by brief captions, and this pattern has been very largely retained to the present day.

This is not to say that no-one cared whether war memorials commemorating those lost in World War Two should be built. At Colchester it was taken for granted that there would be commemoration, and as in the years after the Great War there was disagreement about what form it should take, although the debate was certainly not as extensive or as public as it been in 1918-19. In the end the simple words, "And to the honour also of those who served, worked and died in the further war of 1939-45" were added to the reverse side of the war memorial. However, one innovation did arise out of the debate. In 1946 the Field of Remembrance, two grassed areas on either side and slightly to the front of the memorial, was created at the request of the British Legion. For the first time, in the days leading up to Armistice Day, people were able to place their own miniature crosses in the Field of Remembrance as a more intimate commemoration of lost loved ones and friends.

[13] ECS 18 November 1939.

In the years following 1946 the whole ceremony was consistently downplayed by the local press. Part of this was the fact that the event had lost something of its original, powerfully emotional message. After 1945 the term Armistice Day was replaced by Remembrance Day or Remembrance Sunday, a change in terminology which signified that the day was no longer just a commemoration of the Great War. From this time came the ending of the two minutes silence and the substitution of the Sunday nearest to 11 November instead of Armistice Day itself. Now people had to make a positive effort to participate in the service rather than be a part of the two minutes silence wherever they were. From this time onwards only controversy was sufficient to merit a fuller report on Remembrance Day. In 1964 members of the Colchester branch of the Royal British Legion boycotted the Remembrance Day ceremony at the war memorial because of a rift between the organisation and the town council over the latter's plan to sell the Royal British Legion's headquarters in Crispin Court.[14]

It was not long after 1918 that the battlefield cemeteries on the Western Front, in France and Belgium, became shrines and memorials like the ones which were being built all over the United Kingdom. Various organisations were soon leading journeys to these "sites of mourning" as one historian has described them, in order that grieving parents and relatives might see where their loved ones were buried. Given the often religious nature of these journeys, it is not surprising that those making them were soon being referred to as pilgrims. As early as November 1919 C.W. Butcher, the superintendent of Southend Borough Council, accompanied by his wife, visited Ypres, as members of the first party of "Graven Pilgrims" organised by the Church Army. Its purpose was to allow parents to visit their sons' graves. The Butchers' eldest son was buried at Lyssenthoek.[15] From 1922 the Church Army regularly guided families to the war cemeteries in France and Flanders, assisting with special grants those who would otherwise have been unable to afford it. When the original wooden crosses on the graves were replaced by stone monuments, the Church Army tried to ensure that the crosses were handed over to the families. Another organisation, the Ypres League, had been arranging pilgrimages to the battlefields each Whitsuntide since the Menin Gate was unveiled in 1922. Each year a number of poor widows and mothers were taken free of any expense. In 1934 the secretary to the Ypres League was W.H. Taylor of Colchester. In that year he recommended pilgrims from the Colchester area. They included Mrs E. Bond, whose son had served in the Northamptonshire Regiment and was buried in the Berkshire Cemetery Extension at Ploegstreet. He was killed in action on 7 October 1917, aged just twenty. The pilgrimage was of enormous consolation to Mrs Bond:

> "My son's grave is beautifully and neatly tended," said Mrs Bond. "The flowers planted on and around it are just what I

[14] ECS 13 November 1964.

[15] SST 13 November 1919.

> would have wished, and the sacred words I selected, "The Lord's will be done," are engraved at the base of the headstone, I shall return home much comforted by what I have seen."[16]

All wars leave lasting monuments in one way or another. Colchester has its aptly named Siege House, marked by the shot of royalist soldiers firing from the direction of the East Gate, or by the track of a heavy ball in the vaulting of St John's Abbey, both reminders of the town's ordeal in the great siege of 1648. Memorials of the Napoleonic Wars, the Crimean War, the Indian Mutiny, and the Boer War can be seen throughout Essex. These memorials of earlier conflicts, although largely forgotten today, can still be seen, and to their number hundreds of others were added as a result of the Great War. Unlike earlier conflicts, following which only the larger towns and cities erected monuments, almost every village erected one to its war dead. So many war memorials were to appear after 1918, that one historian, A.J.P. Taylor, felt able to say:

> If the magnitude of an event be judged by the number of monuments to it, the Great War, as men called it, was the greatest event that ever happened.[17]

At the time of writing it is now over ninety years since the start of the Great War, an event which has passed almost beyond living memory. Even in an age of increasing longevity, the number of people still alive who survived the conflict, and particularly those who were young adults when the War began, has inevitably dwindled to a very few. Soon there will be no one left who can recall firsthand what it was like to have lived through this world shattering event, although there are still members of the congregation at St Leonard's, Lexden, who can remember the ceremony in 1924 in which the original war crosses were brought home. However, just thirty-five years ago in 1973, the *Essex County Standard* reported that there had been two members of the Old Contemptibles at the Remembrance Day service at Colchester. Bert Fuller, aged ninety-three, and Fred Baker, aged eighty-four, both of whom lived in the town. The Old Contemptibles was the army of pre-war professionals who saw action in the first weeks of the War, officially between 5 August and 22 November 1914. Two years earlier in 1971, the nine surviving members of the Walthamstow branch of the Old Contemptibles laid up their colours in the Vestry House Museum. Established in 1925, it had at one time numbered 135 members.

Bert Fuller and Fred Baker survived the War and lived to a ripe old age. Of course, many millions of young men did not live to see hostilities concluded in 1918. Jack

16 ECS 25 May 1934.

17 A J.P. Taylor, *From Sarajevo to Potsdam* (1966), 56.

Darrell, a boy telegraphist, was only eighteen when he died in the Gallipoli campaign in 1915. His name is one of those recorded on the memorial tablet at Wivenhoe Congregational Church. Most were buried abroad, near the battlefields where they fell. A few however, those who were wounded in action, were brought home for medical care, which in some cases proved unavailing. Among them are those whose remains still lie in the churchyards and cemeteries of Essex.[18] The simple wooden crosses which were originally placed on the graves were, in due course, replaced by the distinctive, instantly recognisable headstones which are forever associated with those who died in the Great War. In common with the headstones found in their hundreds of thousands in the war cemeteries of France and Belgium, they contain only the serviceman's name and rank, and the badge of his regiment or unit. They are still meticulously cared for by the Commonwealth War Graves Commission, the successor of the Imperial War Graves Commission, which first took responsibility for the graves in the 1920s. There is hardly a burial place hereabouts which does not contain war dead. There are forty-one graves in the churchyard of All Saints', Dovercourt, including the remains of Charles Fryatt, executed by the Germans on 27 July 1916 for daring to attack a German U-boat; there are thirty military graves in Clacton cemetery, together with that of a German airman; the twenty-one in Harwich cemetery includes that of a French naval officer. Other German soldiers were buried at St Andrew's, Marks Tey, Halstead cemetery, and St Edmund's, Tendring. Colchester cemetery is the last resting place of 205 victims of the Great War. They were men who died in the Military Hospital, Eastern Counties Hospital or nearby auxiliary hospitals such as that at Gostwyck. A large stone cross with an inlaid sword at its peak, known universally as the Cross of Sacrifice, informs visitors to the cemetery of their collective presence. Their headstones can be found throughout the cemetery, and at only one spot does there seem to have been a deliberate attempt to concentrate graves together. They include the remains of the single unidentified British soldier whose death so moved Colchester's medical officer in 1915, and whose headstone bears the simple inscription, "A Soldier of the Great War." The graves of Yep Fook, a Chinese labourer, a Russian officer, four Belgian soldiers, Ferdinand Bandour included, thirty-six German soldiers, and one interned German civilian can also be seen. Many were buried here far from home. Private William Bartlett of the Canadian Infantry (Alberta Regiment) was nineteen when he died, a month before the War ended; Private Sidney Barclay originated from Geelong in Victoria, Australia. Some interred soldiers did not remain in the same place for long. In June 1919 Colchester Town Council gave permission for the exhumation of twelve Australian soldiers for reburial. They now lie near the Cross of Sacrifice. Most churchyards and cemeteries containing one, two or three burials, and Colchester too,

[18] A comprehensive list of these burials is in *The War Graves of the British Empire: Cemeteries and Churchyards in North and Central Essex* (1931). A copy is in the Local Studies section, Colchester Central Library. See Appendix 1 for list of war graves in North-east Essex.

often included the interment of men from that place who were brought home wounded and who died near their home. Their families were fortunate to have been able to bury their loved ones where their graves could be visited and tended at any time. One such family buried their boy at Marks Tey:

> Private Oliver Mead, 3rd Battalion Royal West Kent Regt.
> 10 October 1918, son of Mr and Mrs H. C. Mead, Wagstaff
> Cottage, Coggeshall Road, Marks Tey.

These war graves of course, have been of little importance in the public ritual of memory associated with the Great War. However, this is not to say that they were ignored and forgotten. On Anzac Day, 25 April, the day the Australian and New Zealand forces landed at Gallipoli in 1915, the New Zealand military headquarters sent wreaths to Clacton to be placed on the graves of Anzac soldiers. In 1921 there were said to have been many visitors to the graves in Clacton and Colchester cemeteries on Anzac Day. An arum lily was laid on each grave by some anonymous donor, and by the afternoon the graves were completely covered by floral tributes from local people.[19]

Of far greater significance have been the war memorials erected after the War, and which can still be found in practically every town, village and hamlet in the region. In most cases the site chosen for these memorials has changed little in three quarters of a century. This is hardly surprising when one considers that sites were deliberately chosen with a view to their preservation for posterity. That at Colchester was selected so that the memorial formed part of a wider aspect incorporating the magnificent Norman castle and is still beautifully preserved today. When the memorial was being planned the members of the Monument Committee were concerned to achieve perfection:

> The question of the possible discolouration of the stone work by reason of oxidation of the bronze is considered and the hope is expressed that some treatment can be given the figures in order to obviate any such future discolouration.[20]

Alas, their efforts have been in vain. Even today, in spite of numerous attempts to prevent it, the stone work is stained a lurid green, especially in wet weather. It is a problem which seems unlikely to disappear. Other memorials too are well preserved and well cared for. The Remembrance Garden at Clacton still has a delightfully pastoral air; the cross and the Columbine memorial still stare impassively out to sea. Columbine was not forgotten as a plaque which was later attached to the base of the memorial shows:

[19] ECS 1 May 1920, 30 April 1921.

[20] ERO Acc. C4, Monument Committee minutes, 22 March 1921.

> This plaque was affixed in 1957 as a token of the fact that the memory of a gallant comrade is still green in the minds of the members of the 19th Royal Hussars (Queen Alexandra's Own Association).

The modern leisure centre at Clacton bears his name. At Inworth the brass tablet listing the Fallen is still lovingly cared for and periodically removed for cleaning, as I discovered in late 1999. At Layer-de-la-Haye the village cross, dedicated in 1921, was replaced by a stone one in 1997, when the original was worn by the ravages of time. When Colchester's central post office was closed and new premises opened nearby, the war memorial to its post office workers went with it, the second time that it had moved premises since its installation in April 1920. The tablet commemorating the two hundred dead of St John's, Walthamstow, was moved into the new church, built in 1923, when the original church of 1844 was demolished. When Melbourne Road School in Walthamstow was closed, the Jack Cornwell memorial stone was moved to the garden of the Vestry House Museum in the town. The museum also houses the tablet removed from Leyton's Goodall Road School when it was demolished in 1992. Even more recently the Parochial Church Council of Colchester St James rejected a request from the garrison to re-site the 18th Division war memorial in the garrison church. It considered that the original choice of St James's for the war memorial "in perpetuity" had entrusted it with a charge which could not be given up lightly. The book of remembrance at the heart of the memorial is still turned page by page, once a week. There are eighty names on most of its pages; by turning one page a week it would take seven years to go through the whole book.

Several churches, like St Michael's, Myland, still display the roll of honour, now decades old, listing the "glorious" dead. At St Andrew's, Marks Tey, it records the names of the two villagers who died serving in the Royal Navy, the five in the Royal Air Force, and the 111 who lost their lives in the army. The roll of honour of the Leyton Elementary Schools, which listed the names of those former pupils of the borough's seventeen schools who died in the War, was compiled by Doris Flower in 1924. The original manuscript is stored at Leyton Library. At St Peter's, Colchester, the names of five of the Fallen are recorded alongside the warships which they went down with — H.M.S. *Cockchafer*, *Strongbow*, *Good Hope*, *Hogue* and *Princess Irene*. Wivenhoe's Congregational Church has a similar list, and notes how two of the ships on which members of its congregation died were sunk, S.S. *Abusso*, by a U-boat, and H.M.T. *Incoma*, by a mine. Lexden's war memorial is unique in that alongside the names of the Fallen it lists the date of their death. At Colchester Town Hall it is still possible to see the beautifully executed roll of honour, the final result of a methodical campaign to include all of the town's Fallen, in the hope of ensuring that there were no omissions.

Local people still devote great care to 'their' memorials. Walthamstow's cenotaph was moved from Lloyd Park to the grounds of the Town Hall in Forest Road in 1961. It had become too difficult to maintain in its original setting because of the huge increase in road traffic. The records which were used to compile the list of the 820 Fallen at Barking were unfortunately destroyed by enemy action in World War Two, and a new list has only recently been produced. At Elmstead Market, which had only the war memorial inside the church, an outdoor one was erected in 2004. After decades of neglect the roll of honour of Stansted Mountfitchet was located, has been repaired and will hang in its rightful place in St John's Church. The war memorial at Wivenhoe was cleaned and restored in 1993, and that at Great and Little Braxted was restored and re-lettered in 2002. That at Lexden, Colchester, was refurbished in 2003, as was that at Burnham-on-Crouch. Brightlingsea's war memorial was re-dedicated in 1993. In the same year a project requiring £3,000 was launched to restore the memorial to Charles Fryatt at Dovercourt, which today looks as pristine as it did when it was first erected. Some utilitarian memorials such as Ongar War Memorial Hospital are still very much in use today. Even in recent years new war memorials have been erected or are in the process of being planned. On 3 April 1999 a plaque was presented on behalf of the people of Barking and Dagenham to the Cloth Hall Museum at Ypres in Belgium, a town totally destroyed by German shelling and subsequently resurrected from the rubble. The tablet commemorates all those who died in the Great War. Another memorial was presented by the people of these two boroughs in remembrance of all those Sikh soldiers who lost their lives in a conflict far from their homeland. In June 2000 a plaque was placed on the site where Jack Cornwell's birthplace, Clyde Cottages, had stood.

Artefacts from the War found their way back to Essex almost as reliquaries from this holy war. At Copford church in the years after the War, the chalice and paten used in the trenches by the Reverend B.C. Ruck-Keene, prior to his death on 26 September 1917, were used during Holy Communion.[21] When a chapel was built at Canning Town as a war memorial to the men of the Dockland Settlement, the chapel bell was brought from Bruges; the hinge on the large chapel door came from the ruined cathedral of Ypres, and the lock from Bapaume on the Somme; on its smaller doors were relics from Dixmude and Peronne; one of the altar fittings had been rescued from a Greek chapel in no man's land in Macedonia. The reredos installed in Stow Maries church by Gordon Smythe was made of wood brought from Belgium.[22]

There are yet other reminders of the Great War still to be seen in Essex. At Little Wigborough church it is still possible to see a portion of Zeppelin L.33 which was shot down nearby on 23 September 1916. It hangs over the tower arch. What has become of the hundreds of other pieces of the airship, which was cut up and offered to the general public in a hugely popular sale in Colchester a few weeks later, is

[21] ECC 22 May 1920.

[22] ECC 18 September 1920.

perhaps anyone's guess.[23] In the serenely quiet churchyard at Little Wigborough one can still see the grave of Alfred Wright, who died of the injuries he received the night that the airship was downed. The Museum adjacent to the Tiptree Jam Shop and Tea Room at Wilkin's jam factory still has on display the frieze produced by the Belgian refugees who worked in the factory and on the farm. The frieze, poker work on wood, depicts scenes from Belgian history and was done out of gratitude for their stay at Tiptree. Colchester's Avenue of Remembrance, the tree-lined road which formed part of the town's bypass, was opened in 1933, and to this day it remains a lovely entrance to the town for visitors approaching from the west. A new memorial wall has been erected in recent years at the Albert roundabout. At Colchester St Peter's there still hangs the flag of the Essex Royal Horse Artillery Battery, which was carried throughout the Palestine campaign from 1916 to 1918, and which was presented to the church in 1956 by Colonel W.A.B. Daniell, one of the battery commanders in the campaign. Alas, two other flags which used to hang in the church, one of which was brought from the Cenotaph and "deposited for Hallowed keeping" by the Colchester branch of the Old Contemptibles in May 1946, and an American flag from the Great War, were stolen and have not been recovered. The Drill Hall at Chelmsford was home to a German standard taken in 1917 from the Mount of Olives in Jerusalem. It remained in Chelmsford for nearly two decades before being returned to Germany in January 1936.[24] St Michael's, Myland, had a small cross hanging next to the roll of honour. It was found in France by Private William Tipper, and given to the church by his mother. It too was stolen some years ago. Colchester has several street names which recollect the Great War, and which date back to the building schemes of the 1920s when memories were fresher and more fervently in favour of memorialisation. Arras, Cambrai, Flanders, Le Cateau, Messines, Somme, Menin, Ypres, and Mons, all famous names resonating with the echoes of the Western Front, can be found on street maps of the town. Thorp-le-Soken has a Byng Crescent, named after the area's local war hero. The shadows of the past are not easily forgotten, even today, and occasionally a chink of light penetrates them. Only very recently a new plaque was erected on the wall inside St Edmund's, East Mersea, commemorating Private Alfred Edward Russell of the Essex Regiment, who died in hospital in Colchester in 1918. Russell was unjustly denied a position on the church's memorial tablet alongside the other five villagers who died in the Great War. Thanks to the researches of Roger Bullen, military curator at Mersea Island Museum, this eighty-year-old injustice has been put right, and Russell's name now stands alongside those of his comrades.

In recent years the re-introduction of the two minutes silence at 11 a.m. on 11 November, in many public places and schools, has been matched by the increasing numbers of those attending the Remembrance Sunday services. This is a trend partly

[23] The Essex Record Office holds two metal fragments reputedly from the L.33, catalogued as M 55 and M 56, the former worked into a heart-shaped love token.

[24] Essex Review, vol. 45, 1936.

influenced by the advent of modern wars in Iraq and Afghanistan, and the by sense of general crisis in the world resulting from recent economic and political problems. Those ex-servicemen taking part in Remembrance Day services include men who have fought in every conflict involving Britain since 1939, but they do so in a setting created by the survivors of the Great War. Faced with modern anxieties, war memorials from the Great War still provide communities with a focus for their memories, their fears, and their hopes for the future.

Conclusion

CHAPTER SEVENTEEN

Essex at War: Self-Interest, Self-Preservation, Self-Sacrifice

Private Herbert George Columbine, V.C., who gave his life to save those of his comrades.

THERE IS NO DOUBTING the tremendous support for the War which existed in Britain, and this is the impression, so carefully fostered by government propaganda, and assiduously preached by official and semi-official authorities and organisations, of a nation absolutely united behind the war effort, determined to triumph at any cost. This is undoubtedly the view which many people still have of the Great War. However, this rather simplistic impression has to be tempered with a realistic appraisal of the evidence. Self-interest and self-preservation are impulses which are at the heart of the human condition and never more so than in wartime, and both of these impulses were much apparent in Essex at this time.

As in all wars, baser human instincts soon bubbled to the surface. There was widespread consternation in the first two or three days following the outbreak of war, typified by panic buying of foodstuffs. Fears that the War would trigger an economic catastrophe drove those able to afford it into an orgy of hoarding. Some shopkeepers, exploiting the feverish air of crisis, raised their prices and were only too happy to supply the rich at the expense of the poor. Invasion fears wrecked the Essex holiday trade as it was reaching its early August peak, as thousands of would-be holidaymakers cancelled their bookings and left hoteliers and lodging house keepers facing a drastic drop in income. In the frenzied fears of those first few days it is perhaps not too surprising that credulous individuals reported seeing trainloads of Russian troops on Essex railways, or claimed to have seen Belgian Red Cross nurses, their hands severed by sadistic German troops, being ferried to England from the Continent. The fear, panic and confusion were fuelled by a belief that the War was an earthshaking event, and one quite unique in the nation's history. The Bishop of Colchester described the War as "the most stupendous in the history of the civilized world." The *East Essex Advertiser* likened it to a "volcanic eruption."[1] Leading figures added to the air of crisis by issuing dire premonitory warnings about the likely consequences of the conflict. "It means ... unhappily the sacrifice of incalculable life and treasure", wrote the editor of the *Colchester Gazette*, "it means hardship, heroism, suffering, and distress untold".[2]

Loyalty and patriotism were demanded from all, and the accompanying demonisation of the Germans helped to inflate these sentiments. The *East Essex Advertiser*, in its editorial after the torpedoing of the *Lusitania*, said that "the Monarch of the Huns may be best described as the leader of a vast gang of Jack the Rippers."[3] Fighting an enemy which was portrayed as a bloodthirsty barbarian who had spurned Christian values to fight an aggressive war designed to enslave free nations everywhere, meant that anything other than wholehearted support for the War was unthinkable. Those who failed to live up to such a rigid wartime philosophy were vilified as traitors, spies or cowards. Foreigners or individuals of "foreign

1 EEA 8 August 1914.

2 CG 12 August 1914.

3 EEA 15 May 1915.

appearance" were hastily arrested by the police, the military or by over-zealous citizens. Persons of foreign birth with years or decades of residence in Britain, and living impeccable lives, were placed on police "suspect" lists and subjected to anonymous denunciations by the spiteful and the fearful, as well as clandestine police searches of their homes. Police authorities in the prohibited zone were soon expelling German and Austrian aliens as they were considered to pose a threat to national security. Twelve of these subversives were sent packing from Frinton less than three weeks after war broke out.[4] The rioting in parts of metropolitan Essex in 1915 in the wake of the sinking of the *Lusitania* demonstrated the depth of feeling against German aliens in Britain, as well as their vulnerability. Those individuals with German-sounding names often felt that it was prudent to defend themselves in the press against the insinuations that in possessing a "German" surname, they were automatically a potential traitor. Others avoided such complications by adopting English Christian names and surnames. In March 1916 Archibald Shillan of Loughton successfully sued W.T. Garrett who had accused him of being a German and directing Zeppelins from his house.[5] Even a harmless incident such as a pigeon alighting on someone's roof could lead to panic-stricken neighbours becoming convinced that the householder was somehow communicating with the enemy.

Young men who were slow to enlist during 1914-16, regardless of the reasons why, were vilified as slackers, shirkers or standbacks. However, the vilest abuse, which must have been at its worst away from the relatively civilized letters pages of the press or the confines of the military tribunals, was reserved for conscientious objectors. Conchies were despised for lacking patriotism and courage and sometimes even suspected of having purely mercenary motives for avoiding military service. Few in public office, politics or the churches refrained from criticizing them or mocking their beliefs. Some in business and local government were only too happy to drive conchies, and slackers too, out of employment and into the armed forces. In 1919 at the speech day of Colchester Grammar School, the headmaster, Mr Cape, was proud to declare that 419 Old Boys had enlisted, and that the school had not produced one single conchie.[6]

In wartime it was inevitable that people should have tried to hang on to sports, entertainments and leisure activities, particularly the young who had most to lose. However, such pursuits were seen by some as at best inappropriate during wartime, and at worst, as a scandal of national proportions which was indicative of a lack of moral fibre amongst young people. In Essex football was hounded out of existence, and most other sports involving young men jumped before they were pushed by cancelling their activities for the duration. Teachers and clergymen, assuming the role of the major-generals of a modern-day Interregnum, posed as the arbiters of the suitability of sporting activities during the conflict. It was thought inappropriate that

4 ECS 22 August 1914.

5 ECC 24 March 1916.

6 ECS 1 March 1919.

harvest festivals should be anything but muted affairs. Colchester's renowned Oyster Feast was abandoned for the duration. Guy Fawkes Night celebrations, even in small villages where bonfires and fireworks could not possibly have assisted German raiders, were likewise abandoned from 1915 onwards.

For women the War was merely a temporary triumph. The reluctance of employers to hire women as replacements for enlisted men was overcome slowly, and in the case of farmers, very grudgingly, even when the latter faced a critical labour shortage in 1917. The vote for females was obtained in 1918, partly because of women's contribution to the war effort, but then only given to women over thirty. The acceptance of new roles for women was even harder to achieve. Some churches were still opposed to greater female participation in their affairs, and in the Church of England the granting of voting rights and representation on the post-war parochial church councils was not a decision which was universally popular. Women's intrusion into male working life was seen by many as merely a temporary expedient, and in 1919 there was an unseemly rush to replace them with demobilised servicemen. Even this was unacceptable to some ex-servicemen's associations, which maintained a very public and persistent hostility to the continuation of women in most spheres of employment.

Many civilians were prepared to place their own self-interest above the cause of patriotism in order to enjoy a more comfortable war. Some of the better-off elements of society demonstrated little reluctance to pursue successive pay awards, generally well above the pay levels of unskilled workers. Teachers in particular came in for a great deal of criticism for making regular claims that they were facing destitution. Alderman W. Appleby, chairman of the Harwich Education Committee, resorted to Dickens to explain his anger at teachers' pay demands. "It's like *Oliver Twist*", he said, "It doesn't matter what you give, they always want more and more."[7] In 1917 there was a furore over proposals to pay a war bonus to the officers of the Colchester guardians. The proposal, to add ten per cent to salaries of £50 or more, and fifteen per cent to salaries of up to £50, caused a storm of protest and was eventually rejected by ten votes to eight. One guardian, a Mr. Chapman, thought such increases were appalling in view of the fact that servicemen had given up everything to serve for a shilling a day. Chapman said, "He could not understand these continued applications for more money", he raged that, "there seemed to be no pluck or British blood in many of the people at home."[8] In 1917 Essex County Council awarded war bonuses to married staff earning less that £130 a year, after abandoning plans to do the same for higher paid officials because of opposition to the proposal.[9] Some working people of course saw the War as an opportunity to earn wages undreamed of before the conflict began. Many of the women who volunteered to work on the land were said to have been from the better-off element in society. Perhaps this was because in many areas, Billericay for example,

7 HDS 29 January 1916.

8 ECS 12 May 1917.

9 ECC 5 January 1917.

where there was a shortage of women in the fields, working-class women preferred the higher wages being paid in munitions factories.[10] Young men too, saw a double advantage in munitions work. They could earn high wages and simultaneously claim to be performing essential war work as a means of evading conscription.

In retailing there was considerable evidence of self-interest at work. Hundreds of shopkeepers were brought before the courts for contravention of the food regulations. An even larger number of people were hauled up for fraudulently attempting to obtain sugar or fruits, or obtaining petrol for inessential purposes. It was widely suspected that the businessmen who comprised the majority on most food committees were primarily there not to protect public interests, but to safeguard their own businesses. Farmers were criticised for trying to hang on to their labourers, particularly when they were their sons, while other people sacrificed theirs. The drinks trade had no qualms about campaigning robustly against government regulations designed to combat drunkenness in society and absenteeism at work, and continued to claim poverty when annual figures showed most firms were surviving quite well in the circumstances. In 1918 the patriotism of milk suppliers was such that they opted to refuse to deliver their produce to customers rather than accept a cut in their profits. Better-off people used their influence and money to obtain supplies of food and other commodities which were not generally available. In 1914 they could afford to stockpile food, and in 1917 they bypassed the much more severe shortages, in collusion with compliant and mercenary shopkeepers. Farmers, whilst doing their utmost to retain their labourers, spent the entire War attempting to limit their wages, even to the point of resisting the Government's minimum wage proposals.

Military tribunals may have taken a harsh line with conscientious objectors, but there is little doubt that the tribunals were a convenient arena for those who had less than honourable motives for seeking to avoid military service. The arguments of some applicants were, quite frankly, ludicrously far-fetched. The claim of a Braintree barber that he should be exempted because of his contract to cut the hair of the workhouse inmates, or that of the Mayor of Colchester that his chauffeur was performing work vital to the war effort, can hardly be credited. As we have already observed, farmers came in for particularly harsh criticism for the persistency with which they attempted to hang on to their farm workers, but the number of dubious appeals moved well beyond the sphere of agriculture. Women, some of them wives, others mothers or sweethearts, were willing to risk the wrath of the law to shelter conscripted men who were unwilling to serve. When Emmanuel Everitt, a South Weald labourer, failed to report for military service, the law stepped in:

> On arriving at the cottage they heard someone run upstairs. [P.C. Game] went in, leaving P.C. Sturgeon to watch the door.

[10] ECC 24 March 1917.

> On searching the house, witness found prisoner hiding behind the door of the back bedroom. On telling the prisoner that he had a warrant for his arrest, prisoner replied, "I don't want to go and I am not going." Fined £5 and military escort.[11]

However, although there was a great deal of self-serving behaviour on the part of many, it is nevertheless true to say that Essex paid a grievous price for the part it played in the Great War. This cannot be disputed. Eleven battalions of the Essex Regiment served overseas in the Great War, and 8,209 of its men were killed. The 2nd Battalion fought at Le Cateau on 28 August 1914, five days after British troops fired the army's first shots in the War at Mons. This was the Essex Regiment's first action in the conflict. Essex battalions fought in some of the most stirring battles of the War — the retreat from Mons, Ypres in 1915 and again in 1917, Loos in 1915, and at Cambrai in 1917. The 1st Battalion was present at Gallipoli from the first landings in May 1915 to the evacuation in January 1916; 168 men were killed, 750 wounded, and 304 were reported missing. It took part in the disastrous first day of the Battle of the Somme on 1 July 1916, as part of the attack on the German position at Beaumont Hamel. Four battalions fought in Egypt at the Battle of Gaza in November 1917. In total over seventeen thousand of the county's servicemen lost their lives, as well as several hundred of its civilians who were killed in air raids by German Zeppelins and aeroplanes. If we add the two to three thousand people who died of Spanish flu in 1918-19, many of them weakened by years of relative privation and strain brought on by the War, this represents a severe loss of life. Each one is a life cut short, a potential never to be fulfilled, a family devastated. The historian Jay Winter has conducted meticulous research into Britain's war dead, and he has concluded that over seven hundred and twenty-two thousand servicemen died during the conflict.[12] The war dead of Essex would therefore amount to between two and three per cent of this total. It is impossible to grasp what these men endured, what horrors they saw, or how their lives were changed by their military service. However, to try to understand something of what they experienced what we can do is to focus on the War's impact on the men of one community — Hornchurch. For this we owe a debt of thanks to Charles Thomas Perfect, a Hornchurch resident and historian, who with the help of his friends compiled a parish roll of honour and incorporated it into his book, *Hornchurch During The Great War.*[13] He managed to compile information on many of the men who served, and on most of those who lost their lives. Exactly how he achieved this task he does not state, although he admits to "having exhausted all the means in my power to make the lists complete." Perhaps he and his friends made

[11] ECC 7 April 1916.

[12] J. Winter, *The Great War and the British People* (1985), 68-9.

[13] The information upon which the opening part of this chapter is based comes from pages 36-85 of Perfect's book.

harrowing visits to both survivors and families of the Fallen, perhaps he made extensive use of newspaper reports throughout the War. However his roll was compiled, the result is that he has bequeathed to us a remarkable record of the military service of the men of this one community.

Between 1914 and 1918 a total of 1,573 men from Hornchurch served in the army, Royal Navy, Merchant Navy, the Royal Flying Corps, and when its name was changed, in the Royal Air Force. These men served in virtually every theatre of war in this worldwide conflict. They fought in the dogfights over the Western Front, and in the skies above Britain against the German raiders who were sent across the Channel and North Sea. Men who enlisted in the Royal Navy sailed on duty in the Atlantic and Pacific, in the Channel, the North Sea; they helped to keep open the arteries of imperial communication in the Mediterranean, Red Sea and Indian Ocean, and fought in the decisive naval Battle of Jutland in 1916. However, the great majority of Hornchurch men served in the army and they too participated in campaigns which took them all over the globe, from the rain-filled trenches of Flanders to the searing deserts and mountains of Egypt, Mesopotamia, Syria and Palestine: from the jungles of the German colonies in the Cameroons, East Africa and New Guinea to the mountainous regions of the Balkans in Serbia, Salonika, Albania, Macedonia, Dalmatia and Bulgaria: from the West Indies, India and China to the disease-ridden beaches of Gallipoli and on the bone-chilling Russian Front. Those men who performed their duty in the army served in over a hundred regiments and military units, which included dozens of British formations as well as more exotic commands such as the Australian Imperial Force, the Third Toronto Regiment, the Rough Riders, the Alberta Infantry Battalion, the Canadian Cavalry Corps, the New Zealand Rifle Brigade, the Canadian Scottish Regiment, the South Winnipeg Rifles, the Canadian Mounted Rifles, the North Dublin Union, the Chinese Labour Corps and the Punjab Indian Army.

There was no lack of officially recognised gallantry from the men of this Essex town. One man was awarded the Victoria Cross, two the Distinguished Service Order, six the Military Cross, and one the Distinguished Flying Cross. Non-Commissioned Officers and men received a total of six Military Medals, four Distinguished Conduct Medals, one Distinguished Service Medal and a Meritorious Service Medal and the King's Medal. Two were awarded the O.B.E., and one the Military M.B.E. In addition, two men received foreign awards, the Order of the Nile and the Italian *Croce al Merito di Guerra*.

One hundred and ninety seven of these men, about thirteen per cent, made the ultimate sacrifice. Perfect was able to ascertain where 133 of them had died. As one might expect the vast majority, eighty-two, died on the Western Front. Fourteen of them, mostly wounded who had been ferried home to 'Blighty', died in

British hospitals, although a few of these were killed in training accidents before they saw active service. Eleven others perished at Gallipoli, eight at sea, seven in Palestine, four in Egypt, three in Mesopotamia, and one each in Salonika and Dalmatia. One unfortunate man died as a prisoner of war in Germany, and one was killed in Russia in 1919 with British forces which were sent against the Bolsheviks in the Russian Civil War.

Where he was able to, Perfect also meticulously recorded how these men lost their lives. As one might expect most of them, 113 in total, died violent deaths. Sixty-seven of them were killed in action, twenty-one died of wounds received in combat, and fifteen were reported missing, their bodies never recovered, perhaps blown to pieces by shellfire or swallowed up in some mud-filled shell hole in no-man's-land. Five men drowned when their ships were sunk, and more specifically, three died when their ships were torpedoed by German U-boats. One man died as a result of being gassed, one was shot down by enemy fire, another crashed his plane when trying to land when he was injured, one lost his life in a mid-air collision, and yet another in a flying accident. The remaining twenty men died from illness or as a result of circumstances relating to military service. Pneumonia, often brought on by prolonged exposure to appalling weather conditions, claimed seven lives. Dysentery, consumption, malaria, influenza and "illness" each killed one serviceman.

To focus entirely on those who died is to neglect a great part of the story of these men, a story which once again Perfect provides details of. Altogether ninety-eight men on whom he gathered details had been wounded, some slightly, some severely. Fourteen men reported having been wounded twice, and four on three separate occasions. A total of twenty-nine men suffered from the effects of gas, and one man survived being gassed twice. Nine servicemen ended the War disabled to a greater or lesser degree as a result of injuries received. In addition to this, two men had one leg amputated, one man lost his left arm, another lost a foot, yet another an eye, and one man was left nursing a paralysed arm.

Many men did not see out the War in active service. In all twenty-nine men were invalided home having been incapacitated by illness or the effects of wounds. Others were discharged from the services, the men involved suffering from a whole range of complaints including enteric fever, epilepsy, trench feet, dysentery, rheumatic fever, a strained heart, "shell shock and sunstroke", "sick", a nervous breakdown, being gassed and suffering a fractured leg. One man survived being blown up and two men emerged alive after being buried by shellfire. Remarkably in view of the climatic conditions the men were exposed to for long periods, only two of them admitted to having experienced frostbite.

Perfect was able to state the age at death for eighty-six of the men. Nine of them were under twenty years of age, forty-five were aged between twenty and twenty-nine, and twenty-five aged over thirty. Of the latter group, seven men who lost their lives were over forty-one years old. Private William Shield, aged fifty, was the oldest of the Hornchurch men who gave all for King and Country. He had served in the Essex Regiment for fourteen years before the War. Although his period of service had ended, he rejoined the regiment in 1914, but was invalided out in 1916. The War wrecked his health and he died on 12 September 1918, failing to see the Armistice by just two months. The oldest man who was actually killed in action was forty-five-year-old Private Thomas Mayne, a pre-war army reservist who enlisted in the 11th Hussars on 9 September 1914, and who was attached to the Royal Engineers when he was killed on 3 March 1916. His section officer wrote of him that "I could better have spared half my Section than Tom Mayne. He was always bright, willing and good tempered. He died the death of a true soldier." Sadly the youngest to die was Rifleman Harry Parker of the London Rifle Brigade, who was not even old enough to have served in the army. Like so many young men in the War, he lied about his age in order to enlist in April 1916, and six months later he was shot dead by a German sniper while acting as battalion scout on 8 October 1916. He was fifteen years old at the time of his death. Perfect does not specify whether or not any of the 1,573 men who served were married or had children. Presumably some of them were, including some of those who did not return.

Although it might be thought invidious to focus upon the self-sacrifice of particular individuals, the temptation to do so is too great in the case of two young men. Private Herbert George Columbine was twenty-five years old when he was killed in France at the height of the great German offensive in March 1918. He was only seven when his father, a reservist who had been recalled to the colours, was killed in the South African War in July 1900. He and his mother moved from London to Walton five years later when a job opened up for him at the Coast Development Corporation on Walton pier. He worked there for six years until he too joined the army, enlisting in the 19th Hussars in 1911. He arrived in France only six days after Britain's declaration of war. After fighting in the great battles at the start of the War, he was sent home with an arm wound which had become dangerously infected. His arm was saved by timely surgery and he was sent back to France in January 1915. In 1916 he transferred to the Machine Gun Corps, and it was with this unit that he found himself facing what proved to be the last great German offensive in March 1918.

The Germans attacked in great numbers on two sides of the British positions and began a deadly enfilade of their trenches, inflicting serious casualties on the defenders. Part of the British position was a machine-gun post slightly ahead of the main trench. All the men manning it had been killed. Columbine ran forward in the teeth of heavy fire to take charge of the machine gun, and he was soon joined by several others. The position lacked any sort of protective cover and one by one most of the men around Columbine were killed or wounded. Columbine himself was wounded in the arm, but he continued to fire for four hours. The Germans eventually succeeded in working around the flanks of Columbine's position and cut it off except for a narrow gap, through which communications were maintained with the rear. Columbine and his comrades fought off several determined attacks, inflicting heavy casualties on their attackers. By early afternoon it had become obvious that the position was hopeless. Columbine told the only two uninjured men left with him to leave while there was still time. "Save yourselves", he said, "I'll carry on." Reluctantly they left, leaving Columbine to continue operating the machine gun alone. Between midday and one o' clock in the afternoon the Germans tried to overrun Columbine, but he repulsed them eight times. With their whole advance in this sector held up by just one man, the Germans, in desperation, called in aircraft to finish him off. Several German planes appeared, and although they were engaged by British fighters, one broke away, circling Columbine's position at about a hundred feet. Columbine's comrades saw him elevate his gun, then they watched the flight of the bomb which the pilot dropped. There was an explosion and Columbine's gun was silenced. For his astonishing bravery and self-sacrifice he was posthumously awarded the Victoria Cross.

Jack Cornwell was born at Leyton on 8 January 1900. His father Eli was a train driver. Jack tried several times to join the Royal Navy but was rejected as being too young. However, he was finally accepted in July 1915, and on 2 May 1916 he was posted to H.M.S. *Chester*. He was just sixteen and a half years old when his ship took part in the great naval Battle of Jutland at the end of May 1916. Cornwell's job was to stand by one of the ship's heavy guns with earphones on to relay the officer's orders to the gunners. In the first few minutes of the engagement a German shell exploded nearby, killing or incapacitating all but two of the ten-man gun crew. Although seriously wounded and in a dangerously exposed position, Cornwell remained at his post awaiting orders. He survived the battle and was taken to hospital in Grimsby on 1 June, but died the next day. He was buried in a common grave in Grimsby cemetery. However, as news of his courage became public knowledge his body was exhumed and reinterred with great ceremony in Manor Park Cemetery on 29 July 1916. His coffin was borne on a gun carriage with the White Ensign on it, the carriage drawn by boys from Crystal Palace Naval Depot. The funeral route was lined by boy scouts; Cornwell had been one himself before he joined up. Six boy seamen from H.M.S. *Chester* followed the coffin carrying wreaths from the ship's company and there were others from the Lord Mayor of London and Admiral David Beatty, the man who was effectively second-in-command at Jutland.

The experiences, valour and self-sacrifice of Columbine and Cornwell were perhaps quite exceptional. The self-sacrifice of the men of Hornchurch is not unique

— it could be repeated for hundreds of Essex communities during 1914-18. Many fathers must have been left speculating on what might have been, like Colchester's rural dean, Canon Brunwin Hales, when his second son, like his first, was killed in action:

> Had my son lived I believe he would have been at least "a useful man" in this district and county. God has willed that he should serve the town to which he was so much attached by bequeathing — in common with so many other Colchester men — the right spirit for public work, viz. that of sacrifice unstinted. May we the fathers of the borough, be worthy of our children who have reversed the ordinary course of life and become our teachers.[14]

Herbert Columbine and Jack Cornwell were servicemen who laid down their lives in the line of duty. Many civilians too made the supreme sacrifice, and not just those who were killed in air raids. Just after 7 p.m. on 19 January 1917 a fire broke out in the premises of the great Brunner-Mond munitions factory at Silvertown in metropolitan Essex. The fire did not seem too serious and the fire engine from the local fire station arrived to put it out. Hundreds of workers in the nearby factory streamed out of their workplaces as a safety precaution. Then, just five minutes after the fire had been spotted, there was a stupendous explosion. Rows of small houses in the immediate vicinity of the factory were demolished, their occupants buried. The fire engine was destroyed. A forty-ton boiler was lifted and hurled a quarter of a mile away. People were thrown down in the streets and windows were shattered. The concussion from the explosion lifted the top of a gasometer some distance away. The gasometer had contained eight million cubic feet of gas and as it ignited it sent a spectacular column of fire two miles into the air. A fresh breeze fanned the flames which destroyed many surrounding properties, including factories, workhouses and a very large flour mill. The explosion was heard by many people twenty to thirty miles away and the flames from the destroyed gasometer were seen over much of Essex. Evelyn Potter was at a dance at her school nearby. She recalled vividly what happened:

> All of a sudden someone called out "Look at the sky! We all looked. There was a huge glow which gradually increased with flames until bright red. It lit up all our faces in the school hall. Then, turning to look out opposite, the sky was red there also. All round, flaming red! Mr Graham told us to sit down; we all

[14] ECS 28 April 1917.

> thought it was a great fire, or a Zeppelin down very near. About half a minute or so later there was a terrific crash — like a thunderbolt and forty bombs all at once! Many of the school windows smashed and fell. The air was filled with the sound of breaking glass. Somebody said "It's Woolwich Arsenal." A girl fainted. (Her father works there.) One thing — nothing else followed. The sky continued so brilliant that when Lingwood started to play we all danced, with the lights out, as in a flaming limelight.[15]

Sixty-nine people were killed; forty-four men, eleven women and fourteen children. Miraculously, only two of the firemen who had been on the wrecked fire engine lost their lives. Over four hundred people were injured, seventy-two of them seriously. The death toll would have been far more severe had it not been for the five minute interval between the fire and the explosion, which allowed hundreds of people to move to a safer position.[16]

Alongside the self-interest and selfishness of those left at home, there was also much to admire. In spite of the German air raids which inflicted death and destruction on towns and villages, in spite of the portrayal of Germans as inhuman savages, and in spite of horrors such as the sinking of the *Lusitania*, the people of Essex responded to all this with remarkable restraint. The wrecking of German-owned properties in the East End of London was the exception, not the rule. The *Essex County Standard* condemned these outrages and the victimisation of the innocent, accusing the press of having inflamed the situation. "They were largely made up of wasters, shirkers, and some blackguards," said the *Standard*, "out for plunder and personal gain." Those voices calling for retaliation and retribution on Germany's civilian population were few and far between. Most might have heeded the Bishop of Colchester when he urged "prayer without wrath".[17] Leading citizens called for, and on the whole received, an attitude of civilised tolerance towards those of German ancestry in their county, and to their credit there were many individuals who were prepared to stand up and defend their German friends and colleagues in public when they were the targets of bigotry. Some were even brave enough to decry the demands that the German language be abolished in English schools during the War. Although the members of military tribunals gave conscientious objectors a rough ride, their obvious revulsion at their beliefs always seems to have been tempered with a scrupulous observance of the formalities. Tribunals were no hole-in-the-corner affairs. They usually admitted the public to their sittings and there were often full accounts of their proceedings in the press. Hysteria there may have been

15 Potter/Grubb diary, 19 January 1917.

16 ECC 26 January 1917.

17 CG 19 August 1914.

concerning spies and aliens, but there was also a healthy streak of disbelief in the idea that there were widespread enemy conspiracies at work. When William Whitehead of Dovercourt was arrested in August 1914 on suspicion of using carrier pigeons to supply the Germans with information, his friends and customers (he was a publican) refused to believe the charges. When, two weeks later, Whitehead was brought to court at the Harwich Guildhall, a huge crowd of well-wishers besieged the place. When he was acquitted, they celebrated loudly and exuberantly.[18]

Schoolteachers, sharing the patriotism of the country, inevitably inculcated their pupils with such sentiments, but on the whole were successful in resisting the excessively crude jingoism which the military urged them to cram into the heads of children. There was also considerable resistance by education authorities to the releasing of boys at too young an age for important agricultural work, indicating a continued recognition that even in wartime education ought to take priority over military considerations for the young. The political truce between parties which followed rapidly upon the declaration of war in 1914 might have been cast aside with predictable haste in late 1918, but it generally held firm throughout the War. We can appreciate the contrast which the Bishop of Chelmsford made between the war years and the turbulent years of 1911-14, and although his comment that, "The wrath of war, like a hurricane, has driven division and strife from our midst", was rather overstated, in terms of local politics in Essex it does hold true.[19]

Criticism of the War was tolerated to a surprising degree, and newspapers did not hesitate to publish letters which expressed disapproval of aspects of its prosecution. In October 1915 the *East Essex Advertiser* printed a letter by "G.G.G." which criticised the conduct of the War as "muddling on in the same old slipshod way." The letter went on to say,

> Fifteen months of a monstrous war and still undecided, still unorganised, business still uncontrolled, prices without a regulator, commercial thieves allowed to continue the vile robbery of enhanced prices, profits of undertakings greater than ever and no-one to say nay ... What a scandal![20]

In reply, one of the newspaper's readers urged "G.G.G." to keep his feelings to himself. "The great need of humanity today", said the correspondent, "is for the bright and cheery optimists who smile away sorrow and bring bright, buoyant, beautiful hope (as an angel of light) to the sore and tear-stained eyes of humanity."[21] Bright and cheery optimism was expecting too much in this great protracted conflict.

[18] ECT 22 August, 5 September 1914.

[19] ECS 9 January 1915.

[20] EEA 23 October 1915.

[21] EEA 30 October 1915.

However, adapting to the War and continuing their lives as they had always been lived was perhaps the surest form of defence which the people of Essex had in the Great War, as the *Essex County Telegraph*'s Junius Minor recognised:

> Although England is at war, her national life seems to run in ordinary channels ... People pursue their ordinary avocations, buy and sell, make love and marry, amuse themselves in different ways, and generally exhibit a spirit of quiet cheerfulness.[22]

[22] ECT 12 September 1914.

Appendix: Essex Memorials of the Great War

This list records some of the war memorials erected by parishes, churches, chapels, communities and workplaces, as well as those commissioned by individuals, relatives, or friends. Most, but not all, of them are still in existence.

Abbreviations used in the notes:

Capt.	Captain	Pte	Private
Co.	Company	R.A.F.	Royal Air Force
Col	Colonel	R.A.M.C.	Royal Army Medical Corps
Cpl	Corporal	R.A.S.C	Royal Army Service Corps
D.O.W.	Died of wounds	Regt	Regiment
Fl. Cmmdr	Flight Commander	Rev.	Reverend
Gnr	Gunner	R.E.	Royal Engineers
K.I.A.	Killed in action	R.F.A.	Royal Field Artillery
L/Cpl	Lance-corporal	R.F.C.	Royal Flying Corps
L/Sgt	Lance-sargeant	R.G.A.	Royal Garrison Artillery
Lt	Lieutenant	R.H.A.	Royal Horse Artillery
Lt Col	Lieutenant Colonel	R.N.	Royal Navy
Maj.	Major	R.N.V.R.	Royal Naval Volunteer Reserve
M.I.A.	Missing in Action	Sgt	Sergeant

Location	Type	Number of The "Fallen"	Date Unveiled/ Dedicated
Abberton, St Andrew[1]	priests chair & plaque		
Abbess Roding, St Edmund	tablet	2	
Aldborough Hates, St Peter (Ilford)	triptych	18	11 September 1921
Aldham, St Margaret & St Catherine	obelisk	17	
Aldham, St Margaret & St Catherine[2]	organ		
Aldham, St Margaret & St Catherine[3]	tablet		
Aldham, St Margaret & St Catherine[4]	tablet		
Alphamstone, St Barnbas	stained-glass window		1919
Alresford, St Andrew[5]	stained-glass window		1916
Alresford	cross		2 June 1920
Alresford	cross	11	2 June 1920
Althorne	lychgate	18	11 July 1920
Althorne	public shelter	18	
Ardleigh	cross	36	25 September 1921
Ardleigh	tablet	40	

1 In memory of Lt John Geldard, R.E.

2 In memory of John W. Robinson and George S. Robinson.

3 In memory of Henry B. Perry, 1/13th Company, London Regt, K.I.A. 6 November 1918.

4 In memory of Capt. Henry B. Perry, London Regt, (Kensington Rifles), K.I.A. 6 November 1918 at Angre.

5 In memory of Lts Rowland Prichard and Giles Prichard, killed in France, 1915.

APPENDIX: ESSEX MEMORIALS OF THE GREAT WAR

Location	Type	Number of The "Fallen"	Date Unveiled/ Dedicated
Arkesden, St Mary the Virgin[6]	tablet		1919
Ashdon		24	23 October 1921
Ashen	tablet	5	
Ashingdon	panelling	20	20 June 1920
Aveley, St Michael	cross	42	19 September 1920
Aveley Church[7]	litany table		1916
Aythorpe Roding	tablet	7	27 June 1920
Barking Baptist Tabernacle	tablet	19	24 October 1920
Barking	cenotaph	820	25 March 1922
Barking cemetery	cross of sacrifice	820	
Barking, St Margaret	tablet	25	
Barking, St Margaret's Church of England School[8]	tablet	66	
Barking, St Mary and St Ethelburga		63	
Barking, St Mary and St Ethelburga[9]	tablet		
Barking, St Peter and St Paul	tablet	83	17 June 1920
Barking, United Reform Church	roll of honour and tablet	8	
Barking, Wouldham Cement Works		36	29 March 1920
Barkingside, Holy Trinity	tablet	90	
Barling Magna, All Saints	obelisk	11	22 April 1922
Beauchamp Roding, St Botolph	organ & tablet	3	
Beaumont-cum-Moze	stained-glass windows	9	16 May 1920
Beaumont-cum-Moze	tablet		21 September 1919
Beaumont-cum-Moze[10]	tablet	9	1935
Beckton, St Michael	tablet	123	11 June 1922
Beckton Gasworks[11]	plinth, column and lamp	500	June 1922
Becontree Heath Methodist Church	book of remembrance	28	
Belchamp Otten, St Ethelbert & All Saints	cross	6	
Belchamp St Paul	tablet	18	23 April 1921
Belchamp St Paul	tablet /treble bell	17	17 April 1921
Berners Roding[12]	tablet	2	

6 In memory of Lt George W. Beadle, R.A.S.C., died at Euskirchen, Germany, on 8 March 1919, aged twenty-seven.

7 Not strictly a war memorial, it was given by the Sussex Regt "For blessings received during their stay in the parish" (Mee, *Essex*, 19.).

8 Dedicated to former pupils of the school.

9 In memory of Alfred T. Clark, K.I.A. at le Quesnay on 4 November 1918, aged twenty-seven; also Ernest O. Clark, died in France on 5 December 1916, aged twenty-one.

10 In memory of Field Marshal Viscount Byng of Vimy, died in 1935.

11 In memory of former employees of the Gas Light and Coke Company.

12 The church at Berners Roding was declared redundant in 1986 and the memorial is now in St Christoper's, Willingale Doe.

Location	Type	Number of The "Fallen"	Date Unveiled/ Dedicated
Billericay	cross	62	16 October 1921
Billericay, Church of the Holy Redeemer	cross		12 July 1919
Billericay Congregational Church[13]	scroll		11 August 1918
Billericay, St Mary Magdalene[14]	tablet and cross		
Billericay, St Mary Magdalene[15]	tablet		
Birch	cross		
Birch, St Peter[16]	tablet		
Birch (and Layer Breton)[17]	memorial hall		October 1921
Birchanger	cross	37	25 July 1920
Birchanger, St Mary the Virgin	tablet	34	31 October 1922
Birdbrook	cross	11	15 August 1920
Blackmore	cross	20	7 November 1920
Blackmore End, village hall	tablet	20	
Blackstone	cross	120	7 November 1920
Black Notley	obelisk	18	1 April 1926
Bocking, St Mary the Virgin	altar and tablet	51	7 November 1920
Bocking, St Mary the Virgin	tablet	58	7 November 1920
Bocking, St Mary the Virgin	memorial gates		
Bocking, St Mary the Virgin	stained-glass window	26	27 May 1926
Bocking, St Mary the Virgin[18]	tablets		26 November 1916
Boreham, St Andrew	tablet		
Boreham, St Andrew[19]	tablet		
Borley	tablet	6	7 November 1920
Boyton (see Roxwell)			
Bowers Gifford (see Pitsea)			
Boxted, St Peter	brass tablet	16	7 November 1920
Boxted, St Peter	wooden tablet	20	7 November 1920
Boxted, Wesleyan Methodist Church	tablet	16	14 November 1920
Bradfield, St Lawrence[20]	stained-glass windows and tablet		24 August 1919

13 In memory of Cpl O.S. Ladbrook, K.I.A.

14 In memory of Lt H.G. Welham, Royal Sussex Regt, died on 4 November 1918, aged twenty-two.

15 In memory of Edwin W. Cottis, died 28 March 1918, aged thirty-eight, and Cecil J. Cottis, died 18 September 1918, aged twenty-three.

16 In memory of Auriol F. Birch, killed at Le Cateau in 1914, and his two brothers.

17 Dedicated to the men of Birch and Layer Breton.

18 In memory of Capt. John H.J. Savill, killed 5 June 1916 when H.M.S. *Hampshire* sank, and Lt Alfred O. Ollett, Essex Regt, K.I.A. on 27 April 1916 at Calonne, France, aged twenty-one.

19 Dedicated to Lt James H. Seabrook, R.E. and 5th Cavalry Brigade, K.I.A. at the Marne, on 10 September 1914, aged thirty.

20 In memory of Squadron Leader Edwin Harris Dunning, R.N; also Lt Alselan B. Nicholls, Essex Regt, K.I.A. on 25 April 1917, aged twenty-three; also Ralph N.B. Nicholls, died on 17 February 1915, aged seventeen.

APPENDIX: ESSEX MEMORIALS OF THE GREAT WAR

Location	Type	Number of The "Fallen"	Date Unveiled/ Dedicated
Bradfield, St Lawrence	column	21	24 August 1919
Bradwell-on-Sea, St Peter	tablet	13	
Bradwell-on-Sea, St Peter	obelisk	13	
Braintree and Bocking	obelisk	201	6 November 1926
Braintree Congregational Church	tablet	11	
Braintree Grammar School	stained-glass window		3 July 1919
Braintree High School[21]	tablet	19	22 July 1921
Braintree High School[22]	tablet		
Braintree, St Michael	memorial chapel/window	114	26 February 1921
Braintree, St Michael[23]	tablet		
Braintree, St Michael[24]	brass altar cross		
Braintree, Warner Brothers[25]	tablet	7	30 December 1919
Braxted, Beacon Hill[26]	cross	20	27 March 1921
Brentwood	memorial hospital	398	22 January 1921
Brentwood[27]	cross	398	9 October 1921
Brentwood Congregational Church	tablet	17	9 May 1920
Brentwood Grammar School			19 July 1924
Brentwood Grammar School Chapel			
Brentwood Hospital	hospital		4 February 1921
Brentwood, London County Westminster and Parrs Bank	tablet	1	
Brentwood Post Office	tablet	9	20 August 1922
Brentwood St Mary and St Helen Cathedral	cross		
Brentwood, St Thomas of Canterbury	Calvary		2 April 1923
Brentwood, St Thomas of Canterbury[28]	tablet		
Brentwood, Sir Anthony Browne's School[29]	chapel, altar, reredos, and chancel additions	22	9 December 1917
Brightlingsea, Wesleyan Chapel	tablet	13	14 October 1920
Brightlingsea	cenotaph	110	20 October 1921

21 In memory of those former pupils who died in the War.

22 In memory of Cpl George E. Baines, 12th Battalion, Royal Sussex Regt, a former teacher at the school, K.I.A. on 4 July 1916.

23 In memory of Cadet Ralph S. Preston, R.F.A., died 29 March 1916, and Lt Philip S. Preston, R.F.A., died 28 March 1918.

24 Donated by Mr and Mrs E.J. Fuller, in memory of their two sons.

25 In memory of employees of the Warner Brothers firm.

26 The cross was also intended as a memorial of Lt Charles O. Wilson, K.I.A. at Gaza, 26 March 1917. The cross was erected by his parents. The names of seventeen men of Wickham Bishops and three from Great Braxted are also on the cross.

27 The War memorial represents Brentwood, Shenfield, South Weald, Warley, et al.

28 In memory of Lt Basil L. Kimber, Lincolnshire Regt, buried in France, 10 July 1916, aged twenty-two.

29 In memory of the scholars of the school who were killed in the War.

Location	Type	Number of The "Fallen"	Date Unveiled/ Dedicated
Brightlingsea[30]	memorial stone and water garden		
Brightlingsea, Forester's Hall[31]	tablet		
Brightlingsea, The New Church	tablet	14	24 February 1928
Brightlingsea, Forester's Hall	tablet	34	
Brightlingsea, All Saints[32]	tablet		
Brightlingsea, All Saints[33]	tablet		
Brightlingsea, All Saints[34]	tablet		
Brightlingsea, All Saints[35]	tablet		
Broomfield, St Mary & St Leonard	tablet	22	
Broomfield, St Mary & St Leonard[36]	tablet		
Broomfield, St Mary & St Leonard[37]	grave marker		
Broxted and Chickney, St Mary	tablet	17	
Buckhurst Hill	lych gate	127	
Buckhurst Hill	column	84	
Buckhurst Hill, Congregational Church	tablet	7	
Bulmer	cross	18	
Bulphan, St Mary the Virgin	cross	12	
Bumpstead	tablet	16	22 August 1920
Bures St Mary & Bures Hamlet[38]	tablet	42	18 July 1920
Bures St Mary & Bures Hamlet	oak cross	42	17 April 1921
Burnham on Crouch	cenotaph	98	14 August 1921
Burnham on Crouch, St Mary	tablets	98	4 January 1922
Burnham on Crouch; Congregational Church	tablet	22	August 1921
Burnham on Crouch, Forester's Hall	tablet	22	26 October 1922
Burnt Mill (see under Nettleswell)			
Buttsbury (see under Stock)			
Canewdon	chapel & tablet	11	
Canvey Island, Paddocks Garden	tablet		

30 In memory of William H. Osborn, lost with H.M.S. *Natal*, December 1915.

31 Dedicated to the men of the Royal Court of Essex No.5625.

32 In memory of Frederick J. Greenland, lost with H.M.S. *Hogue*, 22 September 1914, aged thirty-three.

33 In memory of Frank H. Mills, lost from H.M.S. *Queen Mary* at the Battle of Jutland, 31 May 1916.

34 In memory of Charles J. Draper, lost with H.M.S. *Margate* in the North Sea, 24 April 1918.

35 In memory of Thomas C. Taylor, lost with S.S. *Woolston*, sunk by an enemy U-boat off Syracuse, Sicily, 14 May 1918.

36 In memory of Lt Llewelyn C. Nash, King's Royal Rifle Corps, D.O.W. on 28 September 1915, aged twenty.

37 In memory of Capt. E.R. Nash, 16th Lancers, K.I.A. at Ypres on 21 February 1915, aged twenty-six.

38 Although located in Suffolk, this village war memorial also commemorates the Fallen from Bures Hamlet, the adjoining village on the Essex bank of the River Stour.

APPENDIX: ESSEX MEMORIALS OF THE GREAT WAR

Location	Type	Number of The "Fallen"	Date Unveiled/ Dedicated
Canvey Island, Royal British Legion Building	tablet	21	
Canvey Island, St Nicholas	tablet	21	
Castle Hedingham	mosaic	34	2 April 1920
Castle Hedingham Church	cross	37	13 November 1921
Castle Hedingham Congregational Church	tablet	23	5 December 1920
Chadwell Heath, St Chad	tablet	97	6 December 1919
Chadwell Heath, St Mary	cross	8	23 May 1920
Chadwell Heath, St Mary	cross	8	
Chadwell Heath, United Reform Church	tablet	4	
Chappel, St Barnabas	tablet	12	
Chelmsford	obelisk	258	11 November 1923
Chelmsford Cathedral[39]	tablet	42	
Chelmsford Cathedral[40]	tablet	258	2 July 1922
Chelmsford Cathedral[41]	tablet	22	23 September 1920
Chelmsford Cathedral[42]	tablet	99	28 May 1922
Chelmsford Cathedral[43]	tablet	44	15 January 1921
Chelmsford Cathedral[44]	leaden panels	55	19 October 1922
Chelmsford Cathedral[45]	tablet		
Chelmsford, Church of our Lady Immaculate	tablet	17	
Chelmsford Conservative Club	tablet	14	October 1921
Chelmsford, County Hall[46]	tablet		
Chelmsford, Essex Regimental Museum[47]	tablet	61	
Chelmsford, King Edward VI School	roll of honour	60	15 June 1920
Chelmsford, Marconi PLC	tablet		
Chelmsford, Police Headquarters[48]	tablet	22	
Chelmsford, Police Headquarters[49]	commemorative stone	62	November 2004

39 In memory of the employees of Hoffmann's Manufacturing Company. The tablet was moved to the cathedral when Hoffmann's closed in 1989.

40 In memory of the men of the Essex Yeomanry.

41 In memory of the members of the Essex County Constabulary.

42 Dedicated to parishioners who died in the War.

43 In memory of those members of the Association of the Essex Change Ringers who died in the War.

44 In memory of the Essex clergy who served as military chaplains, and to the sons of Essex clergy killed in the War.

45 In memory of Marshal S. Straight, Essex Regt, K.I.A. at Gallipoli, 24 December 1915.

46 Dedicated to the members of Essex County Council who lost their lives in the War.

47 In memory of the men of the Order of Achei Brith and Shield of Abraham.

48 In memory of the men of the Essex County Constabulary.

49 In memory of the men of the county's three police forces — The Essex County Constabulary, the Colchester Borough Police Force and Southend Borough Police.

Location	Type	Number of The "Fallen"	Date Unveiled/ Dedicated
Chelmsford, Shire Hall[50]	tablet	22	23 September 1920
Chelmsford, United Reform Church	tablet	10	
Chignall, St James[51]	stained-glass windows, altar, reredos	7	6 June 1919
Chignall Smealy, St Nicholas	tablet	8	
Chignall Smealy, St Nicholas[52]	altar & plaque	8	
Chignall Smealy, St Nicholas[53]	lectern		
Chignall Smealy, St Nicholas	tablet	3	
Chigwell	cross	39	6 November 1921
Chigwell	screen		14 November 1920
Chigwell School	memorial chapel and tablet		11 October 1924
Chigwell School[54]	armoury		1929
Chigwell School	roll of honour		
Childerditch	stained-glass windows	4	19 February 1922
Chingford	cross	240	24 September 1921
Chingford	gardens of remembrance		
Chingford, All Saints	memorial board	18	
Chingford, All Saints	tablet	86	
Chingford, All Saints	memorial panelling	86	
Chingford, All Saints[55]	screen		
Chingford, St Edmund			
Chingford, St Peter and St Paul	roll of honour		
Chingford, St Peter and St Paul[56]	tablet		
Chingford, Winchester Road Methodist Church	tablet	17	
Chipping Ongar, St Martin	tablet	36	
Clacton-on-Sea[57]	tablet		
Clacton-on-Sea, Church of Our Lady of Light (& St Osyth)	gate	6	
Clacton-on-Sea, Rush Green, Wesleyan Chapel	mural tablet	19	3 November 1920

[50] In memory of the men of the Essex County Constabulary.

[51] In memory of Lt Harry Munn R.F.A., Lt Harry W. Mann; also Leon Francis Asnong, K.I.A. on 9 September 1918.

[52] Dedicated to Leon F. Asnong, 4th Carabiniers, Belgian Army, K.I.A. 9 September 1918, also to the men of the parish.

[53] In memory of the men of Mashbury.

[54] In memory of R.E. Hill, R.N.V.R., who died of pneumonia on 1 November 1918.

[55] In memory of Lt Col. V.C. Richmond.

[56] In memory of Lt Francis W. Russell, Queen's Westmorland Rifles, killed in France on 27 August 1918, aged twenty.

[57] In memory of Charles S. Nicholson, K.I.A. on the Somme, 15 September 1916.

APPENDIX: ESSEX MEMORIALS OF THE GREAT WAR

Location	Type	Number of The "Fallen"	Date Unveiled/ Dedicated
Clacton-on-Sea, St James[58]	wooden candlesticks and plaque		October 1921
Clacton-on-Sea, St James	calvary		2 October 1921
Clacton-on-Sea, St Osyth Road School	roll of honour		
Clacton-on-Sea, St Paul	stained-glass window	36	25 January 1921
Clacton-on-Sea Sunday School	garden of remembrance		
Clacton-on-Sea, Wesleyan Church Sunday School	statuary	216	6 April 1924
Clavering	obelisk	27	1921
Clavering Congregational Church	obelisk	28	2 May 1921
Clavering, St Mary and St Clement	tablet	28	
Cliff Town, United Reform Church	memorial hall and tablets	21	1925
Coggeshall	recreation ground		1920
Coggeshall	column and statuary	78	5 September 1920
Coggeshall, St Peter	tablet		17 March 1918
Coggeshall, St Peter	tablet	78	6 October 1920
Colchester	Avenue of Remembrance		1933
Colchester	Avenue of Remembrance, war memorial wall and plaques		1998
Colchester, All Saints	oak panelling	14	4 August 1920
Colchester, All Saints, Shrub End	tablet	17	
Colchester, Ancient Order of Foresters, Court Rangers, Court Room, Butt Road		11	28 March 1923
Colchester, Borough Cemetery[59]	cross	250	22 April 1923
Colchester, Borough War Memorial	statuary	1,248	24 May 1923
Colchester, Cavalry Barracks Square[60]	tablet and panels	206	24 July 1927
Colchester, Christ Church	cross	117	5 May 1921
Colchester, Cooperative Society, Restaurant	tablet	8	
Colchester, Eastern Counties Hospital[61]	hospital bed	1	April 1920
Colchester, Essex and Suffolk Insurance Company	oak doorway	10	15 November 1923
Colchester, Garrison Church[62]	banner		
Colchester, Goat and Boot public house[63]	tablet	34	12 October 1921

58 In memory of six servers at St James, all killed in the War.

59 Erected by the Imperial War Graves Commission, in memory of those men who died of their wounds in Colchester hospitals.

60 In memory of the Fallen of the Queen's Bays Regt.

61 Donated by Richard Hardy, estate agent, in memory of his clerk, Harold Doe, K.I.A. at Beaumont Hamel, 13 November 1916.

62 In memory of the Colchester branch of the Old Contemptibles.

63 In memory of the Fallen of the Court Royal, Ancient Order of Foresters.

Location	Type	Number of The "Fallen"	Date Unveiled/ Dedicated
Colchester, Head St post office	tablet	15	11 April 1920
Colchester, Head St post office, Maw Hall	panel	15	11 April 1920
Colchester, Holy Trinity	tablet	16	26 June 1921
Colchester, Lion Walk Congregational Church	tablets	21	17 October 1920
Colchester, Oddfellows Lodges, Oddfellows Hall	oak panels	106	14 July 1921
Colchester, Old Colcestrians	stone of remembrance and tablet	74	1 May 1924
Colchester, police station[64]	tablet	2	10 November 1995
Colchester, Royal Grammar School	swimming pool	74	5 July 1923
Colchester, Royal Grammar School	stained-glass window	70	
Colchester, St Barnabas	tablet	15	15 November 1925
Colchester, St Botolph	cross	77	10 October 1920
Colchester, St Botolph[65]	stained-glass window		
Colchester, St Botolph[66]	stained-glass window		
Colchester, St Giles[67]	tablet	82	10 September 1922
Colchester, St James the Great[68]	pedestal and memorial book	13,727	1 May 1925
Colchester, St James the Less	memorial chapel and brass gates		1920, 1921
Colchester, St James the Less	Pieta	50-60	December 1919
Colchester St James the Less[69]	tablet		
Colchester, St James the Less[70]	statue, the Virgin Mary		
Colchester, St James the Less[71]	tablet		
Colchester, St John the Evangelist	tablet	21	
Colchester, St Leonard	stained-glass window	80	8 February 1920
Colchester, St Martin	tablet	16	13 June 1920
Colchester, St Martin	war shrine		7 October 1917
Colchester, St Mary-at-the-Walls	memorial chapel	118	26 March 1922
Colchester, St Mary-at-the-Walls[72]	roll of honour	26	11 November 1920

[64] Dedicated to the fallen of the Colchester Constabulary.

[65] In memory of Capt. John B. Hawkins, Essex Regt, K.I.A. on 30 August 1916; Lt Col Arthur H. du Boulay, K.I.A. on 25 October 1918; also Lt Hubert L.H. du Boulay, Wiltshire Regt, K.I.A. on 3 September 1916.

[66] In memory of Edmund Le Spencer, Wiltshire Regt, K.I.A. in Flanders, 20 October 1914.

[67] Now used as the Masonic Hall.

[68] In memory of the Fallen of the 18th or Eastern Counties Division.

[69] In memory of Edward Kirwan, K.I.A. on 26 April 1915.

[70] In memory of prisoners of war from the Leinster Regt.

[71] Dedicated to the men of the Leinster Regt.

[72] In memory of the fallen of the Church Lads' Brigade.

APPENDIX: ESSEX MEMORIALS OF THE GREAT WAR

Location	Type	Number of The "Fallen"	Date Unveiled/ Dedicated
Colchester, St Mary Magdalene[73]	tablet		2 March 1920
Colchester, St Mary Magdalene	tablet, vestries, organ, chamber	53	16 September 1920
Colchester, St Nicholas	reredos	12	3 October 1920
Colchester, St Paul[74]	roll of honour	37	
Colchester, St Peter	tablet	37	31 August 1919
Colchester, St Stephen	oak shrine and tablet		12 June 1919
Colchester Scouts, St George's Club	tablet	26	9 December 1920
Colchester, Shrub End, All Saints	tablet	17	
Colchester, Shrub End, All Saints	cenotaph	17	
Colchester, Spottiswoode and Ballantyne and Company, Hythe	alabaster slab	17	1 May 1922
Colchester, Town Hall	roll of honour	1,248	
Colne Engaine, St Andrew	tablet	18	
Copford, St Michael and All Angels	oak panels	25	16 May 1920
Cornish Hall End, St John the Evangelist	cross	8	
Cornish Hall End, St John the Evangelist[75]	tablet		
Cressing, All Saints	cross	19	14 May 1921
Corringham, St Laurence	tablet	12	
Corringham St Laurence	screen and roll of honour	11	
Crowstone	stained-glass window and tablet	21	16 June 1926
Dagenham Heathway	obelisk		
Dagenham, Methodist Church[76]	tablet		
Dagenham, St Peter and St Paul	tablet	83	17 June 1920
Dagenham, St Peter and St Paul[77]	tablet		
Danbury	cross	24	31 July 1920
Debden	tablets	26	18 January 1920
Debden Chapel	tablet		
Dedham	cross	32	7 August 1921
Dedham, St Mary[78]	tablet		
Dengie	tablet	31	6 June 1920
Doddinghurst Church	tablet		13 April 1919
Dovercourt		187	August 1920

73 In memory of Charles E.C. Bashford, K.I.A. at Ypres on 25 May 1916.

74 St Paul's church building no longer exists. The roll of honour is on display in St James the Great, Colchester.

75 In memory of John W. Whitbread, 4th East Surrey Regt, K.I.A. at Ypres, 29 May 1915, aged twenty-five.

76 In memory of Charles W. Huxtable, died in the Dardanelles on 23 August 1915.

77 In memory of Basil F. Ward, K.I.A. in the Dardanelles on 18 August 1915.

78 In memory of Lt Guy J.H. Ashwin, killed on the Somme, 7 November 1916, aged twenty-two.

Location	Type	Number of The "Fallen"	Date Unveiled/ Dedicated
Dovercourt[79]	tablet		December 1915
Dovercourt, All Saints[80]	memorial stone		18 June 1920
Dovercourt	cross	130	4 August 1920
Dovercourt[81]	obelisk	187	December 1919
Downham	cross	15	1 May 1921
Downham	a nurse's home	15	
Dunmow	cenotaph	84	17 July 1921
Dunmow parish church	tablet	84	17 July 1921
Dunmow[82]	desk, book of the litany		12 November 1930
Dunmow, Philpot End Mission Hall	tablet	6	19 September 1920
Dunmow Priory	mural painting	7	22 September 1920
Dunmow Priory	recreation ground		
Dunmow Congregational Church	tablet	11	16 November 1919
Earls Colne	cross	38	5 June 1921
Earls Colne, Loyal Atlas Lodge Of Oddfellows	tablet		November 1922
Earls Colne, St Andrew	tablet	38	
Earls Colne, St Andrew[83]	tablet		
Earls Colne Grammar School	tablet	36	April 1922
East Horndon	cross	14	21 December 1923
Easthorpe, St Mary the Virgin	tablet	2	
Eastwood	memorial hall	26	8 February 1922
East Donyland	tablet	28	
East Ham	cenotaph	1,824	
East Ham Corporation, Town Hall	board	20	
East Ham, Liberal Club	tablet	102	
East Ham, Methodist Chapel	plaque		
East Ham Old Tramways Shed	tablet		
East Ham, Plashet Grove Baptist Church	tablet		
East Ham, St Mary	obelisk		
East Ham, United Synagogue	roll of honour	250	
East Ham, TAVR Centre[84]	tablets		

79 In memory of Basil M. Ward, Essex Regt, K.I.A. in the Dardanelles on 25 April 1915, aged twenty-seven.

80 Memorial to Charles Fryatt, captain of the S.S. *Brussels*, executed by the Germans on 27 July 1916.

81 Dedicated to the men who lost their lives in minesweeping operations in the Harwich area.

82 In memory of Capt. John C. Dick, K.I.A. at Ypres on 9 May 1915.

83 In memory of Frederick E. Bell, K.I.A. at Ypres on 13 May 1915.

84 In memory of the 281st and 291st Regts, R.F.A: No. 3 T.P. "D" Squadron, Essex Yeomanry; 2nd East Anglian Brigade, R.F.A.; 1st Essex Heavy Battery, R.G.A.; No. 2 Company, Essex and Suffolk R.G.A.; No. 2 Company, East Anglian R.A.S.C.

APPENDIX: ESSEX MEMORIALS OF THE GREAT WAR

Location	Type	Number of The "Fallen"	Date Unveiled/ Dedicated
East Ham, TAVR Centre[85]	tablet		
East Ham, TAVR Centre[86]	tablet		
East Hanningfield	cross	19	
East Horndon	cross	14	31 December 1922
East Mersea, St Edmund	tablet	5	
East Mersea, St Edmund[87]	tablet		
East Tilbury, Coalhouse Fort[88]	obelisk		
East Tilbury, Coalhouse Fort[89]	tablet		
East Tilbury, St Catherine	tablet	54	
East Tilbury, St Catherine[90]	church tower		
East Tilbury, St Catherine	roll of honour	54	
Eight Ash Green	tablet		
Elmstead Market	cross		2004
Elmstead Market[91]	tablet		November 1918
Elmstead Market, St Anne and St Lawrence	tablet	28	6 July 1919
Elmstead Market Wesleyan Chapel	tablet	28	6 July 1919
Elsenham	roadside calvary		
Elsenham, St Mary	tablet	25	
Elsenham, St Mary[92]	tablet		
Elsenham, St Mary	roll of honour	25	
Elsenham, St Mary[93]	tablet		
Epping	tablet	86	10 November 1922
Epping	cross	96	7 May 1921
Epping, All Saints[94]	tablet		
Epping Cooperative Hall[95]	roll of honour		
Epping United Reform Church[96]	cross		

85 Dedicated to the men of London.

86 Dedicated to the 281st and 291st Brigade, R.F.A.

87 In memory of Pte Alfred E. Russell, died in 1918.

88 Built by the Royal Artillery and Royal Engineers to commemorate the Great War.

89 In memory of the men who died in the Great War.

90 Erected by Number 2 Company, London Electrical Engineers, as a memorial to the men of the Coalhouse Fort who lost their lives in the War.

91 In memory of Lt Owen A.F. Allen, killed in an air collision in 1917.

92 Dedicated to William Lankester, died at Hooge, 20 July 1915.

93 In memory of L/Cpl George Woodley, Essex Regt, D.O.W. in France on 12 October 1917, aged twenty-five.

94 In memory of Flying Officer F.L. Collison, R.A.F., killed on flying duty at Kenley Aerodrome on 22 November 1916, aged twenty-eight.

95 In memory of the members of the Temple of Peace Lodge of Oddfellows.

96 In memory of Pte G.W.R. Church, Durham Light Infantry, K.I.A. on 29 August 1917.

Location	Type	Number of The "Fallen"	Date Unveiled/ Dedicated
Epping Upland	column and cross	17	25 May 1920
Epping Upland, All Saints	two screens	17	10 October 1920
Fairstead, St Mary	tablet	8	31 October 1920
Farnham	column	19	28 November 1920
Faulkbourne		5	
Feering, St Martin	tablets	13	6 January 1918
Feering	lychgate	13	6 January 1918
Feering[97]	tablet		17 October 1920
Felsted	tablet	45	27 February 1921
Felsted	village hall	45	
Felsted School	screen, classrooms, library and museum	241	June 1924
Felsted School	screen and stained-glass window	225	June 1921
Finchingfield	cross	27	27 June 1920
Fingringhoe, St Andrew	tablet	16	14 November 1920
Fingringhoe, St Andrew[98]	tablet		14 November 1920
Fingringhoe, St Andrew[99]	reredos		30 November 1920
Fobbing, St Michael	tablet	6	
Fordham	tablet	8	
Fordham	clock tower	18	12 October 1919
Fordham Congregational Church	tablet	8	14 December 1919
Ford End, St John	obelisk	20	
Foulness	tablet	7	
Foxearth, St Peter and St Paul	cross	12	31 January 1920
Frating	memorial hall and tablets	8	24 September 1922
Frinton	men's club and tablet	23	8 October 1921
Frinton Golf Club	tablet	14	20 July 1921
Fryerning[100]	tablet		
Fyfield, St Nicholas	stained-glass window	15	3 July 1919
Fyfield, St Nicholas	tablet		
Galleywood, St Michael & All Angels	tablet	10	
Gidea Park[101]	pavilion and tablet	12	15 October 1921
Goldhanger, St Peter	cross	16	
Goldhanger, St Peter[102]	memorial window		

97 In memory of Capt. Hugh E. Reid and Lt George P.N. Reid, the latter K.I.A. at Ypres on 13 May 1915.

98 In memory of Cpl Robert Page, killed in France on 3 May 1917.

99 In memory of Lt Daniel A. Green, killed near Beaumont Hamel on 13 November 1916.

100 In memory of Capt. Gordon Elton.

101 In memory of the employees of the Great Eastern Railway's Stores Department who died in the War.

102 In memory of Lt Cyril G. Gardner, killed on the Somme on 15 September 1916, aged nineteen.

APPENDIX: ESSEX MEMORIALS OF THE GREAT WAR

Location	Type	Number of The "Fallen"	Date Unveiled/ Dedicated
Goodmayes, All Saints[103]	tablet		
Goodmayes, St Paul	cross		
Goodmayes Congregational Church	roll of honour		
Good Easter, St Andrew[104]	tablet		
Good Easter, St Andrew	tablet	13	1919
Good Easter, St Andrew	cross	13	
Grays	pillar	301	6 March 1921
Greenstead, St John Payne	tablet		
Greenstead, St John Payne	tree or avenue		
Great Baddow[105]	church clock	30	7 June 1920
Great Bardfield	cross		31 October 1921
Great Bentley	column	31	December 1919
Great Bentley School	tablet		
Great Braxted & Wickham Bishops[106]	column	22	
Great Braxted, All Saints	altar and reredos		23 February 1920
Great Braxted, All Saints	tablet	6	2 March 1920
Great Bromley	cross	19	14 September 1919
Great Bromley, St George	tablet	20	
Great Chesterford Congregational Church	tablet	2	4 July 1920
Great Chishill	obelisk	13	
Great Clacton School Board	tablet	156	September 1919
Great Clacton, St John the Baptist[107]	tablet	81	
Great Easton	column		1 May 1915
Great Holland	tablet	20	26 October 1919
Great Holland[108]	tablet		13 April 1919
Great Holland	drinking fountain	20	23 March 1919
Great Holland, All Saints	stained-glass windows	20	11 April 1920
Great Horkesley, All Saints	cross		24 October 1920
Great Horkesley, All Saints[109]	tablet		
Great Horkesley, All Saints[110]	tablet & lecturn		

[103] In memory of Lt Leonard S. Ling, K.I.A. at Avion, France, on 23 April 1917.

[104] In memory of Lt Harry W. Mann, 178th R.F.A., K.I.A. 30 March 1918.

[105] In memory of Maj. Harold Smithers.

[106] Dedicated to the Fallen of both villages; also to the memory of Lt Charles O. Wilson, Essex Regt, K.I.A. at Gaza, Palestine, 6 March 1917.

[107] Dedicated to the men of both Great Clacton and Little Holland.

[108] In memory of Lt Charles H. Hicks, 8th Sherwood Foresters, killed in France on 21 July 1918.

[109] In memory of Cpl Thompson Allen, Essex Yeomanry, K.I.A. 13 May 1915, at Ypres, aged twenty-one.

[110] In memory of Lt Arthur H. Page, Suffolk Regt, K.I.A. at Longueval, on the Somme, 19 July 1916, aged twenty-five.

Location	Type	Number of The "Fallen"	Date Unveiled/ Dedicated
Great Horkesley, St John	tablet	16	24 October 1920
Great Leighs	tablet	19	12 December 1920
Great Maplestead, St Giles	tablet	7	
Great Maplestead, St Giles[111]	tablet		
Great Oakley	cenotaph	25	31 January 1920
Great Oakley, All Saints	tablet	24	
Great Oakley, All Saints[112]	brass plate		
Great Parndon, St Mary the Virgin	cross	9	30 May 1920
Great Parndon, St Mary the Virgin	tablet	9	1920
Great Sampford	tablet	5	May 1920
Great Stambridge	memorial hall		8 January 1922
Great Stambridge	tablet	7	31 January 1920
Great Stambridge[113]	tablet		31 January 1920
Great Tey, St Barnabas	lych gate	18	7 August 1921
Great Totham, St Peter	tablet	14	
Great Totham, St Peter[114]	tablet		
Great Wakering	memorial hall and cross		26 January 1921
Great Wakering[115]	processional cross		June 1918
Great Wakering	cross	45	6 May 1921
Great Wakering, St Nicholas	cross (temporary)		11 November 1917
Great Wakering, St Nicholas	organ	45	2 April 1920
Great Wakering, St Nicholas	triptych	48	
Great Wakering, St Nicholas[116]	tablet		
Great Wakering Congregational Church	tablet		
Great Wakering Methodist Church	organ	28	6 July 1919
Great Wakering United Reform Church	tablet	16	
Great Waltham	cross	36	19 December 1920
Great Waltham, St Mary & St Lawrence	tablet	35	12 December 1920
Great Waltham, St Mary & St Lawrence[117]	tablet		
Great Warley, Christ Church	tablet	c.100	13 June 1920
Great Warley, St Mary	reredos		

[111] In memory of Lt Charles A. Sperling, R.N., K.I.A. at Jutland, 1 June 1916, aged twenty-four.

[112] In memory of Lt Claude L. Harvey, K.I.A. near La Fere, France, on 23 March 1916.

[113] In memory of Col Frank Hilder.

[114] In memory of Capt. Roger D'Arcy Whittaker, Royal Somerset Regt, K.I.A. at Richebourge L'Avoue, 30 June 1916.

[115] In memory of Ernest Barton.

[116] In memory of Edward P.W. Wedd, K.I.A. on 13 July 1918.

[117] In memory of Lt Hugh G. Muschamp Vickers, Indian Cavalry, K.I.A. in Mesopotamia on 30 October 1918.

APPENDIX: ESSEX MEMORIALS OF THE GREAT WAR

Location	Type	Number of The "Fallen"	Date Unveiled/ Dedicated
Great Warley	cross	26	14 November 1920
Great and Little Wigborough, St Stephen and St Nicholas	tablet	9	
Greenstead, St Andrew	tablet	37	14 December 1919
Hadleigh	cenotaph	49	15 October 1922
Hadleigh Methodist Church	roll of honour	13	
Hadleigh Methodist Church	board	50	
Hadleigh, St James the Less	tablet	49	
Hadleigh, St James the Less[118]	tablet		
Hadleigh, St James the Less[119]	altar rail		
Hadleigh, St James the Less[120]	addition to gravestone		
Hadleigh, St James the Less[121]	addition to gravestone		
Hadleigh, St James the Less[122]	addition to gravestone		
Hadleigh, St James the Less[123]	addition to gravestone		
Hadleigh, St James the Less[124]	addition to gravestone		
Hadleigh, St James the Less[125]			
Hadleigh, St James the Less[126]	addition to gravestone		
Hadleigh, St James the Less[127]			
Hadleigh, St James the Less[128]	addition to gravestone		
Hadleigh, St James the Less[129]	addition to gravestone		
Hadleigh, St James the Less[130]			
Hadstock	tablet	18	27 June 1920
Halstead	cross	145	8 May 1920
Halstead, Holy Trinity	lady chapel	145	15 October 1922
Halstead, Holy Trinity[131]	screen, altar, dorsal, chandelier		15 October 1922

118 In memory of Stanley A. Haves, Royal Sussex Regt, M.I.A. at Ypres on 26 September 1917, aged nineteen.

119 Given as a "fervent thanksgiving" for Britain's victory.

120 In memory of Bombardier Sidney C. Allen, died in Carisbrooke Military Hospital on 24 April 1918, aged twenty-four.

121 In memory of Cpl James E. Allen, died on 8 April 1919, aged twenty-two.

122 In memory of Pte S.C. Staines, Coldstream Guards, died on 16 April 1916, aged twenty-two.

123 In memory of Cpl W.J. Staines, K.I.A. on 22 June 1917, aged twenty-six.

124 In memory of Bombardier A. Staines, K.I.A. on 14 August 1917, aged twenty.

125 In memory of John French, drowned on H.M.S. *Formidable* on 1 January 1915, aged thirty-eight.

126 In memory of J.O. Spencer Baldwin. Died on 1 June 1921 "from injuries received in France", aged twenty-two.

127 In memory of Pte William Cowell, died in France on 17 December 1915, aged nineteen.

128 In memory of Pte Richard Cowell, died on 9 November 1918, aged twenty-six.

129 In memory of Lt Alec Charlesworth, Leicestershire Regt, died on 7 February 1917, aged twenty-one.

130 In memory of John Bush, K.I.A. in France on 25 October 1916.

131 In memory of Lt Col Edmund Deacon, K.I.A. at Ypres on 13 May 1915.

Location	Type	Number of The "Fallen"	Date Unveiled/ Dedicated
Halstead, Holy Trinity[132]	stained-glass window		15 October 1922
Halstead, Loyal Courtauld Lodge of Oddfellows	tablet	12	21 March 1921
Halstead railway station[133]	tablet	4	20 November 1920
Halstead, St Andrew	tablet	8	
Halstead, St Francis of Assisi[134]	window		
Harlow, St Mary & St Hugh	cross	74	11 April 1920
Harlow, St Mary & St Hugh	roll of honour		
Harlow, St Mary & St Hugh[135]	addition to gravestone		
Harlow	memorial institute and tablet	74	8 December 1920
Harlow[136]	addition to gravestone		
Harlow Baptist Chapel	reredos	74	9 January 1921
Harlow College	tablet	33	
Harlow, Independent Order of Oddfellows	tablet	40	
Harlow Methodist Chapel		74	6 February 1921
Harlow, St John	tablet		
Harlow St Mary and St Hugh[137]	tablet		
Harlow, St Mary at Latton	roll of honour	2	
Harold Hill	stone of remembrance		
Harold Wood Memorial Hall	roll of honour		
Harold Wood	Memorial Institute	26	15 November 1919
Harwich	column		16 December 1919
Harwich	crucifix		July 1917
Harwich, Harwich Redoubt[138]	tablet	6	
Harwich, St Nicholas	chapel, clock chimes and tablet	133	3 August 1920
Harwich, St Nicholas[139]	tablet		
Harwich, St Nicholas[140]	tablet		

[132] In memory of Capt. Allen P. Adams, K.I.A. in Mesopotamia, 1919.

[133] In memory of the men of the Colne Valley Railway Company.

[134] In memory of the men of the Devonshire Regt.

[135] In memory of James A. Bailey, 11th Royal Fusiliers, K.I.A. in France, 17 February 1917, aged thirty.

[136] In memory of Thomas W. Riley, Essex Regt, died at Malta, September 1915; also of Pte Cecil P. Riley, 5th Batt., East Kent Regt, killed in Mesopotamia, May 1915.

[137] In memory of Lt Alexander G. Swire, Essex Yeomanry, K.I.A. at Potije, Flanders, 13 May 1915, aged eighteen.

[138] In memory of the men of the Harwich, Dovercourt and Parkeston Cooperative Society.

[139] In memory of the men of the 3rd Battalion, Essex Regt, (Essex Rifles).

[140] Dedicated to Thomas J. Denney, 11th Essex R.H.A., who died at Le Havre on his way home for dispersal, 11 March 1919, aged twenty-six.

APPENDIX: ESSEX MEMORIALS OF THE GREAT WAR

Location	Type	Number of The "Fallen"	Date Unveiled/ Dedicated
Harwich, St Nicholas[141]	tablet		
Harwich, St Nicholas[142]	tablet		
Harwich, St Nicholas[143]	scroll		
Harwich, St Nicholas[144]	tablet		
Harwich, St Nicholas[145]	tablet		
Harwich, Trinity House Pilots[146]	tablet	12	21 April 1920
Hatfield Broad Oak St Mary the Virgin	tablet		November 1917
Hatfield Broad Oak[147] St Mary the Virgin	tablet		1917
Hatfield Heath			14 March 1920
Hatfield Peverel	tablet	25	1 August 1920
Hawkwell	stained-glass windows and tablet	7	14 December 1919
Helions Bumpstead, St Andrew	tablet	16	22 April 1920
Hempstead	cross	14	4 July 1925
Henham	cairn	15	6 March 1921
Henham, St Mary the Virgin	tablet	21	March/April 1920
Heybridge	cross	35	10 July 1921
Heybridge Basin, Congregational Chapel	tablet		
Heydon, Holy Trinity	tablet	7	
High Beech	tablet	17	1 June 1919
High Easter	cross	21	31 July 1920
High Ongar, St Mary	obelisk	35	26 July 1921
High Roding	tablet	9	
Highams Park, United Reform Church			
Highwood	tablet and cross	11	
Hockerill, All Saints	tablet		2 January 1921
Hockley	tablet	29	23 May 1920
Hornchurch	cross	290	27 March 1921

141 In memory of Victor Keeble, lost on H.M.S. *Princess Irene* on 27 May 1915, aged twenty-eight; also of William J. Youngs, reported missing 15 October 1916, aged twenty-one.

142 In memory of Sub Lt George M. Paterson, Royal Australian Navy, K.I.A. on board H.M.S. *Defence* at Jutland 31 May 1916 aged twenty-one.

143 In memory of Stoker James Coleman, H.M. Submarine E20.

144 In memory of Pte Lance Bridge, killed in Gallipoli in 1916 aged twenty-eight; also Cpl Hugh D. Bridge, killed in France in 1917, aged twenty-eight.

145 In memory of Sgt Harry G. Gould, K.I.A. on 19 September 1917, aged twenty-four.

146 In memory of the twelve North Channel pilots who lost their lives.

147 In memory of Herbert A. Potter, Surgeon-Probationer, R.N.V.R., and student of the Royal Dental and Middlesex Hospitals, K.I.A. on H.M.S. *Contest* on 19 September 1917.

Location	Type	Number of The "Fallen"	Date Unveiled/ Dedicated
Hornchurch	war memorial institute	26	15 November 1919
Hornchurch[148]	tablet		18 November 1922
Hornchurch, Cornwell Cottages			
Hornchurch, Congregational Church	tablet	6	30 May 1920
Hornchurch, Holy Cross[149]	stained-glass window		
Hornchurch, Holy Cross[150]	font ewer		
Hornchurch, Holy Cross	book of remembrance		
Hornchurch, Holy Cross[151]			
Hornchurch, North Street Baptist Church	tablet and organ	5	20, 30 November 1919
Hornchurch, Royal Britannic Lodge	roll of honour	26	March 1921
Hornchurch, St Andrew	cross	212	27 March 1921
Horndon-on-the-Hill	cross	17	
Horsley Cross, St John	roll of honour		
Horsley Cross, St John[152]	tablet		
Horsley Cross, St John[153]	tablet		
Hutton, All Saints	tablet	27	13 June 1920
Ilford	statue	1,142	11 November 1922
Ilford Baptist Church	tablet	16	
Ilford Baptist Church[154]	organ		
Ilford (Barkingside), Holy Trinity	tablet	90	
Ilford, Buckingham Road Cemetery[155]	addition to gravestone		
Ilford, Buckingham Road Cemetery[156]	addition to gravestone		
Ilford, Buckingham Road Cemetery	cross of sacrifice	13	
Ilford, Buckingham Road Cemetery Chapel[157]	tablet	22	
Ilford, Buckingham Road Cemetery[158]	addition to gravestone		

148 In memory of the 23rd Royal Fusiliers "Sportsmens" Battalion.

149 In memory of Lt Ernest S. Cailes, The Buffs, K.I.A. on 14 June 1917.

150 In memory of George F. White, K.I.A. on 3 October 1918.

151 In memory of Fleet Surgeon W.J. Bearblock, K.I.A. aboard H.M.S. *Invincible* at Jutland in 1916.

152 In memory of Harold Ainger, drowned on H.M.S. *Hawke* on 15 October 1914.

153 In memory of William S. Souter, died 30 May 1915 at Gallipoli; also Wilfred Ainger on 28 March 1917 in Palestine; also Bertram G. Carr on 18 July 1916 in France; also Ernest W. Carr on 26 March 1917 in Palestine; also William Laflin on 17 May 1917 in France.

154 Dedicated as a thanks offering for peace and to the congregation.

155 In memory of Edgar Thomas, K.I.A. on 4 April 1918, aged thirty.

156 In memory of Frederick Thomas, K.I.A. on 22 October 1917, aged twenty-eight.

157 In memory of the men of Howards and Sons.

158 Dedicated to Lt James Battle, K.I.A. in France on 23 April 1917, aged twenty-two.

APPENDIX: ESSEX MEMORIALS OF THE GREAT WAR

Location	Type	Number of The "Fallen"	Date Unveiled/ Dedicated
Ilford, Bus Company offices[159]	tablet	11	
Ilford County High School	tablet	140	9 December 1921
Ilford County High School	memorial book		
Ilford Football Club	roll of honour	4	
Ilford, Gants Hill Congregational Church	tablet		
Ilford, King George Hospital	gardens & statuary		11 November 1922
Ilford, National County and Parrs Bank	tablet	1	
Ilford, private home[160]	roll of honour		
Ilford, Presbyterian Church	tablet	19	1919
Ilford, Redbridge Central Library	roll of honour		
Ilford, St Alban the Martyr	stained-glass window		1922
Ilford, St Alban the Martyr[161]	stained-glass window		
Ilford, St Andrew[162]	tablet	19	
Ilford, St Andrew[163]	stained-glass window		
Ilford, St Andrew[164]	stained-glass windows		
Ilford, St Clement[165]	cross		
Ilford, St Clement	stained-glass window and screen	260	
Ilford, St Luke[166]	statuary		
Ilford, St Luke[167]	crest		
Ilford, St Luke[168]	crest		
Ilford, St Luke[169]	crest		
Ilford, St Luke[170]	crest		
Ilford, St Luke[171]	crest		
Ilford, St Luke[172]	badge		

[159] In memory of Walthamstow Tramway Employees.

[160] In memory of the Merrymeeters.

[161] In memory of Lt Samuel R. Dudley, R.A.M.C., died on 21 December 1915.

[162] Dedicated to the men of the church.

[163] In memory of Stanley J.D. Curnow.

[164] In memory of Capt. Horace E. Griggs, Essex Regt, K.I.A. near Loos on 5 October 1916.

[165] In memory of Lt Herbert M. Beck, R.F.C., K.I.A. on 22 January 1918.

[166] In memory of William J.H. Pain, killed at Messines in 1917.

[167] Dedicated to L/Sgt A.I. Jupp, Cambridgeshire Regt, died 24 September 1918, aged twenty-one.

[168] Dedicated to P.A. Gibbons, killed at Ypres in 1915.

[169] Dedicated to Harold E. Jones, killed at Albert in 1916.

[170] Dedicated to A.L. Gibbons, Essex Regt.

[171] Dedicated to Benjamin H. Halls, killed at Salonika in 1918.

[172] Dedicated to K.C. Harvey George, killed in 1917.

Location	Type	Number of The "Fallen"	Date Unveiled/ Dedicated
Ilford, St Luke[173]	carved stone		
Ilford, St Luke[174]	carved stone		
Ilford, St Margaret of Antioch[175]	tablet	78	
Ilford, St Mary the Virgin[176]			
Ilford, St Mary and St Thomas Hospital Chapel	chapel, roll of honour		1922
Ilford, St Mary and St Thomas Hospital Chapel[177]	aumbry		
Ilford, St Mary and St Thomas Hospital Chapel[178]	tablet		
Ilford, St Mary a St Thomas Hospital Chapel[179]	choir vestries and tablet		
Ilford, St Mary the Virgin[180]			
Ilford, St Mary the Virgin[181]	painting		
Ilford, St Peter and St Paul[182]	tablets	46	
Ilford, St Peter and St Paul[183]	stained-glass window		
Ilford, South Park Junior School[184]	tablet	9	
Ilford, South Park Swimming Club	cup	9	
Ilford, Valentine's Mission[185]	tablet		
Ilford, Valentines Park[186]	shelter & tablet		
Ilford, Wycliffe Congregational Church	roll of honour	22	
Ingatestone	calvary		27 December 1920
Ingatestone[187]	tablet		25 April 1920
Ingatestone Congregational Church	memorial brass		25 May 1920
Ingatestone, St Mary	tablet	75	5 September 1920
Ingatestone, St Mary[188]	tablet		

173 Dedicated to Sgt Walter Fox, killed at Gaza in 1917.

174 Dedicated to E.W. Gulliver, killed in the Holy Land in 1917.

175 Dedicated to the Old Boys of Christchurch School.

176 In memory of the men of the 4th Battalion, Essex Regt, Ilford company.

177 In memory of Lt W.J. Carter, K.I.A. on 21 September 1918, aged thirty-three.

178 Dedicated to Edward W. Smith, assumed killed at Gallipoli on 4 June 1915, aged twenty-seven.

179 In memory of Lt Osborne Montague, K.I.A. at Bucquay on 25 August 1918.

180 In memory of the men of the 4th Battalion, Essex Regt (Ilford Co.).

181 In memory of the men of the 5th Battalion, Essex Volunteer Regt.

182 In memory of the parishioners who died during the War.

183 In memory of O.P. Clarke, K.I.A. in September 1918.

184 Dedicated to the Masters and Old Boys who died in the War.

185 In memory of Belgian refugees who stayed in the area from November 1914 - April 1919.

186 In memory of Cpl H. Cowlin, K.I.A. 1 July 1916; erected by the Ilford Chamber of Commerce.

187 In memory of all the Fallen from the Church and Mission.

188 In memory of Algernon Wood, K.I.A. at Gallipoli.

APPENDIX: ESSEX MEMORIALS OF THE GREAT WAR

Location	Type	Number of The "Fallen"	Date Unveiled/ Dedicated
Ingatestone, St Mary	stone memorial		2006
Ingrave	lych gate and tablets		August 1922
Inworth, All Saints	tablet	6	
Inworth, All Saints[189]	tablet		
Inworth, All Saints[190]	tablet		
Kelvedon	tablet	11	16 November 1920
Kelvedon[191]	tablet		
Kelvedon	cross	47	20 February 1921
Kelvedon Congregational Church	tablet	5	16 November 1919
Kelvedon Easterford, St Mary[192]	screen		
Kelvedon Hatch	obelisk	6	28 August 1920
Kirby Cross	memorial board	34	
Kirby-le-Soken parish church	memorial board	34	
Kirby-le-Soken[193]	tablet		December 1918
Kirby-le-Soken	tablet	31	11 April 1920
Kirby-le-Soken	cross	34	17 July 1921
Kirby-le-Soken Primitive Methodist Chapel[194]	tablet		4 April 1920
Lamarsh, Holy Innocents	tablet	9	
Langford, St Giles	cross	10	29 June 1919
Langham Primary School	gate of honour	19	23 October 1921
Langham, St Mary	tablet	20	
Langholm, St Mary	tablet	25	
Langholm, St Mary[195]	tablet		
Latchingdon church	tablet	5	12 March 1920
Latton and Potter Street	stone	30	23 May 1920
Latton and Potter Street	cross	31	30 May 1920
Layer-de-la-Haye	cross	27	1921
Layer-de-la-Haye, St John the Baptist	tablet	27	
Layer Marney, St Mary the Virgin	tablet	14	
Lawford	cenotaph	7	7 November 1920
Leaden Roding, St Michael[196]	tablet		

[189] In memory of Lt Aubrey F.W. Dickenson, Bedford Rifles, attached to the Royal Irish Rifles, K.I.A. at Ypres, 9 May 1915.

[190] In memory of Capt. Robert G. Worman, died 18 January 1919.

[191] In memory of Richard Galpin, drowned on the troopship *Aragon*, December 1917, aged eighteen.

[192] In memory of Lt Col Harry Wrightson, Essex R.A.S.C.

[193] In memory of Lt David. R.C. Lloyd, R.F.C., K.I.A. on 16 June 1917, aged twenty.

[194] In memory of George F. Grimsey, killed in a munitions works explosion on 14 September 1916; also Bert Grimsey, K.I.A. in France on 27 April 1917.

[195] Dedicated to Lt Harold E. Haddon, the Mooltan Regt, K.I.A. at Kut, Mesopotamia, 24 December 1915, aged twenty-six.

[196] In memory of Ernest Pavitt, Essex Regt, K.I.A. at Gaza, 26 March 1917, aged twenty.

Location	Type	Number of The "Fallen"	Date Unveiled/ Dedicated
Leigh-on-Sea Baptist Chapel	tablet	3	6 June 1920
Leigh-on-Sea, St Clement	calvary and memorial Screen	60	24 August 1921
Leigh-on-Sea, St Clement	chapel	64	24 August 1921
Leigh-on-Sea, St Clement[197]	altar		
Leigh-on-Sea, St Margaret[198]	font		1920
Leigh-on-Sea, Wesleyan Chapel	stained-glass window and board	20	14 April 1920
Lexden	war shrine		7 October 1917
Lexden	cross	37	17 July 1920
Lexden, St Leonard[199]	stained-glass window		11 July 1920
Leyton	fountain and tablet		
Leyton, Emmanuel parish church	obelisk		
Leyton, All Saints[200]	tablet		
Leyton Bus Garage			
Leyton, Cann Hall Road School[201]	tablet		
Leyton, Cann Hall and Harrow Green Baptist Church	tablet	14	
Leyton, Central Library[202]	tablet		
Leyton, County High School	tablet	68	
Leyton, Eton Manor			
Leyton, Farmer Road School	tablet		
Leyton, Goodall Road School	tablet		
Leyton, Newport Road School			
Leyton, postal sorting office	tablet	7	
Leyton, St Andrew	tablet		
Leyton, St Patrick's cemetery			
Leytonstone, Davies Lane Primary School	tablet	80	
Leytonstone, Downsell Road Junior School			
Leytonsone Fire Station[203]	tablet	3	
Leytonstone Football Club[204]	tablet	18	11 June 1922
Leytonstone, Harrow Green			

[197] In memory of Robert C. Joslin, died when H.M.S. *Marmion* sank on 21 October 1917.

[198] Donated by a parishioner as a thank offering for a safe return from the War.

[199] In memory of Lt Roderick H. Gray, R.H.A., D.O.W. on 2 December 1917.

[200] In memory of Jack Cornwell, V.C., mortally wounded on H.M.S. *Chester* and D.O.W. on 2 June 1916.

[201] In memory of the old boys of the school.

[202] In memory of the old boys of Leyton schools.

[203] In memory of those of the Leyton Fire Brigade.

[204] In memory of the club's former players.

APPENDIX: ESSEX MEMORIALS OF THE GREAT WAR

Location	Type	Number of The "Fallen"	Date Unveiled/ Dedicated
Leytonstone, Holy Trinity	tablet	16	
Leytonstone, Mayville Road School	tablet	80	
Leytonstone Methodist Church	scroll and tablet	31	
Leytonstone Methodist Church[205]	plaque		
Leytonstone, postal sorting office	tablet	10	
Leytonstone, St John	tablet		
Leytonstone, St John	roll of honour		
Leytonstone, St Margaret	war shrine	32	
Leytonstone, St Mary the Virgin[206]	stained-glass window		
Leytonstone, St Mary the Virgin[207]	stained-glass window		
Leytonstone, Tom Hood School			
Leytonstone, Trumpington Road School	tablet		
Leytonstone, Whipps Cross Hospital Chapel	tablet	3	
Littlebury	column		17 October 1920
Little Baddow	memorial hall and gate	17	14 January 1922
Little Baddow, St Mary the Virgin	tablet	15	20 June 1920
Little Baddow, St Mary the Virgin[208]	tablet		
Little Baddow, St Mary the Virgin[209]	tablet		
Little Bardfield	tablet	12	11 June 1922
Little Bentley church	tablet	11	2 May 1920
Little Braxted			
Little Burstead	cross	8	18 June 1921
Little Clacton	memorial stone	17	May 1919
Little Clacton, Wesleyan Chapel	column	17	18 April 1920
Little Clacton[210]	memorial window		June 1916
Little Clacton	tablet	17	18 April 1919
Little Dunmow	painting of a memorial	7	
Little Dunmow	painted roll of honour	17	
Little Easton	cenotaph	5	11 September 1921
Little Hallingbury	tablet	33	
Little Hallingbury	cross	33	
Little Horkesley	cross	9	30 May 1920
Little Horkesley, St Peter and St Paul	tablet	9	

205 In memory of Gnr Henry J. Stanton, 291 Brigade, R.F.A., died at Camiers, 3 December 1918.

206 In memory of the fallen of the Boys' Brigade, South Essex Company.

207 In memory of the Rev. John Badenoch, died 11 July 1917, at Baska.

208 In memory of Ft Sub-Lt Mosley G. Woodhouse, R.N., K.I.A. over Flanders 9 August 1917, aged eighteen.

209 In memory of Capt. Lionel M. Woodhouse, R.A.F., K.I.A. in France on 27 September 1918, aged twenty-one.

210 In memory of Charles S. Nicholson, killed on the Somme in September 1916.

Location	Type	Number of The "Fallen"	Date Unveiled/ Dedicated
Little Horkesley, St Peter and St Paul	cross	10	30 May 1920
Little Ilford[211]			September 1922
Little Leighs, St John the Baptist	triptych		22 April 1917
Little Leighs, St John the Evangelist	tablet	12	10 October 1920
Little Maplestead, St John the Baptist	tablet	3	5 September 1920
Little Oakley (see under Ramsey)			
Little Saling, St Peter & St Paul	board	7	
Little Sampford, St Mary the Virgin	tablet	7	December 1924
Little Thurrock	cross	48	
Little Totham, All Saints[212]	memorial window		
Little Wakering	triptych	14	
Little Wakering	triptych/roll of honour	9	November 1936
Little Waltham	cross	23	30 May 1920
Little Waltham	tablet	22	
Little Warley, Essex Regimental Church[213]	tablet	3,429	28 May 1921
Little Warley, Essex Regimental Church[214]	memorial windows		1931
Little Warley, Essex Regimental Church[215]	screen		1932
Little Warley, Essex Regimental Church	pulpit		
Little Warley, Essex Regimental Church[216]	door		
Little Warley, Essex Regimental Church[217]	desk and roll of honour	1,000	21 July 1929
Little Yeldham, St John the Baptist	tablet	9	
Loughton	cross	92	24 June 1920
Loughton, Lincoln Hall[218]	tablet		1 August 1920
Maldon	cross	144	8 May 1921
Maldon	Avenue of Remembrance	144	
Maldon, All Saints[219]	stained-glass window		

[211] In memory of the men of Leyton and the Essex Regt.

[212] In memory of John S. Wakelin, K.I.A. in France on 24 March 1918, aged twenty-five.

[213] In memory of the Fallen of the Essex Regt.

[214] In memory of the men of the 10th Essex Regt, Colchester.

[215] In memory of the men of the Ancient Order of Buffaloes.

[216] In memory of the men of Ilford.

[217] In memory of the men of the 11th Essex Regt.

[218] In memory of the men of the Loughton Brotherhood.

[219] In memory of Lt Cecil D. Bright, killed in Mesopotamia on 22 March 1918.

APPENDIX: ESSEX MEMORIALS OF THE GREAT WAR

Location	Type	Number of The "Fallen"	Date Unveiled/ Dedicated
Maldon All Saints[220]	tablet		1 August 1920
Maldon, Baptist Chapel	tablet	12	21 September 1919
Maldon Council School[221]	tablet		21 June 1922
Manningtree	cross	47	11 June 1919
Manningtree, St Michael	oak shrine		1 July 1923
Manuden	stone of remembrance	18	25 September 1921
Margaret Roding	village hut		
Margaret Roding, St Margaret of Antioch	stained-glass window & tablet		11 August 1920
Margaretting	cross	14	2 October 1920
Margaretting	screen	14	2 October 1920
Marks Tey, St Andrew	obelisk	17	23 January 1921
Marks Tey, St Andrew	tablet	17	
Mashbury[222]	book rest and plaque	7	
Matching	cross	20	26 September 1920
Mayland, St Barnabas	stained-glass window and tablet	11	9 September 1920
Messing	cross	23	13 June 1920
Messing, All Saints[223]	tablet		
Messing, All Saints[224]	tablet		
Middleton, St Peter's Roman Catholic Church	altar and stained-glass window		13 December 1925
Mistley	cross	60	16 January 1921
Mistley Primitive Methodist Church	roll of honour	7	9 April 1920
Moreton	cross	13	1920
Moulsham, St John	cross		7 November 1920
Moulsham, St John[225]	clergy stall		7 November 1920
Mountnessing, St Giles	cross	16	13 June 1920
Mucking, St John		21	
Myland	cross	44	2 January 1921
Navestock, St Mary the Virgin	tablet	25	
Nazeing, All Saints	roll of honour	29	
Nazeing, All Saints	memorial board	29	
Nazeing, All Saints	lych gate	28	
Nazeing, Congregational Church	tablet	29	

220 In memory of Capt. Frederick W. Grantham, Royal Munster Fusiliers, K.I.A. at Richebourg l'Avoue on 9 May 1915, and his son, Hugo F. Grantham, Essex Regt, killed at Gallipoli on 28 June 1915.

221 In memory of the Headmaster, F.W. Moss, and the scholars of Maldon British and Council Schools.

222 Now located in St Nicholas, Chignal Smealy.

223 In memory of Sidney C. Fairhead, Essex Yeomanry, K.I.A. at Ypres on 13 May 1915.

224 In memory of Ralph S. Blyth, K.I.A. at Monchy, 14 April 1917.

225 In memory of Stanley E. Darby, who died in 1915, and Harold E. Darby, who died in 1916.

Location	Type	Number of The "Fallen"	Date Unveiled/ Dedicated
Nettleswell and Burnt Mill	cross	13	1 February 1920
Nevendon	shell-case		
Newland, St Laurence	plaque/roll of honour	3	
Newport	cross	41	12 May 1920
Noak Hill, St Thomas	tablet		
North Benfleet	stained-glass window		8 February 1920
North Fambridge	roll of honour	18	
North Fambridge	cross	16	
North Ockendon, St Mary Magdalene	tablet	21	
North Stifford, St Mary the Virgin	cenotaph	30	
North Weald	cross	34	2 July 1920
Ongar, Congregational Church	Sunday School		14 April 1920
Ongar Hospital		313	
Ongar	roll of honour	313	
Orsett	column	41	20 March 1921
Otten Belchamp	cross	6	16 January 1921
Paglesham	roll of honour	10	
Paglesham	tablet	10	
Panfield, St Mary and St Christopher	roll of honour	10	19 November 1922
Panfield St Mary and St Christopher	tablet	10	19 November 1922
Parkeston	war shrine		27 October 1917
Pebmarsh	stained-glass window	12	6 March 1920
Pebmarsh	cross	12	
Peldon, St Mary	tablet	8	
Peldon, St Mary	roll of honour		
Peldon, St Mary the Virgin	tablet	8	8 April 1920
Peldon, St Mary the Virgin	roll of honour	92	April 1919
Pentlow	stained-glass window and tablet		13 March 1920
Pitsea and Bowers Gifford	statuary		17 November 1928
Plaistow	YMCA, swimming pool, theatre, lounge, restaurant		
Plaistow, Baptist Church[226]	tablet		
Plaistow, Baptist Church[227]	tablet		
Plaistow, Baptist Church[228]	tablet		
Plaistow, Baptist Church[229]	tablet		
Plaistow, Baptist Memorial Church	church, bells and bell tower		16 June 1921
Plaistow, East London Cemetery Chapel	chapel, tablets	230	

[226] In memory of John P. Bourne, K.I.A. in France on 26 May 1918.

[227] In memory of Lt Robert A. Edwards, West Yorks Regt, K.I.A. in Flanders on 14 July 1918.

[228] In memory of Capt. F.J. Poulton, K.I.A. at Gaza on 2 November 1917.

[229] In memory of William M. Bardsley, K.I.A. on 13 November 1916.

APPENDIX: ESSEX MEMORIALS OF THE GREAT WAR

Location	Type	Number of The "Fallen"	Date Unveiled/ Dedicated
Plaistow, East London Cemetery	cross		
Plaistow, East London Cemetery[230]	wall	126	
Plaistow, East London Cemetery	cross of sacrifice	94	
Plaistow, New City Road School	tablet	45	
Plaistow, St Mary	pulpit and tablet	136	
Pleshey, Holy Trinity	cross	9	
Prittlewell	stained-glass window and cross	230	16 December 1922
Prittlewell	cross	1,338	16 February 1922
Prittlewell, All Saints	cross	102	
Prittlewell, All Saints[231]	wooden grave marker		
Prittlewell, All Saints[232]			
Prittlewell, All Saints	remembrance book		
Prittlewell, All Saints Mission Church	unknown		
Prittlewell Priory Park	drinking fountain		
Prittlewell Priory Refectory[233]			
Prittlewell, St Francis	mission church		
Prittlewell, St Mary the Virgin	tablet and roll of honour	225	16 December 1922
Prittlewell, St Mary the Virgin[234]	flag and board		21 September 1919
Prittlewell, St Mary the Virgin[235]	stained-glass window		
Prittlewell, St Mary the Virgin[236]	stained-glass window		
Prittlewell, St Mary the Virgin[237]	stained-glass window		
Purfleet	cross	25	
Purleigh	obelisk	15	
Radwinter	cross	28	3 September 1921
Rainham	clock tower	61	7 November 1920
Rainham	cross	99	12 December 1920
Rainham Congregational Church	tablet	15	13 February 1921
Rainham Council School	tablet		
Ramsden	community oak trees	12	October 1922
Ramsden Bellhouse	community oak trees	12	October 1922
Ramsden Bellhouse	cross	12	2 November 1920
Ramsey, St Michael	memorial hall and memorial stone		

230 Commemorating the troops whose unmarked graves are in the cemetery.

231 In memory of Gnr J.P. Brown, 95th Siege Battery, R.F.A., died on 3 August 1917.

232 In memory of Leslie C.H. Squire, died on 13 May 1915.

233 Dedicated to Sgt W. Redford, R.E., died on 14 May 1916.

234 The flag flew over the Glen Hospital during the War.

235 Referred to as the children's window.

236 Referred to as the Jesus Guild window.

237 Dedicated to Archie Gowing, Australian Imperial Force, missing in action on 11 April 1917.

Location	Type	Number of The "Fallen"	Date Unveiled/ Dedicated
Ramsey with Little Oakley	tablet	23	13 April 1919
Rayleigh	stained-glass window		
Rayleigh[238]	screen		March 1921
Rayne	cross	30	17 October 1920
Rettendon	tablet	13	April 1920
Ridgewell		10	13 November 1927
Rivenhall	cross	24	18 April 1920
Rivenhall and Silver End, St Mary And All Saints[239]	stained-glass window		
Rochford Congregational Church	tablet	14	
Rochford, Holy Trinity	reredos		
Rochford, St Andrew	tablet	41	
Rochford, St Andrew[240]			
Rochford, St Andrew[241]	tablet		23 September 1921
Romford	tablets	260	13 February 1921
Romford[242]	roll of honour	12	1 May 1920
Romford[243]	column	9	
Romford, Albert Road School	roll of honour	31	9 November 1919
Romford, St Andrew	cross	128	
Romford, St Edward the Confessor	board		13 February 1921
Romford, St Edward the Confessor[244]	tablet		
Romford, St Edward the Confessor[245]	tablet		
Romford, St John the Divine	roll of honour		
Romford, St Thomas, Noak Hill		9	12 June 1919
Romford, Town Hall	cross		18 September 1921
Rowhedge	trees of remembrance		15 April 1928
Rowhedge, St Lawrence	gate of thanksgiving		probably post-1945
Rowhedge, St Lawrence	tablet	28	
Roxwell[246]	war shrine		9 August 1918
Roxwell, St Michael and All Angels	tablet	20	5 August 1920
Roxwell[247]	stained-glass window		5 August 1920

[238] In memory of Lt A.E. Chapman.

[239] In memory of Capt. John H.V. Wilmott, 2nd Essex Regt, killed near Arras on 28 March 1918.

[240] Dedicated to Lt John W. Sheridan, Cameron Highlanders and R.A.F., killed on 27 September 1918, aged twenty-nine.

[241] In memory of Capt. Henry C. Stroud, R.E., attached to the R.F.C., K.I.A. on 7 March 1918.

[242] In memory of the men of the Court Rose of Romford, Ancient Order of Foresters.

[243] Dedicated to the men of Scarthin.

[244] In memory of Lt Eric A. Wright, R.A.M.C. Died at Alexandria on 21 June 1918, aged thirty-six.

[245] Dedicated to the Romford branch of the Old Contemptibles.

[246] In memory of Lt Alan Lloyd, R.F.A., and those from the Boyton Estate and Boyton Cross.

[247] In memory of Wilfred R. Millbank, K.I.A. in Flanders on 13 March 1915.

APPENDIX: ESSEX MEMORIALS OF THE GREAT WAR

Location	Type	Number of The "Fallen"	Date Unveiled/ Dedicated
St Osyth	obelisk and recreation ground	56	15 May 1921
St Osyth, St Peter and St Paul	cross	56	19 December 1920
St Osyth, St Peter and St Paul	roll of honour		
Saffron Walden	column and cross	158	7 May 1921
Saffron Walden, Friends School	tablet	24	1919
Saffron Walden, Hoops Hotel, Good Samaritan Lodge of Shepherds	tablet	37	3 October 1921
Saffron Walden, Town Hall	roll of honour	158	7 May 1921
Saffron Walden, Walden Bloom Lodge of Oddfellows	tablet	30	13 May 1920
Salcott-cum-Virley, St Mary The Virgin	tablet	6	17 April 1921
Seven Kings Baptist Church	tablet	4	
Seven Kings Methodist Church	tablet	18	
Seven Kings, St John the Evangelist	chapel		26 September 1954
Shalford, St Andrew	board	7	
Shellow (see under Willingale)			
Shelley (Ongar)	hospital		1933
Shenfield	cross		29 March 1918
Shenfield[248]	parochial hall	46	30 November 1922
Shenfield railway station	tablet	5	28 October 1921
Shenfield, St Mary the Virgin	tablet	46	10 April 1921
Shenfield, St Mary the Virgin	memorial board		
Shenfield, St Mary the Virgin[249]	tablet		
Shenfield, St Mary the Virgin[250]	tablet		
Shoeburyness	obelisk	85	26 May 1921
Shoeburyness Garrison Church, St Peter and St Paul[251]	tablet		
Shoeburyness Garrison Church St Peter and St Paul[252]	tablet	16	25 July 1920
Shoeburyness, Hanguar Street Senior School	tablet	47	22 June 1920
Sible Hedingham	war shrine		1918
Sible Hedingham	cross	52	20 March 1921
Sible Hedingham[253]	roll of honour	33	15 November 1919

[248] This is not strictly a war memorial as such; it was built as "an expression of thanks for victory and peace."

[249] Dedicated to Pte P.E. Basson, Essex Regt, died on 18 August 1918.

[250] Dedicated to Pte L.G.M. Lee, died on 11 May 1917.

[251] In memory of Maj. John H. Massie, D.O.W. on 15 November 1914.

[252] In memory of the men who lost their lives at the Experimental Establishment at Shoeburyness.

[253] In memory of the men of the Loyal Webster Lodge of Oddfellows.

Location	Type	Number of The "Fallen"	Date Unveiled/ Dedicated
Sible Hedingham, St Peter	triptych	52	
Sible Hedingham, St Peter	thanksgiving stone		
Sible Hedingham, St Peter[254]	tablet		
South Benfleet	cross	36	30 May 1920
South Benfleet	stained-glass window		
South Chingford Congregational Church	tablet	6	
South Hanningfield, St Peter	obelisk	8	6 May 1920
South Hornchurch		24	14 December 1919
South Ockendon	cenotaph	45	
South Weald	cenotaph and cross		
South Weald[255]	tablet		20 January 1929
South Weald, St Peter	calvary		
South Woodford	cross		
South Woodford, Holy Trinity	panelling	26	
South Woodford, Holy Trinity	memorial board	117	
South Woodford, Holy Trinity[256]	chairs		
South Woodford, St Mary with St Philip and St Jude	tablet	73	
South Woodford, St Mary with St Philip and St Jude	stained-glass windows		
South Woodford, St Mary with St Philip and St Jude[257]	tablet		
Southchurch, Belle Vue Baptist Church	tablet	4	
Southchurch, Belle Vue Baptist Church[258]	tablet		
Southchurch, Holy Trinity[259]	addition to gravestone		
Southchurch, Holy Trinity[260]	addition to gravestone		
Southend	cenotaph	1,338	27 November 1921
Southend[261]	Victory Sports Ground		
Southend, All Saints	calvary	102	16 November 1919
Southend, Avenue Baptist Church	tablet	15	24 July 1921
Southend Borough Council[262]	roll of honour	1,354	

254 Dedicated to Cpl Alan S. Elsdon, East Surrey Regt, D.O.W. on 1 September 1916, aged twenty-three.

255 In memory of Christopher and Hugh Tower, K.I.A. Hugh Tower was a member of the R.F.C., and was K.I.A. in September 1916.

256 In memeory of L/Cpl H.F. Heritage, K.I.A. in France on 15 March 1917.

257 In memory of G.E. Randall.

258 In memory of Thomas J. Robinson, R.A.M.C., 108th Field Ambulance, K.I.A. at Ledeghen, on 1 October 1918.

259 In memory of Pte George T.R. Taylor, D.O.W. at Suvla Bay, Gallipoli, 7 August 1915, aged nineteen.

260 In memory of Lt Archibald G. Arber, 10th Border Regt, K.I.A. at Gallipoli on 21 October 1915, aged twenty-four.

261 Dedicated to the sportsmen of Southend.

262 Located at Prittlewell Priory Refectory.

Location	Type	Number of The "Fallen"	Date Unveiled/ Dedicated
Southend, Priory Park	drinking fountain		
Southend, Chalkwell Park	Garden of Remembrance		
Southend, Clifftown Congregational Church	tablet	21	4 August 1920
Southend, Hamsted Girls' School[263]	tablet		20 November 1917
Southend High School	organ, panelling and tablet	97	9 June 1923
Southend, police station[264]	bronze plate	9	c.1946
Southend police station	tablet	9	c. 1946
Southend, Park Hotel[265]	tablet	24	6 December 1921
Southend post office	portraits	3	28 January 1920
Southend, St Erkenwald	cenotaph	63	23 July 1919
Southend, St John the Baptist	screen	85	24 June 1919
Southend, York Road Wesleyan Methodist Church	tablet	5	20 June 1920
Southminster	memorial hall		1933
Southminster	cross	70	6 June 1920
Southminster, St Leonard	obelisk, sanctuary stand lights, processional cross	70	8 June 1920
Southminster, St Leonard	roll of honour		
Springfield, All Saints	tablet	63	10 November 1920
Springfield, All Saints[266]	tablet		4 September 1921
Springfield, All Saints[267]	tablet		
Stambridge	memorial hall		17 January 1922
Stambridge, All Saints	tablet		
Stambridge, St Mary	tablet		
Stanford le Hope	cenotaph	83	
Stansted Mountfitchet	stained-glass window		
Stansted Mountfitchet	cross	54	30 June 1920
Stansted Mountfitchet, St Mary	tablet	54	30 June 1920
Stanway, St Albright	lych gate	29	28 November 1920
Stanway, St Albright	roll of honour		
Stapleford Abbotts, St Mary the Virgin	tablet	18	
Stapleford Tawney	tablet	8	

263 In memory of Gladys West, killed in an air raid on Southend on 12 August 1917.

264 In memory of the fallen of the Southend Borough Constabulary.

265 In memory of the Clifftown Lodge of Oddfellows.

266 In memory of Lt Charles T. Paynter, R.N., died aboard H.M.S. *North Star* on 23 April 1918, in the naval attack on Zeebrugge, aged twenty-two.

267 In memory of Capt. Christopher M. Ridley, Essex Regt, K.I.A. at Thiepval 13 October 1916, aged twenty-five; also Capt. Hubert L. Ridley, Royal Dublin Fusiliers, K.I.A. in Flanders on 15 July 1917, aged twenty-two.

Location	Type	Number of The "Fallen"	Date Unveiled/ Dedicated
Stapleford Tawney	roll of honour		
Stebbing	war shrine (crucifix)		July 1918
Stebbing	cross	20	30 May 1920
Stebbing[268]	tablet		9 April 1920
Stebbing	choir stalls		27 May 1923
Steeple Bumpstead	cross	25	12 December 1920
Steeple Bumpstead	tablet and recreation ground	16	15 August 1920
Steeple Congregational Church	tablet	12	19 June 1919
Steeple	organ and tablet	7	16 September 1922
Stifford St Mary	obelisk	29	
Stisted	memorial slab	9	30 May 1920
Stisted Congregational Church[269]	tablet		18 April 1919
Stock, All Saints[270]	tablet		
Stock, All Saints[271]	tablet		
Stock and Buttsbury	cenotaph	40	2 November1920
Stow Maries[272]	school	8	
Stow Maries[273]	propeller		
Stow Maries, St Mary[274]	tablet	8	
Stow Maries, St Mary[275]	aumbry		
Stow Maries, St Mary[276]	illuminated cross		
Stow Maries, St Mary	reredos	8	
Stow Maries, St Mary[277]	carving		
Stratford, Queen Mary's Hospital			11 November 1924
Stratford, St John	tablet		
Takeley	cross	24	18 September 1921
Tendring	column and cross	18	16 November 1920

268 In memory of Edward H. Emery, K.I.A. at Gaza on 26 March 1917.

269 In memory of Arthur Baler and Bertie Saunders, both killed in the War.

270 In memory of Capt. Rae A. Ellis, 1st Montgomeryshire Yeomanry, attached 25th Royal Welsh Fusiliers, D.O.W. received at Ronssoy, France on 22 September 1918, aged thirty-six.

271 Dedicated to Pendarves C. Foll, killed in France on 10 April 1917.

272 Now called the Smythe Hall.

273 Placed in the school and presented by the Air Ministry in memory of the three men of the Stow Maries aerodrome who were killed.

274 This also commemorates the three men of the Stow Maries aerodrome who were killed in flying accidents.

275 In memory of Lee Gordon Fuller Smythe, who died on active service, 26 April 1920, aged twenty.

276 Dedicated to the men of the Stow Maries aerodrome, and presented by Squadron Leader Claude A. Ridley, first commanding officer of the aerodrome in 1916 with "B" Flight, Number 37 Squadron.

277 In memory of Lee Gordon Fuller Smythe, died on active service.

APPENDIX: ESSEX MEMORIALS OF THE GREAT WAR

Location	Type	Number of The "Fallen"	Date Unveiled/ Dedicated
Tendring	roll of honour and village hall	21	2 July 1920
Tendring, St Edmund	column and cross	20	16 November 1919
Tendring, St Edmund[278]	memorial window		
Tendring, St Edmund	tablet	18	
Terling	cross	23	27 March 1921
Thames Haven Oil Refinery	tablet		
Thaxted, St John with Our Lady[279] and St Laurence	tablet	49	
Thaxted, St John with Our Lady and St Laurence	photographic roll of honour	49	
Theydon Bois	cross	27	20 February 1921
Theydon Garnon, All Saints[280]	screen		13 November 1921
Theydon Garnon, All Saints	tablet	27	
Theydon Garnon, All Saints[281]	window		
Theydon Garnon, All Saints	ciborium cover		
Theydon Garnon, All Saints[282]	tablet		13 November 1921
Thorp-le-Soken	cross	37	23 May 1920
Thorp-le-Soken[283]	tablet		16 February 1918
Thorpe Bay, St Augustine	tablet		March 1920
Thorpe Bay, St Augustine	roll of honour	36	17 May 1935
Thorrington Methodist Church	tablet	11	
Thorrington School	roll of honour		
Thorrington, St Mary Magdalen	tablet	11	
Thorrington, St Mary Magdalen	roll of honour		
Tilbury	clock tower	156	
Tilbury, London Cruise Terminal[284]	tablet	403	28 January 1926
Tilbury (East), St Katherine	roll of honour	54	
Tilbury (East), St Katherine[285]	church tower		1917
Tilbury (East), St Katherine[286]	obelisk		

278 In memory of Lt Gerald A. Hervey, Wessex (Hampshire) R.G.A., K.I.A. on 8 August 1917, in Flanders, aged thirty-six.

279 In memory of Eric Makeham.

280 In memory of Capt. Atherton H. Chisenhale, K.I.A. at Wytchete Ridge on 18 September 1918 and Maj. Adam D. Bell, K.I.A. in France on 8 April 1918.

281 In memory of Swaine St George Showers, K.I.A. at Moch Le Preux, 9 August 1917; also of Lt Harold C.M. Lucas, Edward VII's Own Gurkhas, K.I.A. at Neuve Chapelle, 2 November 1914.

282 Dedicated to Capt. Atherton H. Chisenhale, 9th Lancers, K.I.A. on Wytschoete Ridge, 28 September 1918; also of Maj. Adam D. Bell, 4th Hussars, K.I.A. in France, 8 April 1918.

283 In memory of the Rev. C.T. Veryard, killed in France in 1917.

284 Dedicated to the men of the Port of London Authority.

285 Built by No. 2 London Electrical Engineers in memory of the men of the Coalhouse Fort who died.

286 Commemorating the men of the Coalhouse Fort.

Location	Type	Number of The "Fallen"	Date Unveiled/ Dedicated
Tilbury (East), St Katherine[287]	tablet		
Tilbury, St Mary		74	
Tillingham, St Nicholas	tablet	23	2 September 1928
Tillingham	memorial stone		
Tiptree	cross	53	4 July 1920
Tiptree, St Luke	tablet	30	
Tiptree, Wilkin's Jam Factory	land for ex-servicemen and tablet	11	January 1919
Tollesbury Congregational Church	pipe organ	46	22 June 1921
Tollesbury, St Mary	cross	46	
Tollesbury, St Mary[288]	tablet		
Tollesbury, St Mary[289]	stained-glass window		24 October 1921
Tolleshunt D'Arcy, St Nicholas	tablet	26	
Tolleshunt Major, St Nicholas	tablet	37	
Toppesfield, St Margaret	cross	19	
Ugley, St Peter	tablet	8	September 1920
Ulting	cross		
Upminster	cross	66	7 May 1921
Upminster, Albion Road School	roll of honour		
Upminster Congregational Church	tablet	13	26 September 1920
Upminster Congregational Church	community hall		26 May 1923
Upminster, South Essex Crematorium, Garden of Remembrance[290]	tablet		
Uttlesford, All Saints	tablet	5	1921
Vange, All Saints	tablet	21	28 February 1920
Wakering Congregational Church[291]	tablet		
Wakes Colne,	tablet	14	
Wakes Colne, All Saints	tower screen	14	
Waltham Abbey	memorial hospital	190	10 December 1921
Waltham Abbey Jewish Cemetery	tablet	41	1926
Walthamstow	cenotaph	2,500	15 July 1922
Walthamstow, Black Horse Road School[292]	tablet	55	
Walthamstow Cemetery	cross of sacrifice		
Walthamstow, Church Hill[293]	cross		12 November 1921

287 Commemorating the men of the Coalhouse Fort.

288 In memory of Capt. Robert H. Biney, Essex Regt, K.I.A. on 23 March 1918.

289 In memory of Maj. William C. Maskell, D.O.W. in France on 15 December 1917, aged twenty-eight.

290 In memory of Sgt Laurence Calvert, V.C., King's Own Yorkshire Light Infantry.

291 In memory of Capt. E.P.W. Wedd.

292 In memory of the teachers and former pupils of the school.

293 In memory of the men of the 7th Essex Regt and 3rd East Anglian Field Ambulance.

APPENDIX: ESSEX MEMORIALS OF THE GREAT WAR

Location	Type	Number of The "Fallen"	Date Unveiled/ Dedicated
Walthamstow, Forest School	cross, tablets and park	98	3 December 1920
Walthamstow, Goodall Road School	tablet	34-35	
Walthamstow, The Lighthouse Methodist School	tablet	40	
Walthamstow, Marsh Street Congregational Church	tablet	24	3 October 1920
Walthamstow, Melbourne Road School[294]	memorial stone		
Walthamstow, Monoux Grammar School[295]	tablet	72	11 November 1922
Walthamstow, St Barnabas with St James the Great	tablet and rood		19 March 1921
Walthamstow, St John	tablet	200	
Walthamstow, St Mary	screen and painting behind the reredos	2,500	
Walthamstow, St Mary[296]	tablet		
Walthamstow, St Mary[297]	tablet		
Walthamstow, St Mary[298]	tablet		
Walthamstow, St Mary[299]	tablet		
Walthamstow, St Mary[300]	tablet		
Walthamstow, St Michael and All Angels	crucifix and panels		
Walthamstow, St Peter's in the Forest	tablet	41	
Walthamstow, St Peter's in the Forest[301]	tablet		
Walthamstow, St Saviour	triptych	103	
Walthamstow, St Stephen	tablet	100	
Walthamstow, Sybourn Street Primary School	tablet		
Walthamstow, Trinity Congregational Church	tablet		
Walthamstow, Warwick Boys School			
Walton-on-the-Naze	cenotaph	58	12 November 1922
Walton-on-the-Naze, All Saints[302]	tablet	57	18 August 1920

[294] In memory of Jack Cornwell, V.C.

[295] In memory of the old boys killed in the War.

[296] In memory of John S.L. Evans, killed on the Somme, 26 July 1916, aged nineteen.

[297] In memory of Albert L.L. Evans, D.O.W. on 1 May 1917.

[298] In memory of Sgt Vincent P. Bayne, London Rifle Brigade, D.O.W. on 6 November 1917, aged nineteen.

[299] In memory of Henry R. Pracy, Royal West Kent Regt, killed on the Somme on 5 September 1916.

[300] In memory of Lt Percival J. Tattershall, R.A.F., died on 9 January 1918.

[301] Dedicated to the Warner family.

[302] In memory of Lt Commander Harry Craven, died at sea in November 1917.

Location	Type	Number of The "Fallen"	Date Unveiled/ Dedicated
Walton-on-the-Naze Marine Gardens[303]	bust		
Walton-on-the-Naze Memorial Gardens[304]	tablet		
Wanstead	statuary	228	30 April 1922
Wanstead	war shrine		October 1918
Wanstead, Cameron Road Church	tablet	4	
Warley, cemetery	cross of sacrifice		14 November 1920
Warley, Christ Church	tablet	100	4 July 1920
Warley, Christ Church School[305]	oak panels	28	
Warley, Cottage Gardens, Headley Chase[306]	chapel and club room		12 November 1918
Warley, Regimental Chapel	tablet and roll of honour	3,424	28 May 1921
Warley, Regimental Chapel[307]	desk and roll of honour		29 September 1929
Warley, Regimental Chapel[308]	roll of honour		March/April 1929
Warley, Regimental Chapel[309]	stained-glass window		17 December 1930
Warley, Regimental Chapel[310]			19 June 1933
Warley, Regimental Chapel[311]	pew		
Warley Roman Catholic Church	tablet	22	12 April 1919
Weeley	cross	10	26 June 1920
Weeley	mural tablet	10	11 December 1920
Weeley[312]	tablet		3 October 1920
Weeley, Wesleyan Chapel	tablet	10	17 July 1921
Weeley[313]	reredos and almsdish		11 December 1920
Westborough Primary School[314]	tablet		19 July 1915
Westborough Primary School[315]	tablet		
Westcliff-on-Sea, Avenue Baptist Chapel	organ and tablet		24 July 1921
Westcliff-on-Sea Congregational Chapel	stained-glass window	9	May 1919

303 In memory of Private Herbert G. Columbine, V.C., K.I.A. on 22 March 1918.

304 In memory of the crew of H.M.S. *Conquest*, which sank 28 March 1916.

305 In memory of the school's old boys.

306 In memory of Frank E. Sturch. K.I.A. on 14 November 1916, aged twenty.

307 In memory of the men of the 6th Essex Territorial Battalion.

308 In memory of the men of the 5th Essex Territorial Battalion.

309 In memory of the men of the 10th Essex Battalion.

310 In memory of the men of the Essex Militia.

311 Dedicated to the old boys of Brentwood School who served in the Essex Regiment.

312 In memory of Weeley's Fallen, subscribed by the village's ex-servicemen.

313 In memory of Lt Ashton Hill, Essex Yeomanry.

314 Dedicated to Lt Oswald Griffith, R.F.A., K.I.A. in March 1915.

315 Dedicated to Rifleman Ben Dawes and Rifleman William Hynds, ex-pupils of the school, both of them died in 1918.

APPENDIX: ESSEX MEMORIALS OF THE GREAT WAR

Location	Type	Number of The "Fallen"	Date Unveiled/ Dedicated
Westcliff-on-Sea, Essex Bowling Club	tablet	10	
Westcliff-on-Sea, Lindisfarne College	obelisk	55	19 March 1921
Westcliff-on-Sea, Lindisfarne College	tablet		20 November 1949
Westcliff-on-Sea, St Alban	reredos	83	20 June 1920
Westcliff-on-Sea,, Trinity Methodist Church	tablet		1948
Westcliff-on-Sea Westborough Council School[316]	tablet		19 July 1915
West Bergholt	tablet	24	3 October 1919
West Bergholt, Daniell and Sons	tablet	9	30 August 1920
West Bergholt Primitive Methodist Church	tablet	24	5 October 1919
West Ham, Abbey Road Baptist Church	board	8	
West Ham, All Saints	stained-glass windows and tablets	390	9 October 1920
West Ham, All Saints[317]	stained-glass windows and tablets	256	9 October 1920
West Ham, All Saints[318]	tablets	260	
West Ham, The Cedars, T.A. Centre[319]	tablet		
West Ham, Central Baptist Mission Church (Plaistow)	peal of ten bells		14 March 1925
West Ham, Leather Factory	animal figures	24	
West Ham, Russell Road Higher Elementary School[320]			11 November 1922
West Ham Secondary School[321]	tablet	59	19 March 1922
West Ham Tramway Garage[322]	obelisk	53	6 November 1921
West Hanningfield	memorial stone	12	
West Mersea, St Peter & St Paul	cross	44	22 September 1918
West Mersea, St Peter and St Paul[323]	chancel rail		
West Thurrock, St Clement	tablet	67	
Wethersfield, St Mary Magdalene	tablet	19	
Wethersfield[324]	tablet		

[316] In memory of Lt Oswald Griffith, K.I.A. in France; he was a former master at the school.

[317] In memory of the men of the 1/6th Battalion, Essex Regt.

[318] In memory of the Essex Regt.

[319] The London Troops Memorial, the 12th City of London Regt, the Rangers.

[320] Dedicated to the school's old boys.

[321] In memory of former pupils.

[322] In memory of the borough's tramway men.

[323] Commemorates the men of the 54th (Territorial) Division.

[324] In memory of General Gordon, Black Watch, K.I.A.

Location	Type	Number of The "Fallen"	Date Unveiled/ Dedicated
Wethersfield, Chapel of Ease, Blackmore End	tablet	19	
Wethersfield Congregational Church	tablet	19	20 February 1921
White Colne, St Andrew	cross	11	
White Notley	tablet	5	25 January 1920
Whittlesford	memorial hall		29 September 1921
Wickford[325]	cross		
Wickford[326]	pillar		
Wickford[327]	hewn block		
Wickford, Christ Church	tablet	8	
Wickford Congregational Church	tablet	8	21 May 1921
Wickham Bishops, St Bartholomew	tablet	16	
Wickham Bishops, St Bartholomew[328]	tablet		
Widford	cross	14	26 March 1921
Widford[329]	tablet		14 July 1918
Willingale[330]	stained-glass window		21 April 1918
Willingale and Shellow Bowells		15	1 December 1923
Willingale Doe, St Christopher[331]	tablet	2	11 November 1926
Wimbish	tablet	20	13 June 1920
Wiston by Nayland	cross	5	11 July 1920
Witham	cross	79	21 November 1920
Witham United Reform Church	roll of honour	7	
Wivenhoe[332]	tablet		1920
Wivenhoe Congregational Church	obelisk	9	
Wix	obelisk	22	13 March 1920
Wix, St Mary	tablet	23	
Woodford Baptist Church	tablet	8	
Woodford, St Barnabas	calvary	53	22 May 1921
Woodford, St Barnabas	stained-glass window	53	
Woodford, St Barnabas[333]	tablet		

325 In memory of Lt S. Reefe, R.A.F., K.I.A.

326 Dedicated to Capt. Henry C. Stroud, R.F.C., K.I.A. on 7 March 1918. The pillar has an aircraft propeller mounted on the top.

327 In memory of Capt. Alexander Bruce Kynoch, R.A.F., K.I.A. on 7 March 1918, aged twenty-four.

328 In memory of Lt Kenneth C. Herron, Essex Yeomanry, attached to the R.F.C., K.I.A. in France on 24 April 1918.

329 In memory of Lt Col Frederick Taylor. He died in 1915 after an illness. He was an enthusiastic recruiting officer in the county during 1914-15.

330 In memory of Maj. Arthur T. Sauvez, R.F.A., K.I.A. at Arras on 22 April 1917.

331 In memory of Bernard O. Warner.

332 In memory of L/Cpl Felix Squire, Essex Regt, K.I.A. in France on 4 June 1917, aged nineteen years.

333 In memory of Arthur Quelhorst, K.I.A.

APPENDIX: ESSEX MEMORIALS OF THE GREAT WAR

Location	Type	Number of The "Fallen"	Date Unveiled/ Dedicated
Woodford, St Barnabas[334]	tablet		
Woodford, St Mary[335]	tablet		
Woodford, St Mary[336]	tablet		
Woodford Bridge	roll of honour	45	September 1918
Woodford Bridge, private park	tablet	71	
Woodford Bridge, St Paul	tablet	45	1920
Woodford Green, All Saints, St Barnabas with St Andrew	roll of honour	49	
Woodford Green, All Saints, St Barnabas with St Andrew[337]	tablet		
Woodford Green, Bancrofts School	pillar		1919
Woodford Green, Bancrofts School	roll of honour	167	
Woodford Green, Christ Church	tablet	13	
Woodford Green Men's Club	tablet	12	
Woodford Green, postal sorting office	tablet	10	18 July 1920
Woodford Green, St Barnabas	crucifix		
Woodford Green, United Free Church	tablet	27	
Woodford Green, United Reform Church	tablet	20	
Woodham Ferrers, St Mary	obelisk	31	
Woodham Mortimer, St Margaret[338]	tablet		
Woodham Mortimer, St Margaret[339]	tablet		
Woodham Mortimer, St Margaret[340]	tablet	7	
Woodham Mortimer, St Margaret	cross		
Woodham Walter, St Michael the Archangel	clock in church tower		
Woodham Walter, St Michael the Archangel	tablet	20	
Woodham Walter, St Michael the Archangel[341]	tablet		

334 In memory of Charles Eastgate, K.I.A.

335 Dedicated to Clifford J. B. Hunt, Canadian Infantry, K.I.A. at Courcelette on 29 September 1916, aged twenty-six.

336 In memory of Sub-Lt Leslie G. Black, R.N.V.R., died on 13 December 1916, aged thirty-two.

337 In memory of Lt D.J. Geere, killed in France on 23 February 1916.

338 In memory of Lt William L. Parker, R.F.C., K.I.A. 31 October 1917, aged twenty-two.

339 In memory of Capt. & Fl. Cmmdr Greville Oxley Parker, Essex Regt & R.F.C., K.I.A. 24 March 1917, aged twenty-seven, and Lt Henry T. Brunwin Hales, Lincolnshire Regt, K.I.A. at Loos, 13 October 1915, aged twenty-two.

340 Dedicated to Frank Britton, Driver, R.E., K.I.A. near St Jean, Ypres, 28 April 1915.

341 Dedicated to Capt. Arthur N. Falkner, Loyal North Lancashire Regt, D.O.W. 20 July 1916.

Location	Type	Number of The "Fallen"	Date Unveiled/ Dedicated
Woodham Walter, St Michael the Archangel[342]	tablet		
Wormingford, St Andrew	church bells	3	January 1920
Wormingford, St Andrew	tablet	13	27 June 1920
Wormingford, St Andrew[343]	painting		
Wrabness, St Mary[344]	mural tablet		28 March 1920
Wrabness, St Mary	tablet		
Wrabness, St Mary	tablet	5	21 November 1920
Writtle	cross	58	29 May 1920
Writtle, All Saints[345]	tablet		
Writtle, All Saints[346]	tablet		

342 In memory of Pte John A. Campion, Grenadier Guards, K.I.A. near Festubert, 24 December 1914, aged twenty-three.

343 Although not technically a war memorial, this painting is a thanksgiving for the safe return of those villagers who served in the armed forces and survived the War.

344 In memory of Lt Claude L. Harvey, Queen's West Surrey Regt, K.I.A. near La Fere on 23 March 1918, aged twenty-seven.

345 In memory of Lt Edward L. Mildmay Rose, 16th Battalion, Canadian Scottish Regt, K.I.A. at Ypres, 6 June 1916, aged thirty-one.

346 In memory of Sub-Lt Thomas R.G. Usborne, R.N., killed at Kronstadt, Russia, 8 August, aged eighteen. This memorial can be considered to be one that dates from the Great War in that British forces were in Russia engaging Bolshevik forces in consequence of Lenin's withdrawal from the War in January 1918.

Index

INDEX

INDEX